Routledge International Handbook of Restorative Justice

This up-to-date resource on restorative justice theory and practice is the literature's most comprehensive and authoritative review of original research in new and contested areas.

Bringing together contributors from across a range of jurisdictions, disciplines and legal traditions, this edited collection provides a concise, but critical review of existing theory and practice in restorative justice. Authors identify key developments, theoretical arguments and new empirical evidence, evaluating their merits and demerits, before turning the reader's attention to further concerns informing and improving the future of restorative justice. Divided into four parts, the Handbook includes papers written by leading scholars on new theory, empirical evidence of implementation, critiques and the future of restorative justice.

This companion is essential reading for scholars of restorative justice, criminology, social theory, psychology, law, human rights and criminal justice, as well as researchers, policymakers, practitioners and campaigners from around the world.

Theo Gavrielides, PhD, is an international expert in restorative justice, human rights and youth justice. He is the Founder and Director of The IARS International Institute, a user-led NGO that empowers marginalised groups to influence social policy and law internationally. He is also the Founder and Director of the Restorative Justice for All Institute (RJ4All) as well as Adjunct Professor at the School of Criminology of Simon Fraser University and a visiting professor at Buckinghamshire New University. Professor Gavrielides is an expert advisor to the European Commission's criminal justice and equality projects, and has worked with many governments on justice reforms. He has worked as the Human Rights Advisor of the UK Ministry of Justice as well as a researcher at the London School of Economics, and he is the Principal Investigator of numerous EU, UN and UK funded research programmes.

Dr. Gavrielides has published extensively in the areas of restorative justice, legal philosophy youth policy, human rights and criminal justice. He is the Editor of numerous collected editions as well as the Founder and Editor-in-Chief of the *Youth Voice Journal* and the *Internet Journal of Restorative Justice*. He is also the Editor of the *International Journal of Human Rights in Healthcare*.

'This international Handbook grounds itself in the present and past in order to look to the future. It sets for itself an important but challenging goal: to reflect the state of restorative justice in the early 21st century, including not only developments in theory and practice, but also its essential debates and challenges. This is an important collection for anyone who wants to understand and grapple with 21st century restorative justice.'

Howard Zehr, Eastern Mennonite University, USA

'This book is perhaps the most comprehensive and certainly the most up-to-date collection on restorative justice. It goes to some topics rarely addressed in earlier volumes . . . and embraces a wider range of critiques of restorative justice than most volumes on the subject . . . Furthermore, in its geographical coverage, this international Handbook is much broader than older collections . . . We are grateful to Theo Gavrielides for bringing so many voices into the conversation. Many inspiring restorative justice leaders in the past have mobilized convening power toward projects of listening, but none more widely nor in more diverse ways than Theo Gavrielides in recent years.'

John Braithwaite, Australian National University

'A decade after the first two "Handbooks of Restorative Justice", this successor is timely. It is an update of developments in ideas and current debates, and of a great part of the relevant literature. A new generation of authors is emerging. Restorative justice researchers, advocates and critics should have it.'

Lode Walgrave, University of Leuven, Belgium

'In its breadth and depth, this impressive collection represents a new chapter in one of the most remarkable stories in criminal justice of the past century. Restorative justice has grown from the radical, abstract vision of 30 years ago into a fully fledged field of study and practice, worthy of this important international handbook.'

Shadd Maruna, author of Making Good: How Ex-Convicts Reform and Rebuild Their Lives

'This book offers thoughtful and varied approaches to reconciliation and community resilience. As readers, we see that inclusive approaches to justice—involving loved ones, community support systems, and cultural context—offer real hope for renewal and personal peace. This book challenges the punitive aspects of the current criminal justice system, to be sure, but also offers practical tools for transformative leaders to nurture restoration, reformation, and healing. A pathway forward is found through the wisdom of the scholars here, all of whom are committed to restorative justice and a more resilient future.'

Maya Soetoro, University of Hawaii at Manoa, USA

Routledge International Handbook of Restorative Justice

Edited by Theo Gavrielides

Routledge
Taylor & Francis Group

LONDON AND NEW YORK

First published 2019
by Routledge
2 Park Square, Milton Park, Abingdon, Oxon OX14 4RN

and by Routledge
711 Third Avenue, New York, NY 10017

Routledge is an imprint of the Taylor & Francis Group, an informa business

British Library Cataloguing-in-Publication Data
A catalogue record for this book is available from the British Library

Library of Congress Cataloging-in-Publication Data
Names: Gavrielides, Theo, editor.
Title: Routledge international handbook of restorative justice / edited by
    Theo Gavrielides.
Other titles: International handbook of restorative justice
Description: New York, NY : Routledge, 2018. | Includes bibliographical
    references and index.
Identifiers: LCCN 2018005623 | ISBN 9781472480705 (hardback)
Subjects: LCSH: Restorative justice.
Classification: LCC HV8688 .R68 2018 | DDC 364.6/8—dc23
LC record available at https://lccn.loc.gov/2018005623

ISBN: 978-1-4724-8070-5 (hbk)
ISBN: 978-1-315-61351-2 (ebk)

Typeset in Bembo
by Apex CoVantage, LLC

Now in its second generation, restorative justice is not a wild dream: it is a reality, and I for one am energized by the new and younger voices that are emerging.

It is important to open space for these new voices and emerging themes. As a first-generation developer and practitioner, now at the end of my career, it seems appropriate that this may be the last book foreword I write for the field. It is time to make room for others of this new generation. Much appreciation to Theo Gavrielides, himself a representative of this new generation, for leading the way through this Handbook.

Howard Zehr, Eastern Mennonite University, USA

Photograph © Aaron Johnston

Contents

Contents

Figures

Tables

Contributors

Annalise Acorn PhD is a Professor of Law at the University of Alberta. She is the author of *Compulsory Compassion: a critique of restorative justice* (Vancouver: UBC Press, 2004). Her engagement with restorative justice has, indeed, been largely critical as is evident, for example, in her article, "Son Be a Dentist": restorative justice and the Dalhousie Dental School scandal" in the *Harvard Negotiation Law Review*. She is interested in law and literature as well as philosophy of the emotions (particularly compassion and resentment) in relation to conflict and justice. In 2009 she was an H.L.A. Hart Fellow at the Oxford Centre for Ethics and Legal Philosophy and in 2014–2015 she was Visiting Fellow at All Souls College, Oxford. She teaches jurisprudence, professional responsibility and private international law. Since May of 2016 she has been academic mentor to the indigenous students at the University of Alberta Faculty of Law.

David Best PhD is a leading figure in the international research and policy movement around recovery from alcohol and drug problems. He is an experienced addictions and crime researcher and has published around 150 peer-reviewed papers and more than 50 policy and research reports. He has authored three books on addiction recovery. He has worked in academic research at Monash University in Australia, Strathclyde University in Glasgow, the Institute of Psychiatry in London, Birmingham University and the University of the West of Scotland. He has also worked in policy research at the Police Complaints Authority, the National Treatment Agency and the Prime Minister's Delivery Unit. David oversees the Criminology Subject Group within the Law and Criminology Department at Sheffield Hallam University and contributes to the Master's in Applied Human Rights. He also co-chairs the Desistance and Recovery and the Criminal Justice Expert clusters at the same institution.

Jane Bolitho, PhD, is a senior lecturer in Criminology in the School of Social Sciences at the University of New South Wales, Australia. Her research interests include all forms of restorative justice, restorative practices in the civil sphere, mediation and alternative dispute resolution, experiences of violence and innovative justice responses. She is a nationally accredited mediator and facilitates restorative youth justice conferences.

John Braithwaite PhD is Co-Director with Miranda Forsyth of the Centre for Restorative Justice in the School of Regulation and Global Governance (RegNet) at the Australian National University. John founded the School with Valerie Braithwaite. Since 2004 his primary research focus has been on the Peacebuilding Compared project. You can read about his peacebuilding and restorative justice work at johnbraithwaite.com, where most of his writings on these subjects are available as free downloads.

Janine Carroll is the Director of Restorative Now, specialising in Restorative Practice training, implementation and facilitation. She has over 30 years' experience in restorative practice across the criminal justice, education and community sectors, much of this gained in New Zealand and the UK. She is passionate about the life-changing potential of restorative practice in all settings and advocates for its use widely. She is motivated by the empowerment and resolution witnessed at an individual level, alongside the culture change and enduring life skills invested in the future.

Kerry Clamp PhD is Assistant Professor of Criminology at the University of Nottingham. She received her PhD from the University of Leeds in 2010 and also holds degrees from the University of Sheffield and the University of South Africa. Her research agenda focuses on the intersections of restorative justice and policing, and of restorative justice and transitional justice. She has published two monographs and one edited collection with Routledge on these topics. She is the Chair of the Editorial Board and Editor of the *Newsletter* for the European Forum for Restorative Justice, posts which she has held since 2011.

Nestor E. Courakis PhD is Emeritus Professor of Criminology and Penology at the National and Kapodistrian University of Athens, Faculty of Law, and a full-time Professor at the University of Nicosia.[1] He has participated in the committee for the drafting of a new Greek Penitentiary Code and has represented Greece in several criminological meetings at the Council of Europe, the United Nations and the European Union; has also participated in several international conferences and has presented country-reports (e.g. International Congress of Comparative Law, Athens 1994, on Alternative Penal Sanctions in Greece, and at Preparatory Colloquium of AIDP on Organized Crime, Alexandria 1997); scientific counselor on criminological and penological matters at the Ministry of Justice, Athens 1990–93; mem. Bd. Trustees of Hellenic Society of Criminology; has been a member of the European Society of Criminology, International Association of Penal Law (AIDP), Société Internationale de Défence Sociale and the World Society of Victimology. He has also been the director of the Centre for Criminal and Penological Research (2001–2015) as well as the president of the Consultative Body against Corruption (2013–2015).

Janet Davidson, PhD, is Associate Provost for Academic Affairs and Professor of Criminology & Criminal Justice at Chaminade University of Honolulu. Her research interests include recidivism, community corrections, risk and need assessment instruments, and gender and crime. Her work has appeared in *Feminist Criminology, Critical Criminology, Women, Crime & Justice*, and *Federal Probation*. She is the author of the book *Female Offenders and Risk Assessment: Hidden in Plain Sight*. She has been active in applied research on Hawai'i's correctional system for the past 15 years, including work with the Department of Public Safety, Hawai'i Paroling Authority, Hawai'i State Judiciary (Adult Probation), and Girls Court Hawai'i.

Jonathan Doak PhD is Professor of Criminal Justice and Associate Dean for Research at Nottingham Law School, Nottingham Trent University. He completed his LLB and doctoral studies at Queen's University Belfast, and has previously taught at Durham University, the University of Sheffield and the University of Ulster. He has published widely on restorative justice and other non-adversarial justice mechanisms, the rights of victims and survivors, and evidential protections for vulnerable witnesses. He has considerable experience in working with law reform bodies and non-governmental organisations in seeking to improve the experiences of victims, offenders and witnesses who come into contact with the criminal justice system. Jonathan is Editor of the *International Journal of Evidence and Proof* and serves on the editorial boards of the *Journal of Criminal Law*, the *British Journal of Community Justice* and the *International Journal of Law, Crime and Justice*.

Michael Edwards is a senior lecturer in the Department of Law and Criminology at Sheffield Hallam University, joining in September 2015 as a visiting lecturer attached to the Helena Kennedy Centre for International Justice. In May 2016, he was appointed to a permanent position. Michael previously practiced criminal defence law in America for 22 years, overseeing the Eastern Judicial Circuit (Georgia) Public Defenders' Office for 11 years. He has managed several successful externally funded domestic and international research projects and has published several papers for peer-reviewed and professional journals.

Theo Gavrielides, PhD, is an international expert in restorative justice, human rights and youth justice. He is the Founder and Director of The IARS International Institute, a user-led NGO that empowers marginalised groups to influence social policy and law internationally. He is also the Founder and Director of the Restorative Justice for All Institute (RJ4All) as well as Adjunct Professor at the School of Criminology of Simon Fraser University and a visiting professor at Buckinghamshire New University. Professor Gavrielides is an expert advisor to the European Commission's criminal justice and equality projects, and has worked with many governments on justice reforms. He has worked as the Human Rights Advisor of the UK Ministry of Justice as well as researcher at the London School of Economics, and he is the Principal Investigator of numerous EU, UN and UK funded research programmes.

Dr. Gavrielides has published extensively in the areas of restorative justice, youth policy, human rights and criminal justice. He is the Editor of numerous collected editions as well as the Founder and Editor-in-Chief of the *Youth Voice Journal* and the *Internet Journal of Restorative Justice*. He is also the Editor of the *International Journal of Human Rights in Healthcare*.

Ali Gohar is the founder of Just Peace Initiatives, a non-profit working for peace and justice through conflict transformation practices. After receiving a Master's degree in International Relations from Quaid-i-Azam University, Islamabad, he was a Fulbright Scholar at Eastern Mennonite University in Harrisonburg, Virginia, USA. There, Gohar collaborated with Howard Zehr on *The little book of restorative justice* for the Pakistan-Afghan context and has also written a book and a number of articles on Jirga. Gohar has written four plays for television on honour killing, restorative justice, domestic violence and HIV/drug awareness, which have been used by the UN and civil society organisations in Pakistan and Afghanistan and are now on YouTube. He was Additional Commissioner, Social Welfare Cell for Afghan Refugees for 13 years at the UN Refugee Agency. Gohar has also worked with Oxfam UK to end honour killings and address violence against women, and has served as a training specialist and technical advisor to the Ministry of Social Affairs in Afghanistan.

Arthur Hartmann, PhD, is Professor of Criminal Law and Victimology at the University of Applied Sciences in Public Administration in Bremen since 2002 and director of the Institute for Police and Security Research since 2009. He is a doctor (habil.) in law and has a diploma in sociology.

From 1987 till 1989, he evaluated two model projects on victim-offender mediation funded by the Bavarian government. In 1992 he was one of the founders of the ongoing German Federal Statistics on Victim-Offender-Mediation and co-author of the bi-annual reports published by the German Ministry of Justice. From 2004 to 2006 he was a member of COST-Action

A21, 'Restorative Justice Developments in Europe'. He has been partner of several EU-funded projects, including 'Mediation and restorative justice in prison settings', 'Restorative Justice in Europe – Safeguarding Victims and Empowering Professionals', 'Horizontal Crime Prevention', 'Community Policing' and 'Reducing prison population: advanced tools of justice in Europe'. He was also responsible for national and local research projects regarding crime prevention, juvenile violence, the procedure and judgements in cases of rape and an evaluation of the introduction of a restricted area in the city of Bremerhaven. He is responsible for the EU-funded research project 'Victim Analysis and Safety Tool' (VAST), a research project regarding visiting rights of fathers in cases of family violence and a training course for the recently introduced 'Psycho-Social Process or Court Accompaniment' for victims.

Arthur Hartmann has published widely in the field of restorative justice. He contributes to a commentary on German criminal and criminal procedural law, and he is co-author of a German textbook on criminal procedure.

Anne Hayden, PhD, co-founded the Homicide Survivors Support Group (NZ) Inc. and is a member and network coordinator of the Te Oritenga Restorative Justice Group, the first contemporary restorative justice group in New Zealand. She wrote the Restorative Conferencing Manual of Aotearoa New Zealand (2000), and has published *A Restorative Approach to Family Violence: Changing Tack*. She is a member of the committee of the Breast Cancer Advocacy Coalition and holds a BA (double major in Ed and Psych), MA (Hons) in Ed and a PhD (Auckland University of Technology).

Gerry Johnstone, PhD, is Professor of Law at the University of Hull. He is the author of *Restorative Justice: Ideas, Values, Debates* (Routledge, 2011), co-editor (with Daniel Van Ness) of *Handbook of Restorative Justice* (Willan, 2007) and editor of *A Restorative Justice Reader* (Routledge, 2013). He is a member of the editorial board of *The International Journal of Restorative Justice*. He has recently completed a two-year action research project focussed on building bridges – between offenders and victims of crime, between the agencies that work with them and between researchers and practitioners of restorative justice – throughout Europe.

David R. Karp, PhD, is Professor of Sociology and Director of the Project on Restorative Justice at Skidmore College in Saratoga Springs, New York. His scholarship focuses on restorative justice in community and campus settings and on prison programs preparing inmates for return to the community. David has published more than 100 academic papers and six books, including *The Little Book of Restorative Justice for Colleges and Universities* (2013), *Wounds That Do Not Bind: Victim-Based Perspectives on the Death Penalty* (2006), and *The Community Justice Ideal* (1999). David received a BA in Peace and Conflict Studies from the University of California at Berkeley, and a PhD in Sociology from the University of Washington.

Anna Kawalek is a doctoral researcher and Associate Lecturer at Sheffield Hallam University. Before joining Sheffield Hallam, Anna completed her undergraduate degree in Philosophy at Newcastle University followed by a Graduate Diploma in Law at City University, London. She then worked in a number of law firms before returning to academia. Her PhD research is around Therapeutic Jurisprudence and Drug Courts, but she also has research interests around Restorative Justice, the Helena Kennedy Centre Refugee Clinic, and Desistance and Recovery, with several papers (in press) around these topics. Anna teaches across core modules "Criminological Landscapes" and "Criminal Justice" at Sheffield Hallam and is also in the process of completing a Master's in Social Science Research alongside her PhD.

Marian Liebmann, PhD, has worked at a day centre for ex-offenders, with victim support, and in the probation service. She was director of Mediation UK for four years and projects adviser for three years, working on restorative justice. She now works as a freelance restorative justice consultant and trainer in the UK and overseas. She has given presentations at meetings of the United Nations Congress on Crime Prevention and Criminal Justice. She also runs 'Art and Conflict' and 'Art and Anger Management' workshops. She is very involved in helping Bristol, UK, to become a restorative city. She has written/edited 12 books, including *Restorative Justice: How It Works*.

Wendy C.Y. Lui, BA, LLB, LLM, is a lecturer in Law at Department of Law and Business, Hong Kong Shue Yan University. She is currently a PhD candidate at the Department of Applied Social Sciences, City University of Hong Kong. Her areas of interest include mediation and arbitration, negotiation, alternative dispute resolution and restorative justice. Ms Lui is an Accredited Mediator of the Hong Kong Mediation Accreditation Association Limited.

Robert E. Mackay has been a social worker, youth justice policy officer, mediator, restorative practitioner and family dispute resolution practitioner. He also worked as an academic, teaching social work and researching in the field of restorative justice.

Rob has worked in restorative justice since 1985. He established the first victim-offender mediation program in Scotland. He served on the boards of several European and UK restorative justice bodies. He supported practice theoretically, especially through application of Neo-Aristotelian moral theory and Discourse Ethics. He developed the theory of Law as Peacemaking.

In Australia, Rob became a research affiliate at the University of Sydney's Centre for Peace and Conflict Studies. He advocated restorative approaches between churches and the survivors of institutional abuse. He gave evidence to the Australian State of Victoria's Parliamentary Inquiry on Child Sexual Abuse and Australia's Royal Commission into Institutional Child Sexual Abuse.

Giuseppe Maglione is a lecturer in criminology at Edinburgh Napier University and teaches restorative justice at the Strathclyde Law School. He received a PhD in legal theory from the University of Florence and carried out socio-legal research on restorative justice as Visiting Researcher at the universities of Durham, Cambridge and Oslo as well as at the Max Planck Institute in Freiburg and the International Institute for the Sociology of Law (IISL). His recent works have been published in *Criminology & Criminal Justice*, *Theoretical Criminology*, *Critical Criminology* and the *International Journal of Law, Crime and Justice*.

Anna Matczak, PhD, is a lecturer at Collegium Civitas, Warsaw. She holds a PhD from the Department of Sociology, LSE. She also holds Master's degrees in social policy (research) from the LSE and in social policy from the University of Warsaw. Her doctoral research discusses how lay people in Poland understand punishment and justice, and how these understandings can shed light on the viability of restorative justice in the Polish context. Prior to beginning her PhD, she was appointed as research associate at Kingston University & St George's University of London and Anglia Ruskin University, where she was involved in a number of research projects on domestic violence and family interventions. Alongside her doctoral studies, she worked as a qualified legal interpreter in the UK and co-operated with the Home Office, National Crime Agency, London Probation, Social Services, Magistrates and Crown Courts. Her main research interests are: restorative justice, sociology of punishment, lay opinions in criminology, court and police interpreting, penal policies and criminal justice systems in post-socialist countries. She tweets @MatczakAnia and runs a blog entitled: *Lost in Translation: Interpreting the Polish Penality* (www.annamatczak.com). She is currently in the process of preparing her thesis for publication.

Terry O'Connell is an Australian restorative justice pioneer, and a 30-year police veteran [NSW Police] known as the 'cop from Wagga Wagga'. Terry developed the 'restorative conference script' in 1991. He is the recently retired Australian Director for Real Justice, a sister organisation to the International Institute for Restorative Practices (IIRP) based in Bethlehem (PA). A strong advocate for explicit restorative practice, Terry strongly believes that restorative justice/practice provides a 'relational foundation' for everything we do, in our personal and professional lives. Terry was awarded the Order of Australia Medal in 2000. He is a Churchill and Paul Harris (Rotary) Fellow and was a finalist in the NSW Senior Australian of the Year (2016). He was the 2018 Australia Day Ambassador for Wellington (NSW). He has a BA in social welfare and an Honorary Doctorate from Australian Catholic University (2008).

David O'Mahony PhD is Professor of Law at the University of Essex Law School and the university's Human Rights Centre. His research focuses on the meaning of 'justice' in the context of criminal justice systems, with particular sensitivity to the rights of young people and the use of restorative justice and alternative ways of responding to crime. David's work, together with Jonathan Doak (Nottingham Law School), has informed the development of a distinctive critical theory of restorative justice and its application in criminal justice systems. His most recent book is *Reimagining Restorative Justice: Agency and Accountability in the Criminal Process*, Hart Publishing, Bloomsbury, 2017.

George Pavlich PhD holds a Canada Research Chair in Social Theory, Culture and Law and is Professor of Law and Sociology at the University of Alberta. His books include *Justice Fragmented: Mediating Community Disputes under Postmodern Conditions, Critique and Radical Discourses on Crime, Governing Paradoxes of Restorative Justice, Law and Society Redefined* and *Criminal Accusation: Political Rationales and Socio-legal Practice*. He is a co-editor of *Sociology for the Asking*; *Questioning Sociology* (three editions); *After Sovereignty; Governance and Regulation in Social Life; Rethinking Law, Society, and Governance: Foucault's Bequest* and *Accusing Criminals*. He is currently working on a research project outlining a theory of criminal accusation, referring to late nineteenth-century entryways to criminal justice in western Canada.

Ellie Piggott is a doctoral candidate in the School of Criminology and Criminal Justice at Griffith University in Queensland, Australia. In 2013, she graduated with a Bachelor of Psychology (Honours) from the University of South Australia. She was awarded First Class Honours for her thesis examining the psycho-social benefits and effectiveness of police diversion in reducing reoffending by young offenders. The aim of her doctoral research is to examine how and for whom restorative justice conferencing works in reducing recidivism.

Isabel Ximena González Ramírez PhD is a lawyer and mediator of the Pontificia Universidad Católica de Chile, and holds a Master of Criminal Law and Doctorate in Criminal Law from the University of Buenos Aires. She is a teacher of pre- and post-degrees in criminal law, restorative justice and mediation. She has been a director of research projects with publications in restorative justice, for the international organizations Defensoría and Universidad Central. From the Ministry of Justice, she directed the first network of criminal mediation in Chile, and she was director of the Center for Mediation, Negotiation and Arbitration and of the

Master's programme in Mediation, Restorative Justice and Arbitration of the Central University of Chile.

Dan Reisel PhD is an NIHR Clinical Academic Fellow at University College London (UCL). His research is focussed on understanding what leads to clinical safety incidents and how healthcare staff can be best supported to minimise and learn from the clinical errors that occur. He is passionate about personalised, person-centred medicine, and believes that the introduction of restorative practice could transform the way the NHS learns from mistakes.

Megan Schachter graduated from Skidmore College in May 2017 with a BA in Political Science and a minor in Anthropology. She currently works for New York State Governor Andrew Cuomo as a Special Assistant for Briefing.

Ann Skelton PhD has worked as a children's rights lawyer in South Africa for over 25 years. She played a leading role in child law reform through her involvement with the committees of the South African Law Reform Commission that drafted the Child Justice Act and the Children's Act. Her doctorate, obtained in 2005, focused on restorative justice. Ann is Director of the Centre for Child Law and a Professor in the faculty of law at the University of Pretoria. She is an internationally recognised researcher and has published widely in child law and restorative justice. In 2012 she received the Honourary Worlds' Children's Prize. In December 2016 she was awarded the Juvenile Justice Without Borders award presented by the International Observatory on Juvenile Justice. Ann is currently a member of the UN Committee on the Rights of the Child; her term of office started in 2017.

Carl Stauffer, PhD, is Associate Professor of Justice Studies at Eastern Mennonite University. Prior to coming to academia, Stauffer worked as a community activist, organizer and practitioner in restorative justice, transitional justice, peacebuilding and post-war reconstruction in both domestic and international contexts. Stauffer's academic research concentrates on the critique of transitional justice from a restorative frame and the application of hybrid, often parallel indigenous community justice systems. His work has taken him to over 35 countries in Africa, the Middle East, Europe, and Asia. He earned his PhD from the University of Kwa-Zulu Natal in South Africa.

Juan Marcellus Tauri is a member of the Ngati Porou iwi (tribe) of the North Island of New Zealand. He is also a critical criminologist and political activist and currently teaches criminology at the University of Wollongong, Australia. Juan has researched and published on a range of issues, including the settler colonial states response to Indigenous people's critique of crime control, Indigenous responses to social harm, the contradictions of institutional research ethics review processes and critical analysis of the restorative justice industry's utilisation of Indigenous philosophies and cultural practices. Juan recently co-edited a special issue of the *African Journal of Criminology and Justice Studies* on 'Indigenous Perspectives and Counter Colonial Criminology', and with Professor Chris Cunneen, in 2016 published the book *Indigenous Criminology*.

Karen J. Terry, PhD, is Professor in the Department Criminal Justice at John Jay College of Criminal Justice in New York. She holds a doctorate in criminology from Cambridge University. Her primary research interest is sexual offending and victimization, particularly abuse of children in an institutional setting. Most significantly, she was the principal investigator for two studies on sexual abuse of minors by Catholic priests in the United States.

Barb Toews, PhD, is Assistant Professor in criminal justice at the University of Washington Tacoma. She received her doctorate from Bryn Mawr College's Graduate School of Social Work and Social Research. Her research focuses on the relationships among criminal/restorative justice, architecture and environmental design, and psycho-social-behavioral-judicial outcomes for victims, offenders and justice professionals. She has taught restorative justice and design courses inside correctional facilities and co-founded Designing Justice+Designing Spaces (DJ+DS), an initiative that engages incarcerated individuals in the design of justice spaces that promote accountability as well as victim and offender healing. Barb has numerous publications related to restorative justice, including its relationship to design. Prior to joining the academy, she held leadership positions in criminal/restorative justice non-profit organizations.

Johonna Turner, PhD., is Assistant Professor of Restorative Justice and Peacebuilding at Eastern Mennonite University. For over 15 years, she has worked as part of arts collectives, community organizing coalitions and other social movement organizations in the United States to develop youth leadership and cultivate transformational approaches to safety and justice. Her areas of scholarship and teaching include restorative and transformative justice, youth leadership development and organizing, faith-rooted peacebuilding and critical race feminism. Johonna earned her PhD in American Studies and Graduate Certificate in Women's Studies from the University of Maryland, and a Graduate Certificate in Urban Youth Ministry from Fuller Theological Seminary.

Ted Wachtel is the former president and founder of the International Institute for Restorative Practices (IIRP) Graduate School and co-founder of CSF Buxmont schools and group homes for delinquent and at-risk youth. His books include *Toughlove*, for parents of troubled adolescents, *Real Justice* and *The Restorative Practices Handbook*. He is currently founding editor at *BuildingANewReality.com*.

Lorenn Walker, JD, MPH, is a health educator and restorative lawyer. She directs Hawai'i Friends of Restorative Justice, which collaborates with individuals and organizations locally, nationally and internationally, including prisons, courts, schools, law enforcement and non-profits/NGOs to develop, implement and study public health, restorative justice and solution-focused approaches for peace building and addressing trauma. She's the principal researcher of several cited pilot projects, is a lecturer for the University of Hawai'i, has trained thousands on conflict management and communication skills, is a Senior Fulbright Specialist, author of numerous publications, award recipient and speaker at national and international conferences.

Carolyn Boyes-Watson PhD is Professor of Sociology at Suffolk University (Boston, MA) and founding director of the Center for Restorative Justice (CRJ) at Suffolk. Since 1997, the CRJ has fostered community partnerships to implement restorative justice practice. Boyes-Watson holds a PhD from Harvard University and has published numerous articles and books on restorative justice, juvenile justice and the criminal justice system. Her most relevant publications include *Peacemaking Circles and Urban Youth* (2008); *Heart of Hope: A Guide for Using Peacemaking Circles to Develop Emotional Literacy, Promote Healing and Build Healthy Relationships* (2010) and *Circle Forward: Building a Restorative School* (2015), with Kay Pranis.

Dennis S.W. Wong, PhD, is Professor of Criminology at Department of Applied Social Sciences, and Associate Dean of College of Liberal Arts and Social Sciences, City University of Hong Kong. His areas of expertise include juvenile delinquency, bullying studies and restorative justice. Dennis Wong is honorary consultant on youth drugs abuse, school bullying and offenders' rehabilitation for governmental organizations. He is a member of the Executive Board of Asian Criminological Society and Convenor of Asia Pacific Forum of Restorative Justice.

William Wood PhD is a senior lecturer in the School of Criminology and Criminal Justice at Griffith University in Queensland, Australia, and a member of the Griffith Criminology Institute. William holds a PhD in sociology from Boston College. His research focused on restorative justice, youth justice and corrections, and he has published extensively in these areas. He is currently completing a manuscript for Routledge entitled *Race, Crime and Restorative Justice*.

Martin Wright, PhD, is a senior research fellow at the Faculty of Health and Life Sciences, De Montfort University, Leicester. He has been director of the Howard League for Penal Reform, policy officer for Victim Support and a founding member of the Restorative Justice Council and the European Forum for Restorative Justice. He has been a volunteer mediator with two local mediation services in London. His publication include *Making good: prisons, punishment and beyond* and *Restoring respect for justice*, and he is joint editor of *Mediation and criminal justice* and *Civilising criminal justice*.

Preface and acknowledgements

Theo Gavrielides

Handbook's impetus

Public trust in governments and their institutions has been declining globally. This preface is not the grounds for presenting the reasons for this decline, which have been observed and studied by many over the last few decades (e.g. Garland, 1996; Zedner, 2002). As part of our governments' machinery, criminal justice institutions are not exempted from public scrutiny. Courts, the police, probation, prosecution and all related justice services do not exist in a vacuum either. They are developed and function within the societies that they are meant to serve. If they are structured within disempowering governments and democracies, then their users' experience will be one of disappointment.

This decline in trust is also very much linked with users' perceptions and experiences of equality (or inequality). And we do not need scientific evidence to conclude that the criminal justice system has flaws. We have been experiencing these flaws for many decades through its performance, overt or hidden biases, costs and the absence of a feeling of safety that is meant to be felt by everyone, independently of their background (Gavrielides, 2014). Although the majority of the public do not engage in readings about facts and figures on wealth distribution, their living reality is what drives their fear and anxiety about justice and its current system of delivery. This unavoidable truth gradually leads to disengagement and apathy.

But if we do look at published figures, they will tell us that despite the latest economic downturn, the powerful became more powerful, and the powerless increased in numbers. For example, the 2017 Global Wealth Report showed that the wealth of the richest increased from 42.5% at the height of the 2008 financial crisis to 50.1% in 2017. On the other hand, the poor became poorer, with the world's 3.5 billion poorest adults having assets of less than $10,000. Collectively these people, who account for 70% of the world's working-age population, own just 2.7% of global wealth. Shockingly, the globe's richest 1% owns over 50% of the world's wealth.[1]

Concurrently with the decline in public trust and justice performance globally, there has been a rise of community voice and action (Gavrielides and Blake, 2013; Rosenblatt, 2015). In a globalised world where the internet, social media and borderless continents define how we

---

1 The report (eighth edition) is published by the Credit Suisse Research Institute, and it analyses wealth held by 4.8 billion adults across the globe, from the least affluent to the wealthiest individuals, www.credit-suisse.com/corporate/en/research/research-institute/global-wealth-report.html (accessed November 2017).

send and receive information, the notion of community had to redefine itself. It is no longer a place – it is a sense of belonging.

But alas, the modern notion of community lacks the resources to challenge the powerful and the *status quo*. Nevertheless, community leaders, voluntary organisations, campaigners and human rights champions take on active unpaid roles that have now allowed us to talk about informal or community justice. UNDP, UNICEF and UN Women (2012) estimated that in the majority of UN member states, 70% of all disputes are dealt with through informal justice. Indeed, the notion of community now dares to claim ownership, or at least demands joint custody, of justice and criminal justice (Gavrielides, 2013, Wojkowska, 2006). Community voice has been getting louder, and now the powerful have no other option, but to listen.

It is within this transitional global and political framework that I enthusiastically agreed to edit this international Handbook. I hope that it will become part of the aforementioned listening process.

Handbook's structure

Of course, my claim that communities are rising while the powerful are being challenged should not come as a surprise to the reader of this Handbook, given that restorative justice is at its core. There can be no doubt that 'restorative justice' is a contested term with a contested history. This is not surprising, as it emerged within a context of social reform movements and global questioning of extant justice paradigms. Restorative justice also professes to embody the bio-power of community and individual action. This is probably what makes restorative justice timely and appealing to the modern reformists, researchers, students and policy makers.

But for all its goods and promises, restorative justice has flaws like any other human construct. Yes, some may believe that restorative justice is spirited and guided by God, driven by values that are Christian, Buddhist, Muslim, Judaic and so on. Nonetheless, it is a construct. Therefore, the human nature of restorative justice raises the question whether its flaws are as bad as those of the existing criminal justice system. And maybe this question is not as straightforward as it first appears. For example, which elements of restorative justice are not as bad as those of the criminal justice system? Do these relate to certain types of normative claims? Do they relate to practice and certain types of cases or offenders? Are they equally effective globally? Do they relate to finances and charging the public purse less, while achieving better victim satisfaction and recidivism rates?

How can one Handbook answer all these questions? At the same time, I was faced with the challenge of an impressive literature on the topic. Entering online the search terms 'restorative justice' will deliver thousands of results, including research and conference papers, authored and edited books, academic journals, speeches, laws, policy papers, treaties, EU Directives and Recommendations, statutory guidelines, UN Resolutions and Principles, training manuals, press cuttings, videos and even songs, films, pantos and plays. Put another way, what are the normative and empirical questions that remain unanswered and are worthy of investigation by an '*International Handbook on Restorative Justice*'?

Despite my initial hesitation, I proceeded with confidence, knowing that I am in good company. Following discussions with many expert friends (some of whom ended up writing for this Handbook), I divided the volume into four parts that represent the steps I believe we need to take to advance restorative justice internationally.

The first part aims to aid our understanding of the restorative justice normative claims and theories. I have argued many times that this area of work has remained underdeveloped, especially in relation to its philosophical and meta-theoretical questions (Gavrielides, 2005;

Gavrielides and Artinopoulou, 2013). But the advancement of theory alone is insufficient, and thus I proceeded in the second part with a dedicated section on practice bringing to light new evidence. While doing so, I was conscious that the implementation areas of restorative justice are vast. Therefore, I proceeded with caution, focusing only on contested, under-researched and grey areas of practice. Particular attention was given to complex cases such as intimate partner violence and child sexual abuse, where power dynamics are prominent. The Handbook also sheds light on new practice areas such as those with victims and offenders with disabilities as well as the application of restorative practices in healthcare settings and road rage disputes.

But a handbook such as this one would be incomplete without a serious debate that is both critical and up to date. I have always believed that thinking critically about restorative justice not only allows a more balanced and nuanced approach to its theoretical and practical claims, but can also push us to want and ask for more. I was fortunate to work with some well-informed and well-intended critics of restorative justice. In the third part of the Handbook, they present their critical reflections on the claims and potential of restorative justice in an evidence-based and objective manner. I also felt that for an 'international handbook', these critical views had to be spread geographically as much as possible.

Finally, in the fourth part, the empirical, normative and critical contributions of the Handbook are concluded with an articulation of the visions of some of the field's pioneers. I saw these visions of restorative justice as both realistic and aspirational.

Concluding introductory thoughts

This preface aims to invite you onto a journey of questioning, evidence gathering and debate. This journey is timely and much needed, independently of where you are. There can be no doubt (at least in my head) that the shrinking of centralised, top-down, formal structures of justice and the rise of community, bottom-up, informal alternatives is happening now. I will use this Handbook to urge all those who support, or are part of, the *status quo* not to see this shift as a threat. At the same time, I call on all reformists and hopefuls not to treat it as an opportunity to abolish what is and what many have fought for. We must embrace this different Zeitgeist that we are experiencing as a positive shift of our world's justice tectonic plates. Communities want more, and justice's needs and realities are adapting to the fast-moving societal changes of globalisation and new technology.

The experts who wrote for this Handbook aspired to support this global change by presenting new theoretical, empirical and critical works on restorative justice, a concept that has troubled me for almost two decades.

Acknowledgements and personal statement

The editing of this Handbook came at a turning point in my life. I have always wanted to be a dad, even before I even knew what I was going to do with my life and passion for learning, reading, writing and justice. After recognizing that wish, I encountered many wonderful people and had many enlightening experiences that led me down various paths and on several journeys that filled me with joy, sadness and a lot of learning. But my wish to parent never changed, and thus, over the last few years I took a different journey that finally led me to becoming Tommy's dad.

When I gladly accepted Routledge's invitation to edit the *International Handbook on Restorative Justice* three years ago, little did I know how daily life changes once a child is at home. As a single dad with no immediate family around me, the experience is a lot more intense, but the joys and the bond are also stronger and deeper. A relationship between a parent and a child is also a profound, self-learning experience; there is only so much that books can teach you. It is also a relationship that helped me reevaluate my position on restorative justice, which as you will see in this Handbook had been questioned many times in the past. But this time, my shift was not due to intellectual factors, stemming from my narrow legal training and the notion's practical abilities (or inabilities) to materialise its many normative promises.

My new parent role in life created a new intellectual relationship with restorative justice, which, while on the one hand became stronger, on the other, developed to be less intense. It is stronger, because I can now understand better the relational core of restorative justice, and how it can become the driver of both our deviance and restoration. Our human connection, or dis-connection, can bring out the best and worst in us, while society, or the community, try to find their role as regulators or witnesses of our conflicts. As a criminologist, this statement reads rather generic and repetitive of more focused and nuanced approaches to delinquency and control. But as a parent, I read it with hope. If restorative justice can tap into our best and worst selves through self-imposed processes of pain and reconstruction, then there must be hope for our betterment as human beings, as parents, as schoolteachers, as employers and yes, as servants of justice and crimi-nal justice. But I also said that my parenting experience made my relationship with restorative justice less intense, and by this, I mean scaling down the many roles that I have taken as a director, researcher, academic, charity fundraiser project manager, lawyer, author, editor and so on.

It has been a rewarding and intense life journey, and it is by no coincidence that this vol-ume's companions have honoured me with their trust and work. But like Zehr, I must now change my lenses and with them how I view my remaining life path. And I see my contribution to be less ambitious in terms of narrow, legalistic understandings of justice and more hopeful in understanding the core of fairness as this is ingrained in everyone's hearts and minds.

And by definition, journeys should never be walked alone. Therefore, it is fitting for this Handbook's journey to first acknowledge the authors who entrusted me with their work. Conducting new research and creating new paths for theory and practice is a complex task that requires much resources and investment. Having it scrutinised, edited and published in a Handbook such as this one assumes a good and open relationship with the editor, and I could not be more thankful for the prompt and constructive responses that I received from everyone.

Humble and special thanks go to Howard Zehr and John Braithwaite for always supporting me, including writing for this Handbook. It is a great honour to be introduced by Howard, whose vision for restorative justice changed the lenses we use to view justice and life. His writ-ings have inspired me and indeed our generation to ask and want for more, and to never stop questioning ourselves. John's scholarly rigour and excellence have also been my guiding writing principles, setting the standard that anyone who writes and learns about restorative justice and justice will want to achieve. Both have been generous with their time during busy and difficult times, and for that I can only be grateful and honoured.

I am also grateful to all those who have challenged me in both good and bad ways. We all go through various cycles in our life paths, and my recent changes have seen many keen friends with-drawing and new coming forth. To all those whose requirements I cannot fulfil in my new role any-more, I wish all the best and send them my gratitude for what they have taught me. To those who have remained keen champions of my beliefs, and patient with my demands and mistakes, I give my love. These include my mother, sister and her family, my publisher and Alison Kirk, my charity, The IARS International Institute, the volunteers at the Restorative Justice for All Institute, and, of course, Juozas Kelecius. I am also grateful to Jemima Hoffman for spending endless hours volun-tarily preparing the Index for this Handbook as well as for proof reading several chapters. To the new friends that joined my path, I give the promise that I will not let them down, and this includes Mag-gie Scott, who stood by me through some of the most difficult and lonely times of my life.

It is now fitting to close my personal statement by thanking my son, Tom, for inspiring me to continue writing about justice and rights and indeed for helping me to renew my pledge for staying on course. As I dedicated my last work to my late father, I think it is also now fitting to dedicate this one to my son in the hope that I will also inspire him as much as my father inspired me.

In perfect sync – Against all possibilities
Photograph © Maggie Scott

References

Garland, D. 1996. The Limits of the Sovereign State: Strategies of Crime Control in Contemporary Society, *The British Journal of Criminology*, 36(4): 445–471.

Gavrielides, T. 2005. Some Meta-Theoretical Questions for Restorative Justice, *Ratio Juris*, 18(1): 84–106.

Gavrielides, T. 2013. Restorative Pain: A New Vision of Punishment. In T. Gavrielides and V. Artinopoulou (eds.) *Reconstructing Restorative Justice Philosophy*. Farnham: Ashgate, pp. 311–337.

Gavrielides, T. 2014. Bringing Race Relations Into the Restorative Justice Debate, *Journal of Black Studies* 45(3): 216–246.

Gavrielides, T. and Artinopoulou, V. 2013. *Reconstructing Restorative Justice Philosophy*. Farnham: Ashgate.

Gavrielides, T. and Blake, S. 2013. *Race in Probation: Improving Outcomes for Black and Minority Ethnic Users of Probation Services*. London: IARS Publications.

Rosenblatt, F. 2015. *The Role of Community in Restorative Justice*. London: Routledge.

UNDP, UNICEF and UN Women. 2012. *Informal Justice Systems: Charting a Course for Human-Rights Based Engagement*. New York: UNICEF.

Wojkowska, E. 2006. *How Informal Justice Systems can Contribute*. Oslo: United Nations Development Programme.

Zedner, L. 2002. Dangers of Dystopias in Penal Theory, *Oxford Journal of Legal Studies*, 22(2): 577–608.

Foreword

Howard Zehr

This is an important collection for anyone who wants to understand and grapple with 21st-century restorative justice.

In the past four decades, restorative justice has developed into a rich field of practice and study. Some would call it a movement, some a social movement. Either way, there is a growing consensus that it is into its second generation.

This international Handbook grounds itself in the present and past in order to look to the future. It sets for itself an important but challenging goal: to reflect the state of restorative justice in the early 21st century, including not only developments in theory and practice but also its essential debates and challenges.

The concept of restorative justice is so simple, so intuitive – yet, as this collection makes clear – so complex in development and application. It is not only that academics like to complexify things (though they do that sometimes unnecessarily); the issues really are difficult and complex – and so important. Indeed, the integrity of the field and its vision is at stake.

The Western idea and implementation of restorative justice developed initially as a response to problems within the Western legal system, sometimes called the criminal justice system, and by some, the criminal legal system. Working in response to or in conjunction with such a rigid, hierarchical, power- and status-quo oriented system (or non-system, as some have argued), with its inherent self-interests, presents many problems, some of which were acknowledged by early advocates. However, as the theory and practice expanded both within and beyond this arena, whole new layers of challenges and pitfalls emerged.

This Handbook wrestles with many of these developments from a perspective that is both wide and deep: it is international – it reflects the widening circles of application that include areas as disparate as health care, architecture, historical harm, social justice, the nature of democracy – and it digs deeply into the difficulties and dangers inherent in all of these. The writers included here do not answer all the questions that are raised; indeed, there are contradictory voices, as there should be. But they do take the discussion to a new level.

The contributors to this Handbook offer us both hopeful possibilities and worrisome challenges. It will not be an easy read for many restorative justice advocates – not just because of the sometimes-academic language but because the challenges raised are so difficult and fundamental. But as I have often advised, we must listen to – even anticipate – our critics or we will not simply miss opportunities: we may become what we are seeking to reform or replace.

Colorado legislator Pete Lee has been instrumental in introducing restorative justice into law in his state. At a conference some years ago, he claimed that he once said to his wife, Lynn, something like this: "In your wildest dreams, would you ever have imagined that this field would develop like this, and that I would be part of it?" "Honey," she responded, "you aren't even in my wildest dreams!"

Whether apocryphal or not, the story captures something important about the early days of restorative justice: most of us in our wildest dreams would not have imagined it would be what it is today. Now, in its second generation, restorative justice is not a wild dream: it is a reality, and I for one am energized by the new and younger voices that are emerging.

It is important to open space for these new voices and emerging themes. As a first-generation developer and practitioner, now at the end of my career, it seems appropriate that this may be the last book foreword I write for the field. It is time to make room for others of this new generation. Much appreciation goes to Theo Gavrielides, himself a representative of this new generation, for leading the way through this Handbook.

The future of restorative justice

John Braithwaite

A great thing about the rule of law is that we have a universal right to access it, or at least we should. Whether we have been a victim of crime, of an oppressive marriage, of breach of contract or consumer deception, we have a right of access to a court of law to adjudicate that conflict. Historical research on crime and justice, the tradition in which Howard Zehr started as a young scholar, has accumulated helpfully. It has taught us the importance of the rule of law innovations that diffused from the Persian and Roman Empires and beyond. As rights of access to adjudication in courtrooms diffused, blood feuds decreased. It was no longer necessary to deal with serious disputes by confronting our adversary and by carrying a weapon in case the confrontation turned nasty.

This is one reason why European societies are so dramatically less violent than they were half a millennium ago. The rule of law also brought a rights revolution that does not solve all problems but does provide some important tests against which all forms of justice must be measured, as Ann Skelton explores in Chapter 3.

Yet during the centuries when courts of law were near universally absent, diverse informal modalities of justice were more universally present to help make up for this deficiency. Carolyn Boyes-Watson evocatively explores more recent recovery of this history in Chapter 1, as does Ali Gohar in the specific context of Pakistan in Chapter 5. Historical experience has taught us that more universal access both to the rule of law and to disparate types of informal justice (including restorative justice) is likely to be a path to justice and nonviolence. By empowering victims to be able to choose either of these options in a variety of forms, we minimize the likelihood that they will turn to redress by violence against their perpetrator, as the recent evidence on victims indicates (Arthur Hartmann in Chapter 9 and Theo Gavrielides in Chapter 8).

The sad thing about the history of the rise of the rule of law is that it created a wealthy new professional class with a class interest in strengthening the monopoly of the rule of law. Old restorative traditions were construed as barbaric or out of tune. These claims for the attuned modernity of the rule of law were sometimes uttered by men wearing aristocratic black gowns or wigs who insisted on being addressed as 'your honour' or 'your worship'. They asserted authority by thumping a hammer or imploring subjects to swear oaths on bibles or other ancient religious texts. The legal profession became adept at co-opting symbols of aristocratic power and god-like power, as it extracted rents to secure the interests of its professional class.

The poor could not afford their justice. Worse than that, the poor were profoundly oppressed by the criminal justice system in every country. When the legal profession could not fight off competition from more accessible informal justice practices, it reappropriated them as expensive and professionalized mediation services. Large fees had to be paid to accredited mediation professionals to learn the craft. Carl Stauffer and Johona Turner touch upon these dilemmas in Chapter 29 and Isabel Ramirez does so in Chapter 21. Juan Tauri at the same time reminds us in Chapter 23 of pathologies that can arise from marketized models of restorative justice seeking a kind of duopolistic relationship with the state. One of the pathologies at risk is pushing aside genuinely indigenous forms of justice.

So civil society must take back some measure of justice from markets and from sovereigns. It must eke out niches for non-sovereign justice, as Guiseppe Maglione expresses it in Chapter 2. We should want our children to learn at school how to resolve disputes with each other. We should want them to do that without overly quick recourse to the sovereignty of the school principal, the youth court judge or a restorative justice professional, for that matter. I believe that there is a democratic principle at issue here. In Chapter 27, Ted Wachtel discusses this principle and other democratic practices using his experience from the schools where he pioneered restorative justice with inspiring teams of restorative pathbreakers.

This book is perhaps the most comprehensive and certainly the most up-to-date collection on restorative justice. It goes to some topics rarely addressed in earlier volumes, such as restorative justice and disability support (Jane Bolitho, Chapter 11), child sexual abuse (Karen Terry, Chapter 10), intimate partner violence (Anne Hayden, Chapter 13), health (Dan Reisel and Janine Carroll, Chapter 15) and road rage (Marian Liebmann, Chapter 16). It embraces a wider range of critiques of restorative justice than most volumes on the subject, including from some of the most distinguished and thoughtful critics of restorative justice – Gerry Johnstone (Chapter 26), George Pavlich (Chapter 30), Juan Tauri (Chapter 23) and Annalise Acorn (Chapter 25).

Furthermore, in its geographical coverage, this international Handbook is much broader than older collections. It considers restorative practices as they exist beyond Western, predominantly English-speaking, societies. The social movement for restorative justice has been good in the past at forgetting that most of the world's population lives in Asia, discussed by Wong and Lui in Chapter 20 and Gohar in Chapter 5. Africa (Skelton, Chapter 3) and Latin America (Ramirez, Chapter 21) are also hugely important for accomplishing a more just future for the world. There is great learning in this book from the diversity and from the good and bad of restorative justice across this complicated planet of ours. The application of restorative justice in Eastern Europe is another example (Matczak – Chapter 22).

It is not possible to do justice to the diversity of the 31 fine chapters in this Handbook. So I have settled for a taste of just these few themes. Theo Gavrielides admirably integrates them all in his Epilogue, in which he reminds us that restorative justice is ultimately about expanding freedom. This implies a restorative justice implemented with care and responsibility, his way of capturing the spirit of this pathbreaking Handbook. We are grateful to Theo for bringing so many voices into the conversation. Many inspiring restorative justice leaders in the past have mobilized convening power toward projects of listening, but none more widely nor in more diverse ways than Theo Gavrielides in recent years.

One great thing about the complex of lenses across this Handbook is that they show that there are many different versions of restorative justice, as Howard Zehr also points out in his Foreword. The strengths and weaknesses of these versions depend on the contexts in which they are deployed. This in turn shows the silliness of those who frame the problem with restorative justice as one of restorative justice being seen as a solution to all problems. Well, of course, it is a good thing for access to restorative justice to be universally available for the whole range of harms from petty insults right up to genocide.

Being universally available is not the same as being universally chosen. The reasons for the struggle to universalize access to restorative justice are not so different from the reasons that the justice of the courts should be available for all manner of harms from insults up to planetary destruction. Citizens desperately need more universal access to more paths to resolution of problems that oppress them. These must be genuine ways of access rather than fictions of access to justice. In particular, citizens need access to paths that involve formal procedural guarantees and other paths that better protect rights while allowing more flexibility, informality, empowerment and creativity of response. In the great historical struggle to give citizens more options to reject or embrace, a comparative strength of restorative justice is that it is so open to variegated design, even to design by the most marginalized of societal minorities, in ways that are responsive to citizen needs. The project of exploring that design experimentalism to advance human freedom is what is so splendidly advanced by the contributors to this Handbook.

Part I
Restorative justice theory
The next steps

1

Looking at the past of restorative justice

Normative reflections on its future

Carolyn Boyes-Watson

Introduction

A few years ago, I attended a five-day gathering at the Zehr Institute along with 40 or so colleagues to reflect on the future of the restorative justice movement. As a group, we created a timeline of key events ranging from the first victim-offender reconciliation meeting in 1974 to the 1994 Truth and Reconciliation Commission, to the "beginning of time" when humans needed to reconcile themselves with one other in community in a good way. At the time I wondered: were we all talking about the same movement?

Restorative justice is a *contested* concept (Johnson and Van Ness, 2007) with a contested history precisely because it has served as an aspirational paradigm for a variety of different activist movements. For those seeking to create change, restorative justice is the alternative future to a particular aspect of the current reality. The restorative justice movement is far from a unitary movement: it is both a paradigmatic foundation and a banner that different sets of reformers have adopted to frame their agenda in creating social change within a particular context. This can lead to "a blind man and the elephant" problem: depending on which part of the movement you touch – the shape and feel can vary widely.

This chapter makes no attempt to write a history of the global restorative justice movement – that is a massive project chronicling complex developments within different cultural, legal and national contexts. Nor am I able to acknowledge the full roster of activists and scholars who have made substantial contribution to the movement. What I attempt to do for this Handbook is to lay out the basic contours of the restorative justice movement that has emerged within the Western advanced democracies in the late 20th century. The snapshot in this first chapter is developed from my vantage point – as a North American white female sociologist shaped by how, why and for what reasons I became involved in the restorative justice movement. My hope is that this conceptual map will provoke readers to assess the movement from their perspective.

Although some would date the restorative justice movement emerging in the 1970s with victim-offender mediation, I see the start of the modern movement in the 1990s when the term restorative justice came into more widespread use, fuelled by the publication of Howard Zehr's *Changing Lenses* (1990). I identify four relatively independent arenas of activism that have contributed to the modern restorative justice movement. The largest and most influential is a set of justice reform movements targeting the criminal legal system; the second arena is focused on the management of youth behaviour targeting reforms in child welfare, social services, schools and juvenile justice systems; the third arena consists of movements to reinvent post-conflict processes and build conditions for democratic governance and peace; and the final arena contains movements to assert indigenous cultural and political autonomy from colonization and to regenerate these practices within the contemporary context. These arenas develop independently of one another. Although they arose with distinct agendas, they each contributed to the understanding and development of restorative justice theory and practice.

The questions I explore here are: What concerns are motivating activists within this arena? Who are the activists? What are the central ideas and practices promoted by the movement? What are people are trying to change? Where are they concentrating their efforts? Has there been notable achievement or success in creating the desired change? The question of "success" is related to the question of co-optation of the desired changes by the system or structure of power activists are trying to change. The problem of co-optation is a persistent theme within criminal justice reform. As an activist who is also a sociologist, I am mindful that the attempt to build one kind of future can lay the foundation for something else altogether (Boyes-Watson, 1999, 2004).

The final section of the chapter discusses how elements within each of these arenas are influencing current dynamics within the restorative justice movement. Each arena highlights different priorities with the need to engage with a different set of social actors with a distinct agenda. While there are hard truths to be faced about the achievements of the movement thus far, I find reason to be hopeful about the future direction of the movement. This has a great deal to do with the confluence of different agendas in the contemporary landscape – at least in North America – that are reshaping the goals, strategies and practices of the movement in important ways.

The four arenas

Reforming the state justice system

The dominant agenda contributing to the development of the modern restorative justice movement has been reform of the Western legal system. Within this broad stream are several inter-twined reform movements that have contributed to the idea of restorative justice: the "informal justice" movement or Alternative Dispute Resolution (ADR); alternatives to incarceration movement – which includes diversion, community corrections and the restitution movement; and the victims' rights movement (Van Ness and Strong, 1997). The activists here are professionals in the system – legal scholars and criminologists from the academy – and criminal justice professionals working with offenders; advocates from religious communities and victims. In this context, restorative justice is focused on reform of the legal system.

ADR developed in the US in the late 1970s as a means to address a range of concerns from the conservative fear of a "litigation crisis" arising from the threat of overcrowded dockets to the leftist radical critique of the state-centred court (Abel, 1982; Olson and Dzur, 2004). ADR became incorporated into mainstream legal practice and education (McManus and Silverstein, 2011) while the use of mediation in criminal matters remained comparatively underdeveloped until the emergence of the restorative justice movement in the 1990s (Go, 2010).

Critical left theorists rejected liberal procedural justice as substantively unjust and looked to legal anthropologists for alterative systems of dispute resolution outside the formalized Western context. In this context, a 1977 article by criminologist Nils Christie foreshadowed many of the fundamental aspirations of the later restorative justice movement (Christie, 1977). One shared priority between the later restorative justice movement and the leftist scholars of the informal justice movement is the desire to rebalance the relationship between the community and the state as agents of social control (Van Ness and Strong, 1997).

The early development of victim-offender mediation came from activists seeking alternatives to incarceration for offenders (Galaway and Hudson, 1972; Liebmann, 2007). Steven Schafer (1968) in the 1960s linked restitution with restoring victims to the central place within the justice process. Among these was Albert Eglash (1977), who first coined the English phrase "restorative justice," urging the benefits of "creative restitution," in which payment is directly linked to the harm, with positive outcomes for both offender and victim.

According to Mark Umbreit (1985), what distinguished the Victim-Offender Reconciliation programmes that emerged in the late 1970s from correctional restitution programmes was the emphasis on the emotional exchange between the victim and offender. By engaging in an emotional dialogue about the feelings and impact of the offence itself, VORPS sought to facilitate reconciliation in the relationship between the parties. These programmes were housed in community-based religious organizations influenced by values of unity and solidarity expressed within religious doctrine. The goals of reducing recidivism or lowering costs were secondary to the more profound goal of building the beloved community.

The victims' rights movement emerges in the 1970s advocating for a range of reforms such as victim compensation, access to counselling/social support, safety, notification and sentencing reform, generally in support of enhanced sentencing (Elias, 1983). The feminist movement was crucial in shaping the victims' movement: the first victim assistance programmes focused on the crimes of rape and domestic violence (Young and Stein, 2004). Feminist activists asserted key ideas vital to the restorative justice movement: the psychological trauma of crime, the critical importance of empowering victims, the extent to which victims are not treated with respect and dignity by the criminal justice system and the healing journey that involves partnerships between the system and community. Feminists were wary of efforts to apply restorative justice to the crimes of domestic violence and sexual assault (Stubbs, 2002; Ptacek, 2005). The goal of reconciliation in the restorative justice paradigm kept feminists at arm's distance from the restorative justice movement.

Victim activists have been suspicious of the claim that the restorative justice movement is primarily motivated by the needs of victims. Victims who do not wish to engage with their offender, or whose offender has not been apprehended, find most restorative programmes offer few services to meet their needs. What the victims' movement did was to elevate the "needs of victims" as a legitimate political goal (Richards, 2009). The victims' rights movement sensitized the public and thereby politicians to the anger, discontent and unmet needs among crime victims. RJ advocates could then gain support from policy makers by arguing that restorative justice was designed to meet the needs of victims even though many of these needs were not included within the restorative justice agenda.

By the 1990s the label of restorative justice as a strategy for criminal justice reform emerged from this rich confluence of ideas and agendas. Martin Wright and Tony Marshall in the UK and Lode Wolgrave in Belgium promoted the use of victim-offender mediation as a form of restorative justice and alternative to the criminal justice process. The American Bar Association endorsed victim-offender mediation in 1994. In 1996 Dan Van Ness founded the Centre for Justice and Reconciliation as part of Prison International Fellowship. The International Network for Research on Restorative Justice for Juveniles was formed in Leuven, Belgium, in 1997. In the US, Gordon Bazemore and Mark Umbreit joined forces to create a national curriculum that offered comprehensive training to juvenile justice systems with demonstration projects in key states along funding by the National Institute of Corrections and Office of Community Oriented Policing. By 2000, the Canadian federal government began to invest in training and programme development and the European Forum for Victim-Offender Mediation and Restorative Justice (now the European Forum) was formed. In 2002 the UN issued the Basic Principles on the Use of Restorative Justice Programmes in Criminal Justice Matters. Developments in the criminal justice arena multiplied over the next ten years in justice reforms efforts around the world.

Management of youth and families

A second independent powerful arena emerges in the late 1980s from an effort in New Zealand to reshape Western juvenile justice and child welfare systems to engage marginalized families with practices more culturally responsive and empowering for indigenous youth within the system (Maxwell and Morris, 1993; McElrea, 1994). This arena focused on youth with the goal of developing more effective strategies for disciplining, morally educating and rehabilitating delinquent youth. The New Zealand family group conferencing (FGC) model, ostensibly modelled after Maori understandings of conflict resolution and decision-making, captured the imagination of youth-focused policing, juvenile justice criminologists and juvenile justice professionals in Australia and then North America. These ideas aligned with the tenets of positive youth development, empathy development and rehabilitation of youthful offenders.

The main activists here are professionals charged with managing the behaviour of youth and families. The primary context for this second set of reform agendas was first and foremost, the juvenile justice system and then police involvement with youth, child welfare system/social services and schools. The goal of activists within this stream was to make the work of professionals more effective by shifting the way they engage with youth and their families in their professional jobs.

In New Zealand, the 1989 Children, Young Persons and their Families Act established the FGC as a mandatory tool for all important decisions in the Youth Court in which the youth does "not deny" the charge. The process borrowed elements from Maori cultural practice in order to be more culturally sensitive with Maori youthful offenders who make up more than half of youth in the NZ juvenile justice system (Doolan, 1988; Love 1999). In its development, there was no use of the term "restorative justice" and no focus on "victims" as stakeholders in the process. Instead, the focus was on the youth, his or her moral and social development and accountability for their behaviour. Involving families was seen as adding an important dimension to this goal for the culturally communitarian Maori youth.

In 1991 police sergeant Terry O'Connell adapted the FGC as a community policing strategy for responding to minor youth crime (Moore and O'Connell, 1994). By using the Socratic method of asking questions, O'Connell developed the core questions that were later transformed into the "script" widely disseminated by the IIRP. A driving force in the growth and dissemination of family group conferencing is the work of Ted Wachtel. Wachtel heard Terry O'Connell speak about the FGC and recognized the approach as aligned with the practices at his juvenile residential centres. They both contributed to this Handbook by arguing for a different future for restorative justice. Along with Paul McCold, Wachtel later developed the Social Discipline Typology, articulating the balance between support and accountability that constituted a "restorative" approach to discipline using the "script" of the Wagga Wagga model of family group conferencing.

Several other key players contributed to the theoretical underpinning of practices that were increasingly coming under umbrella of "restorative justice." Criminologist John Braithwaite developed the theoretical concepts and empirical research associated with the family group conferencing model beginning with his 1989 seminal book *Crime, Shame and Reintegration*. Braithwaite linked the FGC model with a critique of relational processes within Western societies. Braithwaite articulated the theory of reintegrative shaming, referring to the family group conferencing as a process that condemned the act and not the actor in the context of caring community relationships (Braithwaite and Mugford, 1994).

The work of Sylvan Tomkins (1963, 1964, 1991), a Princeton psychologist, also served as another theoretical basis for the effectiveness of the conference, and particularly the "script" (Nathanson, 1992; Kelly and Thorsborne, 2014). Lauren Abramson entered the field after studying with Tomkins in the final years of his life. For Abramson, the conference process represented the opportunity for human beings to be "fully human" and express emotions in a way that is built into the biological architecture for creating and maintaining social bonds in groups. Abramson rigorously expanded the application of the conferencing model to a wide range of community conflicts in urban Baltimore and brought the practice to schools based on the core ideas of affect theory (Abramson and Moore, 2001, 2002).

In the UK, conferencing, with training by O'Connell, was first adopted by the Thames Valley Police in the mid-1990s as an approach to youth offending (Thames Valley Police Restorative Justice Consultancy, 1997; Hoyle and Young, 2003). In 1998, the Crime and Disorder Act set up interagency Youth Offending Teams (YOTS) as the key preventative strategy for responding to youthful offenders. The experience in New Zealand and Australia was highly influential in shaping the restorative strategies of the Youth Offender Panels and Reparation Orders managed by the Youth Offending Teams (Crawford and Newburn, 2003; Leibmann, 2007).

The expansion of the use of FGC in social services coincided with the spread of family meetings within child welfare. The core agenda was to reform these systems to more effectively fulfil the mission of strength-based family engagement by including the family in assessment, planning and decision-making. Gale Burford and Joan Pennel developed path-breaking pilot projects using family group decision-making for family violence (Burford and Pennel, 1995). Expansion to schools was also a major leap forward in this arena. Marg Thorsborne was the first practitioner to apply the conference model to the realm of school discipline in Queensland, Australia, in 1994 (Cameron and Thorsborne, 2001).

The first conceptual attempt at the idea of a "restorative city" emerged from activists working within the justice reform movement (Van Ness, 2010). The first genuine effort to create a city based on restorative justice principles and practices was in Hull, UK (Mirsky, 2009; Green et al., 2013). It began with implementation of restorative practices in schools followed by training of over 3,000 professionals within schools, police, children's homes, community resource centres and social services across the city (Straker, 2015).

Peacebuilding

The third independent stream is in the arena of peacebuilding, transition to democracy, and conflict transformation in the wake of mass violence, genocide, state violence and civil war. According to Llewellyn and Philpott (2014) the past three decades can be considered the "era of peacebuilding" because of an explosion of efforts around the world to build peace in the wake of massive injustice. These range from the use of international tribunals based on traditional strategies of criminal prosecution to the use of local indigenous practices for forgiveness and reconciliation.

Activists within this stream are NGOs, community-based organizations and religious groups which shift attention away from the diplomacy between representatives of the state (referred to as first track diplomacy) to the promotion of dialogue between ordinary people (second track diplomacy) with the goal of healing and reconciling relationships that have been damaged by the conflict (Montville, 2006). In this arena of peacebuilding and transitional justice, there is a revival of indigenous practices using local customs and processes to promote reconciliation, healing and integration in the wake of civil violence.

In the wake of WWII, the concept of international law grounded in universal principles of human rights and enforced by internationally sanctioned tribunals emerged within a traditional framework of criminal legal prosecution (Minow, 1998). The realm of transitional justice is concerned with issues of power, politics, legitimacy, rule of law and democratic governance. Holding state officials accountable for violations of human rights of their own subjects during war or under authoritarian regimes remains a central objective of the International Criminal Court.

Starting in the 1970s, truth commissions emerged as an alternative process for holding state authorities accountable for atrocities and violent acts by requiring a public record and admission of these violations – the "truth" – in some instances, in exchange for amnesty from retribution or criminal prosecution and/or as a condition for transition to a legitimate democratic government (Minow, 1998; Shriver, 2001). Over 40 such truth commissions have been held worldwide (Llewellyn and Philpott, 2014).

For critics, this approach represents second-class justice – a political compromise abandoning the quest for justice in favour of a settlement of peace or at least the end of physical violence/conflict. (Rotberg, 2000) In the mid-1990s, Desmond Tutu made the prominent and influential argument that the South African Truth and Reconciliation Commission was the realization of a different kind of justice that was called restorative justice (Minow, 1998; Tutu, 1999). Informed both by the indigenous African understandings of "ubuntu" and Christian ideas of forgiveness and redemption, Tutu forged a strong philosophical connection between the global peacebuilding movement and the emerging domestic agenda of the restorative movement.

The focus on victims as key stakeholders in a forum where they tell their stories in the presence of the wrongdoer and the wider moral community resonated with the face-to-face encounters mediated by victim-offender reconciliation programmes (Botchavaria, 2001; Yoder, 2005). Practitioners recognized parallels in bringing parties together face to face in a dynamic process of emotional engagement that transforms emotions and relationships through the dynamic interaction between the parties. The idea that confession, apology, amends, reparations and forgiveness are relevant to "doing justice" in the context of political violence paralleled the "different" meaning of justice and accountability espoused by restorative justice advocates in criminal violations. The issue of reparations for victims – not just for atrocities committed against individuals but also for systemic economic marginalization and oppression of groups – also has become a constitutive, if unrealized, goal of "restoring justice" (Villa-Valencio, 2014).

More recent are efforts to hold established Western democracies accountable for historical and current harms. The Civil Rights and Restorative Justice (CRRJ) Project at Northeastern University, Boston, founded by civil rights lawyer Margaret Burnham in 2008 provides empirical research on anti-civil rights and racialized violence that occurred in the US between 1930 and 1970. This data, available to the public, serves as a basis for remedies for victims participating in criminal prosecution, truth and reconciliation proceedings, public apologies and reparations. The data also is suitable for a national repository for establishing the historical record.

Indigenous rights and regeneration

The fourth independent arena is indigenous justice movements arising from First Nations' mobilization within North America to decolonize, reclaim their cultural practices and heal (Cunnen, 2001; McCaslin, 2005; Sawatsky, 2009). In North America, key actors are indigenous justice movements asserting rights to sovereignty, land return, accountability and reparations for previous and current acts of injustice. First Nations are also addressing challenges of violence, domestic violence, conflict, sexual abuse and addiction through the lens of oppression as well as reclaiming traditional justice and healing practices. The theme of "resisting colonization" in everyday life is combined with the goal of regenerating and reinventing indigenous justice traditions within the modern context. Activists are members of oppressed groups of colour – First Nations and Native Americans, African-Americans, immigrant rights, youth activists and formerly incarcerated men and women.

The development of alternative justice practices in this arena differs from the establishment of family group conferencing in New Zealand that was a state-led initiative (Cuneen, 1997). Activists are challenging racism and privilege within mainstream institutions of policing, corrections criminal justice system, education, welfare, politics and corporations as well as focusing on healing from internalized oppression and creating alternative approaches.

This stream shares with peacebuilding the emphasis on "truth telling" and revising the historical record that denied indigenous people an accurate recounting of the physical and cultural genocide committed against them (McClaslin, 2005; Breton, 2012). There is a need to reclaim language and name realities of ongoing oppression, marginalization and discrimination institutionalized within the current social structure. There is also a need to re-establish the connection between the harms of the past – namely, systemic injustices of slavery, genocide and colonization and ongoing current economic and social inequality.

The Native Law Centre at the University of Saskatchewan, Canada, was founded in 1975 to promote the development of Aboriginal law and legal practitioners. The Aboriginal healing movement began in the 1980s to use traditional practices to deal with the effects of alcoholism and drug abuse within communities (Lane et al., 2005). Healing included understanding the source of the problem in the forced removal of native children to residential schools. In response to Native activists, the Canadian federal government committed to "reconciliation", including a $350 million dollar grant in 1998 to support Aboriginal healing projects, and offered a public apology in 2008 (TRC, 2015).

The Navajo Peacemaker Court was established in 1982 by Navajo judges who wanted to revive traditional peacemaking rooted in Navajo law and custom. Robert Yazzie (1994) explains that in the Navajo world view, an offender is someone who "acts as if he as no relatives" and shows little regard for right relationships; the solution, according to traditional Navajo practice, is to "bring in the relatives" to teach that he or she is connected to and a part of the community. In 2012, the programme dropped the word "court" from its title and renewed its commitment to practice traditional peacemaking that emphasizes education, heroic journeys, expression of emotions and healing (Navajo Peacemaking Program, 2012).

Among the most well-known efforts to use traditional approaches to serious crime is the Hollow Water Community Holistic Circle Healing Programme started in 1987 in an Ojibway community called Hollow Water in Canada (Ross, 1996, 2005). A group of service providers along with lay members from the community recognized the pervasiveness of sexual abuse within the community involving intergenerational cycles of harm, drug abuse and trauma rooted in the destruction of families and community by colonization. The founders of this programme rejected the Western reliance on incarceration, stating that it only made matters worse for the community because "an already unbalanced person is moved further out of balance."

As a justice of the Yukon Territorial Court, Barry Stuart began to collaborate with First Nations communities to use the traditional method of Peacemaking Circles as an alternative for criminal sentencing. In 1996, Stuart connected with Kay Pranis, who was serving as the Restorative Justice planner for the Department of Corrections in Minnesota, in order to bring First Nation teachers from the Yukon to teach the circle process to activists in the restorative justice movement. Pranis became a key teacher of the circle process to Western communities in the restorative justice movement.

My own journey intersected with these developments while I was working with gang and street-involved youth in Boston in 1997 (Boyes-Watson, 2008). I published several books, including *Circle Forward* (Boyes-Watson and Pranis, 2015) with Living Justice Press, a non-profit press founded in 2002 that is dedicated to publications that take the restorative justice dialogue to deeper levels by addressing racism, historic harms, and other conflicts between peoples.

The introduction of peacemaking circles into the restorative justice movement has had the most impact on the growing use of restorative practices within urban schools in Oakland, Boston, Minneapolis and New York City. After 30 years as a civil rights lawyer at the centre of the civil rights movement, Fania Davis enrolled in a PhD programme to study African healers which led to the founding of RJOY – Restorative Justice for Oakland Youth, which promotes school-based restorative justice and court diversion to "interrupt racialized mass incarceration strategies" using healing circles (Davis, 2012).

The whirlpool of restorative ideas

If we take a bird's-eye perspective, the focus of the restorative justice movement has shifted from reform of the justice system to the transformation of practices within civil society to a reconnection with politics, spirituality and social justice. In this discussion, I return to the question of achievement and co-optation of the different priorities and goals within each arena.

The limits of justice reform

As an effort to "reform" the system, it is accurate to say that the amount of "talk" about restorative justice far outpaces the "walk" of practice within the criminal legal system. While it is a common mantra to state that "restorative justice is more than just a programme," for the most part, restorative justice is practised in specialized programmes that have had little impact on "business as usual" of the criminal legal system (Wood and Susuki, 2016).

Co-optation of restorative justice programmes by the needs and interests of the existing system is routine. District attorneys, police and probation serve as gatekeepers and set timelines and criteria for eligibility, participation and completion. Programmes do their best to "bring the community in," but there is an artificial quality to this because relationships are mediated by the legal system, not by naturally occurring connections within the community. Community members play a "scripted" role in the restorative justice process in a sense "trained" by professionals to enact a part in the encounter between the offender and those affected by crime (Rosenblatt, 2015; Rossner and Bruce, 2016).

Much of the restorative justice practice in US juvenile systems gives the outward appearance of restorative practice: youth are assigned "restorative tasks" and required to write apology letters as consequences for misbehaviour; systems professionals deliver curricula that teach youth about the impact of crime on victims, while caseworkers help youth develop empathy for others by helping them think about the impact their behaviour has on others. Low victim participation is a persistent finding in restorative justice programmes.

With historical hindsight we know that "get tough" ideologies accelerated in the 1990s and 2000s, instituting policies that fuel mass incarceration concentrated within minority communities. Expansion has occurred at both the soft end and the hard end of the system. Reform of the criminal legal system requires more than programmatic add-ons – it needs significant political movements for sentencing reform, police, prosecutorial and judicial accountability and justice reinvestment along with shifts in cultural mindsets, political power, resources and priorities.

Taking the justice out of the practice

When we move outside the justice system, we see the most rapid spread of restorative "practices" in the non-criminal justice arena of schools and social services/child welfare.

The measurement of success in this stream is tied to the goals of these systems. In schools, reductions in suspensions and exclusion, increases in attendance and academic achievement and improvements in school climate are key positive outcomes of restorative practices. In social services, outcomes that indicate success are reductions in out of home placements, more family participation and increase in client satisfaction.

It is within this arena that the preference arises for substituting the term "practice" for "justice." IIRP now refers to "Restorative practices is a social science that studies how to build social capital and achieve social discipline through participatory learning and decision-making" (Wachtel, 2017). In some ways, it is an expansive vision. In workplaces, families and schools, people are happier and more productive when people in authority do things "with" others rather than "to" or "for." At the same time, it focuses narrowly on the micro dynamics of the exercise of authority, specifically the relationship between those with authority – teachers, police, parents, managers – and those subject to it.

Green et al. (2015) refer to this development as being in a "downward" direction – away from the state and towards the transformation of everyday activities in schools and workplaces. In this context, the aspiration is to increase the quality of communication in order to build the kind of communitarian society in which ordinary citizens exercise empathy and care in their relationships with one another. The concept of "social capital" is generally invoked here to refer to the rebuilding of community connections and community functions that have atrophied in modern societies.

Within this arena, however, there is little focus on reforming the structure of institutionalized power and privilege embedded within systems themselves. These reforms assume the right of the state to intervene in the lives of poor, marginalized families while attempting to make that intervention more effective, collaborative and less overtly coercive. The dropping of the term "justice" is telling because this arena tends to stand apart from a challenge to the power of the state and from the agenda of doing justice in an "upward" direction by holding the state, elites or corporations accountable or by attempting to address structural inequalities. Focusing on structural injustice points to the limits of the managerial stream of restorative practices that seeks to "give voice" to the governed so that they are more effectively governed.

From practice to politics and spirituality

It is through the concerns of activists within the movements for peacebuilding and indigenous rights that the issue of institutionalized power and privilege is moving towards the centre of the restorative justice movement. Publication of *The New Jim Crow* (Alexander, 2012) and the Black Lives Matter movement has brought more activists of colour with Afro-Centric ideas to the restorative justice movement along with leadership from First Nations activists and incarcerated and formerly incarcerated men and women.

The new wave of restorative justice activism engages with issues of oppression, discrimination and economic injustice. In the US, restorative justice in schools has been fuelled by the political concerns of racial equity and civil rights. For instance, Davis (2016) calls for a Truth and Reconciliation Process in Ferguson and in communities across the US to open space for ordinary people tell the truth about racial oppression through the criminal justice system.

For a new generation of activists, the personal is political. Activists are engaged politically and spiritually, focusing on nurturing oneself and others as a way of living. There is no separation between spirituality and justice (Batley, 2004; Sawatsky, 2009), between heart-thinking and head-thinking (Zion, 2005). There is a greater effort to understand the world view and ethics of Aboriginal justice and to create ways to be true to those values in the Western context. Philosophically, there is resonance between feminist ethics and the vision of justice articulated by Kay Harris (1987) and Carol Gilligan (1982), with a "return of the feminine principles to restore balance with the masculine energy of domination" (Davis, 2016).

These developments bring the movement back to the question of *shalom* that Zehr (1990) identified as the touchstone for the paradigm of restorative justice. A key source of convergence within the North American restorative justice movement is the grounding of the commitment and understandings in essentially spiritual and ethical understandings about "right relationship." There is acknowledgement that values of love and the practice of spirituality cannot be made secondary to the call to struggle against oppression. If there is no vision or aspiration to create a "beloved community" in which relational equity is a condition for all members of the community, then the goals of "restoration" and "participation" seems both hollow and deceptive.

The restorative justice movement has always been more than a "mechanism" or "response to harm." The idea of restorative justice rests on an affirmative vision of how to live in "right relationship" or as Native people would say, "in a good way." Weitkampte and Parmentier (2016) note that the concept of healing justice within Germanic legal philosophy similarly focuses on healthy patterns of everyday life. Restorative justice is about how to create harmony, not just end conflict – how to live in right relationship, not just reconcile over a past harm.

This is in tension with the secular and technical rationality of the social science and legal agenda that frames criteria for restorative justice in terms of efficiency, effectiveness, evidence and outcomes framed by current institutional systems. As Sawatsky (2009) notes, the restorative justice field has overwhelmingly focused on "case management" with little attention to the socio-economic context that generates much of the crisis and harm addressed by the criminal justice and social service systems. Most restorative justice practice ignores the building of a healthy foundation for well-being and focuses on the response to the crisis – the eruption of aggression, violence or harm that is symptomatic of individuals and communities not living in balance or healthy relationship.

Concluding thoughts

People wonder about the future of the restorative justice movement. In my view, it has a very dismal future as a technocratic solution to the inadequacies of the current criminal justice system. Proving through social science evidence that it "works" more effectively to reduce recidivism or suspensions than some other intervention may appeal to funders but does not draw activists into the movement. What inspires people to turn to restorative justice is the connection to humanistic values that have always inspired human beings.

Restorative justice is a big idea that encompasses far more than reform of the criminal justice system. In the long run, ideas change institutions, shape culture and outlast the efforts of individuals. We would do well to remember that race, too, is a big idea – a terrible and oppressive idea that has been institutionalized within modern social structure, institutions and consciousness. Dr Gail Christopher (2017) counselled that as we build a restorative vision about who we are, we must concurrently dismantle the idea of race and practices of privilege and discrimination at the foundation of the current social structure. Opening this international Handbook – diverse in its views and evidence – this chapter argues that the restorative justice movement has always been a vehicle for creating a different future. The expansive growth of the movement is a testament that the big ideas of restorative justice are continuing to draw people to this movement in order to create transformative social change.

References

Abel, R. 1982. Introduction. In *The Politics of Informal Justice: The American Experience*. Volume I. New York: Academic Press, pp. 1–16.

Abramson, L. and Moore, D.B. 2001. Transforming Conflict in the Inner City Community Conferencing in Baltimore, *Contemporary Justice Review*, 4(3–4): 321–340.

Abramson, L. and Moore, D.B. 2002. The Psychology of Community Conferencing. In J. Perry (ed.) *Restorative Justice: Repairing Communities Through Restorative Justice*. Alexandria: ACA, pp. 123–140.

Alexander, M. 2012. *The New Jim Crow: Mass Incarceration in the Age of Colorblindness*. New York: The New Press.

Batley, M. 2004. What Is the Appropriate Role of Spirituality in Restorative Justice? In H. Zehr and B. Toews (eds.) *Critical Issues in Restorative Justice*. Monsey, NY: Criminal Justice Press, pp. 361–374.

Botcharova, O. 2001. Implementation of Track Two Diplomacy: Developing a Model of Forgiveness. In R. Petersen and R. Helmick (eds.) *Forgiveness and Reconciliation: Religion, Public Policy and Conflict Transformation*. Philadelphia: Templeton Foundation Press.

Boyes-Watson, C. 1999. In the Belly of the Beast? Exploring Dilemmas of State-sponsored Restorative Justice, *Contemporary Justice Review*, 2(3): 261–281 2002.

Boyes-Watson, C. 2008. *Peacemaking Circles and Urban Youth*. St. Paul MN: Living Justice Press.

Boyes-Watson, C. and Pranis, K. 2015. *Circle Forward: Building a Restorative School*. St. Paul, MN: Living Justice Press.

Braithwaite, J. 1989. *Crime, Shame and Reintegration*. Cambridge: Cambridge University Press.

Braithwaite, J. and Mugford, S. 1994. Conditions of Successful Reintegration Ceremonies: Dealing with Juvenile Offenders, *British Journal of Criminology*, 34(2): 1–33.

Breton, D. 2012. Decolonizing Justice, *Tikkun*, Winter.

Burford, G. and Pennel, J. 1995. *Family group Decision Making: New Roles for "Old" Partners in Resolving Family Violence*. St. Johns: Memorial University of Newfoundland.

Cameron, L. and Thorsborne, M. 2001. Restorative Justice and School Discipline: Mutually Exclusive? In H. Strang and J. Braithwaite (eds.) *Restorative justice and Civil Society*. Cambridge, MA: Cambridge University Press, pp. 180–195.

Christopher, G. 2017. Racial Healing: The Journey to Sustained Transformation. Keynote speech at 2017 National Association of Community Restorative Justice. Available at www.nacrj.org/index. php?option=com_content&view=article&id=242:dr-gail-christopher-d-n&catid=73&Itemid=1117.

Christie, Nils. 1977. Conflicts as Property, *British Journal of Criminology*, 17(1).

Cunneen, C. 1997. Community Conferencing and the Fiction of Indigenous Control, *Australian & New Zealand Journal of Criminology*, 30(3): 292–311.

Cunneen, C. 2001. Reparations and Restorative Justice: Responding to the Gross Violations of Human Rights. In H. Strang and J. Braithwaite (eds.) *Restorative Justice and Civil Society*. Cambridge: Cambridge University Press, pp. 83–98.

Davis, F. 2012. Whats Love Go To Do With It?, *Tikkun*, Winter.

Davis, F. 2016. This Country Needs a Truth and Reconciliation Process on Violence Against African-Americans – Right Now. *Yes! Magazine*. Available at www.yesmagazine.org/peace-justice/this-country-needs-a-truth-and-reconciliation-process-on-violence-against-african-americans. Accessed 27 October 2017.

Doolan, M. 1988. From Welfare – To Justice: Towards New Social Work Practice with Young Offenders. Nuffield Foundation Study Report. Wellington, New Zealand.

Eglash, A. 1977. Beyond Restitution – Creative Restitution. In J. Hudson and B. Galaway (eds.) *Restitution in Criminal Justice*. Toronto: Minnesota Department of Corrections, Lexington Books, pp. 91–129.

Elias, R. 1983. *Victims of the System: Crime Victims and Compensation in American Politics and Criminal Justice*. New Brunswick, NJ: Transaction Books.

Galaway, B. and Hudson, J. 1972. Restitution and Rehabilitation: Some Central Issues, *Crime and Delinquency*, 18(4): 403–410.

Gilligan, C. 1982. *In a Different Voice*. Cambridge, MA: Harvard University Press.

Green, S., Johnstone, G. and Lambert, C. 2013. What Harm, Whose Justice? Excavating the Restorative Movement, *Contemporary Justice Review: Issues in Criminal, Social, and Restorative Justice*, 16(4): 445–460.

Greensboro Truth and Reconciliation Commission Report. 2006. Presented to the residents of Greensboro, the City. Available at www.greensbororc.org/

Harrington, C. 1982. Delegalization Reform Movements: A Historical Analysis. In R. Abel (ed.) *The Politics of Informal Justice: The American Experience*, Vol. I. New York: Academic Press, pp. 35–63.

Harris, M.K. 1987. Moving Into a New Millenium: Towards a Feminist Vision of Justice, *The Prison Journal*, 67(2).

Hassell, I. 1996. Origin and Development of Family Group Conferences. In J. Hudson, A. Morris, G. Maxwell, and B. Galaway (eds.) *Family Group Conferences: Perspectives on Policy & Practice*. Monsey, NY: Willow Tree Press.

Hoyle, C. and Young, R. 2003. Restorative Justice, Victims and the Police. In T. Newburn (ed.) *Handbook of Policing*. Cullompton and Devon: Willan.

Johnstone, G. and Van Ness, D. 2007. The Meaning of Restorative Justice. In G. Johnstone and Van Ness, D. (eds.) *Handbook of Restorative Justice*. Cullompton: Willan, pp. 5–23.

Kelly, V. and Thorsborne, M. (eds.). 2014. *The Psychology of Emotion in Restorative Practice: How Affect Script Psychology Explains How and Why Restorative Practice Works*. London: Jessica Kingsley Publishers.

Lane, P., Bopp, M., Bopp, J. and Norris, J. 2005. Mapping the Healing Journey: First Nations Research Project. In W. McClaslin (ed.) *Justice as Healing: Indigenous Ways*. St Paul, MN: Living Justice Press.

Lederach, J.P. 1999. *The Journey Towards Reconciliation*. Scottdale, PA: Herald Press.

Liebmann, M. 2007. *Restorative Justice: How It Works*. London: Jessica Kingley.

Llewellyn, J. and Philpott, D. 2014. Restorative Justice and Reconciliation: Twin Frameworks for Peace-building. In Llewellyn and Philpott (eds.) *Restorative Justice, Reconciliation, and Peacebuilding. Studies in Strategic Peacebuilding*. Oxford University Press, pp. 14–37.

Love, C. 1999. Family Group Conferencing: Cultural Origins, Sharing, and Appropriation – A Maori reflection. In G. Burford and J. Hudson (eds.) *Family Group Conferencing: New Directions in Community-Centered Child & Family Practice*. New York: Aldine de Gruyter.

Maxwell, G.M. and Morris, A. 1993. *Families, Victims and Cultures: Youth Justice in New Zealand*. Wellington: Department of Social Welfare and Institute of Criminology.

McClaslin, W.D. 2005. Introduction: Naming Realities of Life. In W. McClaslin (ed.) *Justice as Healing: Indigenous Way – Writings on Community Peacemaking and Restorative Justice from the Native Law Centre*. St. Paul, MN: Living Justice Press.

McElrea, F. 1994. Justice in the Community: The New Zealand Experience. In J. Burnside and N. Baker (eds.) *Relational Justice: Repairing the Breach*. Winchester: Waterside Press.

McManus, M. and Silverstein, B. 2011. Brief History of Alternative Dispute Resolution in the, *CADMUS*, 1(3): 1–10.

Minow, M. 1998. *Between Vengeance and Forgiveness: Facing History and Genocide after Mass Violence*. Boston, MA: Beacon Press.

Minow, M. 2000. The Hope for Healing: What Can Truth Commissions Do? In R.I. Rotberg and D. Thompson (eds.) *Truth v. Justice: The Morality of Truth Commissions*. Princeton, NJ: Princeton University Press.

Mirsky, L. 2009. *Hull, UK; Toward a Restorative City*. 1st ed. [ebook] International Institute for Restorative Practices, pp. 1–2. Available at www.iirp.edu/news/1942-from-the-archives-hull-uk-toward-a-restorative-city. Accessed 25 October 2017.

Montville, J.V. 2006. Track Two Diplomacy: The Work of Healing History, *Whitehead Whitehead Journal of Diplomacy and International Relations*, 7: 15.

Moore, D. and O'Connell, T. 1994. Family Conferencing in Wagga Wagga: A Communitarian Model of Justice. In C. Alder and J. Wundersitz (eds.) *Family Conferencing and Juvenile Justice: The Way Forward or Misplaced Optimism?* Canberra: Australian Institute of Criminology.

Moyle, P. and Tauri, J. 2016. Māori, Family Group Conferencing and the Mystifications of Restorative Justice, *Victims & Offenders*, 11(1): 87–106.

Nathanson, D. 1992. *Shame and Pride: Affect, Sex and the Birth of the Self*. New York: W.W. Norton.

Olson, S. and Dzur, A. 2004. Revisiting Informal Justice: Restorative Justice and Democratic Professionalism, *Law & Society Review*, 38(1): 139–176.

Peacemaking Program of the Judicial Branch of the Navajo Nation. 2012. Institutional History of Hózhóji Naat'aah. Available at www.navajocourts.org/Peacemaking/Plan/PPPO2013-2-25.pdf

Pranis, K., Stuart, B. and Wedge, M. 2003. *Peacemaking Circles: From Crime to Community*. Minneapolis, MN: Living Justice Press.

Ptacek, J. 2005. Guest Editor's Introduction, *Violence against Women*, 11(5): 564–570.

Reeves, H. 1989. The Victim Support Perspective. In M. Whright and B. Galaway (eds.) *Mediation and Criminal Justice: Victims, Offenders and Community*. Newbury Park, CA: Sage Publications, pp. 44–56.

Richards, K. 2009. Taking Victims Seriously? The Role of Victims' Rights Movements in the Emergence of Restorative Justice, *Current Issues in Criminal Justice*, 21(2). pp. 302–320.

Rosenblatt, F. 2015. *The Role of Community in Restorative Justice*. New York: Routledge.

Ross, R. 1996. *Returning to the Teachings: Exploring Aboriginal Justice*. Toronto, ON: Penguin.

Ross, R. 2005. Aboriginal Community Healing in Action: The Hollow Water Approach. In W. McClaslin (ed.) *Justice as Healing: Indigenous Way – Writings on Community Peacemaking and Restorative Justice from the Native Law Centre*. St. Paul, MN: Living Justice Press.

Rossner, M. and Bruce, J. 2016. Community Participation in Restorative Justice: Rituals, Reintegration and Quasi-Professionalization, *Victims & Offenders*, 11: 1–20.

Rotberg, R. 2000. Truth Commissions and the Provision of Truth, Justice and Reconciliation. In R. Rotberg and D. Thompson (eds.) *Truth v. Justice: The Morality of Truth Commissions*. Princeton NJ: Princeton University Press, pp. 3–21.

Sawatsky, J. 2009. *The Ethic of Traditional Communities and the Spirit of Healing Justice*. London: Jessica Kingsley.

Schaefer, S. 1968. *The Victim and His Criminal: A Study in Functional Responsibility*. New York: Random House.

Scull, A. 1982. Community Corrections: Panacea, Progress, or Pretense? In R. Abel (ed.) *The Politics of Informal Justice: The American Experience*, Vol. I. New York: Academic Press, pp. 99–118.

Shriver, D. Jr. 2001. Truth Commissions and Judicial Trials: Complementary or Antagonistic Servants of Public Justice? *Journal of Law and Religion*, 16(1).

Straker, C. 2015. The Restorative City: Emperor's New Clothes or Achievable Paradigm Shift? In *Fifth Restorative Practices International Conference*. March 24, Hobart, Tasmania.

Stubbs, J. 2002. Domestic Violence and Women's Safety: Feminist Challenges to Restorative Justice. In H. Strang and J. Braithwaite (eds.) *Restorative Justice and Family Violence*. Cambridge: Cambridge University Press.

Tauri, J. 2009. An Indigenous Perspective on the Standardization of Restorative Justice in New Zealand and Canada, *Indigenous Policy Journal*, 20(3): 1–24.

Thames Valley Police Restorative Justice Consultancy. 1997. *Restorative Justice, Restorative Cautioning – A New Approach*. Oxford: Thames Valley Police Restorative Justice Consultancy.

Tomkins, S. 1962. *Affect Imagery Consciousness*, Vol. I. New York: Springer.

Tomkins, S. 1963. *Affect Imagery Consciousness*, Vol. II. New York: Springer.

Tomkins, S. 1991. *Affect Imagery Consciousness*, Vol. III. New York: Springer.

Truth and Reconciliation Commission. 1998. Truth and Reconciliation Commission of South Africa Report. Cape Town: Juta & Co. Ltd.

Truth and Reconciliation Commission of Canada. 2015. Honouring the Truth, Reconciling for the Future: Summary of the Final Report of the Truth and Reconciliation Commission of Canada.

Tutu, D. 1999. *No Future Without Forgiveness*. New York: Doubleday.

Umbreit, M. 1985. *Victim Offender Mediation: Conflict Resolution and Restitution*. Valparaiso, IN: National Institute of Corrections, pp. 8–23.

Van Ness, D. 2005. An Overview of Restorative Justice around the World. In *United Nations 11th Congress on Crime Prevention and Criminal Justice*.

Van Ness, D. 2010. *RJ City: Phase 1 Final Report*. RJ City. Washington, DC: Prison Fellowship International, pp. 1–85.

Villa-Vicencio, C. 2014. Living Between Promise and Non-Delivery: Pursuing Inclusive Reparations. In J. Llewellyn and D. Philpott (eds.) *Restorative Justice, Reconciliation, and Peacebuilding: Studies in Strategic Peacebuilding*. Oxford: Oxford University Press.

Wachtel, T. 2009. *My Three Decades of Using Restorative Practices with Delinquent and At-Risk Youth: Theory, Practice and Research Outcomes*. Paper presented at the First World Congress on Restorative Juvenile Justice, Lima, Peru, 5 November.

Wachtel, T. 2016. *Defining Restorative*. International Institute for Restorative Practices, pp. 1–12.

Wachtel, T. 2016. *Governance and the Use of Authority: Encompassing Diverse Definitions of 'Restorative'*. 17th ed. [pdf] European Forum for Restorative Justice, pp. 7–9. Available at www.euforumrj.org/wp-content/uploads/2016/11/Vol_17_3.pdf. Accessed 30 October 2017.

Weitekamp, E. and Parmentier, S. 2016. Restorative Justice as Healing Justice: Looking Back to the Future of the Concept, *Restorative Justice*, 4(2): 141–147.

Wood, W. 2016. Editor's Introduction: The Future of Restorative Justice?, *Victims & Offenders*, 11(1): 1–8.

Wood, W. and Suzuki, M. 2016. Four Challenges in the Future of Restorative Justice, *Victims & Offenders*, 11(1): 149–172.

Yazzie, R. 1994. 'Life Comes From It': Navajo Justice Concepts, *New Mexico Law Review*, 24.

Yoder, C. 2005. *Little Book of Trauma Healing: When Violence Strikes and Community Security Is Threatened*. Intercourse, PA: Good Books.

Young, M. and Stein, J. 2004. *The History of the Crime Victims' Movement in the United States*, 1st ed. Washington, DC: National Organization for Victim Assistance, pp. 1–15.

Zehr, H. 1990. *Changing Lenses: A New Focus for Crime and Justice*. Scottsdale, PA: Herald Press.

Zion, J.W. 2005. Punishment Versus Healing: How Does Traditional Indian Law Work? In W. McClaslin (ed.) *Justice as Healing: Indigenous Way – Writings on Community Peacemaking and Restorative Justice from the Native Law Centre*. St. Paul, MN: Living Justice Press.

2

Pushing the theoretical boundaries of restorative justice

Non-sovereign justice in radical political and social theories

Giuseppe Maglione

Introduction

This chapter is an exercise in political and ethical imagination.[1] It starts from the premise that the recent centralised institutionalisation of restorative justice has outstripped this field of its radical political-ethical potential. The process of incorporating restorative justice into legal frameworks, in fact, equates with the transformation of restorative justice into a mechanism of 'sovereign' justice which limits creativity, produces control and endorses hierarchical relationships. This chapter sets out to re-envision, although in a preliminary way, restorative justice as an emancipatory (non-sovereign) response to transgressions of modes of conducts, embedded in wider social, political and economic vulnerabilities. It advances the thesis that non-sovereign values can help imaging and practicing challenges against institutionalised restorative justice and, more broadly, against exclusionary forms of justice. A range of practical implications can be drawn from this normative exercise.

Institutionalising restorative justice: a diagnosis

Restorative justice has developed historically as a plurality of attempts to rationalise various practices (conferencing, mediation, circles) blossoming at the margins of criminal justice systems. Some of these practices have been increasingly regulated by the state and incorporated in legal frameworks since the 1990s (Aertsen et al., 2006). Similarly, certain understandings of restorative justice have been recognised and prioritised by the state, informing relevant policies and state-funded programmes (Van Ness and Strong, 2003). Three main (and empirically overlapping) approaches to restorative justice are widespread in the Western world: 'enfranchising the victim', 'transforming the offender', 'decentralising conflict management' (Maglione, 2017b). The first two are characterised by a reformist-pragmatic approach to criminal justice and have been underpinning laws and policies on restorative justice widely. The third understanding

1 I wish to thank Kirsty Boutle for her encouragement and support in writing this chapter.

resonates with a radical criminological view, and, whilst often evoked and praised by critical scholars, today appears as a minor theoretical component of state-based restorative justice. The 'enfranchising the victim' approach revolves around the idea that restorative justice endeavours to produce safety and healing for the victim. The restorative encounter is regarded as a time and space where the consequences of a crime are discussed and addressed, restoring the emotional, social, symbolic and material relationships among direct stakeholders (i.e. victim, offender and community), with a specific emphasis on the victim's needs (Dignan, 2005; Strang, 2003; Strang and Sherman, 2003; Zehr, 1990). This view recognises the potential of the restorative encounter to enable participants to express emotions and achieve mutual understanding, healing and closure (Van Ness and Strong, 2003). The idea of 'transforming the offender' (especially youth offenders) is also integral to the restorative justice field. Within this perspective, restorative justice interventions seek to restore human interconnectedness, transforming not just actions which weaken interpersonal relationships but also actors, focussing particularly on the offender's need of change. This approach is backed up by a normative critique of 'punishment as retribution', that is, of the idea of coercing the offender to endure pain commensurate to the gravity of the crime committed. Restorative justice competes with retribution insofar as it entails concrete actions towards transforming the offender through the encounter and the following material/symbolical repair of the harm caused to the victim (Braithwaite, 1999; Walgrave, 2003; Wright, 1996). Finally, the discourse of 'decentralising conflict management', originally resting on radical criminological premises (penal minimalism and abolitionism), stresses the role of community-based and non-professionalised alternatives to the 'conventional' criminal justice. The idea of empowering direct stakeholders by devolving to them the competence to deal with the consequences of their conflicts is characteristic of this perspective.

Institutionalisation

These different approaches have been translated into legislative measures, applicative guidelines, advocacy initiatives and institutional training programmes, with intersections, combinations and tensions. Some recurrent aspects characterise the institutionalisation of restorative justice.

Theoretically, restorative justice enshrined in legislation embraces a functionalist approach to crime (Walgrave, 2017: 97). Crime is seen as a social pathology which needs to be neutralised. Restorative justice aspires to 'cure' this pathology, healing the victim and transforming the offender, whilst neglecting both the emancipatory potential of transgressions of established legal frameworks and the unbalanced power relationships which contribute towards the definition of behaviours as crimes. Additionally, institutionalisation often involves the 'mainstreaming' (O'Mahony and Campbell, 2006), 'flat-pack[ing]' (Blagg, 2017) or 'mcdonaldisation' (Umbreit, 2001) of restorative justice. The centralised regulation, in fact, requires focussing on serving 'conventional' justice goals, such as efficiency, by reducing costs and speeding up the process, as well as on the development of an evidence-based, 'tick the box' approach to justice interventions. This may also have 'colonising' effects considering that, through policy transfer, restorative justice programmes are sold as a 'standardised, homogenised commodity' to non-Western communities (Blagg, 2107: 71).

Operationally, the main concern here is the co-optation of restorative justice by the 'conventional' criminal justice procedures. Restorative justice institutional programmes normally require the offender's admission of responsibility/guilty plea as a condition to enter a scheme (see European Directive 29/12 – i.e. Victims' Directive). This is a form of endorsement of criminalisation processes led by law enforcement agencies and a paradigmatic example of restorative justice being 'defined in' (Mathiesen, 2015) 'conventional' criminal justice with no chance (and no aspiration) to challenge the gatekeepers of criminal justice. Restorative justice works fundamentally as a penal mechanism (Daly, 2016). This means that it is about administering the consequences of a crime whose individual responsibility has been unambiguously decided. Additionally, 'penal' refers to a distinctive understanding of social relationships: dichotomic (victim vs. offender), focussed on personality more than systems, on acts more than interactions, on blame-allocation more than conflict resolution (Hulsman, 1986). In the same vein, the incorporation of restorative justice in law has often been accompanied by the professionalisation and standardisation of restorative practitioners (Johnstone, 2012). This involves the creation of a new professional group which specialises in dealing with crime in a 'restorative way' and/or at the creation of professional bodies overseeing the provision of restorative services (e.g. RJ Councils). Restorative practitioners are new experts with power of control both over the participants' relations during the restorative encounter, and, following it, over the execution of the agreement reached during the encounter (e.g. the youth offender follow-up plans in England and Wales[2] or in Norway)[3]. As Nils Christie sharply noticed (2015: 111), with respect to the new restorative measures for youth offenders in Norway, '[t]he coordinator becomes a judge, a social worker and a police person in one role. There is not much room left for laypeople, the former core members of the boards'. A further element linked to the implementation of restorative justice is the ever-looming net-widening danger. Restorative justice seems to be applied fundamentally as a diversionary measure for youth offenders, or as a stand-alone penal option managed by external professionals to whom 'low tariff' crimes are referred (Crawford and Newburn, 2003). This potentially opens up the co-optation of restorative justice services for a range of cases which would/could not be dealt with by state agencies due to their 'minor' nature of low serious crime (Cohen, 1985). In short, restorative justice, 'despite being based on progressive principles, by locating itself (as an alternative) within the criminal justice system, has found itself being increasingly used in a punitive manner and targeted at people who previously were, by and large, outside the grasp of penal law' (Moore and Roberts, 2016: 130). Furthermore, the legal regulation of restorative justice could be easily bent to coercive practices, for instance, in cases such as the 'restorative caution'[4] or the imposition of pre-sentence 'restorative requirements'[5] in England and Wales. These measures lend themselves to police, judges or facilitators' pressure, especially on youth first time offenders, working as forms of 'low level' responsibilisation of the offender (Crawford and Newburn, 2003). Lastly, institutionalised restorative justice revolves around idealised images of crime stakeholders overlapping with the criminal justice ideal actors (Christie, 1986). The victim appears as disempowered and vulnerable, the offender is presented as the harm-maker and wrongdoer ontologically distinct from his or her victim and the community is depicted as a pro-social parochial collective stakeholder (Maglione, 2017a).

A diagnosis

These rapid institutional developments have outstripped restorative justice's radical theoretical aspirations (encapsulated in the original 'decentralising-conflict management' discourse), letting more conservative elements, indebted with 'conventional' criminal justice, lead its development (Gavrielides, 2013). Restorative justice appears today as a 'positive' reform of

2 Youth Justice and Criminal Evidence Act 1999, Schedule 4.
3 Lov om konfliktrådsbehandling (National Mediation Act) 2014.
4 Criminal Justice and Court Services Act 2000, Section 56, and Code for Crown Prosecutors England and Wales, Sections 7 and 8.
5 Crime and Courts Act 2013 England and Wales, part 2 of Schedule 16.

criminal justice, an alternative justification of the penal consequence for a crime (Christie, 2013; Mathiesen, 2015; Pavlich, 2005) which lacks any 'attitude to say no' (Mathiesen, 2015) to 'conventional' understandings of crime and punishment, and to develop a 'non-penal real utopia' (Scott, 2013).

Looking more closely to the transformation of restorative justice into a state-based penal mechanism, this seems consistent with a range of broad neo-liberal/neo-conservative crime control strategies. First, the relationships between restorative justice and strategies of regulated responsibilisation as a form of crime control should be considered (Garland, 2001). Responsibilisation denotes cautious devolution of decision-making capacity to community-based actors, non-state agencies, non-governmental organisations as well as individual citizens to provide a distinctive type of security. The key aim of restorative justice is, in fact, the direct involvement of a plurality of stakeholders ('victims', 'offenders' and 'communities') (Pavlich, 2005: 81) in order for them to take responsibility for producing their own security. This form of responsibilisation does not rule out the state, since restorative practices are often state-funded, led by state agencies and re-enact the state-based criminal justice language and mindset (dichotomy victim/offender, offender's admission of guilt as a condition to enter restorative justice programmes, etc.) (Davis, 1992: 25).

Additionally, restorative justice interventions seem to be set to perform a 'hybrid' (i.e. beyond the public/private divide) way of crime control (Rose, 2001). Particularly, the production of a virtual arena – the 'community' – as the backdrop of restorative interventions, is an expression of this form of control. Restorative justice, in fact, is about imaging participatory decision-making processes to deal with crimes by (partly) devolving to victims and offenders the power to address the harm experienced, within and through their communities. The 'community', here, is an idealised backdrop for crime control and repression which justifies apparently new forms of controlling individuals and groups, different both from harsh punitive responses and failing rehabilitative instruments. Restorative justice is shaped as a 'third way' community-based form of penal policy, whose cultural background is ostensibly alternative to both the criminologies of 'the self' and of 'the other' (Garland, 2001: 15).

Finally, restorative justice appears integral to trends towards neutralising the moral, political and social character of crime (Rose, 1998: 165). Restorative interventions result in de-activating the political/social content of a variety of problematics by installing a concept of crime stakeholder as an autonomous, self-directing, decision-making agent (Rose, 1999: 499). Here the goal is to offer individuals and groups new opportunities to participate actively in various arenas of action 'to resolve the kind of issues hitherto held to be the responsibility of authorized governmental agencies' (Burchell, 1996: 29). Restorative justice understands crimes as personal choices, avoiding any problematisation of criminalisation processes. Crime is fundamentally a matter of interpersonal conflict or moral wrong deliberately inflicted by an emotionally immature offender, and to be dealt with by the same conflicting parties; the role of social determinants, structures or macro-relations of power in driving the criminalisation of those behaviours or the offender's actions is obliterated. Restorative justice as a penal option appears as an 'inclusive post-social justice' strategy (O'Malley, 2009) seeking to minimise harms, neutralise the public/social dimension of crimes and invest in cohesive and pro-social communities as politico-moral ideals.

Restorative justice between sovereign and non-sovereign relationships

It is my contention that those institutional developments, underpinned by the strategies described previously, configure restorative justice as a 'sovereign' mechanism of justice. 'Sovereignty', in political theory and public law, refers to a state's essential attribute, that is, the exclusivity of political obligation and the monopoly of legitimate violence (Austin, 1954; Hobbes, 2010; Weber, 2004). Differently from traditional political theory, this chapter conceives of 'sovereign' as a distinctive type of social relationship which informs not only specific institutional frameworks but circulates in the social realm, tying individual and groups together. These relationships have certain ontological, epistemological, anthropological and ethical characteristics which can be briefly (and ideal-typically) sketched out. From an ontological viewpoint, sovereign relationships rest on the overdetermination of both subjectivity and social relationships by considering them objective and not merely socially or ethically constructed. Social practices (for instance the defining of 'victim' or 'offender') are natural entities characterised by permanence, homogeneity and stability (Newman, 2010). Social phenomena are the inevitable and necessary consequence of antecedent states of affairs; they are marked by a destiny which unfolds historically towards supposedly better conditions (e.g. the indissoluble link between crime and punishment). This ontological outline ties in with a certain epistemological viewpoint, whereby sovereignty is marked by the idea that objective truth (e.g. the guilty plea or verdict's 'truth'), beyond intersubjective agreements and social constructions, exists and is achievable. Anthropologically, sovereign relationships are characterised by an underlying idea of subjectivity as fixed and stable (e.g. the offender as anthropologically different from the victim). Additionally, they are sustained by the Hobbesian negative view according to which the human condition has an inclination towards egoism, prevarication and violence. Ethically, the main characteristics of these relationships are hierarchy and centralisation; they lack reciprocity, offering minimal space for negotiation and transitivity.

Any institution, group or individual, when exerting top-down command over others, defining or limiting possibilities of being and becoming, is a sovereign machine. 'Conventional' criminal justice institutions are a paradigmatic example of sovereign mechanisms, since they commonly reproduce the type of relationships seen earlier. In a similar vein, institutionalised restorative justice, when endorsing processes of criminalisation, labelling, allocation of blame and dichotomisation of social relationships, re-establishes and diffuses sovereign relationships.

Restorative justice as non-sovereign justice

A possible way to deal with the transformation of restorative justice into a sovereign (penal) mechanism, consists of re-installing, at the core of this field, a generative combination of ethical work, political engagement and social resistance, that is, a commitment to non-sovereign values. 'Non-sovereign justice' is an open-ended ethical-political project of cultivating non-hierarchical and decentralised social relationships, outside a juridical framework (Newman, 2010: 23). It is based on the idea of 'ontological anarchism' (Newman, 2016: xii), that is, on 'a form of thinking and acting without an arché – in other words, without stable foundations or essential identities to determine its course' (Newman, 2016: xii). Non-sovereign justice endeavours to suspend sovereign categories and techniques, since they crystallise social relationships in authoritarian ways and impose hierarchical order upon social indeterminacy. This approach is radical inasmuch as it advocates for subversive and re-significatory justice practices which seek to decentre social norms, and promote transformative sociality. It aims to address transgressions to people's freedoms by offering opportunities to rethink social relationships and political obligations instead of re-establishing sovereign relationships. It is possible to lay out the main themes around which a non-sovereign restorative justice coalesces.

Destituent

Non-sovereign justice attempts to halt and deactivate the sovereign machine (Agamben, 2013) 'by exposing the void that lies at the center of its articulating mechanism, the central fiction that holds the machine together and keeps it running' (Attell, 2014: 164). 'Destituent' means 'a withdrawal of support from the sovereign political order, without the desire to replace it with another sovereign political order' (Newman, 2016: 288). By simply overthrowing the sovereign machine, in fact, this will reconstitute itself but in different forms or shapes, whilst by destitution, that is, by halting sovereign relationships, new relationships will be created. Whilst the constituent power 'refers to the revolutionary capacity [. . .] to constitute a political order', the destituent power embodied by non-sovereign justice 'does not propose to found a new political order, but implies the suspension of all orders' (Newman, 2016: 288). This would open a 'new political dimension' and 'the rediscovery of a form-of-life, the access to a new figure of that political life whose memory the Security State tries at any price to cancel' (Agamben, 2013).

From this perspective, restorative justice should be conceived of as a critique of both 'conventional' criminal justice and the diffused 'penal' mentality, unveiling the contradictions at the centre of these sovereign structures. Restorative justice should expose the criminal justice's focus on acts more than interactions, personality more than systems, breach of social order more than broken human relationships. The mentality of 'pain delivery' (Christie, 1981: 19), as antidote to the violated social order, should be contested as based on metaphysical illusions of sovereign control. This would be possible both by promoting restorative justice as a political movement advocating for an-archist (i.e. without metaphysical origins and authority) forms of sociality and by re-thinking the very restorative process. There is need of more localised, direct and non-representational forms of discussion of transgressions of people's freedoms as symptoms of 'communal inadequacies' (McKinney, 2012). Non-sovereign restorative processes should not be alternative (and apparently less punitive) penal consequences but conflict transformation practices, with no need of admission of responsibility as condition to enter. The only 'requirement' would concern the quality of the process: to neutralise sovereign relationships, that is, domination, hierarchy, violence. Additionally, restorative practitioners should not advocate for state laws or policy regulations. The legalisation, whilst on one hand appears to scale up restorative justice, on the other, ends up transforming it into a mechanism which reproduces authoritarian relationships. Such a critique has the potential to destitute the sovereign relationships that the 'conventional' criminal justice advances, by contesting its dichotomic, de-contextualised and politically neutralising effects. In this way, restorative justice would open up spaces for reinventing social relationships (Critchley, 2007: 113; Hoy, 2004: 89–90) beyond criminal justice institutions, practices and mentalities.

Radically democratic

Non-sovereign justice acknowledges the unequally distributed vulnerability, as a political and social phenomenon, characterising affluent Western democracies (Butler, 2009: 25). It claims attention towards those who struggle to mobilise themselves, because of being disenfranchised, poor and disadvantaged due to the effects of normalised practices of everyday sovereign apparatuses. This requires the recognition of structurally deprived groups and individuals as actors whose agency is mutilated or limited by political, social and economic processes. As Judith Butler suggests, there is need to acknowledge and address the condition of 'precarity' as a form of socio-economic and political vulnerability imposed on certain individuals and groups as well as to accept the vulnerability which pertains to every human being (i.e. 'precariousness') (Butler,

2009). The attempt to deny 'precarity' produces violence since subjects 'immunize [themselves] against the thought of [their] own precariousness' by asserting '[their] own righteous destructiveness' (Butler, 2009: 48). Conversely, the acknowledging of human vulnerability will prevent the violent immune response: 'mindfulness of this vulnerability can become the basis of claims' for non-violent solutions (Butler, 2006: 29). From this perspective, non-sovereign justice promotes, as a form of resistance to sovereign relationships, the mobilisation of precariousness against precarity, the common state of human vulnerability against the socio-economically produced marginalisation.

The way to produce such results within restorative justice is to promote restorative encounters as political-ethical spaces which recognise precariousness and critique of precarity by stressing and encouraging dissent and contentious claims in order to suspend sovereign control. There are no such things as 'victims', 'offenders' and 'communities'; but there are people, more or less deprived or wealthy, gendered and racialised, to be recognised and addressed. In restorative encounters, the 'problematic situations' (Hulsman, 1986: 73), that is, the conflict and harm, would become the material for political and ethical reflection. Individuals would be allowed to rethink the moral relationships questioned or broken by their behaviours, beyond juridical frameworks, and recognise them as related to wider social, economic and political vulnerabilities. It is not the consequences of a 'crime' but the criminalisation process to be the object of discussion. In fact, radically democratic restorative justice would critically engage 'with the relations that: define specific forms of wrongdoing; enable the conditions from which subjects respond as wrongdoers; frame subjects to be considered as the wronged; and generate and sustain identities for both individuals and communities in context' (Pavlich, 2017: 306–307). This also means criticising 'mainstreamed' restorative justice insofar as it individualises conflicts by downplaying their intertwined political, social and cultural drives. From this viewpoint, this approach denounces how restorative justice constitutes parties as victims and perpetrators necessarily in need of reconciliation and healing, overwriting 'other subject positions held by the people' (Renner, 2015: 1110).

Infinitely demanding

From the previous themes, it follows that non-sovereign justice recognises that justice can be only relational, since humans depend on uncontrollable relationships with others, and as such are vulnerable to the other (Kelz, 2015: 3). Non-sovereign justice puts forth an 'ethical appeal that seeks to overstep the boundaries of one's community or personal affiliations' (Kelz, 2015: 6), but at the same time it considers the political and social conditions of precarity. From this angle, ethics is understood as a primary responsibility for the other, instead of as individual accountability for its past actions (Kelz, 2016: 91). Non-sovereign justice poses, to quote Simon Critchley, an 'infinite demand' (2007) of the other that calls on us to act in the name of our 'responsibility to the other, in response to particular injustices and conditions of distress' (Kioupkiolis, 2011: 698). In Critchley's view, this ethical inflection, inspired by Emmanuel Levinas's ethics of an infinite responsibility to the other, facilitates encounters with multiple singularities which could not be contained within a single collective structure. This ethical approach has the potential to articulate 'a demand which is not arbitrary but universal in scope and it is energized by a feeling of anger at a situation of global injustice' (Kioupkiolis, 2011: 698).

The goal of 'infinitely demanding' restorative encounters would be primarily to offer a chance to engage in an activity of 'questioning and adjusting of thought and action in relation to notions of human good and harm' (Christie, 2005: 40). They would not just be an opportunity of 'norm clarification' (Christie, 1977) but political-ethical occasions of norm-creation.

This is possible if restorative encounters are safe and experimental fora, where individuals can participate in the ongoing production of themselves with and in front of others, and where they can be both witness to and resource for the experiments of others. These spaces would allow for critical activities and reflections which aim to intensify our relation with ourselves and with others. This work is as much political-ethical, considering that it is 'not an exercise in solitude, but a true social practice [. . .] an intensification of social relations' (Foucault, 1986: 53). At stake here is the creation of new micro-moral codes as a political act, critically resisting the limited range of possibilities available to those involved in social conflicts and harms offered by the 'conventional' criminal justice but also by 'mainstreamed' restorative justice.

Ethically reflexive

Non-sovereign justice provides opportunities to develop subjectivity whilst limiting subjection, that is, the unilateral and top-down shaping of one's conduct, which characterises sovereign relationships.[6] Michel Foucault defines ethics as the 'reflexive practice of freedom' (1997: 281), that is, the intentional self-forming activities (the 'care of the self') of an individual in order to 'subjectivise' herself, becoming in this way a moral subject (Foucault, 1986). The word 'subject' here entails two different meanings: 'subject to someone else by control and dependence; and tied to his or her own identity by a conscience or self-knowledge. Both suggest a form of power which subjugates and makes subject to' (Foucault, 2000: 331). The first connotation refers to being subjected to someone else but also to intentional and not subjective discourses; the second meaning refers to the activity of subjectivation, that is, the active self-fashioning ethical work. Subjectivation is the attempt to create productive freedom by choosing to shape new truths about oneself, detaching oneself from the normalised identities imposed by others and generating new possibilities of being and becoming. Non-sovereign justice is not grounded on and does not establish a 'fixed' human nature or a 'true' self to be enshrined in moral codes (which would end up promoting another form of domination). The self is instead a ceaseless process of becoming within a cultural and social context rather than a passive being. Accordingly, ethics is conceptualised as a transformative and relational practice of subjectivation (i.e. ethical fashioning of oneself) whose condition and outcome is freedom towards others.

Restorative justice should provide spaces free from the ethical coercion to conform to idealised models of 'law abiding citizens'. Ideas such as 'victim-led' or 'offender-led' interventions and practices such as 'restorative cautions' or the guilty plea as condition to enter restorative schemes, are extremely problematic, insofar as being informed by sovereign coercion. Those spaces should be free in the sense of rejecting the normalising labels offered by 'conventional' criminal justice (e.g. 'victim' and 'offender') as well as of critically re-thinking the labels provided by authoritative discourses of restorative justice ('healing', 'empowerment/disempowerment', 'reconciliation', etc.) (Maglione, 2017b). Therefore, the issue at stake is to think on how to shape restorative justice encounters as pluralistic and creative environments where participants' ethical work can take place, addressing proper responses to 'the other' and to their precariousness (Infinito, 2003: 155). The 'care of the self' would be practised as resistance to that which threatens to control one's identity, considering conversely freedom as the formation of the self (Infinito, 2003: 158). As David Hoy argues, this strategy of desubjugation consists not in our finding our true subjectivity behind ideological masks but in de-subjectifying ourselves, of purging the selves produced by sovereign and authoritarian forces, in order to become

---

6 I have widely developed this point in Maglione, 2017b.

different from the way we normally are (Hoy, 2004: 103). This is not only de-subjectification of individual subject identities but of collective, communal or social subject identities, avoiding entrapment by externally imposed and limiting subjectivities, activating human capacities for self-creation (Infinito, 2003: 159).

Conclusions: restorative justice to come

This chapter is a preliminary effort to envision restorative justice as a critique of sovereign relations. Whilst it provides an up-to-date review of a contested area in this field (i.e. the institutionalisation of restorative justice), it mainly aims to sketch out a restorative justice 'to come', informed by certain political and ethical values. The chapter starts by outlining a quite bleak picture of 'institutionalised' restorative justice as a sovereign form of justice which neutralises conflicts, limits creativity and generates hierarchical relationships. Conversely, the non-sovereign perspective offers 'the possibility to establish new, creative forms of political engagement' (Kelz, 2015: 10) fostering the emergence of new forms of relations between people (Lechte and Newman, 2013: 134). Non-sovereign restorative justice involves the creation of ethically reflexive and radically democratic arenas for norms-production and contestation of social, economic and political harms which feed in individual transgressions. The overarching goal is to 'form a community without affirming an identity' (Agamben, 1993: 86) by detaching individuals from the normalised identities imposed by 'conventional' criminal justice as well as by institutionalised restorative justice. Operationally, a non-sovereign restorative encounter would not be a time and place whereby the 'penal' consequences of the responsibility crystallised by the criminal justice process are decided but would be a space where the criminalisation and its wider context are discussed. The outcome would not be individual 'closure' or 'reconciliation' but ethical reflection and critique of the conditions for individual transgressions of people's freedom as well as political action to address them beyond the encounter. In order to further develop theoretically and implement this approach, a number of actions should be taken. The next step is to focus on the decriminalising and de-penalising of restorative justice, that is, working towards a restorative language truly different and independent from the 'conventional' criminal justice idiom in a bid to re-envision restorative encounters as something better than criminal justice.

References

Aertsen, I., Daems, T. and Robert L., eds. 2006. *Institutionalizing Restorative Justice*. Cullompton: Willan.

Agamben, G. 1993. *The Coming Community*. Minneapolis: University of Minnesota Press.

Agamben, G. 2013. For a Theory of Destituent Power. Available at www.chronosmag.eu/index.php/g--agamben-for-a-theory-of-destituent-power.html. Accessed 10 September 2017.

Attell, K. 2014. *Giorgio Agamben: Beyond the Threshold of Deconstruction*. New York: Fordham University Press.

Austin, J. 1954. *The Province of Jurisprudence Determined*. H.L.A. Hart, ed. New York: The Noonday Press.

Blagg, H. 2017. Doing Restorative Justice 'Otherwise'. In I. Aertsen and B. Pali (eds.) *Critical Restorative Justice*. Oxford: Hart, pp. 61–78.

Braithwaite, J. 1999. Restorative Justice: Assessing Optimistic and Pessimistic Accounts, *Crime & Justice: A Review of Research*, 25(1): 11–127.

Burchell, G. 1996. Liberal Government and Techniques of the Self. In A. Barry, T. Osborne and N. Rose (eds.) *Foucault and Political Reason*. London: UCL Press, pp. 19–36.

Butler, J. 2006. *Precarious Life: The Powers of Mourning and Violence*. London and New York: Verso.

Butler, J. 2009. *Frames of War: When Is Life Grievable?* London and New York: Verso.

Christie, N. 1977. Conflicts as Property, *British Journal of Criminology*, 1(17): 1–15.

Christie, N. 1981. *Limits to Pain.* Oxford: Robertson.

Christie, N. 1986. The Ideal Victim. In E. Fattah (ed.) 1986. *From Crime Policy to Victim Policy. Reorienting the Justice System.* London: Palgrave, pp. 17–30.

Christie, N. 2013. Words on Words, *Restorative Justice: An International Journal,* 1(1): 15–19.

Christie, N. 2015. Widening the Net, *Restorative Justice: An International Journal,* 3(1): 109–113.

Christie, P. 2005. Education for an Ethical Imagination, *Social Alternatives,* 24(4): 39–44.

Cohen, S. 1985. *Visions of Social Control: Crime, Punishment and Classification.* Glasgow: Polity Press.

Crawford, A. and Newburn, T. 2003. *Youth Offending and Restorative Justice: Implementing Reform in Youth Justice.* Collumpton: Willan.

Critchley, S. 2007. *Infinitely Demanding: Ethics of Commitment, Politics of Resistance.* London and New York: Verso.

Daly, K. 2016. What is Restorative Justice? Fresh Answers to a Vexed Question. *Victims & Offenders,* 11(1): 9–29.

Davis, G. 1992. *Making Amends: Mediation and Reparation in Criminal Justice.* London: Routledge.

Dignan, J. 2005. *Understanding Victims and Restorative Justice.* Berkshire: Open University Press.

Foucault, M. 1986. *The History of Sexuality, Volume III, The Care of the Self.* New York: Pantheon.

Foucault, M. 1997. *Essential Works of Michel Foucault: Ethics,* P. Rabinow, ed. New York: New Press.

Foucault, M. 2000. *Essential Works of Michel Foucault: Power,* J. Faubion, ed. New York: New Press.

Garland, D. 2001. *The Culture of Control: Crime and Social Order in Contemporary Society.* Oxford: Oxford University Press.

Gavrielides, T. 2013. Where Is Restorative Justice Heading? *Probation Junior,* 5(1): 79–95.

Hobbes, T. 2010. *Leviathan,* A.P. Martinich and B. Battiste, eds. Peterborough: Broadview Press.

Hoy, D.C. 2004. *Critical Resistance: From Poststructuralism to Post-Critique.* Cambridge and London: MIT Press.

Hulsman, L. 1986. Critical Criminology and the Concept of Crime, *Contemporary Crises,* 10(3/4): 63–80.

Infinito, J. 2003. Ethical Self-Formation: A Look at the Later Foucault, *Educational Theory,* 53(2): 155–171.

Johnstone, G. 2012. The Standardization of Restorative Justice. In T. Gavrielides (ed.) *Rights and Restoration within Youth Justice.* Whitby: de Sitter Publications.

Kelz, R. 2015. Political Theory and Migration Concepts of Non-Sovereignty and Solidarity, *Movements, Journal für kritische Migrations- und Grenzregimeforschung,* 1(2): 1–18.

Kelz, R. 2016. *Non-Sovereign Self, Responsibility, and Otherness: Hannah Arendt, Judith Butler, and Stanley Cavell on Moral Philosophy and Political Agency.* London: Palgrave.

Kioupkiolis, A. 2011. Keeping It Open: Ontology, Ethics, Knowledge and Radical Democracy, *Philosophy and Social Criticism,* 37(6): 691–708.

Lechte, J. and Newman, S. 2013. *Agamben and the Politics of Human Rights: Statelessness, Images, Violence.* Edinburgh: Edinburgh University Press.

Maglione, G. 2017a. *Communities at Large:* An Archaeological Analysis of the 'Community' Within Restorative Justice Policy and Laws, *Critical Criminology,* 25(3): 453–469.

Maglione, G. 2017b. Outlining a Historical and Critical Ontology of Restorative Justice. In I. Aertsen and B. Pali (eds.) *Critical Restorative Justice.* Oxford: Hart, pp. 79–93.

Mathiesen, T. 2015. *The Politics of Abolition Revisited.* London and New York: Routledge.

McKinney, C. 2012. An Anarchist Theory of Criminal Justice. Available at https://theanarchistlibrary.org/library/coy-mckinney-an-anarchist-theory-of-criminal-justice. Accessed 10 November 2017.

Moore, J.M. and Roberts, R. 2016. What Lies Beyond Criminal Justice? Developing Transformative Solutions, *Justice, Power and Resistance,* Foundation Volume: 115–136.

Newman, S. 2010. *The Politics of Postanarchism.* Edinburgh: Edinburgh University Press.

Newman, S. 2016. *Postanarchism.* Cambridge: Polity Press.

O'Mahony, D. and Campbell, C. 2006. Mainstreaming Restorative Justice for Young Offenders through Youth Conferencing: The Experience of Northern Ireland. In J. Junger-Tas and S.H. Decker (eds.) *International Handbook of Juvenile Justice.* New York: Springer. pp. 93–116.

O'Malley, P. 2009. *Risk and Restorative Justice: Governing Through the Democratic Minimization of Harms.* Available at www.researchgate.net/profile/Pat_Omalley/publication/228134124_Risk_and_Restorative_Justice_Governing_Through_the_Democratic_Minimisation_of_Harms/links/00b495350d1d6a9805000000.pdf. Accessed 10 September 2017.

Pavlich, G. 2005. *Governing Paradoxes of Restorative Justice*. London: Glasshouse Press.

Pavlich, G. 2017. Promised Communities, Unrestored Justice. In I. Aertsen and B. Pali (eds.) *Critical Restorative Justice*. Oxford: Hart, pp. 297–313.

Renner, J. 2015. Subjects and Struggles Producing the Subjects of Reconciliation: The Making of Sierra Leoneans as Victims and Perpetrators of Past Human Rights Violations, *Third World Quarterly*, 36(6): 1110–1128.

Rose, N. 1998. *Inventing Our Selves: Psychology, Power, and Personhood*. Cambridge: Cambridge University Press.

Rose, N. 1999. Inventiveness in Politics: Review of Anthony Giddens, The Third Way. *Economy and Society*, 28(3): 467–493.

Rose, N. 2001. Community, Citizenship, and the Third Way. In M. Denise and J. Minson (eds.) *Citizenship and Cultural Policy*. London: Sage, pp. 1–17.

Scott, D. 2013. Visualising an Abolitionist Real Utopia: Principles, Policy and Practice. In M. Malloch and B. Munro (eds.) *Crime, Critique and Utopia*. London: Palgrave Macmillan, pp. 90–113.

Strang, H. 2003. Justice for Victims of Young Offenders: The Centrality of Emotional Harm and Restoration. In G. Johnstone (ed.) *A Restorative Justice Reader: Texts, Sources, Context*. Cullompton: Willan, pp. 286–293.

Strang, H. and Sherman, L.W. 2003. Repairing the Harm: Victims and Restorative Justice, *Utah Law Review*, 1: 15–42.

Umbreit, M. 2001. Avoiding the Marginalization and "McDonaldization" of Victim-Offender Mediation: A Case Study in Moving Toward the Mainstream. In G. Bazemore and L. Walgrave (eds.) *Restorative Juvenile Justice: Repairing the Harm of Youth Crime*. Monsey, NY: Criminal Justice Press, pp. 213–234.

Van Ness, D.W. and Strong, K. 2003. *Restoring Justice: An Introduction to Restorative Justice*. Cincinnati: Anderson.

Walgrave, L. 2003. Imposing Restoration Instead of Inflicting Pain. In A. von Hirsch, J. Roberts, A. Bottoms, K. Roach and M. Schiff (eds.) *Restorative Justice and Criminal Justice: Competing or Reconcilable Paradigms?* Oxford: Hart, pp. 61–68.

Walgrave, L. 2017. Restorative Justice Is Not a Panacea Against All Social Evils. In I. Aertsen and B. Pali (eds.) *Critical Restorative Justice*. Oxford: Hart, pp. 95–110.

Weber, M. 2004. *The Vocation Lectures*, D. Owen and T. Strong, eds. Indianapolis: Hackett.

Wright, M. 1996. *Justice for Victims and Offenders*. Winchester: Waterside.

Zehr, H. 1990. *Changing Lenses: A New Focus for Crime and Justice*. Scottsdale: Herald Press.

3

Human rights and restorative justice

Ann Skelton

Introduction

Justice is underpinned by the idea of each person having an equal right to a fully adequate scheme of equal basic liberties, which is applicable to all (Rawls, 1971). These underpinning liberties were formulated into the Universal Declaration of Human Rights (UDHR) in 1948, the preamble of which indicates that the Declaration was made 'in recognition of the inherent dignity and of the equal and inalienable rights of all members of the human family'. The vision of the drafters of the UDHR was that human rights are 'the foundation of freedom, justice and peace in the world'. Henkin has posited that human rights are derived from accepted principles required by accepted societal ends such as peace and justice, and individual ends such as human dignity, happiness and fulfilment (Henkin, 1990). However, Harvey points out that one of the most frequently heard criticisms of human rights is that they 'perpetuate an individualised, atomistic and inherently selfish form of society' (2012: 70). This perspective views human rights as a 'top-down' set of rules that focus on individual rights at the expense of the collective. It is a view that seems to point in the opposite direction of a restorative justice orientation which favours 'bottom up' norm clarification that allows for democratic participation in justice processes. But Harvey observes that even if human rights seemed to have been delivered from above, their origins can be traced back to a struggle for rights from below.

Amartya Sen has pointed out, with some humour, that human rights activists and practitioners have very little patience for a debate about whether human rights actually exist or from where they are derived, because they are, understandably, getting on with solving the problems of the world (Sen, 2009: 356). Restorative justice practitioners are much the same. They are often somewhat impatient about having to consider whether restorative justice processes are a risk to rights.

Many of the human rights that are important for participants in the criminal justice system arose over centuries as a 'clawing back' of rights, particularly for offenders who found themselves at the receiving end of harsh, punitive measures imposed by the state (Bianchi, 1994; Jacob, 1997). As all restorative justice scholars know, this forms part of the narrative which requires conflicts to be reclaimed from the state and brought back to the people (Christie, 1977). This narrative may be contested by some (Johnstone, 2012), but the need to protect the puny individual against the might of the state was certainly the main reason why fair trial rights and due process rights developed in the criminal justice system and became part of our human rights protections, and why lawyers, in particular, are nervous about letting go of them. Indeed, even in the current criminal justice system, inequalities such as race, gender and poverty exist that stack the odds against certain participants (Gavrielides, 2014a).

This chapter recaps and updates the debates about the risks to rights in restorative justice and the practical means to minimise and manage these, such as through standards setting. It further aims to contribute to the Handbook's ambitions of pushing the boundaries of restorative justice by contrasting the usual vertical state-individual conceptualisation of human rights with a horizontal, relational version of human rights. The chapter ends with some ideas about how the reconceptualised and more compatible view of human rights and restorative justice can advance theory and practice.

What rights are protected in the criminal justice system?

The right to a fair trial

When we talk about rights protection within restorative justice, we often make comparisons with the rights that are available within the criminal justice system. This is a limited framework for discussing human rights, which go far beyond procedural issues. Nevertheless, it is a good place to start because there is a concern that participants may be 'giving up' these rights when they opt for a restorative justice process as an alternative to the criminal justice system. The right to a 'fair trial' or 'due process' includes legal principles that protect the suspect, which are common to most criminal justice systems, irrespective of whether the procedure is adversarial or inquisitorial. In the adversarial model the onus is on the litigants to present their cases before a passive judicial officer, whilst in the inquisitorial system the judicial officer plays an active role in conducting the proceedings. The principles of a fair trial are included in international instruments, Bills of Rights, statutes and common law. They are listed briefly in the following paragraph.

A person charged with a crime has the right to a public trial by a competent and impartial court. The presumption of innocence is considered a primary right, and it is closely linked to the right to remain silent. The suspect has a right to be present and to participate at the trial, and should have adequate notice and time to prepare. The sentence handed down should not include cruel, inhuman or degrading treatment, and should be proportionate to the crime. Any judicial decision which affects a defendant's rights should be open to review, and there should be mechanisms to apply for appeal from the decisions made by the court. A person must not be tried twice for the same offence. The adversarial system is party-based, and the defendant has a right to be placed on an equal footing with the prosecutor. Legal representation is considered to be an important form of assistance to the offender.

The rights of victims

The fair trial principles focus on the defendant, but the rights of victims started receiving attention over the past century, which intensified in the past 50 years. Strang (2001) records how the victim movement developed differently in different parts of the world. She describes the model that developed in the United States as a rights-based one, whilst the European model has been more support-focused, and this may be linked to the differences in the adversarial and inquisitorial approaches to criminal justice, the latter being the dominant model in continental Europe.

The rights movement has concentrated on reforming laws that are detrimental to victims, such as cautionary rules that prejudice victims, particularly women and children, and which weaken the impact of their evidence. The victim's rights movement has also fought for the right of victims to be informed about the developments in their cases. Greater participation in the criminal justice process is something that the victim rights movement has lobbied for, particularly the opportunity to make victim impact statements. The right has been won, but in practice it has done little to promote a sense of participation by victims in the criminal justice process (Erez, 2000; Richards, 2009). Obold-Eshelman has pointed out that victims' rights and voices are often used by the prosecution to determine the just deserts of offenders (2004: 9).

The rights of victims to participate at the sentencing stage is controversial, as some fear that their subjectivity may tip the scales heavily against the offender. Ashworth, for example, says that crime is a matter for the 'public interest' and that this goes beyond whether the victim considers that action should be taken against the offender, or how the offender should be punished (Ashworth, 2002). He cites the New Zealand case of *Clotworthy* and the English case of *Nunn* to illustrate that courts are reluctant to give victims the last word on sentence, due to concerns about proportionality. Braithwaite (2002a), responding to Ashworth (2002), pointed out that cases such as these prove that victims tend to demand less harsh punishments than just deserts theorists expect. Since that time there has been further academic analysis of those judgements (Edwards, 2002; Kirchengast, 2011). There have also been additional judgements from the courts in England and Wales (*R v Roche*; *R v Mills*; *R v Perks*). The courts in these cases have found a way to consider victims' submissions which ameliorate sentences. The standard set by the courts of England and Wales confine this to cases where the suffering of the victims is increased by the sentence set by the courts, or where the forgiveness of the victim indicates that he or she is less negatively affected than might be expected. This approach has carved out a narrow exception and has only led to a reduction in the custodial sentences imposed in the relevant matters, and not a replacement of the custodial sentence with a non-custodial one. Writing elsewhere with a co-author, I have argued that the approach of the appeal courts in England and Wales does not amount to a full application of restorative justice. However, through considering the harms and needs of victims and ameliorating the sentences accordingly, a restorative justice approach is blended with a just deserts requirement for the protection of lower limits (Van der Merwe and Skelton, 2015).

A further aspect to consider is the fact that the victim may not be the only person affected by the crime – the community might also be affected. The victims' rights movement has begun to reconsider who should be included in the definition of being a victim of a crime. One of the observations about a rights approach is that it tends to 'individuate' rather than view effects of crime within a more collective context (Obold-Eshleman, 2004 p. 9).

Unlike the rights of offenders, victims' rights are not expressly mentioned in the UDHR. At the international level, this gap was partially filled by the adoption of non-binding instruments. These include a declaration by the General Assembly on the basic principles of justice for victims of crime and abuse of power in 1985, and the adoption of the guidelines on justice in matters concerning child victims and witnesses, adopted by the Economic and Social Council in 2005. The European Commission issued a directive in 2012, setting out minimum standards on the rights, support and protection of victims of crime, and requiring EU Member States to implement the provisions of the Directive into their national laws by the November 2015 (Gavrielides, 2014b; 2016).

What are the risks to the rights of participants that might occur in restorative justice processes?

Having considered what rights victims and offenders have in criminal justice systems, the obvious next step is to consider what risks there are to the rights of participants in restorative justice processes. I have written about these elsewhere (Skelton and Frank, 2004; Skelton, 2007; Skelton and Sekhonyane, 2007) and will simply re-cap the most important concerns here, incorporating some newer writing by other authors. As I will show in the next part of the chapter, many of these risks have, to some extent, been met with responses through standard setting. Another point to make up front is that it is important to distinguish between normative claims of restorative justice and the gaps or problems that arise through practice. Many of the risks that are listed here will not be experienced if restorative justice is practised properly by experienced facilitators. In other words, the risks may not be inherent in restorative justice processes but may nevertheless be experienced if not actively guarded against through ensuring good practice. A final point to make which permeates the comparative discussion of risks to rights is the fact that many of the same rights are also at risk in the criminal justice system. Indeed, significant rights, such as dignity and freedom, may be even more at risk in the criminal justice system.

Risk to the rights of victims

Starting with the risks to the rights of victims – the beginning point is the risk of coercion to participate. Victims presented with the option of restorative justice may sometimes consent but still feel that they were coerced to do so. Systems where restorative justice processes are a legislated option may sometimes exacerbate the problem of coercion, as there is less choice for the victim (Gavrielides and Artinopoulou, 2012). We should not assume that factual consent dissolves the power imbalances that are inherent in many human interactions (Zehr, 1990; Boyes-Watson, 2000).

Another risk for victims is exposure to offender-biased proceedings. Although restorative justice is usually described as being a victim-centred process, several studies have shown that programmes tend to be offender-focused in practice (Choi et at., 2012: 35). This is a classic case of a gap in practice, rather than a normative problem.

Encounter with the offender can cause a sense of re-victimisation. The prosecution 'stands in' for the victim in criminal proceedings, creating a barrier between the victim and the offender. Although many victims feel less afraid after meeting the offender face to face, this requires careful facilitation of the restorative justice process. There should be support services such as counselling following a restorative justice encounter (Gavrielides and Artinopoulou, 2012).

Restorative justice processes may leave victims without a remedy if there is a failure by offenders to follow through on restitution or compensation agreements. There has been limited attention paid to the question of whether the victim can then turn to the civil system to sue for damages (Skelton and Frank, 2004).

Risks to the rights of offenders

Restorative justice processes start from the position that the offender must acknowledge responsibility, and it may be argued that this effectively removes the presumption of innocence and the right to silence from the suspect. A response to this concern is that the suspect is voluntarily relinquishing these rights in order to benefit from the restorative justice option and does the same in the criminal justice system when opting to plead guilty or enter a plea bargain. Improving the manner in which the options are put to the suspect can reduce the risk of coercion, and proper training is necessary. Ward and Langlands (2008: 361) assert that for restorative justice to be respectful of an offender's rights to autonomy, participation must be voluntary – and in principle this is correct. However, to some extent, there is often some element of coercion in restorative justice because the criminal justice system is a looming alternative.

The right to legal representation is considered an intrinsic part of the right to a fair trial in adversarial criminal justice proceedings. Whilst some restorative justice processes do allow parties to have legal representatives present, there are indications that lawyers who have not been trained in mediation or restorative justice tend to hinder rather than help the process. Braithwaite (2002b: 566) points out that restorative justice is intended 'to transcend adversarial legalism', and he therefore does not support a legal right of the accused to be represented by a lawyer at such proceedings, although he considers it reasonable to allow suspects to seek the advice of a lawyer on whether they should participate in the programme. Harvey (2012: 76–77) points out that lawyers enforcing a 'positivist' view of human rights can have a stifling effect in that they dominate processes and make others who do not know the law feel ill at ease. He does not suggest that lawyers have no role to play, but he is calling for a human rights discourse that is flexible enough to engage with restorative justice in all its complexity and to recognise its legal plurality.

The final two risks to rights lie in the normative rather than the procedural realm. They are proportionality and disparity in outcomes. The principle of proportionality is a major factor in deciding on a particular sentence in a criminal trial. In a criminal trial, a sentence cannot be increased beyond a limit appropriate to the severity of the offence, on the grounds of possible future offending, nor on the grounds of the need to treat the offender (Warner, 1994; Ashworth, 2002). However, these considerations may tend to influence outcomes of restorative justice processes, especially as restorative justice expressly intends to be forward looking as well as backward looking. In restorative justice, the outcome will be influenced by the victim far more than is possible within the criminal justice system. This links to the concern relating to disparities in outcomes, because victims may differ in the specific outcomes that they want to have. There is a risk that not only will there be internal inconsistency between restorative justice outcomes in separate (but similar) cases but that there will also be disparity between restorative justice outcomes and court outcomes for similar offences. Equal treatment before the law is a fundamental tenet of human rights, and it is an issue that is difficult to square with restorative justice's fluid, victim-centred process that values resolution and restoration of relationships over proportionality and equitable outcomes.

In most criminal justice systems, if a convicted person is of the view that his or her sentence is disproportionate to the offence, or if it is not consistent with sentences in similar cases, a remedy lies by way of an application for leave to appeal. This option is generally not available in restorative justice processes. (Skelton and Sekhonyane, 2007). Although one may argue that this is not necessary in a system where everything is done 'by agreement', the concern remains that consent is not always voluntary, and power disparity or even the conciliatory environment of a restorative justice process makes it difficult for participants experiencing unfairness or injustice to speak up about it at the time.

The risks to child defendants require special consideration. Due to their lack of experience, children are highly suggestible and are more likely to be coerced into making false admissions to avoid 'more trouble' (Winterdyk and Jones, 2012: 245). Dumortier (2003) has recorded research that indicates that children are often excluded from mediation due to their inability to pay material reparation, and that once in a process they may concede agreements that they cannot in reality fulfil. Haines has warned against a situation in which a child is 'upbraided' by a room full of adults, and subjected to reintegrative shaming (1998: 99). Ward and Langlands (2008: 363) point out the importance of the competence of the offender to know their rights and to understand what alternatives they have, and they give examples of practice in the well-developed New Zealand youth justice system which show the difficulties of true voluntariness of young offenders' participation. It is clear, then, that when dealing with child offenders, special care must be taken to ensure that the process does not result in domination, or in outcomes that are disrespectful or humiliating. Whilst these concerns should always be kept in mind in any restorative justice process, it appears to be easier for a room full of adults to forget these considerations when dealing with a child.

Standards in restorative justice

As the discussion of risks set out earlier in this chapter indicates, there are some rights issues to be concerned about in restorative justice, but most of them can be resolved. One of the most obvious ways of ensuring rights protection is through the setting of standards that guide practice. There are at least three reasons why such standards are useful – to ensure good practice and thereby protect the integrity of the process, to learn from the practice of others and provide material for training and for programme design, and to promote some similarity in process and outcomes.

Johnstone (2012) has recently reviewed the pro and con arguments about standard setting in restorative justice. He describes the 'ambivalence' that some proponents of restorative justice have about this, and he suggests that this is linked to the way many restorative justice advocates conceptualise restorative justice. Johnstone posits that the movement tells itself and others that restorative justice is a social movement that challenges the professionals and justice institutions that stole the community's conflicts. Johnstone reflects that from this perspective, the standardisation of restorative justice is seen negatively because it may result in restorative justice itself being co-opted by professionals and experts. Johnstone questions that well-rehearsed narrative – he is of the view that restorative justice actually arose due to the advocacy efforts of professionals who were frustrated with the criminal justice system, and he concludes that standard setting is necessary for restorative justice to retain its integrity and credibility. Johnstone has suggested that standard setting is a good idea because it will ensure that actions in the name of restorative justice are consistent with its values, that it will guard against poor or unethical practice and that the rights of participants will be protected (2012: 100).

Johnstone (2012: 100–111) points out that the growth and diversification of restorative justice has presented some challenges. These have given rise to concerns about whether everything that is called 'restorative justice practice' is really restorative, whether it is good practice and whether people's rights are being protected within it. Johnstone believes that standards are necessary.

In any event, even though ambivalence about standard setting may persist amongst some restorative justice writers and practitioners, standards are now part of restorative justice (Van Ness, 2003). At the 11th session of the UN Commission on Crime Prevention and Criminal Justice, Canada put forward a resolution that encourages countries to draw from Basic Principles on the Use of Restorative Justice Programmes in Criminal Matters in developing and implementing restorative justice. The Commission approved the resolution, and the Basic Principles may be seen as guidelines to assist states and organisations in their work. Moore and Mitchell (2009) emphasise the consultative, dialogic process that was followed in the development of these basic principles. The principles were further developed by a UN expert group on restorative justice, drawing on previous recommendations and existing guidelines developed by practitioner groups, and were adopted by ECOSOC in 2002 (Van Ness, 2003).

The Basic Principles deal with many of the risks that were described earlier in this chapter, such as voluntariness, consent, consideration of power imbalances and the parties' age and capacity when referring to, or conducting, a restorative justice process. There are also guidelines on what should happen when the parties fail to reach agreement and when there is failure to implement an agreement that has been made. The remainder of the Basic Principles deal with the recruitment of facilitators and guidelines for how they should carry out their functions, as well as the continuing development of restorative justice programmes and the promotion of research on and evaluation of restorative justice programmes. The principles are not binding. They are intended to provide guidance, and they do not address implementation in detail (Johnstone, 2012::94).

International and regional standards are not specific to the particular country context. Therefore, more detailed standards may be set in individual countries. This is sometimes done through legislation or through codes of conduct. The more prescriptive such standards become, however, the more there is a danger that they begin to destroy the essence of what restorative justice sets out to achieve. For this reason, many restorative justice advocates favour a value-infused approach to standard setting rather than a set of inflexible procedural rules.

There are debates about who should be setting the standards, and through what methods. Ashworth (2002: 581) believes that the state should set the standards because it must 'exercise its power according to established principles that uphold citizens' rights to equal respect and equality of treatment'. Braithwaite (2002b), who is less enthusiastic about standard setting, feels that they should be required only to guard against domination or power imbalance and to ensure upper limits in outcomes. He disagrees with Ashworth about the imposition of standards by the state. He favours a more democratic process of participation by stakeholders in the development of practice principles to ensure protection of rights.

In any event, the Basic Principles and other available standards relate to a narrow set of human rights – mostly procedural rights linked to the parallel and interconnected process of the criminal justice system. The reason for this is that the notion of a restorative justice world, as imagined by Zehr (1990), in which restorative justice stands alone as the only way of doing justice or runs as a parallel but separate track, has not materialised on a wide scale. Although such systems do exist within traditional communities (Shearing 2001), modern restorative justice systems are rarely, if ever, entirely divorced from the criminal justice system. Instead, restorative justice runs along a parallel track that is interlinked with the criminal justice system. This has led to a narrow discourse about rights and restorative justice.

Broadening the discourse around human rights

Human rights protection must be part of developing restorative justice practice. The criminal justice system emphasis on due process rights is, however, a rather narrow construct of rights. It is possible to give up the right to be presumed innocent through acknowledging responsibility and have one's human rights remain intact. Indeed, human rights such as dignity and equality may be enhanced through acknowledging responsibility in a restorative justice process.

Humbach (2001: 41–61) is of the view that depersonalised rights and rules cannot mediate the intricacies of interactions amongst human beings. Humbach refutes the idea that justice is achievable through the protection of individual rights. He believes that what we should be striving for is 'a justice of right relationships'. He contrasts this with the justice of rights, which he characterises as 'a justice of entitlements'. A justice of right relationships, on the other hand, arises out of the human attachments and connections that people form: 'At its core, the justice of right relationships is the intrinsic good that inures to persons who live in interaction with others whose fundamental concern is to maintain the quality and mutual worth of their relationships, instead of insisting on their rights.' (2001: 42).

Harvey argues that human rights should be understood within the social context of the real lives of human beings (2012: 72–74). He identifies a sense of dignity and of autonomy as providing people with the opportunity for discursive engagement. Linked to this is a dialogic conception of rights within which each rights holder can assert their rights equally, thus limiting the 'paternalism' of human rights discourse. Harvey's approach embodies a relational conceptualisation of human rights which considers others in society: 'To advance a normative human rights proposition is to give voice to an intrinsically collective and communal plea for mutual recognition and support' (Harvey, 2012: 73). Van Ness has also pointed out that we live in a relational world, that 'our relationships are who we are' (2012: 5). These arguments articulate a human rights discourse which, properly framed, emphasises dignity and autonomy which allows every individual to advance and claim their own rights. But their rights are enjoyed simultaneously with the rights of others, thus revealing a conception of rights which is ultimately collective and requires processes that will allow for peaceful living together.

The dialogic approach is further elaborated by González (2015: 462–463). She sees restorative justice as defending dignity and demanding empowerment. Drawing on the work of Engel (2012), she asserts the idea of rights-consciousness, and she believes that participants having their rights respected in restorative justice processes will also contribute to those participants' rights-consciousness. She asserts that rights take on meaning through the stories that people tell about themselves and others. In other words, rights can only be fully conceptualised within a real-life context.

Harvey (2012: 72) also sees rights as empowering people so that they 'move from being passive recipients of legal rights to active agents in a contested conversation'. Harvey's critique of formal human rights instruments is that they are legalistic and statist. He is concerned that 'emancipatory discourses can readily be co-opted and absorbed in processes of institutionalisation and codification'. Harvey finds a connection between human rights and restorative justice through a relational conception of human rights that does not seek to 'colonise social and political conversations about the terms of our collective existence'.

This relational and dialogical approach to human rights is also more compatible with indigenous justice conceptualisation of rights. I have previously pointed out that a more communitarian approach to rights is evident in countries that have a history of indigenous conflict resolution (Skelton, 2004). The starting point of this alternative ideation is the moral ethic of collective unity. Whilst modern Western ideation is premised on individualisation, indigenous ideation is based on a theory of collective living (Skelton and Frank, 2004).

These insights add up to a conclusion that a broader conceptualisation of human rights is compatible with restorative justice. A fundamental element of both is the dignity of each person. This should be valued not only singly but within a relational approach, which forms the basis for humans to live in mutually respectful rights relationships with one another. If an incident occurs which disturbs or distorts such a relationship, a restorative justice process would be the optimal method of repairing the harm in meaningful and inclusive ways. This can apply equally well for individual relationships or broader societal ones, which brings us back to the ambitious vision of the drafters of the UDHR, who believed that human rights were the foundation of freedom, justice and peace in the world. Many restorative justice advocates are no less ambitious about the role that restorative justice can play.

Conclusion

Human Rights can be considered on a vertical plane, as a relationship between the individual and the state in which the individual can stake claims or demands for protection, goods and services, and the state is required to desist from using its power to dominate. They can also be considered horizontally, within a contextual conceptualisation of relationships between people, and an understanding that rights are enjoyed simultaneously and that one person's rights may sometimes be limited (wrongly or rightly) by the exercise of another person's rights. The perfect balance is a mutually respectful rights relationship.

The due process rights of the criminal justice system lie mostly in the domain of the vertical relationship, in which the power of the state is constrained. This is particularly important in criminal justice processes which curtail fundamental rights such as freedom. This chapter has recapped some of the concerns that are expressed about the lack of procedural safeguards in restorative justice practice. Standard setting and good ethical practice were seen to be able to resolve some of these problems.

The proximity and interdependence of the restorative justice processes to and with the formal criminal justice process makes genuine voluntariness to participate more difficult – and coercion more likely. Over and above the procedural concerns that linger, there are one or two normative problems that remain, such as proportionality and disparity in outcomes.

The chapter has indicated that there is little point in continuing to debate whether standard setting is advisable, as it is clearly now part of restorative justice discourse and practice. The issue of how and by whom these standards should be set and what they should contain remains a matter for debate. A restorative justice perspective leans in favour of bottom-up norm clarification, and is wary of state-biased, top-down standard setting.

This chapter has also explored the horizontal angle of human rights and identified synergies between human rights and restorative justice through considering relational and dialogic approaches to rights. This conceptualisation retains the idea of individual autonomy but views this within the context of a lived reality in which the individual is part of a community. This shifts rights from the notion of a 'trump' that can be played to resist state power to a communitarian approach in which all participants in a restorative justice process, and indeed in broader society, are living in mutually respectful rights relationships. This accords better with the restorative justice notion that justice itself can be removed from state power, restoring the autonomy and dignity to the participants, who can be agents in the resolution of their own conflicts.

Narrow conceptualisations of rights tethered to comparisons with the 'due process' model of the criminal justice should be transcended. Because restorative justice aims to remove the state from its practices, allowing people to be their own deliverers of justice, it makes sense to be less concerned, going forward, about the vertical plane of rights between the state and the individual. Risks within restorative justice cannot be ignored but can be minimised and resolved through standard setting and good ethical practices. A focus on the horizontal exercise of rights – a consciousness about rights in relationships, will go a long way in achieving this and may even minimise the lingering concerns about normative gaps such as proportionality and disparity in outcomes. The more proportionate the outcomes are, the less disparity there is likely to be.

This chapter has sought to provide an up-to-date resource on restorative justice and human rights. It has aimed to redirect the discussion about human rights away from a vertical, top-down, state-biased, criminal justice tethered and individualistic conceptualisation. It has pointed instead towards a horizontal, mutually respectful rights relationship which allows for dignified rights-conscious participants to be agents in their own justice processes. This reconceptualization can have real effects in practice through the way that standards are developed and by whom, and through the encouragement of a relational rights-consciousness in restorative justice.

References

Ashworth, A. 2002. Responsibilities, Rights and Restorative Justice, *British Journal of Criminology*, 42(3), 578–595.

Bianchi, H. 1994. *Justice as Sanctuary*. Bloomington: Indiana Press.

Boyes-Watson, C. 2000. Reflections on the Purist and Maximalist Models of Restorative Justice, *Contemporary Justice Review*, 3(4): 441–451.

Braithwaite, J. 2002a. In Search of a Restorative Jurisprudence. In L. Walgrave (ed.) *Restorative Justice and the Law*. Cullompton: Willan.

Braithwaite, J. 2002b. Standards for Restorative Justice, *British Journal of Criminology*, 42(3): 563–577.

Braithwaite, J. 2003. Principles of Restorative Justice. In A. von Hirsch, J. Roberts, A. Bottoms, J. Roach and M. Schiff (eds.) *Restorative Justice and Criminal Justice: Competing or Reconcilable Paradigms*. Oxford: Hart.

Braithwaite, J. and Strang, H. 2000. Connecting Philosophy to Practice. In H. Strang and J. Braithwaite (eds.) *Restorative Justice: Philosophy to Practice*. Dartmouth: Ashgate.

Choi, J., Bazemore, G. and Gilbert, M. 2012. Review of Research on Victims' Experiences in Restorative Justice: Implications for Youth Justice, *Children and Youth Services Review*, 34(1): 35–42.

Christie, N. 1977. Conflicts as Property, *British Journal of Criminology*, 17(1): 1–15.

Dumortier, E. 2003. Legal Rules and Safeguards within Belgian Mediation Practices for Juveniles. In E. Weitekamp and H.J. Kerner (eds.) *Restorative Justice in Context: International Practice and Directions*. Cullompton: Willan.

Edwards, I. 2002. The Place of Victims' Preferences in the Sentencing of 'Their' Offenders, *Criminal Law Review*: 689–702.

Engel, D. 2012. Vertical and Horizontal Perspectives on Rights Consciousness, *Indiana Journal of Global Legal Studies*, 19: 423.

Erez, E. 2000. Integrating a Victim Perspective in Criminal Justice Through Victim Impact Statements. In A. Crawford and J. Goodey (eds.) *Integrating a Victim Perspective within Criminal Justice: International Debates*. Aldershot: Ashgate, Ch 8.

Gavrielides, T. 2014a. Bringing Race Relations into the Restorative Justice Debate. *Journal of Black Studies*, 45(3): 216–246.

Gavrielides, T. 2014b. *A Victim-Led Criminal Justice System for Europe: Addressing the Paradox*. London: IARS Publications.

Gavrielides, T. 2016. Repositioning Restorative Justice in Europe: The Victims' Directive, *Victims & Offenders*, 11, ISS. 1: 71–86.

Gavrielides, T. and Artinopoulou, V. 2012. Human Rights-based Restorative Justice for Violence Against Young Women. In T. Gavrielides (ed.) *Rights and Restoration Within Youth Justice*. Whitby: De Sitter Publications. Ch.7.

González, T. 2015. Reorienting Restorative Justice: Initiating a New Dialogue of Rights Consciousness, Community Empowerment and Politicization, *Cardozo Journal of Conflict Resolution*, 16: 475.

Haines, K. 1998. Some Principled Objections to a Restorative Justice Approach to Working with Juvenile Offenders. In L. Walgrave (ed.) *Restorative Justice for Juveniles: Potentialities, Risks, and Problems for Research*. Leuven: Leuven University Press.

Harvey, C. 2012. Reconstructing and Restoring Human Rights. In T. Gavrielides (ed). *Rights and Restoration within Youth Justice*. Whitby: De Sitter Publications, Ch. 3.

Henkin, L. 1990. *The Age of Rights*. New York: Columbia University Press.

Humbach, J. 2001. Towards a Natural Justice of Right Relationships. In B. Leiser and T. Campbell (eds.) *Human Rights in Philosophy and Practice*. Dartmouth: Ashgate.

Jacob, B. 1977. The Concept of Restitution: An Historical Overview. In J. Hudson and B. Galaway (eds.) *Restitution in Criminal Justice*. Lexington Books, Lexington.

Johnstone, G. 2012. The Standardisation of Restorative Justice. In T. Gavrielides (ed.) 2012. *Rights and Restoration Within Youth Justice*. Whitby: De Sitter Publications. Ch.4.

Kirchengast, T. 2011. The Landscape of Victim Rights in Australian Homicide Cases: Lessons from the International Experience, *Oxford Journal of Legal Studies*, 31(1): 133–163.

Obold-Eshleman, C. 2004. Victim's Rights and the Danger of Domestication of the Restorative Justice Paradigm, *Notre Dame J.L. Ethics and Public Policy*, 18: 571.

Rawls, J. 1971. *A Theory of Justice*. Cambridge, MA: Harvard University Press.

Richards, K, 2009. Taking Victims Seriously? The Role of the Victims' Rights Movement in the Emergence of Restorative Justice, *Current Issues in Criminal Justice*, 21(2): 302–320.

Sen, A. 2009. *The Idea of Justice*. London: Penguin Books.

Shearing, C. 2001. Transforming Security: A South African Experiment. In H. Strang and J. Braitwaite (eds.) *Restorative Justice and Civil Society*. Cambridge: Cambridge University Press.

Skelton, A. 2004. For the Next Generations: Remaking South Africa's Juvenile Justice System. In E. Doxtader and C. Villa-Vicencio (eds.) *To Repair the Irreparable: Reparation and Reconstruction in South Africa*. Claremont: David Philip.

Skelton, A. 2007. Restorative Justice and Human Rights. In S. Parmentiar and E. Weitekamp (eds.) *Crime and Human Rights*, Series in *Sociology of Crime, Law and Deviance*, Vol. 9. Amsterdam and Oxford: Elsevier and JAI Press, pp. 171–192.

Skelton, A. and Frank, C. 2004. How Does Restorative Justice Address Human Rights and Due Process Issues? In H. Zehr and B. Toews (eds.) *Critical Issues in Restorative Justice*. Monsey, NY: Criminal Justice Press and Willan.

Skelton, A. and Sekhonyane, M. 2007. Human Rights and Restorative Justice. In D. Van Ness and G. Johnstone (eds.) *Handbook on Restorative Justice*. Cullompton: Willan, pp 580–597.

Strang, H. 2001. The Crime Victim Movement as a Force in Civil Society. In H. Strang and J. Braithwaite (eds.) *Restorative Justice and Civil Society*. Cambridge: Cambridge University Press.

Van der Merwe, A. and Skelton, A. 2015. Victims' Mitigating View in Sentencing Decisions: A Comparative Analysis, *Oxford Journal of Legal Studies*, 35(2): 355.

Van Ness, D. 2003. Proposed Basic Principles on the Use of Restorative Justice: Recognising the Aims and Limits of Restorative Justice. In A. von Hirsch, J. Roberts, A. Bottoms, K. Roach and M. Schiff (eds.) *Restorative Justice and Criminal Justice: Competing or Reconcilable Paradigms*, Oxford: Hart.

Van Ness, D. 2012. Reconstructing and Restorative Human Rights. In T. Gavrielides (ed.) *Rights and restorative justice within youth justice*. Whitby: De Sitter Publications. Ch.3.

Winterdyk, J. and Jones, N. 2012. The Shifting Visage of Youth Justice in Canada: Moving Towards a More Responsive Regulatory Model Within a Human Rights framework. In T. Gavrielides (ed.) *Rights and Restorative Within Youth Justice*. Whitby: De Sitter Publications. Ch.3.

Ward, T. and Langlands, R.L. 2008. Restorative Justice and the Human Rights of Offenders: Convergences and Divergences, *Aggression and Violent Behaviour*, 13: 355–372.

Warner, K. 1994. Family Group Conferences and the Rights of the Offender. In C. Alder, and J. Wundersitz (eds.) *Family Conferencing and Juvenile Justice: The Way Forward or Misplaced Optimism?* Canberra: Australian Institute of Criminology.

Zehr, H. 1990. *Changing Lenses: A New Focus for Crime and Justice*. Scottdale, PA: Herald Press.

Zehr, H. and Toews, B., eds. 2004. *Critical Issues in Restorative Justice*. Monsey, NY: Willan.

Cases

R v Clotworthy (1998) 15 CRNZ 651 (CA).

R v Nunn [1996] 2 Cr. App. R (S) 136.

R v Mills [1998] 2 Cr App R (S) 252.

R v Roche [1999] 2 Cr App R (S) 105.

R v Perks [2001] 1 Cr App R (S) 19.

4

Beyond restorative justice

Social justice as a new objective for criminal justice

Nestor E. Courakis and Theo Gavrielides

From restorative justice to social justice

Following the onset of the 2008 financial crisis, the difficult conditions that most Europeans have been facing have led to the emergence of new challenges in criminal justice policy and to the respective need of new responses. This chapter argues that a possible response to this new demanding situation could be based on the double aim for a greater level of social solidarity in human relations as well as for meritocratic fairness when assessing incidences of inequality.

During the last few decades, criminal justice policy has developed the idea of reconciliation of conflicts between the offender and the victim. Restorative justice has emerged[1] to support these debates and to remind reformists that they must consider the needs of both the victim and the offender. There is also now a need to advocate for relevant methods aiming at extrajudicial settlements and for the reconciliation of the offender and the victim. Restorative Justice is, hence, based on the triptych of the perpetrator assuming responsibility for their actions, of restoring the state of the victim, as far as possible, to what it was before the injurious actions against the victim and, also, of actively expressing the desire for reconciliation with the victim (cf. Gavrielides, 2007: 139). These ideas have already penetrated in legislation. For example, in the Greek Law for Minors, there is provision for the reformatory conciliation measure, pursuant to article 122 of the Greek Penal Code.

Apparently, this trend has reinforced the detachment of criminal law from state authority and from the so-called *jus puniendi*. At the same time, it has brought to the forefront both the decisive role that the victim plays in disputes of a criminal nature and the active participation of the community in resolving differences among its members, for example, through mediation. Therefore, this trend towards restorative justice, has opened up new horizons in the field of criminal policy as well as in the field of criminal science in general.

---

1 Restorative justice owes its origin, and even its name, to Aristotle (Nicomachean Ethics, V 6, 1130 b 38 ff.) (cf. Artinopoulou and Gavrielides, 2013)

At the same time, another significant trend has emerged, one that focuses on the principle of proportionality. This is based on the assumption that the sanction or any other social reaction, caused by the criminal act, must be both proportionate and appropriate to the offence. Known as *"just deserts"* (=deserved punishment or reward), this trend is complementary to restorative justice and draws attention to the gravity of the offence and to the respect of the rights of the perpetrator, either as defendant or as prisoner – cf. von Hirsch, 1986 and von Hirsch and Ashworth, 2005.

However, this chapter argues that both these trends favour only a mere restoration of the *status quo* in the form of a so-called "numerical" equality and proportion (cf. Aristotle, *Nicomachean Ethics*, V 6, 1131 a 33 ff) between the damage caused and the compensation awarded. Yet the characteristics of the perpetrator and the conditions that led him to the criminal act are not taken into account, except for some general considerations regarding his capacity for imputabilty and the degree of his criminal responsibility. Consequently, factors which have led to criminal behaviour, such as the perpetrator's poor financial situation, do not seem to play an important role in his criminal treatment, even though coping with these factors could certainly contribute to the elimination or reduction of such criminal acts in the future.

During times of profound crisis at all levels (financial, moral and ethical), the chapter argues that there is a need for more than simple offender-victim conciliation in the form of restorative justice and just deserts. The chapter aims to contribute to the volume's ambition for pushing the boundaries of criminology and restorative justice by arguing that the need for this spirit of reconciliation and solidarity between persons involved in a criminal act should be extended to the benefit of all those who are experiencing hard times and may, therefore, in their deprivation and frustration, be led to committing crime or to suffering from it. In other words, in view of the current difficult financial conditions, a new form of justice is required to fill this existing gap by embracing the two aforementioned fundamental concepts of social solidarity and meritocratic fairness. Besides, this kind of justice could also be appropriate for healing at a more general level society's wounds relating to crisis and distress. Put another way, when it comes to restorative justice, it should not be just about the victim and the offender in the narrow sense.

The chapter is divided into three main sections. The first aims to unravel the concept of social justice, putting it within the context of our current reality and societies. The second section proceeds to explain how social justice can be achieved by putting an emphasis on socially and economically disadvantaged groups. The third section aims at introducing our social justice notion into contemporary criminal justice policy. The chapter argues that social justice can be incorporated through four routes: legislation, sentencing, correctional services and finally and more importantly, social prevention. We conclude with some critical remarks for the restorative justice movement, which must open up its doors to social justice and its wider aims for addressing economic disparities.

Understanding social justice

Social justice can be described as the shared space where the two concepts of restorative justice and just deserts meet. Social justice "may be broadly understood as the fair and compassionate distribution of the fruits of economic growth" (International Forum for Social Development of the United Nations, 2006: 7).[2] Consequently, social justice has two main aspects and serves, at the same time, two main purposes.

---

2 www.un.org/esa/socdev/documents/ifsd/SocialJustice.pdf.

First, social justice focuses on social solidarity and humanism, having therefore as a main objective the idea of helping others in a spirit of love and "compassion", and even of offering our belongings to those in need.[3] Second, this same notion of social justice contains the idea of meritocratic fairness, which prioritises excellence and encourages each individual to develop their abilities and skills in order to overcome oneself and build a better future at a personal level. Meritocracy contains here a specific sense: According to Aristotle, it provides equality for those who are equal and inequality for those who are unequal (*Politics*, III 5, 1280 a 12 ff. and 1282 b 22 ff.). This kind of "deserved equality" means that emphasis is placed on the specific characteristics of each individual so as to achieve, in accordance with the relevant teaching of the same philosopher, the goal of distributive justice and of a so-called "geometric" equality (*Nicomachean Ethics*, V 6, 1131 b 15 ff, VII, 1132 a 3 ff).

At a more general level, but almost similar in effect, justice, according to David Miller in his book *Principles of Social Justice* (2003: 207 ff., 134 ff., 232), has three major principles and pillars: (a) need (one is lacking in basic necessities and one's capacity to function is being impeded); (b) desert (one earns reward based on performance); and (c) equality (society regards and treats its citizens as equals, so that certain rights should be distributed equally) – (cf. Caravelis and Robinson, 2016, 20 and Capeheart and Milovanovic, 2007, 41 ff.). The idea that equality is also a pillar of justice is in principle correct. However, apart from some specific civil and political rights which must be recognized equally for all citizens, (irrespective of their race, ethnicity, gender, etc.), all other available resources and disadvantages in society have to be distributed on the basis of particular characteristics of these citizens, depending each time on the circumstances – hence mainly on the basis of their needs and their desert.

Obviously, these two criteria and purposes (needs and just desert) conceal in the last analysis two opposing world views. In fact, in their extreme forms, they are contradictory to one another and, when disconnected from each other, create more problems than the ones they solve. The idea of helping others in view of their needs, detached from the motivation of rewarding those who are talented, can lead to a society where citizens have no incentives for excellence and who consequently, instead of working hard, will be expecting help from others and the state. On the other hand, desert and excellence alone encourage an attitude of extreme individualism. This individualistic approach implies, in particular, that everyone must be interested only in themselves, and, essentially, to such an extent that the ideas of social cohesion and social offering are deprived of every substantive content and value. Nevertheless, this view has been particularly expressed by the libertarian Robert Nozick in his book *Anarchy, State and Utopia* (1974: 150 ff.), where he considers the redistribution of income through progressive taxation as "theft" and even "servitude" imposed by the government.

A bridging and creative synthesis of these opposing approaches and world views is therefore essential, also because they are both indispensable for a well-functioning society. Besides, these two counterbalancing views tend to disguise a more general conflict between idealism and utilitarianism, or even between equality and freedom, especially in the form of an opposition between socialism and (neo)liberalism. Furthermore, such controversies can also be detected in the interpretation of legal rules, where the principles of natural law and equitas in the sense of Aristotle (*Nicomachean Ethics*, V 15, 1137 b 16 ff.) contradict the so-called legal positivism.

---

3 Cf. under this aspect: Malekian, 2017: esp. 217 ff. and furthermore Rawls, 1971: 191–192, who considers the so called "love of mankind" as prompting to acts of supererogation and as binding a community of persons together, quoted in Malekian, 2017, 29.

Hence, a crucial question arises: in which way can social justice contribute to the bridging of these contradictions? The chapter argues that this can be achieved if some limits are set concerning both approaches and if the one eventually influences the other in a positive way so as to jointly create an organic whole.

With respect to the *concept of humanism (and social solidarity)*, the limit is to ensure a basic level of living and dignity for our fellow citizens, both at a national and an international level. Obviously, this concerns mainly the vulnerable social groups (e.g. unemployed and homeless people, economic migrants, drug-dependents, inmates that have been released from prison). In the case of these people, solidarity does not constitute a form of generosity within the social state but an important obligation of the state, particularly related to securing citizens' basic social rights, such as education, health and social security services, employment and housing opportunities, protection of children and of the elderly. John Rawls's development of the Difference Principle (*A Theory of Justice*, Harvard University Press, 1971, § 26) provides us with some insight as to how this solidarity in favour of our weak, unqualified fellow citizens can be achieved.

However, this theory was formed back in the 1970s, when economic development in European countries was still unhindered and there was consistent funding of the social state's institutions. Yet nowadays economic conditions have deteriorated dramatically, and a more general phenomenon of impoverished social groups is observed, especially in Southern European countries. Consequently, a new and innovative proposal is required to support these groups and reduce the great economic inequality in society which can lead to crime and to social unrest. This kind of proposal and one with such an objective unfortunately is not found in Rawls's work, even if the influence of this work in modern political philosophy cannot be denied and its ideas are still broadly discussed whenever social justice is at stake (cf. Clayton and Williams (Eds.), 2004, in particular the contributions of Robert Nozick, Ronald Dworkin, G.A. Cohen, Elizabeth S. Anderson and David Miller – Amartya Sen could also be included here!). In particular, the work of Rawls constitutes, according to a pertinent remark, an "ideal theory" and not an approach of how, for example, to organize social institutions in societies with a serious scarcity of resources (Meyer and Sanklecha, 2016: 16).

Furthermore, with respect to the *concept of excellence (and meritocracy)*, the limit is to ensure equal opportunities for all citizens from the beginning of their careers onwards. An important condition for the achievement of this goal is of course to ensure the adequacy of the aforementioned services of education, healthcare and so on, which are related to the social rights and the social state's function. Moreover, what is also crucial is to combat and, if possible, to eliminate the conditions that favour lack of meritocracy, such as clientele relations and corruption. In addition, equally important is to address the factors that give rise to corruption, for instance, the multitude of laws, the bureaucracy, the lack of employee assessment and accountability, maladministration and impunity for duty offences as well as the lack of public sensibilisation, especially of young people, concerning these issues.

Achieving social justice

Social justice attempts to bring together, in a spirit of humanism and meritocracy, (a) a decent standard of living for the members of a society, especially the vulnerable ones, by enhancing their social rights (Kant refers, here, to man's need for being *sui juris*) (1798, in the edition of 1968: 345), and (b) the possibility of equal opportunities at an educational and a professional level for those aspiring to improve their social situation. On this occasion, it is useful to underline here that this equality of opportunity should not be limited to economic equality and justice. Instead, it should also aim, to some extent, at the equality of outcome, even by means of a radical redistribution of income (e.g. by imposing high inheritance taxes). In this way, necessary resources can be provided to offer support, through state scholarships or working capital at the beginning of a professional career, to individuals whose skills and abilities have already become evident during school and higher education. Although this synthesis cannot easily be addressed, one could take into account, on a practical level, the Copenhagen Declaration and Program of Action (1995).[4] This is a thorough and comprehensive programme concerning the ways in which the vulnerable social groups, as well as the countries within which they are found, can be supported without putting economic growth at risk.

It is obvious that the synthesis of these two approaches, (i.e. the humanistic and the meritocratic), within the conceptual framework of social justice, is characterised by fragility, due to difficult balances that must be achieved every time. However, this is a synthesis that constitutes the optimal form of justice, because it combines all the positive aspects of opposing conditions and interests, eventually going back to and even tackling the primary conflict between the community and the individual, or between collectivism and individualism.

At a political level, a substantive form of this Hegelian "synthesis" (or of the "harmony" in the terminology of Heraclitus) could be found in the ideology of social democracy and social liberalism, as a "centrist" reconciliation between socialism and (neo)liberalism. Moreover, at a financial level, a similar form of this synthesis is observed in the successful model of *soziale Marktwirtschaft*, which has been, for decades, the theoretical foundation of the economic policy of the Federal Republic of Germany.[5] Similarly, some of the so-called "mixed economy theories" have been set forth within the same theoretical framework.

However, it should be noted that social justice, although a result of a synthesis between socialism and (neo)liberalism, does not necessarily coincide with the political "centre" and social democracy. Instead, social justice should mainly be understood as overcoming the traditional division between the left and the right, which goes back to the French Revolution in 1789, and as putting the priority on "pragmatic" policies ("Realpolitik"!) that are primarily based on the effective and efficient management of power. This is the case, as it seems, with the governments that the French President Emmanuel Macron formed from 2017 onwards and, to a lesser extent, with the governments of the English statesman Tony Blair: during the ten years of his premiership (1997–2007), and in the spirit of the so-called "Third Way", he advocated social justice, cohesion, the equal worth of each citizen, and equal opportunity combined with an emphasis of personal responsibility.[6]

Social justice is an archetypical notion, having therefore an idealistic character and concerns societies and economies studied by scholars under so-called "laboratory conditions". On the contrary, in real contemporary societies, and especially in societies undergoing an economic crisis or distress, conditions are in a state of flux and, therefore, models are required which would be able to harmonize the proper degree of humanism and meritocracy with the respective given circumstances. When the primary focus in a society is on the economic development and on the increase of the gross domestic product, (neo)liberal policies and wealth accumulation evidently come to the forefront so as to create big, powerful businesses that will not only survive but will also prevail in the intense international competition. But once a country's position in the regional and international economic environment is established, it becomes feasible for socialist, or social-democratic, policies to then be applied in order to achieve a fairer

4 www.un.org/esa/socdev/wssd/text-version/.
5 cf. https://de.wikipedia.org/wiki/Soziale_Marktwirtschaft.
6 – cf. https://en.wikipedia.org/wiki/Third_Way; see also Cook, 2006, esp. pp. 67 ff., where criminal policy of the Blair administration is assessed.

distribution of the already accumulated wealth (i.e. of the big "wealth pie"), especially in favour of the vulnerable social groups.

Finally, if economic development has been established, but its maintenance is put at risk due to conditions of crisis or distress, then a new model becomes essential, which may take a more complex form, combining the two main political systems (i.e. (neo)liberalism and socialism). Such a model would pursue the target of distribution of social wealth with concern to vulnerable social groups so that they do not become impoverished but also without causing any serious impact on the market economy. Achieving this fragile objective is indeed difficult, but it is probably the only solution to the problems triggered by a breaking crisis.

Introducing social justice into criminal justice policy and practice

We are now ready to turn to the question of the possibilities for social justice to help in the planning and implementation of an effective criminal policy at the legislative, judicial (sentencing) and correctional levels as well as in the social prevention of crime. We also ask what the problems are which should be taken into consideration in such an endeavour.

Social justice at the legislative level

At a legislative level, there are institutions that reinforce the idea of social solidarity and humanism, while at the same time there are other institutions that attempt to prevent any unequal treatment of citizens, thus emphasizing the promotion of meritocracy.

With respect to the first part of the issue just mentioned (i.e. social solidarity and humanism), criminal law penalizes the behaviour of any person who does not show solidarity with their fellow citizens and who is not willing to protect them from life-threatening danger, as long as he/she can do it without risking his/ her own life or health (e.g. see – cf. art. 307 Greek Penal Code and art. 422b ff. Belgian Penal Code; see also Feinberg, 1984, 165 ff). Furthermore, the punishment becomes more severe when the person who fails to take such an action has a special legal obligation to do so (e.g. a father who is able to swim and does not do so to save his child from drowning is liable for intentional homicide (cf. art 15 Greek Penal Code and § 13 German Penal Code). In addition, a criminal sanction can be inflicted if a person fails to offer the assistance requested in the case of a fatal accident, of a common danger or of general emergency, provided that this assistance may be offered without putting themselves in substantial danger (cf. art. 288 para. 2 Greek Penal Code and § 323c German Penal Code). Finally, punishment is also imposed on anyone who, in the case of self-defence, exceeds the limits of its proper exercise and badly injures, for instance, a child or a mentally disabled person who steals something from their garden. Apparently, such an act is contrary to the prerequisite of solidarity towards vulnerable persons and furthermore violates the principle of proportionality, which of course plays a decisive role in most legal relations (cf. art. 22 Greek Penal Code and § 32 German Penal Code).

At a more general level, social solidarity and social justice are also recognized as primary principles. In fact, some constitutions, such as the Italian (article 2) and the Greek (article 25 para. 4) ones, stipulate that the state has the right to claim of all citizens to fulfil the duty of social and national solidarity. Moreover, in the existing Treaty of the European Union (article 3 para. 3) there is a clear reference to the obligation of the European Union to promote, *inter alia*, "social justice and protection".[7] Likewise, of particular importance, at the level of soft-law,

---

7 www.lisbon-treaty.org/wcm/the-lisbon-treaty/treaty-on-european-union-and-comments/title-1-common-provisions/4-article-3.html.

is the provision (art. 1) of the Universal Declaration of Human Rights (1948), under which people must treat each other in a spirit of brotherhood.[8] It is noteworthy to recall that brotherhood (fraternité) was also one of the principles of the French Revolution of 1789, along with freedom and equality.

Apart from penal regulations concerning social solidarity, there are also relevant institutions which seek to ensure an equal and meritocratic treatment in the distribution of tax burdens in proportion to the citizens' means (cf. article 13 of the Declaration of the Rights of Man and of the Citizen, 1789)[9]. The violation of the relevant provisions because of tax evasion has serious implications and, in the case of Greece, it can even lead to felony sentencing, especially if it exceeds a certain amount of money (art. 8, Law-Nr. 4337/2015) and/or occurs concurrently with the offence of money-laundering. Under this aspect, legislation on taxation indeed attempts to moderate economic inequality and, therefore to enhance social justice. However, this rule is reversed when legislation leaves room for tax avoidance, as happens, for example, when an offshore company is established, particularly in the so-called "tax havens" (cf. Zucman, 2013). As a result of this legislative loophole, a lot of wealthy taxpayers avoid paying taxes "according to the law", while, on the other hand, the majority of the tax burden is placed on those whose income cannot be hidden (mainly salaried employees and pensioners).

Similar problems of legislative inequality in the treatment of citizens, in the context of criminal legislation, arise with regard to financial crimes. The inequality in this domain was stressed particularly by Edwin Sutherland in his well-known theory of white-collar crime back in 1939 (see his paper "White-Collar Criminality", published in *American Sociological Review*, 5: 1940, 1–12). According to this theory, financial crime, at least in the United States, is not always primarily treated on the basis of criminal provisions (instead, administrative regulations and fines are preferred). In addition, even when treatment is of a criminal nature, the penalties provided are not severe enough and rarely lead to the perpetrators' imprisonment, even in cases where the damage caused may be particularly great.

However, it needs to be acknowledged that over the last few years, due to the financial crisis, this lenient legislative approach towards financial crimes has changed, and several prominent businessmen have already been convicted and imprisoned in the US and elsewhere because of fraud, stock market manipulation and so on.[10] This is a positive evolution, given that society cannot be lenient to persons who, exploiting their high socio-economic situation, violate important laws, thus giving a bad example to the others. In contrast, persons from vulnerable social groups should be treated in a more lenient manner, since they usually do not bear alone the whole responsibility for their illegal acts. Most of them, according to research, have faced problems during their childhood and afterwards, being excluded from school, finding no work as adults and consequently having little or no legal income.[11]

Issues of inequality may also be observed at other levels of criminal repression, thus violating the principles of social justice.

---

8 www.un.org/en/udhrbook/pdf/udhr_booklet_en_web.pdf.

9 https://fr.wikipedia.org/wiki/Imp%C3%B4t_progressif and https://de.wikipedia.org/wiki/Steuerprogression# Deutschland.

10 http://money.cnn.com/2016/04/28/news/companies/bankers-prison/.

11 – cf. a *Home Office* white paper published in February 2001 under the title: Criminal Justice: The Way Ahead, p. 41, also accessible online: www.gov.uk/government/uploads/system/uploads/attachment_data/ file/250876/5074.pdf.

Social justice at the sentencing level

At the level of sentencing, an important question arises as to whether judges, prosecutors, police officers and other law enforcement officials are guided or not in their judgements by a spirit of solidarity and equity in favour of the socially marginalised defendants who belong to vulnerable social groups and deserve some special support so as not to relapse.

According to some scholars, especially those supporting the ideas of "Radical Criminology", the competent law enforcement officials neither treat the less-favoured citizens in a spirit of solidarity, nor behave in a spirit of impartiality and fairness towards the wealthy citizens.[12] However, research in some European countries reveals that things are more complex. In particular, according to the results of various studies on this topic, it seems that a basic "extra-legal" factor that influences the behaviour of law enforcement agencies is whether the suspect or defendant meets the characteristics of a "socially integrated person". This means that judges or other law enforcement officials are more lenient if the defendant has a permanent job (even if the person is poor!), has never before had any issues with the law, has a family and, in general, neither causes any problems in society nor is likely to create such problems in the future by committing new criminal acts (cf. mainly the research findings of Pollück, 1977: 282 ff., of Blankenburg, Sessar, and Steffen, 1978: 268 ff., 292–294, 302 ff. and of Kapardis, 2014, 185–199).

Certainly, this perspective does not satisfy those who would like to see a stronger spirit of solidarity, equity and "gentleness" in the treatment of suffering people by the law enforcement agencies. But even so, it would be difficult for these judicial and police officials to be proved to be prejudiced against a suspect or defendant who simply has a low socio-economic situation. However, the situation seems to be different in the United States, where there are strong indications that "unwarranted racial disparities persist", especially if the perpetrator or the victim is African American (Reamer, 2014, 276 ff.) or Latino (Caravelis and Robinson, 2016, 138 ff., 260 ff; cf. on this topic: Reiman and Leighton, 201210, Wacquant, 2009, Spohn, 2009; see also the findings of a research conducted in Canada: *National Council of Welfare*, 2009).[13]

Furthermore, it seems that the objections of those who believe that the court cases of socially powerful defendants in financial crimes rarely lead to their conviction or severe punishment are rather valid. In fact, during the trial of such cases, the well-paid lawyers of the defendants, who are presumed to be experienced, socially connected and with excellent legal education, usually do have the knowledge to find out and emphasize the deficiencies, obscurities and gaps of the law to be applied. As a result, in such cases the defendant cannot easily be found guilty "beyond a reasonable doubt" and hence be convicted. On the contrary, it is more likely to be declared innocent "because of doubts".

Moreover, in the case of financial crimes, legislation lacks the required vigour to tackle them, while further difficulties also arise during the procuring of evidence, and this mainly for two reasons: Firstly, because, usually, the "objective causal connection" between a defendant's conduct and its result cannot easily and firmly be established (for example, that the sea environment was polluted by wastewater as a result of activities of a specific factory and, further, as a result of activities of a specific individual). Secondly, it is difficult to find plaintiffs, witnesses for the prosecution or experts who are willing to get involved in disputes on economic interests of great importance and to give evidence against powerful businesspersons before the court. Along with these facts, the usually "positive" background of financially prominent defendants

---

12 cf. https://en.wikipedia.org/wiki/Radical_criminology.
13 www.oaith.ca/assets/files/Publications/justice_andthe_poor.pdf

may be taken into consideration by the judges as well, also for the reason that these businesspersons provide employment to dozens or even hundreds of workers and consequently appear as the "pillars of society", even when their actions demonstrate that in essence they are primarily interested only in themselves and in their profit.

Social justice at the correctional level

Finally, at the correctional level (i.e. when the criminal decision is issued and the convicted criminal has to be imprisoned or has to serve a non-custodial sanction), social justice can be essential, both for social solidarity and meritocratic fairness. Indeed, social solidarity may be evinced if convicts are given all the possible opportunities to develop their personality and improve themselves. On the other hand, meritocratic fairness and impartiality are ensured if correctional officers treat the convict the same as they treat other prisoners as well as if convicts' personalities are fully respected, irrespective of their socio-economic situation. In view of this double function of social justice at the correctional stage, one could make a parallel to the two classical models of correctional policy, that is, respectively: (a) the *welfare model*, which places emphasis on the social reintegration of the prisoner through education and appropriate treatment and support by the society, and (b) the *justice model*, which focuses on respecting the prisoner's rights, and, furthermore, on ensuring the conditions necessary for their decent and equitable living in prison or, in less severe cases, on serving properly a non-custodial sanction (for example a community service order).

These remarks should be considered along with the critical question concerning whether the treatment of prisoners is affected by factors relating to their socio-economic situation (i.e. if prisoners facing financial difficulties receive less favourable treatment by correctional officers than those of a higher economic status). At this point, it should be mentioned that research on this topic is, generally, limited due to the "dark figure" of existing evidence. More specifically, prisoners tend to avoid making complaints about any discriminatory behaviour against them in fear of the consequences. As a result, the number of reported incidents of prisoners' unfavourable treatment by correctional officers is usually small. Furthermore, it is just recently –mainly due to the financial crisis – that eminent politicians or businesspersons in the US and elsewhere, even as a result of "scapegoating", have been sent to prison for serious financial crimes, usually connected with fraud or with corruption (rake-off) committed on the occasion of armament programmes or of public works.

Although the number of prisoners that have been sent to prison in such cases is still relatively small, these new developments create the conditions for further, more thorough research as concerns the question whether the way in which prisoners are treated by the correctional officers may be influenced by their socio-economic situation, in violation of the internal and international regulations which protect the rights of prisoners (cf. on such research: Stadler/ Benson/ Cullen, 2013; Logan, 2015).

Social justice at the social prevention level

The two basic principles of social justice (i.e. social solidarity and meritocratic fairness) may contribute decisively in two respective directions: that citizens of vulnerable social groups could be prevented become impoverished, while at the same time talented citizens would gain prominence within a wider framework of opportunities and mobility, similar to what Plato had envisioned in his allegories in *The Republic* (415 a 1 ff.).

Actions that might be taken by governments towards social prevention of crime can move in a double direction. Firstly, actions can improve the opportunities for housing, education, healthcare services, social care and protection of children and of the elderly, while ensuring employment opportunities for all social groups and especially for the vulnerable ones. Secondly, actions can to combat lack of meritocracy, clientele relations and corruption, as well as the factors which lead to these phenomena (cf. Kapardis and Courakis, 2016). In such cases, the recruitment or the promotion of an employee through acquaintances or political intervention, but also the assignment of a public work and the issuance of a permit for investment following a transaction with the state service, can reasonably lead to the malfunctioning of society and eventually to the gradual decline of the whole state, where such situations are fostered.

Among the previously mentioned actions, those concerning the latter issue of fight against lack of meritocracy do not require any significant financial cost. Instead, what is needed is political will for the better functioning of public administration and, mainly, for having a confrontation on the part of political leaders with the mentality of patronage and favouritism, which is primarily promoted by trade-unionists, suppliers of the state and strong local politicians. This ought to be, obviously, an acute confrontation, the outcome of which is uncertain. Yet its undertaking and carrying out is essential, especially in Southern European countries, in order for them to achieve the necessary modernization which will set the pace for the 21st century.

Conversely, the measures aimed at achieving a decent standard of living entail various problems and require a considerable budget, which is, indeed, hard to find in the current time of financial distress. In addition, things are even more difficult in these countries, due to a high level of unemployment and of impoverishment of large groups of the population, even of scholars, which started taking place in the 1990s. This situation has been mainly the result of some new worldwide developments which unfortunately cannot be reversed, such as the further opening of markets (globalisation) and the subsequent growth of multinational enterprises, in connection with the competitive low wages of other countries which are in a state of rapid development (India, China, Korea, etc.) and the predominance of new technologies favouring computerisation/"robotisation" of work and thus eliminating a lot of jobs.

However, the problem of securing resources in favour of vulnerable social groups could be resolved to a great extent, and this could be done without requiring citizens to pay an excessive amount of taxes or suffer retrenchments in salaries and pensions. This would be the case if the public administration could function more appropriately and if patronage together with corruption could be drastically reduced, in accordance with what has been stated earlier. More specifically, a state can certainly attract significant investments, so that thousands of new jobs can be created, if it creates a mechanism by which (a) there are no bureaucracy, clientele relations and corruption, (b) nearly all transactions are done electronically through computers – as seems to occur, for example, in Estonia, (c) there exists a stable, investor-friendly tax system and an equally stable and attractive level of interest rates and (d) all transactions rely on the state's trustworthiness. As a result, these measures may conduce to better standards of living and may equally strengthen citizens' confidence in meritocracy. Besides, from the angle of criminal policy, a great part of offences which can be attributed to bad living conditions and to anomic situations might be diminished.

A redistribution of wealth through progressive taxation may enhance social justice. Nevertheless, special attention needs to be paid to how to achieve this objective. Indeed, there is a danger that, under such political initiatives, the incentives of the individuals who have both the ability and willingness to build wealth and, hence, to contribute to the economic growth of their country will become weaker or will even be wiped out. It is, thus, likely that the continuous and oppressive taxation of those who build the national wealth will result, according to an astute and popular idiom, in "killing the goose that lays the golden egg". Therefore, a pertinent combination of measures is required so that a decent standard of living is ensured without, however, compromising economic growth. This is a difficult undertaking, just like social justice itself, especially in times of distress, when extreme political views and populism may be developed and distort the balance which is necessary for obtaining the optimal result. However, the objective of social justice is worth pursuing, all the more because this is the only way to achieve, in this currently competitive world, a more humane and socially fair society.

Concluding thoughts

We are currently experiencing considerable disparities in the distribution of wealth and power. The recent economic crisis has exacerbated the need for a more equal society. Therefore, the vision for a society that is focused on goals such as combating socio-economic disparities and providing substantial opportunities to all members of society can be a primary objective, worthy of captivating us. Restorative justice has emerged from ancient traditions to teach us in both theory and practice that the victim and the community must also be prioritized alongside the need for just deserts and offender rehabilitation. There has been a plethora of papers and projects on restorative justice, and yet its potential for moving beyond the direct and indirect parties in conflict have been limited. This chapter challenges current thinking and writing by arguing that the new target for criminal justice policy and practice should be social justice. It also argues that restorative justice must move into new project areas – first, for a fairer, meritocratic distribution of social goods, and second, for greater solidarity towards the weaker members of society. We are referring here to all the socially marginalized and often impoverished groups of people, who are scientifically characterized as "weak" or "vulnerable" or "socially excluded" and who try, with great courage, to survive without surmounting the threshold of criminal law, although, according to research, the situation is not always encouraging.[14]

Similarly, there is a need to assist crime victims who suffer from the consequences of an illegal, punishable behaviour against them and who are sometimes unable, due to their financial condition, to participate in a process and claim the restoration of their damage. Apart from securing to these persons a legal aid, so that they can present their claims before the court, a further idea which could be helpful to them is that the state compensate such poor victims via a fund which would be financed by a part of the fines that the convicts pay by court decision to the state for their offences.

If one of the aims of criminal justice policy is to generate solutions to the problems of crime, then it should not solely be limited to facilitating the repair of damage and the conciliation of victim and perpetrator. We have argued that one of the primary aims of criminal justice policy should be to address the causative factors of crime, socio-economic inequalities and other forms of injustice which trigger social reactions, attitudes and a sequence of serious criminal acts (see also Aristotle's *Politics* V. 1301 b 27, 1301 a 32 ff., 1266 b 40). Put another way, restorative justice in its current normative and implementation form is inadequate in helping criminal justice policy to achieve its new goal around socio-economic inequality. We have proposed a "restorative justice plus" version, which we have referred to as "social justice" and extends beyond the criminal justice system.

14 For example in the UK, "crime increased dramatically during the same period that rates of relative poverty escalated" (Garside, 2006, 46).

References

Aristotle. 1932. *Politics*, H. Rackham, trans., Loeb Classical Library 264, Cambridge, MA: Harvard University Press.

Aristotle. 1934. *Nicomachean Ethics*, H. Rackham, trans., Loeb Classical Library 73, Cambridge, MA: Harvard University Press.

Artinopoulou, V. and Gavrielides, T. 2013. Aristotle on Restorative Justice: Where the Restorative Justice and Human Rights Meet (κοινοί τόποι). In: T. Gavrielides and V. Artinopoulou (eds.) *Reconstructing the Restorative Justice Philosophy*. Farnham: Ashgate.

Blankenburg, E., Sessar, K. and Steffen, W. 1978. *Die Staatsanwaltschaft im Prozeß strafrechtlicher Sozialkontrolle*. Berlin: Duncker & Humblot.

Capeheart, Loretta and Milovanovic, Dragan. 2007. *Social Justice. Theories, Issues, and Movements*. New Brunswick, New Jersey and London: Rutgers University Press.

Caravelis, Cyndy and Robinson, Matthew. 2016. *Social Justice, Criminal Justice. The Role of American Law in Effecting and Preventing Social Change*. New York and London: Routledge.

Clayton, Matthew and Williams, Andrew, eds. 2004. *Social Justice*. Malden, MA and Oxford: Blackwell Publishing.

Cook, Dee. 2006. *Criminal Justice and Social Justice*. London, Thousand Oaks, CA and New Delhi: Sage Publications.

Feinberg, Joel. 1984. *The Moral Limits of the Criminal Law*, Vol. One: *Harm to Others*. New York and Oxford: Oxford University Press.

Garside, Richard. 2006. Criminality and Social Justice: Challenging the Assumptions. In Ben Shimshon (ed.) *Social Justice: Criminal Justice*. The Smith Institute, pp. 40–48. Available at www.smith-institute.org.uk/book/social-justice-criminal-justice/

Gavrielides, Theo. 2007. *Restorative Justice Theory & Practice: Addressing the Discrepancy*. Helsinki: HEUNI.

Home Office. February 2001. White Paper Published Under the Title: *Criminal Justice: The Way Ahead*. Available at www.gov.uk/government/uploads/system/uploads/attachment_data/file/250876/5074.pdf.

Kant, Immanuel. 1968, 1st ed. 1798. *Metaphysik der Sitten*. In *W. Weischedel*, Kant Werke, Vol. 7. Darmstadt: Wissenschaftliche Buchgesellschaft.

Kapardis, Andreas, ed. 2014. *Psychology and Law: A Critical Introduction*, 4th ed. Cambridge: Cambridge University Press

Kapardis, Maria and Courakis, Nestor.2016. Anti-Corruption Measures: The Panacea of a Financial Cliff. In M. Dion, D. Weisstub and D.-L. Richet (eds.) *Financial Crimes: Psychological, Technological, and Ethical Issues*. Springer International Publishing as No. 68 in its series 'International Library of Ethics, Law, and the New Medicine', pp. 3–31.

Logan, M.W. 2015. *Coping with Imprisonment: Testing the Special Sensitivity Hypothesis for White-Collar Offenders* [Dissertation], University of Cincinnati.

Malekian, Farhad. 2017. *Judgments of Love in Criminal Justice*. Cham, Switzerland: Springer.

Meyer, Lukas H. and Sanklecha, Pranay. 2016. Philosophy of Justice: Extending Liberal Justice in Space and Time. In Clara Sabbagh and Manfred Schmitt (eds.) *Handbook of Social Justice Theory and Research*. New York: Springer, pp. 15–35.

Miller, David. 2003. *Principles of Social Justice*. Cambridge, MA: Harvard University Press.

National Council of Welfare (Canada). (Spring 2009). *Justice and the Poor*, also Available at www.oaith.ca/assets/files/Publications/justice_andthe_poor.pdf

Nozick, Robert. 1974. *Anarchy, State and Utopia*. Oxford and Cambridge, MA: Blackwell.

Plato. 2013a. *The Republic*, Vol. I, Christopher Emlyn-Jones and William Freddy, Loeb Classical Library 237. Cambridge, MA: Harvard University Press.

Plato. 2013b. *The Republic*, Vol. II, Christopher Emlyn-Jones and William Freddy, trans., Loeb Classical Library 276. Cambridge, MA: Harvard University Press.

Pollück, K.-P. 1977. *Klassenjustiz?*, Diss. Polit. Wissenschaft, Freie Universität Berlin, Bamberg.

Rawls, John. 1971. *A Theory of Justice*. Cambridge, MA: Harvard University Press.

Reamer, Frederic G. 2014. Social Justice and Criminal Justice. In Michael Reisch (ed.) *Routledge International Handbook of Social Justice*. London: Routledge, pp. 269–285.

Reiman, Jeffrey H. and Leighton, Paul. 2012. *The Rich get Richer and the Poor get Prison*, 10th ed. (1st ed. 1979). London: Routledge.

Spohn, Cassia C. 2009. *How do Judges Decide? The Search for Fairness and Justice in Punishment*. Los Angeles: Sage.

Stadler, W.A., Benson, M.L. and Cullen, F.T. 2013. Revisiting the Special Sensitivity Hypothesis: The Prison Experience of White-Collar Inmates. *Justice Quarterly*, 30(16): 1090–1114.

Sutherland, ed. 1940. White-Collar Criminality. In *American Sociological Review*, 5: 1–12.

United Nations. The International Forum for Social Development. 2006. *Social Justice in an Open World: The Role of the United Nations*. New York. Available at www.un.org/esa/socdev/documents/ifsd/SocialJustice.pdf.

von Hirsch, Andreas. 1986. *Doing Justice: The Choice of Punishments*. Boston, MA: Northeastern University Press.

von Hirsch, Andreas and Ashworth, Andrew. 2005. *Proportionate Sentencing: Exploring the Principles*. Oxford: Oxford University Press.

Wacquant, Loïc. 2009. *Punishing the Poor*. Durham and London: Duke University Press.

Zucman, Gabriel. 2013. *La richesse cachée des nations: Enquête sur les paradis fiscaux*. Paris: Le Seuil.

5

Returning to indigenous traditions of peacemaking, peacebuilding, and peacekeeping

From Jirga (TDR) to restorative justice (ADR) in Pakistan

Ali Gohar

Introduction

Since the end of World War II, and particularly after the end of the Cold War, conflicts changed in nature from being inter-state to being intra-state. However, after the 1990s, we observed a reversal of this trend. This is particularly apparent in post 9/11 scenarios where international players jumped in to manage domestic conflicts of another country in the name of international security and peacekeeping or to protect the local inhabitants. Their approach is mostly top-down, as they build state institutions and perhaps unintentionally destroy local institutions prevailing in the countries.

A sustainable peace needs to be based on the indigenous system of peacebuilding as per the wishes of the local people. Such systems are respected, adopted, sustained, and owned by the people on the grassroots level. However, the local people need to follow their own ways and not those imposed by others. This chapter aims to highlight the importance of indigenous systems as a base for introducing modern peacebuilding approaches.

Indigenous systems of conflict resolution

Before the nation-state system was consolidated, each community of the world was governed through its own old traditional methods. The communities with their group of elders, aware of local indigenous values of traditions, customs, and religion, used traditional methods to resolve intra- as well as inter-community conflicts. Such elders, apart from exercising leadership in external affairs, also had a role in representing victims, carrying out offenders' reconciliation, rehabilitation and restoration back to their community. Such interventions mostly resulted in a consensus award or amicable settlement of disputes. This also took care of issues of rehabilitation of the victim as well as the offender

Looking at Pakistan and the available evidence, restorative justice-based systems of governance may provide some of the best tools to update such indigenous systems. The restorative justice system can also be very close to the indigenous system all over the world since it evolved from the same system of the circle of the Native Americans. Societies around the world have developed their own unique ways of overcoming conflict. When the state came into existence, it took away this power from the community. Many communities, however, preserved their indigenous systems. The common examples are Native American Circle, Sulha in Arab countries, Jirga in Pakistan and Afghanistan, Punchayth in India, and gachaca in Africa.

Since the dawn of civilization, human beings have lived according to a set of rules that have changed with the passage of time. Each community developed its own system of rules. Some of these community systems are still preserved in one way of another, a fact that speaks volumes about their resilience in the face of many upheavals and revolutions. The most visible structure of such systems (as mentioned before) are Circles in North America, Gachaca in Africa, Sulha in the Middle East, Family Group Conferencing in New Zealand, and Jirga in the Pukhtoon belt of Afghanistan-Pakistan.

In these systems, the victim, the offender, and the community are all involved in order to resolve conflicts. Therefore, the community becomes a space for all stakeholders in a dispute to come to a mutually agreed resolution. However, when the concept of a state-run system of criminal justice came to fruition, both the victim and the local community lost their right to be involved in decision making, as the state became the victim when a law was broken. With this, the victim and their community, apart from their initial involvement, were not engaged and only the state and offender were parties in the dispute. The state system not only kept the parties separated but served to slow the process down while driving costs up and thus restricting easy accessibility to justice.

Additionally, states tended to manipulate traditional conflict resolution systems in order to further their own interests; an example is in the Pukhtoon community of Pakistan, the FCR (Frontier Crimes Regulations, 1901), which is still in practice. The FCR was introduced by the British Empire in order to control the Jirga system as it was and is still practised in (Federal Administered Tribal Area) FATA and Khyber Pukhtoonkhwa regions of Pakistan. Traditionally, Jirga was community-based; it delivered speedy justice and was accessible to everyone. It did not, however, lose its role due to government interference, and to this day remains intact in the Pukhtoon belt of Afghanistan-Pakistan. Jirga is a name given to the model which in Pakhtoon society is used to resolve issues between individuals, communities, tribes, and even on an international level (Bonn loya jirga of Afghanistan) in order to address concerns and look for solutions acceptable to all the parties having a stake.

What is Jirga?

Jirga is best summarized as a strategic exchange between two or more people to address an issue through verbal communication. The exchange may or may not result in an agreement on the issue, but the process itself leads the parties, including the interveners, to maintain a certain level of formal communication, thus ensuring peace. Jirga is commonly practiced in Khyber Pukhtoonkhwa, Baluchistan provinces, and the Pukhtoon belt of Afghanistan. Jirga is organized by wise, respectable, greybeard elders whose decision is unanimous and acceptable to all community members. There is difference of opinion within the Jirga process, but the final verdict is acceptable to all.

Local scholars claim that Jirga is better than the modern-day democracy, as its decision is acceptable to all, while in the democratic system opposition plays a role both within and outside the Assembly, with representatives taking a stand on their opinions to the end.

Pukhtoon Jirga of the Pustho-speaking belt of Pakistan and Afghanistan is an example of such a case in place since time immemorial. The Pukhtoon tribe is divided between Pakistan and Afghanistan. The majority of Pukhtoon (almost 60 percent) are living in Afghanistan across the international frontier of the Durand line between Pakistan and Afghanistan. These Pukhtoon living cross border in Pakistan-Afghanistan and divided in many tribes, have a code of conduct called Pukhtoonwali with shared values and ethnic, social, and traditional religious linkages. The same tribes are living across the Durand line in both countries, with free access to each other due to porous, mountainous terrain and a difficult border structure. There are many tribes within the Pukhtoon, but the common Pukhtoon code of Pukhtoonwali is the same all over Pakistan and Afghanistan. There are three main institutions of Jirga, Hujra (traditional community centre) in each community of Pukhtoons. These three are used to resolve any conflict or life issue – be it within the community, with other tribes, regionally, or nationally – using Pakhtoonwali (Pukhtoon code is the same with less differences). Jirga is the only mechanism for peacebuilding and conflict transformation wherever there is a Pukhtoon population, not only in both countries but also for Pukhtoon living outside of Pakistan and Afghanistan.

The working principles of Jirga are: (a) it must be community based, (b) it must be fact-finding, and (c) it needs to act like a modern jury system. It intervenes to halt violence, identify the issues, and resolve them through mediation or arbitration and further works for reconciliation and rehabilitation. There are also three aspects of peacekeeping, peacemaking, and peacebuilding in Jirga system. The first one is called Tega (going to the scene with a white flag and declaring a ceasefire). Tega literally means a stone is stuck in a place and a ceasefire is declared, but it can be symbolic also. The second one is Nagha (preventive measure by Jirga, i.e., a ban on arms, fire, and parties' free access to common places, such as Mosque, school, market etc.). The third one is Community Policing (arbakai, shalgoon – keeping law and order in peace and conflict both under the direction of Jirga), and volunteer force (Laskhar – imposing Jirga decision/ punishment by force). The common punishments imposed by Jirga for any violation of the peacekeeping, peacemaking, and peacebuilding process are expelling the perpetrators from the area, confiscating their property, etc. Jirga uses all the three Tega, Nagha, and implements its decision through Community Policing (arbakai, shalgoon) by the Volunteer force (Laskhar).

The main difference between Jirga and the traditional criminal justice system is that the latter punishes, leaving the enmities as they were, while Jirga resolves the enmities by addressing its roots causes, reconciles, and rehabilitates the parties, and also adopts certain rules for preventing a return of hostilities. As mentioned earlier, despite the considerable onslaught of formal state institutions, the Jirga has been able to retain its efficiency, to a large extent as indicated by a comparative preference of the people who often resort to this traditional mechanism of conflict resolution instead of the courts.

Exploring Jirga

Jirga is done at all levels of the society for different purposes and different objectives. For an outsider, the dynamics of Jirga may appear overwhelmingly complex, but upon deeper examination it is clear that a common understanding exists among the members regarding these complexities.

The composition of a Jirga may be categorized in two ways. One is the representative level of a Jirga where the Jirga may represent a party, a village, or an area or region. In the second

Table 5.1 Local meanings of Jirga

Terms used for Jirga	Meanings
Jirga Kawal	Doing a Jirga or literally 'let's sit to talk'.
	Here the parties select their representatives; they give them power to resolve the conflict called waq. The parties decide the conflict and declare it to the parties. Parties are bound to obey the verdict of the Jirga decision.
Pa Jirga talal	Going as a Jirga, or doing an intervention.
	When the jirga members are approached by one or another party to intervene or the jirga elders on their own intervene.
Jirgay ta Khabara workawal	Referring a case to Jirga by parties or one of the parties.
	When the parties in conflict cannot decide an issue on their own, they refer the case to elders and also give them power (waq) to arbitrate.
The Jirgay Khabara	The word of Jirga, opinion of Jirga.
	Decision of Jirga, or verdict of Jirga that is acceptable to all.
Jirga manz ta Ratlal	Intervention by a Jirga, i.e., ceasefire
	When Jirga on their own comes into the middle through parachute diplomacy.

level, the Jirga serves a particular role, which can vary depending on the circumstance. Some examples of these roles are diplomatic missions, peacebuilding interventions, or small juries. Locals use the term Jirga to mean a number of things while interchanging it with various other terms (see Table 5.1).

Each of these terms is used for a variety of meanings related to the organization of local community life, indicating the relevance and importance of Jirga as an integral institution. The nature and scope of a specific Jirga can vary, and there is generally no clear distinction between types of Jirga.

Even the locals will talk about Jirga as the type they best understand, but when questioned, they smile and agree that their definition or understanding of a Jirga is a narrow one. Most writers have divided Jirga into four general types: Sarkari, Qaumi/ Ulusi, Shakhsi, and Loya Jirga.

1   Sarkari or Government Jirga; Government-sponsored jirga under the chair of a political agent, mostly held in tribal areas of Pakistan under Frontier Crime Regulations (FCR). FCR was introduced by the colonial British Government and is still used in the tribal belt. Political Agents are a class of government officials who have combined into their person the authority of executive, judicial, and enforcement powers. Maliks or tribal chiefs assist a political agent in decision making.
2   Qaumi/Ulasi or Local Representative Jirga; This is mostly a tribe, clan, or quam (comprising many tribes' jirga), to discuss and decide local issues/conflicts.
3   Shakhsi or third-party Jirga, when a person in conflict with another refers the case to jirga or jirga members approach an individual to resolve the issues/conflicts.
4   Loya or Grand Jirga, mostly on district, provincial, or national level to address issues of national interest. Afghanistan National Assembly is named as Loya jirga.

Jirga for peacemaking, peacebuilding, and peacekeeping

Jirga is still an active conflict transformation institution playing three different roles, like the present-day modern systems. All the three approaches of modern scientific peacebuilding are embedded in Jirga.

Jirga members intervene on the request of the parties in conflict and start shuttle diplomacy, or in case of an ongoing conflict, come into the middle and act as a mediator. They declare ceasefire by means of Tega (which means a stone is put between the two conflicting parties' properties/houses to signify the immediate cessation of hostilities). The ceasefire is declared for a certain period of time, and then Jirga members start listening to the parties and trying to convince them to sit down for discussion. Jirga members' roles are in flux and change from that of diplomat, to mediator, to arbitrator as appropriate to the situation. They use religious knowledge (e.g. Koranic verses) in favour of conflict resolution as well as to share personal stories of the hardships that conflicts causes (e.g. blood vendettas). All such tactics are used to soften the hearts of the conflicting parties and give them time to think more on the consequences of perpetuating the conflict. When the parties agree to conflict resolution, then they are brought to a common place with a large gathering of friends and community members as witness for reconciliation. The parties put their hands on the Holy Koran making God and community members witnesses in order to get God's blessings. In Islam and traditions there are three systems for resolving any conflict: Qisas, which means an eye for an eye; diyath (blood money); or forgiveness. When jirga is involved, mostly people go for the third option, forgiveness. Later on, after reconciliation, jirga members attend both parties' friends and relatives' parties in order to further strengthen the friendship between the two parties. The ceremony of Jirga mostly started and ended with prayers.

The elders place Tega (stone) symbolically between the parties in conflict and ask for money and weapons to be kept with the Jirga as a guarantee that the parties will not violate the Jirga ceasefire till the final decision of Jirga. Jirga then declares a ceasefire for an interim period before the final decision. If anyone violates the ceasefire, the money and other items that are kept with the Jirga are confiscated by the Jirga. A special volunteer force called Laskhar in such cases imposes the decision of the Jirga by punishing the perpetrator/offender. Such punishments include demolishing of houses and expelling the family or tribe from the area.

Apart from conflict resolution, Jirga also play an active role for the development of the areas. They work closely with government agencies for the welfare of their people and community. Quotas are allocated to each tribe according to their population in government jobs, land, and other resources, and discussions over this take place with the Jirga members from each tribe. To maintain peace, the Laskhar is used, under the elders supervision. Laskhar is further organized into smaller groups called Arbakai (community policing), as well as chagha (Quick reaction force), which is called in case of any emergency.

The three roles of Jirga mentioned earlier are fully manifested among Pukhtoon living in Pakistan – Afghanistan, whereas in settled areas the Jirga can only influence the conflicting parties for resolution of the conflict by means of talks with no recourse to force. They have no Laskhar, or power to confiscate land, demolish houses, or expel someone. The only tool they can employ is social boycott and recourse to intervention of religious scholars who can tell both parties the religious benefits of resolving the dispute, and especially about forgiveness. In the Holy Koran it is mentioned that the victim has the right to approach the court and get revenge of the person, or take money, but if they forgive opponent for the sake of God, the reward is with God here and in the hereafter. That's why mostly people go for the third option, forgiveness.

The law

A law can be considered strong not only if it punishes the criminal but also if it deters others from committing the crime. An example of a law which has high deterrence value is divine law, which, if taken in its real sense, is there to prevent community members from committing crimes in the first place. Then there is traditional law, an example being the Jirga of the Pakistan-Afghanistan Pakhtoon belt.

All indigenous decision-making processes of the world are similar in nature. There is a strong case to be made for easy and speedy access to the justice system. Justice delayed is justice denied. The indigenous system described earlier is one of the oldest justice systems that respond to the needs of victims. Yet there is a great need for such systems to include modern, scientific knowledge that will allow them to incorporate notions of human rights into their methodology.

In these systems, punishment can be in the form of community work. Victim healing must be quite visible in the whole decision-making process, and trauma healing and mental health aspects of the victim are also looked after by various practices. The suffering of the offender's family also needs to be shown to the victim's family in order for the latter to understand the conflict from the offender's perspective.

Jirga and restorative justice

Local and international actors for peacebuilding should understand security and its development in terms of the existing conditions in a country. People who are used to a system since time immemorial can't give it up within a short period of time, as the international community's/donor agency would wish, because change comes slowly over time. The modern justice system in the developing world is also not that strong due to corruption, prolonged process, local indigenous belief of revenge, and the lack of tools for reconciliation, which are most important for any system in tribal life. Without reconciliation, the cycle of violence will continue from one generation to another. Even after courts award heavy punishments like death penalties, the revenge factor still exists and the parties are compelled to take revenge due to shame and honour factors or approach indigenous systems for reconciliation after prolong litigation in the court of law.

Peacebuilders around the globe will have to come up with new ways to resolve conflicts. In these new circumstances, where people due to local conflict are internally displaced or take refuge in another country, they have to start life afresh. What stays with them are their traditions, including their old conflict resolution systems. Such indigenous systems are the foundation for another system to be built. New systems that are compatible with modern human rights values but preserve the indigenous conflict resolution systems are essential in the modern world. A good start is the restorative justice system which has many similarities with many indigenous systems around the world and thus can be acceptable to the practitioners of many indigenous conflict resolution systems.

Human beings from birth to death play many roles. These roles are developed due to the influence of external factors and internal decisions that the person makes. In faith-based communities and religious societies, people link good and bad to fate, the guidance of God or the misguidance of Satan, and even to the soul. But what about those who don't believe in religion and do not have a faith-based approach?

Human nature itself has caused many of the problems humanity faces today. For example, the two world wars have long since ended but still continue to cause pain and suffering today. Human beings can end or find a way out of such problems, but they must start with the self. First, we must bring about a change within ourselves before we can begin the gigantic task of changing others, of bringing peace to this world.

In the Arabic language, the heart is considered the centre of intelligence and affection. Human beings have also been given with the quality of conscience, that is, the ability to make distinctions between right and wrong in regards to one's own conduct (Quran 91:8), and are provided the necessary guidance (Quran 76:3).

The earth will become a place truly worth living in when, following their normal pursuits, people do not become unmindful of keeping their souls' desires in control. Power and resources are the two main reasons for all sort of conflicts, but above all, abusive language, rumours, and propaganda are the immediate causes of individual and group conflict that later leads to national and world conflicts as well. Human ambition to get more by any means is another reason to use power for gaining resources and use resources in order to gain more power. To curb such inner feelings of greed, one needs inner jihad (struggle) against the soul desires.

Inner jihad is man's internal struggle against the evil within, which can only be achieved if we unite the forces of good to fight against the forces of evil. The Holy Prophet (PBUH) in the following Hadith [saying of the Holy Prophet (PBUH)], explains the concept of inner jihad:

> During the return march from the victories of Makkah and Hunayan, the Prophet (peace be upon him) said to some of his companions "We have returned from the lesser Jihad to the greater Jihad. And when one of the companion asked, 'What is the greater Jihad?' He (PBUH) replied, 'It is the war against the soul (Nafs)'."

In our training workshops on restorative justice in Pakistan, we start our presentation by quoting the Koranic injunction about soul: every human soul has three inclinations. One is the inclination towards doing wrong, evil, and is called Nafs-i-Ammarah (12:53). The other is the inclination towards realization and repentance (i.e. to realize immediately if one does something wrong, that what he or she has done is wrong, and repent of it or rather reproach oneself for it). This is called Nafs-i-Lawwamah (75:2). The third is the inclination towards doing good and right-eous deeds. This is called Nafs-i-Mutmainnah (89:27) and also called the soul at peace, because satisfaction and peace of mind are the natural outcome of doing good and righteous deeds.

We also devote a part of the training to human rights, where we first explore traditional and religious rights and link them with modern human rights. Trainees take much interest, as they find modern human rights compatible with in their own religious and traditional systems.

Jirga cannot survive just on good intentions. Jirga will have to recreate its due space if it wants to survive the challenges of the modern world. This will be a process of consolidating what it already has – indigenous systems providing space to the modern systems for bridging the gap between a traditional and more modern systems. Jirga has many similarities with the modern restorative justice system. People have been practicing it for a long time and they have faith in it. It can provide a base for modern systems, i.e. the restorative justice system, to update it and make it on par with modern day human rights values.Growth of such practices will automatically follow clarity and acceptance. The proponents of Jirga will be required to bring a better-reasoned case before the outside world in order to be taken seriously. At the same time, keeping aside the question of a viable substitute for Jirga, the opponents of Jirga will need to undertake a cost-benefit analysis before simply discarding a centuries-old social practice. Restorative justice can be one of the good options.

In 2003, Just Peace Initiatives (JPI) organized the first international conference on a restora-tive justice system with the Federal Investigation Agency (FIA) of Pakistan for three days in Peshawar, Pakistan. Distinguished scholars from all over the world were invited with local intellectuals to shed light on the implementation of the RJ system in the local context.

The most practical steps were taken jointly by JPI and Khyber Pukhtoonkhawa police with the financial assistance of The Asia Foundation and Aus-Aid, the Australian Embassy. These steps included establishment of Muslahathi (reconciliation) committees (MC) in two district police stations of Khyber Pukhtoonkhawa province of Pakistan. In 2008, MC were extended to 12 police stations and now are in almost all 25 districts of Khyber Pukhtoonkhawa (KPK) province of Pakistan. Police and Jirga elders were trained in modern conflict transformation methods with the inclusion of a restorative justice process for implementation in order to avoid human rights violations and minimize heavy punishment. Elders' (MC) offices were established at each police station level. They are performing their duties on a volunteer basis to resolve cases of a petty nature, register cases, and keep proper records. Vulnerable groups, especially women and children who were frightened before because of police brutality, were encouraged by the elders to visit them at the police station. Cases of a petty nature were resolved by MC, while major ones are brought in front of the elders by the police.

Two ways of checks and balances developed within the police station, where elders are to check police corruption and brutality and where police are allowed to check for any human rights violations by Jirga members. Women and children reported being heard by the elders. This was one of the main complaints against indigenous Jirga. Furthermore, verbal decision making was changed to written, and the heavy punishment of Jirga is now changed to community work with the introduction of a restorative justice component. Such practices brought positive change in the behaviour of elders and the police.

Another project[1] was launched in 2009 in five districts of Baluchistan province under the title "ADR and Community Policing". The local Jirga system of Arbakai indigenous community policing was updated with the inception of a restorative justice system and modern community policing components. That development was well received by the law department, the police, and the elders. Bringing such changes in the Jirga system minimizes pressure on the police and judiciary, and such work was well received by those who were formerly against Jirga.

JPI implemented the project "Addressing gender-based violence through ADR (Alternative Dispute Resolution) for Internally Displaced Populations" in 2013. These populations were affected by recent operations in the tribal areas on the Pakistan and Afghanistan borders. The project not only updated the indigenous system of Jirga with the inclusion of restorative justice systems and the establishment of Muslahathi (reconciliation) committees of both men and women but opened up new horizons of trauma healing by overlapping indigenous and modern trauma healing and restorative justice components.

First Muslahathi reconciliation committees (MC), and now the Dispute Resolution Council (DRC), an alternate dispute resolution mechanism, was launched in KP province to help amicably resolve petty disputes mostly of civil nature through a cheap and speedy procedure. The system has been so successful in the province that people now prefer to take their cases to the councils. They provide easy and inexpensive access to justice for ordinary citizens. People of Khyber Pukhtoonkhawa are happy with this easy access to justice. The community members act as a jury, chosen from the civil Jirga and society, and volunteer to hear the disputing parties in the presence of two assisting officials from the police department. The police have no role to play except to inform the parties (victim and offender to attend the Muslahathi committee office at the police station; the police have no other role in decision making) and keep order in the decision-making process if disagreements occur. Restorative justice is included in the Muslahathi committee members' training along with indigenous Jirga knowledge; depending on the situation, both restorative justice or punishment may be used.

MC and DRC are given full support by the government, which has included it in the justice system by amendments to the constitutions of the provincial and national assemblies. Apart from Khyber Pukhtoonkhawa province, other provinces have adopted the same type of MC. In the other larger province of Punjab, where another indigenous system (Punchayath) is in place, MC have been introduced under the direct supervision of the high court.

1 With the financial assistance of The Asia Foundation and the British Embassy.

Elderly men and women enjoy the benefit of their wisdom and age, but younger men also need to come forward, as they are more aware of modern human rights and how they can be incorporated into indigenous conflict resolution systems. The youth also need proper training to equip them in resolving community disputes efficiently. That is a part of modern scientific conflict transformation methods included in restorative justice.

There is a great need that, first of all, in the local community there is a system of decision making that is acceptable to the people. This system can be devised by updating restorative justice. A system imposed will make the situation worse, as local communities are accustomed to their own system, and any change must be slow and gradual. People with urban and rural backgrounds have different systems which they follow. Urban communities are more used to state law, but rural population will stick to their religious and traditional values and systems, so both should be addressed separately.

The introduction of a restorative justice system is easier in the more rural as compared to the urban educated class. The rural population already has such practices more deeply entrenched into their customs and are familiar with it.

The training of women should be arranged separately according to the customs, traditions, and religious beliefs. Women participate in Muslahathi committees (MCs) and dispute resolution council (DRC) but don't know much of Jirga dynamics. Women in MC and DRC are greatly needed because they have a better understanding of women's issues than do men. Most of the cases of women are resolved by men because there fewer women have the training needed. Cases of MC and DRC need publicity and sharing with all stakeholders in order to promote both modern and traditional ways of resolving disputes and building peace. For cases resolved in 2017 by DRC and MC, see Annex I. The other major province, Punjab, followed the Khyber Pukhtoonkhawa province model. In Punjab, DRC is working under the Lahore High Court branch, which has direct supervision in the whole province.

Conclusion

All over the world there are indigenous systems/practices which have a lot of potential in terms of conflict resolution. The only problem is that these indigenous practices are not codified for use in peacebuilding or as a subject of learning for future generations. The "criminal justice system" is under tremendous pressure to provide speedy justice to the masses, particularly in countries where conflict is going on. Indigenous conflict resolution systems can play a major role, as they utilize community-based approaches to minimize pressure on the police and judiciary.

If we want a peaceful environment around us in the community, the country, and the world, we will need to look for such approaches to help both the community and governments. The indigenous systems of the world and restorative justice based on traditional indigenous peacebuilding practices are the best example for all of us. We need to explore, train, implement, and develop the traditional systems of different communities where the same indigenous systems exist.

Dispute resolution resources can help these grassroots approaches for peacebuilding, which can be updated in order to face modern challenges, as we did in Pakistan with the indigenous system of Jirga.

Annex I

Dispute Resolution Council (DRC)

(Prepared by Dr. Shah Jehan and Dr. Mustafa Tanveer SSP)[2]

Restorative justice, also sometimes called reparative justice, is an approach to justice that focuses on the needs of the victims and the offenders as well as the involved community, instead of satisfying abstract legal principles or punishing the offender. Victims take an active role in the process, while offenders are encouraged to take responsibility for their actions, "to repair the harm they've done – by apologizing, returning stolen money, or community service". Restorative justice involves both victim and offender and focuses on their personal needs. In addition, it provides help for the offender in order to avoid future offences. It is based on a theory of justice that considers crime and wrongdoing to be an offence against an individual or community, rather than the state. Restorative justice that fosters dialogue between victim and offender shows the highest rates of victim satisfaction and offender accountability.

The process of restorative justice necessitates a shift in responsibility for addressing crime. In a restorative justice process, the citizens who have been affected by a crime must take an active role in addressing that crime. Although law professionals may have secondary roles in facilitating the restorative justice process, it is the citizens who must take up the majority of the responsibility in healing the pains caused by crime.

There are six guiding questions:

1   Who has been hurt?
2   What are their needs?
3   Whose obligations are these?
4   What are the causes?
5   Who has a stake in the situation?
6   What is the appropriate process to involve stakeholders in an effort to address causes and put things right?

2 www.facebook.com/shaman52/posts/10154954101886332 (Oct. 1, 2017)

Restorative justice is defined as:

> a growing social movement to institutionalize peaceful approaches to harm, problem-solving and violations of legal and human rights. These range from international peacemaking tribunals such as the South Africa Truth and Reconciliation Commission to innovations within the criminal and juvenile justice systems, schools, social services and communities. Rather than privileging the law, professionals and the state, restorative resolutions engage those who are harmed, wrongdoers and their affected communities in search of solutions that promote repair, reconciliation and the rebuilding of relationships. Restorative justice seeks to build partnerships to reestablish mutual responsibility for constructive responses to wrongdoing within our communities. Restorative approaches seek a balanced approach to the needs of the victim, wrongdoer and community through processes that preserve the safety and dignity of all."

To begin from Peshawar city on an experimental basis the DRC is organized on the following lines:

Aims and objectives

1   To introduce concept of restorative justice in capital city Peshawar
2   To avoid unnecessary litigation among public
3   To reduce conflicts at local level
4   To empower community and strengthen the concept of community policing
5   To bridge gap between public and police
6   To ease the burden on police

Structure of DRC

1   The committee shall consist of 21 members representing a cross section of the community belonging to the city division, Peshawar.
2   The overall working of DRC will be organized and planned by the coordinator elected/selected from among the members as per the procedure laid down hereafter.
3   Each committee will be divided in different panels consisting three members.
4   The lower superordinate of the concerned police station will be appointed as a support staff for maintain record of working and decisions of the committee.
5   These committee will function on close liaison with concerned SDPO.

Qualification of members of DRC

1   A member of the DRC should be at least 35 years old.
2   He/she should not have any criminal record, and should be of respectable repute in the community he/she lives in.
3   He/she should have reasonable education, and should be well aware of the community's prevailing values.
4   He should be known for his/her impartiality in decision making.
5   He/she might be from non-controversial NGO, retired government/pak.forces/senior professor/well-known social worker.
6   He/she should not have any official affiliations or be a political office holder.

Selection of DRC coordinator

1　A coordinator will hold his office for a period of three months.
2　No member will offer his services for the post of coordinator, rather he will be appointed after mutual consultation.
3　There will be no convincing efforts for candidature for the post of coordinator.
4　Coordinator will be elected through a secret ballot.
5　Every member can propose a choice of two names for coordinator position.
6　The election will be held under the supervision of concerned SDPO.

Roles and responsibilities of the coordinator

1　He shall be responsible for overall coordination of various activities of the DRC.
2　He will be responsible for forming different panels of the members and equal distribution of cases to the panels.
3　He will receive the applications marked to the DRC from the SDPO and refer them to the panel members.
4　He will prepare the timetable and schedule for hearing cases by different panels of DRC.
5　He will maintain a proper register containing a complete record of all decisions of DRC.
6　The coordinator may change the members of the panel if any of the party in a case has any reservation against member(s) of the panel.
7　He would ensure that each panel of members should consist of people from different walks of life.
8　He will be responsible for arranging a monthly meeting of the DRC for discussing progress and other issues concerning the working DRC.
9　A summary report of all activities of DRC will be prepared by the coordinator and sent to the CCPO's office on the 7th day of every month.
10　He will be responsible for maintaining a complete file of each case.
11　The coordinator will ensure that no case is given to any of the party members unless the Sub Divisional Police officer (SDPO) deems it necessary.

Code of Conduct for Members of DRC

1　The committee will take up only those applications which are referred through the office of CCPO, SSP (operation) or SP (city).
2　The committee will take up any case on its own.
3　Every application will be disposed of within shortest possible time, which should not be more than 15 days.
4　Every application will be taken up by the complete panel, not by any individual member of the committee.
5　An application referred to a panel will be finalized by the same panel except under special circumstances.
6　If any member of the panel approached/influenced by any party will be withdrawn from the panel and the coordinator will replace such member by another impartial member.
7　If any party has any reservation on decision of the DRC, it may apply to SDPO for review.
8　A review committee consisting of 5 members will review the finding. Their decision shall be considered as final.
9　The police liaison officer will be appointed by the concerned SDPO to help the coordinator in record keeping and other issues of the committee.

10   The CCPO will conduct a monthly meeting of the DRC to review the performance of the committee and to discuss the progress of applications referred to the committee and any problems faced by the committee.

11   The DRC would order the SHO for the facts findings report within a stipulated time. Once the party if found guilty, the DRC would suggest preventive actions against the party.

12   The DRC would be a silent observer in cases of contested investigations during the hearings of both the parties.

13   The DRC would resolve domestic/petty yet cognizable disputes amicably and practically keeping in view the cultural and traditional norms that are not against the prevailing law.

14   The police liaison officer will guide the committee about the panel's decision if it is against the law.

15   The committee will not entertain those cases that are supposed to be decided in the court of law unless both parties give written agreement.

Venue: The meeting of DRC will be held in a designated place inside the police station, where they will have support from the concerned police officer. Instead of offender and victim the DRC members will have to take an oath of impartiality and honesty.

Reconciliation committees

Dispute Resolution Council: www.facebook.com/PTIOfficial/videos/10154097353299952 7/?pnref=story

An example of reconciliation by Jirga in Afghanistan: www.economist.com/blogs/banyan/ 2014/05/feuding-afghanistan

References

Baya sahar sha! True TV Play on Honor killing and Positive Roe of Jirga! with English Captions www. youtube.com/watch?v=eztVuVfN3j8#t=27My

Bocock, Robert. 1974. *Ritual in Industrial Society: A Sociological Analysis of Ritualism in Modern England.* London: Allen & Unwin.

Braithwaite, John and Gohar, Ali. 2013. Restorative Justice, Policing and Insurgency: Learning from Pakistan. RegNet Research Paper No. 2013/14, Peacebuilding Compared, Regulatory Institutions Network, Australian National University.

Driver, Tom Faw. 1991. *The Magic of Ritual: Our Need for Liberating Rites That Transform Our Lives and Our Communities.* San Francisco, CA: Harper.

Easwaran, Eknath and Flinders, Timothy. 1985. *A Man to Match His Mountains: Badshah Khan, Nonviolent Soldier of Islam.* Plough Publishing House.

EMU New 12 peacebuilder of the world http://emu.edu/now/news/2015/09/special-issue-of-peace builder-features-12-international-peacebuilding-institutions-led-by-emu-linked-

Gohar, A. and Schirch, L. 2016. Indigenous Storytelling as a Peacebuilding Process. In H. Tuso and M.P. Flaherty (eds.) *Creating the Third Force: Indigenous Processes of Peacemaking* Lanham, MD: Lexington Books, pp. 455–470.

LaDuke, Winona. 1999. *All My Relations: Native Struggles for Land and Rights.* Cambridge, MA: South End Press.

Nonviolent News, Nonviolence and campaigning news from INNATE 1 The extended edition – and more – is at www.innatenonviolence.org Number 184 Belfast 11th November 2010 (www.innate nonviolence.org/news/184nn.shtml).

Reviews

BBC News. Pakistani Women Use Jirga to Fight for Rights. Available at www.bbc.co.uk/news/world-asia-23453243. Accessed 25 July 2013.

"Last Rites for the Jirga?" Reviewed by Muqaddam Khan, 13 August 2006

Schirch, Lisa. 2005. *Ritual and Symbol in Peacebuilding*. Bloomfield, CT: Kumarian Press.

Tribal Liaison Office, Kabul, Afghanistan. March 2009. Between the Jirga and the Judge: Alternative Dispute Resolution in Southeastern Afghanistan. Available at www.usip.org/sites/default/files/file/jirga_judge.pdf

Turner, Victor. 1969. *The Ritual Process: Structure and Anti-Structure*. Chicago: Aldine.

van Gennep, Arnold. 1960. *The Rites of Passage*. Chicago: University of Chicago Press.

Yoder, Carolyn. 2005. *Little Book of Trauma Healing*. Intercourse, PA: Good Books.

Yousufzai, H.M. and Gohar, A. 2012. *Towards an Understanding of Pukhtoon Jirga: An Indigenous Way of Peacebuilding and More*. Lahore: Sang-e-Meel Publications.

Zehr, H. 1990. *Changing Lenses: A New Focus for Crime and Justice*. Scottsdale, PA: Herald Press.

Zehr, H. and Gohar, A. 2003. Little Book of Restorative Justice. Peshawar: Uni- Graphics. The Asian Vision of Change-Kosmos journal. Available at www.kosmosjournal.org/reader-essay/the-asian-vision-of-change/

6

Finding a normative place for a recast restorative principle of peacemaking

Peacemaking and conflict responses in a threefold typology of temporal focus, level of formality and locus of conflict – with an application to Shakespeare's *Romeo and Juliet*

Robert E. Mackay

Background

Restorative justice has suffered from diffuseness in its conceptualisation and dilution of its focus through the breadth of claims made for it about its relevance in domains beyond the criminal and juvenile justice arenas (e.g. education, workplace, international and post-conflict situations) (Gavrielides, 2007, 2008; Mackay, 2007a, 2007b). The conclusions of this analysis of the state of restorative justice theorising were that (1) the restorative principle of justice occupies a position within a legal framework of conflict responses and that its focus is retrospective; and (2) the broader restorative principle (reparation/restitution and reconciliation) belongs to the social and political arena. However, the aspiration (or aim) of a number of restorative justice advocates is to address future relations between the parties in a criminal case, and between them and the community at large. This is reflected in the debate between 'Maximalists', represented by Walgrave and communitarians such as Wright (Walgrave, 2008; Wright, 2003, 2007). Whilst rejecting the notion that the restorative principle can from an epistemological perspective coherently encompass such an aim, it was acknowledged that this aim is laudable, and a conceptual framework is needed to permit such a widening of the scope of criminal and civil justice as well as recognising diverse temporal perspectives in conflict responses generally.

Finding a normative place for a revised restorative principle within a broader conceptualisation of conflict responses has led to the construction of a comprehensive three-dimensional typology within an overarching model of peacemaking. The purpose of this chapter is to propose this legal-ethical model and framework, and to provide evidence of its relevance for making sense of approaches dealing with disputes and conflicts.

The concept of 'restorative justice' is freighted with a number of claims made on its behalf, which it cannot sustain. In order to preserve 'restorative justice' as a term of art it needs to be pruned by the recognition of three limitations: (1) its role as a social principle and as principle of justice within a wider typology that refers to the locus of dispute/conflict (an axis from the individual to the international level); (2) its relevance to an enforcement continuum proceeding from the voluntary level, through a regulatory level to a level of enforcement (cf. Braithwaite's model, 1989); and (3) its primary focus on dealing with what has happened between people – in the past) (the past in a continuum of past, present and future).

The method is to justify this approach to peacemaking using legal-ethical arguments and to demonstrate the implications that this model holds for social institutions, and then to locate institutional arrangements and practices dedicated to handling disputes, conflicts and social infractions in a comprehensive framework. The first part of the argument involves examining peacemaking as an overarching *ethos* in different types of institution (Finnis, 1980; MacIntyre, 1985, 1988) and peacemaking institutions in a framework of '*Lifeworld*' and '*System*' (Habermas, 1986, 1995). The second part develops the typology of conflict responses in three dimensions: the *temporal perspective*, the *sociopolitical locus* (individual – state – international), and thirdly the *axis of consent-coercion* (voluntary – regulatory – enforcement).

After this theoretical presentation, it is argued that this typology has some relevance to the analysis of conflict responses themselves. It can show how the application and misapplication of conflict response can be mapped onto the three-dimensional grid. So, it is proposed, a proper analysis of a conflict or dispute will help to determine what type of response is indicated. This is illustrated by an analysis of conflict responses in *Romeo and Juliet* (Shakespeare, 2005).

Peacemaking: conceptual framework

In developing a conceptual framework for peacemaking, it should be stated that in the development of my theoretical research on restorative justice (Mackay, 2007a, 2007b), it became apparent that the legal-ethical justifications that I had previously put forward for restorative justice (Mackay, 1993) still held good despite the increasing evidence that the concept of restorative justice was too limited or even too weak a vehicle to carry the weight of the aspirations of its advocates. In fact, these arguments were more aptly applied to peacemaking. However, the range of reference of these arguments takes us into broader areas than the justice and legal system, to encompass a broad swathe of social institutions and activities. The exposition here is therefore brief.

Peacemaking as ethos

Peacemaking provides a goal or purpose not only for social institutions but also for social life. It also provides a way of thinking about how people should conduct themselves. This combination of goal and attitude constitutes an ethos. This can be recognised as MacIntyre's teleological approach to ethics (1985, 1988). The virtues of the citizen and of the office-bearer embody the values and goals of the community, which are reflected in individual public and private conduct. Societies in which homogeneity of ethos is contested may have difficulty in sustaining harmony, and sometimes even minimal conditions of social stability, but it is argued that most societies make a claim that a major purpose of their coming into being is the provision of the conditions of peace for their members.

In this approach (as an ideal-typical model), peacemaking means the creation, maintenance and repair of the conditions of peaceful life for members of society. The task of peacemaking is distributed in a variety of functions relating to different domains of the life of society. Thus we see law, as an institution, and social policy, as an activity of government, interacting with the social life of citizens and others, with law regulating behaviour and providing the framework by which social policy creates and maintains conditions for peace and human flourishing (see Figure 6.1) (cf. Finnis, 1980).

This approach provides us with both an overarching ethos for conflict responses and an intimation of the dimension of connection between different levels of social structure encompassing individual, social and political groupings.

Peacemaking in a framework of discourse ethics (Habermas)

By way, not of contrast, but of complementarity, discourse ethics places emphasis on legitimate methods of coming to consensus about how the community should make agreements about how to manage social life, handle disputes and conflicts. What are legitimate aims, goals, institutions, rules and conduct can only be discerned through a judgement about the integrity of the means by which the decisions on which all of these are based. The rules of practical discourse are reflected in Habermas's view of how negotiation should operate (1990).

Habermas (1987) depicts law as having intermediate status, part of the System, that structure of institutions that governs human societies, but also operating within informal life (Lifeworld), inasmuch as law both affects human conduct by its external operations and also because its principles are incorporated into individual and group values, attitudes and assumptions. Furthermore, although for the most part people do not overtly calculate during the carrying-on of their daily life whether their social acts are lawful or not, from an external viewpoint, all acts in life may, from the perspective of law, be deemed 'lawful' or 'unlawful' (see Figure 6.2).

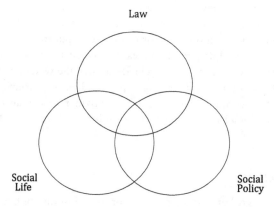

Figure 6.1 The interrelationship between Law, Social Life and Social Policy

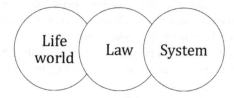

Figure 6.2 The positioning of Law between Lifeworld and System

This immersion of law in the Lifeworld leads us to a recognition that conflict responses will take a variety of forms depending upon the agreement of free individuals about how different types of conflict or dispute are to be managed or resolved. The variety of forms will also include different levels of formality to the extent that people's expectations about how to resolve and manage disputes and conflicts will be affected by the seriousness with which they are viewed (Habermas on resentment on the commission of crimes [1990: 45, 48]). The practical discourses that Habermas invokes, developed in practices such as negotiation, eschew all forms of manipulation and violence. They are designed to create consensus (Habermas, 1990: 72).

The distinction between Lifeworld and System provides the distinction on which we are able to construct the dimension of formality of conflict responses, with at one end of the axis the informal world of private social life through to the intervention of state authority at the other.

Both MacIntyre and Habermas see Law as connected to social life. Fuller (1969) and Finnis (1980) argue that Law is a product of Morality and Ethics. These views of Law are antithetical to Luhmann's autopoietic theory of law (2004). That theory sees law as having such a discrete function that it reproduces, organises and reforms itself from within, as if had had not only autonomy within the state but also its own autochthonous status.

The development of this theory of peacemaking is partial. Whilst it may be seen to hold good within the 'Western' tradition, it lacks a broader formulation that can be tested against other traditions of law and conflict response. That project is necessary for any future advancement of conflict responses at inter-communal and international levels. To that extent, this chapter must be read as a provisional and limited account.

Typology for conflict responses

The typology of conflict responses is articulated in three dimensions: a *temporal perspective*, the *social locus* (individual – state – international), and lastly an *axis of formality* (*consent – coercion*, or voluntary – regulatory – enforcement).

Conflict responses in a temporal framework

The development of a temporal focus for peacemaking is stimulated by reference to Durkheim's views about the evolution of law in relation to his theory of the development of societies from mechanical to organic solidarity and his evaluation of the role of peace in the development of social rules (Durkheim, 1984). Durkheim's thought has not appeared to have had much influence in the development of contemporary restorative justice thinking. As argued later, his main analysis of the nature of restitutory function of law is flawed as to the timing of its emergence in history.

Durkheim argued that the law is divided into two main types, restorative and repressive (op. cit.). Of these two functions, the repressive function is seen to have developed first in ancient societies. He saw ancient law as almost totally repressive with 'restitutory law and co-operative law playing very little part' (ibid: 92–93). However, a number of anthropological studies (Mackay, 2002; Evans-Pritchard, 1956; Malinowski, 1961; Vergouwen, 1964) show that restitution has played an important part in dispute and conflict settlement alongside religious expiation.

Durkheim is inconsistent in the development of his typology. At one point (op. cit.: 87) he distinguishes 'negative and abstaining relationships' from 'positive or co-operative relationships' as the two components of 'rules with a restitutory sanction determining different relationships'. However, later he distinguishes restitutory and co-operative law as two categories without explanation (ibid: 93).

However, there is one aspect of Durkheim's account of restorative law which, although it would not find favour with some advocates of restorative justice (who see it as having forward looking and even therapeutic value), is clearly correct. The principle of restoration relates to the rectification of harm done to the enjoyment of legally established rights and expectations within social relationships. In addition, setting aside his inconsistent usage of restitutory and co-operative law, Durkheim makes a crucial point for advocates of restorative justice, which is that the restorative principle refers to non-criminal matters as well as to criminal matters, which can be inferred from his conclusion that 'the obligations that arise from an offence or a quasi-offence are of exactly the same character' (ibid: 75). The implications of this are that it exposes a fundamental issue for restorative justice, which is that the commission of a crime brings down upon the offender the attentions of both the restitutory and the repressive functions of Law.

What we can take from this is that there is a clear distinction to be drawn between responses that focus on past action (restitutory) and those that deal with the future (repressive), and that legal and social infractions share the same framework of conflict responses.

For the sake of completion, it is also necessary to deal with Durkheim's views of peace. In developing his account of how people come together to make rules to live together, Durkheim suggests that it is not the desire for peace which brings people together. Indeed, some societies clearly thrive on war, peace being merely a product of temporary lassitude or distraction in a warrior society. Rather, he argues, 'men need peace only in so far as they are already bound by some bond of sociability' (ibid: 76). However, his further remarks about the emergence of a sense of the dependence of European nations upon each other indicated that they were part of a common society already, and that the balance of power 'marks the beginning of the organisation of that society' (ibid: 77). Although this suggestion has been tragically refuted by two world wars, the Cold War confrontation and the conflicts in the former Yugoslavia, we do see now the emergence of a common society in Europe, notwithstanding the United Kingdom's decision to leave the European Union. Furthermore, despite continuing wars and other forms of violent conflicts engulfing whole communities, there is some recognition internationally of the need for worldwide institutions to help to promote peace and to manage and resolve conflicts. This has some bearing upon the construction of the dimension of the social locus of conflict resolution. It also reveals something about the motivation of protagonists in conflict and of those who institute conflict responses.

In Figure 6.3, three principles for the functioning of conflict responses both within and outside legal frameworks are illustrated with regard to their relationship with Time. It is suggested that these principles are inherent in legal and political systems.

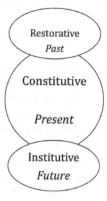

Figure 6.3 The three temporal elements of peacemaking focus, with the Constitutive Present as the lens

In responding to conflict, attention needs to be paid to dealing with issues from the past (restorative), how to handle the relationship in the present (constitutive) and how to plan the handling of relationships in the future (institutive). The constitutive principle will have to incorporate both restorative and institutive elements. However, it is clear that some modes of conflict or dispute management and resolution are better suited to the aims of one principle rather than to another, whilst others are suited to each of the principles. (See Table 6.1.)

Before analysing this question further, it is important to reflect upon the dual aspects of restoration. Following Habermas's distinction between Lifeworld and System and his construction of the role of law in both, it is suggested that the restorative principle has a role both in the Lifeworld and in the System (Law and Politics) (Habermas, 1987, 1995; Orts, 1993).

This analysis helps us to recognise that restoration in the Lifeworld is concerned with informal relations. Reconciliation is the primary concern for some advocates of restorative justice, but this aim is sometimes given priority over the justice claims of restoration which are the proper business of legal systems and politics. What is suggested here is that both have a place in the task of peacemaking but that we need clarity in determining the ways in which different aspects of restoration can be worked upon and within what domain (see Figure 6.4).

Conflict responses by level of formality and social locus (see Table 6.1)

It is important to recognise that in the relations between states (as states), there is an element of voluntariness. Can one speak of a Lifeworld existing between states which is separate from an international System? Whatever the answer to this question, it is clear that relations between states have some components which are obligatory and others which are not. It is therefore possible to map out two dimensions, a consent – coercion axis and a hierarchy of social structures in which disputes and conflicts are handled. Some of the cells are left empty because it has not been clear which interventions most clearly fit the typology. There is also scope for debate about the placement of some of the conflict response types.

The consent – coercion axis is fairly self-evident. However, there is the potential for overlaps and gradations, particularly on the boundary of voluntary and regulatory practices. Thus, entering into a contract is a voluntary act, but a contract once in place regulates the relationship between parties.

The hierarchy of social structures is also fairly clear, but there is one complication not explicitly covered here, namely, the situation, frequent enough in current times, of conflicts in the international environment involving nation states, international groupings and parties within states in a condition of civil war or breakdown. This can also be reflected in the concept of asymmetrical conflicts. Technically this hybrid type falls within the heading 'Multi-state environment'. In this hierarchy, the state is taken to mean a sovereign state. The relations between states within a federal union are to be considered in the heading 'Societal-State'. An 'inter-state grouping' is a body such as NATO or the European Union that is an international grouping that is not global. Of course, an inter-state grouping may be in dispute with a particular state outside the group. Groupings

LIFEWORLD	SYSTEM
Reconciliation	**Restitution**
Healing relationships	**Restoring right**

Figure 6.4 Distinguishing the relational and justicial elements of peacemaking

Table 6.1 Mapping conflict responses by social locus and axis of voluntariness – coercion

	Individual – private	Societal – state	Inter-state bilateral	Inter-state grouping	Multi-state environment
VOLUNTARY PRACTICES	Negotiation				
	Mediation – Conciliation – Alternative Dispute Resolution				
	Promises And Agreements				
	Healing Rituals – Forgiveness		Diplomacy		
	Peacemaking Circles				
		Politics		Politics	
REGULATORY PRACTICES	Contracts	Codes Of Practice	Treaties (Including Trade Agreements)		
	Mediation-Arbitration	Audit/Inquiries		Audit/Inquiries	
	Arbitration/Ombudsmen				
	Adjudication, including Executive Decision-making, both by states and autonomous bodies, e.g. professional bodies			Adjudication (European Court of Human Rights; War Crimes/Genocide Tribunals, UN Resolutions)	
	Legislation, Secondary Legislation, Directives				UN Charters
		Truth & Rec. Coms.	UN Resolutions		
ENFORCEMENT PRACTICES	Policing – (including Crime prevention)		UN Mandates		
	Security Activities				
	Enforcement of Judgements				
	Penalties (including 'Shunning')		Sanctions/[Collective punishments]		
	[Duel/Revenge]	[Blood-feud, Lynch law, Extra-judicial punishments, Terror, Assassination]	Defence/Peacekeeping/[Military aggression, Terror, Assassination]		

will have different purposes and different types of structure and levels of formality. Some of the conflict responses are placed in square brackets. This is because they are deemed illegitimate by most communities, even if they may have been legitimate in former times (e.g. blood-feud), or even be thought to be legitimate still in some quarters (e.g. collective punishments and military aggression). Military aggression excludes military action taken as a result of a UN decision or in proportionate self-defence. Shunning as a social practice of avoidance is a damaging activity, but it is often the case that the most common practice of conflict response is avoidance, or ignoring the conflict. 'Pocketing an insult' is a common reaction to social or political unpleasantness.

This table covers almost the full range of possible responses to conflicts and disputes. The choice of response depends on the perceptions of the parties as to where the conflict sits within the framework, but also on their intentions. For instance, an international grouping may feel that diplomacy is the most appropriate method, believing that there is room for voluntary or regulatory action, whereas another party may think that some form of enforcement is required. The intentions will be reflected in the choice of method. Thus, a party that seeks an advantage in the short term at the expense of mending a relationship, or wishes to deter the other party, may move towards coercion, rather than have recourse to a voluntary or regulatory method. Finally, the intention and choice of response will be reflected in a strategy which may be derived from a number of models, for instance, the Prisoner's Dilemma (Fisher and Brown,

1989). What is important here is that the choice of response can be distinguished within a dimension of consent and coercion, and that these choices reveal a great deal about the intentions and strategies of actors. Several of these methods have wide application across the range of social locus, such as negotiation and mediation. However, it is important to note that, particularly in the field of voluntary dispute resolution, there is a range of hybrid methods under the general label of mediation – conciliation and alternative dispute resolution.

Conflict responses by temporal focus and axis of voluntariness – coercion

The final correlation of dimensions of peacemaking processes relates to the temporal focus and the level of formality (see Table 6.2).

Table 6.2 draws out a number of responses that operate generically across the social locus dimension. This representation of the typology demonstrates the interdependence of different types of institutions in the function of peacemaking, whether it be the activities of political institutions, executive government and its agents, legislators, courts or other legal officers. These interventions may be carried out at every level of the social scale.

If we look at the temporal dimension, what stands out is the ontological difference of the present. It is in the present that our knowledge and understanding is shaped, our motives emerge and our actions are manifested. Even reinterpretation of the past is a present act. In conflicts, these elements of mind and action are brought forth in relation to the 'Other', either face to face or with them in mind. How we perceive the 'Other' is critical to our conflict response. As Buber has put it:

> The present – not that which is like a point and merely designates whatever our thoughts may posit as the end of "elapsed" time, the fiction of the fixed lapse, but the actual and fulfilled present – exists only insofar as presentness, encounter and relation exist. Only as the You becomes present does presence come into being.
>
> (Buber, 1970: 63)

Table 6.2 Mapping conflict responses by temporal focus and axis of voluntariness – coercion

	All domains private – societal – international		
	Past only restorative	*Past – present- future constitutive*	*Future only institutive*
VOLUNTARY	Making amends Reparation / Restitution Making apologies	Conciliation Negotiation Mediation	Agreeing terms of future relations Promises Assistance/Aid
REGULATION	Arbitration of law Adjudication of responsibility Compensation Settling claims	Arbitration of interests Mediation-arbitration Mediation-adjudication	Contracts & Treaties Arbitration of interests Adjudicated rehabilitation Legislation

ENFORCEMENT	Imposing penalties and
	    sanctions retributively
		Policing, including
		    military action
		Security activities
			Crime prevention
			Security activities
			Imposing penalties as risk
			    management and/or
			    deterrence

So the quality of the outcome of the conflict is directly dependent on the motivations and capacities of the actors. Within that nexus, the role of the neutral or the interlocutor with the actors may be to moderate or ameliorate each party's perception and feeling towards the 'Other'. We will return to this in the light of the exploration of *Romeo and Juliet*.

Relevance of the framework for conflict and dispute resolution practice

The typology shows that conflict responses have different ranges of application across the three dimensions. When a party in conflict or a third party considers how to respond, whatever their intentions, they may face a limited range of options. In an ideal conflict response environment, the parties would be able to construct a conflict response using a range of methods that encompass the restorative, constitutive and institutive agendas identified in the case. However, in practice, what methods are available, and the capacity to link different methods in a package of conflict response, may be limited.

Thus, using a criminal justice example, in one jurisdiction, a prosecutor may be able to refer a case for a restorative conference and thereby avoid prosecution. In another jurisdiction, they have to prosecute in order to access a restorative response. The implication is that whilst in both cases the restorative agenda may be met, the constitutive and institutive implications may be different. For instance, an accused may be far more willing to accept responsibility for an offence they have committed if there is no danger of prosecution but may be reluctant if they are sent to court, at least until the finding of guilt. That may mean that the potential for restoration of relationships and the setting of good relations in the future may be impaired. Punishment as a response to conflict can be interpreted on the temporal dimension in two ways. Restoratively, in a negative sense, it is retributive. It holds a person to account for what they have done in the past. Prospectively, or institutively, it serves either to manage risk to the public, or to deter. Constitutively, all it succeeds in doing is to condemn, and in many cases, to remove the offender from the community. This example illustrates how a conflict response, although it can be primarily focused on one or two points on the temporal dimension, can have other consequences at different points, some of which may be contradictory or unintended.

Another type of difficulty arises when the range of options available is not appropriate to the nature of the conflict. Thus, the prosecutor in the first example may think that criminal proceedings are far too heavy a response to the case in question. Thus, the constitutive and institutive agendas are sacrificed to a negative restorative-retributive agenda. A practical example of this might be the prosecution of an older person with depression for shoplifting. Alternatively, the methods may not be appropriate to the socio-legal environment. An example of this kind might be that the dominant justice system of a state may be seen as lacking legitimacy or relevance to an indigenous community because it does not engage with that community's sense of justice, either in terms of accepting the state's definition of the activity as an offence, or as to the justice, or indeed the intelligibility, of the procedure. It is suggested that whilst Western systems of justice are still primarily retributive (in the negative sense), indigenous systems tend to include more restorative, constitutive and institutive approaches (whilst also having some punitive elements). So in this type of case, there is a meta-constitutive agenda, that the individual accused and the victim, the indigenous community and the state are not even engaged in a common understanding of the present. So legitimacy is an integral element of the constitutive principle, making links with the principles of practical discourse in community that have been identified earlier.

The example of asymmetrical conflict is particularly challenging for third parties. Many conflict responses are designed to operate between parties who occupy a defined status in relationship with each other either of similarity (citizens before the law, the community of nations) or defined difference (employer – employee; state – citizen). However, when the disputants are not only different in status but also do not occupy a common ground for conflict response, it becomes more difficult to discern non-aggressive conflict responses. Thus, there is no court room or political arena in which a non-state group outside a state can raise a grievance against that state. How can, for instance, the small farmers of a state that has consigned a considerable proportion of its agricultural land to the interests of business in another state find a way of working out their conflict with the foreign state – absent the capacity to engage with their own state? Another significant example of this issue is emerging over the adjudication of the status of EU citizens in the United Kingdom (UK) and those of British citizens in EU countries after the UK leaves the European Union. If the UK declines to accept the European Court of Justice as the appropriate site for adjudicating issues on an even-handed basis, on the grounds that it compromises UK sovereignty, or if the UK and the EU fail to agree on the provision of another common judicial forum, people who are living as Britons in the EU, or EU citizens in the UK, will experience a lack of legal reciprocity in the application of whatever treaty agreement is made over their future status.

The recognition that each party in any dispute has different agendas that can be analysed in relation to how each sees the past, present and future of the conflict in which they are engaged helps us to make sense of the conflict response in which parties engage. The mapping of disputants' responses on the temporal dimension enables neutrals to interpret intentions of disputants. However, this mapping may also reflect a limit of imagination of, or confidence in, alternative responses. This has implications that go wider than the case of asymmetrical conflict. Thus, a family involved in a neighbourhood dispute in a violent and marginalised community which has led to a serious wounding or killing may engage in blood-feuding because they do not have knowledge of an alternative model, or because, if they do, they do not have confidence in its efficacy. If one does not have confidence that a report to the police will lead to a helpful outcome, or, worse, one has the fear that going to the police may lead to retaliatory action, disputants may well respond from their interpretation of present needs. The negative but accurate analysis of such a family's constitutive agenda is that it has a need to secure its current survival in adverse social conditions.

Turning again to the situation of EU and British citizens after 'Brexit', there is a need to address how a treaty can be enforced in a way that is even-handed for all those affected (institutive principle). There is also a need to address the changed legal relationship between the UK and the EU (institutive principle). There is a question of whether historic rights associated with movement of labour across the EU are sustainable, either on account of Brexit, or as a result of developing thinking and concern about this question across the EU itself (constitutive and restorative principles). Thus, negotiators need to find ways both to recast the principle of freedom of movement in a way that is fit for purpose for the EU itself (an internal EU process, and a bilateral EU-UK process), and to craft an institution that can manage future questions arising from the exercise of citizen's rights across the EU/UK boundary. The obvious potential examples for the latter are a joint commission with delegated judicial powers or the appointment of UK judges to the European Court of Justice for the purpose (*ad hoc*) of constituting a judicial panel. In this negotiation, we may see that if a UK government insists on dealing with EU citizens in UK solely within the UK court system, this could reflect the 'limit of imagination of, or confidence in, alternative responses', mentioned earlier, driven by political fears of being seen to be weak on the question of sovereignty.

We can see how some forms of intervention can operate in a constitutive way, that is, they have a bearing upon the past, present and future within a dispute or potential dispute. We can also begin to consider amalgamations of methods to deal with a particular conflict. Thus we can consider conflict responses within the framework of project management and practical reasoning. This is particularly important when conflicts have a political dimension. We can also see how a package for dealing with a conflict can both deal with rectifying harm (restorative) and with reducing or managing risk (institutive) whilst motivating the parties to engage in conflict response (constitutive). However, it will be argued that without attentive focus on the present, the response will be incomplete.

We can also examine particular conflicts using this analytic framework to examine how particular conflicts have been managed. Although the example is fictional, the universality and fame of the story allows us to consider Shakespeare's play *Romeo and Juliet* (2005) not so much as a tale of doomed love but rather in its other guise of *The case of the Prince against Capulet and Montague*, as a useful object lesson in failed conflict responses. Although it might be argued that the application of the model is anachronistic, inasmuch as the play was written about 400 years ago, it is a feature of drama that it can reveal insights across generations. This approach is presented as an exercise in Law and Literature. Briefly, this model adopts a dual approach to the study of Law, namely, that first, Law can be examined through the lens of literary criticism (Dworkin, 1986), and second, legal issues can be illuminated from the way they are represented in literature (White, 1985; Mackay, 2003).

When we look at the attempts by different characters to deal with the escalating conflict in the play, we can see examples of interventions that occupy all the cells in the grid of *Degree of Formality* by *Temporal Focus* and Axis of Voluntariness-Coercion (Table 6.2).

In Table 6.3 we see the various types of conflict response in which characters in the play engage. These are presented by *Degree of Formality* and *Temporal Focus*.

(The reference in Roman numeration refers to the location of the incident by act and scene of the play.)

What we see in the play are the effects of having a very weak political and legal structure alongside an ineffective but explosively charged social structure. It is clear that the state as personated by the Prince, a common feature of early modern and mid-modern times, is incapable of imposing the rule of law. Indeed, it is unclear what the rule of law means in the Verona of Prince Escalus. Unlike Louis XV of France who was able to state with superb conviction, 'L'Etat, c'est moi', the Prince can only strut petulantly in the market place. He makes threats that he cannot enforce (I,i). He imposes the requirement for the heads of household to engage in mediation-adjudication, but does not follow through on this (I,i). Even at the end of the play, in the face of a genuinely shared distress, when leadership could be exercised with an easy gravity, he is incapable of bringing clarity to his judgements, stating that some will be pardoned and some punished, but without saying whom (V,iii).

In addition to this, and perhaps unsurprisingly, there seems to be confusion in the community about what is the basis of the legal order. Sentences are issued extempore by the Prince, in the immediate aftermath of a riot (when he admits he is in a moved state of mind as a result of his relative, Mercutio's death), and not by independent judges sitting in a court of law (I,i). The sentence is not a judicial sanction, but a threat of future punishment (capital execution of the heads of the Capulet and Montague households for future breaches of the peace, which of course, are never carried out). Appeals are made to the *lex talionis* as a way of mitigating the increasing bloodshed (III,i). The Prince's response is pragmatic: to avoid further bloodshed he arbitrarily banishes Romeo from Verona, a solution that not only did not satisfy anyone, it did not make sense, for in the same breath that he exiles Romeo, he states that mercy encourages

Table 6.3 Mapping conflict responses in *Romeo and Juliet* by temporal focus and axis of voluntariness – coercion

	Restorative	Constitutive	Institutive
VOLUNTARY People minded to fight	Heads of Capulet and Montague households give each other their hands and promise statues to Romeo and Juliet (V,iii).	Lord Capulet welcomes Romeo and tries to calm Tybalt at the feast (I,v). Benvolio attempts to intervene to prevent violence (I,i & III,i); Romeo, (III,i). Benvolio advises withdrawal and avoidance (III,i)	Heads of Capulet and Montague households fail to control servants (I,i). Heads of household fail to control followers (all the time).
REGULATION Partiality No independent judge (The Prince) No effective mediator (The Friar). Failure to engage parties in dialogue and test solutions. Un-clarity about meaning of justice. Absence of 'capable guardian'	Lord Montague asking The Prince to see exchange of dead as a blood-feud accounting (III,i).	Prince orders shuttle mediation-adjudication but this never happens (I,i). Friar marries Romeo and Juliet: 'reconciling your friends' without engaging the main parties. Methods too instrumental (II,iii & III,iii). Prince banishes Romeo, whilst declaring himself to be an interested party (III,i).	Threats by Prince (I,i).
ENFORCEMENT Absence of 'capable guardian'. Reliance on violence (all).	Lady Capulet plans to poison Romeo (III,v). Duels (several).	Policing dependent on the crowd of citizens (I,i & III,i) Prince threatens to punish and pardon, but whom (V,iii)?	Prince's collusion: 'winking at your discords' (V,iii).

murder (III,i). He allows his judgement to be moved by the loss of his relative. He acknowledges at the end of the play that he has avoided the issue of handling the dispute, he had 'winked at your discords' (V,iii,294).

In a state wherein loyalty to family is greater than loyalty to the wider community (for which one may interpolate for modern times strong sectional non-state interests such as businesses), conflicts of interest abound. One of the Prince's relatives, Mercutio, is among the dead. Juliet has a terrible conflict of interest between loyalty to her Montague husband and loyalty to her cousin, Tybalt (III,v). Her mother, Lady Capulet, relieves Juliet of these painful scruples by taking a leaf out of the Milanese Borgia ladies' approach to law enforcement by attempting to poison Romeo (III,v). Juliet has no difficulty in the idea of taking revenge, it is just inconvenience of the person of the perpetrator that places her in the dilemma. But the main issue is that third parties faced with conflicts of interest are not free to make a decision about the correct form of conflict response.

If we turn to the analysis of the case itself, the conflict is chronic ('ancient grudge' [Prologue]). The causes of conflict are not explained. It is just a given. The past is inaccessible. The Prince avoids the issue (absent from a constitutive perspective). From a restorative perspective, there is nothing to prevent this conflict continuing. It has never been addressed. It is being handled by tolerance of the repeated brawls between the retainers of the conflicting houses. From a crime prevention (institutive) perspective there is no capable guardian who can deter the parties or alert the forces of law and order.

There are four types of conflict response which might be deemed to be potentially constructive in the play.

Near the beginning of the drama, after the Prince has harangued the heads of household (I,i), Lord Capulet attempts to use a combination of diplomacy and authority to downplay the arrival of Romeo Montague and his friends at the Capulet party, refusing to allow this to be seen as grounds for outrage (I,v). In this he is overtly obeying the edict of the Prince, recognising the legitimacy of his authority. He also invokes the rule of courtesy towards a genteel guest. He tries to assert the authority of a head of house towards his nephew, but he is no more successful in this than the Prince is towards his subjects. Capulet's conduct is both constitutive and institutive, trying to reframe his nephew Tybalt's view of Romeo from being an enemy to a young man who is of good character and therefore worthy of a courteous reception (I,v). He is also institutive in invoking a rule about how people ought to conduct themselves at family feasts.

From then on, the conflict is sustained in immediate and life-threatening encounters. The very immediacy of these scenes evokes powerful constitutive behaviour on the part of Benvolio and Romeo; after all, it is a drama to be experienced and beheld. This behaviour involves trying to break up blade fights: Benvolio tries to break up a fight twice, Romeo once (I,I; III,i; III,i). There is an attempt by Romeo to invoke a sense of honour ('Gentlemen, for shame!', III,i,85) However, these attempts are not successful, and in one case leads to Mercutio being killed (III,i).

The role of immediate crime prevention (constitutive and institutive principles) devolves upon the People. On two occasions in the play the assumption of the characters is that the People have the power to intervene to restrain public violence (I,i & III,i). This is plainly a vain hope. Nevertheless, there is a recognition that, in the absence of specialised policing, the community itself has authority, if not capacity, to police. Verona's finest were 'ancient citizens' who had three times to

> Cast by their grave-beseeming ornaments
> To wield old partisans, in hands as old,
> Cankered with peace, to part your cankered hate
> (I,i,92–95)

The other main theme of conflict response is the potential function of the marriage of Romeo and Juliet in healing the rifts between the two families.[1] The protagonist is the Franciscan Friar (Lawrence). In medieval and early modern times in Catholic countries, friars often played the role of mediators, so the Friar Lawrence's role is almost institutional. Mediation (or Alternative Dispute Resolution) takes many forms and, from the typology presented here, operates at the level of voluntary action, as well as a constitutive practice in the temporal dimension, which operates over the full range in the social locus dimension. Friar Lawrence's perspective is to

---

1 No doubt on the Hapsburg principle: *Bella gerant alii, tu felix Austria nube* – 'Let others wage war: thou, happy Austria, marry'.

see in the marriage of a Capulet and a Montague a voluntary present act that heals the past and regulates the future relationships of the families (II,iii). So far, so good, but however sincere the Friar is and however passionate the couple, the marriage as sacrament (or action with symbolic power) to heal a conflict is a mechanism that cannot work. The Friar is indulging in almost magical thinking. He confuses the level at which the conflict is played out. The love problems of two Veronese teenagers (private, social levels) are irrelevant to the concerns of family and civic leaders. Lord Capulet is interested in brokering an alliance between his family and the house of the Prince through the marriage of his daughter Juliet with County Paris, a relative of Prince Escalus, as Juliet is only too keenly aware (I.iii) (social, political levels). Not only does Friar Lawrence confuse the locus of the dispute but he fails to engage the real parties in resolving it. He tries to manipulate the parties into peace ('reconcile your friends' (III,iii,161) by a *fait accompli*, 'For this alliance may so prove/ To turn your households' rancour to pure love' (II,iii,87–88). Because he does not engage with what is really happening outside the love story, he is driven to the dangerous expediency of simulating death in trying to manage the crisis of the unravelling situation (IV,i). His strategy only deals with the past by way of seeking to impose a new reality – the marriage of a Montague and a Capulet – rather than by addressing what caused the problem in the first place (restorative principle). He does not address what is happening in the present, except through crisis management. He does not reality-test his stratagem in any way to establish whether it will indeed bring about the end of peace (institutive principle). In short, the Friar's intervention demonstrates that even if a conflict response addresses the past and the future, it is not necessarily constitutive. In this case, the Friar did attempt to address both agendas, but incompetently, by most standards of mediation practice, and he did not address the contextual present, that is, what is happening between the actual parties in dispute.

Reflection on the present personal, relatedness and recognition

In order to resolve conflicts, we have to take seriously the task of being in the present, whether we are negotiators, parties or mediators. This means we have to appraise our own involvement in the conflict and to seek to understand the involvement of the 'Others'. Understanding of oneself is critical for all actors in conflict, but it is especially so for mediators, because they have the task of facilitating change, which often means helping the parties and negotiators to shift their own perceptions of (*inter alia*) their own needs and the motivations of their 'Others'. This means stripping one's perception of the veils of stereotyping, and de-ascribing to oneself and others the trappings of social roles, or at least reflecting on them self-critically and reflectively. In other words, we have to be congruent, acting as ourselves in role, but not simply as a role-holder.

Buber alludes to this strikingly in *Between Man and Man* (2002):

> When imaginings and illusions are over, the possible and inevitable meeting of man with himself is able to take place only as a meeting of the individual with his fellow-man – and this is how it must take place. Only when the individual knows the other in all his otherness as himself, as man, and from there breaks through to the other, has he broken through his solitude in a strict and transforming meeting.
>
> *(p. 239)*

Consider, for example, a family mediator working with a couple which is in conflict and whose behaviour towards each other causes distress to their children. The mediator hears about and evaluates this historic and continuous situation in the present. At the same time, the mediator may be affected emotionally or psychologically by their own experience of their own parents' conflict. They should be aware as a professional of the potential impact of this on their own capacity to work effectively with the couple. What we are witnessing here is the potential for countertransference, whereby the therapist imposes their own experience onto the therapeutic process, thereby defining the way they see the parents' conflict and affecting the way they respond to it. Here we can see the potential impact of the past upon the present. The mediator, from a restorative perspective, needs to have disarmed the trigger of their own experience in order to act with a clear mind in the present, that is, constitutively. Thus the therapist will have recognised and distinguished their own experience from those of the 'Others', the children, and will thereby become capable of empathy towards them, albeit vicariously, which is the strongest quality in mediation. How then to transfer that capacity for empathy towards the conflicted parents? Instead of being driven by their own hurt, to blame the parents, the mediator must deal with their own feelings about their own parents. This may involve recognition that their own parents had mixed motives, to protect even whilst driven to act destructively, weakening but not destroying completely the protection needed by a child. This reflection may encourage the mediator to seek to access inner motives of the parents to protect their own children. This process is institutive or re-institutive, in that it sets up or recovers a benchmark for the parents' future way of parenting. But that will most likely take place if the parents learn to recognise each other as having these positive motivations for parenting.

This entails trust. The presence or absence of trust determines the mode of conflict response, relating to temporal focus and mode of conflict response. Where trust is high, there is less need for focus on healing the past (restorative) and voluntary agreements are likely to be more useful than in situations where there is low trust (mode of response). Trust may be developed through work in the present (constitutive). This may lead to a more voluntary outcome. However, if such work is unsuccessful, regulation of relationships may be needed.

Buber argues that in order to meet truly, individuals need to transcend their own spheres to communicate 'in a sphere which is common to them' (p. 241). This Buber calls 'the sphere of "between"' (ibid.). In our examples we see that there are often hidden connectors between actors in a conflict.

A model for harnessing the insights derived from the typology

In the literature of ADR (Alternative Dispute Resolution) there is reference to the concept of the Multi-door Courthouse (Moody, 1995; Mackay, 1995).

The key element of this concept is that when a dispute or conflict is identified, there should be a process of discernment as to how to respond to the dispute. This process is usually related to whether a case should be allowed to proceed to litigation or to some form of ADR. Thus, one can use quasi-legal tests to decide whether a case should be directed to litigation. Thus, cases should not go to court 'except when the level of harm done, the risk of further harm, issues of public policy, disagreements about the facts or the appropriate outcome, requires open court action' (Mackay, 2000, 2006: 213; Restorative Justice Consortium, 2002).

More dynamically, we can also use the threefold typology to assist in the discernment process. The application of the typology will help not only to understand what has happened in a case but to realise how we need to address previous harms, future needs and the current relationship. We could develop a role of 'civil procurator', as complement to the office of procurator as public prosecutor in Scotland and some mainland European jurisdictions (Mackay, 1995). A civil procurator, with skills in the analysis of conflict and the creative application of conflict responses, would be able to assist parties to choose the most effective way forward in addressing their dispute.

Conclusion

In this chapter, a theoretical framework for analysis of conflicts and discernment of appropriate conflict responses has been developed. This has drawn upon strong theoretical roots in ethics, sociology and the multidisciplinary work of Buber. The three-dimensional framework of temporal focus, sociopolitical locus and level voluntariness/coercion has been used to explore a rich fictional literary scenario and has also been applied to a reflection of a practice vignette in family mediation.

The main conclusion to be drawn from this exercise is that in order to address conflicts effectively, we need to analyse them and understand them not only correctly – and not only from our own perspective as decision makers and practitioners – but also dialogically, from the perspectives of the parties involved. We also need to apply that analysis and understanding to the practical work of developing and deploying appropriate conflict responses. Professionals often have recourse to default options, which are known and accredited within their own culture or legal environments. However, we sometimes do not recognise that a particular response, by its particular orientation in time, focus and location in the voluntariness – coercion continuum, or its position in the sociopolitical dimension, may actually serve to frustrate the overt aim of the decision maker: the prosecutor, judge or parole adjudicator.

Indeed, the issue may be more complex still. Sometimes a dispute may have asymmetric qualities for different parties in the dispute. Some parties in a dispute may be more concerned about dealing with past issues (retribution) whilst others may be concerned with the future (political stability). For some, the conflict has a primary focus on their personal lives or social networks, whilst for others the conflict has major political implications, whether local, national or international (e.g. human trafficking). Again, there may be disparities in people's perceptions about the level of consent or coercion required in dealing with a particular dispute or conflict.

Those who decide which approach to follow in dealing with the conflict or dispute need to find creative ways to address the disputants' aspirations and needs. We need to find ways not to be trapped by the available antinomial models (Truth and Reconciliation Commissions with amnesty *versus* post-conflict trials; Public Inquiries *versus* Coroners Inquests in English Common Law jurisdictions; tagging restorative practices to one or several but not all sectors of a criminal justice system). This means being creative in designing conflict resolution practices.

The application of the threefold typology creates a disciplined structure in which important questions concerning the deployment of conflict response can be addressed. It is hoped the arguments and examples in this chapter have demonstrated how such a process can be undertaken.

References

Braithwaite, J. 1989. *Crime, Shame and Reintegration*. Cambridge: Cambridge University Press.
Buber, M. 1970. *I and Thou*, W. Kaufmann, trans. New York: Touchstone and Simon and Schuster.
Buber, M. 2002. *Between Man and Man*, Friedmann, trans. London and New York: Routledge Classics.
Durkheim, E. 1984. *The Division of Labour in Society*, W.D. Halls, trans. London: Macmillan.
Dworkin, R. 1986. *Law's Empire*. London: Fontana.
Evans- Pritchard, E.E. 1956. *Nuer Religion*. Oxford: Clarendon Press.
Finnis, J. 1980. *Natural Law and Natural Rights*. Oxford: Clarendon Press.

Fisher, R. and Brown, S. 1989. *Getting Together – Building a Relationship That Gets to Yes*. London: Business Books.

Fuller, L.L. 1969. *The Morality of Law*, 2nd ed. New Haven and London: Yale University Press.

Gavrielides, T. 2007. *Restorative Justice Theory and Practice: Addressing the Discrepancy*. Helsinki: HEUNI

Gavrielides, T. 2008. Restorative Justice: The Perplexing Concept. Conceptual Fault Lines and Power Bsattles Within the Restorative Justice Movement, *Criminology and Criminla Justice Journal*, 8(2): 165–183. ISSN 1748–8958.

Habermas, J. 1987. *The Theory of Communicative Action: Lifeworld and System: A Critique of Functionalist Reason*, Vol 2, B. McCarthy, trans. Boston, MA: Beacon Press

Habermas, J. 1990. *Moral Consciousness and Communicative Action*, C. Lenhardt and S.W. Nicholsen, trans. Cambridge: Polity.

Habermas, J. 1995. *Justification and Application*, transl. by C. Cronin. Cambridge, UK: Polity

Luhmann, N. 2004. *Law as a Social System*, K. A. Ziegert, trans. Oxford: Oxford University Press.

MacIntyre, A. 1985. *After Virtue*. London: Duckworth

MacIntyre, A. 1988. *Whose Justice? Which Rationality?* London: Duckworth.

Mackay, R.E. 1993. A Humanist Foundation for Restitution, *Ratio Juris*, 6(3): 324–336.

Mackay, R.E. 1995. The Future of ADR in Scotland. In S.R. Moody and R.E. Mackay (eds.) *Alternative Dispute Resolution in Scotland*. Edinburgh: W Green and Sweet & Maxwell.

Mackay, R.E. 2000. Ethics and Good Practice in Restorative Justice. In European Forum for Victim-Offender Mediation and Restorative Justice (eds.) *Victim-Offender mediation in Europe – Making Restorative Justice Work*. Leuven: Leuven University Press.

Mackay, R.E. 2002. Punishment, Guilt and Spirit in Restorative Justice – An Essay in Legal and Religious Anthropology. In E. Weitekamp and H.-J. Kerner (eds.) *Restorative Justice: Theoretical Foundations*. Cullompton: Willan.

Mackay, R.E. 2003. Noble Delinquence and Kind Complicity: Themes in Restorative Justice from Twain's *Tom Sawyer* and Chopin's *A Night in Acadie*, *British Journal of Community Justice*, 2(2): 67–80.

Mackay, R.E. 2006. The Institutionalization of Principles in Restorative Justice – A Case Study from the UK. In I. Aertsen, T. Daems and L. Robert (eds.) *Institutionalizing Restorative Justice*. Cullompton: Willan.

Mackay, R.E. 2007a. Law as Peacemaking – Beyond the Concept of Restorative Justice. In R. Mackay, M. Bosnjak, J. Deklerck, C. Pelikan, B. van Stokkom and M. Wright (eds.) *Images of Restorative Justice Theory*. Frankfurt: Verlag für Polizeiwissenschaft.

Mackay, R.E. 2007b. Ethical Justification for the Theory of Law as Peacemaking, *Acta Juridica* 'Restorative Justice: Politics, Policies and Prospects': 73–90.

Malinowski, R. 1961. *Crime and Custom in Savage Society*. London: RKP.

Moody, S.R. 1995. An Overview of Alternative Dispute Resolution in Scotland. In S.R. Moody and R.E. Mackay (eds.) *Alternative Dispute Resolution in Scotland*. Edinburgh: W Green and Sweet & Maxwell.

Orts, E.W. 1993. Positive Law and Systemic Legitimacy, *Ratio Juris*, 6(3): 245.

Restorative Justice Consortium. 2002. *Principle of Restorative Justice*. London: Restorative Justice Forum.

Shakespeare, W. 2005. *Romeo and Juliet*, T.J.B. Spencer ed. and commentary. Penguin Shakespeare Series. London: Penguin

Vergouwen, J.C. 1964. *The Social Organisation and Customary Law of the Toba-Batak of Northern Sumatra*, J. Scott-Kimble, trans. The Hague: Martinus Nijhoff.

Walgrave, L. 2008. *Restorative Justice, Self-interest and Responsible Citizenship*. Cullompton: Willan.

White, J.B. 1985. *Heracles' Bow: Essays on the Rhetoric and Poetics of the Law*. Madison: University of Wisconsin Press.

Wright, M. 2003. Is It Time to Question the Concept of Punishment? In L. Walgrave (ed.) *Repositioning Restorative Justice*. Cullompton: Willan.

Wright, M. 2007. Punishment and Restorative Justice: An ethical comparison. In R. Mackay, M. Bosnjak, J. Deklerck, C. Pelikan, B. van Stokkom and M. Wright (eds.) *Images of Restorative Justice Theory*. Frankfurt: Verlag für Polizeiwissenschaft.

7

Recovery and restorative justice
Systems for generating social justice

Anna Kawalek, Michael Edwards and David Best

Introduction

This chapter aims to contribute to the Handbook's central objectives by providing an original, theoretical contribution that compares two related paradigms predicated upon similar principles: restorative justice (RJ) and addiction recovery. We believe that whilst the parallels have been recognised, previous literature has not yet demonstrated clearly how they align and where they can learn from one another. Throughout the chapter, we – as adherents of Positive Criminology theory – focus upon the concept of community reintegration by arguing that this is where the two paradigms most coherently parallel one another. Both seek to create positive social bonds in which the well-being of all those involved, on micro (individual), meso (social/community) and macro (broader systems of social justice) levels (Gavrielides, 2015), are restored through the formation of a generative virtuous cycle, which creates resources to facilitate further positive change. We argue that RJ and Recovery-Oriented Systems of Care (ROSC; Sheedy and Whitter, 2009; White, 2008) are ultimately "levers" that power individuals towards reintegrative forces, although it is ultimately wider societal structures (both meso and macro levels) that enable the full reintegration process to occur. We believe UK Restorative Cities (such as Hull and Leeds) are, arguably, a demonstration of this process functioning fully, generating community well-being and enhancing social justice by challenging exclusion and stigmatisation of marginalised groups who are attempting to reintegrate. We therefore suggest the construction of a "Recovery City", based upon the infrastructures, principles, and culture of "Restorative Cities".

The paradigm shifts: human potential within a strengths-based genre

Recently there has been a paradigmatic shift that represents a recognition amongst scholars, researchers and practitioners that the Risk Need Responsivity (RNR) model of rehabilitation should be remoulded in the light of the Good Lives Model (GLM) (Ronel and Segev, 2015; Gavrielides and Worth, 2015). Whilst both approaches are fundamentally rehabilitation-focused, the RNR model is ultimately concerned with pathological deficits at biological, psychological and social levels, and focus on individual rather than contextual factors, whilst the GLM is positive, holistic and restorative (Gavrielides and Worth, 2015). In the criminal justice field, the GLM is often associated with the Positive Criminology school, yet it extends to other domains such as positive psychology (Seligman, 1998) and recovery (Best and Laudet, 2010), with authors demonstrating that the model is a vehicle to enable these distinct but related disciplines to enrich one another (Vyver, et al., 2015; Gavrielides and Worth 2015). Maruna and Lebel (2015) distinguish between risks-based, needs-based and strengths-based strategies to prisoners within the prison re-entry context. Risks-based approaches are typically associated with managing behaviours as well as broader recidivism rates, whilst needs-based approaches are associated with helping prisoners gain independence through treatment enforcement, yet both assign control, restrictions and management to offenders and their behaviours and thus fit better under the RNR umbrella (Maruna and LeBel, 2015). Conversely, rooted in a humanistic school, a strengths-based approach implements a restorative ideology, treating prisoners as individuals with talents, abilities and indeed strengths, and as valued members of the community to which they can make a positive contribution (Maruna and LeBel, 2015). There are complexities to this analysis, as some scholars from the RNR school posit that the model is in fact strengths-based (Andrews Bonta and Wormith (2011) cited in Gavrielides and Worth, 2015). However, more commonly, a strengths-based approach is associated with the GLM, whereby a positive starting point is thought to bring about better results and less harm to those that come in contact with social, legal or justice institutions or interventions (Ronel, 2015). A strengths-based approach thus looks to engender social justice for individuals, families and broader communities and cultures. These approaches form key themes of this chapter.

Addiction recovery

In line with this broad paradigmatic shift, there has recently been a theoretical and practical shift within the alcohol and other drugs (AOD) recovery domain which has reconsidered both the parameters and possibilities of addiction recovery. Until recently, addiction was framed as weakness of the will and body, rooted in human pathology and occurring at brain level as a chronic relapsing brain disease (White, 2007). Consequently, many intervention approaches were rooted in the RNR school by being "problem and treatment"-driven (Chen and Gueta, 2015: 221) with low aspirations, assuming both the powerlessness of the addict and the central role of experts for deploying psychological and pharmacological therapies (Best and Savic, 2015). The premise was a need to correct human flaws through deficit and clinical-based intervention models, in which professionals handled addiction as if it were a genetic disease, implying that recovery is a difficult (if not impossible) state to achieve (White et al., 2003; White, 2007). Empirical evidence has emerged challenging the disease model by demonstrating that, on average, over half of AOD addicts will recover from addiction (White, 2012; Sheedy and Whitter, 2009), many without clinical interventions. As studies continue to show high rates of recovery, the implication is that addiction recovery must be something beyond a diseased-based pathology of the mind – if not at the point of onset, then certainly through the process of resolution.

To help explain these trends, the "recovery capital" model has been developed. Recovery capital has been defined as the "sum of resources necessary to initiate and sustain recovery from substance misuse" (Best and Laudet, 2010: 2), which can be accumulated and/or exhausted when attempting cessation (Granfield and Cloud, 2001; Cloud and Granfield,

2009, Best and Laudet, 2010). The model has been used to illustrate how (theoretically and empirically) individuals are able to garner the resources needed to support them in their recovery (Best, 2012; Granfield and Cloud, 2001; Cloud and Granfield, 2009). Recovery capital represents a significant shift in rhetoric; instead of characterising addiction as a disease within a negative clinical doctrine, recovery becomes a strengths-building exercise. This has given the discipline new-found optimism, with similar effects on family members, profession-als engaged in recovery support and the wider public through hope-based narratives. Whilst the recovery capital model has been groundbreaking for transferring AOD addiction recovery into a positive, strengths-based arena, it is also predicated on the idea of something that can be measured and counted and that is open to rigorous testing (Groshkova et al., 2013; Best and Laudet, 2010). This also creates a framework for translating ideas of recovery capital to clinical practice as a "currency" that can be measured and improved. As the discipline moves from a disease-based conceptualisation, the relational (social and community) aspects of recovery capital continue to be emphasised, with evidence strongly indicating that access to these dimensions makes individuals better placed to overcome addiction (Best and Laudet, 2010). As a method for assessing well-being, recovery capital also provides opportunities for bridging beyond specialist treatment care contexts, supporting the movement away from professional and medicine-based interventions and settings into strength-building, community and social driven models for supporting and sustaining addiction recovery (McKnight and Block, 2010; Humphreys, 2004). In other words, the transition to a strengths-based model through the capital framework removes the medicalisation of recovery and bolsters the relational compo-nents of recovery.

Restorative justice and restorative practices

Whilst not limited to the criminal justice (CJ) field (Liebmann, 2015), RJ has most commonly found itself developing new ideologies and related practices within offender, victim and com-munity harm resolution (Bazemore and Walgrave, 1999; Huang et al., 2011). Although there is no single definition of RJ, with experts struggling to form a consensus upon this (Llewellyn et al., 2013), Zehr and Gohar (2002: 40) define RJ as "a process to involve those who have a stake in a specific offense to collectively identify and address harms, needs and obligations in order to heal and put things as right as possible". RJ is therefore a holistic and collective process which relies upon experience with the broader community, although intrinsically interpersonal and predicated on assumptions of de-professionalisation and a commitment to social justice. RJ is as much a system of ideals and principles underlying practices than a system of practices themselves; it is, as Gavrielides has articulated, an "ethos". (Gavrielides, 2007: 139; Gavrieldes, 2014). Whilst "modern" RJ has its roots in CJ, and it is within that milieu that it has had global application (Gavrielides, 2014, 2005), RJ lends itself to translation into other contexts, as we demonstrate. We do not set out to align either with those who argue for a purist approach to RJ (McCold, 2000), nor with those who argue for a wider application, for example, Walgrave's (2000) "maximalist". Rather, we posit that RJ is a single contextual application of restorative principles, and that those principles and thus its underlying principles have broader application.

RJ has led to a refocusing upon reintegration, reducing recidivism and validation within the justice process (as opposed to punishment, shame and depreciation) (Braithwaite and Mugford, 1994), and so to greater openness, community ownership and accessibility to justice practices. RJ theory assumes that offenders hold potential to heal "those who have a stake in the offence" (Zehr and Gohar, 2002: 4); they are able to put right, repair harm and make up for wrongdo-ing. This has changed the narratives associated with offenders; they become individuals with capabilities, abilities and no longer innately "bad" or atomistic people (Llewellyn et al., 2013). This creates a possible transformation of the CJ field itself into a strengths-based genre, a paradigmatic shift that resembles the AOD recovery doctrine (Braithwaite, 1989; Zehr and Gohar, 2002; Braithwaite and Mugford, 1994). This has implications for professional-service user relationships and status, for locus of power and control, and for assessing and interpreting impact and effectiveness of the justice process. Both paradigms offer an egalitarian approach in which those who had previously been labelled as problematic individuals to whom things are done become individuals with strengths and capabilities able to flourish under positive circumstances, and who are empowered to do so. There is a further drive towards self-determination shaped by prosocial activities shaping reparation and community re-engagement. Both on theoretical and practical levels, RJ and recovery have embraced interpersonal change as an intrapersonal, holistic and relational phenomenon (Llewellyn et al., 2013; Best and Laudet, 2010), and they rely upon mechanisms within broader communities to leverage change at a personal level by providing forums in which positive change is made a reality through strengths-building exercises.

Recovery and restorative justice as relational theories

As ROSC (Sheedy and Whitter, 2009; White, 2008) are founded upon social and community predicators, abstinence is not considered the only or even necessarily the primary goal of care (Best and Laudet, 2010; Granfield and Cloud, 2001). Newer care models consider success within life-course perspectives to include health and well-being, social networks, employment, finance (Wittouck et al., 2013) education and training, mental and/or physical health, relationships, criminal justice, social engagement and meaningful activities, and these are personally articulated (Manning et al., 2016; Savic et al., 2014; Laudet et al., 2009; Kodner and Kyriacou, 2000). Recovery is further seen as a process rather than a state (and one which typically takes around five years, expecting that these objectives will not only differ between people but will also change over the course of a recovery journey) (Betty Ford Institute Consensus Group, 2007). The underpinning assumption is akin to Maslow's (1943) Hierarchy of Needs in which the achievement of lower-order objectives generates the capacity to aim higher for more complex aspirational goals.

In the same way, RJ's measurement parameters move beyond traditional CJ analyses by considering community, subculture and relationship successes (Llewellyn et al., 2013) as well as democracy building (Braithwaite, 2016). Llewellyn (2013) has argued that this creates challenges for evaluation and comparative assessment, as it is much more difficult to demonstrate effects and indeed causes when the desired outcomes involve relationships and community-level domains such as safety and connectedness. As the relational components are emphasised, experts have applied the notion of "social capital" to the recovery domain (Bourdieu, 1986; Coleman, 1988, Putnam, 2000; Granfield and Cloud, 2001; Best, Irving and Albertson, 2016). Relationships are valuable assets for initiating recovery success, and the model provides a lens for examining both the positive/negative roles that social networks play in enabling/disabling recovery (Granfield and Cloud, 2001; Best, Irving and Albertson, 2016). The "capital" aspect of the model refers to a dynamic process of exchanging social networks, bolstering motivation to change and building capacity to inaugurate recovery through social control/networks, mutual acquaintances, family support, group membership and expectations of others (Granfield and Cloud, 2001; Cloud and Granfield, 2008; Best, 2016). In other words, social capital refers both to the sum of groups and networks that individuals can call upon and to the extent of those individuals' bonding and commitment to those groups. Within the recovery literature, there is an assumption that accessing prosocial groups generates social recovery capital by creating role models for "social learning" and through the norms and values of the group referred as "social control" (Moos, 2007). Indeed, recovery chances are enhanced when addicts engage in social networks concordant with a non-using lifestyle, with the literature showing that those with a stake in "conventional" life have greater capacity to control drug use (Blomqvist, 2002; Murphy and Rosenbaum, 1999; Granfield and Cloud, 2001).

Granfield and Cloud (2001: 1545) first explored this idea by evidencing that individuals leading a "double life" with a "stake" in the non-drug using world had higher chances of natural recovery success. Possession of "conventional" social assets, which generally referred to employment, financial security, relationships, information, expectations, institutions and lifestyle, was maintained alongside associations with alternative drug-using cultures (Granfield and Cloud, 2001). Individuals embedded in networks comprised of norms, values and activities consistent with a using lifestyle were likely to adopt negative behaviours (Granfield and Cloud, 2001). Litt and colleagues used the "gold standard" of randomised controlled methods, to evaluate 187 individuals going through either: (i) standard aftercare; or (ii) aftercare with a social support component (establishing a relationship with a non-drinking peer) (Litt et al., 2007). The researchers found that those with additional social capital derived from a new prosocial network engagement (condition 2) had a 27% higher chance of increasing abstinence one year later in comparison to those administered standard aftercare (condition 1) (Litt et al., 2007). Likewise, Longabaugh et al. (2010) reported that the strongest predictor of long-term recovery stability, in a cohort of problem drinkers, was successfully making the transition from a social network supportive of drinking to a social network supportive of recovery. Elsewhere, research shows that social capital is strengthened via exposure to social networks/communities that hold positive values/attitudes/beliefs which strengthen control capacity and social connectedness (Buckingham et al., 2013; Best, Bird et al., 2015; Granfield and Cloud, 2001; Best 2014). Best et al., (2008) demonstrated that ex-heroin addicts remained abstinent due to movement away from using networks into non-using recovery circles, and that whilst psychological change and life experience may have been the catalyst for initial change, it was a combination of social factors that were most strongly associated with sustained abstinent recovery over time. These studies each imply that overcoming addiction strongly correlates to social context and the existence of social recovery capital, generated by moving from excluded groups (who have limited access to community resources) towards prosocial groups (who can provide not only practical support and resources but also access to knowledge and information about the local community). Recovery-positive group membership is crucial, as positive social platforms facilitate social contagion in which norms, values and culture are spread through social control, social learning (Moos, 2007), reciprocity, connectedness, acquaintances, emotional support, expectations and obligations (Best, Bird et al., 2015). One possible mechanism is around social identity encapsulated by the Social Identity Model of Recovery (SIMOR; Best, Beckwith et al., 2015), which suggests that access to prosocial groups offer attractive and viable models of recovery, engage and motivate change, and promote recovery success. It also exposes individuals to new values and group norms that bind them to the group and in doing so help them internalise the rules and behaviours of the group. What is important about social capital is the emphasis upon the relational aspect of recovery capital formation, which is also central to RJ. Restorative conferencing acts as: (i) family group conferences; (ii) victim-offender meetings; (iii) neighbourhood accountability boards and; (iv) peace-making circles (Bazemore and Umbriet, 2001). RJ processes rely upon a joint dialogue between stakeholders (Zehr and Gohar, 2002), which builds trust and reciprocity (Bazemore, 2005). Bazemore (2005: 136) considers restorative processes as "forums for community members to share and affirm norms and values as means of developing social cohesion" in a model that mirrors aspects of SIMOR. Similarly, Braithwaite (2000) defines RJ as multi-sectorial processes that bring together victims, offenders, friends, loved ones and representatives of the state. Llewellyn et al. (2013) argue that RJ should be considered in terms of "equality of relationship" parameters, such as mutual care, concern, respect and dignity (Llewellyn et al., 2013). The relational aspect is the cornerstone of both systems.

Perhaps the best practical examples to illustrate relational components of these processes are 12-step recovery fellowships such as Alcoholics Anonymous (AA) and Narcotics Anonymous (NA) (AA, 1943; NA, 1992; Kaskutas, 2009) and circles of support and accountability (COSA; Thomas et al., 2014). During fellowship meetings, attendees join together, often forming an acutal circle, and share their experiences. Each individual in turn becomes the core member, who is given the opportunity to discuss progress, failures and successes, the 12 steps and 12 principles and so on with the AA members present. AA meetings are both open and closed (the former open to anyone, but the latter restricted to members), and there are meetings dedicated to particular groups (e.g. women, young people, addicted doctors) and for particular purposes (such as "Big Book" meetings, where there are readings from the key text of the organisation). COSA (a circle model that operates RJ principles) has been widely applied in the UK, for example, with sex offenders attempting to rehabilitate (Thomas et al., 2014), in which the offender also becomes the core member of a supportive circle and members collaborate to discuss strategies for prevention of further sexual offending. Many of the group will be volunteers, although professionals may also be included in the circle, as well as a coordinator for the meetings. In both cases, positioning the individual at the centre of a generative circle facilitates the construction of meaningful relationships and positive social ties with other stakeholders to oversee sustainable prosocial behaviour (whether that is relationship building, desistance, recovery or something broader). Both models are concerned with "making good", a concept affiliated with the desistance paradigm (Maruna, 2001; Maruna and LeBel, 2015). Within RJ processes (such as COSA) "offenders' obligations are to make things right as much as possible" (Zehr, 2003: 83); for instance, through apology, change and restitution (Umbreit and Roberts, 1996; Walker, 2015). Similarly, within fellowships, Steps 8 and 9 state: "[We] made a list of all persons we had harmed, and began to make amends to them all" and "make direct amends to such people wherever possible, except when to do so would injure them or others" (Alcoholics Anonymous, 1939). "Making good" bolsters social reintegration and strengthens social capital ties through the broader relational dimension (Maruna and LeBel, 2015). It is clear that both models assume that change strategies extend beyond individual choices/incentives, require a wider pool of social resources and, therefore, establish practical responses where recovery/ restoration can be contextually negotiated. If strong empirical research suggests social capital impacts practical outputs within recovery groups (Best and Savic, 2015), similar conclusions can be applied to RJ platforms given their theoretical, practical and methodological similarities.

Extension of the relational component: community capital and reintegrative shaming

Common characteristics between recovery and RJ paradigms are most salient within discussions around stigma and exclusion and the resulting pressures individuals face when attempting to reintegrate and access resources within their local community (Best and Laudet, 2010). Ideas around reintegration can be found within recovery's "community capital" model and RJ's "reintegrative shaming" theory respectively (Best and Laudet, 2010; Braithwaite, 1989). In the former, recovery groups themselves can be characterised as a mechanism for building social capital whilst enabling and facilitating access to community resources. The latter focuses on the ritual processes of reintegrating individuals following sentencing or punishment to ensure that they are enmeshed within society. In both cases, it is assumed that: (i) the community responses to the offender can expedite reintegration by creating bridges into non-stigmatised groups, or that; (ii) community attitudes can debilitate reintegration through stigma and discrimination leading to exclusion by prolonging stigmatising labels, processes and structures. In this sense, both discourses sit within Positive Criminology theory, which is concerned with how positively construed reintegrative experiences help to generate prosocial behaviours (whether that be in context of the addict or the offender) (Ronel et al., 2013). We argue therefore that recovery and RJ overlap within their discussions around reintegration. Best and Lubman (2016) explore the "dark side" of social contexts, indicating that social ties are not inherently positive/prosocial forces and may entice drug-using behaviours through isolation from positive networks. This builds on work with homeless populations in Australia by Jetten et al. (2014) in which it was argued that strong binding ties to excluded populations could act as barriers to effective reintegration in spite of the benefits they may confer in terms of a sense of belonging and well-being. Similarly, in a study of members of an Australian therapeutic community, Dingle and colleagues (2015) found that maintaining social identification with a substance-using population even whilst engaged in recovery-oriented activities resulted in poorer outcomes. Putman's (2000) differentiation between "bridging" and "bonding" capital is relevant; whilst "bonding" capital refers to the quality/intensity of relationships (positive or negative), "bridging" capital refers to connections ("bridges") to wider positive community structures (Putnam, 2000). Strongly bound marginalised groups may be highly valued by members yet act as barriers to reintegration through their exclusion from community capital and a lack of bridges to community resources.

This "bridging" synergy has been most famously demonstrated by McNeill's (2016) tripartite model, building on Maruna and Farrall's (2004) earlier articulation of primary and secondary desistance, in which the tertiary stage of desistance from offending involves community acceptance. Within this approach, change relies not only on the acceptance of the immediate social networks such as family but also on the absence of structural barriers to being able to access key community resources such as housing, jobs and positive relationships. In the recovery field, this idea was first applied in Cloud and Granfield's (2009) cultural capital concept and was adapted latterly into Best and Laudet's (2010) three-pronged recovery capital model (which included personal, social and collective) (see Figure 7.1). It is within the latter part of the model that Best, Irving, Collinson et al. (2016) have demonstrated the significance of community attitudes for supporting the process of reintegration. By extending to wider community structures/attitudes, "capital" becomes a powerful force to combat entrenched community stigma that impedes

Figure 7.1   Best and Laudet's three-pronged recovery capital model

individual recovery progress and the viability, visibility and accessibility of recovery groups, thereby enhancing reintegrative efforts (Best et al., 2015). Treatment outcomes are more positive for those who are able to overcome stigma by accessing community capital, augmenting their "recovery" identity through participation in meaningful activities and social groups that have the most positive recovery outcomes (Best et al., 2011; Best, Lubman et al., 2014; Zywiak et al. 2009). In the Glasgow Recovery Study (Best et al., 2011), the strongest predictors of higher levels of recovery well-being were predicted by social capital (time spent with others in recovery) and community capital (being able to access meaningful activities such as work, education and volunteering). *The World Health Organisation (2001)* found drug addiction to be the most stigmatised health condition across the globe, with alcohol addiction the fourth most stigmatised.

Braithwaite (1989) provided an explanation for RJ's effectiveness within his reintegrative shaming theory (Ray et al., 2011; Harris, 2006). Braithwaite separates "reintegration" from "disintegration" as a shame management tool within CJ systems (Braithwaite and Mugford, 1994; Braithwaite, 1989; Zehr and Gohar, 2002). Reintegrative shaming processes (such as RJ) ritually reaccept offenders by directing shame towards the act rather than towards the offender, whilst disintegrative shaming (i.e., "typical" CJ practices) outcasts individuals through shame so that perpetrators internalise "offender" as their master status (Braithwaite, 1989). As reintegration becomes the locus of the restoration process, RJ therefore intends to strengthen support within communities (Braithwaite, 1989). What is important is that the factors are structural rather than individual, indicating the importance of community-level processes and their role in creating the environments that can facilitate bridging capital to positive groups with the resulting impact on personal resources and well-being. Reintegrative shaming ceremonies, such as RJ, rely upon two structures: (a) presence of individuals to support the offender (social capital) and; (b) confrontation within a wider pool of individuals from the community to enable reintegration via positive acts of inclusion (community capital) (Brathwaite and Mugford, 1994). However, they also provide "bridges" to communities and professionals and mechanisms for managing exclusion and the adverse consequences of stigmatisation. The core synthesis of these reflections on recovery and reintegration capital is summarised in the Figure 7.2, which shows that the personal, social and community aspects of capital are linked and that RJ and ROSC involve organisational and structural requirements at a locality level.

A gear system model to represent reintegration and future directions

The "restoration" process is therefore equally applicable to RJ and ROSC, and both can be thus considered "restorative practices". Both re-establish a connection between perpetrating individuals and close relationships such as family (on micro level) and the wider community (on meso level) by representing a broader change in belief system (on macro level), thus creating a virtuous cycle in the form of a therapeutic landscape as shown in Figure 7.2 (Llewellyn et al., 2013). Restorative practices themselves operate as gears on the X Axis that power individuals towards reintegration or disintegration via the shaming or inclusion process, generating positive (reintegrative) or negative (disintegrative) power. However, it is ultimately the wider community that provides the structure and the space to harness the power initiated by the gears, making reintegration (or disintegration) a reality. In other words, reintegration occurs through a reciprocal relationship with the community, which accepts the individual and by doing so, strengthens itself. As the X Axis produces positive energy (though reintegrative shaming), the micro, meso and macro levels rise, creating a virtuous cycle of social justice at systems level.

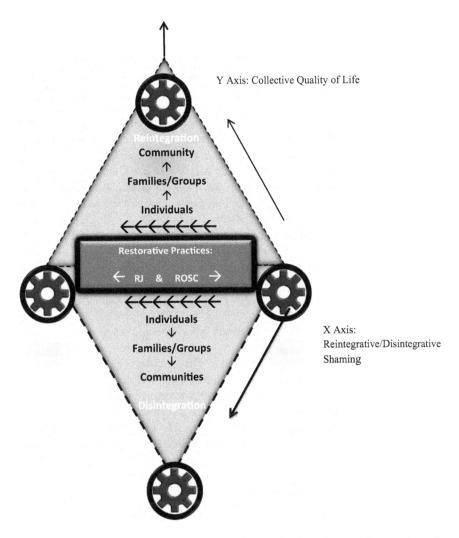

Figure 7.2 Linking personal, social and community mechanisms for enabling reintegration

This is represented by the Y Axis, which enhances (or diminishes) quality of life on a collective level. If the X Axis produces negative (disintegrative) energy, the power draws down and quality of life on the Y Axis also drops. As the power rises or drops, the effect is felt at rising (or falling) levels from the individual (micro) to families and community levels (meso) and to a broader culture of social justice (macro). Whilst restorative practices (represented by the gears on the middle band) are crucial for generating restoration, they have limited power when practised in isolation. Instead, they reach full capacity when drawing upon assets (or gears) found within wider communities, a change that must be reflected at policy level. Embedding restorative practices into policy, as the UK has done with recovery (UKDPC, 2008), is a critical step which must be sustained in order to enhance the power of the system.

The virtuous cycle has the potential to grow, strengthen and gain power as success at all levels continues during this cumulative healing process, and to make communities more inclusive by minimising marginalisation of sub-groups. As more participants are engaged, active and empowered by RJ/ROSC methods and accepted into the wider community, it becomes a functioning reintegration platform, bolstering quality of life collectively. As the process repeats itself, the community gets stronger, and so do the individuals within it, including (but not limited to) those being reaccepted. Continued movement up the Y axis increasingly bolsters overall quality of life for those both within and outside of RJ/ROSC through the networks of inclusion and support from community members, professionals and peer champions of recovery and RJ. However, the reversal of this process moves downwards on the Y axis, creating a negative cycle for each of the micro-meso-macro dimensions. The idea of the figure is that there is a constant tension between the pressures towards punishment and exclusion, often driven by community fears and populist political rhetoric on the one hand, and the commitments to neighbourhood, social justice and inclusion on the other. In principle, this is an empirically testable question around structures and systems linked to community attitudes and beliefs about reintegration and their effects on individual attempts at doing so. The diagram further depicts the idea that RJ and recovery should be understood and measured in terms of this model's relational component and as a broad experience that relies upon restoration or relationship building with the community rather than simply individual visions of success or prosperity on a smaller scale (Llewellyn et al., 2013).

Best and Laudet (2010) posit that community recovery capital includes the visibility, accessibility and acceptability of recovery groups. When recovery groups are seen as valuable in the community, when the champions of recovery are visible and when they are linked to a diverse range of community resources, the space can be characterised as a "therapeutic landscape for recovery" (Wilton and DeVerteuil, 2006). The idea is that spaces can be transformed to accept and engage with recovery groups/communities, and that this is an emerging property of community life (not only for those in recovery but also for the broader community). This is something which accumulates over time, increasing the likelihood that future generations will consider the transformed community viable and realistic. The gear model implements this idea by characterising the positive or negative impetus to reintegration that results from the implementation and visibility of these processes. The system level creates the space for individual growth and relational development through providing access to assets in the community, to visible and positively valued recovery and reintegration groups, and to role models of successful change.

The idea of a therapeutic landscape has already been implemented with success in the recovery sphere within the Asset-Based Community Development model (ABCD; McKnight and Block, 2010; Kretzmann and McKnight, 1990). ABCD is a mechanism for identifying positive assets in the community, creating links to them and deploying community assets to support the recovery journeys and pathways of individuals who had previously been excluded and marginalised. It works by identifying indigenous community resources (community capital) and linking them together to create support networks for vulnerable individuals (social capital). By looking inwards to their own assets, such as people, informal groups and formal organisations (who represent community capital), networks of community resources and recovery champions are created and held together by local people who already have established links and connections to wider community groups. These in turn act as "community connectors" (generating bridging capital) (McKnight and Block, 2010; Putnam, 2000). Our own work in Sheffield around identifying the levels of social capital of drug and alcohol users to determine the extent to which they will need assertive linkage to community assets (Best, Irving, Collinson et al., 2016) is an attempt to utilise asset models to target community partnerships to support recovery and, in doing so, to encourage recovering individuals to make active and sustained contributions to their lived communities. It is important that the group does not work in isolation but instead engages with wider community networks to facilitate reintegration. As Best, Irving and Albertson (2016) have shown, this is a model that energises communities by activating their resources through supporting the growth of connectors, improving the opportunities and well-being for excluded groups and increasing the pool of those who are active champions. As depicted in Figure 7.2, as this process repeats, the power of the community becomes stronger, thereby producing the virtuous cycle.

In many ways, RJ has already developed a piecemeal approach to this process through development of Restorative Cities, both in the UK and internationally. Over the past decade, Restorative Cities have developed as a loose coalition, although their definitions tend to be more amalgamations of intangible principles than tangible criteria. Hull in the UK was the first Restorative City (Macdonald, 2012; Green et al., 2013), and was developed to create "social and economic restoration of an entire city" by extending beyond the resolution of individual harms (Green et al., 2013). The aim was for restorative language to become commonplace, not only in justice settings, but also in social services and education contexts, thus providing families, children, young people and communities with the appropriate tools for resolving problems and conflicts in everyday life (Green et al., 2013). In the UK, Restorative Cities have since been extended to Leeds (Wachtel, 2012), also aiming to use models that share "'power' across communities and with families" so that solutions lie within broader relational dimensions (Finnis, 2014). Again, "restorative" values have extended beyond the CJ sector by changing attitudes as well as behaviours (Finnis, 2014), representing a broader change in culture. Another more quantifiable approach comes from a recent proposal put forward by The Institute for the Future, which provides a futuristic model for Oakland, California, also with the purpose of creating their city as a Restorative City. The rationale was to provide a service of peace centred on RJ principles to move away from a culture of punitivism and the associated stigma brought to offenders. The authors provided a map as "an attempt to reimagine the urban landscape through a restorative lens, bringing people out of prisons and the criminal economy, into productive and useful work in the service of their own communities" (Ross, 2016). The proposed model has been premised upon six basic principles: (i) healing the city; (ii) community focus; (iii) listening; (iv) food sovereignty; (v) positive contact, and (vi) environmental justice. Most significant to each of these three cities is a change in culture around social justice by embodying a new way of thinking. In turn, this generates sustainable reintegration for individuals passing through RJ models as a more accepting broader community premised upon an egalitarian philosophy.

We propose the piloting of Recovery Cities to enhance the reintegration journeys for those in recovery based on the same ideology around activating social justice. Changes in systems and processes at the community level would increase active engagement with marginalised groups through the promotion of recovery groups and communities and their engagement with a diverse range of community assets. However, the broader objective of this model is to create social and community capital to kickstart a contagion of connection and participation by a wide range of stakeholders who sign up to the Recovery Cities model. The proposed model adapts features from the ROSC and parallels the Restorative Cities model by providing a community space in which recovering individuals can be supported in an equal way to RJ participants within Restorative Cities. We believe that Sheffield should be construed under this title, as it contains a group of active researchers attempting to engage individuals in recovery, a range of ROSC based around relational principles and is increasingly breaking down the stigma attached to addicts from the overly medicalised model. That is no reason not to look to Restorative Cities to provide an outline of what a recovery city would be; indeed, the very opposite is true. As with Restorative Cities, we suggest that Recovery Cities are more about culture and ethos than specific guidelines processes, with the latter being merely the manifestations of the former within the context and confines of the given community. However, what is important is to recognise that these cities might provide the fundamental gear that reintegrates individuals in recovery through stigma management and community reacceptance, which research strongly demonstrates is the cornerstone of any recovery journey.

Conclusion

As the history of principles underlying and debates concerning RJ are extensively discussed throughout the other chapters of this Handbook, our intention was to bring the readers up to date with the recovery literature by giving a comprehensive overview of its newer, older and more contested areas. Furthermore, we aimed to show how the recovery movement's growth has been co-occurring with RJ, as the two align to one another by virtue of: (i) their strengths-based approaches and their positive reconceptualisation of "deviant" individuals; (ii) their holistic outlook on success indicators; (iii) the significance of the relational component and the importance of considering outcomes at the level of networks, relationships and communities, and; (iv) their similar ideologies around reintegration/disintegration.

Even where they are not overlapping, the scaffolding that supports both RJ and recovery processes shares many elements, making the theoretical borders between them blur, or rather, interlock. The gear model depicts a cumulative process which gains power as the process repeats itself and the community gets stronger. Each of the "micro", "meso" and "macro" components can be seen as gears that power the full restoration process, but as soon as one cog stops working, so do the others. As the paradigm shift within the addiction recovery domain gains momentum, we posit that both RJ and ROSC facilitate a reciprocal relationship between the gears, generating a virtuous cycle that enables full restoration for the individual, families and the community, and a broad change in culture. This is a mechanism and model for generating community participation by marginalised populations through creating social and community capital from which the entire community will benefit as a result of increased community cohesion and improved social integration (Sampson and Laub, 2003). It is at the level of community that RJ and recovery efforts create the pathway to reintegration, and according to both desistance and recovery theories, there can be no full recovery or restoration without reacceptance from the community. This chapter has therefore proposed a unique model to integrate principles of RJ and addiction recovery, looking at the practices through new lenses to support innovation.

We posit that reintegration is equally foundational to both type of restorative practice, and thus that these platforms must work with the community to improve and enhance both the private and public good through this virtuous cycle. Reintegration by definition necessitates community action and involvement. Community involvement, in turn, is constructed on the scaffolding of the structure and ethos of the organisational components of the community (i.e. the governing, social support, economic and ecological systems). Stated differently, effective reintegration, which we have argued is the hub of the restorative and recovery-focused action, has as a predicate part the existence of strong community capital. The aims of reintegrative communities are about improving community cohesion for all, not targeting only those who are marginalised and excluded. Best, Byrne et al.' (2014) reciprocal community development concept illustrates the process and value of it, and is based on the idea that vulnerable groups should not only tap into the assets in communities through linkage but should engage in a Hobbesian social contract by ensuring that they have a commitment to giving back and enhancing existing assets as part of the process of engagement. These well-researched principles help also to explain the workings of reintegrative shaming theory within RJ and create a model for improving the attractiveness of engagement to the wider community. Furthermore, bringing these paradigms together creates a strong partnership whereby research, theory and practice can be fine-tuned through mutual acquaintance across the disciplines.

References

Alcoholics Anonymous. 1939. *Alcoholics Anonymous* (The Big Book). New York: Anonymous Press.

Andrews, D.A., Bonata, J. and Wormwith, J. 2011. The Risk-Need-Responsivity (RNR) Model: Does Adding the Good Lives Model Contribute to Effective Crime Prevention? *Criminal Justice and Behavior*, 38(7): 735–755. Doi: 10.1177/0093854811406356.

Bazemore, G. 2005. Whom And How Do We Reintegrate? Finding Community in Restorative Justice. *Criminology & Public Policy*, 4: 131–148. Doi:10.1111/j.1745–9133.2005.00011.x.

Bazemore, G. and Umbriet, M. 2001. *A Comparison of Four Restorative Conferencing Models*. U.S. Department of Justice, Office of Justice Programs, Office of Juvenile Justice and Delinquency Prevention.

Bazemore, G. and Walgrave, L. 1999. *Restorative Juvenile Justice: An Exploration of the Restorative Justice Paradigm for Reforming Juvenile Justice*. Monsey, NY: Criminal Justice Press.

Best, D. 2012. Drug Nation: Patterns, Problems, Panics & Policies, *Drug and Alcohol Review*, 31(1).

Best, D., Beckwith, M., Haslam, C., Haslam, S.A., Jetten, J., Mawson, E. and Lubman, D.I. 2015. Overcoming Alcohol and Other Drug Addiction as a Process of Social Identity Transition: The Social Identity Model of Recovery (SIMOR), *Addiction Research and Theory*, 24(2): 111–123.

Best, D., Bird, K. and Hunton, L. 2015. Recovery as a Social Phenomenon: What Is the Role of the Community in Supporting and Enabling Recovery? In N. Ronel and D. Segev (eds.) *Positive Criminology*. London: Routledge, pp. 194–207.

Best, D., Byrne, G., Pullen, D., Kelly, J., Elliot,K. and Savic, M. 2014. Therapeutic Communities and the Local Community: Isolation or Integration? *Therapeutic Communities: The International Journal of Therapeutic Communities*, 35(4): 150–158. Doi: 10.1108/TC-07-2014-0024.

Best, D., Ghufran, S., Day, E., Ray, R. and Loaring, J. 2008. Breaking the Habit: A Retrospective Analysis of Desistance Factors among Formerly Problematic Heroin Users, *Drug and Alcohol Review*, 27(6): 619–624.

Best, D., Gow, J., Taylor, A., Knox, T., Groshkova, T. and White, W. 2011. Mapping the Recovery Stories of Drinkers and Drug Users in Glasgow: Quality of Life and its Associations with Measures of Recovery Capital, *Drug and Alcohol Review*, 31(3): 334–341.

Best, D., Irving, J. and Albertson, K. 2016. Recovery and Desistance: What the Emerging Recovery Movement in the Alcohol and Drug Area Can Learn from Models of Desistance from Offending, *Addiction Research & Theory*, 25(1): 1–10. Doi: 10.1080/16066359.2016.1185661.

Best, D., Irving, J., Collinson, B., Andersson, C. and Edwards, M. 2016. Recovery Networks and Community Connections: Identifying Connection Needs and Community Linkage Opportunities in Early Recovery Populations, *Alcoholism Treatment Quarterly*. Doi: 10.1080/07347324.2016.1256718.

Best, D. and Lubman, D. 2016. Friends Matter but So Does Their Substance Use: The Impact of Social Networks on Substance Use, Offending and Wellbeing Among Young People Attending Specialist Alcohol and Drug Treatment Services, *Drugs: Education, Prevention and Policy*, 24(1): 111–117. Doi: 10.3109/09687637.2016.1149148.

Best, D., Lubman, D.I., Savic, M. and Jetten, J. 2014. Social and Transitional identity: Exploring Social Networks and their Significance in a Therapeutic Community Setting, *Therapeutic Communities: the International Journal for Therapeutic and Supportive Organizations*, 35(1): 10–20.

Best, D. and Laudet, A.B. 2010. *The Potential of Recovery Capital*. London: Royal Society of the Arts.

Best, D. and Savic, M. 2015. Substance Abuse and Offending: Pathways to Recovery. In R. Sheehan and J. Ogloff (eds.) *Working Within the Forensic Paradigm. Cross-Discipline Approaches for Policy and Practice*. London: Routledge, pp. 259–271.

Betty Ford Institute Consensus Panel. 2007. What Is Recovery? A Working Definition from the Betty Ford Institute, *Journal of Substance Abuse Treatment*, 33: 221–228.

Blomqvist, J. 2002. Recovery With and Without Treatment: A Comparison or Resolutions of Alcohol and Drug Problems, *Addiction Research & Theory*, 10: 119–158.

Bourdieu, P. 1986. The Forms of Capital. In J. Richardson (ed.) *Handbook of Theory and Research for the Sociology of Education*. New York: Greenwood, pp. 241–258.

Braithwaite, J. 1989. *Crime, Shame and Reintegration*. Melbourne, Australia: Cambridge University Press

Braithwaite, J. 2016. *Restorative Justice and Responsive Regulation: The question of evidence*. RegNet No. 51 (revised), School of Regulation and Global Governance (RegNet).

Braithwaite, J. and Mugford, S. 1994. Conditions of Successful Reintegration Ceremonies, *British Journal of Criminology*, 34(2): 139–171.

Buckingham, S., Frings, D. and Albery, I. 2013. Group Membership and Social Identity in Addiction Recover, *Psychology Of Addictive Behaviors*, 27: 1132–1140. Doi: 10.1037/a0032480.

Chen, G. and Gueta, K. 2015. Application of Positive Criminology in the 12-Step Program. In N. Ronel and D. Segev (eds.) *Positive Criminology*. London: Routledge

Cloud, W. and Granfield, R. 2009. Conceptualising Recovery Capital: Expansion of a Theoretical Construct. *Journal of Substance Use and Abuse*, 43: 1971–1986.

Coleman, J.S. 1988. Social Capital in the Creation of Human Capital, *American Journal of Sociology*, 94: Supplement: Organizations and Institutions: Sociological and Economic Approaches to the Analysis of Social Structure: S95–S120.

Dingle, G., Stark, C., Cruwys, T. and Best, D. 2015. Breaking Good: Breaking Ties with Social Groups May Be Good for Recovery form Substance Misuse, *British Journal of Social Psychology*, 54(2): 236–254.

Finnis, M. 2014. *Towards a Restorative City, County, Authority or Community*. Available at: https://restorativejustice.org.uk/sites/default/files/resources/files/Towards%20a%20restorative%20city%2C%20county%2C%20authority%20or%20community%20-%20Mark%20Finnis_0.pdf

Garland, D. 2013. Penalty and the Penal State, *Criminology*, 51(3): 475–517.

Gavrielides, T. 2005. Some Meta-theoretical Questions for Restorative Justice, *Ratio Juris*, 18(1): 84–106.

Gavrielides, T. 2007. *Restorative Justice Theory and Practice: Addressing the Discrepancy*. Helsinki, Finland: HEUNI.

Gavrielides, T. 2014. Reconciling the Notions of Restorative Justice and Imprisonment, *The Prison Journal*, 94(4): 479–505. Available at: http://tpj.sagepub.com/content/early/2014/09/01.0032885514548010.

Gavrielides, T. 2015. Introduction. In T. Gavrieldes (ed.) *The Psychology of Restorative Justice: Managing the Power Within*. London: Routledge.

Granfield, R. and Cloud, W. 2001. Social Context and Natural Recovery: The Role of Social Capital in the Resolution of Drug-Associated Problems, *Substance Use & Misuse*, 36(11): 1543–1570.

Green, S. Johnstone, G. and Lambert, C. 2013. What Harm, Whose Justice?: Excavating The Restorative Movement, *Contemporary Justice Review*, 16(4).

Groshkova, T., Best, D. and White, W.L. 2013. The Assessment of Recovery Capital: Properties and Psychometrics of a Measure of Addiction Recovery Strengths, *Drug and Alcohol Review*, 32: 187–194.

Harris, N. 2006. Reintegrative Shaming, Shame, and Criminal Justice, *Journal of Social Issues*, 62: 327–346. Doi:10.1111/j.1540–4560.2006.00453.x

Hser, Y-I. 2007. Predicting Long-Term Stable Recovery from Heroin Addiction Findings from a 33-Year Follow-Up Study, *Journal of Addictive Diseases*, 26(1).

Huang, L.-Y., Sheu, C.-J., Huang, T.-W., Tseng, T.-C., Teng, L.-W., Lin, W.-T. and Hsieh, H.-C. 2011. *Evaluation Report on Application of Restorative Justice Application in the Criminal Justice System*. Taipei, Taiwan: Ministry of Justice, Taiwan.

Humphreys, K. 2004. *Circles of Recovery: Self-Help Organizations for Addictions*. Cambridge: Cambridge University Press.

Jetten, J., Haslam, C., Haslam, S.A., Dingle, G. and Jones, J.M. 2014. How Groups Affect Our Health and Well-Being: The Path from Theory to Policy, *Social Issues and Policy Review*, 8: 103–130.

Kaskutas, L.A. 2009. Alcoholics Anonymous Effectiveness: Faith Meets Science, *Journal Addictive Disease*, 28(2): 145–157.

Kodner, D. and Kyriacou, C.K. 2000. Fully Integrated Care for the Frail Elderly: Two American Models, *International Journal of Integrated Care*, 1(1).

Kretzmann, J.L. and McKnight, J. 1990. *Mapping Community Capacity*. Center for Urban Affairs and Policy Research, North Western University.

Liebmann, M. 2015. *Restorative Justice: How It Works*. London: Jessica Kingsley Publishers.

Litt, M.D., Kadden, R.M., Kabela-Cormier, E. and Petry, N. 2007. Changing Network Support for Drinking: Initial Findings from the Network Support Project, *Journal of Consulting and Clinical Psychology*, 75(4): 542.

Llewellyn, J., Archibald., B, Clairmont, D. and Crocker., D. 2013. Imagining Success for a Restorative Approach to Justice: Implications for Measurement and Evaluation, *Dalhousie Law Journal*, 36(2): 281.

Longabaugh, R., Wirtz, P.W., Zywiak, W.H. and O'Malley, S.S. 2010. Network Support as a Prognostic Indicator of Drinking Outcomes: The COMBINE Study, *Journal of Studies on Alcohol and Drugs*, 71(6): 837.

Macdonald, J. 2012. *World's First "Restorative City": Hull, UK, Improves Outcomes of All Interventions with Young People, Saves Resources*. Available at: www.iirp.edu/news/1981-world-s-first-restorative-city-hull-uk-improves-outcomes-of-all-interventions-with-young-people-saves-resources

Manning, V., Garfield, J.B., Best, D., Berends, L., Room, R., Mugavin, J., . . . and Lubman, D.I. 2016. Substance Use Outcomes Following Treatment: Findings from the Australian Patient Pathways Study, *Australian and New Zealand Journal of Psychiatry*, online early.

Maruna, S. 2001. *Making Good: How Ex-Convicts Reform and Rebuild Their Lives*. Washington, DC: American Psychological Association.

Maruna, S. and Farrall, S. 2004. Desistance from Crime: A Theoretical Reformulation, *Kölner Zeitschrift für Soziologie und Sozialpsychologie*, 43.

Maruna, S. and LeBel, T. 2015. Strengths-Based Restorative Approaches to Reentry: The Evolution of Creative Restitution, Reintegration and Destigmitization. In N. Ronel and D. Segev (eds.) *Positive Criminology*. London: Routledge.

Maslow, A.H. 1943. A Theory of Human Motivation, *Psychological Review*, 50: 370–396.

McCold, P. 2000. Toward a Holistic Vision of Restorative Juvenile Justice: A Reply to the Maximalist Model, *Contemporary Justice Review*, 3(4): 357–414.

McKnight, J. and Block, P. 2010. *The Abundant Community: Awakening the Power of Families and Neighborhoods*. San Francisco, CA: Berrett-Koehler Publishers Inc.

McNeill, F. 2016. Desistance and Criminal Justice in Scotland. In H Croall, G. Mooney and R. Munro (eds.) *Crime, Justice and Society in Scotland*. London: Routledge, pp. 200–216.

Moos, R.H. 2007. Theory-Based Active Ingredients of Effective Treatments for Substance Use Disorders, *Drug and Alcohol Dependence*, 88(2–3): 109–121.

Murphy, S. and Rosenbaum, M. 1999. Pregnant Women on Drugs: Combating Stereotypes and Stigma, *Contemporary Sociology*, 29(1): 248.

Narcotics Anonymous. 1992. *An Introductory Guide to Narcotics Anonymous*. New York: Narcotics Anonymous World Services, Inc.

Putnam, R.D. 2000. *Bowling Alone: The Collapse and Revival of American Community*. New York: Simon & Schuster.

Ray, B., Dollar C.B. and Thames, K.M. 2011. Observations of Reintegrative Shaming in a Mental Health Court, *International Journal of Law and Psychiatry*, 34(1): 49–55. Doi: 10.1016/j.ijlp.2010.11.008.

Ronel, N. 2015. How Can Criminology (and Victimology) Become Positive? In N. Ronel and D. Segev (eds.) *Positive Criminology*. London: Routledge.

Ronel, N., Frid, N. and Timor, U. 2013. The Practice of Positive Criminology: A Vipassana Course in Prison, *International Journal of Offender Therapy And Comparative Criminology*, 57(2): 133–153.

Ronel, N. and Segev, D. 2015. 'The Good' Can Overcome 'the Bad'. In N. Ronel and D. Segev (eds.) *Positive Criminology*. London: Routledge.

Ross, C. 2016. *Examining the Ways Art and Culture Intersect With Public Safety*. Available at www.urban.org/sites/default/files/publication/79271/2000725-Examining-the-Ways-Arts-and-Culture-Intersect-with-Public-Safety.pdf

Sampson, R. and Laub, J. 2003. Life-Course Desisters? Trajectories of Crime Among Delinquent Boys Followed to Age 70, *Criminology*, 41(3): 301–340.

Savic, M., Grynevych, A., Best, D. and Lubman, D.I. 2014. Review of Integrated Working Strategies. Doi: 10.13140/RG.2.1.1280.2167.

Seligman, M.E.P. 1998. Building Human Strength: Psychology's Forgotten Mission. *APA Monitor*, 29(1).

Sheedy, C.K. and Whitter, M. 2009. *Guiding Principles and Elements of Recovery-Oriented Systems of Care: What do We Know From the Research?* HHS Publication No. (SMA) 09–4439. Rockville, MD: Center for Substance Abuse Treatment, Substance Abuse and Mental Health Services Administration.

Thomas, T., Thompson, D. and Karstedt, S. 2014. *Assessing the Impact of Circles of Support and Accountability on the Reintegration of Adults Convicted of Sexual Offences in the Community*. Centre for Criminal Justice Studies, School of Law, University of Leeds.

UK Drug Policy Commission. 2008. *The UK Drug Policy Commission Recovery Consensus Group: A Vision of Recovery*. London: UK Drug Policy Commission.

Umbreit, M.S. and Roberts, A.W. 1996. *Mediation of Criminal Conflict in England: An Assessment of Services in Coventry and Leeds*. St. Paul: Center for Restorative Justice and Mediation, University of Minnesota.

Vyver, J., Travaglino, G., Vasijevic, M. and Abrams, C. 2015. The Group and Cultural Context of Restorative Justice: A Social Psychological Perspective. In T. Gavrieldes (ed.) *The Psychology of Restorative Justice: Managing the Power Within*. London: Routledge.

Wachtel, J. 2012. *Hull and Leeds: A Tale of Two Restorative Cities*. Available at www.iirp.edu/news/2147-hull-and-leeds-a-tale-of-two-restorative-cities

Walgrave, L. 2000. How Pure Can a Maximalist Approach to Restorative Justice Remain? Or Can a Purist Model of Restorative Justice Become Maximalist?, *Contemporary Justice Review*, 3(4): 415–432.

Walker, L. 2015. Applied Positive Criminology: Restorative Re-Entry and Transition Planning Circles for Incarcerated People and Their Loved Ones. In N. Ronel and D. Segev (eds.) *Positive Criminology*. London: Routledge, pp. 128–139.

White, W.L. 2007. Addiction Recovery: Its Definition and Conceptual Boundaries, *Journal of Substance Abuse Treatment*, 33(3): 229–241.

White, W.L. 2008. Recovery: Old Wine, Flavor of the Month or New Organizing Paradigm? *Substance Use and Misuse*, 43: 1987–2000.

White, W.L. 2012. *Historical Perspectives on Addiction Recovery Support*. Presented at the 2012 BFI/UCLA Annual Recovery Conference, February 21–23, Rancho Mirage, CA.

White, W.L., Boyle, M. and Loveland, D. 2003. Addiction as Chronic Disease: From Rhetoric to Clinical Application, *Alcoholism Treatment Quarterly*, 3(4): 107–130.

Wilton, R. and DeVerteuil, G. 2006. Spaces of Sobriety/Sites of Power: Examining Social Model Alcohol Recovery Programs as Therapeutic Landscapes, *Social Science & Medicine*, 63(3): 649–661.

Wittouck, C., Dekkers, A., Ruyver, B., Vanderplasschen, W. and Laenen1, F.V. 2013. The Impact of Drug Treatment Courts on Recovery: A Systematic Review, *The Scientific World Journal*, 2013, Article ID 493679, http://dx.doi.org/10.1155/2013/493679.

World Health Organisation. 2001. The World Health Report. *Mental Health: New Understanding, New Hope*. Geneva: World Health Organisation.

Zehr, H. and Gohar, A. 2002. *Little Book of Restorative Justice*. Pennsylvania: Good Books.

Zywiak, W.H., Neighbors, C.J., Martin, R.A., Johnson, J.E., Eaton, C.A. and Rohsenow, D.J. 2009. The Important People Drug and the Alcohol Interview: Psychometric Properties, Predictive Validity, and Alcohol Treatment Outcome, *Journal of Substance Abuse Treatment*, 36: 321–330.

Part II
Restorative justice practice
The evidence

8

Victims and offenders' perceptions and experiences of restorative justice

The evidence from London, UK

Theo Gavrielides

Introduction

Over the last 20 years, restorative justice has gained substantial ground in policy and law-making, while the volumes on its research continue to accumulate. One of the important claims of restorative justice is that, despite all that divides them, victims and offenders have some common interests. In fact, many have claimed that the labels "victim" and "offender" are fluid in nature and that the line between them is movable (Shpungin, 2014; Gavrielides, 2015).

As the interest in restorative practices continues to grow and more public money is spent on their development and mainstreaming, this chapter raises the question of how aligned restorative justice is with victims and offenders' realities and experiences. To answer this question, we carried out primary fieldwork with victims and offenders in London, UK. The research was undertaken from September through December 2016, with data analysis in January 2017. We combined knowledge from the extant literature with various research methods of fieldwork, including surveys, in-depth interviews and a focus group. Before starting the fieldwork, a review of the extant literature was carried out, paying particular attention to local and national material, including policies, legislation, third-sector publications and academic writings. Following this, we designed a research plan, the central feature of which was the establishment of a User Scrutiny Panel (USP) consisting of eight victims and practitioners with lived experience in restorative justice. Members were openly recruited based on location, experience, commitment and willingness to sign up to the Terms of Reference. We consulted with them on our research design, draft questionnaires and emerging data.

London, UK, provided a unique locus for our investigation for at least three reasons. Practically, it gave us immediate geographical access to our sample. Being based in London meant that the research team could carry out face-to-face interviews as well as contextualise the environment a lot easier. Secondly, England and Wales have been a particularly interesting case study in terms of legislative developments in restorative justice. After the 2010 change in government, key reforms took place in the adult and youth justice sentencing philosophy (Ministry of Justice, 2012) in the hope of reducing costs and increasing efficiency. This included the first national government strategy on restorative justice and the investment of considerable funds. This started in 2013, with £29 million that went to Police and Crime Commissioners[1] to help deliver restorative justice for victims over three years. The money was part of a wider allocated funding for victims of at least £83 million through 2015–16.

Another important development was the passing of the Crime and Courts Act 2013, as it inserted a new section 1ZA into the Powers of the Criminal Courts (Sentencing) Act 2000. Since December 2014, the courts have had the power to defer the passing of a sentence to restorative justice provided that all parties agree. The Act also requires that anyone practising restorative justice to have regard to the guidance issued by the Secretary of State. In May 2014, non-statutory guidance was issued by the Ministry of Justice that provides an overview of the processes involved in the delivery of pre-sentence restorative justice in accordance with section 1ZA.

The chapter is divided into three parts. The first presents some key definitions that were used for consistency in the research analysis as well as our sampling demographics. Subsequently, the chapter presents the key themes as they arose from the content analysis of the triangulated data. Finally, it proceeds with some critical reflections and conclusions for future policy and investment in restorative justice. Although the research data are limited in their ability to be generalised, and the conclusions must not be read as universal truths, they offer timely and robust insights into victims' and offenders' realities and perspectives on restorative justice.

Definitional agreements and sampling demographics

Definitional agreements

In the interest of data consistency, we used the extant literature and governmental guidance to define certain key terms, including restorative justice and victims. For restorative justice, we used the definition of the Victims' EU Directive: "Restorative justice is any process whereby the victim and the offender are enabled, if they freely consent, to participate actively in the resolution of matters arising from the criminal offence through the help of an impartial third party" (Article 2, para 1.d). We were mindful of broader definitions such as Gavrielides's "Restorative justice is an *ethos* with practical goals, among which is to restore harm by including affected parties in a (direct or indirect) encounter and a process of understanding through voluntary and honest dialogue" (2007: 139). The word "ethos" was defined as "A way of living; a new approach to life, interpersonal relationships, and a way of prioritising what is important in the process of learning how to coexist" (Gavrielides, 2007: 139). For Braithwaite (2002), the principles underlying this "ethos" are victim reparation, offender responsibility and communities of care. In a similar vein, Daly and Curtis-Fawley (2006) said that restorative justice places "an emphasis on the role and experience of victims in the criminal process" (237), and that it involves all relevant parties in a discussion about the offence, its impact and what should be done to repair it. The decision making, Daly said, has to be carried out by both lay and legal actors.

We also used the Victims' Directive for the definition of "victim": (i) a natural person who has suffered harm, including physical, mental or emotional harm or economic loss which was directly caused by a criminal offence; (ii) family members of a person whose death was directly caused by a criminal offence and who have suffered harm as a result of that person's death.

---

1 The Police Reform and Social Responsibility Act 2011 established a Police and Crime Commissioner (PCC) for each police force area across England and Wales. In London, the elected Mayor is the equivalent of the PCC and is responsible for the totality of policing in the capital.

The survey and its sampling

Two separate surveys were developed with the aim of collecting data both from victims and offenders in regards to their experience and preferences at key stages of the restorative justice process. Respondents were able to complete the survey either online or via hard copy, which could then be returned by post. Using the extant literature, we assumed that awareness of, engagement with, restorative justice amongst victims and offenders is extremely low. We were also mindful that it is complicated and time-consuming for those working with victims of crime to contact past service users to disseminate surveys. The research undertook an ethics approval process, which adjusted certain tools and recommended that a variation of recruitment methods is adopted.

Of the 136 responses received, only 110 were fully completed, and thus 26 were discarded. There were 66 responses from victims of prosecuted crimes and 44 responses from unrelated prosecuted offenders.

Demographics for victims of crime

GENDER

- 67% of respondents identified as female
- 31% of respondents identified as male
- 2% of victim respondents identified as other

AGE

- 12% of respondents were 18–24 years old
- 25% of respondents were 25–34 years old
- 21% of respondents were 35–44 years old
- 21% of respondents were 45–54 years old
- 12% of respondents were 55–64 years old
- 9% of respondents were 65 or more years old

ETHNICITY

- 55% identified as White English/Welsh/Scottish/Northern Irish
- 12% identified as Black/African/Caribbean/Black British
- 9% identified as Asian or Asian British: Indian
- 9% identified as White Any other White background
- 4% identified as Black/African/Caribbean/Black British
- 5% identified as "other"
- 2% identified as White Irish
- 2% identified as White Gypsy or Irish Traveller
- 2% identified as Mixed or Multiple ethnic groups.

NATIONALITY

- 84% identified as being British
- 4% identified as being Irish

- 2% identified as being Australian
- 2% identified as being Lithuanian
- 2% identified as being Jamaican
- 2% identified as being a New Zealander
- 2% identified as being Polish
- 2% identified as being Nigerian

GEOGRAPHIC COVERAGE

Respondents were all based in the capital and came from 24 out of 32 London boroughs.

OFFENCE TYPE

The majority of respondents reported that the offence had occurred in the last 6–12 months (32%). Thirty-one percent said the offence had occurred in the last five years, 15% said it had occurred more than ten years ago, 11% said in the last ten years, 7% said in the last month and almost 2% said in the last week (Figure 8.1).

Demographics for offenders

GENDER

- 100% of respondents identified as male.

AGE

- 40% were 18–24 years old
- 31% were 25–34 years old
- 14% were 35–44 years old
- 10% were 45–54 years old
- 0% were 55–64 years old
- 5% were 65 and over years old

ETHNICITY

- 38% identified as White English/Welsh/Scottish/Northern Irish
- 19% identified as Mixed or Multiple ethnic groups
- 10% identified as Black/African/Caribbean/Black British
- 7% identified as Black/African/Caribbean/Black British
- 5% identified as White Gypsy or Irish Traveller
- 5% identified as Mixed or Multiple ethnic groups
- 5% identified as Black/African/Caribbean/Black British
- 2% identified as White Irish
- 2% identified as White Any other White background
- 2% identified as Mixed or Multiple ethnic groups
- 2% identified as Asian or Asian British: Indian
- 2% identified as Asian or Asian British: Bangladeshi

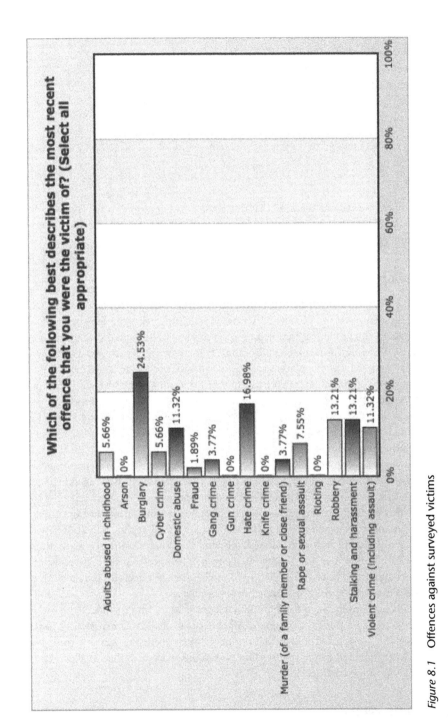

Figure 8.1 Offences against surveyed victims

NATIONALITY

- 88% identified as being British
- 3% identified as being of mixed nationality
- 3% identified as being Caribbean
- 3% identified as being Somalian
- 3% identified as being German

GEOGRAPHIC COVERAGE

Respondents were all based in the capital and came from 18 out of 31 London boroughs.

OFFENCE TYPE

The majority of respondents reported that the offence had occurred in the last five years (46%) followed by in the last 6–12 months (44%). Eight percent said the offence had occurred more than ten years ago and 3% said it had occurred in the last five to ten years (Figure 8.2).

The follow-up interviews, focus group and their sampling

Follow-up, in-depth, semi-structured interviews were planned to capture deeper insights into key areas critical to the victim-led service design and delivery. This method, alongside the USP focus group, aimed at complementing the surveys by capitalising on their emerging trends and by allowing for further exploration via qualitative discussions. To ensure consistency and to maximise time and resources, it was decided that the interview sample will be drawn from survey respondents who had indicated that they would be willing to participate in further research. Twenty-six survey respondents indicated such interest and were contacted to schedule an interview. Eleven individuals subsequently responded. All interviews were recorded, and written notes were taken during the conversations, the longest of which lasted approximately 3.5 hours.

All interviewees were victims of prosecuted crimes. Seven participants identified as female, three identified as male and one identified as other. Five participants were aged between 45 and 54 years old, four were between 35 and 44 years old and two were between 25 and 34 years old. The crimes that participants had been victims of were wide-ranging and had occurred between sometime in the last six months to more than ten years ago. They included burglary, robbery, hate crime, stalking and harassment, abuse in childhood, domestic violence, rape, sexual assault and murder of a family member. Two participants had been offered restorative justice and had agreed to take it up, two had been offered restorative justice but declined to take it up and seven had never been offered restorative justice but would like to be.

The USP focus group lasted for approximately two hours and included two male victims, two female victims and three practitioners. All participants had lived experiences in restorative justice. The USP were given in advance the data display from the survey results. No critical reflections were included in the report. The discussions were recorded, analysed and fed into the final analysis of the findings.

Our analysis method

A content analysis was then completed using the records of each interview, the written responses from the surveys and the focus group. This technique was preferred, as it allowed us to interpret

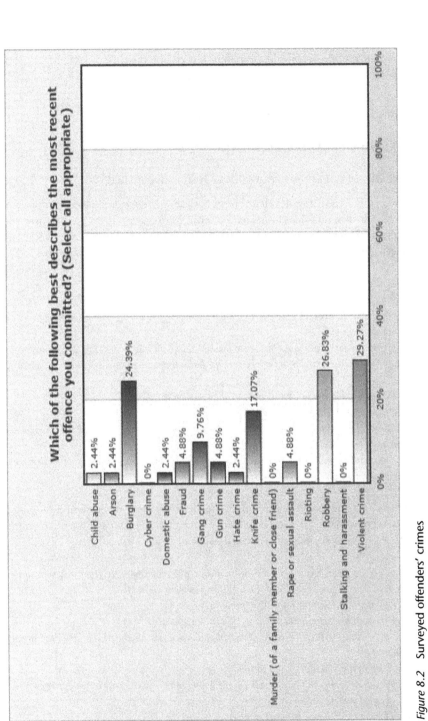

Figure 8.2 Surveyed offenders' crimes

and identify trends in our written material produced via our chosen communication methods. It is a way of applying a degree of quantitative rigour to the analysis of qualitative data. This process involved reading through each interview record, identifying interesting or relevant points of information, reviewing these points and coding them into different categories, and then analysing the occurrence of each category to identify the major trends.

Victims and offenders' experiences and realities

Key themes emerging from the surveys

1. Do victims and offenders know about restorative justice?

As expected, there were low levels of awareness about restorative justice amongst victims. When asked whether they had heard of the term "restorative justice", 69% answered negatively, while 31% said they had. Those who had heard of restorative justice were then asked what it means to them. A representative selection of responses is provided below:

> "Community-led response to helping victims to have their voice heard."
> "Reclaiming power back for the victim."
> "The ability of the victim to take power back from the perpetrator by communicating with them how they made them feel."
> "The opportunity for victim and offender to meet so that both can move on with their lives."
> "Getting the chance to explain to the offender the harm they caused and ask questions about why they did it."
> "Making the offender understand the impact they had on the victim."
> "Trying to address the harm caused by the crime."
> "Where the victim has a chance to be listened to and the person who committed the crime have a chance to understand and learn from mistakes."
> "A way to manage crime that recognizes that the current punitive system doesn't work for victims, or for reducing crime."

Awareness of restorative justice amongst offenders was evenly split, with 50% having heard of it. Those who had heard of restorative justice were then asked what it means to them. A representative selection of responses is provided below:

> "To say sorry, to give back, to give the victim a chance to understand, to repair relationships."
> "The chance to meet your victim and apologise and explain yourself."
> "Building a new life, turning your life around."
> "To give the victim a better understanding of why it happened."
> "To get the victim involved, looking at the impact crime has on the victim, making amends in the community."
> "Giving back to the community and victim."
> "Getting together, trying to find out what went wrong to find some constructive outcomes."
> "Giving you an understanding of the effect of the crime on others."
> "Chance for both victim and criminal to meet and share."
> "Where I sit down and have a discussion with the victim over my crime."

2. Are victims and offenders being offered restorative justice?

Amongst the victims surveyed, the vast majority had never been offered restorative justice. In fact, 85% were never offered the chance to communicate with their offender, either directly or indirectly, and only 15% said that they had.

For the 15% of victims who were offered restorative justice, when asked at which stage of the criminal justice system this happened, the most common answers were during probation (50%) and post-release (17%). In regards to who offered them restorative justice, 50% said probation, 17% said victim support, 17% said a community/volunteer organisation and 17% said they had initiated restorative justice themselves outside of any service.

Fifty percent of victims said they had been given information about restorative justice via a telephone conversation, 33% said they received information via a face-to-face discussion and 17% said they had received information via a mobile text message. This is broadly in line with what victims said their preferred methods of receiving information would be. For example, 50% said they would prefer a telephone conversation, 17% would prefer a face-to-face conversation, 33% would prefer a letter or email but only 17% would prefer a leaflet. Eighty-three percent of victims said that they received the right amount of information, and 17% would have preferred to have received more information. When asked what form of additional information would have been helpful, one respondent said they would have liked a leaflet or a website address where they could look up information.

Amongst the offenders surveyed, the vast majority had never been offered restorative justice. In fact, the number was lower than that of victims, reaching only 12% of them. In regards to the stage of the criminal justice system at which they were first offered restorative justice, 50% said in prison, 25% said before trial and 25% said post-release. In relation to who offered them restorative justice, 43% of respondents said probation, 30% said "other" and subsequently identified community/volunteer services, 14% said victim support and 14% said a court. Sixty-seven percent of respondents said they had been given information about restorative justice via a face-to-face conversation, and 33% said they received information via a leaflet or booklet. This is broadly in line with what offenders said their preferred methods of receiving information would be, as 80% said they would prefer a face-to-face conversation. Sixty percent of respondents said that they received the right amount of information, and 40% would have preferred more. Leaflets were not a preferred option.

3. If offered, do victims and offenders opt for restorative justice?

Uptake of the offer of restorative justice amongst victims was evenly split, with 57% choosing to participate in restorative justice and 43% declining the offer. As illustrated by Figure 8.3, in regards to the reasons for participation, the majority said "to bring closure" (60%), equally followed by "to have their say and explain the impact of the offender's actions" (40%), "to ask the offender questions" (40%) and "other reasons", which included "because I am passionate about restorative justice" (40%).

For offenders, the uptake of restorative justice was much higher, with 80% deciding to participate and only 20% declining the offer. As illustrated by Figure 8.4, the majority of offenders said that they opted for restorative justice in order to give the victim the opportunity to ask questions (75%), equally followed by to have their say and explain their actions (50%), demonstrate that they are working to stop offending (50%) and to offer an apology or compensation (50%).

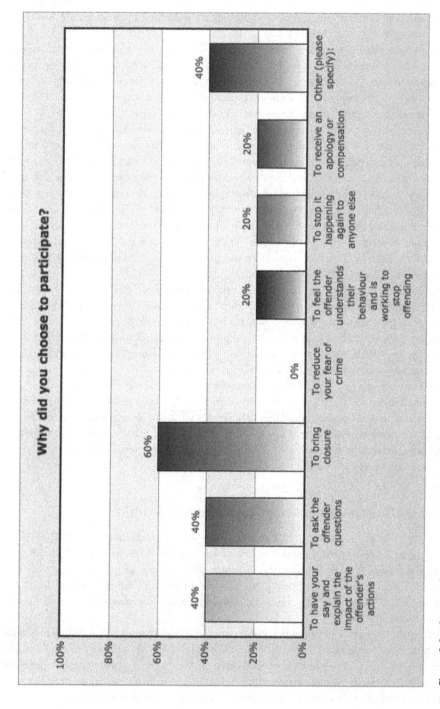

Figure 8.3 Surveyed victims' reasons for participating in restorative justice

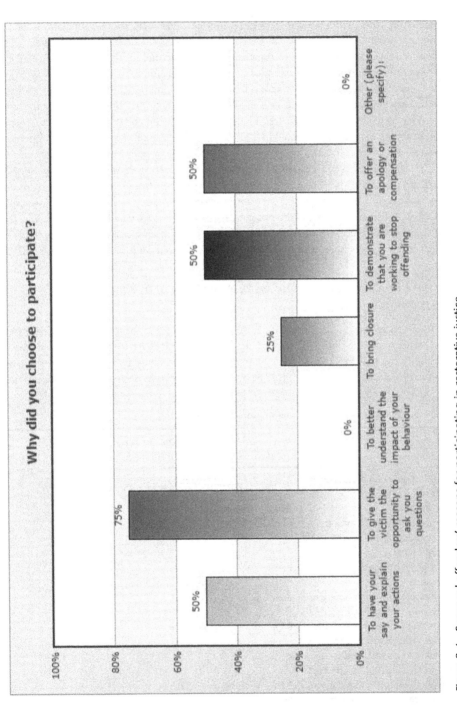

Figure 8.4 Surveyed offenders' reasons for participating in restorative justice

4. How satisfied are victims and offenders from restorative justice and why?

Of the victims who participated in restorative justice, 50% were offered mediation (face-to-face meeting with their offender), 25% were offered a face-to-face meeting between them, the offender and others connected to the crime (e.g. family members) and 25% were offered a telephone conversation with their offender. They were then asked how satisfied they were with certain elements of the restorative justice process they had experienced. Two respondents were unable to answer these questions as one was yet to undertake the meeting and for the other, the offender had refused to participate. The levels and reasons for satisfaction for the victims who were able to answer are recorded in Table 8.1. When asked if they would recommend this process to other victims, 60% of respondents said yes and 40% said they didn't know.

Of the offenders who participated in restorative justice, 50% were offered letter writing, 25% were offered mediation (face-to-face meeting with their victim) and 25% were offered a meeting with victims of crime but of other offenders (surrogate victims). They were then asked how satisfied they were with certain elements of the restorative justice process they had experienced. The levels and reasons for satisfaction for the offenders who were able to answer are recorded in Table 8.2. When asked if they would recommend this process to other offenders, 50% said they would.

5. Is there an unmet demand for restorative justice and what does this look like?

The survey results indicate that there is a level of unmet demand for restorative justice amongst victims, with over two-thirds of respondents (68%) who had never been offered restorative justice indicating that they would have liked to have been offered it. In relation to the stage at which victims would have liked to have been offered restorative justice, police diversion (29%)

Table 8.1 Surveyed victims' satisfaction with restorative justice

	Very Satisfied	Quite Satisfied	Neither Satisfied or Dissatisfied	Quite Dissatisfied	Very Dissatisfied
Information provided about the process	67%		33%		
Facilitator	67%	33%			
The extent to which the process was tailored to your specific circumstances	67%	33%			
Support given throughout the process	67%		33%		
Your physical safety (how safe you felt throughout the process)	33%	33%	33%		
The extent you could control the process (you were able to decide what would happen and were able to say what you needed to)	67%		33%		
Venue (e.g. comfort, intimidation)	33%	33%	33%		
Convenience (e.g. timing and location)	67%		33%		
Overall satisfaction	**33%**	**33%**	**33%**		

Table 8.2 Surveyed offenders' satisfaction with restorative justice

	Very Satisfied	Quite Satisfied	Neither Satisfied or Dissatisfied	Quite Dissatisfied	Very Dissatisfied
Information provided about the process	75%	25%			
Facilitator	100%				
The extent to which the process was tailored to your specific circumstances	100%				
Support given throughout the process	50%		50%		
Your physical safety (how safe you felt throughout the process)	33%		33%	33%	
The extent you could control the process (you were able to decide what would happen and were able to say what you needed to)	33%		67%		
Venue (e.g. comfort, intimidation)	50%	25%			25%
Convenience (e.g. timing and location)			67%		33%
Overall satisfaction	**75%**		**25%**		

and during probation (21%) were the top preferences. The next highest category chosen was "other", where 18% of respondents said that they would like it to be offered at all stages. When asked who they would expect to offer them restorative justice, the majority of respondents said victim support services (67%), followed by police (46%) and probation (43%). Under the option of "other", 7% of respondents indicated that they thought that all the services mentioned should offer restorative justice to victims of crime. A very low proportion indicated that they would expect to self-refer to restorative justice (4%).

When asked what their preferred method for receiving information about this type of service would be, the majority of victims said via a face-to-face conversation (32%), followed by a telephone conversation (25%), referred to website (18%) and then via a leaflet or booklet (14%). Under the category of "other", 11% of respondents said they would prefer the combination of a leaflet or email with the option to follow this up with a telephone conversation.

When asked what kind of restorative justice process they would like to participate in, a significant majority of victims said victim-offender mediation (face-to-face meeting with the offender) (71%). The preferences of the remaining respondents were quite evenly spread amongst the other options (e.g. letter writing, telephone call, email, online video call and a face-to-face meeting with the offender and others connected to the crime, such as family members).

With regards to our offenders' sample, the survey results indicate again a level of unmet need for restorative justice services, with over two-thirds of respondents (66%) who had never been offered restorative justice indicating that they would have liked to have been offered it. The preference of the criminal justice stage at which offenders would have liked to be offered restorative justice was evenly spread, with the prison stage as the top preference (30%), followed by the probation stage (21%). The next highest category chosen was "other", where 18% of respondents said that they would have liked restorative justice to be offered at all stages. When asked who they would expect to offer them restorative justice, the majority of respondents said probation officers (75%), followed by victim support service providers (25%) and community and voluntary organisations (15%). No one said that they would like to self-refer.

When asked what their preferred method for receiving information about this type of service would be, the majority of respondents said via a face-to-face conversation (62%). Only 5% said they would prefer a telephone conversation (25%), and no one said they would prefer to be referred to website. However, under the category of "other", 10% of respondents said they would prefer the combination of a face-to-face or telephone conversation as well as a leaflet or booklet.

When asked what kind of restorative justice process they would like to participate in, a significant majority of respondents said victim-offender mediation (a face-to-face meeting with the victim) (74%). The preferences of the remaining respondents were quite evenly spread amongst the other options such as letter writing, telephone call, email, online video call and a face-to-face meeting with the offender and others connected to the crime (e.g. family members).

6. What are the reasons victims and offenders may reject restorative justice?

Thirty-two percent of our victims who had never been offered restorative justice said they wouldn't like to be offered it anyway, and of those who had been offered it, 43% said they decided not to participate. Figure 8.5 presents their reasons. The top factors were: no desire to meet the offender and being too traumatic as the top factors (under the option of "other" victims said: They just wanted their offender locked up (one person), they were not ready at the time it was offered but would have liked to have had it offered again (one person), they didn't feel that the offence had been taken seriously enough by the police).

Victims were given the option to provide more qualitative responses some of which are included here:

> "I might want to meet the offender for maybe more serious crimes. It depends how I am affected. If burglary, then no, as I am not affected so much. . . . Murder maybe. Possibly more inclined to say yes in certain physical violence scenarios"
> "I had no desire to meet the offender due to my circumstances (burglary). In general, I think it is a good idea to meet the offender."
> "I would consider meeting the offender if I feel that I am going to make a difference to the offender (positively)."
> "I really like the idea and would be very interested if I felt that it could be done safely. Domestic violence is very complex and ongoing even after the relationship has split. There is such a poor understanding about it amongst professionals. I would be concerned that the facilitator would collude with his cohesive control etc.
> "If I feel that I could do it safely . . . then I would be interested, but I would take some convincing because of experience of so called professionals knowing so little about domestic violence, and colluding with the offender."

Moving on to our offenders' sample, of those who had never been offered restorative justice, 34% said they wouldn't like to be offered it anyway, and of those who had been offered it, 20% said they decided not to participate. Figure 8.6 presents their reasons. The top factors were lack of information and no desire to meet the victim (one offender answered "other", under which he subsequently said that there was no victim for their crime).

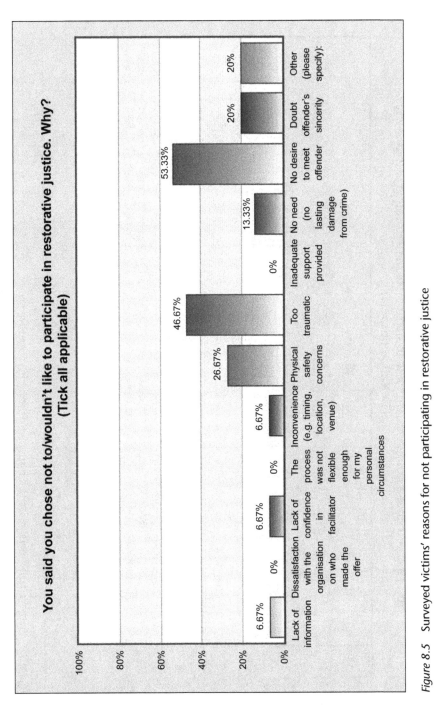

Figure 8.5 Surveyed victims' reasons for not participating in restorative justice

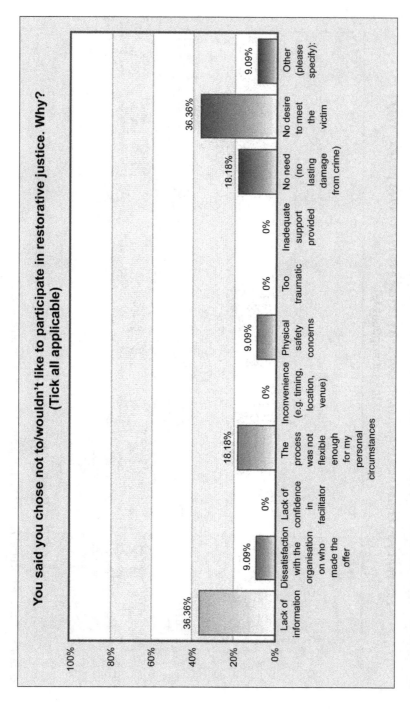

Figure 8.6 Surveyed offenders' reasons for not participating in restorative justice

7. What do victims and offenders value the most in the pursuit of justice?

For our victims' sample group, the following were valued the most in the pursuit of justice for what had happened to them: To have their say and explain the impact of the offender's actions (51%); To feel that the offender is making up for the crime in some way (17%); To ask the offender questions (11%); Other (9%) (this included sentiments such as to change the way victims are treated, to help offenders understand what they have done and promote desistence from reoffending, and to identify and punish offenders); To bring closure (6%); To reduce your fear of crime (6%)

For our offenders' sample group, the following were valued the most when caught in the criminal justice system: To have their say and explain their actions (44%); To bring closure (25%); To allow the victim to have their say and explain the impact of the crime (11%); To feel that they are making up for the crime in some way (8%); Other (8%) (this included answers indicating that respondents felt that all of the answers were important); To better understand the impact of the crime (3%).

8. What does an ideal victim-led restorative justice look like?

Our survey respondents were asked, in an open-ended manner, what in their view are the key indicators of success for a victim-led restorative justice.

For our victims sample, the following were recorded in order of preference: For the offender to understand what they did and the impact it had so they will be less likely to reoffend; To heal/move on/get closure; To not feel victimised anymore but empowered and to have the opportunity to be heard; A high degree of preparation before any meeting takes places so that each party knows what to expect; To be able to feel safe again; To see that the offender has remorse for what they did; For the process to be voluntary and for each party to be able to opt out at any time; For those dealing with complex cases, in particular domestic violence, to be adequately experienced to deal with the specialised needs of such cases; A low level of bureaucracy and for the service to be independent, professional, individualised, patient and not tied to contract targets.

For our offenders sample, the following were recorded in order of preference: To be able to understand what they did and the impact it had so they will be less likely to reoffend; To heal/move on/get closure; For it to be widely available and for more people to be aware of it; For the process to be beneficial to both parties and for both parties to be supported; For the offender to have the chance to explain their actions; Effective communication between both parties.

Key themes emerging from the follow-up interviews

The overwhelming trend amongst those interviewed was that people only found out about restorative justice via their own efforts rather than being made aware of it via any of the services they had engaged with. This included being aware of it already via their pre-existing work within the criminal justice system and mental health agencies or because they had a friend who knew about it or just because they read about it online (e.g. websites, Facebook, YouTube). This is consistent with the survey findings that most victims are not offered information about restorative justice.

In regards to how they preferred to be offered restorative justice, the interviewees said that they wanted the offer to come from someone they had already built up trust with. For many, this was the police contact they had had the most contact with. We noted a range of views in regards to when information about restorative justice should be provided, with some saying it should be when the crime is first reported, others saying a week or two afterwards and some saying that they wouldn't be open to information until much later. There was consistency, however, that information needs to be available/provided in multiple formats. Victims also noted that it was common for them to receive information about other services they could access via the provision of a business card or a text with the name of whom they could contact. They all said that this approach gave them time to consider whether they wanted to access the services, so they didn't feel pressured to make a decision. They also suggested that this approach should be taken up by all available services (e.g. police, Victims Support, restorative justice services, community-based organisations for people wary of engaging with statutory services, doctor's surgeries and other community hubs).

Again, there was a strong theme that in order to increase awareness, information needs to come from people/organisations who have a trusting relationship with local communities, as people will be more likely to listen and take the information on board if it comes from someone they know. This information needs to be easy to find. Many interviewees reported looking for information online for significant periods of time and still not finding what they need.

The complexity of language and the terminology that is being used for offering restorative justice was also criticised. Some victims also pointed out that it is important to strike the right balance by not making them feel patronised by the dumbing down of the language, but at the same time not expecting them to be legal experts. Translation was also brought up by our victims, some of whom did not have English as their first language. Attached to this was the issue of cultural competency and being able to sympathise and understand their respective cultures without assumptions.

Furthermore, some victims felt that they were being approached by practitioners as commodities through a "sales pitch". They often felt pressured to opt for restorative justice and that the benefits were highlighted more than the risks. Victims suggested that when being approached, it should just be about answering their questions and explaining how restorative justice directly relates to their specific circumstances. Several interviewees also said that it would be good to explain how restorative justice is different to the police and court system and that it would be good to hear about real examples/cases of positive outcomes and what other victims have got out of it.

The reasons our interviewed victims opted for, or would have opted for, restorative justice included their desire to: feel empowered and have their voice heard; ask questions of the offender about the crime; get the offender to understand the impact of the crime so that they might not do it again. The interviewees also reported dissatisfaction with, or distrust of, criminal justice processes and agencies as reasons they would be interested in participating in restorative justice. Feelings of dissatisfaction stemmed from not feeling like they had been given a chance to be heard, not having the chance to hear anything from the offender, or needing something else in order to heal and move on. Feelings of distrust stemmed from previous negative experiences with statutory services resulting in people not wanting to invite such services further into their lives, as well as people being wary of the public nature of CJS processes. Hence they would prefer an alternative process to address the crime and its impact. For example, one interviewee who identified as being from a BAME background and being "queer", disabled, suffering from mental illness and having previously experienced significant periods of homelessness, said that:

> Independence, anonymity and confidentiality will make community services a more attractive option for people wanting to access restorative justice. For marginalised people, it be would be better to have restorative justice delivered via a system which has not put you where you are. People won't trust it otherwise – especially people with bad experiences of statutory services. I know lots of other

marginalised people who would never go near police or mental health services and risk further contact with the system.

In regards to circumstances which might lead them to not want to participate in restorative justice, the majority said that they would feel that way if they did not have enough information about the process or they were pressured. We also discussed with our interviewed victims their experiences with restorative justice services as well as any other services they had engaged with (e.g. police, victims support services), and those factors most important in regards to satisfaction and having their needs met. Our participants agreed that restorative justice services should be tailored and personalised to their individual and specific circumstances if they are to be victim-led. They did not want to feel that they are just another "number" in the system. This also included appropriate service delivery to children (e.g. one interviewee reported dissatisfaction with her nine-year-old son being given the same information and advice from a victim support service about coping and recovering that she received as an adult and that it was completely inappropriate and confusing to him). Victims also pointed out the significance of setting appropriate expectations and meeting them. Service providers not following through on what they said they would do or providing incorrect information was a common reason for dissatisfaction. For example, one interviewee said about their experience:

It was like they didn't care at all. They sent individual letters to each family member including my young children that had all our names spelled wrong. My son needed support.

Furthermore, victims agreed that having a single point of contact is critical to building trust and confidence and that not having to repeat information is important for their satisfaction and confidence in restorative justice. They also said that patience in service delivery is key to satisfaction levels, as it makes them feel less anxious. Our interviewees also noted the significance of being kept updated regularly, even in regards to small matters or just checking in (even when there are not any specific developments). Having consistency in how and when this is done, as well as by whom, is also important for reassuring victims and building trust and confidence. High levels of frustration were reported when victims had to chase service providers for updates and information.

In addition, our interviewed victims noted that having confidence in the confidentiality provided by the restorative justice service is crucial. Participants reported that when it is obvious that organisations have shared their personal information, it destroys their trust in that service. Some participants reported high levels of doubt that their information would not be shared more widely, resulting in their not having trust in restorative justice. Anxiety about confidentiality also led them to wanting to avoid engagement with restorative services or where they did so, not sharing all the details of their case. To address this, our interviewees recommended ensuring that victims be fully informed about who will receive their information and what information will be shared. They further stressed that they wanted their consent for the sharing of information to be obtained before any information about them is given to anyone else. Having the option to edit what is shared was also reported as being preferable. Providing victims with information as to why the information is being shared was also suggested as good practice (e.g. for evaluation purposes or to inform service improvement). One participant framed it in the following way:

Victims are always asked for all the details of their lives as if people are entitled to it without saying why they need it.

Furthermore, interviews argued that being well prepared and knowing what will happen throughout the process is important for confidence and reducing anxiety and stress about participating. Ensuring that restorative justice is available at any stage was also thought to be important for victims. All interviewees said that restorative justice should be made available whenever the victim is ready and wants to access the service.

Participants also pointed out the importance of perseverance and patience on behalf of the restorative justice provider. In fact, some shared that at first they rejected restorative justice (or indeed any other options to address their crime), as they wanted the whole thing to be over as soon as possible.

> *Services need to have patience as victims may change their minds once the immediate situation has calmed down.*

Others said that this may be a much longer process, with some not wanting to access restorative justice until many years later. Once accessed, victims said that timeliness of the process is important so that it doesn't drag on and keep them stuck in that moment of trauma. Signposting to other support services and working well with those other services was also thought to be important for a successful and holistic restorative justice service. Having a single point of contact to coordinate multi-agency service delivery rather than the service user having to coordinate everything was considered crucial for victim satisfaction. Similarly, the training, experience and quality of practitioners was very important for victims.

In regards to independence, there was disagreement amongst the interviewees. Some preferred that restorative services are offered via the formal criminal justice system, while others could trust only community-based services. In particular, some said that they wouldn't have confidence in a service delivered by a community organisation, as they wouldn't perceive it to have the necessary weight behind it, like the formal system has. Other people preferred the idea of accessing a community organisation, as they didn't want to be further engaged with the criminal justice system.

However, there was consistency in that equality of access was important. Interviewees pointed out the significance of being able to access the service regardless of where you live. They also argued that the quality of service received must be consistent regardless of location. This also extended to wider support services that they should be referred to as part of a holistic approach to what happened to them. If equal access and quality cannot be offered, then the restorative service providers need to be honest with victims from the outset. Setting clear expectations with victims in honesty and without agendas was key in creating trust. The importance of effective cross-borough working was also raised in this context. Interviewees recommended that a mechanism by which victims can provide direct feedback anonymously about the service they received is important in ensuring transparency and honesty.

Critical reflections

This chapter aimed to contribute to the Handbook's ambition of progressing our knowledge around restorative justice and crime prevention by presenting new evidence on victims and offenders' experiences and perceptions of restorative justice. London was used as our locus of investigation.

One of the clearest messages coming out of the fieldwork is that the most important thing for both victims and offenders in the pursuit of justice is their empowerment though having a voice (e.g. by explaining what happened to them/why they committed the crime). This resonates with restorative justice, and thus it could be read as a demand for more empowering justice processes that do not simply process individuals through the "system" as mere numbers.

If victims are approached for a restorative justice offer, their wish is that this is done by someone they know or trust. It is worth pointing out victims' warning for restorative justice practitioners to stop approaching them as commodities through a sales pitch. Victims also identified interests that are being served within the restorative justice movement and which are unrelated to what happened to them. In the end, what victims really want is to feel that their individual circumstances have been considered and that if they are to spend time seeking justice through an emotional and risky process, that a holistic service is available.

In relation to offenders, two of the most noticeable surprises of our London-focused research was that the number who had been offered restorative justice was significantly lower than that of victims. It was also surprising to hear that when it was offered to them, it was only after they had been incarcerated. This is despite the new UK law allowing for pre-sentence restorative justice as well as what was thought a well-structured and well-funded restorative justice provision within London CRC. We could conclude from this that legislation and resourcing the public sector might not be the answers to offenders' low uptake of restorative justice.

Furthermore, it must be noted that restorative justice is not seen as a panacea. For example, our evidence and the extant literature point out that there is a good proportion of victims who simply do not want to engage with it at all (Johnstone, forthcoming). This must be respected, and any attempt to tick boxes for the sake of numbers will backfire.

As for the buzz term "victim-led restorative justice", this remains academic and controversial. The chapter has argued that both victims and offenders seem to want the same things from the justice process, and thus whether victim- or offender-led, the restorative justice service will do well just by simply listening to their individual circumstances. This also goes to the variety of the practices that need to be engaged to meet their needs. In fact, although most research participants opted for victim-offender mediation, there was a clear message that the selling of a specific model will again be seen as serving alternative means. The same applies to when the restorative justice offer is actually made to victims and offenders. The consensus seems to be the earlier, the better, or to just make it available at any stage the parties feel it should be initiated.

Interestingly, and contrary to statements in the media and political speeches, according to our research, the more complex and serious the crime is, the more likely victims would opt for restorative justice. This is aligned with the reasons they would prefer restorative over criminal justice. These include making a difference not so much for them but for the offender and the community. It is also apparent that it is more likely for offenders to opt for restorative justice than victims. Again, unlike what many tabloids have reported, this is not to get "off the hook" but to help make a difference for the victim. According to our research, offenders also want closure for themselves and to be able to move on and heal. It must be pointed out that restorative justice engages with offenders who had admitted guilt and are genuinely ready to engage in dialogue. It must also be remembered that any restorative justice service that does not factor the costs and time of preparation will simply be in breach of both statutory guidance as well as the very values of the restorative norm and the parties' wishes and assumptions.

What was not surprising from the research were the low levels of awareness about restorative justice. However, it was useful to hear the types and mediums of information that users prefer, and this did not include adverts on buses or leaflets. The preference was for information that would come directly from a trusted contact. If victims and offenders felt that they wanted to know more after this initial trusted contact was made, then referral sources were deemed to be useful (including leaflets). Finally, the impact of language, culture and the various accessibility barriers should not be underestimated when offering restorative justice. In fact, one of the most consistent findings from the research was the need to provide equal access to all, and this included those with hearing and visual impairments, those whose first language is not English or those who simply cannot read. Isn't restorative justice an individual promise after all?

From the outset, we have accepted the inherent limitations of our research, which was bound by a tight timeline and carried out within a specific location. Although the sample numbers are too small to be able to draw any generalisable scientific conclusions, they provide a qualitative picture of victims and offenders' wants and needs, awareness and experiences in restorative justice in London. These are lessons that can be of use to the international reader of the Handbook.

Bibliography

Braithwaite, J. 2002. *Restorative Justice & Responsive Regulation*. Oxford: Oxford University Press.

Daly, K. and Curtis-Fawley, S. 2006. Restorative Justice for Victims of Sexual Assault. In K. Heimer and C. Kruttschnitt (eds.) *Gender and Crime: Patterns of Victimization and Offending*. New York: New York University Press, pp. 230–265.

Gavrielides, T. 2007. *Restorative Justice Theory & Practice: Addressing the Discrepancy*. HEUNI: Helsinki.

Gavrielides, T. 2015. *Offenders No More: An Interdisciplinary Restorative Justice Dialogue*. New York: Nova Science Publishers.

Johnstone, G. Forthcoming. Restorative Justice for Victims: Inherent Limits?, *International Journal of Restorative Justice*.

Ministry of Justice. 2012. *Criminal Justice Statistics Quarterly Update to September 2012 Ministry of Justice Statistics Bulletin*, www.gov.uk/government/uploads/system/uploads/attachment_data/file/220090/criminal-justice-stats-sept-2012.pdf. Accessed 13 July 2014.

Shpungin, E. 2014. The Fluidity of Victimhood. In T. Gavrielides (ed.) *A Victim-Led Criminal Justice System: Addressing the Paradox*. London: IARS Publications.

9

Victims and restorative justice
Bringing theory and evidence together

Arthur Hartmann

Introduction

The chapter aims to analyze restorative justice from the victims' perspective. The first section assesses historic and ethnological roots, especially those that serve as examples for modern restorative practices and contrasts restorative justice theories with historical and ethnological research. The second section discusses the terms "victims" and "stakeholders", and compares restorative justice theories with positions on the European Victim's Directive and the women's movement. The third section presents available research regarding victims in restorative justice procedures and distinguishes research on satisfaction and participation on the one hand, and research about the effects those practices can have on victims on the other hand.

The chapter contextualizes research from within the restorative justice scientific community, victimological and psychological research. Aligned with the Handbook's ambition to provide readers with an up-to-date picture of restorative justice, the chapter provides the latest overview of available qualitative, quantitative and experimental research that is needed for a balanced assessment. Of course, the presentation cannot be exhaustive, and the selection may have some subjective bias from the author's side, although the central idea was to assess restorative practices *sine ira et studio*, and specifically from the perspective of victims of crime.

The last section presents unpublished results from an ongoing survey on restorative practices in Germany. It analyzes the cases of nearly 50,000 victims who became involved in restorative justice between 2010 and 2016 all over Germany and reveals the position of restorative practices within the whole criminal justice system. The chapter closes with a résumé reflecting the main results of the previous sections, generating some lessons for the international reader of this Handbook.

Historic and ethnological roots of restorative justice

Scholars present restorative justice as a major development in criminological thinking and emphasize its grounding in traditions of justice from the ancient Arab, Greek and Roman civilizations as well as Hindus, Buddhist, Taoist and Confucian traditions (van Ness, 1989: 64–68; Weitekamp, 1989; Braithwaite, 1998: 323, Gavrielides, 2001).

Besides these historical foundations, the preserved traditions of first nation societies have a great influence on restorative justice. This is especially true for New Zealand, where the Maori contributed the model of restorative conferencing and for Canada, where healing and sentencing circles were developed according to native peoples' practices (Braithwaite, 1998).

So far, we know that restorative practices have been widely used since the Neolithic period (Lee and DeVore, 1976; Evans-Pritchard, 1956; Sigrist, 1967: 21; Wesel, 1985: 185; Gavrielides, 2011; Braithwaite, 1998: 323), but not necessarily with restorative values in a modern sense. Especially from the perspective of victims, one should emphasize that practically all of the just-mentioned ancient urban societies and proto-states had a patriarchal political order refusing women fundamental rights, and they widely used and justified slavery and wars (Finley, 1968). At least the latter is true also for the Maori, according to available sources (Vayda, 1961); litigious marginals do exist (Todd, 1978). Throughout history, restorative practices had been used as a preferable alternative to feuds or court decisions (Spittler, 1980; Merry, 1982), and many offenders possibly needed this threat or motivation by feuds or court decisions to accept restorative practices..

These amendments should not oppose restorative justice but point to the problem that restorative practices do not necessarily hinder any kind of injustice (for contemporary examples, see Johnstone and van Ness, 2007b: 11) Therefore, evaluating procedures and effects of restorative practices is an ongoing task.

Victims and stakeholders

The restorative justice perspective

Restorative justice has come to mean many things to many different people (McCold, 1998), but still there may be concordance on the main principles and values, such as voluntariness, active participation, inclusion and equality of the parties, non-domination, future-orientation, restoration, respect and empowerment (Vanfraechem et al., 2015: 52–53; Johnstone and van Ness, 2007a: 11). Restorative justice serves as an alternative to mainly retributive criminal justice systems that aim to repay harm and prevent further crimes by inflicting additional harm. Furthermore, legal theory and court practice define crime as a breach of the law that evokes a conflict between the offender and the state, whereas the harm done to victims serves at best as a criterion for a proportional punishment. Courts need the victims as witnesses but do not care about their needs. This causes a considerable danger for secondary victimization (Zehr, 1990; Johnstone and van Ness, 2007b; Trenczek, 2013; Pelikan, 2007; Hartmann, 1995: 99; Wright, 1991: 24). Instead, restorative practices focus on the possibilities for restoring losses, injuries and relationships (Wachtel, 1997; Zehr, 1990; Wright, 1991: 42). In addition, restorative procedures require and allow an active participation of the persons who are affected by a crime (Pelikan and Trenczek, 2008). Therefore, with regard to the theory of procedural justice, restorative justice is "fair" (Rawls, 1958; Hartmann, 1995: 122; Hartmann and Trenczek, 2016), provided that the participants have equal power and resources. Therefore, "empowerment" is an important concern of restorative practices (Pelikan and Trenczek, 2008; Johnstone and van Ness, 2007b: 9; Christie, 1977).

Besides individual victims and offenders, the "community" is a central and highly debated concept in restorative justice theory (Vanfraechem, 2007: 77). One kind of "community" called "community of care" includes relatives, partners and the broader personal network of victims and offenders (McCold and Wachtel, 2002). Another category is the "local community", which consists of persons that reside in a specific locality (McCold, 1996). Besides these "micro-communities", some scholars also regard "communities at large" that include persons, who became aware of a crime in any way, as "stakeholders" of that crime (McCold and Wachtel, 2002).

Although key values and concepts are widely consented, so far a consensual definition of restorative justice does not exist. A project using a Delphi technique ended with a minimum working definition introduced by Tony Marshall: "*Restorative Justice is a process whereby all the parties with a stake in a particular offence come together to resolve collectively how to deal with the aftermath of the offence and its implications for the future*" (McCold, 1998: 20).

Another well-known and contrasting definition is: "*Restorative Justice is every action that is primarily oriented toward doing justice by repairing the harm that has been caused by a crime*" (Bazemore and Walgrave, 1999: 48). This view does not limit restorative justice to a face-to-face communication process. To stress this point, Walgrave later defined restorative justice as "*An option for doing justice that is primarily focused on repairing the harm that has been caused by a crime*" (Walgrave, 2005: 4).

With these definitions, we limit restorative justice to practices dealing with specific crimes. This decision is due to the topic and the limitations of this chapter and explicitly does not include a negative assessment of other restorative practices. Concerning the definitions, astonishingly, both do not mention victims. The proposal of Marshall includes victims in the big "melting pot" of stakeholders, with the consequence that restorative processes do not require direct victims when other stakeholders are available. The definition of Walgrave does not refer to victims. Modern measures and sanctions such as community service, compensation orders, paying money to a charity organization may be assessed as "restorative" regardless of the involvement of a victim. Furthermore, both definitions do not mention the voluntary nature of participation for victims and offenders. Therefore, from these well-known definitions some uncertainties are created about the status of victims in restorative justice.

Some scholars present restorative justice as a new paradigm of criminal justice, which should re-establish a kind of justice where the stakeholders, and not a centralized state, lawyers and other professionals, deliberate how to deal with the consequences of a crime and prevent its recurrence. Harmony and social support should be restored and the gathering around friends during a time of crisis institutionalized (Braithwaite, 1998: 329; Christie, 1977; Zehr, 1990). Such far-reaching concepts evoke concerns that restorative justice will take advantage of victims in order to transform the society in a way that scholars may appreciate but perhaps a majority of victims would not support if they had a chance to discuss it.

Braithwaite illustrates his considerations with an example of a homeless teenager, who knocked an aged lady over and stole her purse. After a difficult beginning, the participants of a conference found an amicable agreement meeting all the aims of restorative justice mentioned earlier, including financial restitution, restoration of broken relationships and human dignity (Braithwaite, 1998: 326–328). Braithwaite had composed this story from several real examples in order to explain how restorative justice can work. Therefore, especially from the perspective of victims, it is astonishing that he did not even mention a number of problems included in this case. First, the facilitator tried hard to find three people who supported the teenager, but the aged lady was supported only by her daughter. This is an obvious imbalance caused by the intervention of the facilitator. Second, although his parents had abused the teenager according to the story, neither an offer for psychological treatment nor further social services is mentioned. Here, a claim from victim support agencies that better cooperation between restorative justice and victim support is needed becomes relevant (Lázaro and Moyano Marques, 2008: 95). Third, the case also raises questions regarding the confidentiality of conferences in severe cases.

Perhaps there are other children still abused by the parents? Has the facilitator or anybody else a duty to check this point, and must he or she eventually inform the police? Fourth, the teenager and his supporting sister incriminated their absent parents during the conference. Should third parties get an opportunity to present their view when participants are seriously reproaching them? Fifth, the facilitator and the other participants seemingly believed the teenager and his sister that their parents abused them. What if offenders or even victims invent stories in order to achieve a favourable outcome? Investigations are completely outside the focus of restorative justice theory and practices. In modern criminal justice systems, the state and its police and prosecutors mainly take this burden ex officio. For example, the Inter-American Court of Human Rights emphasizes the duty of states to investigate, identify and prosecute perpetrators of human rights violations (Antkowiak, 2011: 303). Without regulations concerning investigations, restorative justice cannot completely replace the criminal justice system from the perspective of victims. All in all, the case is both a good example for the benefits of restorative justice and for problems that call for a close cooperation between restorative practices, the existing systems of social care and the criminal justice system.

Restorative justice and the European Victim's Directive

The European Victims' Directive (EUVD; OJEU 2012 L 315: 57–73; November 14, 2012) comprises 72 considerations and 32 articles (see Gavrielides, 2014). According to Art. 1 EUVD, the Directive safeguards that victims of crime receive appropriate information, support and protection so they are able to participate in criminal proceedings. The Member States shall ensure that victims are recognized and treated in a respectful, sensitive, tailored, professional and non-discriminatory manner in all contacts with victim support or restorative justice services or competent authorities. The following articles elaborate these rights and provisions. The central regulation concerning restorative justice is article 12 EUVD, which obliges the member states to take measures safeguarding victims from secondary and repeat victimization, from intimidation and from retaliation when providing any restorative justice services. According to Art. 12 para 1 (a) EUVD, restorative justice services should be used only if they are in the interest of the victim, subject to any safety considerations and based on the victim's free and informed consent, which may be withdrawn at any time. Restorative justice services have to provide the victim with full and unbiased information about the process and the potential outcomes as well as information about the procedures for supervising the implementation of any agreement before the victim agrees to participate in the restorative justice process (Art. 12 para. 1 (b). Furthermore, it is necessary that the offender has acknowledged the basic facts of the case before a referral to restorative justice services is possible (Art. 12 para. 1 (c) EUVD). Additional regulations of Art. 12 EUVD assure that discussions in restorative meetings are confidential and that the member states facilitate the referral of cases. The directive does not provide a right for victims to access restorative justice services as it does, for example, with victim support services (Art. 8 EUVD) and legal aid (Art. 13 EUVD).

From these regulations, one can recognize an attitude that acknowledges restorative justice and its benefits for victims and offenders but at the same time remains very cautious and tries to protect victims from unsafe services (Kilchling, 2014; Hartmann and Haas, 2014). A similar cautious position formulates the "Convention on preventing and combating violence against women and domestic violence" (Istanbul Convention) of the Council of Europe from 11th of May 2011. Art. 48 forbids mandatory alternative dispute resolution processes or sentencing in cases of violence against women and domestic violence. It becomes clear from these cautious positions of two important international regulations that there is obviously some uncertainty in the political sphere and society regarding the position and treatment of victims in restorative justice services.

Two implications of the Victim's Direction need further attention. In contrast to the stakeholder concept, Art. 2 EUVD defines "victim" either (1) as a natural person, who has suffered harm, including physical, mental or emotional harm or economic loss, which was directly caused by a criminal offence, or (2) as a family member of a person, whose death was directly caused by a criminal offence and who has suffered harm as a result of that person's death. Furthermore, according to art. 4 par. 1j and art. 6 par. 4 EUVD, authorities have to inform the victims at first contact about all available restorative justice services. Consequently, the informed victim in accordance with the offender decides which setting seems to be "fully restorative" and suitable in his or her case (Hartmann and Haas, 2014: 122). Concepts which assess only practices as "fully restorative" that include members of the closer and wider community (McCold and Wachtel, 2002) do not comply with the directive.

The directive gets support from the finding that different settings serve different victims best (Bolivar et al., 2009: 141). According to a recent pilot to introduce peacemaking circles in Belgium, Germany and Hungary, direct victims welcomed participants from the closer and wider community when they were really involved in the case, but not when the position as "stakeholder" was more or less artificial. The "threat to privacy and confidentiality" that results from a larger number of participants was a major reason why victims and offenders rejected circles and preferred victim-offender-mediation (Weitekamp and Kerner, 2015: 339).

Perspective of women's movement

There is rapidly growing evidence that also in cases of family violence and sex-related crimes restorative practices can be safe and helpful for the victims, when considering their special needs and vulnerabilities (Jülich and Landon, 2014; Zinsstag and Keenan, 2017; Pelikan and Hofinger, 2017; Hayden et al., 2014; Koss, 2014; Angel et al., 2014; Pelikan, 2002; Pelikan, 2009; Bals, 2010). Nevertheless, latent critical attitudes on the part of the women's movement against restorative justice are visible (e.g. in the EU Victim's Directive). The primary goal of "first wave" feminism was to achieve the right to vote (suffrage) for women and to secure an equal share of power and influence for women within the state. "Second-wave feminism" (early 1960s through late 1980s) added the cultural perspective, which uncovered the link between everyday discrimination and political inequalities. Discrimination derives not only from state regulations, but rests in the traditional culture that assigns women to serving positions such as in the home (Freedman, 2002). Considering this, the communitarian mindset in restorative justice theory and the role models of women in many ancient and contemporary first nation societies may not be very promising for the women's movement. And indeed the problems of modern conferences and circles used in indigenous societies in cases of family violence or with offenders from strong families have already come to the surface of research (Daly and Stubbs, 2007: 161–164). "Third wave" and contemporary feminism are very diverse and have developed in many directions (Gerhard, 2004; Budgeon, 2011; Hudson, 2003: 123), and it is therefore not possible to find a single feminist position regarding restorative justice. But it is safe to say that the notion of criminal law is not mainly negative in the women's movement.

Feminist scholars acknowledge retribution in the sense of a reaction to crime, which is limited by a proportionality of harm but clearly expresses the wrongfulness of the offence and vindicates the value of the victim (Hampton, 1998: 39). Regarding empirical research, Daly found evidence in South Australia that conferences are highly gendered events, as few offenders were female (15%), women were the majority of offenders' and victims' supporters (52%; 58%) and more mothers than fathers were present at conferences. She found that 25% of victims present were treated with disrespect or were re-victimized in conferences; this occurred, for example, when victims were outnumbered by offenders and their supporters (Daly and Stubbs, 2007: 157). Similar problems were observed with further studies in New Zealand and Australia (Daly and Stubbs, 2007: 158). Therefore, scepticism regarding the use of restorative practices continues, although feminist engagement with restorative justice is evolving (Daly and Stubbs, 2007: 164).

Evidence from research

Victims' satisfaction with restorative justice

There is evidence from widespread research that relatively high numbers of victims are willing to participate in restorative practices and reveal subsequently high satisfaction rates (Dignan, 2007; Shapland et al., 2007; Strang, 2006; Umbreit et al., 2004; Wemmers and Canuto, 2002). Some victims particularly valued the opportunity to participate actively (Umbreit, 1994), some the experience of meeting the offender (Coates and Gehm, 1989) and some especially the preparation process (Umbreit, 1994; Bolivar et al., 2009; Strang, 2002a). Research also shows that satisfaction depends on the quality of restorative practices and declines when, for example, victims feel badly prepared (Strang, 2002a), regard the mediator/facilitator as biased (Strang, 2002a), the offender as insincere (Daly, 2006; Wemmers and Canuto, 2002), miss the opportunity to participate actively (Bolivar et al., 2009: 2) or miss a follow-up (Coates and Gehm, 1989; Shapland et al., 2007).

The benefit of satisfaction rates has been criticized, as satisfaction depends not only on the quality of services but on many other aspects, for example, the personal nature of contact, the knowledge of the service. (Bouckaert and Van de Walle S., 2003). Furthermore, satisfaction has shown to be a poor measure of therapeutic benefit and the well-being of victims (Biffi et al., 2016: 27; McNally et al., 2003). Nonetheless, the generally high rates of participation and satisfaction of victims are remarkable. Undoubtedly, there is a need for restorative practices from the side of victims of crime.

Victims' needs and their fulfilment in restorative practices

Protection from and prevention of crimes is a general need of people, victims in particular, and a paramount concern in cases of chronic abuse such as stalking, domestic violence and sexual exploitation (Campbell, 2002; Jordan, 2004; van der Aa, 2010). In such situations, victims report the crime to the police primarily in order to stop violence (Biffi et al., 2016: 31; Bachinger and Pelikan, 2009: 36). Stalking, especially, is a contra-indication for usual restorative practices, because they would help the offender to stay in contact and continue the stalking behaviour (see e.g. www.stalking-kit.de).

Besides these specific cases, in general, restorative justice helps the victims to reduce the fear of further victimizations, to regain a feeling of safety and control and to leave their victimization behind (Mesmaecker, 2011; Angel, 2005; Beven et al., 2005; Gustafson, 2004; Strang, 2002a; Umbreit, 1989, 1994; Wemmers and Cyr, 2005; Bolivar et al., 2009; Berndt, 2016). Where possible and the victim wishes, the involvement of members of the victim's family and/or community can give additional support (McCold, 1996; McCold, 2000). According to research in

Austria, most victims and offenders had been integrated in families and communities and re-integration was not needed (Bachinger and Pelikan, 2009: 51).

An obvious impact of crime very often lies in financial and material consequences. To which extent they become a topic in restorative practices depends on private and public insurances, public welfare institutions and the provisions of the criminal justice system. Therefore, in industrialized countries, financial reparation often may serve a more symbolic function (Strang, 2002a; Beven et al., 2005; Biffi et al., 2016: 57). Furthermore, financial restitution has become a growing concern of the criminal justice system in many countries; see, for example, the Directive 2014/42/EU on the freezing and confiscation of instrumentalities and proceeds of crime (OJEU L 127, 29.04.2014: 39; L 138, 13.05.2014: 114). Nevertheless, restorative practices enable victims to receive compensation from the offenders in a fast and unbureaucratic way (Bachinger and Pelikan, 2009: 45). And it has a specific value that the offender him- or herself is actively repairing the harm (Biffi et al., 2016: 54; van Ness and Strong, 2014).

Psychological and emotional consequences of victimization have received high attention because many victims experience at least some symptoms of post-traumatic stress. For most of them, these symptoms pass within a period of weeks or months (Bonanno et al., 2011), but a large minority, amongst them especially victims of severe, repeated or chronic victimization, develop a post-traumatic stress disorder that needs adequate therapy (Brewin et al., 2000). Nevertheless, besides the therapeutic dimension, coping with severe victimization includes also efforts to rebuild relationships, respect, control and status (Biffi et al., 2016: 34; Pemberton et al., 2017). The experience of social support is one of the strongest predictors of recovery from victimization (Biffi et al., 2016: 35). In this respect, restorative practices can help victims in regaining a positive self-perception, in establishing a feeling of respect and dignity and in restoring their relationships and trust in the world surrounding them (Zehr, 1990; Brenda et al., 2006; Morris, 2002; Daly, 2006). It is especially helpful when the offender takes responsibility, acknowledges the harm done and doesn't blame the victim (Koss et al., 2003).

A recent randomized experiment with victims of burglary and robbery in London found a significant reduction of post-traumatic stress symptoms for those victims who participated in restorative conferences compared to victims that participated in normal court procedures (Angel et al., 2014; Angel, 2005). There is some critique that victims, who are able to confront an offender may be those victims who probably would recover without treatment (Biffi et al., 2016: 53). Nevertheless, the evidence that restorative practices can help to recover from post-traumatic stress symptoms is available now.

Furthermore, victimological research distinguishes three main procedural needs: information, participation and respectful treatment (Strang, 2002a). Criminal justice has neglected these needs for a long period and restricted participation to the reporting of a crime and the burdensome role of a witness. Finally, the treatment at the police and in the courts all too often caused secondary victimization (Biffi et al., 2016: 38; Vanfraechem et al. 2015; Frazier and Haney, 1996; Wemmers and Canuto, 2002). Therefore, one of the main justifications for a turn to restorative justice is the active involvement of victims and offenders, the possibility to become better informed, to tell one's story, express one's feelings and needs, and finally to settle claims (Zehr, 1990; Larson Sawin and Zehr, 2007; Vanfraechem et al., 2015). However, we have to consider that the whole criminal justice system is changing. The aforementioned EU Victim's Directive is only one example. Common law systems have introduced a victim's impact statement, civil law jurisdictions give victims the possibility to participate as a *parti civile* (Kilchling and Kury, 2011). Information, participation and respectful treatment should no longer be a quality of restorative justice alone but a concern of the whole criminal justice system.

Victims of severe crimes often suffer especially by a shake-up of trust in the moral order as well as a (symbolic) removal of power caused by the wrongdoing of the offender. Therefore, the first intuitive reaction to the wrongdoing may be an urge to pay back the offender "eye for eye". However, victim surveys show that victims of crime are as equally punitive as non-victims, and most prefer outcomes such as compensation, support or a sincere apology from the offender (Biffi et al., 2016: 36; Pfeiffer, 1993; Sessar, 1990; Strang, 2002a). Further research reveals, however, that the need for repair does not necessarily replace the desire for payback and that the more severe the impact of a crime, the less likely the desire for retribution might be circumvented by other means (Alter et al., 2007; Biffi et al., 2016: 36). Victims of more severe crimes prefer modes of participation with more retributive features and feel that an acquittal of suspects can and does impede recovery (Pemberton, 2015). Concluding this, traditional juris-prudence seems at least not completely based on false assumptions, as, for example, Strang and Sherman claim (Strang and Sherman, 2003: 15). For severe crimes it seems to be a necessary backbone serving also the interests of victims especially in cases with a high impact or cases with a considerable imbalance of power.

Social ecology

Restorative justice does not exist on an "island". Many external factors are relevant, as are, for example, the criminal justice system, crime rates, incarceration rates and victim support services. This so-called "societal ecology" (Biffi et al., 2016: 15) should be considered especially regarding research. Most of the findings mentioned earlier reflect the situation in common law jurisdictions, some results come from EU-funded projects in Europe, and only scattered and isolated scientific evidence is available from many other regions of the world. Therefore, this chapter should not conclude without explicitly mentioning this weakness.

Evidence from German restorative justice statistics

Restorative justice in Germany in its modern form developed from the implementation of the first experimental projects in 1985 that triggered a foundation boom (Hartmann, 1995: 194; Lenz et al., 2010, 121, 125; Schreckling, 1990: 13; Bannenberg, 1993: 86). National surveys indicate that restorative practices are offered to about 25,000 victims and offenders per year (Wandrey and Weitekamp, 1998: 131–133; Kerner and Weitekamp, 2013: 12–19). The stormy development of the early years did not continue, although the legal basis for restorative practices has been increasingly expanded (Lenz et al., 2010: 123; Hartmann, 2010: 126).

Methodology

The German Victim-Offender-Mediation Statistics (VOM-statistics) has documented cases since 1993 (Hartmann, 2008). The following evaluations combine all cases documented from 2010 until 2016. As participation is voluntary, these statistics have similar limitations as many surveys because the return is not a random sample and therefore not representative in a strict sense. In substance, however, all criteria we can use indicate that the VOM-statistics gives an at least valuable, if not valid and reliable, impression (Lenz et al., 2010: 130).

If a VOM-scheme takes part, it has to document all its cases – whether successful or not – with a standardized questionnaire implemented in a computer program that contains about 60 items for every case, regarding (a) data about the scheme (b) the case and its progress, (c) particularities of the victims, and (d) the offenders; an English version is available at (Hartmann,

2008: 61). VOM, including extended mediation, is still the predominant practice of restorative justice in Germany despite recent initiatives to introduce conferences and circles (Weitekamp and Kerner, 2015).

Referring and selection

In order to assess the place of restorative justice in society, an interesting point is the initiative. As Figure 9.1 shows, the prosecutors refer the biggest part of cases. The overall picture has not much changed since the starting period of restorative justice in Germany in 1985 (Hartmann, 1992: 213; Hartmann, 1995: 186; Lenz et al., 2010: 136).

According to German law, police have no discretionary power and thus have to transfer all cases to the prosecuting services after preliminary investigations. Therefore, the influence of police is mainly informal and underestimated in Figure 9.1 (Jacob, 2015: 211; Hartmann et al., 2016a: 19).

Most victims obviously prefer to report criminal offences to the police and do not directly involve VOM-schemes, although this is possible and not prohibited. After 30 years of restorative practice in Germany, it is remarkable that only a very tiny amount of victims and offenders try to circumvent the police and with it the criminal justice system in order to get support from a VOM-scheme.

The following figures give a comparison between the amount of cases reported to the police and the cases of VOM-schemes. The first come from the German Police Statistics (PKS), and the latter are from the VOM-statistics. The PKS includes all crimes reported to the police with the exception of security-related offences, specific traffic offences like driving without a licence and some further minor exceptions (Bundesministerium des Innern: 5).

Table 9.1 shows the total number of offences, the detection rate and the resulting cleared cases. According to the PKS, a "cleared case" is defined by the fact that the police could find a

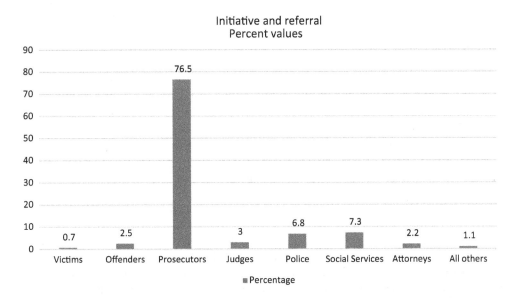

Figure 9.1 Initiative and referral regarding RJ cases in Germany 2010–2016 – victim-based cases N = 51,189 (victims); missing cases 7,526; valid cases 42,969 (victims)

Arthur Hartmann

Table 9.1 German Police Statistics (PKS) and VOM-statistics – offender-based cases, 2010–2016

Offences including attempted cases	PKS Cases in total	Detection rate	Cleared cases	VOM – statistics cases in total
All registered cases	41,777,446	54.5%	22,783,060	49,051

(Bundesministerium des Innern)

Table 9.2 Procedural decision of prosecutors in the year 2013

Procedural decisions	No. of Cases
Cleared cases reported to prosecutors by police	3.25 Mio.
Cases closed because reported facts did not meet the requirements of a criminal offence or the evidence was not sufficient	1.3 Mio.
Cases dismissed without any sanction or measure, mainly because the guilt or fault of the offender was slight or even minimal	1.1 Mio.
Cases dismissed on the condition of fulfilment of a measure	183,333
Order of summary punishment	527,228
Offenders charged at a criminal court	455,510
Offenders convicted by criminal courts	596,000
Offenders sentenced to prison without parole	38,000

(Baumann, 2015: 77–82).

suspect who may have committed the offence (Bundesministerium des Innern: 136). This does not necessarily imply that the prosecutors or the courts value the existing evidence as sufficient. Especially in cases of rape and sexual assault, the conviction rates are rather low, mostly because of insufficient evidence (Hartmann et al., 2016b).

First, we can presume that in uncleared cases, which make on average about 50% of all cases reported to the police, neither a traditional criminal procedure nor a fully fledged restorative practice is possible. Second, we can see from Table 9.1 that only very few cleared cases find their way to VOM-schemes. Even if we consider that the VOM-statistics does not contain all VOM-cases and use instead the earlier estimate of 25,000 cases a year, the total sum would be only 175,000 compared to 22,783,060 cleared cases in the relevant period. However, the picture changes if we consider the prosecutors.

The latest published data on prosecuting is for the year 2013. Table 9.2 shows the procedural decisions for this year.

The number of convicted offenders is larger than the number of charged offenders, because the courts had to deal with cases from previous years.

Measures in dismissed cases can be, for example, a payment to the treasury or a charitable organization (149,216 cases in 2013), a "Täter-Opfer-Ausgleich" (11,659 cases in 2013), which is commonly translated by victim-offender-mediation but actually not identical (Hartmann and Haas, 2014: 132), the reparation of a damage (9,123 cases) and a number of other measures including, payment of alimonies (Baumann, 2015: 81).

It is beyond question that much more than about 25,000 cases per year should be suitable for restorative practices (Bundesministerium des Innern, Bundesministerium der Justiz, 2006: 95). But the mentioned figures demonstrate that some narratives in restorative justice literature about the criminal justice system do not really meet the realities at least in Germany, because an exclusively revenge-oriented criminal justice system would produce different figures.

Another scenario appears when we look at the share of significant crimes in the total case-load, shown in Figure 9.2.

Cases with violent offences are highly overrepresented amongst VOM-cases compared to the PKS. Obviously, the prosecutors see the best use of restorative justice in cases of personal violence, and they refer most of these cases in the pre-trial stage, usually dismissing criminal procedures when victims and offenders reach an agreement.

Results of RJ procedures

The ratio of victims that accept VOM against those who reject participation comes close to 3:1 or 75% to 25% over the years, which is impressively high when considering the large share of violent cases referred to VOM. However, as it takes "two to tango" in restorative justice and the share of cases with both victims and offenders accepting VOM is only 38.9%. These rates are rather stable regarding different kinds of offences, age and gender of victims and offenders.

An essential point of the concept of restorative justice is that victims meet face to face with their offenders. However, victims or offenders can reject this on a variety of reasons, for example, when the offence appears negligible or when it had a traumatizing impact to the victim. In the Figure 9.3, we calculated only cases when both the victim and the offender accepted VOM.

Figure 9.3 shows higher rates of face-to-face meetings with more serious crimes, and it seems reasonable to assume that victims of severe crimes, who want to participate in restorative practices, have a specific interest to meet with the offender.

Regarding the results, 85% of the victims came to a full and complete agreement and 4.5% came to a partial agreement, based on cases where both victims and offenders agreed to VOM. This result is stable, with only small variations over the years since 1993; also, the kind of crimes, the age and gender of victims and offenders, and other available data, make no significant difference.

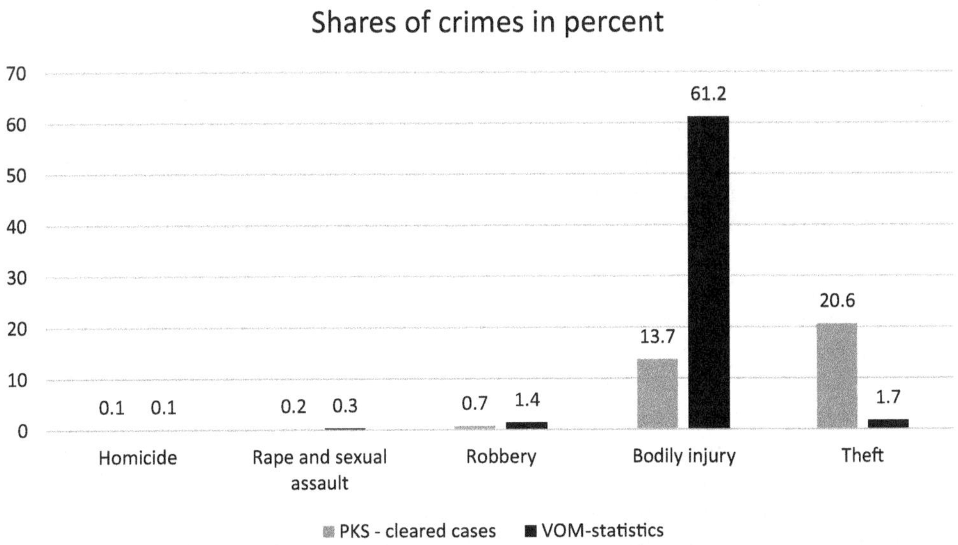

Shares of crimes in percent

Figure 9.2 Share of significant crimes in German PKS and the German VOM-statistics; 2010–2016

German PKS: N = 3.25 Mio. offenders – cleared cases; German VOM-statistics; N = 49.051 offenders

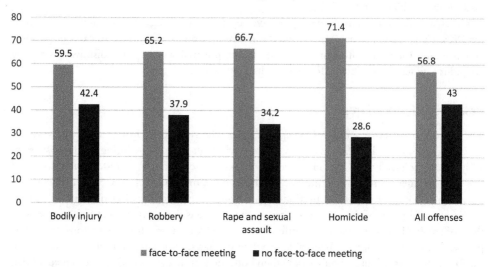

Kind of meetings in percent

Figure 9.3 Kind of meetings; 2010–2016

N = 19,898 victim-based cases with victims and offenders accepting a RJ practice.

Conclusions

We could find a bulk of evidence that restorative practices can have very positive effects on victims. Indeed, victims can be highly satisfied if the practice follows restorative values. However, the nature of restorative practices alone cannot guarantee this, as historical sources and contemporary research show. Therefore, ongoing research is necessary to give warnings when wrong turns happen.

The well-informed victim, in accordance with the offender, should decide whether and if so, in which kind of restorative practices they want to participate. Concepts which assess only practices as "fully restorative" that include members of the closer and wider community comply neither with the European Victim's Directive nor with the restorative value of voluntariness and can neglect the voice of the direct victims to a significant degree.

The analyses from the German VOM-statistics give a double-sided picture. From the perspective of mediators, we see a great acceptance of restorative practices amongst victims and offenders, even with serious crimes, and if both participate, they mostly find a settlement. However, from the perspective of police, prosecutors and judges, restorative practices help only in a small part of their caseload. First, they cannot reduce the large amount of uncleared cases. Second, referrals require offenders that accept their responsibility. These are the greater part of juvenile offenders, a considerably smaller part of adult offenders and especially in some serious crimes, only a small fraction of the offenders. Finally, only a bit more than one-third of the referred cases ended with a settlement at least in Germany.

Both perspectives are justified, and it seems to be a safe conclusion, at least for Germany, that restorative justice cannot replace the criminal justice system. But it can offer great opportunities and advantages when both victims and offenders want to participate. A choice only exists, if there are alternatives, and so far we can see there is no political impact from the side of victims to replace the criminal justice system with a restorative justice system. It's the option that provides the benefit.

Finally, from the perspective of the victims, we should add that victim support agencies, insurances and effective health care are as important as restorative justice is because they can also offer support in cases where no offender was identified or willing to accept responsibility. On the other hand, restorative practices can overcome the ongoing specialization of services for victims, offenders, justice, social support and other entities, and provide an option to solve the problems and conflicts directly where they originated. These are all lessons that hopefully can be of value to the international reader whether for research, social policy or practical purposes.

References

Aertsen, I. and Peters, T. 1998. Mediation for Reparation: The Victim's Perspective, *European Journal of Crime, Criminal Law and Criminal Justice*, 6: 106–124.

Alter, A.L., Kernochan, J. and Darley, J.M. 2007. Transgression Wrongfulness Outweighs its Harmfulness as a Determinant of Sentence Severity, *Law and Human Behavior*, 31(4): 319–335.

Angel, C.M. 2005. *Crime Victims Meet their Offenders: Testing the Impact of Restorative Justice Conferences on Victims' Post-Traumatic Stress Symptoms*. Dissertation.

Angel, C.M., et al. 2014. Short-Term Effects of Restorative Justice Conferences on post-Traumatic Stress Symptoms among Robbery and Burglary Victims: A Randomized Controlled Trial, *Journal of Experimental Criminology*, 10(3): 291–307. Accessed 16 November 2016.

Antkowiak, T.M. 2011. An Emerging Mandate for International Courts: Victim-Centered Remedies and Restorative Justice, *Stanford Journal of International Law*, 47: 279–332. Available at www.brandeis.edu/ethics/pdfs/internationaljustice/JustPerformance/Antkowiak_Emerging_Mandate.pdf. Accessed 30 November 2017.

Bachinger, L.M. and Pelikan, C. 2009. Chapter 1. Victims and Restorative Justice in Austria. In *Victims and Restorative Justice: An Empirical Study of the Needs, Experience, and Position of the Victim within Restorative Justice Practices*. Leuven: European Forum for Restorative Justice, pp. 19–54.

Bals, N. 2010. *Der Täter-Opfer-Ausgleich bei häuslicher Gewalt: Vermittlung und Wiedergutmachung auf dem Prüfstand*, 1st ed. Baden-Baden: Nomos.

Bannenberg, B. 1993. *Wiedergutmachung in der Strafrechtspraxis: Eine empirisch-kriminologische Untersuchung von Täter-Opfer-Ausgleichsprojekten in der Bundesrepublik Deutschland*. Bonn: Forum-Verl. Godesberg.

Baumann, T. 2015. *Staatsanwaltschaftliche Ermittlungstätigkeit in Deutschland: Umfang und Struktur der Verfahrenserledigung* [online]. Statistisches Bundesamt. Available at www.destatis.de/DE/Publikationen/WirtschaftStatistik/2015/03/StaatsanwaltschaftlicheErmittlungstaetigkeit_032015.pdf?__blob=publicationFile. Accessed 30 November 2017.

Bazemore, G. and Walgrave, L., eds. 1999. *Restorative Juvenile Justice – Repairing the harm of Youth Crime*. Monsey, NY: Willow Tree Press, Inc.

Berndt, A.F. 2016. *Der Täter-Opfer-Ausgleich aus Sicht des Opfers*. Dissertation: Lit-Verlag; Universität Heidelberg.

Beven, J., et al. 2005. Restoration or Renovation? Evaluating Restorative Justice Outcomes, *Psychiatry, Psychology and Law*, 12(1): 194–206.

Biffi, E., et al., eds. 2016. *IVOR Report-Implementing Victim-Oriented Reform of the Criminal Justice System in the European Union*. Lissabon.

Bolivar, D., Aertsen, I. and Vanfraechem, I. 2009. *Victims and Restorative Justice: An Empirical Study of the Needs, Experience, and Position of the Victim Within Restorative Justice Practices*. Leuven: European Forum for Restorative Justice.

Bonanno, G.A., Westphal, M. and Mancini, A.D. 2011. Resilience to Loss and Potential Trauma, *Annual Review of Clinical Psychology*, 7: 511–535.

Bouckaert, G. and Van de Walle S. 2003. Comparing Measures of Citizen Trust and User Satisfaction as Indicators of 'Good Governance': Difficulties in Linking Trust and Satisfaction. Indicators', *International Review of Administrative Sciences*, 69(3): 329–344.

Braithwaite, J. 1998. Restorative Justice. In M.H. Tonry (ed.) *The Handbook of Crime & Punishment*. New York: Oxford University Press, pp. 323–344.

Brenda, Morrison and Eliza Ahmed. 2006. Restorative Justice and Civil Society: Emerging Practice, Theory, and Evidence, *Journal of social Issues* (62).

Brewin, C.R., Andrews, B. and Valentine, J.D. 2000. Meta-Analysis of Risk Factors for Posttraumatic Stress Disorder in Trauma-Exposed Adults, *Journal of Consulting and Clinical Psychology*, 68(5): 748–766.

Budgeon, S. 2011. *Third Wave Feminism and the Politics of Gender in Late Modernity*. Houndsmill, Basingstoke: Palgrave Macmillan.

Bundesministerium des Innern, Bundesministerium der Justiz. 2006. *Zweiter Periodischer Sicherheitsbericht: Unterrichtung durch die Bundesregierung*. Köln: Bundesanzeiger.

Campbell, J.C. 2002. Health Consequences of Intimate Partner Violence, *The Lancet*, 359(9314): 1331–1336.

Christie, N. 1977. Conflicts as Property, *British Journal of Criminology*, 17: 1–15. Available at Christie, Conflicts as Property.

Coates, R.B. and Gehm, J. 1989. An Empirical Assessment. In B. Galaway and M. Wright (eds.) *Mediation and Criminal Justice: Victims, Offenders, and Community*. London and Newbury Park: Sage Publications, pp. 251–263.

Daly, K. 2006. Justice for Victims of Sexual Assault: Court or Conference? In K. Heimer and C. Kruttschnitt (ed.) *Gender and Crime: Patterns of Victimization and Offending*. New York: University Press, pp. 230–265.

Daly, K. and Stubbs, J. 2007. Feminist Theory, Feminist and Anti-Racist Politics, and Restorative Justice. In G. Johnstone and D.W. van Ness (eds.) *Handbook of Restorative Justice*. Cullompton and Portland, OR: William Publishing, pp. 149–170.

Dignan, J. 2007. The Victim in Restorative Justice. In S. Walklate (ed.) *Handbook of Victims and Victimology*. Cullompton: Willan, pp. 309–332.

Evans-Pritchard, E.E. 1956. *The Nuer: A Description of the Modes of Livelihood and Political Institutions of a Nilotic People*, 2nd ed. Oxford: Clarendon Press.

Finley, M.I., ed. 1968. *Slavery in Classical Antiquity: Views and Controversies*. Cambridge: Heffer.

Frazier, P.A. and Haney, B. 1996. Sexual Assault Cases in the Legal System. Police, Prosecutor, and Victim Perspectives, *Law and Human Behavior*, 20(6): 607–628.

Freedman, E.B. 2002. *No Turning Back: The History of Feminism and the Future of Women*. London: Profile Books.

Gavrielides, T. 2011. Restorative Practices: From the Early Societies to the 1970s, *Internet Journal of Criminology* (ISSN 2045–6743). Available at www.researchgate.net/publication/265247294. Accessed 22 December 2017.

Gavrielides, T. 2014. The Victim's Directive and the project Perstorative Justice in Europe: Saveguarding Victims and Empowering Professionals: An Overview. In T. Gavrielides (ed.) *A Victim-Led Criminal Justice System: Addressing the Paradox*. London: Independent Academic Research Studies, pp. 83–102.

Gerhard, U. 2004. Diversity and Internationality. In H. Rømer Christensen (ed.) *Crossing Borders: Re-Mapping Women's Movements at the Turn of the 21st Century*. Odense: University Press of Southern Denmark, pp. 337–345.

Gustafson, D. 2004. Exploring Treatment and Trauma Recovery Implications of Facilitating Victim Offender Encounters in Crimes of Severe Violence: Lessons from the Canadian Experience. In E. Elliott and R. Gordon (eds.) *New Directions in Restorative Justice: Issues, Practice, Evaluation*. Cullompton: William Publishing, pp. 193–227.

Hampton, J. 1998. Punishment, Feminism, and Political Identity: A Case Study in the Expressive Meaning of the Law, *Canadian Journal of Law and Jurisprudence*, 11: 23–45.

Hartmann, A. 1992. Victim-Offender-Reconciliation – Program and Outcomes. In H. Messmer and H.-U. Otto (eds.) *Restorative Justice on Trial: Pitfalls and Potentials of Victim Offender Mediation; International Research Perspectives [Proceedings of the NATO Advanced Research Workshop on Conflict, Crime, and Reconciliation: The Organization of Welfare Interventions in the Field of Restitutive Justice, IlCiocco, Lucca, Italy, 8–12 April 1991]*. Dordrecht: Kluwer, pp. 211–224.

Hartmann, A. 1995. *Schlichten oder Richten: Der Täter-Opfer-Ausgleich und das (Jugend-)Strafrecht.* München, München: Fink; Bayerische Staatsbibliothek.

Hartmann, A. 2008. Federal Statistics of Victim-Offender-Mediation in Germany, *British Journal of Community Justice*, 6(2): 43–68.

Hartmann, A. 2010. Legal Provisions on Restorative Justice in Germany. In Afford Ltd., M. Gyökös, and K. Lányi (eds.) *European Best Practices of Restorative Justice in the Criminal Procedure: Conference Publication.* Budapest: Ministry of Justice and Law Enforcement of the Republic of Hungary, pp. 125–129.

Hartmann, A., et al. 2016a. *Täter-Opfer-Ausgleich in Deutschland: Auswertung der bundesweiten Täter-Opfer-Ausgleich-Statistik für die Jahrgänge 2013 und 2014: Bericht für das Bundesministerium der Justiz und für Verbraucherschutz.* 1st ed. Mönchengladbach: Forum Verlag Godesberg GmbH.

Hartmann, A., et al. 2016b. Untersuchung zu Verfahrensverlauf und Verurteilungsquote bei Sexualdelikten in Bremen, *Rechtspsychologie*, 2(1): 7–22.

Hartmann, A. and Haas, M. 2014. The Victim's Directive and Restorative Justice in Germany. In T. Gavrielides (ed.) *A Victim-Led Criminal Justice System: Addressing the Paradox.* London: Independent Academic Research Studies, pp. 119–141.

Hartmann, A. and Trenczek, T. 2016. Vermittlung in strafrechtlich relevanten Konflikten – Fachliche Standards unter Berücksichtigung des Mediationsgesetzes und der EU-Opferschutzrichtlinie, *Neue Justiz*, 8: 325–333.

Hayden, A.E., et al., eds. 2014. *A Restorative Approach to Family Violence: Changing Tack.* Farnham Surrey and Burlington, VT: Ashgate.

Hudson, B. 2003. *Justice in the Risk Society.* London: Sage Publications.

Jacob, O. 2015. *Täter-Opfer-Ausgleich und Polizei.* Dissertation: Verlag für Polizeiwissenschaft.

Johnstone, G. and van Ness, D.W., eds. 2007a. *Handbook of Restorative Justice.* Cullompton and Portland, OR: William Publishing.

Johnstone, G. and van Ness, D.W. 2007b. The Meaning of Restorative Justice. In G. Johnstone and D.W. van Ness (eds.) *Handbook of Restorative Justice.* Cullompton and Portland, OR: William Publishing, pp. 5–23.

Jordan, C.E. 2004. Intimate Partner Violence and the Justice System. An Examination of the Interface, *Journal of Interpersonal Violence*, 19(12): 1412–1434.

Jülich, S. and Landon, F. 2014. Restorative Justice and Sexual Violence: Overcoming the Concerns of Victim-Survivors. In T. Gavrielides (ed.) *A Victim-Led Criminal Justice System: Addressing the Paradox.* London: Independent Academic Research Studies, pp. 41–56.

Kerner, H.-J. and Weitekamp, E.G.M., 2013. *Praxis des Täter-Opfer-Ausgleichs in Deutschland. Ergebnisse einer Erhebung zu Einrichtungen sowie zu Vermittlerinnen und Vermittlern.*

Kilchling, M. 2014. Entwicklungsperspektiven für den Täter-Opfer-Ausgleich nach der neuen EU-Opferrechtsrichtlinie: Recht auf TOA?, *TOA Magazin*, 2: 36–39.

Kilchling, M. and Kury, H. 2011. Accessory Prosecution in Germany: Legislation and Implementation. In E. Erez, M. Kilchling and J.-A. Wemmers (eds.) *Therapeutic Jurisprudence and Victim Participation in Justice: International Perspectives.* Durham: Carolina Academic Press, pp. 41–65.

Koss, M.P. 2014. The RESTORE Program of Restorative Justice for Sex Crimes, *Journal of Interpersonal Violence*, 29(9): 1623–1660.

Koss, M.P., Bachar, K.J. and Hopkins, C.Q. 2003. Restorative Justice for Sexual Violence. Repairing Victims, Building Community, and Holding Offenders Accountable, *Annals of the New York Academy of Sciences*, 989: 384–396; discussion 441–445.

Larson Sawin, J. and Zehr, H. 2007. The Ideas of Engagement and Empowerment. In G. Johnstone and D.W. van Ness (eds.) *Handbook of Restorative Justice.* Cullompton and Portland, OR: William Publishing, pp. 41–58.

Lázaro, J. and Moyano Marques, F. 2008. What to Do With these Victims?, *British Journal of Community Justice*, 6(2): 93–97.

Lee, R.B. and DeVore, I. 1976. *Man the Hunter: The First Intensive Survey of a Single, Crucial Stage of Human Development – Man's Once Universal Hunting Way of Life.* New York: Aldine.

Lenz, S., Weitekamp, E.G.M. and Kerner, H.-J. 2010. Depicting the Development of Victim-Offender Mediation. Empirical Research on Restorative Justice in Germany. In I. Vanfraechem, I. Aertsen and

J. Willemsens (eds.) *Restorative Justice Realities: Empirical Research in a European Context*. The Hague: Eleven International Publishing, pp. 121–147.

McCold, P. 1996. Restorative Justice and the Role of Community. In B. Galaway and J. Hudson (eds.) *Restorative Justice: International Perspectives / Edited by Burt Galaway and Joe Hudson*. Monsey, NY: Criminal Justice Press, pp. 85–101.

McCold, P. 1998. Restorative Justice – Variations on a Theme. In L. Walgrave (ed.) *Restorative Justice for Juveniles: Potentialities, Risks and Problms for Research: A Selection of Papers Presented at the International Conference Leuven, May 12–14, 1997*. Leuven: Leuven University Press, pp. 19–53.

McCold, P. 2000. Towards a Mid-Range Theory of Restorative Criminal Justice: A Reply to the Maximalist Model Source, *Contemporary Justice Review*, 3(4): 357–404.

McCold, P. and Wachtel, T. 2002. Restorative Justice Theory Validation. In E.G.M. Weitekamp and H.-J. Kerner (eds.) *Restorative Justice: Theoretical Foundations*. Cullompton: Willan, pp. 110–142.

McNally, R.J., Bryant, R.A. and Ehlers, A. 2003. Does Early Psychological Intervention Promote Recovery From Posttraumatic Stress?, *Psychological Science in the Public Interest : A Journal of the American Psychological Society*, 4(2): 45–79.

Merry. 1982. The Social Organization of Mediation in Non-industrial Societies: Implications for Informal Justice in America. In R.L. Abel (ed.) *The Politics of Informal Justice*. New York: Academic Press, pp. 17–45.

Mesmaecker, V. de. 2011. *Perceptions of Justice and Fairness in Criminal Proceedings and Restorative Encounters: Extending Theories of Procedural Justice*. PhD dissertation: KU Leuven.

Morris, A. 2002. Critiquing the Critics. A Brief Response to Critics of Restorative Justice, *British Journal of Criminology*, 42(3): 596–615.

Pelikan, C. 2002. Victim-Offender-Mediation in Domestic Violence cases – A Comparison of the Effects of Criminal Law Intervention. The Penal Process and Mediation, *Doing Qualitative Research*, 3(1).

Pelikan, C. 2007. The Place of Restorative Justice in Society: Making Sense of Developments in Time and Space. In R. Mackay, et al. (eds.) *Images of Restorative Justice Theory*. Frankfurt am Main: Verlag für Polizeiwissenschaft, pp. 35–55.

Pelikan, C. 2009. *Die Möglichkeiten und die Bedingungen einer wirksamen Stärkung (Mächtigung) der Opfer von Gewalt in Paarbeziehungen durch den Außergerichtlichen Tatausgleich*, 1st ed. Wien: Institut für Rechts- und Kriminalsoziologie.

Pelikan, C. and Hofinger, V. 2017. An Interactional Approach to Desistance. Expanding Desistance Theory Based on the Austrian Mediation Practice in Cases of Partnership Violence, *Restorative Justice*, 4(3): 323–344.

Pelikan, C. and Trenczek, T. 2008. Victim Offender Mediation and Restorative Justice: The European Landscape. In D. Sullivan (ed.) *Handbook of Restorative Justice: A Global Perspective*. London: Routledge, pp. 63–90.

Pemberton, A. 2015. Changing Frames. Restorative Justice in the Netherlands. In I. Vanfraechem, D. Bolivar and I. Aertsen (eds.) *Victims and Restorative Justice*. London: Routledge, pp. 126–152.

Pemberton, A., Aarten, P.G.M. and Mulder, E. 2017. Beyond Retribution, Restoration and Procedural Justice. The Big Two of Communion and Agency in Victims' Perspectives on Justice, *Psychology, Crime & Law*, 23(7): 682–698.

Pfeiffer, C. 1993. Opferperspektiven. Wiedergutmachung und Strafe aus der Sicht der Bevölkerung. In P.-A. Albrecht (ed.) *Festschrift für Horst Schüler-Springorum: Zum 65: Geburtstag*. Köln: Heymann, pp. 53–80.

Polizeiliche Kriminalstatistik [online]. Bundesministerium des Innern. Available at www.bka.de/DE/AktuelleInformationen/StatistikenLagebilder/PolizeilicheKriminalstatistik/pks_node.html. Accessed 1 December 2017.

Rawls, J. 1958. Justice as Fairness, *The Philosophical Review*, 67(2): 164–194.

Schreckling, J., ed. 1990. *Täter-Opfer-Ausgleich nach Jugendstrafen in Köln: Bericht über Aufbau, Verlauf und Ergebnisse des Modellprojekts "Waage"*, 1st ed. Bonn: Bundesministerium der Justiz.

Sessar, K. 1990. Strafbedürfnis und Konfliktregelung. Zur Akzeptanz der Wiedergutmachung im und statt Strafrecht. In E. Marks (ed.) *Täter-Opfer-Ausgleich: Vom zwischenmenschlichen Weg zur Wiederherstellung des Rechtsfriedens*. Bonn: Forum-Verl. Godesberg, pp. 42–56.

Shapland, J., et al. 2007. *Restorative Justice: The Views of Victims and Offenders the Third Report from the Evaluation of Three Schemes.* London: Ministry of Justice.

Sigrist, C. 1967. *Regulierte Anarchie: Untersuchungen zum Fehlen und zur Entstehung politischer Herrschaft in segmentären Gesellschaften Afrikas.* Olten: Walter.

Spittler, G. 1980. Streitregelung im Schatten des Leviathan, *Zeitschrift für Rechtssoziologie,* 1(1): 4–32.

Strang, H. 2002a. *Repair or Revenge: Victims and Restorative Justice.* Oxford: Clarendon Press.

Strang, H. 2002b. *Repair or Revenge: Victims and Restorative Justice.* Oxford: Clarendon Press.

Strang, H. 2006. *Repair or Revenge: Victims and Restorative Justice.* Oxford: Oxford University Press.

Strang, H. 2014. The Morality of Evidence: The Second Annual Lecture for Restorative Justice: An International Journal, *Restorative Justice: An International Journal.* Available at www.repository.cam. ac.uk/bitstream/handle/1810/247836/Strang%20and%20Sherman%202015%20Restorative%20 Justice.pdf?sequence=1. Accessed 22 March 2016.

Strang, H. and Sherman, L. 2003. Repairing the Harm: Victims and Restorative Justice. *Utah Law Review* (15): 15. Available at http://heinonline.org/HOL/LandingPage?handle=hein.journals/utahlr 2003&div=9&id=&page=.

Todd, H.F. 1978. Litigious Marginals: Character and Disputing in a Bavarian Village. In L. Nader and H.F. Todd (eds.) *The Disputing Process: Law in Ten Societies.* New York: Columbia University Press, pp. 86–121.

Trenczek, T. 2013. Beyond Restorative Justice to Restorative Practice. In D.J. Cornwell, J.R. Blad, and M. Wright (eds.). *Civilising Criminal Justice: An International Restorative Agenda for Penal Reform.* Hampshire: Waterside Press, pp. 409–441.

Umbreit, M.S. 1989. Crime Victims Seeking Fairness, Not Revenge: Toward Restorative Justice, *Federal Probation,* 53: 52–57.

Umbreit, M.S. 1994. *Victim Meets Offender: The Impact of Restorative Justice and Mediation.* New York: Willow Tree Press, Inc.

Umbreit, M.S., Coates, R.B. and Vos, B. 2004. Victim-Offender Mediation: Three Decades of Practice, *Conflict Resolution Quartely,* 22(1–2): 279–303.

van der Aa, S. 2010. *Stalking in the Netherlands: Nature and Prevalence of the Problem and the Effectiveness of Anti-Stalking Measures.* Apeldoorn: Maklu.

van Ness, D.W. 1989. *Crime and Its Victims: What We Can Do/Daniel W. Van Ness.* Leicester: Inter-Varsity.

van Ness, D.W. and Strong, K.H. 2014. *Restoring Justice: An Introduction to Restorative Justice.* Waltham, MA: Anderson Publishing.

Vanfraechem, I. 2007. Community, Society and State in Restorative Justice: An Exploration. In R. Mackay, et al. (eds.) *Images of Restorative Justice Theory.* Frankfurt am Main: Verlag für Polizeiwissenschaft, pp. 73–91.

Vanfraechem, I., Bolivar, D. and Aertsen, I. (eds.). 2015. *Victims and Restorative Justice.* London: Routledge.

Vayda, A.P. 1961. Maori Prisoners and Slaves in the Nineteenth Century, *Ethnohistory,* 8(2): 144.

Wachtel, T. 1997. *Real Justice.* Pipersville, PA: Piper's Press.

Walgrave, L. 2005. Towards Restoration as the Mainstreem in Youth Justice. In E. Elliot and R. Gordon (eds.) *New Directions in Restorative Justice: Issues, Practice, Evaluation.* Collumption: William Publishing, pp. 3–25.

Wandrey, M. and Weitekamp, E.G.M. 1998. Die organisatorische Umsetzung des Täter-Opfer-Ausgleichs in der Bundesrepublik Deutschland – eine vorläufige Einschätzung der Entwicklung im Zeitraum von 1989–1995. In D. Dölling (ed.) *Täter-Opfer-Ausgleich in Deutschland: Bestandsaufnahme und Perspektiven.* Mönchengladbach: Forum-Verl. Godesberg, pp. 121–143.

Weitekamp, E.G.M. 1989. *Restitution: A New Paradigm of Criminal Justice or a New Way to Widen the System of Social Control?* Dissertation: University of Pennsylvania.

Weitekamp, E.G.M. and Kerner, H.-J. 2015. *Developing Peacemaking Circles in a European Context: Main Report.* Tübingen: Universitätsbibliothek Tübingen.

Wemmers, J. and Cyr, K. 2005. Can Mediation be Therapeutic for Crime Victims? An Evaluation of Victim's Experiences in Mediation with Young Offenders, *Canadian Journal of Criminology and Criminal Justice,* 47(3): 527–544.

Wemmers, J.-A. and Canuto, M. 2002. *Can Mediation Be Therapeutic for Crime Victims? An Evaluation of Victim's Experiences in Mediation with Young Offenders*. Department of Justice Canada. Available at www.justice.gc.ca/eng/rp-pr/cj-jp/victim/rr01_9/rr01_9.pdf

Wesel, U. 1985. *Frühformen des Rechts in vorstaatlichen Gesellschaften: Umrisse einer Frühgeschichte des Rechts bei Sammlern und Jägern und akephalen Ackerbauern und Hirten*, 1st ed. Frankfurt am Main: Suhrkamp.

Wright, M. 1991. *Justice for Victims and Offenders: A Restorative Response to Crime*. Milton Keynes: Open University Press.

Zehr, H. 1990. *Changing Lenses: A New Focus for Crime and Justice*. Scottdale PA: Herald Press.

Zinsstag, E. and Keenan, M. 2017. *Restorative Responses to Sexual Violence: Legal, Social and Therapeutic Dimensions*. London and New York: Routledge.

10

Restorative justice and child sexual abuse

Karen J. Terry

Introduction

Sexual assault is a pervasive problem globally. Much of this sexual victimization is perpetrated against children and adolescents, and most often by individuals they know well (Kilpatrick, Saunders and Smith, 2003). The effects of child sexual abuse (CSA) can be devastating, leading to physical, psychological and/or emotional trauma (Kilpatrick et al., 2003). These problems can be exacerbated by the criminal justice system, which has the potential to re-victimize abuse survivors through an arduous process in which their agency, dignity and power are challenged. Despite the potentially traumatic effects of this process, there have been few victim-centred alternatives implemented to replace or supplement the current criminal and civil processes for survivors of sexual abuse.

One such alternative is restorative justice, which provides an opportunity for offenders, victims and the community to come together and acknowledge the harms caused and determine a way forward to repair those harms (Bolitho and Freeman, 2016). In cases of CSA, some jurisdictions have begun to offer restorative justice alternatives, which have traditionally been applied in non-violent cases or in cases of youth offending. Though restorative justice alternatives for youth sexual offending are rare, evaluations show promising outcomes for both offenders and survivors who have participated (e.g., Daly, 2006; Bolitho and Freeman, 2016).

This aim of this chapter is to discuss the benefits and limitations of restorative justice programmes in cases of CSA. It begins with an overview of the prevalence and effects of CSA, the difficulties encountered by sexual abuse survivors throughout the criminal justice process and the restorative justice initiatives globally that are available to survivors of CSA. It then provides an overview of the efficacy of these initiatives, as evaluated through qualitative and quantitative measures, and the potential future directions of such programmes. Finally, it poses questions about what still needs to be studied in regard to restorative justice programmes for survivors of CSA. Evidence to date indicates positive outcomes for restorative justice practices for CSA offenders and survivors; however, future research in this area should include methodologically rigorous evaluations of existing programmes to better understand what initiatives are successful, when and for whom.

Prevalence of child sexual abuse

It is impossible to accurately estimate rates of sexual victimization because of the varying definitions of CSA and the delay in, or lack of, reporting (Wiseman, 2015). Estimates of CSA vary greatly depending on the source of information. Sources include official data sources, for example, the Uniform Crime Reports (UCR) in the US or the European Sourcebook of Crime and Criminal Justice Statistics, both compiled from reported offences; victimization surveys, for example, the National Crime Victimization Survey (NCVS) in the US or the International Crime Victimization Survey (ICVS); social service data, for example, the National Incidence Study (NIS) and the National Child Abuse and Neglect Data System (NCANDS) in the US; or empirical studies. However, a meta-analysis by Bolen and Scannapieco (1999) shows that as many as 30% of girls and 13% of boys are sexually victimized in their lifetime. Additionally, multiple scholars have found that those who are sexually assaulted in childhood experience more than one form of direct (assault, maltreatment, sexual victimization) or indirect (witnessed) victimization (Horwitz et al., 2001; Kilpatrick et al., 2003; Finkelhor et al., 2005; Finkelhor, 2008; Widom et al., 2008).

All sources of data about CSA indicate that there has been a decline in abuse cases in the 1990s in the US and other countries (see Child Maltreatment Report, 2001; Hanson and Morton-Bourgon, 2004; Jones and Finkelhor, 2004). For example, NCANDS data show a 63% decline in the rate of child sexual abuse between 1990 and 2011. This trend is supported by other sources, including the NCVS, which shows that sex offences against children ages 12–17 declined 56% between 1993 and 2000. The Minnesota Student Survey, which includes more than 100,000 student respondents each year, also showed that sexual abuse by family and non-family perpetrators decreased by 22% from 1992 to 2001. There is no clear explanation for the decline in rates of CSA. However, common explanations include awareness campaigns; education and training to those in organizations such as schools, churches and youth organizations; prevention programmes; criminal justice interventions, such as lengthier sentences, increased incarceration and registration and notification; and, treatment of offenders (Finkelhor, 2004). These strategies were apparent in the US, Australia, the UK, Sweden, Spain, New Zealand and other Western countries.

Despite the declining incidence of CSA, victimization surveys indicate that sexual victimization continues to be highly prevalent. These surveys are insightful in that they not only provide an understanding of the "dark figure" of abuse, or the rates of unreported offences, but also help to explain the reasons for underreporting. For instance, in the US, the NCVS is a collection of self-report data on all crimes against the household and individuals in the household who are over the age of 12. According to the NCVS, only about 37% of all crimes are reported to the police. Respondents stated that they do not report for various reasons, including that the offences are personal (particularly domestic violence and sexual offences); they do not believe the police could identify or arrest the perpetrator; they do not trust the police; they fear their own criminal behaviour (e.g., drug use) would be exposed; they fear their reputation would be damaged or they think the perpetrator will retaliate (Terry, 2013: 12). In regard to sexual victimization specifically, data from the NCVS indicate that sexual assault survivors are more likely to report their victimization if the perpetrator is male rather than female; if the perpetrator is black rather than white; if the perpetrator was young; if there were multiple perpetrators; if the abuse was committed by a stranger and if the perpetrator used a weapon (Hart and Rennison, 2003).

When CSA is reported, it is often years after the abuse occurred. Through adult retrospective studies of CSA survivors, scholars have provided data on rates of disclosure and reasons for the delay in disclosure of abuse. Though there are some validity and reliability concerns with adult retrospective studies of CSA, these studies provide insight into the variables related to abuse disclosure. For example, in a study of 228 adult female CSA survivors, Roesler and Weissmann-Wind (1994) found that one-third of the victims reported the abuse to authorities before age 18, and the average age of disclosure was 25.9. In a study of 204 female victims of child sexual abuse, Arata (1998) found that the average age of CSA victims was just over eight, and approximately 41% of victims disclosed the abuse at the time it occurred. Similarly, in their study of 45 adult female and 12 adult male CSA survivors, Lamb and Edgar-Smith (1994) found that CSA occurred on average at age ten, and 64% of the victims disclosed the abuse as adults. Smith, Letourneau, and Saunders (2000) also found that the majority of female CSA survivors waited more than eight years to report their victimization.

Researchers have identified various personal factors relating to the likelihood of disclosing abuse. These include: the age of the victim at the time the abuse occurred; the victim-perpetrator relationship; the gender of the victim and perpetrator; the cognitive abilities of the victim; the type of sexual abuse that occurred and the chance of negative consequences related to disclosure. A significant factor in whether a child will disclose abuse contemporaneously is whether that child thinks the person they report to will believe them (Lawson and Chaffin, 1992). The most important factor in whether a victim discloses abuse at all appears to the the victim-perpetrator relationship. Victims are less likely to report abuse and more likely to delay the report of child sexual abuse if the perpetrator is well known to the child, (Wyatt and Newcomb, 1990; Arata, 1998; Smith et al., 2000), and this relationship is most significant if the perpetrator is a relative or step-parent (Roesler and Weissmann-Wind, 1994; Arata, 1998; Goodman-Brown et al., 2003).

Effects of child sexual abuse

Scholars have extensively studied the impact of victimization, and research shows that sexual abuse during childhood often causes severe, irreparable harm to victims. Survivors of CSA may experience a range of adverse effects as a result of their victimization. In the short term, children who are sexually abused may experience feelings of guilt, shame, anxiety, fear, poor self-esteem and self-blame (Finkelhor, 1984). They also tend to show poor concentration in school, may act out physically and/or sexually against their peers or exhibit antisocial and delinquent behaviour generally.

CSA can lead to long-term psychological problems as well, and the consequences are cumulative over time (Papalia et al., 2017). Those who experience fear during the abusive acts themselves may later experience nervousness, specific anxiety about future sexual assaults and ultimately a generalized anxiety (Calhoun and Atkeson, 1991). As adults, survivors of CSA may develop anxiety-related disorders, such as phobias, panic disorders, obsessive-compulsive disorders and sleep disturbances (Lundberg-Love, 1999). Depression is particularly common in those who experienced ongoing abuse and where the perpetrator was someone close to the victim (Lundberg-Love, 1999). Survivors may also experience feelings of guilt, worthlessness and a sense of hopelessness, all of which may lead to suicidal thoughts and tendencies (Calhoun and Atkeson, 1991; Dube et al., 2005). As a result of their low self-esteem and self-blame, survivors of CSA may withdraw from social interaction and further perpetuate the cycle of depression. CSA also affects how survivors develop and maintain relationships, and may result in increased promiscuity, loss of satisfaction with sex or confusion over sexual identity (Ellis, Atkeson, and Calhoun, 1981; Kendall-Tackett et al., 1993; Bensley, Van Eenwyk and Simmons, 2000; Thompson et al., 2001).

Those who were sexually abused as children may adopt self-harming techniques as a result of their victimization. Many adolescents who were abused develop eating disorders and weight regulation practices such as anorexia and bulimia (Kendall-Tackett, Williams and Finkelhor, 1993; Dube et al., 2005; Wolfe et al., 2006). Other self-harming techniques include behaviours such as pulling out hair, cutting and burning themselves (Lundberg-Love, 1999). Though these behaviours are more common amongst females who are abused, male victims may also internalize their responses to abuse and behave in self-harming ways. As adults, both male and female survivors of CSA have an increased likelihood of developing substance abuse and alcohol addictions (Heffernan et al., 2000; MacMillan and Munn, 2001; Simpson and Miller, 2002; Dube et al., 2005; Wolfe et al., 2006).

By definition, survivors of CSA have been abused by those in positions of power over them. Perpetrators could include relatives, child care providers, sports coaches, teachers and clergy, amongst others. The dynamics of this relationship could lead to additional negative outcomes for the survivors. For example, research shows that those sexually abused by priests during their childhood have experienced particularly devastating consequences (Rosetti, 1995; Schmitz, 1996). Fater and Mullanney (2000) and van Wormer and Berns (2004) show that in addition to the above psychological effects of CSA, those abused by clergy feel a deep sense of betrayal and spiritual harm, and many victims distance themselves from God and the Catholic Church or renounced their faith altogether (Rosetti, 1995; McMackin, Keane and Kline, 2008). This can be particularly distressing for victims who typically turned to religion or spirituality for support in times of need or crisis. Gavrielides (2012: 625) identifies six themes of spiritual trauma resulting from CSA by clergy, including theological conflict, idiosyncratic silencing strategies, spiritual identity, existentialism, political anger and re-traumatization by the church.

CSA does not just affect the actual (primary) victim; it also affects the family of the victim and others who are close to them (secondary victims) (Ward and Inserto, 1990). These individuals can help the primary victim to cope with the abuse and respond to the psychological reactions that emerge. The parents and siblings of those who were abused, in particular, may experience emotional reactions to the abuse such as denial, disbelief, remorse, regret and even trauma. When the abuse is interfamilial, the family is likely to go through significant changes, because in most cases either the victim or perpetrator will be removed from the home (Ward and Inserto, 1990). This uprooting may cause disruption for the entire family, and disruption may create emotional trauma for all involved – particularly the victim, who may feel responsible for the upheaval. CSA within an institutional context may result in additional types of trauma for secondary victims. For instance, clergy abuse could lead the families of victim-survivors to question their spirituality and the role of the church in society. This could even cause a breakdown of family relationships, as families of victims struggle to understand the abuse in the context of the sacraments and rituals previously performed in the church (Gavrielides, 2012)

In sum, a large percentage of the population are sexually victimized as youths, and this victimization can lead to significant harms. The psychological, emotional, physical and behavioural effects of CSA can be debilitating to some survivors and permeate all aspects of their lives in both the short and long term (Fater and Mullaney, 2000). Many victims of CSA do not report the abuse contemporaneously, if at all, and the psychological harms of victimization may increase over time. It is critical to understand ways in which these harms can be repaired, which rarely happens through the criminal justice system alone.

Responding to child sexual abuse: retributive versus restorative justice approaches

Most individuals who are sexually abused as children do not ever disclose the abuse to anyone, let alone civil authorities. Those who do report often do so years after the abuse took place.

Whether victims of CSA report their abuse as children or years later in adulthood, the criminal justice process is a psychologically taxing experience for most survivors of CSA. The criminal justice system follows a retributive process, and the goals of this system – retribution, deterrence, incapacitation and rehabilitation – focus primarily on offenders. In this process, a crime is considered an act against the state, and the state punishes offenders for wrongdoings. Actors in the system (the police, prosecutors and judges) represent the state and the best interests of the state, and victims have little or no say in the process. Additionally, many jurisdictions have statutes of limitation for certain crimes, and a delay in disclosure may render the crime unprosecutable. When victim-survivors do report CSA within the time allowed by the statutes of limitation, the criminal justice process that follows causes many to feel re-victimized. Gutheil (2000) calls this feeling of re-victimization "critogenesis", or the exacerbation or genesis of a condition by legal processes; rather than addressing, helping and reducing victimization, the criminal justice system leads to further harm for survivors of sexual abuse. The question then becomes, if the retributive process alone is not sufficient to address and repair the harms done to victims of CSA, what other initiatives can be implemented to assist them? One possible approach is restorative justice, though any such programmes initiated for cases of CSA must be done with caution.

Unlike the retributive focus of the criminal justice system, restorative justice is a theoretical approach to wrongdoing that focuses on repairing victim harm. While the criminal justice system views crimes as an act against the state, restorative justice approaches considered crimes to be acts against a person. This gives the victim-survivor agency that is lacking in the criminal justice system. And, while the criminal justice system gives the state all of the decision-making power for how to respond to an abuser, restorative justice approaches are a cooperative process in which all parties of a wrongdoing – including the offender, the victim and the community – work together to repair that harm. Restorative justice is not a single programme; rather, it is a process that varies depending on the type of crime, type of offenders and needs for reparation. There is no single consistent definition of restorative justice, but the most comprehensive definition is "an ethos with practical goals, amongst which is to restore harm by including affected parties in a (direct or indirect) encounter, and a process of understanding through voluntary and honest dialogue" (Gavrielides, 2012: 621).

Restorative justice programmes are delivered in various forms, such as face-to-face meetings, circles or conferences; restitution; community service and other emotional and/or spiritual programmes (Jones and Compton, 2003; Center for Justice and Reconciliation at Prison Fellowship International, 2005). Whichever process is utilized, the goal is to reach an agreement about how an offender will make amends for the harm caused to the victim. This is not done through forced apologies or through offender blaming and shaming, which can lead to withdrawal, avoidance or further offending. Rather, a truly restorative process includes building relationships, creating connections, listening, understanding and responding to the needs of the situation. Importantly, this process should also reduce the likelihood that the offender will recidivate and will help the offender reintegrate into society (Bennett, 2006). According to Braithwaite (1989; Braithwaite and Petit, 1990), the reintegrative shaming process of restorative justice is more likely to reduce the reoffending than state-imposed sanctions through the conventional retributive justice process.

In theory, restorative justice should be applicable to all types of crimes, from vandalism to sexual assault to genocide. Yet it has traditionally been used most often in cases of youth offending, and rarely in cases of gendered or sexual violence. It is particularly rare in cases of CSA, and there are no published studies of restorative justice programmes with adult perpetrators of sexual violence where those abused are still minors. Restorative programmes are most common in Australia, New Zealand, Canada and the UK, with some jurisdictions in the US and other countries adopting individualized restorative programmes. In the UK, for example, restorative justice programmes are now offered by at various points in the criminal justice process. Pre-sentence guidelines, however, note that restorative justice should be applicable to nearly all offences except for those involving domestic violence, hate crimes and sexual offences (Ministry of Justice, 2014). Leaders in New Zealand have stated that child sexual offences and other forms of family violence are the least likely to be a good fit for restorative justice practices, given the power imbalance between the perpetrators and the victims (Jülich, 2006; Proietti-Scifoni and Daly, 2011). Daly (2006) noted that restorative justice has rarely been applied to cases of sexual assault for youths or adults, and as such there is little empirical evidence about its efficacy. Additionally, Daly (2008) stated that it is difficult to compare established and alternative justice responses to sexual assault because there are so few jurisdictions in the world where such pro-grammes exist. The question then remains, should restorative justice programmes be offered to adults who were sexually abused as children, and in what cases would this be an effective alternative to the current criminal and/or civil justice processes?

As part of the Royal Commission's investigation into institutional responses to child sex-ual abuse in Australia, Bolitho and Freeman (2016) evaluated the restorative justice initia-tives involving CSA that have been implemented globally. They found only 15 sites that offer restorative justice programmes in combination with the criminal justice response to repair the harm following child sexual abuse or similar crimes, and they summarize the 30 evaluations of these programmes. Of these 15 programmes, only three were geared specifically towards sexual offending, and none of them were specifically for victims of institutional abuse (e.g., abuse within the Catholic Church, schools or other organizations). The programmes varied in aim, scope, length and when they are delivered. Programmes were delivered as diversion out of the criminal justice system, following plea negotiations, after conviction or upon release from custody, when the offender is reintegrated into the community. The evaluations of these programmes varied in terms of methodological pedagogy and rigour. The limited empirical evidence indicates positive outcomes for those who participated in the programmes; for victim-survivors, this included a feeling that the process was procedurally fair and worthwhile, and it ultimately led to an improved feeling of well-being (Bolitho and Freeman, 2016). Outcomes were more likely to be positive when certain conditions were met, the most important of which were: specialization and expertise of the facilitator; vigilant screening for suitability to the programme; understanding of participant needs and readiness; and inclusion of sex offender-specific treatment for the offenders (Bolitho and Freeman, 2016).

The most rigorous of the studies in the Royal Commission report was the Sexual Assault Archival Study (SAAS) in South Australia. In the SAAS, Daly (2006) compared outcomes of youth sexual violence cases that were finalized either through family conferencing, formal cau-tion or in youth court over a six-year period. The SAAS produced several important findings, most notably that the family conferencing model leads to an early admission of guilt from the offender. This is advantageous to both the victims (as the admission of guilt provides vindica-tion for their experience) and for the youth offenders (who receive referral to a conference and avoid detention) (Daly, 2006). Daly also noted that court cases take twice as long to finalize as family conferencing cases, and the court cases were also more likely to shift jurisdiction or require the victim to attend a court proceeding an average of six times. The recidivism out-come, however, did not vary by type of action taken; rather, future reoffending was predicted by offence history (Daly, 2006).

The other two restorative justice programmes that Bolitho and Freeman (2016) identified that are specifically geared towards sexual offending are RESTORE (in Arizona, in the United

States) and Project Restore (in New Zealand). RESTORE is a restorative justice programmes for adults convicted of misdemeanour and felony sexual assaults. Though it is a prosecutor-referred programme, it is voluntary and requires that perpetrators acknowledge their offences, meet with relevant primary and secondary victims and create a plan for redress for the harms they caused (Koss, 2014). Inspired by RESTORE, Project Restore is also geared towards the reparation of harm for victims of sexual assault, but it was formed by survivors of sexual violence (Jülich et al., 2010). Both are primarily geared towards adult victims of sexual violence, though they include some adults who were sexually abused as children. The evaluations of both programmes involve small samples (22 cases for RESTORE and four cases with 18 participants for Project Restore), but the evidence indicates positive outcomes for those who participate (Jülich et al., 2010; Koss, 2014). Both studies include extensive qualitative evaluations of the experiences of the participants, and indicate that participation in conferences improved the well-being of the survivors. Additionally, survivors perceived the conferences as worthwhile and procedurally fair (Bolitho and Freeman, 2016).

Most restorative justice programmes are either independent of the criminal justice system or are managed by non-profit organizations but accept referrals from the criminal justice system (Stothart, 2011). Bolitho and Freeman (2016: 48–50) identified 29 programmes globally that are parallel with, or located independently of, the formal criminal or civil justice systems. Of these, eight of the programmes are specifically for adult victims of sexual assault and four are geared towards victims of comparable harms (e.g., hate crimes). Some of the programmes are linked to single institutions where abuse occurred (e.g., the abuse by Christian Brothers at Mount Cashel Orphanage in Canada; see Hughes 1991), while others are linked to a single case of abuse (e.g., the case of "Lucy" in the UK, an adult survivor of CSA; see McGlynn, Westmarland and Godden, 2012).

Some of the programmes described by Bolitho and Freeman (2016) focus primarily on reducing the likelihood of recidivism for sexual offenders. One example of such a programme is Circles of Support and Accountability (COSA), established in Canada in 1994 and since expanded to various parts of the United Kingdom and the US (Hannem and Petrunik, 2007). The goal of COSA is for family, friends, social agencies and other community volunteers (e.g., faith groups) to provide support to ex-offenders and reduce their chances of reoffending (Wilson and Prinzo, 2001). The programme is evidence-based and reduces recidivism for offenders by approximately 70% (Wilson, Picheca and Prinzo, 2007). Though some reports have been critical of the methodology used in COSA evaluation studies (Elliot and Zaiac, 2015), it is clear that COSA is beneficial for sexual offenders who are trying to re-enter the community. For example, since the Department of Corrections in Minnesota implemented COSA, it has found a 40% reduction in rearrests for any offense (and a non-significant reduction in sexual offense recidivism) (Duwe, 2012).

Approximately a third of the programmes described by Bolitho and Freeman (2016) are specifically geared towards reparation for abuse within an institutional context, and several of these are associated with, or run by, the Catholic Church or other faith-based institutions.[1] Historically, the majority of cases of sexual abuse within the Catholic Church have been resolved through either criminal offences or torts (Gavrielides and Coker, 2005). Yet few survivors of clergy abuse feel that the harm they experienced has been repaired after participating in those processes. Gavrielides (2012) notes that many survivors of clergy abuse continue to experience feelings of pain and neglect after pursuing justice through state laws.

---

1 It is likely that additional restorative justice programmes exist in addition to these 29 listed. However, they may not have any published material or evaluations of their programmes and thus were not included in this analysis.

The Catholic Church, it seems, would be the ideal institution in which to establish restorative justice programmes for victim-survivors since harm was established by both the individual priests who committed the abuse and the Catholic Church hierarchy who did not act expeditiously to remove abusive priests or care for the victims who were harmed. Additionally, restorative justice aims to realize forgiveness and reconciliation, which are both principles and values found in Christianity (Gavrielides and Coker, 2005.) As knowledge about the nature and scope of sexual abuse crisis in the Catholic Church started to become apparent in 2002, many in the Catholic community began calling for an increase in the implementation of restorative justice programmes.[2] The Albany Catholic Worker Community (2002: 389), for example, stated that "the Church is broken" and called for each diocese to implement Victim-Offender Reconciliation Programmes (VORPs) and family group conferences. They noted that restorative justice processes have led to personal and communal healing for centuries (p. 391), and that such a process could help to heal their broken church.

Many dioceses began to implement restorative justice programmes based on abuse cases that happened within those dioceses or within institutions run by the Catholic Church. Gavrielides (2012: 633–636) published case studies of five such programmes: Mount Cashel Orphanage in Newfoundland, Canada; the Milwaukee Archdiocese in Wisconsin, US; the Restorative Justice Council on Sexual Misconduct in St Paul, Minnesota, in the US; The Netherlands, as a result of the Deetman Commission; and Faith Communities Affirming Restorative Experiences Programme in Ontario, Canada. Gavrielides outlines the principles, goals and structures of each programme and provides outcome information where available. However, he notes that restorative justice initiatives such as these are largely untested and evaluation is limited (Gavrielides: 636.) It is also worth noting that all of the victim-survivor participants in these programmes are adults, and their abuse occurred years earlier. It is not clear, however, how the delay in disclosure of abuse affects the efficacy of the programmes for those who participate.

Restorative justice: what works

Traditionally, scholars have raised some concerns about restorative justice as it is applied to gendered and family violence (Curtis-Fawley and Daly, 2005; Daly, 2006; Jülich, 2006), and these concerns are also applicable to survivors of CSA. One such concern is the inherent power differential in a perpetrator-victim relationship (Cossins, 2008). Some adult survivors of CSA have stated that the abuser maintains the control and power in the relationship, and they do not believe restorative justice programmes can help to alleviate this differential (Jülich, 2006). Survivors have also said they believe offenders can manipulate the process, saying what they think others want to hear without really meaning the apology. Another hesitation with survivors is their distrust of the community, or those who stood by as they were being abused as children (Jülich, 2006). This criticism could apply to a diverse group of people, from the family members to the Catholic Church hierarchy. Members of the community may also inadvertently reinforce the victim-blaming, or may feel some loyalty towards the offender (Daly, 2006). Either of these can undermine the restorative process for victim-survivors. And finally, feminists have expressed a concern for victim safety in the informal restorative justice programmes (Proietti-Scifoni and Daly, 2011).

Despite these challenging dynamics of restorative justice programmes for adult survivors of CSA, it is important to consider the potential benefits of creating and expanding such

---

2 For an exhaustive review of the sexual abuse crisis in the Catholic Church, see: John Jay College (2004); Terry et al., (2011); and Terry, 2015.

programmes. There is a substantial body of literature on the benefits of restorative justice programmes generally (e.g., see Strang, 2002; Strang et al., 2006), and the few restorative justice
initiatives in place for sexual assault survivors have shown the potential to repair harm while
also reintegrating offenders into society. And, when survivors of CSA are asked what they want
from the justice process, they are primarily interested in restorative justice-based responses
(Gavrielides, 2012). These include factors such as full disclosure of the wrongs done to them,
prevention and assurance that the offender will not abuse again, empowerment, validation and
an open process without prejudgements (Gavrielides, 2012; Pelikan, 2012). Most importantly,
victim-survivors want an opportunity for their stories to be heard (Jülich, 2006), and restorative justice programmes provide a forum for that to happen (Daly, 2006). Additionally, these
programmes allow victim-survivors to express their feelings and fears and have these truths
validated by others. Having their voices heard is empowering to the victims (Pelikan, 2012),
and is often not possible during the criminal justice process (Daly, 2006.) Restorative justice
programmes may also be beneficial to the offenders. Not only is the offender required to accept
responsibility in restorative justice programmes, but other members of the community – often
their family members – witness the offenders assuming responsibility and taking accountability
for their actions (Jülich, 2006).

Future directions for restorative justice and child sexual abuse

Despite the observed benefits of restorative justice programmes for both offenders and survivors of CSA, it is necessary to proceed with caution when considering implementing them on
a wider basis. CSA causes a unique set of harms, and restorative justice programmes cannot
be uniformly implemented in response to all CSA offences. Additionally, restorative justice
programmes for CSA should only be administered to adult survivors, and only in cases that
are initiated by the victim. Given the reasons for the delays in disclosure, the close relationship
between most victims and perpetrators, the power differential between adult perpetrators and
the children they abused, and the potentially devastating effects of CSA on children, it would
be irresponsible to have children participate in any programmes in which they face adult abusers. To do so would inevitably exacerbate the harms that had been caused by the abuse itself.
And, when restorative justice programmes are administered for adult survivors of CSA, they
should be mediated by an independent party (e.g., not a Catholic Church official in cases of
clergy abuse), with a skilled facilitator, and should provide extended psychological care for the
survivors once the programme is complete. Only through such a holistic approach can restorative justice programmes fulfil their goals of reparation.

One of the most significant barriers to implementing restorative justice programmes more
systematically for survivors of CSA is the lack of empirical support for such initiatives. The few
programmes that have been evaluated show that restorative justice has the normative potential
to repair the harms done to survivors of CSA in cases where the offenders, victims and communities are willing to work together. However, the empirical studies evaluate small samples
or involve specific types of offenders, and are not generalizable to the larger population of CSA
offenders and survivors. The positive outcomes from these studies, however, indicate that such
programmes may be an appropriate mechanism for reparation given certain conditions. Perhaps
the strongest case can be made to implement further restorative justice programmes for cases
of institutional abuse where members of the larger community (e.g., hierarchy of the Catholic
Church) also participate in the reparation process. These programmes can be complementary
to criminal and civil justice options, when viable, and should be user-led, voluntary and confidential (Gavrielides, 2012). The emotional and spiritual trauma survivors experienced may best

be repaired through the open, honest and supportive dialogue of restorative justice programmes rather than civil and criminal pathways alone.

Many empirical questions remain in regard to how effective restorative justice programmes are, for whom, in what time frame and in what context, and these questions should be addressed in future studies. For example, how is "success" defined when discussing restorative justice programmes? It can (and should) include factors as diverse as reparations for individuals who were sexual abused as children to successful reintegration of offenders into society without reoffending. A second question is, for whom is restorative justice most likely to be successful, and what variables should be considered? For instance, are restorative justice programmes more successful for those who report at different times (e.g., within ten years of the abuse occurring, compared to after 30 years) and is it dependent on the victim-perpetrator relationship (e.g., intra- or extra-familial, within an institutional context)? A third question is, when do you measure whether a programme is successful? A survivor may feel empowered, for example, immediately after face-to-face conferencing but years later may begin experiencing traumatic effects of the abuse. This leads to the question of what resources are available to survivors after the completion of restorative justice programmes and who provides such resources? Restorative justice is a holistic approach that requires myriad resources to repair the long-term harms of abuse, and those needs will vary greatly by survivor. And finally, do the punitive laws against sex offenders in most Western cultures have an effect on the provision of, or efficacy of, restorative justice initiatives? It is possible that offenders in the US, for example, are less likely to accept responsibility for committing a sexual offence if that means they are required to remain on a sex offender registry for life (along with notification to the community and residence restrictions in most jurisdictions). With so few programmes to evaluate globally, it is not yet possible to answer these questions.

Though rigorous, quantitative evaluations of restorative justice programmes are limited, the published case studies of individual restorative justice programmes indicate that restorative justice approaches are advantageous in the few cases of CSA in which they have been utilized. Restorative justice programmes can help survivors to take an active role in holding offenders accountable for their actions, participate directly in the condemnation of wrong and gain a sense of closure to their abuse (Anderson, 2015). Importantly, the limited number of survivors of CSA and offenders who have participated in restorative justice programmes have generally viewed it as a positive experience. Such programmes can serve as a tool of empowerment for survivors of CSA, restoring both their human dignity and repairing the feelings of neglect and pain that can sometimes result from criminal and civil law processes (Gavrielides, 2012). Restorative justice and CSA are a contested area of practice, however, and scholars recommend that "the development of restorative justice in cases of sexual violence must, necessarily, be cautious at this stage, and must be preceded by further debate, evaluations and careful planning," (McGlynn, Westmarland and Godden, 2012: 230).

Additionally, the benefits of restorative justice programmes must be weighed against any risk of future harm (Bolitho and Freeman, 2016). According to Bolitho and Freeman (2016: 45), restorative approaches at a minimum are doing no worse than standard criminal justice approaches to reduce rates of reoffending. But these programmes require buy-in on a local level, resources to provide the programmes and long-term care, as well as increased awareness about what restorative justice is and how it can positively affect change (Ministry of Justice, 2014). What is clear is that the criminal and civil justice options are not sufficient at repairing the harm experienced by victims of CSA, and restorative justice initiatives may be able to provide survivors with agency and restore their human dignity, provide them with a greater sense of empowerment and repair the devastating harm that results from such a personal violation. As scholars and practitioners look towards the future of restorative justice programmes, they should consider the true potential of such initiatives for survivors of CSA.

References

Anderson, J. 2015. Comprehending and Rehabilitating Roman Catholic Clergy Offenders of Child Sexual Abuse, *Journal of Child Sexual Abuse*, 24: 772–795.

The Albany Catholic Worker Community. 2002. Wiping Away the Tears: A Faith Community Responds to Clergy Sexual Abuse in the Roman Catholic Church, *Contemporary Justice Review*, 5(4): 389–391.

Arata, C.M. 1998. To Tell or Not to Tell: Current Functioning of Child Sexual Abuse Survivors Who Disclosed their Victimization, *Child Maltreatment*, 3: 63–71.

Bennett, C. 2006. Taking the Sincerity Out of Saying Sorry: Restorative Justice as Ritual, *Journal of Applied Philosophy*, 23(2): 127–143.

Bensley, L.S., Van Eenwyk, J. and Simmons, K.W. 2000. Self-reported Childhood Sexual and Physical Abuse and Adult HIV-Risk Behaviors and Heavy Drinking, *American Journal of Preventative Medicine*, 18(2): 151–158.

Bolen, R. and Scannapieco, M. 1999. Prevalence of Child Sexual Abuse: A Corrective Meta-Analysis, *Social Service Review*, 73: 281–313.

Bolitho, J. and Freeman, K. 2016. *The Use and Effectiveness of Restorative Justice in Criminal Justice Systems Following Child Sexual Abuse or Comparable Harms*. Sydney, Australia: Royal Commission into Institutional Responses to Child Sexual Abuse.

Braithwaite, J. 1989. *Crime, Shame and Reintegration*. Cambridge: Cambridge University Press.

Braithwaite, J. and Petit, P. 1990. *Not Just Desserts*. Oxford: Clarendon Press.

Calhoun, K.S. and Atkeson, B.M. 1991. *Treatment of Rape Victims: Facilitating Psychosocial Adjustment*. Elmsford, NY: Pergamon.

Child Maltreatment Report. 2001. Washington, DC: Children's Bureau, Administration on Children, Youth and Families.

Cossins, A. 2008. Restorative Justice and Child Sexual Offences, *British Journal of Criminology*, 48(3): 359–378.

Curtis-Fawley, S. and Daly, K. 2005. Gendered Violence and Restorative Justice: The Views of Victim Advocates, *Violence Against Women*, 11(5): 603–638.

Daly, K. 2006. Restorative Justice and Sexual Assault, *British Journal of Criminology*, 46(2): 334–356.

Daly, K. 2008. Setting the Record Straight and a Call for Radical Change: A Reply to Annie Cossins on Restorative Justice and Child Sexual Offences, *British Journal of Criminology*, 48(4): 557–566.

Devoe, E.R. and Coulborn-Faller, K. 1999. The Characteristics of Disclosure among Children Who May Have Been Sexually Abused, *Child Maltreatment: Journal of the American Professional Society on the Abuse of Children*, 4: 217–227.

Dube, S.R., Anda, R.F., Whitfield, C.L., Brown, D.W., Felitti, V.J., Dong, M. and Giles, W.H. 2005. Long-Term Consequences of Childhood Sexual Abuse By Gender of Victim, *American Journal of Preventative Medicine*, 28(5): 430–438.

Duwe, G. 2012. Can Circles of Support and Accountability (COSA) Work in the United States? Preliminary Results from a Randomized Experiment in Minnesota, *Sexual Abuse: A Journal of Research and Treatment*, 25(2): 143–165.

Elliot, I.A. and Zaiac, G. 2015. The Implementation of Circles of Support and Accountability in the United States, *Aggression and Violent Behavior*, 25: 113–123.

Ellis, E.M., Atkeson, B.M. and Calhoun, K.S. 1981. Sexual Dysfunction in Victims of Rape. *Women and Health*, 5: 39–47.

Family Life Development Center, Cornell University. National Child Abuse and Neglect Data System (NCANDS), Detailed Case Data Component (DCDC). *National Data Archive on Child Abuse and Neglect*. Available at www.ndacan.cornell.edu/ndacan/Datasets/Abstracts/DatasetAbstract_NCANDS_General.html

Fater, K. and Mullaney, J. 2000. The Lived Experience of Adult Male Survivors Who Allege Childhood Sexual Abuse by Clergy, *Issues in Mental Health Nursing*, 21: 281–295.

Finkelhor, D. 1984. *Child Sexual Abuse: New Theory and Research*. New York: Free Press.

Finkelhor, D. 2004. Church News Obscures Overall Decline in Abuse. *USA Today*, p. 13a

Finkelhor, D. 2008. *Childhood Victimization: Violence, Crime, and Abuse in the Lives of Young People*. New York: Oxford University Press.

Finkelhor, D., Ormrod, R.K., Turner, H.K. and Hamby, S.L. 2005. The Victimization of Children and Youth: A Comprehensive, National Survey, *Child Maltreatment*, 10(1): 5–25.

Gavrielides, T. 2012. Clergy Child Sexual Abuse and the Restorative Justice Dialogue, *Journal of Church and State*, 55(4): 617–639.

Gavrielides, T. and Coker, D. 2005. Restoring Faith: Resolving the Roman Catholic Church's Sexual Scandals Through Restorative Justice, *Contemporary Justice Review*, 8(4): 345–365.

Goodman-Brown, T.B., Edelstein, R.S., Goodman, G.S., Jones, D.P. and Gordon, D. 2003. Why Children Tell: A Model of Children's Disclosure of Sexual Abuse, *Child Abuse and Neglect*, 27: 525–540.

Hannem, S. and Petrunik, M. 2007. Circles of Support and Accountability: A Community Justice Initiative for the Reintegration of High Risk Sex Offenders, *Contemporary Justice Review*, 10(2): 153–171.

Hanson, R.K. and Morton-Bourgon, K. 2004. *Predictors of Sexual Recidivism: An Updated Meta-Analysis: (Research Rep. No 2004–02)*. Ottawa: Public Safety and Emergency Preparedness Canada.

Hart, T.C. and Rennison, C. 2003. *Reporting Crime to the Police, 1992–2000*.Washington, DC: U.S. Department of Justice, Bureau of Justice Statistics.

Heffernan, K., Cloitre, M., Tardiff, K., Marzuk, P.M., Portera, L. and Leon, A.C. 2000. Childhood Trauma as a Correlate of Lifetime Opiate Use in Psychiatric Patients, *Addictive Behaviors*, 25(5): 797–803.

Horwitz, A.V., Widom, C.S., McLaughlin, J. and White, H.R. 2001. The Impact of Child Abuse and Neglect on Adult Mental Health, *Journal of Social Behavior*, 42: 184–201.

Hughes, S.H.S. 1991. *Royal Commission of Inquiry into the Response of the Newfoundland Criminal Justice System to Complaints*. Newfoundland: Office of the Queen's Printer.

John Jay College Research Team. 2004. *The Nature and Scope of Sexual Abuse of Minors by Catholic Priests and Deacons in the United States, 1950–2002*. Washington, DC: United States Conference of Catholic Bishops.

John Jay College Research Team. 2006. *The Nature and Scope of Sexual Abuse of Minors by Catholic Priests and Deacons in the United States, 1950–2002: Supplementary Data Analysis*. Washington, DC: United States Conference of Catholic Bishops.

Jones, L.M. and Finkelhor, D. 2004. *Sexual Abuse Decline in the 1990s: Evidence for Possible Causes* (Juvenile Justice Bulletin No. NCJ1999298). Washington, DC: Office of Juvenile Justice & Delinquency Prevention.

Jones, T.S. 2003. Restorative Justice Programs in Schools. In T.S. Jones and R. Compton (eds.) *Kids Working It Out: Stories and Strategies for Making Peace in Our Schools*. San Francisco, CA: Jossey-Bass.

Jülich, S. 2006. Views of Justice among Survivors of Historical Child Sexual Abuse, *Theoretical Criminology*, 10(1): 125–138.

Jülich, S., Buttle, J., Cummins, C. and Freeborn, E. 2010. *Project Restore: An exploratory Study of Restorative Justice and Sexual Violence*. Auckland: Auckland University of Technology. Available at www.academia. edu/274691/Project_Restore_An_Exploratory_Study_of_Restorative_Justice_and_Sexual_Violence

Kendall-Tackett, K.A., Williams, L.M. and Finkelhor, D. 1993. Impact of Sexual Abuse on Children: A Review and Synthesis of Recent Empirical Studies, *Psychological Bulletin*, 113: 164–180.

Kilpatrick, D.G, Saunders, B.E. and Smith, D.W. 2003. *Youth Victimization: Prevalence and Implications: NIJ Research in Brief*. Washington, DC: U.S, Department of Justice, Office of Justice Programs.

Koss, M.P. 2014. The RESTORE Program of Restorative Justice for Sex Crimes: Vision, Process, and Outcomes, *Journal of Interpersonal Violence*, 29(9): 1623–1660.

Lamb, S. and Edgar-Smith, S. 1994. Aspects of disclosure: Mediators of Outcome of Childhood Sexual Abuse, *Journal of Interpersonal Violence*, 9: 307–326.

Lawson, L. and Chaffin, M. 1992. False Negatives in Sexual Abuse Disclosure Interviews: Incidence and Influence of Caretaker's Belief in Abuse in Cases of Accidental Abuse Discovery by Diagnosis of STD, *Journal of Interpersonal Violence*, 7: 532–542.

Lundberg-Love, P.K. 1999.The Resilience of the Human Psyche: Recognition and Treatment of the Adult Survivor of Incest. In M.A. Paludi (ed.) *The Psychology of Sexual Victimization: A Handbook*. Westport, CT: Greenwood.

MacMillian, H.L. and Munn, C. 2001. The Sequelae of Child Maltreatment, *Current Opinion in Psychiatry*, 14(4): 325–331.

McGlynn, C., Westmarland, N. and Godden, N. 2012. 'I Just Wanted Him to Hear Me': Sexual Violence and the Possibilities of Restorative Justice, *Journal of Law and Society*, 39(2): 213–240.

McMackin, R.A., Keane, T.M. and Kline, P.M. 2008. Introduction to Special Issue on Betrayal and Recovery: Understanding the Trauma of Clergy Sexual Abuse, *Journal of Child Sexual Abuse*, 17(3–4): 197–200.

Ministry of Justice. 2014. *Pre-Sentence Restorative Justice*. Available at www.gov.uk/government/uploads/system/uploads/attachment_data/file/312426/pre-sentence-restorative-justice.pdf

National Institute of Justice. 1992. *When the Victim Is a Child*, 2nd ed. Washington, DC: U.S. Department of Justice, Office of Justice Programs.

Papalia, N.L., Luebbers, S., Ogloff, J.R.P., Cutajar, M. and Mullen, P.E. 2017. The Long-Term Co-Occurrence of Psychiatric Illness and Behavioral Problems Following Child Sexual Abuse, *Australia and New Zealand Journal of Psychiatry*, 51(6): 604–613.

Pelikan, C. 2012. Restorative Justice and Partnership Violence: Austria. In T.Gavrielides (ed.) *Rights and Restorative within Youth Justice*. Whitby, ON: de Sitter Publications.

Roesler, T.A. and Weissmann-Wind, T.A. 1994. Telling the Secret: Adult Women Describe their Disclosures of Incest, *Journal of Interpersonal Violence*, 9: 327–338.

Rossetti, S.J. 1995. The Impact of Child Sexual Abuse on Attitudes Towards God and the Catholic Church, *Child Abuse and Neglect*, 19: 1469–1481.

Schmitz, R.E. 1996. Of Dinosaurs, Carrier Pigeons and Disappearing Priest, *America*, 175(10): 7–11.

Simpson, T.L. and Miller, W.R. 2002. Concomitance Between Childhood Sexual and Physical Abuse and Substance Use Problems: A Review, *Clinical Psychology Review*, 22: 27–77.

Smith, DW, Letourneau, E.J. and Saunders, B.E. 2000. Delay in Disclosure of Childhood rape: Results from a National Survey. *Child Abuse and Neglect*, 24: 273–287.

Sorenson, T. and Snow, B. 1991. How Children Tell: The Process of Disclosure in Child Sexual Abuse, *Child Welfare*, 70: 3–15.

Stothart, C. 2011. Restorative Justice for Young Sex Offenders, *Community Care* (1867): 20–21.

Strang, H. 2002. *Repair or Revenge: Victims and Restorative Justice*. Oxford: Clarendon Press.

Strang, H., Sherman, L. Angel, C.M., Bennett, S., Newbury-Birch, D. and Inkpen, N. 2006. Victim Evaluations of Face-to-Face Restorative Justice Conferences: A Quasi-Experimental Analysis, *Journal of Social Sciences*, 62: 281–306.

Summit, R.C. 1983. The Child Sexual Abuse Accommodation Syndrome, *Child Abuse and Neglect*, 7: 177–193.

Terry, K. 2013. *Sexual Offenses and Offenders: Theory, Practice and Policy*. Belmont, CA: Cengage.

Terry, K.J. 2015. Child Sexual Abuse within the Catholic Church: A Review of Global Perspectives, *International Journal of Comparative and Applied Criminal Justice*, 39(2): 139–154.

Terry, K.J., Smith, M.L., Schuth, K., Kelly, J., Vollman, B. and Massey, C. 2011. *Causes and Context of the Sexual Abuse Crisis in the Catholic Church*. Washington, DC: United States Conference of Catholic Bishops.

Thompson, K.M., Wonderlich, S.A., Crosby, R.D. and Mitchell, J.E. 2001. Sexual Victimization and Adolescent Weight Regulation Practices: A Test across Three Community Based Samples, *Child Abuse and Neglect*, 25: 291–305.

U.S. Department of Health and Human Services. 2010. Fourth National Incidence Study of Child Abuse and Neglect (NIS-4), 2004–2009. Available at www.nis4.org/nishome.asp

van Wormer, K. and Berns, L. 2004. The Impact of Priest Sexual Abuse: Female Survivors' Narrative, *Affilia*, 19: 53–67.

Widom, C.S., Czaja, S.J. and Dutton, M.A. 2008. Childhood Victimization and Lifetime Revictimization, *Child Abuse & Neglect*, 32(8): 785–796.

Wilson, R.J., Picheca, J. and Prinzo, M. 2007. Evaluating the Effectiveness of Professionally Facilitated Volunteerism in Community-Based Management of High-Risk Sex Offenders: Part Two – A Comparison of Recidivism Rates, *The Howard Journal of Criminal Justice*, 46(4): 327–337.

Wilson, R.J. and Prinzo, M. 2001. Circles of Support: A Restorative Justice Initiative. In M.H. Miner and E. Coleman (eds.) *Sex Offender Treatment: Accomplishments, Challenges and Future Directions*. Binghamton, NY: Haworth Press, pp. 59–77.

Wiseman, J. 2015. *Incidence and Prevalence of Sexual Offending (Part I): SOMAPI Research Brief*. Washington, DC: US Department of Justice, Office of Sex Offender Sentencing, Monitoring, Apprehending, Registering and Tracking.

Wolfe, D.A., Francis, K.J. and Straatman, A.L. 2006. Child Abuse in Religiously-Affiliated Institutions: Long-term Impact on Men's Mental Health, *Child Abuse and Neglect*, 30: 205–212.

Wyatt, G.E. and Newcomb, M.D. 1990. Internal and External Mediators of Women's Sexual Abuse in Childhood, *Journal of Consulting & Clinical Psychology*, 58: 758–767.

11

Complex cases of restorative justice after serious crime

Creating and enabling spaces for those with disability[1]

Jane Bolitho

Introduction

This chapter explores the potential of restorative justice to meet the needs of participants in complex cases following crime. What is meant by 'complex'? The Oxford dictionary defines 'complex' as 'consisting of many different and connected parts' and 'not easy to analyse or understand; complicated or intricate' (English Oxford Living Dictionary, accessed 2017). Most simply, what makes something 'complex' is the increased number of components, the nature of those components and the subsequently multifarious network that exists between components. In one sense, all crime is 'complex' because each event involves different individuals, different harms, different circumstances and impact; each event is completely idiosyncratic. In the restorative justice literature, 'complex' is generally understood to mean cases where in addition to a crime having occurred, there are particular risks in addressing the harm (e.g. see Gavrielides, 2012). This may be because there is little practice in that area, or there is less established about what works. Usually though, complexity is seen to relate to situations where the differentials in power (inherent in some crimes, and in some cases) make the potential for further harm more likely. This chapter focuses on restorative justice and disability, which is an area where little is known and the potential for further harm does exist because of the particular power dynamics in the restorative space.

In the *Convention on the Rights of Persons with Disabilities*, the United Nations recognises individuals with disabilities as 'those who have long-term physical, mental, intellectual or sensory impairments which in interaction with various barriers may hinder their full and effective participation in society on an equal basis with others' (Article 1). As a signatory to this Convention, in Australia at least, legally there is an obligation that the principles on which the Convention rests frame societal responses to disability. Article 3 of the Convention sets out these

1 This work was supported by an Australian Research Council Linkage Project [grant number LP100100382]. Thanks to Professor Janet Chan, Ms Jenny Bargen and Dr Jasmine Bruce for their contributions to the design of the study and fieldwork and to Holly Blackmore for research assistance during the data collection.

principles to include 'respect for inherent dignity, individual autonomy including the freedom to make one's own choices, and independence of persons; non-discrimination; full and effective participation and inclusion in society; respect for difference and acceptance of persons with disabilities as part of human diversity and humanity; equality of opportunity and accessibility'. Of relevance to this chapter, the Convention (Article 13) makes specific provisions relating to accessing 'justice'. Article 13 states:

> Parties shall ensure effective access to justice for persons with disabilities on an equal basis with others, including through the provision of procedural and age-appropriate accommodations, in order to facilitate their effective role as direct and indirect participants, including as witnesses, in all legal proceedings, including at investigative and other preliminary stages.

Furthermore,

> In order to help to ensure effective access to justice for persons with disabilities, States Parties shall promote appropriate training for those working in the field of administration of justice, including police and prison staff.

The prevalence of disabilities in the criminal justice sphere (for both perpetrators of crime as well as victims) is higher than in the general population both in Australia (Baldry, 2014; Baldry et al., 2013; Herrington, 2009; Dias et al., 2013; Butler et al., 2011) and internationally (see for example Fazel and Danesh, 2002; Hughes et al., 2012, Einarsson et al., 2009, Forrest et al., 2000). Yet, at least in Australia, the Australian Human Right Commission found in their assessment of disability and the criminal justice system that much disability remains hidden and that, routinely, relevant adjustments within criminal justice interventions were *not* made, which contributed to a 'cycle of violence'. In the criminological literature, very little has been established about the impact of specific disabilities (if any at all) on the process or effectiveness of its programmes, and in the restorative justice sphere it has been noted there is simply less known about what works with participants that are 'other than' (see for example Drennan et al. 2015 on forensic mental health). At a conceptual level, Baldry (2014: 370) has argued that there needs to be 'a wholesale change in the way the law, the criminal justice system, and human and social agencies work together to support people with mental and cognitive disability'.

Inherently, restorative justice has the trappings of a framework that may avoid some of the usual critiques in the field. After-all, the bedrock of restorative justice is a series of values, of relationship, dignity, participation, voice, informed and consensual decision making (Zehr, 2005; Pranis, 2007). Restorative justice is a philosophy that specifically does things 'with' and not 'for' or 'to' individuals (see Wachtel's (1997) social discipline window). Furthermore, it has been 15 years since Braithwaite's (2002: 569) seminal paper on standards for restorative justice made clear that 'non-domination', 'empowerment' and 'respect for fundamental human rights' (amongst other values) are the foundation of good practice. Since then, the interplay of human rights with restorative justice has been explored by those such as Gavrielides (2012), Harvey (2012), Johnstone (2012) and Walgrave (2012). However, to date there has been no empirical work done assessing whether the process and outcome of restorative justice meets its potential for participants with a disability. This gap in the justice sphere is all the more noticeable given the work done in the broader sphere of restorative practice in schools where a comprehensive guide on working restoratively with special needs was recently published (Burnett and Thorsborne, 2015).

Aligned with this Handbook's key objective of pushing the barriers for restorative justice theory, research and practice internationally, this chapter begins to address the gap in empirical work on restorative justice in the criminal justice setting and disability. The chapter draws from a larger study of 74 victim offender conferences (VOC) completed post-sentencing in the aftermath of serious (primarily violent) crime in the state of New South Wales, Australia. However, the lessons and our findings are relevant to all practitioners, researchers and theoreticians internationally.

The specific research aims were to find out how (if at all) disability affects the process of restorative justice, what strategies (if any) were used by facilitators to ensure safe and effective practice, the overall impact of disability (if any) on the VOC success and what might be learnt from these cases in reflecting on future directions for restorative justice in Australia and internationally.

The chapter is an attempt to better engage with the 'hidden' topic of disability (Becroft, 2012). It is also an attempt to move beyond the usual 'hegemonic normalcy' assumed in much criminological research (Meekosha and Dowse, 1998: 49). However, this contribution has some natural limits. I am writing from the position of being outside of the direct experience of disability, impairment and 'otherness'. I am writing from the privileged position of being white, able-bodied, neuro-typical and educated. Furthermore, the research sample includes very few voices of those actually affected by disability. Genuinely understanding what full citizenship in criminal justice processes (including in restorative justice spaces) looks like for those with disability and impairment will only come when the voices of those experiencing otherness are brought to the fore (Meekosha and Dowse, 1998). This, then, is a direction for future research. By admission, this is a weakness but also a strength highlighted by this chapter and indeed a Handbook which aims to pave the way for new research in the field.

The remainder of this chapter will be structured as follows. Literature in the field of restorative justice and disability will be canvassed, the research design and method will be described, the findings outlined and then implications considered.

Background to restorative justice and disability

For the purposes of this chapter, I will define restorative justice to be one application of the broader movement and philosophy of restorative practice bringing together individuals that have been directly affected by a harm formally identified by the criminal justice system. I accept Gavrielides' (2007: 139) definition of restorative justice as being an 'ethos with practical goals among which is to restore harm by including affected parties in a (direct or indirect) encounter and a process of understanding through voluntary and honest dialogue'. My understanding of restorative justice also draws from Pavlich's (2002 p. 3) conceptualisation of restorative justice whereby the 'ethics' of restorative justice is framed as 'specific cases of hospitality in which subjects imagine new ways to be with others'. Pavlich writes that 'the language together with the subjects, of ethics is produced through responses generated when a 'host' welcomes – opens up to – a 'guest'' (ibid.). Pavlich (ibid..) suggests that viewed in this way, restorative justice does not assume that ethical subjects are natural or fixed (as say, victim, offenders, etc.). Paralleling this idea, in the field of disability, Dowse (2017) has written that respect and dignity for all parties comes in an acceptance of identity and behaviour as 'embodied, emergent, relational and historically contingent' (Dowse, 2017: 447). Put another way, this means that identity is not immutable or defined narrowly through labels but is better understood as multifaceted and dynamically emerging in relation to and with others.[2] Understanding restorative justice this way

2 See Mandelin (2016) for an interesting discussion of the label of 'offender'.

is important because, as the Australian Human Rights Commission (2014) found, many offenders have been themselves victims of violence and/or have struggled with undiagnosed disability with little relevant intervention. Thus, this chapter begins with the assertion that restorative justice is a space where each person's past, present and future can be brought to bear on an issue and where avenues for new ways of being emerge during, and because of, the process.

Viewed through a health lens, each and every 'disability' needs to be understood within the medical contexts of symptoms, diagnosis and treatment. However, in the criminological sphere, whilst labels may give a sense of patterns of characteristics, much disability is hidden (that is, it has simply not been realised, detected or diagnosed), comorbidity of issues is common (Dias et al., 2013; Einarrson, 2009) and there is variance in the severity of symptoms. Here, medical labels or diagnoses (where they exist) are just a starting point. It is more important to consider the effects or impact of issues (as they are identified by the relevant parties) on everyday functioning, and functioning under some stress and emotional duress (as is likely when participating in a VOC addressing violent crime). Thus, whilst acknowledging the possibility of individual differences and differences in severity, in brief, disability can affect the internal processing of information and experiences and the external responses an individual makes. The impact of disability is seen to affect cognition (thinking and feeling), communication and behaviour (Burnett and Thorsborne, 2015). For some, information may be processed more slowly; for some, words may be taken literally, but for others it may be difficult to slow down speech and there may be excessive talking, interrupting, trouble with ordering thoughts and speech logically, and impatience. For some, it may be difficult to 'filter out' distractions (such as environmental noise). There may be inflexible thinking, unwillingness to tell a story or an over-developed desire to please and therefore change a story; for some there may be difficulty coping with change such as deviations from what was expected (such as pre-empted in a scripted restorative justice process). If working memory is affected, it can be hard work for some to quickly articulate a past sequence of events, or inconsistent memory; for some, sequencing of events may be more easily done visually than verbally. Some disability changes the 'affect' of an individual; for example, there may be a lack of eye contact and/or less visible emotion; for some there may be involuntary and/or repetitive bodily movements particularly in situations perceived as stressful (where it is self-soothing). For some, it may be hard to read others' body language, and the sense of personal space (and boundaries) may be different, affecting the physical proximity of parties in the room. For others, emotional processing may be different, for example, identifying and understanding the needs of others and genuinely feeling something such as empathy may be hard (psychopathy), or having the words to describe emotion may be difficult or impossible (alexithymia). For others, there may be hyperactivity, impulsivity and hyper-vigilance; there may be paranoia, underlying anxiety and for those with post-traumatic stress disorder (PTSD), anxiety linked to particular 'triggers'. In some cases, neurological differences will make some things difficult, if not impossible.[3] In many cases where a novel event is to be experienced there can be a high degree of stress and anxiety because of the additional work being done internally to process and cope with what is going on around one.

3 See Reisel (2015) for a discussion of the field of neuroscience and the potential of restorative justice in cases where there are differences in emotional processing. Increasingly research is finding links with early childhood neglect and abuse and neurological differences that make the processing and display of emotion difficult. This research is relevant to those in the restorative justice field given the prevalence of neglect and abuse in the early childhoods of many offenders (see for example Driessen et al, 2006).

There is a paucity of literature linking the *effect* of disability on restorative process. A notable exception is the work of Snow (Snow and Powell, 2007; 2011; Snow and Sanger, 2010; Hayes and Snow, 2013). Originally trained as a speech and language pathologist, Snow has conducted a number of studies into the language competencies of incarcerated youth and has raised specific (though at this point theoretical) concerns about the harm (for victims and offenders) of 'verbally mediated interventions' such as restorative justice, where oral language competency is not acknowledged and appropriately managed (Snow and Sanger, 2011; Hayes and Snow, 2013). Snow & Sanger note that offenders 'run the risk of appearing lazy, rude, or unmotivated' (2011: 8) and harm may be caused to a victim because of things that are said or not said or said in a different way to what was expected. For offenders, not being able to easily or effectively verbalise what happened and why, to describe the impact, what has happened since and how they were and are feeling (all typical parts of restorative justice processes) may be frustrating and could compound existing feelings of inadequacy (Hayes and Snow, 2013). In the UK, similar findings and concerns have been reported by Bryan et al. (2007: 505). However, a core assumption underpinning the argument in these papers is that *verbal* communication is integral to restorative justice processes. Undoubtedly *communication* is critical, but whether other non-verbal forms could suffice is at this stage empirically unknown.

In terms of the actual practice of restorative justice with participants with a disability, there have been just a few pieces of writing. In the criminal justice sphere, Cook et al. (2015) drew from ten interviews to explore the experience of restorative justice where forensic mental health issues were present. They concluded that whilst a number of the restorative aspects supported psychological goals, a high level of facilitator skill was imperative. In 2012, Holland travelled around Australia as part of a Churchill Fellowship to find out how restorative practitioners worked with individuals with special needs, with a particular focus on cognitive impairment. A range of creative practices were found, and Holland (2012) concluded that, though there were cases where individuals were not able to safely participate, in many cases, with enough preparation, special needs could be met. Building on this work, the scope of restorative practice in schools and on participants with special needs (including ADHD, autistic spectrum disorder, foetal alcohol spectrum disorder, intellectual disability, social and emotional and behavioural difficulties, trauma and attachment disorders, and speech, langage and communication needs) was comprehensively covered by Burnett and Thorsborne (2015).

Burnett and Thorsborne discuss a range of strategies used by practitioners already working in this area, including, where there is cognitive impairment, the use of visual props, storyboards, timelines and 'cueing in' participants, asking individuals to repeat back in their own words what has been said, allowing for extra time to process and listen, and during preparation and the process, supporting parties via normalising how they may be feeling. Burnett and Thorsborne (ibid.) highlight how, when communicative competence is in question, adjustments can include modifications in script (framing questions purposefully to avoid acquiescence and using more closed-ended questions), keeping sentences short and language simple and precise, avoiding jargon, irony and metaphor. Adjustments relating to behavioural issues include modifying the space (seating layouts, considering lighting and potential ways to reduce auditory interference), building more time into preparation to really develop the relationship with the facilitator and making behavioural contracts (ibid., pg 142–150).

Thus, supporting Holland's work, the authors found that restorative practice with participants with special needs was entirely possible but that good practice rested on adjustments being made to the preparation and process, which is necessarily predicated on sufficient time, sufficiently skilled practitioners and adequate resourcing (ibid., pg 40). The chapter will now turn to the current study.

Programme description, research design and method

Programme description

This chapter draws from a large qualitative dataset relating to a long established (1999-present), post-sentencing programme known as Victim Offender Conferencing (VOC) in New South Wales (NSW), Australia. It is attached to the formal criminal justice system and run by a small unit of staff that form the Restorative Justice Unit; for a history of this Unit see Milner, 2012. Akin to the *Victims Voices Heard* programme in Delaware, USA (Miller, 2011), the programme specifically aims to meet the needs of victims of crime (for a comparative analysis see Miller and Hefner, 2015). There can be a lengthy period of time from sentencing to VOC (averaging 3.6 years with a range of one month to 15 years and a median of 23 months), and an extensive preparation phase (the average length of time from referral to VOC was 11 months, the range one to 43 months and a mode of ten months). The use of facilitators with particular skills that might be described as advanced is standard (Bolitho and Bruce, 2017).

The Restorative Justice Unit accepts referrals from both victims and offenders following serious crime, post-sentencing, with no other criminal matters pending and generally pre-release from prison. Both offenders and victims have to agree to participate for a VOC to go ahead, and participation in a VOC plays no role in later decisions about parole. In addition to these eligibility requirements, there is a suitability screening process undertaken by one of the two facilitators in conversation with the Unit manager. Suitability rests on assessments of the victim's needs against the offender's capacity to meet those needs; it includes assessments of empathy and the degree of responsibility assumed (Milner, 2012, Bolitho, 2015).

In addition, and of relevance to this chapter, the Restorative Justice Unit has a series of Practice Guidelines, including on the assessment of suitability where an offender has been classified as a 'forensic patient' (Restorative Justice Unit, 2013). The guideline defines three categories of forensic patients: those found unfit to plead (based on mental illness or intellectual disability), those found not guilty on the grounds of mental illness, and those inmates that begin a prison sentence but subsequently are found to be mentally ill. In the first and second cases, an offender cannot be found suitable for VOC because (respectively) the lack of capacity to understand legal processes, to tell their story and to take responsibility for the crime (core components of restorative justice) is seen to render restorative justice impossible. For the same reasons, if an offender is psychotic at the time of referral, it is automatically deemed unsuitable. In the third case, there is some discretion and the staff of the Restorative Justice Unit coordinate with prison health staff to consider whether VOC is (or could be in the future) 'in the best interests' of the offender (ibid.).

Between programme inception to the end of the research project (1999–2013) there were 926 referrals and 76 VOC completed. The most common reason for not going ahead with a VOC was the victim not being contactable or interested (41%), the offender not being contactable or interested (27%) and offender suitability (17%) (Bolitho, 2015). There are no legislative or internal time limits on the length of time from referral to VOC and on average de-briefing continued for six months post VOC. Just over half (40/76, 53%) of VOC were completed after death (murder, manslaughter, driving causing death) followed by armed robbery (13/74, 17%) and a small number of sexual violence matters (5/74, 9%). In just over half the cases, the victim was known to the offender (44/76, 58%) (ibid.).

Research design

The empirical study into the practice of VOC was conducted between 2010–2013. As only a small number of cases are completed each year (approximately eight to ten), the research also drew from historical cases completed. The first component of study consisted of a census of past completed VOCs. For cases completed between 1999–2010, ethics approval was sought and approved to access and thematically analyse the case files kept by the Department on each matter. Case files consisted of the notes kept by the facilitator at referral, suitability and de-briefing; copies of court sentencing notes (including psychological reports tendered) and reports from prison psychologists and correspondence with, for example, supporting parties such as Victim Advocacy groups. Case files varied in terms of how much detail was recorded. To supplement these case file notes, one in-depth qualitative interview with the original facilitator of each case was completed (n = 60). Facilitators were given their original case file in preparation, and asked a series of questions to understand the dynamics of the process. Because the length of time from the original VOC to the research interview varied, some individual biases might have affected the recall and the retelling of each case.

The second component of the study involved an in-depth study of the VOC completed between 2010–2013. Whilst 16 were completed in two cases, both involving historical child sexual assault, no approval was given to access any detail; in one additional case, consent was given for access to only some parts of the data. For this component of study, the case files were analysed (n = 73). Two researchers from a four-person research team observed the VOC (n = 13) and completed pre-and post interviews with victims and offenders (19 victims, 14 offenders). The facilitator was also interviewed (n = 14). The third component of data involved a longitudinal five-year follow-up of cases completed in 2005, 2006 and 2007 (yielding interviews with five victims, seven offenders and 20 other participants).

This study

For this chapter, a series of word searches were conducted (e.g. psychiatrist, forensic, disability) across each of the forms of data (case files, interviews, and observation notes) to get a baseline number of cases where disability was present. Sixteen cases were identified for analysis. In the majority of cases, a diagnosis was recorded in the case file material; in a few cases, the terms used were not diagnostic but general, for example, 'neglect and trauma as a child, emotionally disturbed'. Where it was clear from the case file that mental health was an issue (for example, notes recording regular stints in the forensic health unit within prison), these cases were included. Table 11.1 gives a brief overview of the 16 cases. It is possible that disability was not always recorded in the case files and not always obvious to a facilitator; thus, the 16 cases are likely to be an underestimate of the actual number of restorative justice cases completed with a participant that had a disability. Thematic coding of the qualitative material[4] was done manually by the author. Quotes have been chosen because they are indicative of a particular theme or because they exemplify a different perspective.

---

4 Across the 16 cases identified there were 35 in-depth interview transcripts (made up of interviews with victims n = 7, with offenders n = 9, with offender supporters n = 3 and facilitators n = 16), seven sets of ethnographic observation notes, and 15 case files.

Table 11.1 Cases with disability and adjustment(s) to restorative process

Case #	Offence type	Participant(s)	Disabilities identified	Adjustments	Brief description of adjustments
002	Assault	Offender (male) Victim (female)	Depression (prison notes) Cognitive impairment	Yes	For the victim, facilitator checked in re need for additional support party in the Conference, rehearsal (offender and victim had a number of telephone cases prior to VOC)
007	Murder	Offender (male)	Schizotypal and/or avoidant personality disorder and/or personality disorder with prominent depressive schizoid traits (pre-sentence report, prison psychologists report)	Yes	More than usual 'intensive' preparation with the victim to prepare for the potential lack of empathy and difficulty showing emotion (offender)
008	Armed robbery	Offender (male)	Agoraphobia, exacerbated by alcohol and drug use (pre-sentence report)	Yes	Extra preparation in order that the relationship with the facilitator was solid & certain level of trust was developed
009***	Murder	Offender (male)	ADHD, severe alcohol & drug abuse (sentencing notes)	Yes	Additional preparation with the facilitator working with Correctional Staff to ensure offender was ready for the VOC
012	Murder	Offender (female)	Undiagnosed psychiatric issues; delusions, 'emotional disturbance' (departmental case notes)	Yes	Offender's psychiatrist was brought into the decision about proceeding with VOC. Additional preparation with facilitator reality tested and rehearsed responses to prepare for the victim's anger
021	Robbery, grievous bodily harm	Offender (male)	ADHD, alcohol and drug abuse (pre-sentence report)	Yes	Extra preparation; facilitator worked with offender on slowing down thoughts, rehearsing the sequence of the VOC as well as sitting, listening and turn taking
075***	Manslaughter	Victims (females)	Long-term drug abuse (amphetamines, cannabis, other) (Departmental case notes)	Yes	Extra preparation (many more meetings than usual), a verbal/behavioural contract around not attending the VOC under the influence of drugs
037	Armed with intent	Offender (male) Victim (male)	Personality disorder, possible acquired brain injury due to alcohol abuse (pre-sentence report) Cognitive impairment	Yes	During preparation facilitator recalled checking back frequently on understanding and using simple, clear language

048	Murder	Offender (male)	Emotional disturbance -childhood abuse & neglect (sentencing notes)	Yes	Additional preparation, before the VOC was held other RJ interventions were held (3 x exchange of letters); the timing of the VOC was considered, VOC held when psychiatric condition stabilised (monitored by prison staff and discussed with facilitator)
062***	Malicious wounding with intent to cause grievous bodily harm	Offender (male) Victim (male)	Depression, alcohol abuse, emotional disturbance re childhood abuse & neglect (sentencing notes) PTSD (relating to crime)	Yes	Additional preparation including contingency plans for during the VOC if particular triggers meant the process felt unsafe
063***	Historical child sexual assault	Offender (male) Victim (male)	Emotional disturbance (case notes) PTSD	Yes	The preparation was described as lengthy and intensive, verbal/behavioural contracts were made in conjunction with both offender and victim psychologists that were brought in to support
071***	Historical child sexual assault	Offender (male) Offender support Victim (female)	Depression (sentencing notes) Physical disability-quadriplegic Depression, anxiety, eating disorder (case notes)	Yes (for victim)	Additional preparation in the form of pre-VOC meetings with psychologists to ensure awareness triggers, additional preparation with offender & prison psychologist (VOC held off until prison treatment program had begun)
018	Murder	Offender (male)	Cognitive impairment-IQ 76, schitzoid avoidant type personality disorder (sentencing notes)	Yes	Additional preparation with the victim for the offender's possible presentation
026**	Murder	Offender (male)	Cognitive impairment, emotional disturbance – childhood neglect & abuse (case notes)	Yes	More preparation done to work out the offence story and capacity to take responsibility
046	Aggravated driving-grievous bodily harm	Offender (male) Victim (male)	Acquired brain injury, severe alcohol abuse (pre-sentence report) Neurological disorder (Parkinson's disease) worsened by physical impact of crime, poor working memory (case notes)	No	Noticed the disabilities but accepted the extra time it might take and implicitly trusted in the RJ maxim 'let the circle regulate itself'
073***	Manslaughter	Offender (male)	Learning difficulties, depression & other emotional disturbance (case notes)	Yes	Additional preparation with psychologist from Violent Offenders Program, additional sessions developing trust with the facilitator

*Part of the census study, **Part of the five-year follow up study, ***Part of the current case study

Findings

The nature of disability in this sample of VOC

In this sample just over a fifth of cases (16/74, 22%[5]) involved at least one party with a disability; this supports the literature on the high rate of persons with a disability involved with criminal justice systems. In 15/16 (94%) cases, it was the offender that presented with a disability. However, there were seven cases (44%) where a victim presented with a disability. In six cases, *both* the victim and offender had identified disabilities (38% of the sample). The majority of offenders and victims with a disability were male (94% and 57%, respectively), and no participant with a disability identified as Aboriginal or Torres Strait Islander. In all 16 cases (100%), there was at least one party with a mental illness (including depression, anxiety, personality disorders, PTSD, ADHD). There were six cases (38%) where disability related to cognition (intellectual disability or impairment) and one case (6%) where a participant had a physical disability. In 6/16 (38%) cases at least one of the parties had more than one disability identified, supporting the literature on comorbidity (Dias et al., 2013).

Complexity

It was clear from the analysis of qualitative material that the primary concern for facilitators remained the complex harm from the offence; disability was identified and considered but was never the overarching concern. This is perhaps not surprising given the seriousness of offence types facilitated in VOC. In terms of what complexity looked like in practice, there was some variance. Concern was noted more often in cases where disability related to a lack of capacity for feeling and talking about emotion, as generally this was perceived to be potentially harmful for a victim. In Case 062, the facilitator recalled 'partly expecting the offender to lose his capacity to engage and blow his stack', in Case 018, there was concern that in the VOC 'he may lie, he may not, he may clam up completely', in a case involving sexual violence, there was concern 'that the offender's own trauma as a victim of child sexual abuse would affect his ability to be empathic to the victim' (Case 063). In Case 026, there was:

> concern about his capacity to own his behaviour . . . he wasn't a particular insightful man, there was a lot abuse and neglect in his younger years and he'd grown up in the juvenile justice system, drug addicted, living a pretty tragic life, so he wasn't emotionally connected, he wasn't particularly articulate, and there were concerns about his capacity to own his behaviour. We didn't want him going into the conference 'umming' and 'ahing' about what happened because that would be distressing or upsetting to the victim.

In a similar case, the facilitator recalled being:

> concerned that the VOC may feel almost superficial, that he may not connect emotionally and then maybe (the victim) would sense that he didn't feel it and wasn't carrying it which could have been very distressing. The offender . . . had spent his early 20s in prison so he wasn't particularly mature, not particularly insightful, not particularly articulate, not

---

5 For the purposes of this chapter, all decimal points have been rounded up to the nearest whole number.

particularly capable of expressing emotion and affect. He is quite guarded. He's a ball of muscle but feels like he's about to pop at any stage.

(Case 009)

In cases where intellectual impairment was present, other issues were of concern. For example, one facilitator recalled feeling 'quite nervous, as (the offender) seemed to know what was going on but he just didn't have anything to say. I couldn't get two words out of him' (Case 018). Whilst the majority of concern related to potential harm to a victim, there was also cognisance of the vulnerability of offenders with a disability. Thus, in Case 012, the facilitator noted feeling worried about the offender's capacity to hear 'information that didn't come out in court, the level of wrath, (to see) the fairly big group of support people compared to her side'. In Case 007, the offender 'was so isolated within the prison community . . . I had concern for him that he would just be abused and then go back to his cell to serve the rest of his days in prison, (I wondered) could he be hurt through the process'. In one of the few cases where an offender with a disability was interviewed as part of our research, there is some evidence that the process was indeed overwhelming. The offender commented that he found the start of the VOC hard: "I was confused because I didn't know who was who, yeah I was confused and bewildered" (Case 073).

Facilitators recognised that for both offenders and victims, disability brings to the fore questions of consent and the concept of best interests. Thus, in Case 048, the facilitator noted:

> the offender has chronic mental health issues and, with his illness he'll have periods where he's stable, compliant with medication, he's coherent but then he'll also have periods where he's acutely unwell. So, this was about finding a time when he was stable and prepared, could consent, and had appropriate support, and it was in his best interests.

Similarly, in Case 037, the facilitator recalled concern around informed consent for victims:

> as I was talking about process and what was involved, I started to have some concerns about their (victims) capacity to understand the concept of conferencing. I really had to articulate it clearly and slowly and ask a lot of questions to check back to see if they'd understood what I was saying. Whether they were consenting to participate genuinely.

Case 037 reveals an additional complexity for facilitators; whilst departmental case files give facilitators a sense of the disabilities an offender may have, no such notes are available on victims before the first meeting. Thus, the first meeting becomes critical in terms of accurately and sensitively identifying issues of concern. In summary, the findings suggest that disability is acknowledged by the facilitators of VOC as an important though not pivotal feature of cases; it brings additional complexity, and issues of concern for best practice relate to gaining informed consent and working within the 'best interests' of parties.

Adjustments

Supporting the work of Burnett and Thorsborne (2015) on the need for adjustments in restorative practice and special needs in the school setting, in 15/16 (94%) cases, completed accommodations were made to the preparation and/or process of VOC. Whilst all the adjustments described were specific to the case, some patterns relating to the impact of specific disabilities were noted. For example, with cases where there was concern around the capacity to cope with the intensity of emotion, facilitators described thinking the offender might become furious 'if he thought he wasn't being listened to and working with the psychologist to have a "Plan B" in the VOC' (Case 062). In other cases, verbal contracts around acceptable behaviour were negotiated, and in one notable case, a facilitator recalled:

> many of the participants in the VOC came from a drug using and drug dealing background. If the victim's family were unable to follow the process, I had a real concern that they might just lose it (so) in the lead-up to the conference I flagged time and time again – that if people turned up intoxicated, drug affected we would not be able to work with them – that was very much part of the negotiation in the preparation phase of the VOC.

Similarly, in Case 063, where there was concern that the victim might 'punch the offender', the facilitator recalled there was a 'handshake on that, me and the victim, and he is a man of his word'.

In cases where anxiety was a feature, facilitators recalled working with psychologists to 'reality test the conference process, working through together with the psychologist, what might be the stresses and developing ways for him to manage the anxiety and distress' (Case 007). Similarly, in a case where PTSD was present, a facilitator recalled saying "[W]e will go as fast or slow as you need to and I'll be 100 per cent guided by you and your psychologist in terms of if anything triggers" (Case 071). Other strategies to ameliorate the impact of anxiety included giving as much information as possible about the process as early as possible in order to reduce ambiguities. In Case 008, the facilitator recalled the offender being 'outside smoking a cigarette like he was going to the gallows' and noted the importance of having two staff present on the day – one for each side – in case of last minute jitters. Another strategy mentioned related to the timing of the VOC, and in a number of cases VOCs were put off whilst trust was further developed with the facilitator. For example, one facilitator recalled:

> it took such a long time because we waited until he felt some rapport between us, he trusted the process, he was feeling confident with me as a facilitator, and his level of anxiety had decreased from the level it reached when he knew the meeting was going to happen, and he felt he was ready and it was the right moment.
>
> *(Case007)*

In cases where intellectual impairment was present, strategies included working with the help of psychologists on the offence narrative to 'connect with what he was thinking and feeling at the time so that he could actively take responsibility' (Case 006). In another case, the seating plan was different:

> she actually sat outside the circle, she just sat there kind of quietly watching the interaction. She was very introverted to the point of not being able to make eye contact.. She wanted to hear what the offender was going to say, but didn't want to be involved in the process, it just felt too much for her and it had became apparent that she wasn't ready, able, mature enough to participate but she simply wanted to sit there on the outside and hear it – so that's what we did.
>
> *(Case 037)*

In another case, the strategy was to focus on what the victim needed and to work in a targeted way to achieve this. Thus, in Case 018, the facilitator knew the victim's mother was aware of the offender's cognitive impairment and was not interested in a show of emotion or an apology, but she did desperately want some more specific information about her daughter's death. The facilitator asked the psychologist to work with the offender specifically towards being able to answer those questions during the VOC. In other cases where disability resulted in behavioural differences such as ADHD and hyperactivity, the strategies were again different. For example, in Case 021, the facilitator recalled preparing the participant by rehearsing the pace: 'stopping, taking your time, telling your story and then allowing the victim to tell his story and just being able to sit there and hear it'.

In summary, whilst the range of accommodations were diverse and specific to the individual, common features were the use of other professionals (primarily psychologists and psychiatrists) in the assessment, lead-up and actual VOC process, and extra time in the preparation of cases. Supporting Burnett and Thorsborne's (2015) work, strategies used in preparation (and the VOC) related to language, rehearsal, having contingency plans, spending more time developing trust and having behavioural contracts. Interestingly, in the only case where a facilitator specifically recalled *not* making any particular adjustment in preparation, it is clear that (in the facilitator's view) the restorative justice maxim of 'the circle regulating the circle' is paramount:

> (Researcher) In your running notes you say the collision affected his brain and he can't easily communicate and sometimes he speaks in German, sometimes in English. Was that a problem at the conference? (Facilitator) No, you just had to go, well, he's a person who just gets frustrated, and sometimes it's easier in his own language. . . . In the conference I think there might have been a feeling he could ramble on, but I think the circle has its own moderation. So, you know, if someone says, hey, you're talking too much, someone else says, no, no, this is important, so, I think, often, I have faith in the circle.
>
> *(Case 046)*

Impact on success of VOC

In no case was disability a determining feature in the overall perceived success of the VOC. There were just two cases where disability was mentioned at all in the commentary around the overall success of a case. In Case 026, there was concern for the offender, with the offender support person recalling (five years later), "I don't think he knew how to process exactly what happened. I thought there was some relief in his face but I think it was absolutely overwhelming for him, I really do". In the other case, and the only case involving physical disability, two different perspectives were gathered, and both came from participants in more peripheral (supporting) roles at the VOC. The participant with a disability noted that 'in a wheelchair you don't have the opportunity to turn your body like an able-bodied person', and this became an issue when, as the VOC progressed, they were 'profoundly unhappy with the way things were going' and 'frantically trying to use eye contact to get the facilitator's attention to let them know' (Case 071). This was the only case where an overtly prejudicial view was present (and the participant knew this!), as the support person noted it was this participant's physical difference that was challenging:

> you know their disability was obvious. Look, I have – I don't have much to do with disabled people so I guess you're very wary about how to approach. It is a bit biased or ignorant maybe on my part but – it's very hard to just be able to direct questions at them and maybe to see them as available to answer questions. If I was more comfortable around that sort of thing and realised that they don't want to be treated differently maybe that would have helped. It was a hard situation anyway.

In VOC, the focus is on preparing victims and offenders for the process, and there is generally less time given to those in supporting roles. However, Case 071 highlights how important preparation is for everyone. For the participant in a wheelchair, preparation and the forming (for example) of a plan to check in regularly could have pre-empted the frustrations that arose. For other participants, the preparation phase of RJ is an opportunity for education around what disability means and is important so that a genuine lack of knowledge or experience of disability does not cloud the process. This preparation would not need to be lengthy or overly detailed; a statement such as, 'In the VOC you will notice that Person X is in a wheelchair. This means they may not be able to turn easily to look at who is speaking, and sometimes eye contact will be difficult. This will not affect Person's X's ability to take part fully in this VOC; they will be thinking, feeling and interacting just like you will be, and they will expect you to treat them no differently than as you would others' – would likely provide enough context.

Concluding thoughts

Our research explored the population of VOC cases across the first 15 years of practice (1999–2013) with a view to understanding post-sentencing practice and more broadly what, why and how restorative justice works. Whilst the research did not set out to specifically explore disability, using a variety of lenses (observation, participation interview, case file documentation), every component of VOC practice was considered, and from the 74 cases completed, for this chapter, the 16 that explicitly referenced disability were drawn out for further analysis. The findings from this analysis support domestic (Baldry, 2014) and international research (Fazel and Danesh, 2002) on the presence of disability for individuals accessing the criminal justice system, whether as perpetrators or victims of crime. In a number of cases, disability affected more than one participant in the circle. Furthermore, the presence of more than one type of disability (that is, comorbidity) was not unusual; again, this supports prior research in this area (Dias et al., 2013; Einarrson, 2009). The kinds of disability varied, but many involved difficulties with the processing, feeling and expression of emotion. Whilst the number of case studies in this chapter is relatively small, the links between a childhood history of abuse and neglect and particular emotional difficulties in perpetrators of crime supports the emerging literature in this area (Reisal, 2015). If disability is an everyday reality for many accessing criminal justice intervention, then restorative justice practitioners need to take it as given that some practice will involve this complexity. If this is the reality, what evidence is there that practitioners shape restorative processes to ensure the safety and well-being of all parties?

Disability was routinely identified during the preparation phase for a case and in many cases was of some concern to the facilitator, but in no case was disability perceived by a facilitator to be a reason for not proceeding. In 15 of the 16 cases explored, the evidence suggests that there was full and active participation from all participants. The findings from this study suggest then that restorative practitioners can and do work intuitively and effectively to enable fair access to the process and proceedings. However, an important caveat is that in the vast majority of cases, adjustments were made to the preparation and process phases of VOC. The kinds of adjustments made were similar to those identified by Burnett and Thorsborne (2015) as being in use in the restorative practices and education sphere. Thus it would seem that restorative practitioners (in VOC at least) inherently have a can-do, problem-solving, creative approach in thinking through how to make complex cases work. Difference is noticed and adjustments are routinely made that would seem to be consensual, specific and effective. This is in keeping with current human rights frameworks, specifically the obligations set out in the United Nations *Convention on the Rights of Persons with Disabilities*.

What might explain these positive findings? In NSW, there is no particular training on disability and VOC, though it is highly likely as government employees (public servants) that the staff of the Restorative Justice Unit had completed some professional development in this area. It is possible that the philosophy of restorative justice engenders a natural sensitivity to different parties' needs. As noted earlier, the philosophy of restorative justice takes seriously the principles of the inherent rights and dignity of all parties, of active participation and non-domination. Alternatively, or in addition to this, it may be that the particular practice of VOC in NSW engenders good practice even when complexity in the form of disability is present. In VOC, the guiding principle is 'to do no harm', and the severity of offences means ample time and consideration must be given for every case. Other professionals (such as psychologists and victim support) are routinely involved at all stages of the process (Bolitho, 2015), and there is the capacity and desire to 'innovate' to meet victims needs (Chan et al., 2016). The VOC practice also uses a small number of highly skilled facilitators within a small team where difficult decisions are undertaken after rigorous discussion (Bolitho and Bruce, 2017).

Realistically, the features that engendered success in these cases may not be routinely present in other restorative justice practices, such as those constrained by time, the use of less skilled/experienced facilitators and/or a lack of resources. Indeed worldwide, pre-sentencing, restorative practices for young people are many times more common than post-sentencing, victim-focused, VOC-type programs following serious crime committed by adults. And the number of cases completed in pre-sentencing programmes is often substantially higher. For example, in NSW, the restorative practice utilised for young people that have committed crime ('youth justice conferencing') must be completed within a 28-day time frame, facilitators are employed from the community, with no prior mediation skills, on a casual basis (*Young Offenders Act* 1997) and over 1,000 cases are completed each year (NSW Government, accessed 10th October 2017). It becomes important, then, to consider how the techniques that enabled fair access to the VOC process could be achieved in other programmes.

Even if practitioners intuitively practise safely because they are working towards a restorative justice ethic of care, Article 13 of *Convention on the Rights of Persons with Disabilities* suggests it is necessary for those working in the justice sphere to develop some specialist knowledge via training. This is, then, a recommendation for restorative practitioners. Training does not need to be done in a bureaucratically 'standard' manner; as Braithwaite (2002) cogently argued, there is a natural risk as time goes on for restorative practices to become overly standardised and bureaucratised, contrary to the movement's beginnings. Whilst some basic descriptive information on disability would be useful, training could also be about strengthening the core restorative skills that are needed even more in complex cases: deep listening, careful observation, active conversation with other relevant professionals, and an abiding respect for the human condition. Knowledge of the kinds of adjustments that can and are being made in other restorative practices across the globe would also be of value. For this reason, a more concerted effort to share experiences, build knowledge and develop resources around restorative practice and disability is a priority.

This chapter is based on a small number of cases; larger and more targeted research needs to be conducted to really understand what best practice might look like. The voices of those with a disability that have participated in restorative justice are important to developing best practice. The facilitator of Case 073 noted that "we shouldn't shy away from matters which on the face of it might look really problematic or difficult". Normatively, we should indeed be doing more to ensure that those with a disability have fair access to the process and proceedings of restorative practice. We should be doing this because disability is an everyday reality, because active participation is what restorative justice is about and because everyone has the right to equal access to justice. We should be doing this because it is the 21st century, and the restorative movement is roughly half a century old (at least in Western democracies); it is the right time to move on from some of the early debates to grapple with new complexities. Were these kinds of complexities to be embraced, and practitioners were to know why and how they were working with disability and to what effect, the restorative movement would be a genuine frontrunner amongst its criminal justice programme counterparts in living up to its ideals.

References

Australian Human Rights Commission. 2014. *Equal Before the Law, Towards Disability Justice Strategies*. Available at www.humanrights.gov.au/sites/default/files/document/publication/2014_Equal_Before_the_Law.pdf. Accessed 2 August 2017.

Baldry, E. 2014. Disability at the Margins: The Limits of the Law, *Griffith Law Review*, 23(3): 370–388.

Baldry, E., Clarence, M., Dowse, L. and Troller, J. 2013. Reducing Vulnerability to Harm in Adults with Cognitive Disabilities in the Australian Criminal Justice System, *Journal of Policy and Practice in Intellectual Disabilities*, 10(3): 222–229.

Becroft, A. 2012. *Special Report: 'Nobody Made the Connection: the Prevalence of Neuro-Disability in Young People Who Offend'*, Issue 60: 2–3. Available at www.youthcourt.govt.nz. Accessed 2 August 2017.

Bolitho, J. 2015. Putting Justice Needs First: A Case Study of Best Practice, Victim Offender Conferencing in New South Wales Australia, *Restorative Justice: An International Journal*, 3(2): 256–281.

Bolitho, J. and Bruce, J. 2017. Science, Art and Alchemy: Best Practice in Facilitating Restorative Justice, *Contemporary Justice Review: Issues in Criminal, Social and Restorative Justice*, 20(3): 336–362.

Braithwaite, J. 2002. Setting Standards for Restorative Justice, *British Journal of Criminology*, 42: 563–577.

Bryan, K., Freer, J. and Furlong, C. 2007. Language and Communication Difficulties in Juvenile Offenders, *International Journal of Language and Communication Disorders*, 42(5): 505–520.

Burnett, N. and Thorsborne, M. 2015. *Restorative Practice and Special Needs: A Practical Guide to Working Restoratively with Young People*. London: Jessica Kingsley Publishers.

Butler, T., Indig, D., Allnutt, S. and Mamoon, H. 2011. Co-occurring Mental Illness and Substance Use Disorder among Australian Prisoners, *Drug Alcohol Review*, 30(2): 188–194.

Chan, J., Bolitho, J. and Bargen, J. 2016. Innovative Justice Responses to Violence. In J. Stubbs and S. Tomsen (eds.) *Australian Violence*. Annandale: Federation Press, pp. 230–247.

Cook, A., Drennan, G. and Callanan, M. 2015. A Qualitative Exploration of the Experience of Restorative Approaches in a Forensic Mental Health Setting, *The Journal of Forensic Psychiatry and Psychology*, 26(4): 5110–5151.

Dias, S., Ware, R., Kinner, S. and Lennox, N. 2013. Co-Occurring Mental Disorder and Intellectual Disability in a Large Sample of Australian Prisoners, *Australian and New Zealand Journal of Psychiatry*, 47(10): 938–944.

Dowse, L. 2017. Disruptive, Dangerous and Disturbing: the 'Challenge' of Behaviour in the Construction of Normalcy and Vulnerability, *Journal of Media and Cultural Studies*, 31(3): 447–457.

Dowse, L. 2009. 'Some People Are Never Going to Be Able to Do That'. Challenges for People with Intellectual Disability in the 21st Century, *Disability and Society*, 24(5): 571–584.

Drennan, G., Cook, A. and Kiernan, J. 2015. The Psychology of Restorative Practice in Forensic Mental Health Recovery. In T. Gavrielides (ed.) *The Psychology of Restorative Justice: Managing the Power Within*. London: Taylor & Francis.

Driessen, M., Schroeder, T., Widmann, B., von Schonfeld, C. and Schneider, F. 2006. Childhood Trauma, Psychiatric Disorders and Criminal Behavior in Prisoners in Germany: A Comparative Study in Incarcerated Women and Men, *Journal of Clinical Psychiatry*, 67(10): 1486–1492.

Einarsson, E., Sigurdsson, J, Gudjonsson, G., Newton, A. and Bragason, O. 2009. Screening for Attention-Deficit Hyperactivity Disorder and Co-Morbid Mental Disorders Among Prison Inmates, *Nordic Journal of Psychiatry*, 63(5): 1–7.

English Oxford Living Dictionary. 2017. Available at https://en.oxforddictionaries.com/definition/complex. Accessed 10 August 2017.

Fazel, S. and Danesh, J. 2002. Serious Mental Disorder in 23000 Prisoners: A Systematic Review of 62 Surveys, *Lancet*, 359(9306): 545–550.

Forrest, C., Tambor, E., Riley, A., Ensminger, M. and Starfield, B. 2000. The Health Profile of Incarcerated Male Youths, *Pediatrics*, 105(1): 286–291.

Gavrielides, T. 2007. *Restorative Justice Theory AND Practice: Addressing the Discrepancy*. Helsinki: Heuni.

Gavrielides, T. 2012. Contextualising Restorative Justice for Hate Crime, *Journal of Interpersonal Violence*, 27(18), pp. 3624–3643.

Gavrielides, T. 2016. A Human Rights Vision of Restorative Justice: Moving Beyond Labels. In T. Gavrielides (ed.) *Offenders no More: An Interdisciplinary Restorative Justice Dialogue*. New York: Nova Science Publishers.

Harvey, C. 2012. Reconstructing and Restoring Human Rights. In T. Gavrielides (ed.) *Rights & Restoration within Youth Justice*. Whitby: de Sitter Publications.

Hayes, H. and Snow, P. 2013. Oral Language Competence and Restorative Justice Processes: Refining Preparation and the Measurement of Outcomes, *Trends & Issues in Crime and Criminal Justice*: 463. Available at www.aic.gov.au/publications/current%20series/tandi/461-480/tandi463.html. Accessed 10 October 2017.

Herrington, V. 2009. Assessing the Prevalence of Intellectual Disability among Young Male Prisoners, *Journal of Intellectual Disability Research*, 53(5): 397–410.

Holland, B. 2012. Inclusive Restorative Justice: An Investigation and Exploration. London: Winston Churchill Memorial Trust. Available at www.wcmt.org.uk/sites/default/files/migrated-reports/1035_1.pdf. Accessed 20 August 2017.

Hughes, N., Williams, H., Chitsabean, P., Davies, R. and Mounce, L. 2012. *Nobody Made the Connection: The Prevalence of Neuro-Disability in Young People Who Offend*. Available at www.childrencommissioner.gov.uk. Accessed 06 October 2017.

Johnstone, G. 2012. The Standardization of Restorative Justice. In T. Gavrielides (ed.). *Rights & Restoration within Youth Justice*. Whitby: de Sitter Publications.

Mandelin, J. 2016. How I Became an Offender and What I Did to Remove this Label. In T. Gavrielides (ed.) *Offenders no More: An Interdisciplinary restorative Justice Dialogue*. New York: Nova Science Publishers.

Meekosha, H. and Dowse, L. 1998. Enabling Citizenship: Gender, Disability and Citizenship in Australia, *Feminist Review*, 57(1): 49–72.

Miller, S. 2011. *After the Crime: The Power of Restorative Justice Dialogues between Victims and Violent Offenders*. New York: New York University Press.

Miller, S. and Hefner, K. 2015. Procedural Justice for Victims and Offenders? Exploring Restorative Justice Processes in Australia and the US, *Justice Quarterly*, 32(1): 142–167.

Milner, K. 2012. Restorative Justice and Adult Offending: Twelve Years of Post-Sentence Practice. In J. Bolitho, J. Bruce and G. Mason (eds.) *Restorative Justice: Adults and Emerging Practice*. Annandale: Federation Press, pp. 80–99.

New South Wales Government, Department of Justice, *Juvenile Justice Year in Review 2015–2016*. Available at www.juvenile.justice.nsw.gov.au/Pages/Juvenile%20Justice/publications/2015-16%20Year%20in%20Review.pdf. Accessed 10 October 2017.

Pavlich, G. 2002. Towards an Ethics of Restorative Justice. In L. Walgrave (ed.) *Restorative Justice and The Law*. London and New York: Routledge.

Pranis, K. 2007. Restorative Values. In G. Johnstone and D. Van Ness (eds.) *Handbook of Restorative Justice*. USA: Willan.

Reisel, D. 2015. Towards a Neuroscience of Morality. In T. Gavrielides (ed.) *The Psychology of Restorative Justice: Managing the Power Within*. London: Taylor & Francis.

Restorative Justice Unit. 2013. *Victim Offender Conferencing Procedures Manual*. Corrective Services New South Wales, Unpublished document accessed during research project.

Rugge, T. and Cormier, R. 2013. Restorative Justice in Cases of Serious Crime: An Evaluation. In E. Elliot and R. Gordon (eds.) *New Directions in Restorative Justice: Issues, Practice, Evaluation*. London and New York: Routledge, pp. 266–277.

Snow, P. and Powell, M. 2007. Oral Language Competence, Social Skills and High-Risk Boys: What Are Juvenile Offenders Trying to Tell Us? *Children and Society*, 22(1): 16–28.

Snow, P. and Powell, M.B. 2011. Oral Language Competence in Incarcerated Young Offenders: Links with Offending Severity, *International Journal of Speech-Language Pathology* 13(6): 480–489.

Snow, P. and Sanger, D. 2011. Restorative Justice Conferencing and the Youth Offender: Exploring the Role of Oral Language Competence, *International Journal of Language and Communication Disorders*, 46. DOI: 10.3109/13682822.2010.496763.

Umbreit, M.S., Vos, B., Coates, R.B., et al. 2006. Victims of Severe Violence in Mediated Dialogue with Offender: The Impact of the First Multi-Site Study in the US. *International Review of Victimology*, 13(1) pp. 27–48.

United Nations, General Assembly, *Convention on the Rights of Persons with Disabilities, adopted by the General Assembly*, 24 January 2007, A/RES/61/106. Available at www.un.org/development/desa/disabilities/convention-on-the-rights-of-persons-with-disabilities/convention-on-the-rights-of-persons-with-disabilities-2.html. Accessed 2 August 2017.

Wachtel, T. 1997. *Real Justice: How to Revolutionize our Response to Wrong- doing*. Pipersville, PA: Piper's Press.

Walgrave, L. 2012. Restorative Justice and Human Rights in a Democratic Society. In T. Gavrielides (ed.) *Rights & Restoration Within Youth Justice*. Whitby: de Sitter Publications.

Zehr, H. 2005. *Changing Lenses: A New Focus for Crime and Justice*, 3rd ed. Ontario: Herald Press.

12

Restorative policing for the 21st century

Historical lessons for future practice

Kerry Clamp

Introduction

At the end of the 1980s, the introduction of family group conferencing in New Zealand and the publication of the seminal text *Crime, Shame and Reintegration* (Braithwaite, 1989) dramatically altered the global restorative justice landscape in two principal ways (Umbreit and Zehr, 1996a). First, those who were involved in delivering restorative processes were no longer exclusively trained volunteers but increasingly became trained practitioners. Second, the number of participants in the process expanded beyond the victim, offender and facilitator to include friends, family members and other interested parties. As scholarship on restorative justice became increasingly popular, it also became possible to distinguish restorative scholars based on their intellectual and philosophical orientations (Dignan, 2005).

First, *abolitionists* campaigned for the replacement of the criminal justice system with an alternative restorative system of justice (e.g. Zehr, 1990). Second, *separatists* believed that criminal justice and restorative justice were incompatible and that any interaction between the two would result in the usurpation of restorative justice for criminal justice aims. Thus, they campaigned for restorative justice to exist as a completely distinct twin-track system (e.g. Wright, 1991). Third, *reformists* believed that restorative justice principles, values and processes had the potential to transform criminal justice from the 'inside-out' and thus campaigned for its integration within the criminal justice process (Dignan and Lowey, 2000).

Of course, the criminal justice system has remained robust, and there is widespread agreement that it will remain the dominant formal response to crime and deviance for the foreseeable future. While the ambitions of reformists have had a number of promising starts,[1] the fears of separatists have also been apparent, as Umbreit explains:

> As any reform moves from its early stage of development and attempts to become accepted and institutionalized, the probability of 'losing its soul' is increased. As the primary focus of

---

1 This has included the integration of restorative outcomes (such as reparation, compensation and community service) into sentencing. 'Mainstreaming' has also been evident, whereby restorative principles and processes

the process shifts from offering an experience of healing and closure for those most affected by crime to serving justice system goals, the initial passion and creativity of the movement can be quickly lost.

(1999: 214)

The insemination of restorative justice into the criminal justice system in neoliberal states has reflected this pattern. In particular, the obsession with legislating behaviour criminal, holding offenders to account and managing the performance of criminal justice agencies through targets and audits has resulted in a rather limited presence of *qualitatively* 'restorative' solutions to the crime problem. Instead, these initiatives have often been characterised by low victim participation rates and a neo-correctionalist[2] agenda whereby the '"don't make matters worse" philosophy of the minimum intervention approach' has been rejected 'in favour of a policy of *zero tolerance*' (Cavadino and Dignan, 2007: 320, emphasis original). Thus, managerialist concerns over 'effectiveness' have constrained the expansion of restorative justice within the criminal justice system (Miers, 2004).

The outcome of this for restorative policing in its contemporary guise, particularly within England and Wales, is that it is primarily used as an early interventionist response to minor offending committed by juveniles (Shewan, 2010). This is in stark contrast to the aims and practice of the original restorative policing model which sought to find a way of effectively dealing with crime *outside* of the criminal justice process and in *partnership*[1] with the community. This chapter interrogates the reasons for this and makes two key arguments. The first is that the operationalisation of restorative justice within contemporary policing environments, with the pressures of austerity and public accountability, naturally lends itself to quantity over quality resolutions that can be interrogated and repackaged in the form of statistics.

The second is that both the champions and evaluators of contemporary restorative policing schemes have prioritised learning from perceived risks rather than the key successes secured during pilots. If we return to the origins of the restorative policing model, we learn that good practice takes time, investment and community-police partnerships. Only once these resources are secured can a form of restorative policing take place that benefits all stakeholders. Limits to that realisation come from surprising quarters and raise some uncomfortable questions about the state of the field if restorative policing was 'allowed' to work.

This chapter thus forms an important part of a collection that focuses on contentious applications of restorative justice framed by a forward-looking orientation. Restorative policing (only matched by the application of restorative justice to domestic and sexual violence) has received significant resistance from commentators who believe that the risks involved in allowing such practice far outweigh the benefits (see Clamp and Paterson, 2017 for a broad overview of this debate). In seeking to meet the Handbook's aims, this chapter begins by explaining what restorative policing is, for those who are unfamiliar with this area of practice, by looking at its emergence in Australia at the beginning of the 1990s. Next, a short history of the international experimentation of restorative policing is presented before drilling down into why the Wagga Model worked and why it has not been replicated elsewhere. The chapter ends by arguing that a strategy of 'learning fast' and 'doing fast' can only end in 'fast failure' (Braithwaite, 2016).

---

have shaped new policy and legislation (i.e. in diversion programmes or within the reform of the system itself in relation to young offenders, as in New Zealand, Northern Ireland and South Africa. See further Clamp 2008).

2 See Cavadino and Dignan (2007) for a full discussion of the characteristics of this.

The 'Wagga Model' of restorative policing: a brief overview

It should be noted that all police work in common-law countries takes place prior to the prosecution of offences, and therefore the use of restorative justice processes within this context takes place as a diversionary option, or in other words, an informal resolution of the case without prosecution. Given the range of due process concerns that arise from such interaction, most restorative justice schemes used within these settings first require the offender to admit responsibility for the offence and then for both the victim and the offender to consent to their participation in the process. Reportedly, such an inclusionary approach results in (more often than not) participants experiencing a sense of 'procedural justice' – that they are satisfied that they have been dealt with in a fair and equitable manner (see Tyler, 2006).

In contrast, in civil law jurisdictions, such as Europe, police officers do not hold the same level of discretion as their neoliberal counterparts (Daly, 2001). Decision making about the offences that are channelled into and away from the criminal justice process is often determined by prosecutors rather than police officers (Clairmont and Kim, 2013). As such, the opportunity for restorative practice to be used by police officers is restricted because they are unable to decide on how a case should be dealt with on their own or in consultation with the affected parties (Vynckier, 2009). For this reason, this chapter deals exclusively with common-law jurisdictions given the focus is on the Wagga Model.

Restorative policing in common-law jurisdictions, in particular, has been underpinned by three innovative developments in criminal justice (McCold and Wachtel, 1998). The first was the emergence of community and problem-oriented policing which sought to alter the dominant and ineffective reactive policing style by increasing partnerships between the police and the community they served. The second was the emergence of the theory of reintegrative shaming (Braithwaite, 1989) that argued informal social networks were more effective in bringing about remorse and actions to repair harm caused than were remote legal authorities (see further Moore et al., 1995). Finally, the restorative justice movement offered a *process* through which the objectives of community/problem-oriented policing and reintegrative shaming could be realised. Thus, the emergence of the restorative policing model has offered the police a framework through which to engage victims, offenders and communities in dealing with crime, an aspect that has largely been missing from community-oriented and problem-oriented policing (Clamp and Paterson, 2017).

Restorative policing practice[3] emerged during the early 1990s in New South Wales, Australia. Terry O'Connell (a Senior Sergeant with NSW Police) and John McDonald (Advisor to the Police Commissioner on Youth and Juvenile Justice) played instrumental roles in the development of what became known as the 'Wagga Model' of police cautioning (see Moore and O'Connell, 1994). Traditional responses were seen to perpetuate a criminal cycle due to the stigmatising and often humiliating nature of the process, and therefore alternative approaches were explored to contest the 'revolving door' of youth crime that was blighting the community (Moore, 1995). The only offences that were automatically disqualified from the conferencing

---

3 Restorative policing can be discussed in one of two ways. First, as the 'Wagga Model', which refers to the practice of police officers facilitating conferences between victims, offenders and their supporters (i.e. the processes themselves are police-led). Second, as the 'New Zealand Model' which not only rejects the active role of police officers as facilitators but also expands the notion of restorative policing beyond the conferencing process to include the integration of restorative principles into routine policing practice and referrals to conferencing schemes that exist outside of the police agency altogether. For the purposes of this chapter, only the police-led scheme or the Wagga Model is discussed.

scheme were serious indictable offences (i.e. those offences that were punishable by imprisonment for a minimum term of five years or more). Instead, the amount of individual and social harm caused (rather than the type of offence committed) was the primary criterion used in selecting cases. For a detailed explanation of the history and practice of the Model, please see Chapter 28, in this Handbook, written by Terry O'Connell.

Moore and Forsythe (1995) evaluated the scheme by analysing the Model, gathering the views of conference participants (including police officers and other government officials) and grounding their findings within a theoretical model. The research revealed a number of extraordinary findings. First, the numbers of cases being processed by the courts declined by 50 percent *without any net-widening* (i.e. the amount of cases reported to the police began to decrease – they were not dragging less serious offences into the conferencing process). Second, this occurred *without increasing the recidivism rate* (in fact, there was a 40-percent reduction in repeat offending overall). In addition, 93 percent of offenders fulfilled the agreements that they had participated in creating during the conference, and high levels of satisfaction amongst all participants (i.e. the police, victims and offenders) was reported (see Moore, 1994).

The restorative policing 'movement'[4]: trials and tribulations

These results unsurprisingly soon garnered the attention of practitioners further afield, and other states across Australia adopted the Wagga Model, including the Australian Capital Territory (see Sherman et al., 1997), the Northern Territory (see Fry, 1997), Queensland and Tasmania (see O'Connell, 1998). However, towards the middle of the 1990s, intense academic debate[5] and political distaste arose about the legitimacy of police-led conferencing (see Moore and Forsythe, 1995; Daly, 2001). This has resulted in the visible absence of police-led conferencing in Australia. Ultimately, in 1998, the running of conferences fell under the jurisdiction of juvenile justice agencies with police officers referring suitable cases on to restorative justice schemes run outside of police forces (Richards, 2010). However, around the same time as the demise of restorative policing in Australia, it began to gain ground internationally.

The first country outside of Australia to experiment with the Wagga Model was the United States (O'Connell, 1998). The most well-known scheme is the 'Bethlehem Family Group Conferencing Project' in Pennsylvania because of its experimental evaluation (McCold and Wachtel, 1998). The primary purpose of the experiment was to assess the model by randomly diverting suitable cases to conferencing or through the normal adversarial (i.e. court) process (Hines and Bazemore, 2003). Eligible cases included a high percentage of first-time felony cases and repeat offenders charged with misdemeanour violations in which the offender was willing to admit responsibility and the victim and family agreed to participate.

Early findings indicated that some of the 18 police officers who had received training to facilitate conferences did not carry them out according to the benchmarks of the Wagga Model, and further training and support had to be delivered. McCold and Wachtel (1998) report that officers were able to facilitate conferences in a manner consistent with due process and restorative

---

4 It is important to note that while only two examples of the Wagga Model have been presented here, it was implemented in a range of different forces within the US, in Canada and a number of counties within the UK. This representation has been necessarily selective due to space constraints. For a more more detailed overview, please see Clamp and Paterson (2017).

5 There is a wide body of literature that is critical of an increase in restorative practice within the criminal justice sector generally and, more specifically, police-facilitated restorative processes (see, for example, Ashworth, 2001; McCold, 1998; Umbreit and Zehr, 1996a, 1996b; Young, 2001).

justice principles (most of the time) where further ongoing support and training was offered. All outcomes were agreed to by the victim and were perceived to be reasonable in relation to the nature of the offence committed. This research showed that victims (96 percent) and offenders (97 percent) were satisfied with the process, just as much as other victim-offender mediation programmes facilitated by non-police officers, and nearly all respondents confirmed that they would opt to participate in a similar process again and recommend it to others (McCold, 2003). Much like in Wagga Wagga, the vast majority of offenders (94 percent) fulfilled the contents of the agreements reached during the conference (McCold and Stahr, 1996).

However, unlike in Wagga Wagga, McCold and Wachtel (1998) reported that they did not perceive a cultural shift across the force, only a moderate change amongst those actually delivering conferencing towards a more community-oriented problem-solving approach (McCold, 2003). This lack of cultural transformation was thought to be a result of the marginalisation of the pilot, which was kept separate from the broader policing activities taking place on a day-to-day level. Both officers and supervisors saw conferencing as an additional task to be undertaken which interfered with patrol and responding to calls for service, thus attracting limited organisational and managerial support (McCold, 2003). As a result, despite the positive findings that the evaluation yielded, practice was soon marginalised in favour of referring cases out to community-based restorative justice organisations.

A few years later, another notable case study emerged in England and Wales. Sir Charles Pollard, who was the Assistant Chief Constable at Thames Valley Police at the time, sought to reduce crime through a force-wide rollout of the Wagga Model (1998–2001). His approach departed from previous restorative policing experiments in that a headquarters-based 'Restorative Justice Consultancy' was established to oversee the training of police officers across the force to ensure consistent practice by police officers in a more transparent and accountable manner against specific aims and standards. This acknowledged some of the objections raised by critics of police officer involvement in facilitating restorative processes (see further Clamp and Paterson, 2017). Furthermore, two distinct practices emerged – restorative *cautions* (which only involved the offender and his or her supporters) and restorative *conferences* (which also involved the victim and his or her supporters).[6]

The scheme was evaluated using an action research methodology whereby the police could benefit from interim findings and alter their practice as the evaluation went on (Young and Hoyle, 2003). This proved to be useful given that evaluators found a number of implementation issues that included officers dominating discussions, prioritising their own agendas rather than those of the participants, reinvestigating the offence, engaging in intelligence gathering and behaving as if the offender had to account to them personally, with the other participants reduced to little more than passive observers (Hoyle et al., 2002). Furthermore, a significant procedural problem was identified in that over a third of participants received no pre-conference preparation.[7] In response to this, researchers were able to arrange top-up training for officers, and the introduction of a revised script insisted officers not pursue a policing agenda during the conferencing process, which resulted in a dramatic reduction of the issues outlined (Hoyle et al., 2002).

---

6 Pollard's tenacity in lobbying for a more pronounced role of restorative justice in response to crime committed by youths received backing by the government through the eventual introduction of the Crime and Disorder Act 1998 and the Youth Justice and Criminal Evidence Act 1999 (Hoyle, 2007, 2009).

7 These findings are not unusual for English restorative justice schemes (see, for example, Crawford and Newburn, 2003 in relation to juvenile referral orders or Meadows et al., 2010 on community justice panels).

Nevertheless, in 2001, shortly after Charles Pollard left the force, the government began putting significant pressure on Thames Valley to improve their performance figures for detections (whereby an offender is prosecuted for an offence). Without strong leadership and support for restorative justice from within, restorative cautioning and conferencing began to decline, and soon traditional cautions were once again being utilised (Hoyle, 2007). The legacy of restorative policing in England and Wales is that conferencing has been mainly used for cases that would not have been prosecuted (Hoyle, 2002), thus resulting in net-widening – a feature that had been absent in most of the case studies up until this point.

These two key examples of international experimentation (US and UK) with the Wagga Model demonstrate both stark and complementary findings in comparison to the original pilot. While police leaders (post-Wagga Wagga) were keen to associate their forces with the restorative policing experiment and drive forward some changes in restorative practice at the frontline, ultimately their legacy withered and normal policing resumed. In many respects, this is unsurprising. The role of senior police officers is to provide vision and a sense of mission for the force, and these individuals were certainly successful in introducing restorative concepts and setting force priorities in favour of a restorative, as opposed to a crime control, response. However, 'vision among the lower ranks is more operationally focused', with officers reluctant to change their approach and practices unless such change also suits their perceived purpose and functions (Pearson-Goff and Herrington, 2013: 19). In many respects, then, the initial 'boom' of restorative practice within these forces can be attributed to subordinate officers following orders, while the subsequent collapse provides evidence of a veneer of change rather than any meaningful change within the cultural meaning of police work at the local level.

Some have suggested that the key to longer-term change lies in a move from a transactional leadership style to a transformational leadership approach. The former, said to be a traditional or conventional approach to managing forces, involves the leader specifying not only the expectations of subordinates but also the conditions under which such expectations should be met and the rewards and penalties on offer (Engel and Worden, 2003). In recent years, this approach has fallen into disrepute and transformational leadership styles have become increasingly popular which emphasise 'participation, consultation and inclusion' in a bid to get subordinates to buy into the 'vision' that is being proposed (Silvestri, 2007: 39), much like that witnessed in Wagga Wagga.

While approaches to motivate cultural change within police forces are clearly important, it is questionable whether this would result in sustainable change in the long term. Rather et al. (2013) suggest that in order for meaningful and sustainable change to take place, a twin-track approach is needed whereby leadership from above is informed by restorative principles that not only allow, but also actively encourage, transformational leadership by frontline officers. Contemporary attempts to drive this change occur within a top-down approach that unfortunately has not resulted in a significant transformation of policing itself or police relations with the communities that they serve more generally. So while restorative policing presents a radical shift in the expectations of how police officers should approach their job, and indeed the resistance felt in response to restorative policing confirms how radical a shift it is, it has not been implemented through a larger process of reform.

Instead, a short-term view of restorative justice has been adopted – one that offers a cost- and time-effective response to low-level offending – which has doomed it to the margins of police business. In addition, the resistance to viewing restorative policing as an important transformative shift has hampered the potential of restorative approaches not only for policing but for offending behaviour as well. This has been reinforced by the perception that restorative justice is a 'soft option' and one that should be viewed by offenders as a last chance (as outlined by the welfare approach) before punitive action is taken (as outline by the zero-tolerance approach). This repackaging of restorative justice has enabled neoliberal governments to 'sell' a perceived 'soft option' for dealing with offending behaviour in a manner that more comfortably sits with the punitive attitudes of the public.

The 'politicization' of crime and a 'bifurcated' approach (see Cavadino and Dignan, 2007) to dealing with offending reflects the growing intolerance and fear of crime amongst the public, sensationalist media reporting and the exploitation of the subject by politicians (Garland, 2001). In both the United States and the United Kingdom, there is a much greater demand for accurate crime data to demonstrate that something is 'being done' and a greater emphasis placed on accountability. As such, statistics have become an important part of public policy to highlight and describe the nature of social problems and also to monitor and inform the policies and practices designed to remedy them (Simmons et al., 2003). The significant challenge with this reality is a need to transcend both the cultural and political belief that punishment is necessary. The Wagga Model, to a large degree, provided the evidence-base to show that there are effective alternatives to the *status quo*. What is needed is a long-term view of crime reduction and an overhaul of the relationship between the police and the public, as the following section will now demonstrate.

Learning from the past: the Wagga model

The problem with subsequent iterations of restorative policing is threefold. First, previous and contemporary programmes continued to operate without altering the role of policing in reducing crime. Offending behaviour or 'crime' is viewed as an offence against the state that needs to be punished in line with both reductivist and retributive principles. This has led to a number of critics to question the utility of current justifications for punishment, particularly in light of evidence that challenges the main rationales that underpin contemporary criminal justice approaches (see further Braithwaite, 1997; Cavadino and Dignan, 2007; Lacey, 2003). Cavadino and Dignan (2007: 61), in particular, suggest that there is '[n]o morally legitimate aim of punishment that cannot be achieved just as well and more humanely by the use of non-custodial punishment'. This leads them to ask: 'Why – unless we are all closet reductivists or retributivists – should not offenders be formally denounced with words and ceremony and then set free?' (2007: 48)

In Wagga Wagga, police officers were convinced that the criminal justice process was *the problem* and that they needed to alter their approach in order to disrupt offending behaviour that was blighting the community. They did this not only by creating an alternative approach for cautioning but also (and perhaps most importantly) by forging a strong partnership with local community members.[8] This has been missing from subsequent iterations of the Model, which have largely been implemented through a 'top-down', rather than a 'bottom-up' approach. The distinction between the two approaches is that the former is superimposed *onto* the community whereas the latter is conducted in conjunction *with* the community.

More often than not, community-based schemes are devised as a means to further engage the public in the administration of criminal justice in an attempt to increase confidence in the criminal justice system (see Clamp and Paterson, 2017) rather than to reduce reliance on it as in Wagga Wagga. Moore (1993) regards this is a mistake. For him, consultation with the geographic community is essential and only once full consent and cooperation is achieved should

---

8 It is important to note that this Model, unlike others, was not informed by local 'indigenous' justice practices, nor were local indigenous communities involved in its development. The community referred to here refers to a geographic one.

any scheme be established. Indeed, subsequent schemes have located ultimate failure as the result of a lack of community ownership (see, for example, Hines and Bazemore, 2003; Roberts and Masters, 1999). As Johnstone (2002) warns, 'restorative' schemes are inherently more difficult to implement because there is a lack of consensus about the roles (both traditional and those newly created) of individuals within the process.

Second, crime in Wagga Wagga was redefined as a breakdown of relationships (rather than an offence against the state), and conferencing or restorative dialogue, with its focus on harm and relationships, became an opportunity for changing the experiences and lives of *all* stakeholders. As such, the principle of 'parsimony' guided policing in Wagga Wagga along with a shift in practice whereby breaches of obligation to the law were 'addressed as if they were breaches of obligation to the family and community' (Grimshaw, 2004: 7). However, this shift has not been achieved in later cases. In fact, the imposition of restorative policing on police officers has created important unintended consequences, as Braithwaite predicted many years ago when he said:

> If the police do not support conferencing and are not involved, and listened to in the development of conferencing policies, then conferencing is not a good idea. This is not just because police resistance will effectively kill the reform. If police do not believe in conferencing and are required to refer young people to someone else to run a conference, they will not refer many cases. Worse, the cases they do refer will be cases they do not regard as serious enough to justify laying a charge themselves.
>
> *(1994: 208)*

A wide range of empirical studies investigating police decision making in referrals to independent restorative justice schemes have demonstrated that they have widened the net rather than reducing it, as in Wagga Wagga. The most common factors cited that influence whether or not police divert cases has included the seriousness of the offence, offending history and attitude – particularly evidence of remorse and responsibility (see Carrington, 1998; Crocker, 2013; Doob and Cesaroni, 2004; Doob and Chan, 1982; Marinos and Innocente, 2008; Meadows et al., 2012). This ultimately results in bias given that oppressed minorities often benefit less because of cultural differences in interaction (police not being able to interpret remorse) and over-policing (and thus having prior criminal records). This approach further reinforces that restorative justice schemes are perceived as yet another fad in police reform by officers rather than a completely new way of perceiving and reacting to crime.

Third, restorative policing was not perceived to be a programme or a scheme but rather a new way of being. A canvass of local officers prior to the implementation of conferencing revealed that, not unlike other forces who experimented with restorative justice, the approach was perceived as a 'soft option'. In an attempt to get sceptics to support a trial of the proposed scheme, a sergeant's review committee met once a week to review all juvenile matters, to decide which cases would be eligible for caution and to invite officers to observe the process (Moore and Forsythe, 1995; O'Connell, 1998). This slow and considered approach to developing the new cautioning process is acknowledged for helping the police to accept the merits of the Model and subsequently actively support its implementation (see O'Connell, 1998). The review committee had a further unintended consequence in that it challenged bias in case selection, as O'Connell explains:

> Previously young people were too often inappropriately arrested for an offence, which might be called 'contempt of cop'. Quality control was being exercised for the first time,

with supervisors reviewing all juvenile arrests in a collegial way, establishing 'benchmarks' for the seriousness of offences. This, and not necessarily the conferencing process itself, accounted for much of the considerable reduction in the number of cases placed before the court between 1991 and 1993.

(1998: n.p.)

Review committee meetings were also transparent in that they were open to interested parties (police and community) who wanted to attend. Developing oversight mechanisms and encouraging external community participation served to provide an additional set of checks and balances that were not always available in later iterations of the Model. The current 'on the spot/ street RJ' that takes place by police officers in England and Wales and Northern Ireland does not serve to drive down the amount of cases dealt with by the criminal justice process but often further increases the net of cases. As demonstrated by O'Mahony and Doak:

[S]ome 80% of cases . . . examined were for offences concerning property of less than £15. It was not uncommon to come across cases where a considerable amount of police time had been invested in arranging for a full conference for the theft of a chocolate bar or a can of soft drink.

(2004: 495)

So what can we take from the Wagga Model to inform current practice? I have grouped these under three headings: time, investment and community-police partnerships.

Time

As research has shown (see, for example, Hoyle et al., 2002; McCold and Wachtel, 1998), some officers find the transition to restorative policing a relatively easy one, whereas others are unable to easily grasp the implications of restorative practice for their roles. When O'Connell first developed the Wagga Model, it took time to learn what worked and what did not. While this groundwork has been laid, there is still a need for this learning to take place in each implementation site. A common theme running across all US and UK restorative policing pilot sites is that training has been done either 'intensively' through a three-day course or through a one-day session (also see Justice Committee, 2016). This does not work. In the words of John Braithwaite (2016): '[L]earning fast and doing fast can only lead to fast failure.'

As such, success in this area requires constant reinforcement through training, monitoring and mentoring. Getting police officers to embrace this role and to understand it presents the biggest obstacle. The Wagga Model has demonstrated that involving officers in case selection and/or having them observe conferences facilitated by their colleagues appeared to have a significant impact on subsequent attitudes towards the Model (see Clamp and Paterson, 2017). As highlighted by developmental theorists, notably William James, John Dewey, Lewin and Piaget, people learn best through 'doing', which can be fostered by having a supportive structure in place to facilitate understanding (see Landry, 2011 for an overview of police officer learning styles). As such, in many respects, it is inevitable that mistakes will be made and that 'old habits will die hard' until officers gain insight into what is required during the process and hold an appreciation of what it means to act in a restorative way – a radical shift from traditional institutional practice.

Shapland (2009) speculates that the manner in which practice is implemented can have a significant impact on whether police-led schemes are successes or failures. Drawing on her own experience, she suggests that the best models are characterised by specialised units undertaking restorative justice facilitation on a full-time basis. The importance of this approach is that officers are able to 'up skill' on a continuous basis; they are relatively autonomous (and therefore somewhat shielded from the operational pressures experienced throughout the force more widely); they can 'develop and maintain a proper restorative culture'; they have sufficient time for follow-up; and no conflicts arise in terms of the facilitating officer also being the arresting officer (2009: 128). These assumptions appear to be consistent with the experience of schemes in both Australia and the United States and explain the varied experience in the United Kingdom.

However, this also has the unfortunate consequence of marginalising restorative practice, which then has no impact on the wider organisation. Furthermore, as other initiatives have shown, these small units are subject to the changing whims of force priorities. Real sustainable restorative policing needs to be a force-wide initiative that starts with a few and slowly expands outwards, integrating other force members through a ripple effect. The key to the success of the short-lived Wagga Wagga pilot, was that both the community and police officers were exposed to restorative justice through a slow and considered approach, and a safety net was implemented through the review committee, who were committed to community policing (Moore and Forsythe, 1995; O'Connell, 1998). Once this had been done and a conference arranged, officers were offered the opportunity to observe the process. This has been a key feature of convincing sceptical officers (not only in Australia but worldwide) that restorative justice is not a soft option and that there is high value in dealing with offences in a restorative manner.

Investment

Many of the studies on the Wagga Model have identified officers as being committed to restorative justice values, demonstrating genuine concern for the future welfare of offenders, treating participants with respect and encouraging active participation (see, for example, Sherman and Strang, 1997; Young and Gould, 2003). Criticism of police involvement in restorative practice that use police culture as the frame of analysis struggle to pick up the nuances that emerge from the mixed economy of policing (Crawford, 2005). Contemporary policing is resourced via a mixture of traditional reactive police officers who work alongside more community-oriented officers who may be funded by local authorities, private agencies or even acting as volunteers. Each organisation will have its own distinct working culture, and close collaborative working has the potential to produce new hybrid cultures.

As such, Young (2003) argues that traditional police culture can certainly pose a challenge to the implementation of restorative policing but that the evidence suggests that the threat that police will act as 'judge and jury' when facilitating cases might be overstated. A more pressing issue is that senior officers become complacent when implementing restorative practices within their forces, believing that police facilitation poses no problems and can be carried out without the investment of resources. As Sherman and Strang note:

> When RJ (or any programme) is rolled out quickly on a wide scale, there is a risk that many conferences will just 'go through the motions' to 'tick off a box', rather than treating each case as a kind of surgical procedure requiring careful advance planning, preparation and follow-up.
>
> *(2007: 21)*

As such, in a climate of austerity, it is harmful to promote restorative justice on the basis of its cost savings. It is not an easy solution to a crime problem. If done properly, it is actually very resource intensive. The cost savings come after the conference in the form of a reduction in recidivism. There appears to have been a misinterpretation of how savings were made in Wagga Wagga. Ultimately, it was police oversight and management of cases that were being brought into the system as many of them, as outlined previously, were for 'offences' that should not have been considered 'offences' at all.

Community-police partnerships

Kathy Daly (2016) has argued that we should perceive restorative justice as a mechanism, because if we think of it as anything beyond this, it is doomed to failure. The problem with this assessment is that restorative policing/conferencing becomes yet another tool in the police officer's toolbox. The outcome is that restorative processes are subject to operationalisation in a way that fits with overriding norms and values of the system. Restorative justice is not about responsibilising offenders, reducing recidivism or a quick fix. Only once officers understand that it is not a tool and rather a completely new way of viewing the crime problem, engaging with people that they come into contact with (both inside and outside of the police organisation) and viewing success, will long-lasting change come about. Change, as the Wagga Model has shown, could be revolutionary not only for the criminal justice system but for communities as a whole.

Restorative policing offers a completely different way to respond to crime. Individuals and groups within communities are not only important stakeholders but also essential actors in determining what behaviour falls outside of tolerable limits. This creates a dramatic shift in the *status quo*. In order for policing priorities to be set, the community has to be engaged in a conversation about what the priorities should be. Furthermore, the community has to be actively engaged so that they play a key role in responding to behaviours that are unacceptable. Policing thus becomes a community-police issue that requires strong partnerships to be forged.

Conclusion

This chapter has argued that we have learnt little from previous iterations of restorative policing. It does seem strange that we appear to have been successful in creating a revolutionary policing model but that despite the reported successes, it has failed to be taken seriously by senior criminal justice practitioners. The Wagga Model was so successful because it viewed 'success' in a different light. Many years ago, Peel (1829, *emphasis original*) argued that '[t]he test of police efficiency is the *absence* of crime and disorder, not the *visible evidence* of police action in dealing with it'. Many of the key restorative policing proponents have understood this and made a case for the reform of the way in which policing is viewed and how that shift would alter police-community responsibilities.

Unfortunately, in practice, the visible evidence of police action has usurped restorative processes whereby cases are brought into contact with the criminal justice process that ultimately should not be there. Some six years ago, Bazemore and McLoed (2011) provided an alternative framework through which restorative processes could, and should, be evaluated. They suggested that we should ask:

> whether the intervention process, and subsequent follow-up steps, created or strengthened relationships; increased participants' sense of capacity and efficacy in community skills in problem-solving and constructive resolution; promoted individual awareness of and commitment to the common good; and expanded informal support systems or 'safety nets' for victims and offenders.

> *(2011: 162)*

The Social Discipline Window (Wachtel, 1997, 2000; Wachtel and McCold, 2000) provides a visual to demonstrate how restorative justice is distinct from other approaches. If any initiative or programme is going to be successful, we have to involve all stakeholders in the process so that we do things *with* them rather than *to* or *for* them. Perhaps stated more explicitly, the police should involve all stakeholders (in our case community members, victims and offenders as well as their supporters) through a process of co-construction of practice in the negotiated space of justice realisation that seeks to confront and reduce power imbalances.[9] Through empowerment, knowledge co-construction and the validation of 'lived experiences', all involved would be able to propose new crime responses rather than applying standardised solutions to injustices by outside 'experts' (i.e. the government or policing hierarchies).

As such, restorative policing should become an iterative process (as demonstrated by the Wagga Model) whereby it is used as a reflective process of progressive problem solving to improve the way the police and community address issues and solve problems collectively. Instead of viewing restorative justice as a *tool* for achieving the functions of policing (i.e. upholding and enforcing the law, promoting and preserving public order, protecting the public and preventing crimes), restorative policing should be perceived as an entirely different *framework* through which officers can develop an effective partnership *with* the community. Through such an approach, restorative policing can ultimately result in a way to transform the way we view crime, our responses to it and to reduce social distance (Braithwaite, 2003; Christie, 2004; Johnstone and Van Ness, 2007).

Ultimately, where officers are trained fast and do fast, they can only fail fast, too. Restorative policing is so much more than a mechanism that should be evaluated according to the criminal justice systems key performance indicators (such as reducing recidivism, satisfaction and cost-benefit analyses). Ultimately, the Model has demonstrated strong outcomes in this regard, but that did not frame why O'Connell and his colleagues designed and implemented it. They knew that the current approach to dealing with offending was faulty and that change had to be initiated within the force along with their community's help first. Imagine, for a moment, what society would be like if restorative policing was allowed to work as intended.

Note

1 The author would like to thank Professor David O'Mahony for his helpful comments on an earlier draft of this chapter.

References

Ashworth, A. 2001. Is Restorative Justice the Way Forward for Criminal Justice?, *Current Legal Problems*, 54: 347–376.

Braithwaite, J. 1989. *Crime, Shame and Reintegration*. Cambridge: Cambridge University Press.

Braithwaite, J. 1994. Thinking Harder About Democratising Social Control. In C. Alder and J. Wundersitz (eds.) *Family Conferencing and Juvenile Justice: The Way Forward or Misplaced Optimism?* Canberra: Australian Institute of Criminology.

Braithwaite, J. 1997. *Restorative justice: Assessing an immodest theory and a pessimistic theory*. Available at www.aic.gov.au/rjustice/braithwaite.html

Braithwaite, J. 2000. Republican Theory and Crime Control. In S. Karstedt and K. Bussmann (eds.) *Social Dynamics of Crime and Control: New Theories for a World in Transition*. Oxford: Hart.

9 Often used in public health; see, for example, Shannon et al. (2008).

Braithwaite, J. 2003. Principles of Restorative Justice. In A. von Hirsch, J. Roberts, A. Bottoms, K. Roach and M. Schiff (eds.) *Restorative Justice and Criminal Justice: Competing or Reconcilable Paradigms?* Oxford: Hart.

Braithwaite, J. 2016. Learning to Scale Up Restorative Justice. In K. Clamp (ed.) *Restorative Justice in Transitional Settings*. London: Routledge.

Carrington, P. 1998. *Factors Affecting Police Diversion of Young Offenders: A Statistical Analysis*. Ottawa: Solicitor General of Canada.

Cavadino, M. and Dignan, J. 2007. *The Penal System: An Introduction*. London: Sage Publications.

Christie, N. 2004. *A Suitable Amount of Crime*. London: Routledge.

Clairmont, D. and Kim, E. 2013. Getting Past Gatekeepers: The Reception of Restorative Justice in the Nova Scotia Criminal Justice System, *The Dalhousie Law Journal*, 36(2): 359–391.

Clamp, K. 2008. Assessing Alternative Forms of Localised Justice in Post-Conflict Societies – Youth Justice in Northern Ireland and South Africa. In D. Frenkel and C. Gerner-Beuerle (eds.) *Selected Essays on Current Legal Issues*. Athens: ATINER.

Clamp, K. and Paterson, C. 2013. An Exploration of the Role of Leadership in Restorative Policing in England and Wales. In A. Normore and N. Erbe (eds.) *Collective Efficacy: Interdisciplinary Perspectives on International Leadership*. Bingley: Emerald.

Clamp, K. and Paterson, C. 2017. *Restorative Policing: Concepts, Theory and Practice*. London: Routledge.

Crawford, A. 2005. *Plural Policing: The Mixed Economy of Visible Patrols in England and Wales*. Bristol: Policy Press.

Crawford, A. and Newburn, T. 2003. *Youth Offending and Restorative Justice: Implementing Reform in Youth Justice*. Cullompton: Willan.

Crocker, D. 2013. The Effects of Regulated Discretion on Police Referrals to Restorative Justice, *The Dalhousie Law Journal*, 36(2): 393–418.

Daly, K. 2001. Conferencing in Australia and New Zealand: Variations, Research Findings and Prospects. In A. Morris and G. Maxwell (eds.) *Restoring Justice for Juveniles: Conferencing, Mediation and Circles*. Oxford: Hart.

Daly, K. 2016. What Is Restorative Justice? Fresh Answers to a Vexed Question, *Victims & Offenders*, 11(1): 9–29.

Dignan, J. 2005. *Understanding Victim and Restorative Justice*. Maidenhead: Open University Press.

Dignan, J. and Lowey, K. 2000. *Restorative Justice Options for Northern Ireland: A Comparative Review*. Research Report 10. March. Belfast, Northern Ireland: Criminal Justice Review Group.

Doob, A. and Cesaroni, C. 2004. *Responding to Youth Crime in Canada*. Toronto: University of Toronto Press.

Doob, A. and Chan, J. 1982. Factors Affecting Police Decisions to Take Juveniles to Court, *Canadian Journal of Criminology*, 24(1): 25–37.

Engel, R.S. and Worden, R.E. 2003. Police Officer Attitudes, Behaviour and Supervisory Influences: An Analysis of Problem-Solving, *Criminology*, 41(1): 131–166.

Fry, D. 1997. *A Report on Community Justice Program: 'Diversionary Conferencing'*. Northern Territory Police: Alice Springs.

Garland, D. 2001. *The Culture of Control: Crime and Social Order in Contemporary Society*. Oxford: Oxford University Press.

Grimshaw, R. 2004. *Whose Justice? Principal Drivers of Criminal Justice Policy, Their Implications for Stakeholders, and Some Foundations for Critical Policy Departures*, vol 7. London: British Society of Criminology conference.

Hines, G. and Bazemore, D. 2003. Restorative Policing, Conferencing and Community, *Police Practice and Research: An International Journal*, 4(4): 411–427.

Hoyle, C. 2002. Securing Restorative Justice for the 'non-participating' Victim. In C. Hoyle and R. Young (eds.) *New Visions of Crime Victims*. Oxford: Hart.

Hoyle, C. 2007. Policing and Restorative Justice. In G. Johnstone and D. Van Ness (eds.) *Handbook of Restorative Justice*. Cullompton: Willan.

Hoyle, C. 2009. Restorative Justice Policing in Thames Valley. In T. Peters, P. Ponsaers, J. Shapland and B. Van Stokkom (eds.) *Restorative Policing*. Netherlands: Maklu-Publishers.

Hoyle, C., Young, R. and Hill, R. 2002. *Proceed with Caution: An Evaluation of the Thames Valley Police Initiative in Restorative Cautioning.* York: Joseph Rowntree Foundation.

Johnstone, G. 2002. *Restorative Justice: Ideas, Values, Debates.* Collumpton: Willan.

Johnstone, G. and Van Ness, D. 2007. The Meaning of Restorative Justice. In G. Johnstone and D. Van Ness (eds.) *Handbook of Restorative Justice.* Collumpton: Willan.

Justice Committee. 2016. *Restorative Justice Inquiry: Report.* House of Commons: UK Parliament.

Lacey, N. 2003. Penal Theory and Penal Practice: A Communitarian Approach. In S. McConville (ed.) *The Use of Punishment.* Cullompton: Willan.

Landry, J. 2011. *Learning Styles of Law Enforcement Officers: Does Police Work Affect How Officers Learn?* Unpublished PhD thesis, Capella University, Minneapolis.

Marinos, V. and Innocente, N. 2008. Factors Influencing Police Attitudes Towards Extrajudicial Measures Under the Youth Criminal Justice Act, *The Canadian Journal of Criminology and Criminal Justice,* 50(4): 469–489.

McCold, P. 1996. Restorative Justice and the Role of Community. In B. Galaway and J. Hudson (eds.) *Restorative Justice: International Perspectives.* Monsey, NY: Criminal Justice Press.

McCold, P. 1998. *Police-Facilitated Restorative Conferencing: What the Data Show.* Paper presented to the Second Annual International Conference on Restorative Justice for Juveniles, Florida Atlantic University, and the International Network for Research on Restorative Justice for Juveniles, Fort Lauderdale, FL, 7–9 November. Available at: fp.enter.net/restorativepractices/policeconferencing.pdf.

McCold, P. 2003. An Experiment in Police-Based Restorative Justice: The Bethlehem (PA) Project, *Police Practice and Research: An International Journal,* 4(4): 379–390.

McCold, P. and Stahr, J. 1996. *Bethlehem Police Family Group Conferencing Project.* Paper presented to the American Society of Criminology Annual Meeting, Chicago, 20–23 November.

McCold, P. and Wachtel, B. 1998. *Restorative Policing Experiment: The Bethlehem Pennsylvania Police Family Group Conferencing Project.* Pipersville, PA: Community Service Foundation.

Meadows, L., Albertson, K., Ellingworth, D. and Senior, P. 2012. *Evaluation of the South Yorkshire Restorative Justice Programme.* Sheffield: Hallam Centre for Community Justice.

Meadows, L., Clamp, K., Culshaw, A., Cadet, N., Wilkinson, K. and Davidson, J. 2010. *Evaluation of Sheffield City Council's Community Justice Panels Project.* Hallam Centre for Community Justice. Sheffield: Hallam Centre for Community Justice.

Miers, D. 2004. Situating and Researching Restorative Justice in Great Britain. *Punishment and Society,* 6(1): 23–46.

Moore, D. 1993. Facing the Consequences. In L. Atkinson and S. Gerull (eds.) *National Conference on Juvenile Justice Conference Proceedings.* Canberra: Australian Institute of Criminology.

Moore, D. 1994. Evaluating Family Group Conferences. In D. Biles and S. McKillop (eds.) *Criminal Justice Planning and Coordination.* Canberra: Australian Institute of Criminology.

Moore, D. 1995. *A New Approach to Juvenile Justice: An Evaluation of Family Conferencing in Wagga Wagga:* A Report to the Criminology Research Council. Wagga Wagga, AUS: Center for Rural Social Research, Charles Sturt University – Riverina.

Moore, D. and Forsythe, L. 1995. *A New Approach to Juvenile Justice: An Evaluation of Family Conferencing in Wagga Wagga:* A Report to the Criminology Research Council. Wagga Wagga, AUS: Centre for Rural Social Research, Charles Stuart University – Riverina.

Moore, D., Forsythe, L. and O'Connell, T. 1995. *A New Approach to Juvenile Justice: An Evaluation of Family Conferencing in Wagga Wagga.* Wagga Wagga, AUS: Charles Strut University.

Moore, D. and O'Connell, T. 1994. Family Conferencing in Wagga Wagga: A Communitarian Model of Justice. In C. Alder and J. Wundersitz (eds.) *Family Conferencing and Juvenile Justice: The Way Forward or Misplaced Optimism?* Canberra: Australian Institute of Criminology.

O'Connell, T. 1998. *From Wagga Wagga to Minnesota.* Paper presented at the First International Conference on Conferencing, Minneapolis, MN, USA. Available at www.iirp.edu/article_detail.php?article_id=NDg5

O'Mahony, D. and Doak, J. 2004. Restorative Justice – Is More Better? The Experience of Police-Led Restorative Cautioning Pilots in Northern Ireland, *Howard Journal of Criminal Justice,* 43(3): 484–505.

Pearson-Goff, M. and Herrington, V. 2013. Police Leadership: A Systematic Review of the Literature, *Policing: A Journal of Policy and Practice*, 8(1): 14–26.

Peel, R. 1829. *Sir Robert Peel's Principals of Law Enforcement*. Available at www.durham.police.uk/About-Us/Documents/Peels_Principles_Of_Law_Enforcement.pdf

Richards, K. 2010. *Police-Referred Restorative Justice for Juveniles in Australia*. Trends & Issues in Crime and Criminal Justice no. 398. Canberra: Australian Institute of Criminology.

Roberts, A. and Masters, G. 1999. *Group Conferencing: Restorative Justice in Practice*. Minneapolis, MN: University of Minnesota, Centre for RJ and Mediation, School of Social Work.

Shapland, J. 2009. Restorative Justice Conferencing in the Context of Community Policing. In L. Moor, T. Peters, P. Ponsaers, J. Shapland and B. van Stokkom (eds.) *Restorative Policing*. Netherlands: Maklu-Publishers.

Sherman, L. and Strang, H. 1997. *The Right Kind of Shame for Crime Prevention*, RISE Working Paper No. 1. Canberra: Australian National University, Research School of Social Sciences. Available at www.aic.gov.au/rjustice/rise/index.html

Sherman, L. and Strang, H. 2007. *Restorative Justice: The Evidence*. London: The Smith Institute.

Sherman, L., Strang, H. and Barnes, G. 1997. *Reintegrative Shaming Experiment for Restorative Community Policing*. Canberra: Australia National University.

Shewan, G. 2010. *A Business Case for Restorative Justice*. Available at www.restorativejustice.org.uk/resource/the_business_case_for_restorative_justice_and_policing/

Silvestri, M. 2007. Doing Police Leadership: Enter the New Smart Macho, *Policing and Society*, 17(1): 38–58.

Simmons, J., Legg, C. and Hosking, R. 2003. *National Crime Recording Standard (NCRS): An Analysis of the Impact on Recorded Crime*. Companion Volume to Crime in England and Wales 2002/2003. Home Office Occasional Paper 31/03. London: Home Office.

Tyler, T. 2006. Restorative Justice and Procedural Justice: Dealing with Rule-Breaking, *Journal of Social Issues*, 62(2): 307–326.

Umbreit, M. 1999. Avoiding the Marginalization and 'McDonaldization' of Victim – Offender Mediation. In G. Bazemore and L. Walgrave (eds.) *Restorative Juvenile Justice: Repairing the Harm of Youth Crime*. New York: Criminal Justice Press.

Umbreit, M. and Zehr, H. 1996a. Family Group Conferences: A Challenge to Victim-Offender Mediation?, *VOMA Quarterly*, 7(1): 4–8.

Umbreit, M. and Zehr, H. 1996b. Restorative Family Group Conferences: Differing Models and Guidelines for Practice. *Federal Probation*, 60(3): 24–29.

Vynckier. 2009. A Comparative View on the Role of Police in Different Restorative Practices in Flanders. In L. Moor, T. Peters, P. Ponsaers, J. Shapland and B. van Stokkom (eds.) *Restorative Policing*. Netherlands: Maklu-Publishers.

Wachtel, T. 1997. *Real Justice: How to Revolutionize our Response to Wrongdoing*. Pipersville, PA: Piper's Press.

Wachtel, T. 2000. Restorative Practices with High-Risk Youth. In G. Burford and J. Hudson (eds.) *Family Group Conferencing: New Directions in Community Centered Child & Family Practice*. Hawthorne, NY: Aldine de Gruyter.

Wachtel, T. and McCold, P. 2000. Restorative Justice in Everyday Life. In J. Braithwaite and H. Strang (eds.) *Restorative Justice in Civil Society*. New York: Cambridge University Press.

Wright, M. 1991. *Justice for Victims and Offenders: A Restorative Response to Crime*. Milton Keynes: Open University Press.

Young, R. 2001. Just Cops Doing 'Shameful' Business? Police-led Restorative Justice and the Lessons of Research. In A. Morris and G. Maxwell (eds.) *Restorative Justice for Juveniles Conferencing, Mediation and Circles*. Oxford: Hart.

Young, R. 2003. Just Cops Doing 'shameful' Business? Police-Led Restorative Justice and the Lessons of Research. In A. Morris and G. Maxwell (eds.) *Restorative Justice for Juveniles Conferencing, Mediation and Circles*. Oxford: Hart.

Young, R. and Gould, B. 2003. Restorative Police Cautioning in Aylesbury – From Degrading to Reintegrative Shaming Ceremonies. In E. McLaughlin, R. Fergusson, G. Hughes and L. Westmarland (eds.) *Restorative Justice: Critical Issues*. Thousand Oaks, CA: Sage Publications.

Young, R. and Hoyle, C. 2003. New Improved Police-Led Restorative Justice? In A. von Hirsch, J. Roberts, A. Bottoms and M. Schiff (eds.) *Restorative Justice and Criminal Justice Competing or Reconcilable Paradigms*. Oxford: Hart.

Zehr, H. 1990. *Changing Lenses*. Scottsdale, PA: Herald Press.

13

Restorative justice and gender differences in intimate partner violence

The evidence

Anne Hayden

Introduction

Dealing with IPV (intimate partner violence) by using restorative justice is a subject which continues to raise eyebrows and debate. This is despite frequent comments from around the world (Mills, 2008; Goel, 2010; Gavrielides et al., 2014; Gavrielides, 2017) which show that IPV is not decreasing or becoming less serious, *and* that there is general dissatisfaction with the criminal justice system (Gelsthorpe, 2014). It seems logical to me that if the status quo is not always working, then careful consideration and research into alternative ways of dealing with this type of violence needs to be carried out. In this subject, however, there is a serious impediment of "blinkered vision" in a variety of sectors, particularly victim advocacy.

This chapter concerns alternative ways of thinking about IPV and what can work. It is based on the premise that mainstream remedies for dealing with IPV have proved inadequate in their majority. While much of the data focuses on the New Zealand situation, its implications relate to the wider community. The chapter will use a three-pronged approach, including a relatively brief literature review about the definition of IPV, victim precipitation, and relevant research. Because most literature cites women as being most frequently abused by men and most affected by IPV, and only occasionally acknowledges that men may also be subjected to IPV, the voices of men are seldom heard. Earlier research (Hayden, 2010) produced some data not previously discussed in depth and will form the basis of my attempt to help fill the literature gap. The same research will develop findings relating to (1) dissatisfaction with the criminal justice system and its approach to IPV, and (2) using restorative justice as a potential course of action in some cases.

Where we currently stand with IPV

It is agreed that there is little consensus among researchers on how to define IPV. Terms such as IPV, domestic violence, gender(ed) violence, family violence, and spousal violence have been used interchangeably. Intimate partner violence, though, has been used more recently. Some terms are used politically. For example, the word battering has consistently been used by the anti-domestic violence movement.

There are numerous feminist analyses of many aspects of IPV, including possible causal factors, incidence, and implications. Two of those are by Nancarrow and Stubbs. Addressing causal factors, Nancarrow (2006) described IPV as a consequence of patriarchal power, with social and economic structures making women dependent upon men and therefore vulnerable to abuse by them. Using gender-neutral language, Stubbs (2002) discussed IPV as control-based, comprising features such as:

- A range of behaviours and coercive tactics, not always recognisable to others;
- Being often repetitive, meaningful and strategic, reflecting deeply held beliefs rather than an isolated incident; and,
- Social and cultural norms giving meaning to the violence, possibly authorizing or sustaining gender-based violence which may constrain women's options for dealing with the violence. (Stubbs, 2002, pp. 43–44)

Gender differences have been seen in studies of the impact of IPV. New Zealand research by the Ministry of Justice (Morris et al., 2003) reported that although women's violence to men was similar in proportion to men's, it had a significant difference in its impact. Women reported that they were affected very much or quite a lot, whereas men were not. Dobash and Dobash (2004) made similar observations.

Mackenzie (2009), of Safer Homes in New Zealand Everyday, studied arrested women in Auckland. Out of 60 women, Mackenzie found 40 had offended against male victims (2009: 11–15). Of these, almost 50% were intimate partners and had a history of being the victim of the same male intimate partner (p. 11). A quarter (25%) of the women offended against their intimate partner and had no known history, whereas 15% women had a history as a perpetrator against the intimate partner, and 12.5% had perpetrated violence against other male victims. This finding is consistent with theory about victim precipitation (Muftic et al., 2007b), discussed later in this chapter.

Homicide is a known outcome of some IPV. For example, a 1991 study by Fanslow, Chalmers and Langley, cited in Anderson (1997: 6), found 47% of female homicide victims were killed by an existing or former male partner. A report by the Family Violence Death Review Committee in New Zealand (2014) found that between 2009 and 2012 an average of 13 women, 10 men, and nine children were killed each year as a result of family violence. The World Health Organization (2013), which examined global and regional estimates of violence against women, found that globally, 38% of the murders of women were committed by their intimate partners. In data reported by The Huffington Post (2014) in the US, 1,509 women were murdered by men they knew during 2011. Of that number, 926 were killed by an intimate partner.

As we focus on gender differences in IPV, it is necessary to examine the term "gender violence" in greater detail. Earlier international covenants referred to IPV as gender violence, generally considered to be violence by men against women. For example, the General Assembly of the United Nations, in its "Declaration on the Elimination of Violence Against Women" (1993), in Article 1, defined violence against women as:

> any act of gender-based violence that results in, or is likely to result in, physical, sexual, or psychological harm or suffering to women, including threats of such acts, coercion or arbitrary deprivation of liberty, whether occurring in public or private life.
>
> *(United Nations, 1993)*

In Article 2, the General Assembly further defined violence against women as including but not limited to:

> Physical, sexual and psychological violence occurring in the family, including battering . . . (and) marital rape
>
> *(United Nations, 1993)*

These covenants were formed only a few years after the New Zealand police (and police in other parts of the world) became aware of the need to change its attitude to domestic violence from "just a domestic" to it being a serious offence against women (see Ford, 1993). Accordingly, it is not unreasonable to consider the term "gender violence" as the basis of the common belief that men abuse women rather than it going both ways or the other way around. Nor is it unreasonable to think gender violence relating to men's violence is now a habitual way of thinking. IPV against women needed to be countered and the UN Covenant, largely driven by the domestic violence movement, evolved as part of that objective. As far as I am aware, there is no equivalent for male victims. The Oxford English Reference Dictionary, however, states the word "gender" refers to a "person's sex . . . belonging to such a class . . . sex as expressed by social or cultural distinctions" (Pearsall and Trumble, 1995) It does not use the word in solely feminine terms.

However, as long as abuse remains unreported, there is little chance of accurately establishing its prevalence in our communities, or the genders affected. Taking us nearer to this knowledge is an important and recent New Zealand survey conducted by Auckland University by Clark et al. (2015) which examined the sexual and reproductive health of secondary school students. As we know, intimate partner (or "gender violence") includes sexual abuse. Around 8,500 students from around New Zealand were surveyed about their experiences of unwanted sexual contact, sexual and reproductive health, and ethnic factors. Even though out of the total number of boys (N = 184), 25% had experienced bad, really bad, or terrible sexual contact, only 9% reported it to anyone. Similarly, with the girls (N = 622), where 40.1% had experienced bad, really bad, or terrible sexual contact, 19.5% reported it. Thus, less than half of those boys and half of the girls reported their experiences. Furthermore, the study showed that males also experienced abuse, in this case, sexual abuse. Therefore, it casts doubt, in my view, on the prevalent assumption that women and girls are the only victims of this type of violence.

For example, a number of researchers and some literature (e.g. Curtis-Fawley and Daly, 2005; R.E. Dobash et al., 2007; Enander, 2010; Hester, 2004) and common usage by practitioners in the field also indicate that gender violence is violence perpetrated by men against women. Gelles (2004: 412) acknowledges that women are the most likely to be injured. He qualifies this, however, by stating that society focuses so much attention on battered women that male victims become invisible. "The real horror is the continued status of battered men as the "missing persons" of the domestic violence problem." (Gelles (2004: 412).

New Zealand's Crimes Act (1961) has a crime called "male assault female", a very serious offence. However, if a female assaults a male, it is a common assault, which has a lesser penalty. This implies that women's violence against men is something different, unrelated to gender and requires less accountability. Linda Mills describes this common perception as follows.

> Whether we as a society are comfortable admitting it or not, many men are physically abused. Ironically, many of our assumptions, whether unspoken or otherwise, about battered men are similar to those we once held about battered women: "Why don't you fight back? Why do you stay? You're so pathetic to put up with this."
>
> *(Mills, 2008: 35)*

Merry (2009) summarized gender violence as a diverse set of actions ranging from interpersonal violence within the home to the rape of men or women. It was violence whose meaning depended on the gendered identities of the parties. Merry acknowledged the wide range of issues and approaches used to define gender violence, noting the risks associated with a movement-generated definition. She stated:

> [The movement] has produced a very broad definition of gender violence that has some conceptual incoherence and builds on a wide variety of theories about [gender violence] and modes of intervention.

Gender has, according to Murray A. Straus (2006), influenced the way research has been reported. He gave examples of research that collected data about the violence of men and women but published only that which related to men's violence against women. Straus explained that this could be due to an ideological commitment to the idea that men are almost always a sole perpetrator, and, significantly, to avoid "vitriolic denunciations and ostracism". Furthermore, Straus raised a possibility of progress towards equality between men and women leading to more equality in the perpetration of crime (Straus, 2006).

Fortunately, some research has found limitations in the term. For example, Fergusson et al. (2005) in a Christchurch (New Zealand) birth cohort of 25 year olds, which examined both victimization and perpetration of IPV, found "considerable similarity in the range of responses and levels of domestic violence reported by men and women" (Fergusson et al., 2005: 1113). Fergusson et al. suggested this could indicate that IPV was more a function of violent partnerships rather than violent individuals. Johnson (2005) suggested Fergusson's results were the result of situational couple violence, because it was the most common type of IPV. Johnson (2006) identified four types of IPV: (1) intimate terrorism (gross misuse and imbalance of power by one party against the other), (2) violent resistance (when one party fights back), (3) situational couple violence (when neither is controlling but each can be violent or non-violent), and (4) mutual violence (both are equally violent).

The differences in intimate partner experiences are crucial when considering an appropriate response. They should not all be treated as one phenomenon. As Johnson (2006) stated, to make useful policy recommendations, these distinctions need to be made. In other words, each case of IPV needs to be assessed on its own merits rather than using a blanket approach for all, both in policy and practice.

Another way of looking at the involvement of two parties in IPV is victim precipitation.

In contrast to an innocent victim (Hollander, 2009) who lacked an ability to resist violence perpetrated against them and who was weak and defenceless, some victims have had something to do with the incident. When victims' actions were a contributing factor, Muftic, Bouffard, and Bouffard (2007a), attributed this to victim precipitation, or "the victim . . . act[ing] as a direct, positive precipitator in the crime" (citing Wolfgang, 1967; Muftic et al., 2007a: 328). Victim precipitation was referred to as "unplanned or spontaneous" by Koons-Witt and Schram (2006). Their research on the relationship between co-offending groups, victims, and the conditioning of these by the offender's race, found that aggravated assaults committed by women were usually retaliatory and involved a personal relationship with the victim. Citing research by Wolfgang (1967), Muftic et al. (2007a) discussed a sample of homicides involving many victims and offenders who were in interpersonal relationships. In 26% of the homicides, victims had been first to use physical force. Wolfgang referred to these as victim precipitated, or examples of victims who had used their agency, possibly to defend themselves. Muftic et al. (2007a) suggested that victim precipitation could provide new insights into the use of violence among intimates, especially the contextual differences between men's and women's use of violence.

Downey (1997; cited in Daly and Nancarrow, 2010, in Ptacek, 2010:153) stated that violence in families is often recursive or mutually shaping. Most people working in the field would agree that it is not unusual for adult perpetrators of abuse to have been victims of parental abuse, thus perpetuating intergenerational violence. Thus, it is clear IPV is very complex. Is restorative justice, then, one option for sorting out who did what and why and where to go from here?

Restorative justice and intimate partner violence: the new debate

Like other countries where restorative justice has been practised, there has been considerable debate in New Zealand about the use of restorative justice for IPV. This global discussion has been explained by Frederick and Lizdas (2010) as a result of the crossing of paths of two reform movements, the battered women's movement and the restorative justice movement, each of which were challenging the Western criminal justice system. These "both . . . [held] the promise of being truly effective responses to domestic violence" (Frederick and Lizdas, 2010: 39). In this section, I consider the implications of using restorative justice for IPV. A starting point is to determine whether current criminal justice practices improve victims' safety.

Gelsthorpe (2014: 116) summed it up:

> [E]stablished criminal justice practices and the law have not speedily, convincingly or uniformly succeeded in ensuring women's safety and there are some promising results from empirical studies relating to the use of restorative justice in the context of violence . . . [however] it is important to take account of women's preferences.

Gelsthorpe highlights the need to take into account the specific needs of individual cases, careful planning, and cultural perspectives, while noting that the new Victims' Code, in Section 7 states that police must, where appropriate, offer or direct victims to information about restorative justice, ensuring the victim is not re-victimized, particularly victims of domestic or sexual abuse or violence (Ministry of Justice, 2013).

Restorative justice offers more to victims and perpetrators of IPV than they have at present. As highlighted by Christie (Llewellyn and Philpott, 2014: 120, cited in Van Ness), state control of domestic criminal justice is now so complete that it has amounted to a "theft of crime" from victims and offenders, thus excluding them from meaningful roles in resolving crimes and decision making. Restorative justice offers a way to correct this. Kay Pranis explained how listening respectfully to a person's story gives them a positive kind of power; it gives them dignity and worth (Pranis, 2002 cited in Goodmark, 2012), an essential ingredient of resolving conflict.

Participating in a restorative justice conference, while giving couples an opportunity for a facilitated discussion, may also pose risks. The focus of this section is on the latter, a subject about which victim advocates have been vocal. People dealing with IPV have often found it necessary to balance safety with considerations of their future together. Most battered women do not want their partners prosecuted (Frederick and Lizdas, 2010; Morris and Gelsthorpe, 2000). One possible reason is that separation has presented substantial risks for victims before, during or within a few months of separation (Busch, 2002; Stubbs, 2002). Hooper and Busch (1996) stated that a characteristic of men who are violent towards their partners is that their violence often escalates at the time of separation, or within 12 months of that date. Intimate partner violence has been considered too serious for mediation (Carbonatto, 1995; Curtis-Fawley and Daly, 2005), because it could provide the offender with another opportunity to abuse the victim emotionally or physically (Cameron, 2006; Hooper and Busch, 1996). This has been frequently attributed to an abuse of power.

Critiques have included the fact that apology was frequently used by perpetrators to reinstate their power over the victim (Stubbs, 2007); the risk of re-privatizing IPV after the years that have been spent bringing this type of offending out into the open (Curtis-Fawley and Daly, 2005; Edwards and Haslett, 2003; Stubbs, 2002); and the inability of restorative justice to prevent imbalance of power between the victim and perpetrator (Curtis-Fawley and Daly, 2005). However, there are ways to reduce this imbalance.

In addition to well-informed facilitators, procedures can be adopted to address unequal power. Morris and Gelsthorpe (2000) suggested using procedural fairness, supporting the less powerful, and challenging the most powerful. They also suggested that the presence of friends and families could prevent recurrence of violence and help monitor a safety plan. It is vital that the community present at a restorative justice conference had a deep understanding of the dynamics of IPV, the past and potential harm to the victim, the perpetrator's likely response, and other personal and political dynamics which could affect the process or the result. Curtis-Fawley and Daly (2005) cautioned that any legal response to gendered violence needed to consider different victim-offender relationships and victims' needs, factors relevant for the use of restorative justice. Furthermore, cultural factors needed to be taken into account, a possible strength of restorative justice usually absent in Western criminal justice systems.

So here is the problem. As a former victim support volunteer and victim of IPV in New Zealand, I was aware of the need for victims of IPV to have more options than to accept the status quo or report to the police. My experience as a restorative justice facilitator dealing with cases involving IPV with positive results encouraged me to seek empirical data. The promoters of the New Zealand Court-Referred Restorative Justice Pilot initiated in 2001[1] declined my request to the then-Minister of Justice, the Hon. Matt Robson, to include a small empirical study relating to family violence. I decided that it was up to me to do my own research to create some empirical data. This led to the beginning of a doctoral research which focused on non-reporting of IPV using non-randomized participants who were either victims, perpetrators of IPV, or key informants working in related fields. Although none had experienced restorative justice, I questioned them about their views on using restorative justice for IPV after giving each participant an overview of restorative justice as comprising facilitated meetings between victims and perpetrators in a safe environment. How I carried this out is described next.

Fieldwork findings on IPV and restorative justice

Research methodology

Intimate partner violence is an issue largely affecting women, so the research used methodology based on feminist literature, as appropriate to that population. Therefore, mostly qualitative data from in-depth interviews, observation, and autoethnography formed the triangulated approach.

Although a small amount of quantitative (often regarded as a patriarchal approach) data was reported, the weight of the results reported were the voices of the participants, in keeping with feminist research principles.

I had intended to use focus groups, but because of gatekeeping by victim agencies, this was not possible. The sample, therefore, was obtained in three ways by adopting a "convenient sampling strategy". Key informants were selected from my network and agencies or victim advocates I knew had anti views about using restorative justice for IPV. Perpetrators were selected as volunteers from my attendance at a men's group meeting, and by word of mouth. One perpetrator was also a key informant and an anger management group leader who offered to be a perpetrator as well. Victims were selected from my networks, word of mouth, and people I knew had been victims of IPV.

While this was a small sample, which was non-randomized, the research was justified by the use of a triangulated approach, including in-depth interviews, autoethnography, and observation. It was largely qualitative but did include simple quantitative analysis. Data was collected from both victims and perpetrators, when it is more common for research relating to IPV to be focused on either victims or perpetrators. Six case studies added depth to the experiences of people experiencing IPV.

Findings

People are classified within the judicial process as being either victim or perpetrator, yet there are situations where it is not clear who is the victim and who is the perpetrator, or even when their designated role is wrong.[2] An example of this situation was an Iranian man I called Kaveh.

Kaveh explained:

> We were not happy with each other the way that things were but there was never violence, not once. I came to the conclusion that I had to move out of there . . . So I made the arrangement for 50/50 custody [of our daughter] . . . there was never violence . . . If there had not been a child involved, I would have walked away from [my partner] in 2002, 2003. But I was worried about my daughter. I was worried about [my partner's] psychology . . . [my partner] is not a normal person. When she says, 'I'm ugly, no-one loves me, I'm miserable,' . . . Pausing on those words . . . that's what pisses me off about the Family Court or the lawyer for the child, they should examine these things! None of them came to the attention of the court . . . [Before I indicated I wanted us to separate] I said, 'I'm going to be around, I'm going to be a good Dad. Teach her the right things.' Then I realized she was abusing [my daughter]. She felt rejected and she made it clear to me she didn't want me to leave . . . She said, 'No, no. I'm going to fight if you leave me.' I said, 'Why?' She said 'Because you've destroyed my life. Who is going to come into a relationship with me?'

His wife physically fought back because he told her he wanted them to separate. She hit him repeatedly, and to make her stop he held her wrists up against the wall. Within 24 hours she laid a complaint to the police that he had abused her, which resulted in his having to spend thousands of dollars defending himself in both the Family and Criminal Courts. Despite the case being dismissed in the Criminal Court, he lost unsupervised access to his daughter as a result of a ruling by the Family Court.

This case raises the question: "Who was the victim?" It was Kaveh's view that he was the victim even though he had been arrested and charged. Supporting his claim was the fact that he was eventually found not guilty in the Criminal Court. His situation was, as far as I could tell from hearing only one side of the story as well as viewing relevant documentation, an abuse of power by his former wife. It highlights the need for greater information being available to decision makers after offending has occurred. Even though Kaveh was officially in the perpetrator group of participants in the research, he was a victim in more ways than one. His experience illustrates the potential for people to abuse the power of the criminal justice system negatively. Kaveh told me he wished a restorative justice conference had been offered. If it had, the court could have been provided more information in the conference report about both parties' views and recollection of events, emotional aspects, and the context of the offending. The outcome could have been quite different.

Another example of the negative use of power was Fraser, a victim who self-referred and was possibly the most vulnerable of all the victims in the study. He advised that at times when they argued, his wife punched, kicked, and/or threw things at him, on one occasion lacerating his head with a stiletto heel of a shoe thrown at him. The worst, he said, was being slapped, which he described as:

> . . . so degrading . . . and worse than a punch . . . an action of contempt . . . It wasn't like, she would just attack me. She would get really, really angry. And then I would want to leave and she saw that as a power and control thing . . . that I would control her by leaving and not saying when I was coming back . . . and I'd say I'd call her in the morning.

She thought his leaving the house was an exercise of "power and control" over her. Others might see it as the only non-violent means he could have used to claim back some control over his life at the time. Once Fraser telephoned the police to report his wife's abusive behaviour towards him. The policewoman answering his call asked him if he was afraid of his wife. He said he wasn't. She replied, "Then be the man and leave the house." Fraser has a police record now through the domestic violence procedures due to his wife's repeated false allegations about him. This means that the police can enter his home as and when they consider it necessary. Fraser made a very interesting observation, in fact quite a telling one.

> As a man, in some ways, it's easier to be a perpetrator. Because then you are fulfilling a stereotypical role that everyone can relate to.

Other participants also had negative comments about the criminal justice system, often related to the Family Court, where custody of children was dealt with. One perpetrator, the male spouse of an alcoholic, commented,

> The domestic violence hearing taught me that the Family Court didn't see me as an equal parent for my children. In my opinion, my being unable to access the family court to try to protect my children has destroyed my older son's 3rd and 4th years at school. . . . Gender bias is not as bad in the criminal court – people can usually laugh about it., whereas with the Family Court the impact stays.

Another man, charged with breaching a protection order for using misogynist language in an email about his wife to a lawyer, requested Family Court counselling to help them sort out custody issues told me,

> You are treated as though you are guilty before any of the evidence is presented. You are herded into the dock even before you have pleaded. . . . And the complainant is always referred to as the victim. So there's an automatic assumption that this male probably has an excess of testosterone and is assumed to be violent and that the female is the innocent victim, rather than both being parties to a dispute or conflict.

Yet another perpetrator tried to explain the complexity of the situation.

> *In my case you've got a lawyer and a police officer that are wanting to interpret a situation in a way that supports their actions. So the officer is trying to achieve a conviction. The lawyer is trying to achieve parental rights. Anything that strays from that disrupts what they see their role as. It's an adversarial system so their incentive is to be adversarial.*

One perpetrator put forward the suggestion that perpetrators could benefit from some help rather than judgement. He said,

> *I think that if the offender realises that other people are concerned about what is happening to him . . . because I think offenders often have pressures that cause them to commit crimes . . . even where a man strikes a woman, there's a certain amount of provocation and he reacts to it . . . sometimes the wrong way.*

Restorative justice offers the opportunity for couples to have a facilitated meeting which can include revisiting the incident, its context, and emotional aspects. What led to it all happening? Could it have been dealt with in another, better, way? In controlled situations, each party could actually listen to and hear the other's view and experience. Together with support people, they could consider how to deal with it if a similar situation arose again.

An example of what some could describe as provocation was Heeni, a Maori victim. She advised,

> *When I knew he was on [methamphetamine] and before we actually started talking about it . . . I couldn't control myself. I just went anti. I'd be negative and was at him all the time which caused us to fight more.*

Ian, a perpetrator, called it a mutual problem:

> *To me it is a mutual problem. It is not just one hitting on the other. Extreme cases . . . maybe in one hitting on the other. But often it is not. It is a conflict which reflects the power struggle between the male and female. The man's reaction, usually, is to get a bit physical. The female's tactic is usually a lot more subtle. But it's the actual issue. And simply to deal with one part of that conflict and to demonise one half of that conflict is not dealing with the issue, with the fundamentals.*

Neville, another perpetrator, commented that it was not only men who used violence in an intimate relationship:

> *I've got two friends now, where the female is the perpetrator of violence. But . . . they'll never get reported . . . well, they probably wouldn't . . . describe it as domestic violence . . . a guy can stick up for himself most times. . . . but that doesn't stop the female partner displaying violence, but the guy's gonna be pretty unlucky if he comes off second best, if you know what I mean . . . it's just part of the relationship, you just keep going.*

Also significant was Neville's comment, which indicated resignation and acceptance of the status quo, with his comment that "you just keep going."

Recently (July 2016) I conducted an interesting exercise around the issue of gender(ed) violence. I was fortunate enough to be invited to participate in the Third Restorative Justice

Symposium 2016, held on Skopelos Island, Greece.[3] As part of my presentation on the use of restorative justice for IPV, I included an exercise to be completed by the multidisciplinary group of 18 leading scholars, academics, and practitioners. In groups of two or three, they had five to ten minutes to share with their group one time when they were "really, really angry". Following this, I asked them to then discuss the reasons. Were they angry because the person(s) they were angry with:

(a) was of a particular gender – that is, their behaviour was inappropriate for a boy/girl or man/woman?
(b) was related to you? – that is, it was ok for someone else's family member to do it but not yours?
(c) had done something wrong?

Their responses were unanimous in favour of (c), that is, they had been angry because of what the subject of their anger had done. It had not been gender or the relationship that had prompted the intense emotion. Clearly this data is not generalizable, but it does lend some weight to the need to reconsider the current trend/practice of using the term gender(ed) violence. Furthermore, it provides an invitation for in-depth research into the subject of intense anger to determine whether or not the gender bias as is present today is relevant or indeed, appropriate. I will now discuss what I consider are the implications of my doctoral research, supplementing this discussion with some newer material related to this troubling topic for communities here in New Zealand and abroad.

Implications

Cases

Both Fraser's and Kaveh's case studies illustrate that men are reluctant to report incidents of IPV. In behavioural terms, it could be argued that this virtually reinforced their wives' abusive behaviour towards them. The implications of the low reporting are numerous. Men will continue to be victimized and their experiences minimized or marginalized as unimportant or irrelevant when compared to the abuse of women. Women will continue to be considered the only or main victims of IPV. Under New Zealand's legislation where women can only be charged with "common assault", women will be included as perpetrators of violence but will not be accountable for their violence towards their partners in the same way men are under the "male assaults female" offence. Modelling theory suggests that boys will learn from their fathers and peers that it is unmanly or inappropriate to report abuse, while girls will learn that it is the prerogative of women to abuse their men.

There will continue to be inadequate support for men who are being abused. On the other hand, it is possible for support for men to be available personally, through the community, or institutionally. My research showed that reporting IPV need not be confined to the police alone. Instead I identified five levels of support: a family member or friend; employer, acquaintances or colleagues; professionals such as counsellors, school teachers, health providers; victim support, men's groups or women's refuge; and ultimately, the police (Hayden, 2010).

Generally, when we talk about reporting, we think of telling the police, but each of these levels is an opportunity to get help or support and to make a safety plan. Unfortunately, men rarely ask for support. This, coupled with the heightened probability that they will become perpetrators later in life, has a negative impact on any attempts to reduce family or intimate partner violence. Furthermore, there are few agencies to support men who are victims of IPV. There are no men's refuges. One key informant in my research (Hayden, 2010) told me that some years previously one men's refuge was established in New Zealand which could not be maintained for lack of funding.

The nearest attempt to remedy this is work is being carried out by New Zealand community leader Rick Houghton, Chief Executive Officer of He Korowai Trust. Houghton is in the process of establishing a home where men involved in IPV, the majority of whom are perpetrators, are able to take time out from their situation. When the full meaning of the definition of IPV was canvassed, he advised that everyone including the men, women, and children were victims. The reasons for this in many cases are socio-economic, often as a result of colonization (see Hayden, 2014).

Houghton described the demographic of the Far North of New Zealand as including 37% single parent families with 25% living below the poverty line. The situation could be described as a vicious cycle, where poverty created hardship, frustration, dysfunction, and abuse, which in turn led to the men being arrested and incarcerated. As a result, they lost their jobs; their wives were then given sole custody of the children, the responsibility of the state-owned house and were supported by the state. As he put it, "The [state] has taken over the men's role".[4] Consequently, any hopes of reconciliation were strongly disadvantaged because the men were dependant, frustrated, and suffering from low self-esteem.

The Trust's approach to these men tends to be clinical rather than providing a refuge. Men are assisted to address their health and communication issues, and/or to "unlearn [undesirable] learned"[5] behaviours. Sometimes the partners are included in this process, using restorative language and communication skills. Because of minimal government support, He Korowai focused on healing its own community, rather than taking a corrections approach. Therefore, a significant step in a healing approach has to be to address intergenerational violence.

The cycle of intergenerational violence is maintained by offspring and youths witnessing and modelling abusive behaviour of their parents and other family members, be they men or women. This includes parental behaviour intended to correct or reprimand their children's behaviour by using abusive means, similarly "acting out" violently to their partners, or other family members. Intergenerational violence self-perpetuates violence between and of both genders. New Zealand's Domestic Violence Act 1995 includes in its definition of domestic violence, allowing children or young people to witness it. I am uncertain, however, how often witnessing IPV on its own is considered sufficient to either report or lay charges on those who ignore it. It has similar connotations to Fraser's case when he reported. It appears to be a situation of when there is no physical evidence to substantiate it, no further action is taken.

As long as men's victimization by their intimate partners is ignored, minimized, or marginalized, they are being denied access to the same human rights to safety, and so on, as women. Unfortunately, existing gender-free conventions provided for in the purposes and principles of the United Nations Charter, for example, appear to be disregarded. Article 1(3) provides for the:

> promot[ion] and encourag[ment of] respect for human rights and for fundamental freedoms for all without distinction as to race, sex, language, or religion.
>
> *(www.un.org/en/documents/charter/chapter1.shtml)*

New Zealand has a Commission for Human Rights where Commissioners are required to promote understanding of measures to ensure equality and freedom from discrimination (see Hayden, 2014:74). Commissioners are required to promote and encourage understanding and compliance with the New Zealand Bill of Rights Act 1990. Among other things, this Act in section 9 provides that:

> Everyone has the right not to be subjected to torture or to cruel, degrading, or disproportionately severe treatment or punishment.

The New Zealand Victims Rights Act 2002 requires that victims be treated with courtesy and compassion; and their dignity and privacy be respected (Part 2, 7 (a) & (b). Thus, in New Zealand the infrastructure and legislation are there but are virtually forgotten when it comes to men's rights. Perhaps this is a clue to why there is so much dissatisfaction with the criminal justice system, both here in New Zealand and elsewhere. One of the reasons violence is intergenerational could be public dissatisfaction with the state's dealing with crimes. The next section will briefly address some of the consequences of this dissatisfaction.

Dissatisfaction with criminal justice systems

As long as people are dissatisfied with the criminal justice system, they will be reluctant to report IPV to the police. This, as illustrated earlier, this is especially so for men. They can almost surely assume that they will be blamed, ignored, or their victim experience will be minimalized. Their manhood will be even more under threat and their self-esteem shattered. Fraser's comment that it was easier to be the perpetrator was indicative of the demeaning effect of (a) the abuse, and (b) the result of reporting to anyone, but especially to the police.

This could almost certainly increase their frustration levels and their likelihood of striking back. Thus, couples could find themselves experiencing situational couple violence or mutual violence as defined by Johnson (2005) earlier. Their families will have increased opportunities to witness the violence perpetuated by either or both parties, and intergenerational violence will become increasingly likely. There will be little opportunity for the criminal justice system to demonstrate justice and fairness to *all* parties to the abuse. Laws prohibiting violence will be considered a waste of time by perpetrators and victims alike as long as it is all right for women's violence to continue.

Criminal justice systems exist because states have taken on the responsibility of making people accountable for their wrongdoing. However, the current trend of women being assumed innocent does not achieve that objective. Many women are just not being held accountable, and as a result may be of the impression that they (and their violence) are untouchable. Whereas the "innocent until proven guilty" ethic seems to apply to women without full and objective investigations taking place, the reverse appears to be happening for men. It seems to me that they are predominantly seen as guilty unless proven innocent.

The exercise I carried out at the Symposium gave an indication that gender is not always, indeed ever, an issue with violence generally. While the questions I asked did not specify anger with intimates, it would be a useful exercise for future research to explore this option, thus gaining more information about the significance of gender in IPV. Are women abusive towards their men because they are men, or abusive towards their children because of their gender? Similarly, are men abusive towards their partners and children because of their gender? I think not. While the imbalance in criminal justice remains as it is, so will the level of violence. I was once told my views risked turning the family violence movement on its head. I accept that to effect changes in these widely held views about gender will take time. However, many families and couples do not have that time as they move towards self-destruction. One way to improve accountability of all participants in IPV is taking away the prejudice and making restorative justice more available.

What RJ has to offer

As long as emotions and context are ignored, current interventions for dealing with these situations have limited capacities. Does the criminal justice system adequately deal with the emotional side of IPV or the context in which IPV has occurred? I asked my research participants what they thought. Most key informants, including members of the judiciary, agreed that the criminal justice system falls short in this regard.

Restorative justice has been practised in situations of IPV for some years. One key informant, a judge, when asked if he supported the use of restorative justice for IPV, responded with a resounding "yes". His work in Rotorua entailed making regular referrals of these cases to restorative justice service provider Mana Social Services. He added that the judges in his court frequently found that in the majority of cases after an assault was over; the victim would want to recant, in whole or in part. He considered that if the victim knew of the possibility of restorative justice which could, if there was a positive outcome, reduce the punishment of the perpetrator, the victim was more likely to seek help in the first place.

Reporting similar experiences in the courts, Mather (2005) commented that frequently perpetrators will remain in the relationship or relationships will resume shortly after an incident. This is likely to influence the co-operation of victims within the criminal justice system. However, on the subject of restorative justice for IPV, a key informant (Judge O) was slightly more conservative, coming from a provisionally positive point of view:

> *The ethical dilemma remains for the intervener, especially when the violence is repeat and/or serious. Because we have such a poor success rate with [family violence] prosecutions, where victims don't carry through, from a wider perspective, we might in fact get better interventions with a less coercive approach in some cases.*

Victims in my research (2010) were also positive about the potential of restorative justice. For example, recently separated Gayle, who had moved on, saw it as having benefits for her ex-partner and adult children, and she would participate in a conference for their sakes. She stated:

> *I think it would be great if, um, both parties are willing. Fantastic. It could be hugely helpful, I'm sure. Um, whether or not you're talking about IPV, whether or not they're getting back together again, I think it would be hugely helpful to help them move on, understand their behaviour, understand their partner's behaviour, and air any grievances and um, . . . and . . . probably give them tools to get on with their lives and heal themselves. . . . healing of what made them aggressive. . . . To help him move on, get some self awareness, and you know, help him in future relationships . . . If he's genuinely wanting to help himself, yes I would. Um, I imagine, though, in that situation . . . I could possibly get quite angry. Um, but yeah, if it helped him out, if he genuinely wanted to sort himself out . . . He's not all bad, you know, and also, he's my children's father . . . And him having some insight into himself is going to be helpful for their relationship with him. Because at the moment, especially with [my son] it's not good at all . . . And it's not good for [my son] not to have a good relationship with his father . . . So if [my ex partner] can come to some self awareness it would help them as well. . . .*

Brenda, who is Chinese, in hindsight felt attending a restorative justice conference would have been preferable to reporting the abuse to the authorities. She considered restorative justice could resolve issues without the perpetrator losing face. She considered restorative justice had much to offer the Chinese community because it prevented shaming of the perpetrator. In hindsight, she wished she had known about restorative justice, as it was a way she could have avoided the Western confrontational form of approach to IPV.

The Judge's enthusiasm was largely supported by recent New Zealand research by Kingi et al. (2008). They researched the delivery of restorative justice in the family violence context, based on the definition of family violence in the Domestic Violence Act 1995. It is useful to compare the data from their research, which involved 24 key informants, including violence intervention programme providers, victim advisers, judges, police, and lawyers. My study consisted of 16 key informants, including judges, victim advisors, cultural advisers, restorative justice practitioners (one of whom was a lawyer), and men's group and violence intervention programme providers. Key informants in Kingi et al. (2008) were closely divided into three groups in their support or non-support for using restorative justice for IPV. That is, a third expressed unconditional support, almost two-fifths (38%) expressed conditional support, and more than a quarter (29%) were against the use of restorative justice in family violence cases (Kingi, et al., 2008: 85). On the other hand, key informants in my research showed greater approval, the figures being just under a fifth (19%) against, a quarter (25%) were provisionally positive, and over half (56%) were positive. It is important to note, however, that the higher approval in my research was likely to be influenced by the inclusion of restorative justice practitioners in the group. Notwithstanding this, it might, to some extent, have been balanced by the inclusion in Kingi, et al. of lawyers, some of whom could have been defence counsel and therefore more likely to hold positive views on this subject. But this is uncertain.

Participants in my research considered attending counselling and/or anger management programmes to be important. What varied, however, was the timing of these. Two key informants, both victim advocates, regarded it vital for both victim[6] and perpetrator to attend, and possibly complete a programme before the restorative justice process. Furthermore, victim advocate R thought perpetrators should attend a restorative justice conference after they had attended a stopping violence programme, so that one objective would be to show the victim what they had learnt. She stated:

> They need to have attended "X" number of sessions. I think they need to be able to say what they learnt, how it applied to them. What they are able to change themselves, the awareness they have gained, what they are prepared to do to break the cycle.

Another key informant, a restorative justice practitioner and lawyer, believed, however, that making attendance at a stopping violence programme compulsory prior to a restorative justice conference would be likely to prejudice their commitment to the programme. He said perpetrators were more likely to willingly participate if attendance was an agreement made at a restorative justice conference. All victims acknowledged the need for the conference to be a safe process. One perpetrator considered intense preparation of perpetrators was an issue.

This man, speaking from the dual perspectives of perpetrator and anger management programme leader, made clear the need for appropriate preparation, including the provision of reasonable expectations of the process and outcomes as stated in the Government's restorative justice (Ministry of Justice, 2004). Zeddy said:

> I don't know whether to go or not. You know I don't know what it's going to be like. Well I'd need to be really informed about what goes on in there. I'd need to know, I'd have to have experienced several so that I could speak from a place of knowledge or experience with him. And I'd prep him for that quite a lot . . . that support person I think needs . . . I dunno, I haven't been to restorative justice, you know. I'd be concerned the support person wouldn't know how to support, you know? . . . And I'd need to

understand, I'd need to be prepped around being defensive. 'Cos if you start being defensive in an environment like that, you're stuffed. I think . . . It sort of changes the dynamics . . . [if we were to reconcile] I guess a lot of that would come out. But if we weren't together, yeah I'd be sort of – it'd be a bloody emotional experience actually. . . . It might bring up all the shame and guilt and anger again, at myself. You know, feelings at myself . . . Because sometimes it's just plain old arrogance that stops me talking about stuff. A lot of the time it's shame . . . And it's self-hate . . . [Women can ask] questions or tricky stuff where he feels trapped. . . . If I answer that, that way, she's going to come back with that, "Oh fuck you" . . . you become defensive . . . [I'd go to a restorative justice conference] if I care for her enough, and she needs to go through this, then I'd go. But it would be a scary place for me to be, an intimidating place.

One of the critiques of restorative justice is the observation that it tends to minimize the violence and focus more on reconciliation. Victim advocate T commented as follows:

We are concerned that restorative justice processes may place victims of domestic violence in more danger and may not be a safe process for them to participate in. And our concerns about that are largely due to the fact that we cannot see how a two hour restorative justice conference is going to be significantly different from the types of discussion that the perpetrator of violence and the victim might have had in the past. And that we understand that the perpetrators of violence have apologised ongoingly throughout relationships for the violence they commit. The saying "sorry" part has probably already occurred many times in the relationship, and also, talking about change and wanting to change may have happened continually throughout the relationship.

While the frequency of apologies and discussions about behaviour are undoubtedly true, these are almost without doubt occurring in a very private situation. The advantage restorative justice has over this includes the presence of support people, which, in turn, increases perpetrators' accountability and ongoing support for both victim and perpetrator (Morris and Gelsthorpe, 2000). In addition, this argument has often been countered by the view that giving the victims the opportunity to speak freely to the perpetrator in a controlled environment gives the perpetrator greater insight into the effects of their behaviour, which hopefully will lead to change (D. Coker, 2006; Edwards and Sharpe, 2004).

Although there was an opportunity to observe the effect of restorative justice in cases of IPV, when the New Zealand Court-Referred Restorative Justice Pilot was conducted, family violence was specifically excluded, as stated earlier. However, one of the main findings of this research was that there was a small overall decrease in the reconviction rate of those participants who had attended a restorative justice conference, compared with those who had not (Triggs, 2005: 7). This, at least, suggests that restorative justice could play a positive part in some IPV cases, or at least not making the situation worse.

Conclusion

In a field of much debate here in New Zealand and overseas, there is consensus that reported IPV is just the tip of the iceberg. Furthermore, most agree that the present criminal justice systems are having little impact in attempts made to reduce the incidence of this type of offending. The findings of my research support this view: out of eight victims, only four reported the IPV they experienced to the police. Of those four, only two were satisfied with the assistance provided, and one of these was in the UK. This is, at the very least, an indication that an acceptable alternative means of dealing with these situations is required. Restorative justice for these cases has been supported by positive feedback from victims and perpetrators in Kingi et al. (2008),

Tisdall et al. (2007), the majority of participants in this research, and the opinions of victim advocates in Australia.

The challenge is to encourage reporting so that IPV can be dealt with more constructively. One way would be to provide an option that could better cater for *all* victims' emotional needs and provide opportunities for both parties to put the offending into context. The incident-based arrest process found in the criminal justice system completely disregards the contexts and/or foundations of the abuse and how victims and perpetrators feel about their situations. Furthermore, it is unrealistic to expect courts to address the context and emotional side of IPV for couples, let alone do so satisfactorily.

Most participants in my research were positive about the prospect of restorative justice. As illustrated by Brenda, cultural needs presently not met by the criminal justice system could be met at a restorative justice conference. I acknowledge that research and practice must explore the potential of restorative justice with care, but I emphasize the need to be particularly mindful of the realities of research, gender, and victim advocacy biases while also being fully informed about the nature of IPV.

Opponents to using restorative justice for IPV urge the restorative justice movement to be realistic about the nature of IPV. It seems, however, that few are realistic about the abusive behaviour of women. Therefore, I urge all people working in the field of IPV to remove their blinkers on the perpetual innocence and frailty of women and the brutality of men. *It does take two to tango, and two or more to untangle the mess.*

Notes

1 For an evaluation of this Pilot, see Triggs 2005.
2 See Gavrielides, T. 2016. *Offenders No More: An Interdisciplinary Restorative Justice Dialogue.* New York, Nova Science Publishers, pp. xviii.
3 3rd International Symposium on Restorative Justice: "Disciplining and Taking Restorative Justice Forward" 2016, 17th–24th June Skopelos Island, Greece.
4 Telephone interview with CEO Rick Houghton, Te Korowai Trust, New Zealand on 22 August 2016.
5 Telephone interview with CEO Rick Houghton, Te Korowai Trust, New Zealand on 22 August 2016.
6 For victims it was suggested they attend a course which explains the dynamics of IPV and power and control (Key Informant, Interview T).

References

Anderson, T. 1997. Murder Between Sexual Intimates in New Zealand 1988–1995, Masters Thesis, Victoria University of Wellington.

Busch, R. 2002. Domestic Violence and Restorative Justice Initiatives: Who Pays If We Get It Wrong? In H. Strang and J. Braithwaite (eds.) *Restorative Justice and Family Violence*, 1st ed. Cambridge: Cambridge University Press, pp. 223–248.

Cameron, A. 2006. Stopping the Violence: Canadian Feminist Debates on Restorative Justice and Intimate Violence, *Theoretical Criminology*, 10(1): 49–66.

Carbonatto, H. 1995. Expanding Intervention Options for Spousal Abuse: The Use of Restorative Justice [Occasional Papers in Criminology New Series: No 4], *Occasional Paper in Criminology New Series: No. 4*, pp. 1–19.

Christie, N. 1977. Conflict as Property, *British Journal of Criminology*, 17 (8).

Clark, T., Moselen, E., Dixon, R., The Adolescent Health Research Group and Lewycka, S. 2016. *Sexual and Reproductive Health and Sexual Violence Among New Zealand Secondary School Students: Findings From the Youth'12 National Health and Wellbeing Survey.* Auckland, New Zealand: The University of Auckland.

Curtis-Fawley, S. and Daly, K. 2005. Gendered Violence and Restorative Justice: The Views of Victim Advocates, *Violence Against Women*, 11(5): 603–638.

Dobash, R.E., Dobash, R.P., Cavanagh, K. and Medina-Ariza, J. 2007. Lethal and Nonlethal Violence Against an Intimate Female Partner: Comparing Male Murderers to Nonlethal Abusers, *Violence Against Women*, 13(4): 329–353.

Dobash, R.P. and Dobash, R.E. 2004. Women's Violence to Men in Intimate Relationships: Working on a Puzzle, *British Journal of Criminology* (Advance Access), pp. 1–26.

Downey, L. 1997, cited in Daly, K. and Nancarrow, H., 2010. Restorative Justice and Youth Violence Towards Parents. In J. Ptacek (ed.) *Restorative Justice and Violence Against Women*, 1st ed. New York: Oxford University Press, pp. 223–248.

Edwards, A. and Haslett, J. 2003. *Domestic Violence and Restorative Justice: Advancing the Dialogue*. Available at www.sfu.ca/cfrj/fulltext/haslett.pdf. Accessed 4 November 2006.

Enander, V. 2010. 'A fool to keep staying': Battered Women Labelling Themselves Stupid as an Expression of Gendered Shame, *Violence Against Women*, 16: 5–31. Doi: 10.1177/1077801209353577.

Family Violence Death Review Committee. 2014. *Fifth Report: January 2014 to December 2015*. Wellington: Family Violence Death Review Committee, pp. 1–140.

Fanslow, J. Chalmers, D. and Langley, J. 1995. Homicide in New Zealand: An Increasing Public Health Problem. *Australian Journal of Public Health*, 19(1): 50–57

Fergusson, D.M., Horwood, L.J. and Ridder, E.M. 2005. Partner Violence and Mental Health Outcomes in a New Zealand Birth Cohort, *Journal of Marriage and Family*, 67 (December): 1103–1119.

Ford, G.W. 1993. *A Review of the 1987 Police Policy on Domestic Violence*. Auckland: Policing Developing Group, Police National Headquarters.

Frederick, L. and Lizdas, K. 2010. The Role of Restorative Justice in the Battered Women's Movement. In J. Ptacek (ed.) *Restorative Justice and Violence Against Women*. New York: Oxford University Press, pp. 39–59.

Gavrielides, T. 2017. Structured & Unstructured Restorative Justice: The Case of Violence Against Women. In D. Halder and K. Jaishankar (eds.) *Therapeutic Jurisprudence and Overcoming Violence Against Women*. Pennsylvania: IGI Global Publications.

Gavrielides, T., Loseby, G. and A. Ntziadima, A. 2014. *Restorative Justice and Domestic Violence: A Critical Review*. London: IARS Publications. ISBN: 978-1-907641-28-2.

Gelles, R. 2004. Family Violence Against Men Is a Serious Problem. In K.F. Balkin (ed.) *Violence Against Women*. Farmington Hills, MI: Greenhaven Press.

Gelsthorpe, L. 2014. The Promise and Possibilities of Restorative Justice. In A. Hayden, L. Gelsthorpe, V. Kingi and A. Morris (eds.) *A Restorative Approach to Family Violence: Changing Tack*. Surrey: Ashgate.

Goel, R. 2010. Aboriginal Women and Political Pursuit in Canadian Sentencing Circles: At Cross Roads or Cross Purpose? In J. Ptacek (ed.) *Restorative Justice and Violence Against Women*. New York: Oxford University Press, pp. 60–78.

Hayden, A. 2010. *Why Rock the Boat? Non-Reporting of Intimate Partner Violence*. PhD. Auckland University of Technology.

Hayden, A. 2014. Achieving Balance: Towards Rights-Centred Justice. In T. Gavrielides (ed.) *A Victim-Led Criminal Justice System: Addressing the Paradox*. London: IARS, pp. 57–79.

Hayden, A., Gelsthorpe, L., Kingi, V. and Morris, A., eds. 2014. *A Restorative Approach to Family Violence: Changing Tack*. Surrey: Ashgate.

Hester, M. 2004. Future Trends and Developments: Violence Against Women in Europe and East Asia. *Violence Against Women*, 10(12): 1431–1448.

Hollander, J.A. 2009. The Roots of Resistance to Women's Self Defence, *Violence Against Women*, 15(5): 574–594.

Hooper, S. and Busch, R. 1996. Domestic Violence and the Restorative Justice Initiatives: The Risks of a New Panacea, *Waikato Law Review: Taumauri*, 4(1): 101–130.

The Huffington Post. 2014. *30 Shocking Domestic Violence Statistics That Remind Us It's an Epidemic*. Available at www.huffingtonpost.com/2014/10/23/domestic-violence-statistics_n_5959776.html. Accessed 23 February 2017.

Johnson, M.P. 2005. Domestic Violence: It's Not About Gender – Or Is It?, *Journal of Marriage and Family*, 67: 1126–1130.

Johnson, M.P. 2006. Conflict and Control: Gender Symmetry and Asymmetry in Domestic Violence, *Violence Against Women*, 12(11): 1003–1018. Doi: 10.1177/1077801206293328.

Kingi, V., Paulin, J. and Porima, L., 2008. *Review of the Delivery of Restorative Justice in Family Violence Cases By Providers Funded By the Ministry of Justice: Final Report*. Wellington: Victoria University of Wellington.

Koons-Witt, B.A. and Schram, P.J. 2006. Does Race Matter? Examining the Relationship Between Co-Offending and Victim Characteristics for Violent Incidents Involving Female Offenders, *Feminist Criminology*, 1(2): 125–146. Doi: 10.1177/1557085105285971.

Mackenzie, D. 2009. *Arrested Female Offenders in Auckland City: April–September 2008*. Auckland: Safer Homes in New Zealand Everyday.

Merry, S.E. 2009. *Gender Violence: A Cultural Perspective*. Chichester: Wiley-Blackwell.

Mills, L.G. 2008. *Violent Partners: A Breakthrough Plan for Ending the Cycle of Abuse*. New York: Basic Books.

Ministry of Justice. 2004. *Restorative Justice in New Zealand: Best Practice*. Wellington: Ministry of Justice.

Ministry of Justice. 2005. *New Zealand Court-Referred Restorative Justice Pilot: Evaluation*. Wellington: Crime and Justice Research Centre, Victoria University of Wellington.

Ministry of Justice. 2013. *Draft Code of Practice for Victims of Crime (Published in Accordance with Section 33 of the Domestic Violent Crime and Victims Act 2004)*. Available at Http://www.gov.uk/government/uploads/system/uploads/attachment_data/file/182037/victims-code-consultation.pdf

Morris, A. and Gelsthorpe, L. 2000. Re-Visioning Men's Violence Against Female Partners, *The Howard Journal*, 39(4): 412–428.

Morris, A., Reilly, J., Berry, S. and Rayson, R., 2003. *The New Zealand National Survey of Crime Victims 2001*. Wellington: Ministry of Justice.

Muftic, L.R., Bouffard, J.A. and Bouffard, L.A. 2007a. An Exploratory Analysis of Victim Precipitation Among Women Arrested for Intimate Partner Violence: Violent Women or Violent Resistance?, *Feminist Criminology*, 22(6): 753–774. Doi: 10.1177/0886260507300756.

Muftic, L.R., Bouffard, J.A. and Bouffard, L.A. 2007b. An Exploratory Study of Women Arrested for Intimate Partner Violence: Violent Women or Violent Resistance?, *Journal of Interpersonal Violence*, 22(6): 753–774. Doi: 10.1177/0886260507300756.

Nancarrow, H. 2006. In Search of Justice for Domestic Violence and Family Violence: Indigenous and Non-Indigenous Australian Women's Perspectives, *Theoretical Criminology*, 10(1): 87–106.

Pearsall, J. and Trumble, B. eds. 1995. *The Oxford English Reference Dictionary*, 2nd ed. New York: Oxford University Press.

Pranis, K. 2002. Restorative Values and Family Violence. In H. Strang and J. Braithwaite (eds.) *Restorative Justice and Family Violence*. Cambridge: Cambridge University Press.

Straus, M.A. 2006. Future Research on Gender Symmetry in Physical Assaults on Partners, *Violence Against Women*, 12(11): 1086–1097. Doi: 10.a077/1077801206293335.

Stubbs, J. 2002. Domestic Violence and Women's Safety: Feminist Challenges to Restorative Justice. In H. Strang and J. Braithwaite (eds.) *Restorative Justice and Family Violence*. Cambridge: Cambridge University Press, pp. 42–61.

Stubbs, J., 2007. Beyond apology? Domestic violence and Critical Questions for Restorative Justice, *Criminology & Criminal Justice*, 7(2): 169–187.

Tisdall, M., Farmer, S., Robinson, M., Wells, A. and McMaster, K. 2007. *Review of the Use of Restorative Justice in Family Violence Cases in the Rotorua District*. Wellington: Ministry of Justice.

Triggs, S. 2005. *New Zealand Court-Referred Restorative Justice Pilot: Two Year Follow-Up of Reoffending*: Ministry of Justice. Available at www.justice.govt.nz/pubs/reports/2005/nz-court-referred-restorative-justice-pilot-2-year-follow-up/chapter-2.html

United Nations. 1993. *Declaration on the Elimination of Violence Against Women: General Assembly*. Available at www.un.org./documents/ga/res/48/a48r104.htm

Van Ness, D. 2014. Accountability. In *Restorative Justice, Reconciliation and Peacebuilding*. Llewellyn and Philpott. New York: Oxford University Press.

World Health Organization. 2013. *Global and Regional Estimates of Violence Against Women: Prevalence and Health Effects of Intimate Partner Violence and Non-Partner Sexual Violence*. Available at apps.who.int/iris/bitstream/10665/85239/1/9789241564625_eng.pdf. Accessed 23 February 2017.

14

Evaluating the success of restorative justice conferencing

A values-based approach

Jonathan Doak and David O'Mahony

Introduction

Restorative justice literature is replete with references to 'benchmarks' or 'indicators' of good practice. As with many other criminal justice interventions, statistics on the use of conferencing are commonly used to attest its success (or, in some cases, failures). Over the past three decades, commentators have proposed a range of frameworks concerning what restorative processes should look like, what values and practices they ought to espouse and indeed whether or not they ought to be classed as forms of restorative justice at all (Daly, 2002; O'Mahony and Doak, 2017; Zehr, 2005). As restorative conferencing becomes more widely adopted, evaluations have sought to measure practice on the ground in order to better understand whether or not a particular programme 'works'. Yet there still is no common view of what constitutes 'success'. The concept is necessarily in the eye of the beholder and is dependent not only on the desired outcome(s) but also the way in which evidence is gathered and interpreted to measure against particular benchmarks. Some organisations, including criminal justice agencies, may measure success in terms of crime prevention and reduced reoffending, often from a standpoint of managerial efficiency and cost/benefit analysis; practitioners may measure it in terms of levels of participation and agreed outcomes; individual stakeholders may measure it according to whether they had a satisfactory experience of the process. Academic proponents may look through a wider collective lens to explore, for example, whether underlying relationships are repaired (e.g. Llewellyn et al., 2013), or communities are healed (e.g. Crawford and Clear, 2001). Beyond these, there are conceptual measures of success, depending on whether a scheme aims to be retributive, rehabilitative or reparative.

Aiming to contribute to the Handbook's objectives, this chapter critiques evidence relating to five common benchmarks which are frequently invoked in restorative conferencing research: success by rates of participation, engagement, satisfaction, restoration and reducing recidivism. In particular, we consider the operation of youth conferencing in two jurisdictions, Northern Ireland and New Zealand. These jurisdictions are unique because the restorative conference is mainstreamed within the youth justice system; prosecutors and courts are under a statutory obligation to make referrals. We were both part of a team that undertook an extensive evaluation of the Northern Ireland scheme shortly after its roll-out (Campbell et al., 2006). As with other chapters within this section, we critically review the evidence as to 'what works'. However, we argue that much of the discourse around what constitutes success needs to be more finely attuned to take into account the nuances of restorative conferencing practices and outcomes. We propose that it may be beneficial, in terms of evaluating and understanding the success of conferencing, to use an overarching framework of values which could help inform these benchmarks, which we have labelled elsewhere as the 'agency-accountability framework' (O'Mahony and Doak, 2017).

Restorative conferencing: an overview

In order to understand the specific measures of success, we begin with the unique history of restorative conferencing. Modern restorative conferencing originated in New Zealand; its initial roll-out stemmed from a drive to confront issues surrounding the treatment of juveniles in the criminal justice and welfare systems, particularly among the Maori and Pacific Island minorities (Maxwell and Morris, 1993). As with the very concept of restorative justice itself, conferencing lacks a universally accepted definition or prototype, and this is reflected in a diversity of practice. However, broadly speaking, the approach involves a range of actors, including parties beyond the victim and offender, and is facilitated by an independent convenor. Its overarching aim is to involve participants in a non-adversarial dialogical process to collectively deal with the aftermath of crime and how it is resolved (O'Mahony and Doak, 2017).

Restorative conferencing may be used as either a diversionary mechanism or alongside conventional approaches to prosecution and sentencing. Like most other forms of restorative justice, and in line with international benchmarks of best practice, conferencing can only proceed if the offender admits to the offence and consents to participate in the process (Braithwaite, 2002a)

The theoretical framework which underpins the model lies in its focus on inclusive participation and collective decision making as well as its apparent capacity to facilitate the participation of offenders, their families and the community more effectively than the conventional criminal justice system (O'Mahony and Doak, 2017; O'Mahony and Doak, 2007). As such, conferencing is arguably better positioned than other forms of intervention to undertake a holistic enquiry into the circumstances of the offence and tailor the most effective outcomes for the stakeholders involved.

The perceived strengths of the model over more punitive approaches led to its adoption in other places; it became the lynchpin of four studies of restorative justice as a form of youth diversion in Canberra (Strang, 2001), and from there rapidly spread to a number of Australian states (see generally Larsen, 2014). Likewise, restorative interventions based around family group conferencing were widely replicated across the United States, whilst a cautioning scheme in England and Wales acted as a catalyst for its diffusion across the United Kingdom (Wilcox and Young, 2007). Although in many jurisdictions the police, prosecution or courts are empowered to refer certain juvenile cases to conferencing, in others referral is mandatory. For example, in New Zealand and Northern Ireland, an automatic statutory trigger is activated whereby the prosecution and/or the courts are required to make referrals (O'Mahony and Campbell, 2006). Increasingly, conferencing is also used in certain cases involving adult offenders, with New South Wales, Queensland and South Australia having made statutory provision for its use for certain offences and subject to conditions (Larsen, 2014). The New Zealand Victims' Rights Act 2002 provides that all victims have the right, in principle, to request a restorative justice conference at any time during criminal proceedings.

In contrast to its rapid expansion across the common law world, Belgium is currently the only European civil law jurisdiction which offers restorative justice for both juveniles and adults for all types of offences, and is the first civil law jurisdiction to have introduced conferencing as a mainstream option for juvenile offenders. In 2000, *Hergo* (based on the New Zealand conferencing model) was piloted across five judicial districts in Flanders to deal with more serious young offenders. Under the Youth Justice Act 2006, mediation and conferencing are the primary disposals for youth crime and must be offered to the offender in every case where a victim has been identified (Put et al., 2012). Conferencing is also practised in the Netherlands. Although no legislative provision is in place, referrals are accepted for a range of low-level offences by private organisations, welfare agencies, the courts and affected communities (Van Pagée et al., 2012).

Unlike many other forms of restorative intervention, conference participants include not only the victim and offender but also a 'micro-community' or 'community of care' comprising those who have been touched in some way by the offence (Braithwaite, 2002b; McCold, 1996). Such communities may comprise family members, friends, neighbours, teachers, social/youth/community workers, religious leaders and others. Conferences are considered to be less formal than orthodox court proceedings and are designed to empower participants to actively engage in a dialogical exchange free from domination by criminal justice professionals (O'Mahony and Doak, 2017; Doak and O'Mahony, 2011). Discussions are structured around a loose script and are convened by a trained facilitator. The typical process will begin with an opening statement by the facilitator, followed by a summary of the facts by the police officer. Agreement of these facts is confirmed by the young person; if disputed, the case will be referred back to the court. The conference then usually hears first from the victim, who explains how the offence affected him or her, and then from the offender, who explains the circumstances surrounding the offence and why he or she committed the offence. Participants are encouraged to describe how the offence impacted them and the steps that could be adopted to address the needs of victims and prevent further offending. The facilitator will assist the group in formulating and agreeing what measures might be most effective. Common plans may include an apology, reparation/compensation to the victim, rehabilitative measures (such as involvement in programmes dealing with issues such as alcohol/ substance abuse, family issues or anger management) or community work and restrictions on the offender. The plan is then recorded and may – depending on the nature of the scheme – be subsequent to approval or oversight by the police, court or other criminal justice agency.

Measuring success

Although there are many potential 'yardsticks' for measuring success (see e.g. Braithwaite, 2002a; United Nations, 2006; Zehr, 2005), the following five types of measures tend to be widely utilised as indicators of success in international evaluations of restorative justice: rates of participation, the nature and extent of engagement, participant satisfaction, restoration and the impact upon recidivism rates. Each of these are considered now.

Success through participation

The levels of participation of eligible victims and offenders, and the underlying reasons for opting to participate or not, can grant a useful insight into how both sets of stakeholders perceive the utility of restorative conferencing. Although some early evidence from emerging programmes suggested that only around half of victims invited to conferences had opted to participate, this was attributable to the fact that programmes had to grapple with a number of logistical and organisational problems in their infancy (see e.g. Daly, 2002; Maxwell and Morris,

1993; McCold and Wachtel, 1998). However, as the evidence base concerning 'what works' continued to expand, and public understanding of what restorative justice entails continues to grow, more victims have been willing to participate. Shapland et al.'s (2007) evaluation of three programmes in England adopting different methods had very high levels of victim participation, with up to 77 percent victim participation in cases involving adult offenders and up to 89 percent victim participation in cases involving young offenders. Participation rates in New Zealand have also improved significantly (Maxwell et al., 2004), whilst research in Northern Ireland found some form of victim participation in 69 percent of youth conferences (Campbell et al., 2006). Similarly high participation rates have been reported in New South Wales (Trimboli, 2000) and in conferences organised under the RISE experiment in the Australian Capital Territory (Braithwaite, 1999).

Whilst high participation rates are widely viewed as a 'good thing', it is important to bear in mind that not all victims want the opportunity to participate. Hartmann's and Gavrielides's chapters in this Handbook present new empirical evidence on victim participation. The extant literature has also suggested that some victims may feel it is not worth their time and effort, particularly if the offence had little or no impact on their lives, or they may simply wish to move on. Conversely – and particularly in more serious cases – other victims may not wish to meet the offenders at all (Campbell et al., 2006; Maxwell et al., 2004). They may be traumatised, fearful or angry, and international benchmarks of best practice recognise that the decisions of victims who do not wish to participate should be respected. Sometimes participation is simply impractical; maybe due to inadequate notice, preparation, the unavailability of a nearby venue or suitable time, which can all act as barriers to participation (Campbell et al., 2006; Maxwell and Morris, 1993; Maxwell et al., 2004).

However, for the majority of victims who do opt to participate, common findings emerge, although these may differ according to different types of victims and for different types of offences. In general, however, victims consistently report that their primary reason is to express their feelings to the offender and ask questions of them in a safe environment (Achilles and Zehr, 2001; Doak and O'Mahony, 2006; Strang et al., 2006; Umbreit et al., 2006). Victims often seek to gain a better understanding of why the offence happened; they want to hear and understand the offender and to explain the impact of the offence to them (Campbell et al., 2006; Hayes and Daly, 2004; Shapland et al., 2007; Strang et al., 2006). Victims also want to have an input into how the injury/damage they suffered will be redressed and how the offender is dealt with (Herman, 2004; Strang et al., 2006). In contrast to conventional court proceedings where the victim is sidelined as 'evidentiary cannon fodder' (Braithwaite, 1992: 4), conferencing offers victims an opportunity to pursue these aims through empowering them as active participants in the criminal process.

Such findings, beyond seeing success through levels of participation, reveal how victims can move beyond their own immediate needs and experience their capacity to offer forgiveness and support. Interestingly, there is very little evidence that participants in restorative conferencing seek out the traditional justifications for sentences such as retribution or punishment. Whilst some victims may enter conferences with punitive motives, the evidence suggests that most victims do not opt to participate in conferencing (or in the criminal process more generally) in order to vent anger or to seek onerous punishments. Rather, it seems that victims have strong altruistic reasons for participating, reporting that they value the opportunity conferencing provides in seeing something good come out of the harm that was caused (Doak and O'Mahony, 2006; Herman, 2004; Strang, 2002). These findings are in line with broader victimological research which shows that victims of crime are no more punitive than the general public (Hough and Park, 2002).

Offenders, too, can be empowered through the conferencing process. Unlike conventional court proceedings, conferencing holds offenders to account through a dialogical exchange with others affected by the offence; this will often include reflecting on the reasons underlying their harmful behaviour, telling their side of the story and – crucially – apologising for their actions. The evidence suggests that whilst a minority of offenders state that they participated simply to avoid court, the majority recognise it as an opportunity to accept responsibility for their actions and to repair the harm they caused (Campbell et al., 2006; Shapland et al., 2011; Wood and Suzuki, 2016). Whilst the opportunity to apologise also features strongly, many offenders express a desire to take more concrete steps to make amends for the broader impacts of the offence and assist victims in the recovery process (Campbell et al., 2006; Doak and O'Mahony, 2006; Shapland et al., 2007; Van Camp and Wemmers, 2013).

However, the decision to participate may not always be entirely voluntary, particularly in cases involving young offenders. Our own research in Northern Ireland revealed that around a quarter (24 percent) of those who attended also said their decision to participate was made under some pressure, especially from their parents, or that they felt the court had 'made' them come (Campbell et al., 2006). Similarly, a quarter (25 percent) said they felt they had to agree to the conference plan and also felt they had no real choice, as the court 'expected' a plan. This underscores the need for thorough preparation in advance of the process; offenders should be familiar with what it entails and what will be expected of them. Where offenders feel coerced to attend a conference against their will, there is little prospect for a positive outcome (Haines and O'Mahony, 2006; Strang, 2002). Indeed, it will often be counterproductive for the victim, too, who may be confronted with a defiant or disinterested offender.

Although some offenders may opt for conferencing on the grounds that they perceive it as a more lenient option than court, the converse is often the case. Some offenders are undoubtedly aware that it is an emotional and challenging process that may probe sensitive and personal areas of their lives, and there is an expectation that they will engage accordingly. Whilst court hearings often involve little more than confirming one's name and address, conferencing will usually entail a direct face-to-face meeting with the victim and others affected by the offence. Irrespective of the underlying reasons for declining to participate, any such decision should be fully respected. Thus, it is important to appreciate that measuring success in restorative conferencing through rates of participation does not actually give us any real insight into whether it works, why individuals participated and what they got out of the process.

Success through engagement?

Even when the victim and offender opt into conferencing, gathering participants together in a circle marks the beginning of a demanding and potentially emotional process. The face-to-face encounter is widely held to be a keystone for the effective delivery of conferencing; without meaningful engagement of the parties, a viable plan is unlikely to emerge. Generally, all participants value the opportunity to speak and interact directly with each other (Maxwell and Morris, 1993; Petrucci (2002); Scheff, 1998; Shapland et al., 2007). Overall, the research evidence suggests that victims are generally more willing and more able to engage in discussion than offenders. For example, the Northern Ireland research showed that almost all (98 percent) of victims were observed to be talkative in conferences (Campbell et al., 2006). Whilst a minority showed some signs of nervousness in the early stages of the meeting, this tended to fade as facilitators put them at ease. Victims were keen to tell their stories and ask questions, with very few displaying overt hostility towards the offender. Notably, there was also a clear correlation between the degree of preparation prior to the conference and the extent to which victims felt comfortable participating. Over four-fifths of victims (83 percent) were rated as 'very engaged' during conference observations, whilst 92 percent reported that they had said everything that they wanted to during the conference. Similar findings have been arrived at in other programmes (Strang, 2002; Maxwell et al., 2004; Shapland et al., 2007; Trimboli, 2000; People and Trimboli, 2007).

High levels of engagement of offenders can prove more difficult to achieve. This is particularly evident in cases involving young offenders, the majority of whom are being held to account in an environment dominated by adult authority figures (Haines and O'Mahony, 2006). In many conferencing programmes, police officers, probation officers, social workers and teachers may be in attendance in addition to the facilitator, the young person's parents and, of course the victim and his or her supporters. In Northern Ireland, almost three-quarters of young people (71 percent) displayed some degree of nervousness at the beginning of the conference; this was evident through their posture and body language, for example, avoiding eye contact, looking at the floor, fidgeting and shaking (Campbell et al., 2006). In most cases, offenders have significantly less developed verbal skills to articulate their feelings than the other participants and may feel reticent to speak in a group environment (Daly, 2003). This may be attributable to a combination of age, stress, shame, embarrassment, lack of recall, or unfamiliarity with the process (Hoyle and Noguera, 2008; Lynch, 2008; O'Mahony and Doak, 2017), though offenders with histories of substance abuse and learning disabilities may be additionally impaired in their ability to empathise and understand alternative viewpoints (Cunneen, 2010).

Despite such limitations (and in common with many victims), initial apprehensiveness often gives way to more confident engagement, with offenders more willing to discuss the offence and its circumstances in a full and frank manner (Campbell et al., 2006; Maxwell et al., 2006; Maxwell and Morris, 1993). Body language, eye contact and verbal articulacy generally improve as conferencing progresses, with offenders showing signs of being receptive to the accounts of victims and showing various degrees of empathy and understanding in the dialogue. Interviews carried out with the young people after conferences in Northern Ireland revealed that most felt involved in the decision-making process and almost all said that they understood the decisions that were made (Campbell et al., 2006).

But as Roche (2003: 33) reminds us, accounts of restorative justice describing 'how people should respond are confused with the reality of how people do respond'. Ultimately, successful outcomes will hinge on a successful process, which in turn depends upon a high level of active engagement of all participants. Research has shown how offenders are more likely to engage in conferencing and positively contribute to the decision making if they have been well prepared and know what is expected of them (Choi et al., 2012). The onus thus falls on facilitators to ensure that offenders – particularly the young and vulnerable – are thoroughly prepared for the conference and feel comfortable expressing themselves within the conference (Choi and Gilbert, 2010; Rossner, 2013; Wood and Suzuki, 2016). Therefore, in assessing success through engagement, it is important not to lose sight of the quality and nature of the engagement, rather than the amount of engagement.

Success through satisfaction?

'Success' may also be measured in terms of participant satisfaction. Restorative justice is consistently compared favourably to orthodox forms of criminal disposal (Shapland et al., 2011; Sherman et al., 1998; Strang et al., 2013; Van Camp and Wemmers, 2013). Indeed, in an international meta-analysis of seven evaluations, Poulson (2003) found that restorative justice outperformed court procedures on almost every variable (including judgements of fairness, accountability, increased respect, emotional well-being and reductions in fear) for both victims and offenders.

Measures of satisfaction broadly relate to either *procedural* or *distributive* justice. Whilst procedural justice reflects the extent to which participants consider the process to be fair, distributive justice bears on the question as to whether the specific outcomes are fair. Whilst both forms of justice are important in their own right, they are also difficult to bifurcate. It may be the case that perceived deficiencies in one form of justice are offset by the perceived fairness of another. As such, satisfaction appears to be connected to not only the way victims and offenders feel they were treated but also how fairly they rate both the process and the outcome (Strang et al., 2013; Rossner, 2013).

Procedural justice is often equated with the concept of 'voice'; the more participants feel that they have been able to exercise their voice and have been heard, the more likely they are to perceive the process as 'fair' (Lind and Tyler, 1988). This is generally borne out in restorative conferencing research, where offenders who generally perceive the process to be fair state that they value being able to have their say and gain a better understanding of the offence and its consequences (Sherman et al., 1998, Strang et al., 2013). Many report being treated with respect, by having their rights acknowledged and their input into the process taken seriously (Tyler et al., 2007; Sherman et al., 1998).

High levels of victim satisfaction have been reported in most of the research concerning restorative conferencing. Our own evaluation of the Northern Ireland youth conferencing arrangements found that perceptions of fairness and satisfaction were especially high. Almost all victims (92 percent) experienced the process as 'fair', and 98 percent stated that their views were taken seriously (Campbell et al., 2006). The vast majority of studies also reveal that victims who have taken part are happy to recommend conferencing to another person in similar circumstances (Campbell et al., 2006; McCold and Wachtel, 1998; McGarrell, et al., 2000).

For offenders, the face-to-face encounter helps them to realise the impact of their actions and the harm they have caused, whilst for victims it gives them the opportunity to have their say, to hear from the offender and understand more about why the offence happened and to hold the offender to account for the harm they caused. In this way, conferencing can help offenders realise the impact of the harm and gain a sense of closure, as well as allow them to think about the future in a positive way (Shapland et al., 2007). In Northern Ireland, almost three-quarters (71 percent) of the young offenders were satisfied with the process (Campbell et al., 2006). The active involvement of families in the process would also seem to correlate with offender satisfaction rates (Clairmont, 2005; Maxwell et al., 2004). More broadly, satisfaction with the conferencing process has also been found to increase levels of offenders' respect for the criminal justice system, perhaps owing in part to positive interactions they may have with criminal justice personnel in conferences (Doak and O'Mahony, 2011; Sherman and Strang, 2007; Triggs, 2005). In turn, this may serve to legitimise the law and the criminal justice system in their own eyes and even help them to desist from future offending (Tyler, 2006).

The true value of the face-to-face encounter is its capacity to foster participants with a sense of ownership in their case and its helping them feel empowered by being actively involved in the resolution of the conflict (O'Mahony and Doak, 2017). For this empowering potential to be fully realised, however, rigorous preparation is essential. Generally, offenders report being more satisfied with the process when they are well prepared because it helps them to be involved and integrated in the decision-making process. Similarly for victims, research shows them to be much more able to contribute to the conferencing process, as well as having more realistic expectations of what they will get out of it, when they are well prepared (Morris et al., 1993; Shapland et al., 2011; Vanfraechem, 2015). The early research that emerged from New Zealand highlights that procedural justice cannot be taken for granted. Maxwell and Morris (1993) reported that just a third of young people felt involved in the process and only nine percent felt that they ultimately decided the outcome. In addition, just half of all victims reported that they were satisfied, whilst over a quarter (27 percent) felt worse. The most frequent reasons cited were that the young person did not come across as being genuinely remorseful or that victims felt unable to express themselves fully.

However, later research suggests that many of these issues had been subsequently addressed through improved practice, with only five percent of those victims interviewed saying that they felt worse after the conference and 81 percent of victims saying they felt better (Maxwell et al., 2004). Enhanced preparation, better training and more comprehensive follow-up have helped to ensure that the needs of victims and offenders have been more effectively addressed and that they are have more realistic expectations of what can be achieved. In particular, offenders and their families reported that they felt that their voices were genuinely taken into account in devising the plan, with the majority of young people saying they had the opportunity to say what they wanted and almost all saying they understood the nature of the decisions that had been made. Satisfaction rates also showed a marked improvement among victims. Around 60 percent found the conference to be helpful, positive and rewarding. Aspects of the conference that they found particularly rewarding included being given the opportunity tell the young person what they had felt as a result of the crime and being able to contribute to the decision process on what should happen to the young person. Providing victims with a voice in conferences is obviously important for victims, as is being able to come face to face with the young person and his or her family so they can better understand why the offence happened.

Yet, as Van Camp and Wemmers (2013) observe, procedural justice is just one (albeit an important) factor in overall satisfaction. Their own interviews with victims of violent crime who had been engaged with some form of restorative intervention reveal that flexibility, the provision of care, the opportunity for dialogue and the capacity to address 'pro-social' motives were also deeply valued by the participants. Similar findings were uncovered in relation to Northern Ireland conferencing; whilst notions of procedural justice were important, so too were the practicalities such as the location, timing and the lapse in time from the date of the offence to the actual conference (Campbell et al., 2006: 102). These findings highlight the complexity of understanding the meanings of satisfaction in relation to restorative conferences and the need to be cautious in using them as a blunt measure of success.

Success through restoration?

As indicated earlier, overall satisfaction rates also hinge on questions of whether participants feel that justice is actually 'done'; in other words, that the outcomes of the process are regarded as a fair means of dealing with the offence. Levels of outcome satisfaction broadly mirror those of process satisfaction, and generally these are have been found to be high (McGarrell et al., 2000; Vanfraechem, 2005 Shapland et al., 2011; Campbell et al., 2006).

The findings on outcomes are particularly pertinent, however, insofar as they give us an insight into the types of outcome which participants favour or perceive as fair. For victims, the desire for compensation or indeed retribution seems to be of much less importance to them than some form of symbolic reparation, for example, through admission of harm, a sincere apology or undertaking to desist from future offending (Campbell et al., 2006; Shapland et al., 2011; Doak and O'Mahony, 2006). Generally, these kinds of outcomes help victims feel more secure and gain a sense of closure (Shapland et al., 2011). In Northern Ireland, most of the agreed plans focused on delivering reparative and constructive outcomes, often addressing the needs of the offender rather than seeking to impose punitive sanctions (Campbell et al., 2006). Plans often incorporated elements like support with drug and alcohol problems, or help with anger management, rather than curfews or punitive sanctions. In fact 73 percent of plans primarily sought to address the needs of offenders and elements of restitution for the victim. Importantly, victims often reported that they wanted to see something positive come out of the conference and to help the offender in some way, particularly if it could help them to stop offending.

In terms of redress, offenders generally offered token amounts of financial or proprietary reparation. This stems primarily from the fact that most young offenders simply lack the means to make any substantial material recompense; to oblige them to do so might only serve to heighten the chances that they return to crime (Campbell et al., 2006; Hoyle et al., 2002, Shapland et al., 2006). More importantly, however, both the punishment of the offender and financial compensation seem to be of secondary importance. Rather 'victims put much greater stress on the symbolic reparation of offenders taking control of their lives and deciding to change their life patterns away from offending' (Shapland et al., 2011: 164).

By far the most common form of symbolic reparation is the apology, which is arguably both the most difficult but also the most fundamental ingredient of any restorative process. This is because apologies often act as 'turning points', when feelings of anger and shame are transformed to feelings of understanding and empathy (Rossner, 2014). In this way, they can help bring about a sense of closure for both parties and enhance overall levels of satisfaction with the process (Campbell et al., 2006; Hoyle et al., 2002; Sherman et al., 2005).

Apologies are certainly commonplace, and are often expected in restorative conferences. They are also frequently used as one of the proxy measures for restoration in the research literature. Yet they are complex and are intertwined with subtle cues and interactions that make their interpretation difficult – particularly as a measure of success. For instance, it is apparent that apologies must be genuine and be perceived as such. A genuine apology should include a visible expression of remorse, which signals to the victim that the offender really regrets his or her behaviour and wishes to make amends (Petrucci, 2002). Findings have been mixed on this issue. In Northern Ireland, the vast majority of victims (85 percent) felt that the apology was genuine (Campbell et al., 2006), whilst in Shapland et al.'s (2011) evaluation of RJ schemes in England, that figure fell to two-thirds. An evaluation of youth conferencing of South Australia reported that whilst just under a third of victims perceived the apologies that offenders gave to be genuine, almost twice that proportion felt that the apologies were insincere (Daly, 2002). Victims may be particularly suspicious about the sincerity of apologies given in conferences, especially where offenders are particularly young and where there may be social and intellectual barriers between the parties (Strang, 2002, Daly, 2003; Haines and O'Mahony, 2006). It is also clear that some offenders are better equipped both to understand and articulate what seems to be a genuine apology, and some victims are more open to accepting the sincerity of an apology, irrespective of how it is communicated or received (Cunneen, 2010; Daly, 2008).

Success through reducing reoffending?

Perhaps the most common measure of success – particularly within policy circles – is the extent to which conferencing can succeed in reducing recidivism. Criminal justice policymakers face pressure from stretched resources and a creeping culture of performance-based targets to introduce fresh mechanisms to respond to age-old problems (Lister, 2013). They are thus keen to assess whether restorative interventions can be 'sold' on the basis that they pass the 'cost/benefit analysis'; that is to say, that they are a more cost-effective measure of addressing crime than other processes. Certainly, there is a growing body of research that demonstrates restorative conferencing can have some positive impacts in reducing reoffending. Wood and Piggott write about this issues in this Handbook.

Conferencing can be a useful tool in reducing levels of reoffending, particularly when it is used in combination with other rehabilitative interventions that help offenders to move away from crime (Bonta et al., 2006, McGarrell et al., 2000; Strang et al., 2013). Other non-stigmatic interventions may complement restorative justice, including education and training, counselling and support, anger management, victim awareness, building capacity to resist peer pressure and treatment for substance abuse. Reviews of the research evidence point to the conferencing model being most effective for more serious and violent of offences, as opposed to minor property offences (Bergseth and Bouffard, 2007; Bonta et al., 2006; Luke and Lind (2002); Lynn (2007); McCold and Wachtel (1998); Sherman and Strang, 2009; Strang et al., 2013). However, reliable studies report modest favourable reductions in reoffending, similar to those achieved through other offender-focused interventions (Luke and Lind, 2002; Strang et al., 2013).

But much of the research that shows differences between restorative conferencing and more traditional criminal justice interventions, in terms of reducing crime, reveals very little about how or why such interventions work. Indeed, it is counter-intuitive to measure the success of restorative conferencing simply on the basis that it appears to reduce the probability of reoffending, particularly because it doesn't indicate why it was successful. More detailed research, which has looked beyond reoffending and specifically at factors associated with reduced reoffending rates, shows that restorative conferences which result in genuine expressions of remorse, where the outcomes are consensual, where the process is inclusive and where participants experience solidarity, are more likely to see reductions in recidivism (O'Mahony and Doak, 2017; Hayes and Daly, 2003; Shapland et al., 2008). In other words, what the participants experience in the restorative conference, such as their sense of involvement and ownership in the process and the extent to which they are able to take responsibility for the consequences of their actions, are the indicators of success behind the reoffending figures.

Conclusions: reflecting on the meaning of success

Ultimately, the question of 'success' in restorative conferencing hinges on what it is we purport to be measuring. Restorative conferencing is first and foremost a non-adversarial criminal justice mechanism for repairing harm. It is not a crime prevention tool, a substitute for therapy or a rehabilitative measure. It can certainly be evaluated as a mechanism through various lenses; the measures of success above all constitute legitimate lines of inquiry, but care must be taken not to conflate these individual measurements with grander claims.

In our view, it is overly simplistic to brand conferencing as a 'success' story (or, conversely, one of failure), and by the same token it is not a panacea to the crime problem. Like other forms of restorative justice, it clearly works in the eyes of many victims, and many offenders, under a variety of circumstances. We can go so far as to say it is more likely to be a successful mechanism than conventional sentencing procedures. Though restorative conferencing is more normatively attractive than adversarial forms of justice, not all cases are inherently suitable. Some victims may not be ready or willing to participate, and some offenders will remain defiant. Moreover, conferencing is not designed to be a fact-finding mechanism and thus cannot be applied where the evidence is in dispute. As with any criminal justice intervention, resources are finite and a balance must be struck between the need for high-quality fully restorative interventions and the types of offences that merit these interventions (O'Mahony and Doak, 2017).

It is evident in this Handbook and the literature that much of the existing empirical data only gives us a particular line of insight into how practice is working. Llewellyn et al. (2013: 286) observe that '[a]ll that is of value may not be quantifiable or measurable'. Indeed, many of the key values widely held to underpin restorative justice, such as respect, equality, fairness, inclusivity, truth telling, honesty, voluntariness, empathy, repair and reintegration do not readily lend themselves to simple empirical investigation, nor are they adequately reflected in the current benchmarks of success.

As Gavrielides (2008) suggests, it may be more useful to think of restorative justice not only in terms of what works but also in terms of what happened. Thus, we contend that by looking at what *happened* we can also elicit the key values that contribute towards 'successful' restorative encounters. Indeed, such values can be consolidated and clarified within an 'agency-accountability framework' to allow for a clearer and more accurate explanation of how restorative justice works and the normative goals it ought to propel in practice (O'Mahony and Doak, 2017). In other words, success should also be calibrated taking into account the extent to which individuals are empowered to gain a sense of agency, whereby they are able to make choices, actively participate and engage with the process and its outcomes. Similarly, it should assess how it empowers them to accept accountability for their actions and towards others, thus creating and accepting obligations, as opposed to having them imposed. Indeed, we argue elsewhere that restorative conferencing should be both designed and evaluated in such ways that agency and accountability are recognised as underpinning goals (O'Mahony and Doak, 2017). Aligned with this Handbook's vision for a better restorative justice future, we call for a reappraisal of how we measure success in restorative conferencing. Such a reappraisal would allow for the benchmarks to reflect the underlying goals of providing agency to the participants and allowing them to be accountable to each other and for the consequences of crime.

References

Achilles, M. and Zehr, H. 2001. Restorative Justice for Crime Victims: The Promise, the Challenge. In G. Bazemore and M. Schiff (eds.) *Restorative and Community Justice Cultivating Common Ground for Victims, Communities and Offenders*. Cincinnati, OH: Anderson Publishing, pp. 87–100.

Braithwaite, J. 1999. Restorative Justice: Assessing Optimistic and Pessimistic Accounts. In M. Tonry (ed.) *Crime and Justice: An Annual Review of the Research*, Vol. 25. Chicago: University of Chicago Press.

Braithwaite, J. 2002a. Setting Standards for Restorative Justice, *British Journal of Criminology*, 42(3): 563–577.

Braithwaite, J. 2002b. *Restorative Justice and Responsive Regulation*. Oxford: Oxford University Press.

Campbell, C., Devlin, R., O'Mahony, D., Doak, J., Jackson, J., Corrigan, T. and McEvoy, K. 2006. *Evaluation of the Northern Ireland Youth Conference Service*, NIO Research and Statistics Series: Report No. 12. Belfast: Northern Ireland Office.

Choi, J.J., Bazemore, G. and Gilbert, M.J. 2012. Review of Research on Victims' Experiences in Restorative Justice: Implications for Youth Justice, *Children and Youth Services Review*, 34(1): 35–42.

Choi, J.J. and Gilbert, M.J. 2010. 'Joe everyday, people off the street': A Qualitative Study on Mediators' Roles and Skills in Victim – Offender Mediation, *Contemporary Justice Review*, 13(2): 207–227.

Crawford, A. and Clear, T. 2001. *Community Justice: Transforming Communities Through Restorative Justice?* In G. Bazemore and M. Schiff (eds.) *Restorative Community Justice: Repairing Harm and Transforming Communities*. Cincinnati: Anderson Publishing Company, pp. 127–149.

Cunneen, C. 2010. The Limitations of Restorative Justice. In C. Cunneen and C. Hoyle (eds.) *Debating Restorative Justice*. Oxford: Hart.

Daly, K. 2002. Restorative Justice the Real Story, *Punishment and Society*, 4(1): 55–79.

Daly, K. 2003. Mind the Gap: Restorative Justice in Theory and Practice. In A. von Hirsch, J.V. Roberts, A.E. Bottoms, K. Roach and M. Schiff (eds.) *Restorative Justice and Criminal Justice: Competing or Reconcilable Paradigms*. Oxford: Hart, pp. 219–236.

Daly, K. 2016. What Is Restorative Justice? Fresh Answers to a Vexed Question, *Victims & Offenders*, 11(1): 9–29.

Doak, J. and O'Mahony, D. 2006. The Vengeful Victim? Assessing the Attitudes of Victims Participating in Restorative Youth Conferencing, *International Review of Victimology* 13(2): 157–177.

Doak, J. and O'Mahony, D. 2011. In Search of Legitimacy: Restorative Youth Conferencing in Northern Ireland, *Legal Studies*, 31(2): 305–325.

Gavrielides, T. 2008. Restorative Justice – The Perplexing Concept: Conceptual Fault-Lines and Power Battles Within the Restorative Justice Movement, *Criminology & Criminal Justice*, 8(2): 165–183.

Haines, K. and O'Mahony, D. 2006. Restorative Approaches, Young People and Youth Justice. In J. Muncie and B. Goldson (eds.) *Youth Crime and Justice*. London: Sage, pp. 110–124.

Hayes, H. and Daly, K. 2004. Conferencing and Re-Offending in Queensland, *Australian and New Zealand Journal of Criminology*, 37(2): 167–191

Herman, S. 2004. Is Restorative Justice Possible Without a Parallel System for Victims, *Critical Issues in Restorative Justice*: 75–83.

Hough, M. and Park, A. 2002. How Malleable Are Attitudes to Crime and Punishment? Findings From a British Deliberative Poll. In J. Roberts and M. Hough (eds.) *Changing Attitudes to Punishment*. Cullompton: Willan, pp. 163–183.

Hoyle, C. and Noguera, S. 2008. Supporting Young Offenders Through Restorative Justice: Parents as (in) Appropriate Adults, *British Journal of Community Justice*, 6(3): 67–85.

Larsen, J.J. 2014. *Restorative Justice in the Australian Criminal Justice System*, Research and Public Policy Report No. 127. Sydney: Australian Institute of Criminology.

Lind, E.A. and Tyler, T.R. 1988. *The Social Psychology of Procedural Justice*. New York: Springer.

Llewellyn, J.J., Archibald, B.P., Clairmont, D. and Crocker, D. 2013. Imagining Success for a Restorative Approach to Justice: Implications for Measurement and Evaluation, *Dalhousie Law Journal*, 36(2): 282–316.

Lynch, N. 2008. Youth Justice in New Zealand: A Children's Rights Perspective, *Youth Justice*, 8(3): 215–228.

Maxwell, G., Kingi, V., Robertson, J., Morris, A. and Cunningham, C. 2004. *Achieving Effective Outcomes: Youth Justice in New Zealand*. Wellington: Ministry of Social Development.

Maxwell, G. and Morris, A. 1993. *Families, Victims and Culture: Youth Justice in New Zealand*. Wellington: Victoria University of Wellington.

Maxwell, G., Morris, A. and Hayes, H. 2006. Conferencing and Restorative Justice. In D. Sullivan and L. Tifft (eds.) *Handbook of Restorative Justice: A Global Perspective*. Abington: Routledge.

McCold, P. 1996. Restorative Justice and the Role of Community. In B. Galaway and J. Hudson (eds.) *Restorative Justice: International Perspectives*. Monsey, NY: Criminal Justice Press, pp. 85–102.

McCold, P. and Wachtel, T. 1998. *Restorative Policing Experiment: The Bethlehem Pennsylvania Police Family Group Conferencing Project*. Washington, DC: U.S. Department of Justice.

McGarrell, E., Olivares, K., Crawford, K. and Kroovand, N. 2000. *Returning Justice to the Community: The Indianapolis Juvenile Restorative Justice Experiment*. Indianapolis, IN: Hudson Institute.

O'Mahony, D. and Campbell, C. 2006. Mainstreaming Restorative Justice for Young Offenders Through Youth Conferencing: The Experience of Northern Ireland. In J. Junger-tas and S. Decker (eds.) *International Handbook of Youth Justice*. Amsterdam: Springer Academic Press, pp. 93–116.

O'Mahony, D. and Doak, J. 2007. The Enigma of 'Community' and the Exigency of Engagement: Restorative Youth Conferencing in Northern Ireland, *British Journal of Community Justice*, 4: 9–25.

O'Mahony, D. and Doak, J. 2017. *Reimagining Restorative Justice: Agency and Accountability in the Criminal Process*. Oxford: Hart.

People, J. and Trimboli, L. 2007. *An Evaluation of the NSW Community Conferencing for Young Adults Pilot Program*. NSW Bureau of Crime Statistics and Research.

Petrucci, C.J. 2002. Apology in the Criminal Justice Setting: Evidence for Including Apology as an Additional Component in the Legal System, *Behavioral Sciences and the Law*, 20(4): 337–362.

Put, J., Vanfraechem, I. and Walgrave, L. 2012. Restorative Dimensions in Belgian Youth Justice, *Youth Justice*, 12(2): 83–100.

Roche, D. 2003. *Accountability in Restorative Justice*. Oxford: Oxford University Press.

Rossner, M. 2013. *Just Emotions: Rituals of Restorative Justice*. Oxford: Oxford University Press.

Scheff, T. 1998. Community Conferences: Shame and Anger in Therapeutic Jurisprudence, *Revista Juridica Universidad de Puerto Rico*, 67: 97–119.

Shapland, J., Atkinson, A., Atkinson, H., Chapman, B., Colledge, E., Dignan, J., Howes, M., Johnstone, G. 2007. *Restorative Justice: The Views of Victims and Offenders: The Third Report From the Evaluation of Three Schemes*. Sheffield: Centre for Criminological Research, University of Sheffield.

Sherman, L., Strang, H., Barnes, J., Braithwaite, J., Inkpen, N. and Teh, M. 1998. *Experiments in Restorative Policing: A Progress Report on the Canberra Reintegrative Shaming Experiments*. Canberra: Australian Institute of Criminology.

Strang, H. 2001. *Restorative Justice Programs in Australia, Report to the Criminology Research Council*. Canberra: Australian Institute of Criminology.

Strang, H. 2002. *Repair or Revenge: Victims and Restorative Justice*. Oxford: Clarendon Press.

Strang, H., Sherman, L., Angel, C.M., Woods, D.J., Bennett, S., Newbury-Birch, D. and Inkpen, N. 2006. Victim Evaluations of Face-to-Face Restorative Justice Conferences: A Quasi-Experimental Analysis, *Journal of Social Sciences*, 62(2): 281–306.

Strang, H., Sherman, L.W., Mayo-Wilson, E., Woods, D. and Ariel, B. 2013. *Restorative Justice Conferencing (RJC) Using Face-to-Face Meetings of Offenders and Victims: Effects on Offender Recidivism and Victim Satisfaction: A Systematic Review*. Oslo: Campbell Collaboration.

Trimboli, L. 2000. *An Evaluation of the NSW Youth Justice Conferencing Scheme*. Sydney: NSW Bureau of Crime Statistics and Research.

Tyler, T.R., Sherman, L., Strang, H., Barnes, G.C. and Woods, D. 2007. Reintegrative Shaming, Procedural Justice, and Recidivism: The Engagement of Offenders' Psychological Mechanisms in the Canberra RISE Drinking-and-Driving Experiment, *Law and Society Review*, 41(3): 553–585.

Umbreit, M., Vos, B., Coates, R. and Armour, M.P. 2006. Victims of Severe Violence in Mediated Dialogue with Offender: The Impact of the First Multi-Site Study in the US, *International Review of Victimology*, 13(1): 27–48.

United Nations. 2006. *Handbook on Restorative Justice Programmes*. Vienna: United Nations Office on Drugs and Crime.

Van Camp, T. and Wemmers, J.A. 2013. Victim Satisfaction with Restorative Justice More Than Simply Procedural Justice, *International Review of Victimology*, 19(2): 117–143.

Van Pagee, R., Lieshout, J. van and Wolthuis, A. 2012. Most Things Look Better When Arranged in a Circle. Family Group Conferencing Empowers Society Developments in the Netherlands. In E. Zinsstag and I. Vanfraechem (eds.) *Conferencing and Restorative Justice: International Practices and Perspectives*. Oxford: Oxford University Press, pp. 217–230.

Vanfraechem, I. 2005. Evaluating Conferencing for Serious Juvenile Offenders. In E. Elliott and R. Gordon (eds.) *New Directions in Restorative Justice*. Cullompton: Willan, pp. 278–295.

Wilcox, A. and Young, R. 2007. How Green Was Thames Valley? Policing the Image of Restorative Justice Cautions, *Policing and Society*, 17(2): 141–163.

Wood, W.R. and Suzuki, M. 2016. Four Challenges in the Future of Restorative Justice, *Victims & Offenders*, 11(1): 149–172.

Zehr, H. 2005. *Changing Lenses: A New Focus for Crime and Justice*, 3rd ed. Waterloo, ON: Herald Press.

15

Introducing restorative practice in healthcare settings

Janine Carroll and Dan Reisel

Introduction

Though doctors and other healthcare professionals have been exhorted from ancient times to 'first do no harm', harm inevitably happens in the complex endeavour that is modern medicine. Some of this harm is due to overt negligence. However, in the vast majority of cases, harm is caused by systemic errors and minor oversights that are not intentional. According to the National Reporting and Learning System (NRLS), there are around 80,000 safety incidents in the NHS per year that result in moderate/severe harm or death, yet only a fraction of these lead to disciplinary proceedings or criminal charges. It is our contention that the methodology of Restorative Practice (RP) is uniquely suited to the healthcare setting, because the harm that is caused within the normal practice of medicine is almost always unintended.

Although intentional errors are rare, the harm these incidents cause is real. Yet when patients seek procedural or legal redress, they are often met with bureaucracy and lengthy legal claims. As healthcare professionals, we have spoken to numerous patients who felt forced to seek monetary compensation through court proceedings when all they wanted was to be heard and for the healthcare system to ensure that the harm that befell them would not be repeated.

The term Restorative Justice, whilst more widely known than RP, is thought by many to carry strong connotations of its arena of origin: the criminal justice system. It is associated with a readiness to address parties with labels such as the wrongdoer, the victim, the perpetrator and the harmed. However, the principles of Restorative Justice are not exclusively beholden to this domain. Restorative Practice has in recent years become a wider, more accessible way to speak about the needs of all impacted parties being voiced with dignity and heard with respect, and responded to with a view to seeing a conflict fairly addressed and resolved. RP now has application with schools, housing associations, care homes, community service agencies and in a variety of international aid settings. This approach addresses the quality of relationships between staff and service users and also between staff within the organisational teams.

The aim of this chapter is to set out the case for RP in the healthcare sector, where RP so far has been slow to gain traction. Our objective is to give the reader an up-to-date evidence-based and critical overview of how RP could work within a national health system like the NHS. To this end, the chapter draws on our own direct experiences of introducing RP within a Maternity Care setting. The principles we review are universal and so should be applicable as well to the interested international reader of this Handbook.

Restorative practice in the health setting

One of the ways in which RP can be invaluable in the healthcare setting is by acknowledging that each involved party suffers following a harmful incident. The patient and their family suffers most acutely, but incidents also weigh heavily on healthcare professionals. In addition, the strain of patient safety incidents and their management is a severe burden on an already struggling health service. It is therefore timely to consider the impact RP might bring to addressing adverse outcomes within the healthcare setting. Through direct engagement at a personal level in the immediate aftermath of an incident, the individuals have the opportunity for resolution.

Clinicians working in a setting where blame culture is prevalent will not only experience distress and shame but might also be unwilling or unable to address patient concerns. A culture which increasingly recognises the importance of openness and dialogue not only harnesses the learning that such events offer but also presents both clinicians and patients with an opportunity for resolution and reintegration, with the event ceasing to define them.

Organisations are only ever as effective as the health of the relationships within their teams. A Restorative culture provides a template for addressing issues of tension as they arise. A workplace which values open communication, learns from mistakes and knows how to engage and listen when it matters, will then reflect those qualities in the relationships afforded to the users of their service. The health setting pivots on relationships of trust between staff and patients, and evidence of an open responsivity when situations occasionally but inevitably go wrong is the hallmark of a safe, effective service.

Which problem are we trying to solve?

Errors and conflicts occur throughout the health sector. A 'patient safety incident' is defined as 'any unintended or unexpected incident which could have, or did, lead to harm for one or more patients receiving NHS care' (NPSA, 2011). In most cases, the errors are minor and may not even be noticed. Yet at times, errors accumulate and become endemic, with a resultant breakdown of trust between healthcare users and providers.

When serious errors occur, the most common way this is dealt with is through a Serious Incident review. This usually entails senior doctors and nurses performing a root-cause analysis following a clinical error, or in some cases, a near miss. The clinicians leading in the Incident Review are nearly always not the same healthcare professionals that were involved in the incident. Those involved may be asked to submit a statement about their experience, but many do not feel included in the process.

Moreover, patients are not always part of the Incident Review process. A report looking at the cerebral palsy claims in the NHS from 2010–2015 (NHS Resolution, 2017) found that out of 50 investigations into the causes of cerebral palsy, only 40% had included the patient or their family in the review. Only around 4% had included any external experts in their review panel.

The introduction of a statutory duty of candour

Patients who decide to opt for the legal route do so from a number of different motivations. However, in many cases, patients feel compelled to enter into a legal dispute because they feel it's the only way to achieve some kind of redress. Many say that they just want to make sure what happened to them doesn't happen to another family. For this to be achieved, the learning from the event must be embedded in process change, and this requires an open approach to exploring the event, with all parties involved in that task.

Whilst there have been cases where legal proceedings have impacted on the way care is delivered, it is not always clear whether legal proceedings result in changes in clinical practice. Very often, once the hospital's legal team gets involved, the healthcare professionals implicated have less of a say in terms of how the case is pursued.

This situation was further complicated by the fact that a statutory 'Duty of candour' was introduced for NHS bodies in England in 2014. First suggested by Robert Francis QC in his report into the calumny of errors at the Mid Staffordshire Hospital (Francis Report, 2013). Both the General Medical Council and the Royal College of Surgeons of England have for decades stated in their guidance that it is a doctor's duty to admit errors and explain fully to the patient if a clinical error has occurred. With the introduction of new legislation, this is now enforceable by law.

The implementation of the Duty of Candour was hampered by two main issues. One was the definition of what constitutes a serious incident. According to Section 81 of the *Health and Social Care Act 2014*, incidents that qualify as requiring a Duty of Candour are those that lead to death or severe/moderate harm. However, it remains an open question what constitutes moderate harm, and so individuals and hospital trusts will work according to slightly different sets of criteria.

The second issue that has impeded the implementation of the statutory Duty of Candour is that little guidance has been issued about how to actually conduct these conversations with patients. The aim of transparency is laudable, but there also needs to be room to listen to the patient's account of events, and mechanisms need to be put in place to support patients and staff following disclosure, and to ensure appropriate lessons are learnt at the organisational level. What is lacking is a methodology of restorative practice.

Changes in clinical and legal practice

Larger trends look positive. In recent years, there has been a move towards placing greater emphasis on the autonomy of the individual patient. In the past, medical colleagues may have been able to defend a colleague who failed to disclose an error, based on the 'Bolam test', which stated that professional standards relied on what was commonly accepted practice (*Bolam v Friern Hospital Management Committee [1957]*).

This medical and surgical paternalism has already been challenged in court rulings for several decades, leading judges to rely instead of what the 'reasonable patient' might expect with regards to their care. A case in point would be the *Pearce v United Bristol Healthcare NHS Trust (1998)* lawsuit, where the judge in conclusion noted that if '*there is a significant risk which would affect the judgement of a reasonable patient, then in the normal course it is the responsibility of a doctor to inform the patient of that significant risk*' (*Pearce v United Bristol Healthcare NHS Trust [1998]*).

The most recent legal development in this area is the Supreme Court case *Montgomery vs Lanarkshire Health Board (2015)*, which further reduced the reliance on the 'Bolam test'. Here, a woman was inadequately consented for a Caesarean section, her wishes were not listened to and she went through a vaginal delivery that resulted in a child affected by cerebral palsy. The Court decided that the 'Bolam test' was obsolete in this case, because the test should not be whether this would be expected of a 'reasonable doctor' but whether the process of consent was adequate and fully informed as judged by a 'reasonable patient'.

The Supreme Court emphasised that: "*The doctor is therefore under a duty to take reasonable care to ensure that the patient is aware of any material risks involved in any recommended treatment, and of any reasonable alternative or variant treatments. The test of materiality is whether, in the circumstances of the particular case, a reasonable person in the patient's position would be likely to attach significance to the risk, or the doctor is or should reasonably be aware that the particular patient would be likely to attach significance to it*" (Montgomery v Lanarkshire Health Board [2015]).

When it comes to patient safety incidents, this shift towards patient autonomy means that healthcare professionals face a new reality both in terms of the consent process and the Incident Review and complaint resolution process. Medical paternalism is now considered anathema, and renewed emphasis is placed on patient–centred care, which attempts to include the patient and their family in the resolution of a conflict.

An opportunity for restorative practice?

It is amidst these changes that RP might be introduced as a tool that can be used in the correct circumstances. An overview of some of the key advantages of the RP approach is presented in Table 15.1.

Table 15.1 Five reasons to enhance staff and patient opportunity for dialogue in addressing shared situations of concern

1 **Offers participants a chance to address and understand the event**	When all parties to an event participate in dialogue, the shared perspectives and impact provide answers and a reduction in the potential sense of shame and resentment. In reinforcing this sense of interconnectedness, all parties recognise they are part of a larger whole.
2 **Gives the patient (and their family if relevant) a voice and the ability to participate in dialogue to address the scope for resolution**	When patients and their families engage in direct dialogue with staff, the forum provides an opportunity for empowerment and resolution, reduces the sense of victimhood and provides an opportunity to consider the learning contributing to the greater good.
3 **Gives the staff member the ability to integrate the event into ongoing safe practice as a valued clinician**	When clinicians engage in direct dialogue with patients and their families, the clinician gains clarity and reassurance in their professional value and an opportunity to declare a commitment to ongoing learning and safe practice. To deny this risks a damaged sense of self-worth and competence.
4 **Enhances life skills for conflict situations for both parties**	When an organisational culture values direct dialogue, it models an approach which enhances all parties' capacity to talk and resolve. These skills are enduring, and in the clinical setting will additionally inform communication expectations between team members.
5 **Maximises opportunity for organisational learning**	At an organisational level, safe clinical practice relies upon an open responsivity to adverse outcomes with dynamic process modification as a result.

We might summarise the potential gains from this approach by looking at three main parties: the patient, the healthcare professional(s) and the healthcare organisation. For the patient that has been harmed in some way, being able to have their story listened to, to be taken seriously, to be given the time of day by a busy clinical service, is invaluable. Patients often feel disempowered when seeking redress from an institution as large as the NHS. The current process of Patient Advice and Liaison Service (PALS), which exists in nearly every British hospital, has its role, but it is hard not to suspect that the message doesn't always get through to the people who need to hear it. If the patient was able to actively take part in a dialogue with the aspect of the service that they feel let them down, this would give them a direct way to impact change and to do what they can to prevent repetition of such events in the future.

For healthcare staff involved in a harmful incident, it can be frustrating to be advised that they are not allowed to make contact with the harmed party. Whether it is to seek clarification or offer an apology, far too often staff are told that the matter will be dealt with by other professionals. In midwifery there is even a tradition of removing the implicated midwife from the clinical area and placing them on probation. If instead there was a local system that could contain both the harmed and the (usually unintentional) cause of the harm, and to allow them to meet and both tell their narrative of events, this is likely to be beneficial for both parties.

Finally, for the healthcare service, there are considerable gains to be had. First, it is envisaged that the direct encounter with the harmed party will, in the majority of cases, cause the individual staff member to learn from their mistakes in a completely new way. Rather than just filling in an incident form and, in many cases, never hearing any more about it, they will have to engage with the patient who was harmed on their watch. It is appreciated that this is not for everyone, and there might be times when a Risk Manager or senior clinician takes the place of a junior staff member, but the narratives and the lessons could easily be summarised and shared in a safe manner.

Some progress towards this has already occurred. Following an apt name change from 'NHS Litigation Authority' to 'NHS Resolution', a new strategic framework was published in 2017 (NHS Resolution, 2017) that aims to diversify the ways in which individual and organisational learning can occur. NHS Resolution envisages that learning should occur immediately after an incident has occurred in a proactive rather than reactive way—through patient complaints and the lengthy legal route (see Figure 15.1).

In our own sector, Maternity Care, there is abundant scope to introduce RP, if only because the clinical errors that occur perinatally are extremely serious and very costly. In fact, the most recent figures suggest that within Obstetrics & Gynaecology, legal claims by value are equal to all other medical and surgical specialties combined (see Figure 15.2).

The appeal of RP in the healthcare setting is likely to become even more relevant if current proposals for a 'rapid resolution and redress (RRR) scheme', proposed by the Health Secretary in October 2016, are approved. As part of the government's action plan for implementing a new safety culture with Maternity services, the RRR scheme would enable eligible families to opt into the scheme without the need to bring a claim through the courts. Families would receive help, including counselling, case management and legal advice.

The scheme, which was welcomed by patient support groups, including Action for Victims of Medical Accidents, would offer timely access to financial support without the current obligation on families to launch a formal legal process, which at present on average takes over a decade to resolve. An approach that focused on resolution in the immediate aftermath of the incident, with patient narratives complemented with additional information and lessons learnt at the individual and organisational level, would work well with a no-claim rapid redress scheme.

The previous model of incident-to-resolution.

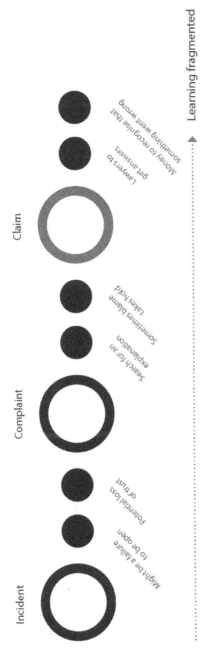

Incident

Complaint

Claim

Might be a failure to be open
Potential loss of trust
Search for an explanation
Sometimes blame takes hold
Lawyers to get answers
Money to recognise that something went wrong

Learning fragmented

The new model of incident-to-resolution.

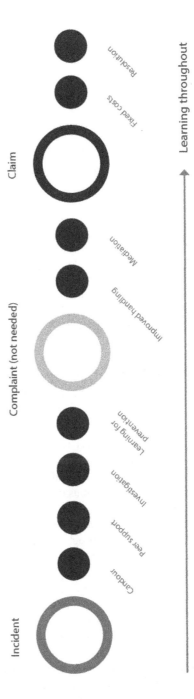

Incident

Complaint (not needed)

Claim

Candour
Peer support
Investigation
Learning for prevention
Improved handling
Mediation
Fixed costs
Resolution

Learning throughout

Figure 15.1 The new model of incident-to-resolution, as proposed by NHS Resolution (figure adapted from NSH Resolution, 2017).

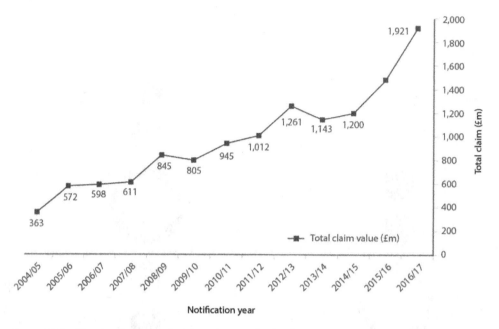

Figure 15.2 The total value of claims for cerebral palsy and neonatal brain damage has increased sevenfold over the last 12 years

(Adapted from NHS Resolution, 2017).

Introducing restorative practice in the maternity care setting

Prior to commencing training in RP, we surveyed all members of staff at our tertiary teaching hospital (6,500 deliveries per year). A questionnaire was distributed electronically to all doctors and midwives in July 2017, with a response rate of approximately 40% (n=105). We established that staff members, irrespective of their level of seniority, had on average been involved in two serious safety incidents in the past year. In Maternity, examples of such safety incidents would include neonatal and maternal death, unexpected admission of a neonate to the Neonatal Intensive Care Ward and serious untoward incidents such as birth trauma or other harm to either the mother or the baby.

Whilst most healthcare professionals had been involved in a safety incident, only 30% had received individual feedback relating to the incident. Many staff members felt unsupported in the aftermath of a serious incident, and almost all indicated that they would be interested in receiving both individual feedback and further training in how to conduct better conversations with affected patients. Only a handful of staff surveyed had received any training in how to conduct Duty of Candour conversations with patients following an incident.

Supported by a Maternity Safety grant from Health Education England (HEE), we then created bespoke teaching sessions for NHS staff working on the labour and postnatal ward. Participants included midwives and doctors of every level of seniority. Learning from the implementation of RP in schools and other settings outside of criminal justice, we sought to train a cohort of doctors and midwives in the methodology of RP. The first thing we realised was the need to alter some of the language used – away from blaming and the binary approach of right and wrong, and to a concern with the impact of an event on all parties and their needs in the present as well as going forward.

Key steps in facilitating a restorative process adapted to the health setting are summarised in Table 15.2. Arranging a practice conference is merely the start, and the more patients' voices can been heard, and the more staff are able to take part in meaningful discussions, the greater the chance that individual learning can occur. There are also key gains to be had in terms of a

Table 15.2 How to convene a restorative practice conference in a health setting

Clarify the key parties involved in the event	Gather information from key parties as to the circumstances of the event and their knowledge of others who may wish to be involved.
Determine whether these parties are to be grouped in their involvement	Clarify with these individuals whether they are part of a group, e.g. perhaps an individual is closely supported by their family, who are also affected by the event, or a clinician may be part of a close team.
Hold individual restorative enquiry meetings with the parties	Undertake separate Restorative Enquiry meetings with the key individuals, noting perceptions, impact and need. Capture their points of engagement, curiosity and need. Also explore whether there are others they perceive are important to be included.
Hold individual restorative enquiry meetings with any additional groups	Undertake a separate Restorative Enquiry meeting with the additional groups, e.g. families or team colleagues, and capture their points of engagement, curiosity and need.
Assess the level of engagement evidenced by the parties	Artful Facilitation skills will elicit points of engagement during these individual Restorative meetings with parties and groups, questions they need answered, statements they need heard and reassurances they need met. These points of engagement are then enhanced with the individuals actively nominating who needs to be part of the dialogue and what value they perceive in this involvement.
Consider the safety and risk in bringing the parties together	Apply a Risk and Safety assessment to the situation, considering readiness to engage, emotional/behavioural factors of the parties, timing and venue.
Determine whether there is to be a two-tiered approach or one large meeting	A decision is made regarding progressing with a smaller focused Joint Restorative Meeting between key individuals and any silent support people. And once they have completed their meeting, they then meet with the larger involved group. Alternatively, it may be appropriate to directly progress to the Joint meeting with the larger group of participants.
Facilitate the joint meeting	Welcome and give context to the Joint Restorative Meeting by introducing participants and outlining the format for the meeting. Select parties one at a time and ask the Restorative Questions clarifying perceptions of the event, thoughts and feelings at the time, feelings now and the link to needs. Once each participant has spoken invite consideration of the voiced needs and encourage collaboration on the joint task of addressing these needs. Facilitate clarity and points of agreement and ensure all matters have been addressed.
Record agreements	Record the agreement between the parties and ensure any relevant time frames and measures referred to are quantified.
Assist the parties to determine who else needs to know of this resolution	Lastly, consult with the meeting group to clarify whether there are others more widely associated with the event whom they wish to now make aware of the joint agreement. Clarify the method of that information delivery e.g. perhaps a larger circle forum for a joint presentation of the clarity reached and agreement determined.

change in organisational culture, including a move away from a blame culture to one where disputes and conflicts become a source for reflection and growth. It remains to be seen whether this effort will result in a reduction in the spiralling costs of legal claims.

The two fundamental principles of RP remain intact when translated into the healthcare setting. The Practice works by trained practitioners talking separately with the parties and giving them the opportunity to reflect upon events, recognise the impact they have experienced and the needs they now have as a result. Inevitably, these needs will focus upon a necessity to have important statements understood, to have questions answered and to gain resolution through direct dialogue with those key to the event. This participation in the individual Restorative Enquiry will bring some clarity and perspective. There will be those who choose not to pursue such an opportunity for direct dialogue, but there is still merit in the Restorative Enquiry.

Concluding thoughts

This chapter has argued that restorative meetings can provide a space for both parties of a dispute to voice their perspective and make their needs known. In sharing this information, they can recognise each other's difficulties and see each other as part of their solution. The result can be collaboration to address remedies and actions that will represent resolution for them all.

In conclusion, it seems to us that the introduction of RP in the healthcare setting is timely, and it may lead to a number of beneficial outcomes. As we have attempted to lay out, the healthcare service has a number of features that make it a potentially excellent arena for RP, yet there are no current academic evaluation programmes looking at the implementation of RP in this setting. It seems to us that there is great opportunity here both for practitioners and academics interested in RP, to create joint ventures in order to assess implementation of RP in the health service. For policy makers, the appeal should be obvious: there is clearly both human cost and real monetary cost to be saved by allowing some of the many safety incidents to be resolved before the legal route is considered.

We have also found RP to be uniquely suited to addressing incidents of harm within the Maternity Care setting. If other medical and surgical specialties take up the challenge, perhaps we could contribute to fulfilling the government's aim of transforming the NHS into the world's largest learning organisation. Our lessons and evidence are preliminary, but they are also relevant to the international restorative justice movement as it proceeds to explores new areas of application.

References

Bolam v Friern Hospital Management Committee. 1957.1 WLR 582.
Francis, R. 2013. *Report of the Mid Staffordshire NHS Foundation Trust Public Inquiry*. London: TSO; 2013.
Montgomery v Lanarkshire Health Board. 2015. UKSC 11.
National Patient Safety Agency. 2011. *What Is a Patient Safety Incident?* Available at www.npsa.nhs.uk/ nrls/reporting/what-is-a-patient-safety-incident/. Accessed 21 May 2014. *Five Years of Cerebral Palsy Claims*. NHS Resolution, 2017. *Delivering Fair Resolution and Learning from Harm*. NHS Resolution, 2017.
Pearce v United Bristol Healthcare NHS Trust. 1998. 48 BMLR 118 (CA).

16

Traffic congestion and road rage

A restorative case study to road sharing

Marian Liebmann

Introduction

The evidence for this chapter come from 'Road Sharing – A Restorative Approach'. This was an innovative project funded by the Office of the Police and Crime Commissioner through Bristol City Council, linked to Bristol's status as European Green Capital for 2015. Bristol is a large industrial city in the UK with a reputation for innovative social enterprises but suffers from extreme traffic congestion owing to its eighteenth century street pattern and hilly terrain. The project was undertaken by Bristol Mediation, an established charity providing both restorative justice and community mediation services.

Restorative Bristol is a meeting place for all those in the city using restorative approaches in a variety of ways. Its vision is a city where individuals, agencies and services see restorative approaches as the first option for dealing with conflict. It builds connections and networks between organisations and individuals who work across the spectrum of restorative justice, restorative interventions and restorative philosophies. It recognises and values the diversity of work on this issue and also recognises the common principles which underpin restorative work.

Its members include the local youth offending team, victim support, probation, restorative approaches in criminal justice, mediation services (neighbour and workplace), primary and secondary schools, nurseries, trainers, academics and City Council officers. The Restorative Bristol Board meets quarterly to take forward proposals and new initiatives for restorative work in the city. The project is supported and administered by a Bristol City Council officer in the crime reduction section who is allocated a small amount of time for this work amidst competing priorities. From time to time, the project organises conferences and events to involve the wider public and promote restorative values and work (Restorative Bristol, 2017).

The proposal for the restorative road sharing project was a contribution to Bristol's European Green Capital status for 2015: to tackle the conflict experienced on the roads between different users. Although the number of people killed or seriously injured on Bristol roads declined during the years prior to 2014, there was still concern at the numbers: in 2013, there were 12

Figure 16.1   Bristol's traffic congestion

people killed and a further 94 people seriously injured (Garmston, 2014). Moreover, the perception of many citizens is that Bristol's roads are dangerous places, and would-be cyclists are deterred from entering the fray. Incidents of 'road rage' in Bristol's narrow, congested streets are commonplace. Figure 16.1 shows some aspects of the congestion. There was a sense of curiosity within the Restorative Bristol Board – could a restorative approach offer something new, an alternative to prosecution or undealt-with conflict?

This chapter's aim fits in with the focus of this Handbook in that it explores a new area where the relevance of restorative work has not yet been identified and provides a case study showing how innovative practice can forge new pathways.

Methodology and context

Project outcomes and outputs

It was thought the best mechanism to start the project would be an application from Bristol Mediation to the Office of the Police and Crime Commissioner for this innovative piece of work (Police and Crime Commissioners [PCCs] are elected officials in England and Wales charged with securing efficient and effective policing of a police area. They are elected for four-year terms). Accordingly, Bristol Mediation applied to the Avon & Somerset OPCC [Office of the Police and Crime Commissioner] for £20,000 and was awarded £10,000. The agreement included the preparation to enable a facilitated restorative conference between different road users in the city and to create a six-minute short film to promote the work to wider communities.

Expected outcomes were:

- Improved communication between different and diverse groups of road users across the city

- Empowerment of road users in finding a way to move forward with this issue
- Improved understanding from different groups' perspectives of road use in the city
- Enablement of different groups to have had a voice and to have felt heard
- Enablement of groups to have had input from development stage through to post-conference
- Increased input from a diverse range of people from across the city
- Development of restorative champions who can continue to develop and promote the work so that it goes wider
- Increased confidence in neighbourhoods/communities/roads across the city

The outputs were to be measured quarterly:

Quarter 1 (April to June 2015): Recruitment of project coordinator; creation of road user groups

Quarter 2 (July to September 2015): Meetings with each group to prepare for conference

Quarter 3 (October to December 2015): Host and facilitate a conference with all working groups

Quarter 4 (January to March 2016): Create a six-minute video.

As the project progressed, it was interesting to see how well these outputs were achieved and the reasons for needing to change the focus.

Resourcing and sampling

Two project coordinators were appointed from June 2015 to work half a day per week each for 10 months. Annali Grimes and I were jointly appointed to take on this role, as we had complementary skills, to cover the work entailed. As with many such projects, the work involved took far longer than the allocated paid time. The last third of the time we were unpaid; fortunately, I was in a position to continue voluntarily, although my colleague was not.

Our first task as project coordinators was to produce a project outline to attract participants, with the help of Julie Cox, director of Bristol Mediation. We produced a flyer for the project and an 'expression of interest' form to enable accurate collection of personal details, diversity information and so on. Both these documents were uploaded on to the Bristol Mediation website.

We envisaged separate group meetings for different road users (e.g. a meeting for cyclists, a meeting for car drivers, a meeting for pedestrians and so on). We hoped to include organisations as well as individuals. We saw each of these road user groups as a 'stakeholder' with a coherent view of road issues which could be expressed by representatives of the group. We expressed this as follows on our project flyer:

> *Each small group will attend a two-hour meeting in November 2015, and will then choose two or three people to represent their interests at a larger all-day meeting in February 2016.*
>
> *The large meeting in February will be run using a restorative approach. This means that the focus will be on expression of concerns, dialogue between different groups of road users and finding a constructive way forward. It is hoped that those who attend will gain greater awareness and understanding of other road users' perspectives.*
>
> *(Liebmann et al., 2016, Appx 2)*

We researched, through our own networks, links and internet organisations, contacts and individuals in the following categories:

- Pedestrians
- Cyclists
- Motorcyclists
- Car drivers
- Disabled/elderly people
- Bus and taxi drivers
- Lorry drivers
- Other street users (e.g. Playing Out – an organisation promoting street closures to traffic so that children can play in the street)

We made contact with identified organisations and groups, and we promoted the project through Voscur (the local network for voluntary-sector community organisations and groups), the Restorative Bristol website, the Bristol Mediation website, social media and existing networks using various forms of contact. Whilst there was initial disappointment at the low level of responses (only nine from 100 contacts), we later understood that this is the expected rate of response to e-mail and web-based requests.

It became clear that it would be a challenge to recruit equal numbers of participants from the different road user groups with similar availability, especially within the time and resources of the project, so we needed to revise the original idea of single road-user groups. The 'expressions of interest' forms showed that many prospective participants used several forms of transport. It also became clear that the people interested in our project led very busy lives and had limited availability.

We therefore decided to invite participants from all the road user groups to mixed meetings to fit in with their schedules, with morning, afternoon and evening groups arranged. Meetings planned with little take-up were then cancelled. We were very grateful for the help from Mark Parry (Bristol City Council), who coordinated these room bookings for us in Brunel House, a set of offices belonging to Bristol City Council.

Based on these amendments, the original invitation was revised to include the following changes:

> There will be separate meetings taking place during October, November and December. We hope to include organisations and individuals. These will be run using a restorative approach. This means that the focus will be on expression of concerns, dialogue between different groups of road users and finding a constructive way forward. It is hoped that those who attend will gain greater awareness and understanding of other road users' perspectives and enable people to work together and provide recommendations which will be considered in future developments in the city.
>
> Each small group will attend a two-hour meeting, and will then express interest to participate in the larger meeting in February 2016.

We continued to make additional contacts, and also re-contacted the organisations we had not heard from. This resulted in further expressions of interest, with more starting to come in, so that by December 2015 the total had risen to 61. Many of these were from pedestrians, cyclists and car drivers. But we also managed to recruit disabled people, taxi drivers and bus drivers.

In addition to the 71 people who took part in the small groups, a further 25 people expressed interest but were unable to attend due to their other commitments. The groups included a mixture of road users: cyclists, pedestrians, car drivers, motorcyclists, taxi drivers, bus drivers, disabled people, blind people, young, middle-aged and older adults. This included individuals as well as representatives of other groups in the city.

Whilst cyclists, car drivers and pedestrians presented themselves readily for the groups, we had to work hard to ensure that taxi drivers, bus drivers, motorcyclists and disabled people were represented. We were ultimately successful in finding these, and the only unrepresented group was lorry drivers, despite our sustained efforts with haulage and waste management organisations. However, this categorisation is only part of the picture, as many participants used several forms of transport as appropriate (e.g. pedestrian/ bus/ bike/ car). See figure 16.2.

We also gathered data on areas of Bristol where people lived, gender, age, disability and ethnic background. Most participants were of working age, evenly spread between 25–49 and 50–64, with a small number of older and younger people. The participants were not very diverse ethnically, with a preponderance of white British people, and much smaller groups of diverse origins; however, these proportions reflect the structure of Bristol's population. Most participants were not disabled, but we did manage to include a substantial minority. More encouraging was the picture of where participants lived in Bristol. The areas of the city by postcode showed a fairly even spread across those postcodes with easy access to the city centre, including inner city districts; outlying districts were poorly represented. This may reflect one of Bristol's most pressing transport difficulties – the inadequate and expensive bus service.

We were keen to involve organisations as well as individuals. In all, 34 people were involved as individuals and 37 as members of an organisation. There were also several participants who, whilst working for an organisation, attended the groups as individuals. The organisations represented included general transport, cycling, motorcycling, taxi, energy, children's play and disability organisations.

Additional group meetings

We realised that some groups of people were not represented, particularly disabled and young people, because of difficulty taking part in the mixed sessions. We therefore liaised with

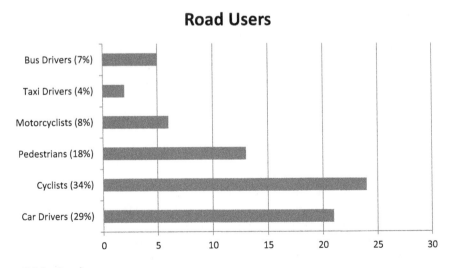

Figure 16.2 Road users

appropriate agencies and managed to hold separate sessions for two groups which had not been included.

We had wanted to include the voices of younger people, but had been unable to persuade any university student groups to come forward – all too busy! In the end, we approached a secondary school contact and were able to hold an informal group with school students aged 14–16. They had plenty to say about traffic and road issues, especially as pedestrians and cyclists.

In one of the early groups, we became aware that an elderly deaf man was not able to take a meaningful part in the group due to his poor hearing. We thought that deaf people might experience particular problems with traffic, so we decided to try to arrange a special group for them. We were able to do this with the help of Trish Vallance of Bristol City Council and Clive Gray of the Restorative Bristol Board. Trish (deaf herself) e-mailed deaf people known to Bristol City Council and arranged a BSL interpreter for the evening. The participants were very appreciative of the opportunity to give their views and take part in discussion.

We also liaised with LinkAge (an organisation for older adults) with a view to holding a group with their service users, but in the end they were not able to arrange this within the timescale of the project. However, we already had several participants in the older age bracket, so we felt their voices had been included.

We spent a large amount of time between September and December 2015 coordinating and running the small groups. These went well and gave us lots of food for thought (see later in the chapter). We also made contact with other linking agencies, such as Sustrans (a Bristol-based national voluntary organisation promoting cycling), who were working on a Good Transport Plan for Bristol, and other organisations in the transport field. We had hoped to engage actively with these organisations, but their funding and time frames differed from ours, so our liaison remained at a 'friendly information' level. We were able to attend the launch of their plan, and one of their senior staff joined our last group and took part in the filming at the end.

By January we were planning the large conference for February and researching suitable venues to ensure that there was a larger space as well as additional break-out spaces for smaller groups and for filming. An event page was created via Eventbrite and circulated to all who had attended the smaller meetings and shown interest in attending the larger meeting. We also sent it to additional expressions of interest received. The response was low, with limited availability from participants. In addition there were clear financial implications through the need for additional facilitators for a larger meeting, for BSL (British Sign Language) interpreters for the day, and the increased cost of a fully accessible and suitable venue.

We had received an encouraging visit from the OPCC in October. They were pleased at the number of people we were engaging and the way the groups were going. They emphasised the importance of bringing people together for dialogue, but were not concerned whether or not the project resulted in a large meeting.

So, in January, after consultation between the coordinators, the director of Bristol Mediation, Bristol City Council and the OPCC, we reconsidered the large group event. We had so much positive information from the small groups that people felt it would be a better use of the limited resources to concentrate on evaluating the data we had and to proceed with one final small group meeting which would be filmed.

The additional group to be filmed took place in February and went very well with eight participants. Our film-maker Lee Cox also filmed several participants from the previous groups, to ensure representation from the different road user groups and to elicit their views on the value of this work. We all met to look at the film material, and then Lee and her colleague Frank edited it into an eight-minute film which was shared with the OPCC and Bristol City Council (and other agencies involved in the project) and placed on Bristol Mediation's website and YouTube.

The restorative justice meetings and offer

The ground rules

For each of the 11 small groups, the aims were posted on the wall:

- Use a restorative approach – all to have a voice and feel heard
- Get people talking and listening to each other
- Make suggestions to take forward to a larger meeting in February
- Feed ideas to Bristol City Council

This last aim was an important motivation for many of the group participants, who were eager to take an opportunity to influence the City Council to make improvements in traffic and road issues.

The ground rules were also posted on the wall:

- Mobile phones off or on silent
- Uninterrupted time to talk
- Respect for each other
- Give others space to speak
- Speak for yourself
- Acknowledge and respect our differences
- Ask if anything else.

We started the small groups by introducing ourselves, saying how the meeting would be run and setting out the ground rules. We had also asked participants to send in any issues they specifically wanted to discuss ahead of attending the group. We asked all attendees to introduce themselves and their issues and then let the group choose which issues to pursue in exchange and dialogue.

The restorative model used was a peacemaking circle (Fellegi and Szegő, 2013), in which participants hold a talking piece passed round the circle, enabling everyone to have a voice. We provided an attractive stone (in keeping with the theme of roads) as the 'talking piece' held by each participant as he or she spoke and then passed to the next person. After sharing and discussion, we rounded off each group by asking what people had learnt and what they might do differently in the future. Annali and I shared the tasks – for the most part I facilitated the group, whilst Annali recorded the discussions on a flipchart, visible to all. We also used a recording device to capture the final round of learning and differences that people might make. Figure 16.3 shows one of the groups in action.

Evaluating the interventions

We evaluated the group sessions in several ways (with assistance from Nikki McKenzie of the University of the West of England [UWE] in developing the following methods):

- Before-and-after forms on attitudes to other road users
- A feedback sheet at the end of the group on their experience of the group
- A final round in which we asked all participants to say one thing they had learnt, and one thing they might do differently

Figure 16.3 Running the groups

The points made in the final round depended on the make-up of the group. For instance, in a group which included motorcyclists, someone said 'I learnt about issues for motorbikes, I didn't know about them before' and then 'I will have more respect for motorbikes on the road.'

For each participant, we had a form with basic data, a 'before-and-after' form concerned with attitudes to different road user groups and responses to a questionnaire about their experience in the small groups.

A university student from UWE volunteering with Bristol Mediation worked with us to analyse this data, linking the before-and-after scores to each group's make-up. This data was then matched with the target outcomes set at the beginning of the project.

Findings from the project

Promotion and media interest

In September, whilst we were promoting the project to gain expressions of interest, the *Bristol Post* (the local paper for Bristol) interviewed Annali and wrote an excellent and thoughtful article about the project (Ashcroft, 2015). The article quoted Annali as saying:

> *What we are doing is promoting a non-confrontational, restorative approach to the issues surrounding our road usage in Bristol. This is something which affects every single person in the city, from parents*

who are too scared to let their children walk to school because of traffic to people who do not want to take public transport because of the cost and reliability factors. The point is to get different road users together to listen to each other and to put themselves in each other's shoes.

The assistant mayor of the City Council contributed:

We were keen to support this project as part of our ongoing commitment to reducing congestion and encouraging more active modes of transport, particularly during our year as European Green Capital. Bristol has the highest proportion of cycling commuters compared to the other core cities and we are always supportive of any project that encourages positive relationships between all different road users.

This article engendered further media interest, including national newspapers and local television – unfortunately, the slant of these other media outlets, without factual information or contacting Bristol Mediation to clarify, had a negative impact on the project. Some of them portrayed the project as confrontative, whilst others ridiculed its aims. We felt this might well put off potential participants. This was upsetting for us, for Bristol Mediation, for the OPCC and for Bristol City Council, despite the fact that we had little control over the various misrepresentations. Nevertheless, it certainly put the project on the map. There was also much traffic on social media, including a wave of anti-cyclist diatribes. Bristol Mediation posted a response on social media, giving the facts and encouraging people to sign up so that their voices could be heard, but none of those expressing strong views on Facebook came forward to the project.

As a result of this experience, we refused all further media invitations until the end of the project, with any additional media contact going through Bristol City Council Communications Department. Bristol Mediation published the project report and the film on its website, after approval by Bristol City Council (Liebmann et al., 2016; Cox, 2016)

Being listened to

The small groups took place during November, December and January. Five of these took place in the morning, two in the afternoon and four in the evening. The best-attended groups were the morning sessions.

Each group experience was different, according to the composition of the group, and different issues were aired. Some groups had a preponderance of cyclists (Bristol experienced an increase in cycle commuters of 94% between 2001 and 2011, and was named Bristol's first 'cycling city' in 2008) (Lake, 2015). Other groups had more mixed composition. Two groups including motorcyclists helped to change other participants' views of motorcyclists. A group containing two bus drivers told how they were educating older bus drivers in cyclist-awareness. A group including two taxi drivers heard how out-of-town taxi drivers were stealing their work. Several car drivers learnt about the difficulties of pedestrians.

For one meeting, we had an observer (the film-maker, who wanted to get an idea of the nature of the meetings before planning the filming of the last group). She wrote:

The restorative meeting I attended as part of the Road Sharing project was very interesting in content and process. People with differing needs seemed to settle once they realised the meeting would be held as a safe process and they wouldn't be vulnerable, once making their points, however controversial. The introduction made it very clear that each person would have time to speak in detail. At times I thought some might lose patience with how long others spoke for. But, having listened, they then understood that they too would be listened to. I felt they appreciated the restorative approach. The summaries given were also very clear, which allowed people to move on, as they understood that their points had been noted and everyone's views included.

Thus the results from the small groups were very positive. Instead of regarding different road users as enemies and competitors, this project harnessed listening and consideration of other views, leading to a cooperative ethos. We conclude that this model of restorative working could be applied to many other situations, such as focus groups, hard-to-reach groups with fixed views and incidents of road rage.

Concerning the process of the group, people said the workshops met their expectations, were well organised, and they appreciated the opportunity to work with others to find possible ways forward. They had a greater understanding of other road users in the city, and they felt they had had a voice and felt heard. However, they did not feel more confident using the roads in the city. Thus the project fulfilled all the expected outcomes except the last one (see list in the section 'Project outcomes and outputs').

From the 'before-and-after' forms, we hoped to map any shifts in attitude. Although one two-hour group might not be expected to produce much change, if any, eight of the groups showed a positive shift, whilst two showed a small negative shift. (There were only ten groups to be evaluated this way, as we did not use the 'before-and-after' questionnaire with the school group, as we deemed it too formal and off-putting for the young people).

Attitudinal change

Our research assistant analysed the figures from the 'before-and-after' forms and produced graphs based on these. Figures 16.4–16.7 show the results from four of the small groups. These showed positive changes in attitude towards road users who were present in the group, suggesting that this method can improve attitudes towards other road users.

Meeting 1: Within this first meeting, we can see that the attitudes towards car drivers have become more negative; this is interesting, as there were several car drivers in the group. The attitudes towards pedestrians have improved; with only one pedestrian being represented in the group, they have had a clear impact. What is most interesting about this group is the conflicting views between car drivers and other road users; possibly the car users in this group have

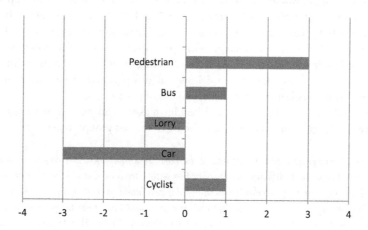

Figure 16.4 Graph analysis: Meeting 1

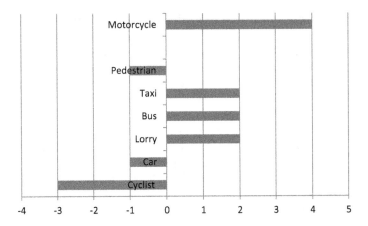

Figure 16.5 Graph analysis: Meeting 4

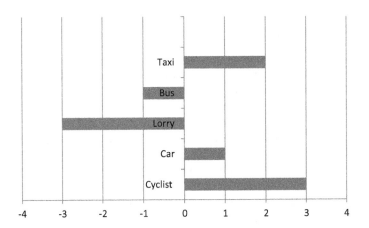

Figure 16.6 Graph analysis: Meeting 5

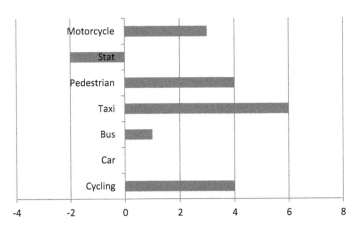

Figure 16.7 Graph Analysis: Meeting 10

realised the impact their driving can have on other road users, and this has added to the views of other road users.

Meeting 4: The attitudes towards cyclists have become more negative – this could be due to having no cyclists in the room to put forth their point of view. By contrast, the presence of a motorcyclist led to more positive attitudes towards them as road users. This suggests that views may vary depending on who is at the meeting. Road users speaking for themselves seem to have a positive impact on other road users' views, as one might expect.

Meeting 5: In complete contrast to Meeting 4, there were cyclists at this meeting and the views of them became more positive, notably from a car driver, so this shows how the meeting can have a positive impact. The same situation happens here with taxi drivers, as there were two in attendance. On a further note, attitudes towards lorry drivers became more negative, but with no one to represent them, they could not share their issues.

Meeting 10: This group included several cyclists and a motorcyclist; the attitudes towards both these groups have improved significantly. This shows that people airing their views has a positive impact, counteracting the often-expressed annoyance of car drivers with other road users. Meetings like this can thus have a positive impact on attitudes.

Changing perceptions and attitudes

Our question to participants, 'Is there one thing you have learnt?', elicited some specific things, such as a new appreciation of motorcyclists, as mentioned earlier, or the issues about out-of-town taxis or information about issues for particular groups. But many of the answers to this question were about awareness of others and the way issues could be addressed through listening and dialogue.

The final question, 'Is there one thing you might do differently?', led to some interesting answers, and showed that, even in a two-hour group session, learning can take place which may result in people changing their behaviour. Again, there were particular intentions, for example, to pay more attention to motorcyclists, to undertake training for mobility scooters, to cycle more, to look into the Playing Out scheme – but also for many a resolve to pay more attention to the needs of other road users and be more considerate towards them.

The groups also resulted in a huge amount of data on people's views and thoughts that they were keen to have shared within the group, then taken forward to Bristol City Council and other groups that might be able to influence change in the city. We organised these suggestions into themes so they would be readable and user friendly:

- Attitudes on the roads
- Infrastructure
- Sustainability issues
- Cyclists
- Motorcyclists
- Cars
- Buses
- Taxis
- Children, older adults and disabled people
- Shared paths and spaces
- The Highway Code
- Particular danger spots

Discussion

Our original approach – small stakeholder groups feeding into a larger dialogue process – was based on an assumption that there would be a coherent view from each group, and that this view would be in conflict with other groups, as in a standard large-scale dispute scenario. However, we did not find that to be the case. There was much variation of issues within each group of road users, and considerable agreement between different groups of road users. This made for interesting group processes and much learning from each other. As facilitators, we also learnt from each group as different issues were presented and discussed.

There is also the point mentioned previously that many people use a variety of modes of transport, as appropriate, so they are able to see issues from several points of view. And many times participants emphasised that we are all human beings who sometimes make mistakes and need to develop tolerance and empathy for each other.

What is clear from the responses is that the groups were appreciated by almost everyone who took part as a safe and welcoming space where they could air their issues and be heard.

It is interesting to compare these findings with those of more 'traditional' restorative justice interventions (in criminal settings). Research by the University of Sheffield in the UK between 2001 and 2008 showed that direct meetings between victims and offenders were more effective than indirect meetings in terms of enhanced communication and satisfaction (Shapland et al., 2011). There were parallel experiences in our project, in that there were positive shifts in attitude towards types of road user where such users had been part of the group. The changes in attitude seemed to result from direct meetings of participants sharing their views and issues. However, whilst it is clearly valuable to provide processes which enable individual change, this may not be enough to effect system change.

This observation leads us to suggest that a restorative approach would be useful for many situations where contentious issues are at stake – using mixed groups to bring problems to the fore in a way that is not adversarial and can engender a change of attitude. This could also have applications for hard-to-reach groups with fixed opinions or for incidents of 'road rage'.

At some point, it would be useful to involve decision makers in a larger group including some of the small group participants to share the findings of the project using a restorative approach. It would also be useful for planners to be involved, in order to let people know why things are planned in certain ways and how things are taken forward. Judging by the results of the project, such a move could result in greater understanding from road users.

Conclusion

This project took off in a different direction from the one originally envisaged. We started with a traditional 'stakeholder model' and finished with a more flexible restorative model. The project has shown the power of small groups of different road users meeting to share their issues using a restorative approach. The model used a peacemaking circle with a talking piece, which worked well and provided the environment for people to feel safe airing their issues.

The results showed that people found the groups useful and enjoyable, and learnt something which enabled them to consider how they might make a change towards other road users.

There are many possible applications for these groups, in terms of using a restorative approach in different situations where contentious issues are at stake. We hope the project will provide a blueprint for further work in this area and for further consultations and developments locally.

Cities all over the world suffer from similar problems of traffic chaos and conflicts, so we also hope that international readers may be inspired to try similar methods to alleviate the tensions and encourage a restorative approach.

References

Ashcroft, E. 2015. Council Funds Scheme to Find Peace Between Cars and Bikes, *The Bristol Post*, 29 September.

Cox, L. 2016. *Road Sharing: A Restorative Approach*. Video for Bristol Mediation. Available at www.bristol-mediation.org

Fellegi, B. and Szegő, D. 2013. *Handbook for Facilitating Peacemaking Circles*. Available at http://euforumrj.org/assets/upload/peacemaking_circle_handbook.pdf

Garmston, G. 2014. Bristol Road Casualty Review (2013) Summary. Unpublished report.

Lake, A. 2015. Bristol: A Cycling City in Name Alone? *The Bristol Cable*, 13 February issue. Available at https://thebristolcable.org/2015/02/bristol-a-cycling-city-in-name-alone/. Accessed 14 October 2017.

Liebmann, M., Grimes, A. and Cox, J. 2016. *Road Sharing: A Restorative Approach*. A Bristol Mediation project. Bristol: Bristol Mediation. Available at www.bristol-mediation.org

Restorative Bristol. 2017. Available at www.restorativebristol.co.uk. Accessed 14 October 2017.

Shapland, J., Robinson, G. and Sorsby, A. 2011. *Restorative Justice in Practice: Evaluating What Works for Victims and Offenders*. London: Routledge.

17

Restorative justice in universities
Case studies of what works with restorative responses to student misconduct

David R. Karp and Megan Schachter

Introduction

College students know how to get in trouble. At a large university in the United States, a conduct office will manage thousands of cases each year. In 2015–2016, for example, the University of Colorado at Boulder handled 6,143 conduct violations (University of Colorado, 2016). Many conduct administrators have incorporated restorative practices into their work (Karp and Frank, 2016b). At Boulder, a restorative justice approach was used for 417 of those violations. An RJ approach to college student misconduct is an inclusive process in which students who have caused harm, those who have been harmed, support persons, and other campus community members engage in a decision-making process that helps identify and repair harm as well as rebuild trust and strengthen campus relationships. A variety of restorative practices are used, with their own cultural and historical origins. Most typically, restorative conferences are used to manage individual incidents of misconduct. Restorative conferences, which have their origins in New Zealand and Australia, are convened by a facilitator who guides the process using a protocol of questions that allow the participants to share their perspective and collaboratively decide on an outcome (Karp, 2009a). Restorative circles, which are based on Native American and First Nations Canadian practices, are often used for incidents that have caused widespread harm or are linked to ongoing conflicts (Llewellyn, MacIsaac, and Mackay, 2015). Circle practices make use of a "talking piece" that is passed around the circle to establish who is to speak and to ensure equal participation.

In this chapter, we share how restorative justice (RJ) cases were successfully resolved on campuses across the United States. Some were minor violations, such as a student who vandalized a sprinkler system. A graduate student aspiring to work in higher education asked for a restorative process to make amends for falsifying data so that he could still pursue his chosen career. Others were serious. A restorative circle was used to resolve a conflict between football players after a white player called a black player the "N word." A sexual assault survivor sat down with the student who assaulted her three years earlier after he read through her extensive writing about the assault. In a restorative conference with two students who drove through campus firing BB guns, a facilities worker explained that he chased them down to prevent them from being shot by police. Despite their variety, all of the cases involved students who wished to take responsibility for their misconduct and harmed parties who had important stories to share and specific needs they wanted addressed through a restorative process. This chapter also examines what we know about what works when employing RJ for college student misconduct. We begin with a brief review of published studies that focus on "Campus RJ" and then examine six case studies from universities across the United States that illustrate how RJ benefits harmed parties and enhances student learning.

Restorative justice in campuses: the evidence from the extant literature

Our literature review suggests that studies of Campus RJ are divided into five categories: (1) general proposals for a restorative approach, (2) analyses of cases, (3) descriptions of campus programs and best practices, (4) applications of RJ to specific types of violations, and (5) empirical studies of effectiveness.

Sebok and Goldblum (1999) published the first article on Campus RJ, which described their project to build a programme at the University of Colorado at Boulder. After learning about a community-based RJ program in nearby Longmont, Colorado, the authors and other university staff developed the first Campus RJ program: "As far as we knew, if we proceeded, we were moving into uncharted waters . . . if we were to try RJ on campus, it would be up to us to do it" (p. 15). As of 2016, Boulder's Program, known as CURJ (Colorado University Restorative Justice), continues to thrive, with 417 student offenders participating in RJ conferences during the 2015–2016 academic year (CURJ, 2016).

Karp et al. (2002) mapped out the theoretical basis for a Campus RJ approach, based on a restorative approach they developed at Skidmore College one year after Boulder implemented its pioneering program. Subsequently, several others have provided theory and practice-based proposals for implementing Campus RJ (Clark, 2014; Goldblum, 2009; Kara and MacAlister, 2010; Karp, 2009a; Karp, 2013; Karp and Frank, 2016b; Sebok, 2006; Warters et al., 2000). Implementation models vary from campus to campus, with most adopting the conferencing model or circle practices. Traditionally, student conduct cases are adjudicated by hearing boards or, more simply, a one-on-one hearing between a student and conduct administrator. Some campuses have tried to infuse these hearing models with restorative questions and the restorative goals of repairing harm and rebuilding trust.

Karp and Allena (2004) published an edited collection of essays describing various models of practice and cases studies from several campuses such as vandalism, drug and alcohol abuse, bias incidents, and hazing. In-depth case studies have also been published exploring restorative responses to various violations, including theft (Karp, 2011), disorderly conduct (Rinker and Jonason, 2014), academic dishonesty (Karp, 2009b), and sexual harassment (Llewellyn et al., 2015b; Llewellyn et al., 2015a; see also Karp, 2015). Blas Pedreal (2015) examines the implications of Campus RJ for students of colour. Wachtel explores how RJ practices can be used to build community in residence halls (Wachtel and Wachtel, 2012; Wachtel and Miller, 2013). Several authors have considered the potential of RJ for sexual assault (Brenner, 2013; Coker, 2016; Harper et al., 2017; Kaplan, 2017; Karp et al., 2016; Kirven, 2014; Koss et al., 2014; Koss and Lopez, 2014).

We are aware of only eight empirical studies of Campus RJ (Ahlin et al., 2015; Gallagher et al., 2014; Karp and Sacks, 2014; Karp and Sacks, 2013; Karp and Shum, 2009; Karp and Conrad, 2005; McDowell et al., 2014; Meagher, 2009). Technically, Ahlin et al. (2015) did not study Campus RJ, but they did examine college students' support for the philosophy of RJ and whether they would be willing to participate in an RJ process themselves. The researchers conducted an online survey of 195 students at a large public university in the northeastern US. They found that students were generally supportive of RJ, with higher support among female students, those further along in their education, and those who are more involved in their community. Karp and Shum (2009) conducted a survey of members of the Association for Student Conduct Administration to identify the extent of RJ implementation across the US. Among the 245 responding institutions at that time, 14% offered RJ as a conduct resolution option. We suspect many more institutions are using Campus RJ now but do not know of any more recent surveys.

Gallagher et al. (2014) studied what motivated student offenders to choose a restorative-based conduct process. They also looked at what benefits the students received from participating in an RJ dialogue and how the outcomes related to their original motivations. The study was conducted in the midwestern US at a large public university. At that school, 191 students completed the survey instrument after participating in an RJ conference: Ninety-two percent of the students were satisfied or very satisfied with the RJ process. Eighty-one percent reported that meeting with harmed parties was somewhat to very beneficial. Eighty percent believed the process helped strengthen their sense of community at the university. Ninety-five percent agreed that if they had to do it over, they would again choose the RJ process. The researchers also conducted a cluster analysis to categorize the participants into four groups based on their initial motivation to participate in the RJ process. Motivations ranged from self-oriented (e.g., "remove the offense from my record") to other-oriented (e.g., "help the harmed party"). The most common motivations were having their offense removed (82%), "take direct responsibility for making things right" (78%), and "offer an apology" (66%). Students were rarely motivated by the need to "satisfy my parents" (3%) or because they "felt pressured to participate" (7%). The study also found, perhaps not surprisingly, that the students with the most restorative or community-minded motivations also reported that they benefitted the most from the process.

McDowell et al. (2014) measured the impact of a set of restorative justice community-building circles in a university residence hall. Five circles were facilitated by peer resident advisors over the course of a semester with groups of primarily first-year students. Topics of the circles included "communication styles, phenomenology, vandalism issues, student open discussion circles, and celebration circles" (p. 351). A survey was administered at the end of the semester to 66 residents who had participated in the circles compared with 36 residents who did not. It is unclear from the study how well trained the facilitators were or if the participating students who completed the survey needed to have participated in all of the circles or only one of them. Generally, results did not show statistically significant differences in community building between the two groups. However, students who did participate in the circles were more likely to say that they "attempt[ed] to see the perspectives of professors and family members" and "were more willing to listen to the perspectives of others regarding a conflict situation" (p. 353).

For his dissertation research, Meagher (2009) interviewed 16 student offenders who participated in Campus RJ processes on three public university campuses in the western and midwestern US. He found that the process helped these students transform their view of themselves in relation to others by broadening their awareness of who was harmed and how their actions affected others. They also changed their view of the harmed parties and about the incidents themselves. The process helped them come to a sense of resolution and learn new skills, such as how to live harmoniously in a residential community, how to better manage alcohol consumption, and how to resolve conflicts. The students viewed the process as engaging, inclusive, and respectful.

Karp and Conrad (2005) assessed the restorative justice program at Skidmore College in New York State. They reviewed 257 cases that appeared before a campus restorative justice board from Fall 2001 to Spring 2004. Their findings indicate that the process typically led to restorative outcomes such as apologies, restitution, and community service. They also led to reintegrative outcomes such as research or writing projects, counselling or educational training, and campus presentations or programming. Outcomes often included more traditional sanctions such as written warnings and placement on probation, meaning that the students would be suspended if they were to get in trouble during the probationary period. Of the 257 cases, two students were expelled, and 21 students were suspended. The suspended students all had to complete restorative and reintegrative tasks to prepare them for a successful return to the college. Recidivism was calculated to be 10.5%, but this was not measured against the rate for a traditional conduct process.

Karp and Sacks (2014) conducted a study called the STARR Project (Student Accountability and Restorative Research Project) that compared three types of conduct processes for 659 cases adjudicated at 18 higher-education institutions across the US. They compared 403 traditional conduct hearings with 91 RJ processes that included harmed parties in conference, circle, or board practice. They also compared 165 hybrid hearings that involved a one-on-one traditional conduct hearing with a student and conduct administrator but with restorative questions included. Although this was a large data set, the vast majority of cases included were for minor conduct violations, with conduct administrators rating them as not serious or mildly serious (87%). Thirty-four percent of the cases involved violations of the campus alcohol policies. A separate analysis focusing only on these alcohol cases was also conducted, which found similar results (Karp and Sacks, 2012). Karp (2013) reported STARR findings on harmed party satisfaction with their participation and the restorative outcomes. Mean scores were consistently positive across a range of satisfaction measures.

The STARR Project's primary focus was on student offender learning and development, which is summarized in Figure 17.1. Students completed a survey instrument with several indicators for each learning outcome. Their mean scores for each outcome were compared

Just Community/Self-Authorship: "I had a voice"
- We want students to be able to build community by having a voice in establishing and enforcing norms.

Active Accountability: "I took responsibility"
- We want students to take responsibility for their misbehavior and demonstrate their commitment to the community.

Interpersonal Competence: "I talked it out"
- We want students to communicate effectively face to face under difficult circumstances.

Social Ties to Institution: "I belong here"
- We want students to feel connected to their school communities.

Procedural Fairness: "That was fair"
- We want students to abide by the rules because they understand their purpose.

Closure: "I'm ready to move on"
- We want students to face difficult issues head-on, but then get back to their studies.

Figure 17.1 Six learning goals for a campus conduct process

across the three types of conduct process. The results demonstrated that student learning was improved when restorative questions that focused on identifying and repairing harm were incorporated into the traditional hearing process. The scores were further improved with students participating in the restorative process that included harmed parties. These results were consistently found across all six of the learning outcomes.

In sum, a limited number of studies have been conducted on Campus RJ. Most focus on the impact for student offenders, and these are generally positive, especially when compared with traditional conduct processes. In the next sections of this chapter, we highlight each of the six STARR Project learning outcomes by sharing restorative justice case studies from campuses across the US. We interviewed conduct administrators at six institutions ranging from small liberal arts colleges to large public universities. The cases provide a variety of conduct violations and restorative practices, revealing how harm was repaired and trust rebuilt between the participants. Each focuses on a different learning outcome.

First learning outcome from fieldwork: just community/ self-authorship: "I had a voice"

The first learning outcome draws on two related student development theories to emphasize the importance of having students develop self-efficacy through community involvement. Ignelzi's (1990) "just community" model focuses on student participation in campus community governance while Baxter Magolda's (2008) "self-authorship" concept focuses on how such participation helps students locate their own behaviour within the context of community. While a traditional conduct process may tell students of their violation, it does not provide a space for students to actively participate as key decision makers in the process. Active participation allows students to realize their obligations to their community and reaffirm the values the community holds. Having a meaningful voice in the conduct process is illustrated in a case at a small, rural, liberal arts college in the midwestern United States.

A female student, Jenna (all names in these case studies are pseudonyms), was one week into her first year of college when she got in trouble. Jenna, along with her friend, Gabby, went to an on-campus party. Jenna and Gabby had gone to high school together. They got high on marijuana, but Jenna had a bad reaction to it. She had a panic attack and her friends were unable to help her. A campus security officer saw that Jenna was in a state of distress. Since Jenna was flailing and screaming, he held on to her to keep her from running or hurting others. With her fighting him off and hitting him, all he could do was hold tight; he asked Gabby to push his radio call button so he could get assistance. While waiting, Jenna's roommate, Beth, happened to walk by. Beth was able to calm Jenna down and when the ambulance came, Jenna was able to go peacefully to the hospital for evaluation and observation overnight.

Jenna's background further complicated this incident. Although almost all students new to campus feel out of place, Jenna was an African-American, first-generation student from a big city who had just arrived at a small, rural, predominantly white college. Even at an institution committed to diversity and inclusion, students of colour can be made to feel as if they are "guests" generously hosted by whites rather than intrinsic members of the community (Blas Pedreal, 2015). Jenna's actions caused harm to herself and to the officer who tried to help her, but her behaviour was triggered by her perception of herself as an outsider and not really welcome at the institution.

By Monday, Jenna had already apologized to the associate dean and expressed embarrassment about her behaviour. In fact, Jenna had cut off her long hair so that people might not associate her with the girl who had acted out that Friday night. The dean referred Jenna's case to an RJ facilitator, hoping the process would address concerns she had for Jenna's well-being as well as an accountability plan for the harm caused to others.

When Jenna met with two co-facilitators and learned about RJ, she looked at them with disbelief that there was actually a process that could support her, include who she wanted to join her, and give her a voice in what would happen. For the restorative conference, the facilitators convened Jenna, her roommate Beth, her friend Gabby, the campus security officer, and the associate dean.

When they all met, Jenna explained that she had smoked weed once before and did not have any adverse reaction, so she was not expecting what happened. On the night of the incident, she thought she was going to die. Afterward, she was convinced that she was going to get herself and her friends kicked out of school. She was also ashamed that her parents were informed about the incident. She said that she felt hopeless and discouraged. She explained to the officer that she was brought up to distrust police. Her high school friend, Gabby, agreed and said they were always told the police were out to get them. The officer replied that he had just wanted to make sure she was okay, that he worked at the school because he cared about the students and hoped to keep them safe, not get them in trouble. Both Jenna and Gabby were moved by this; it was unlike anything they had heard growing up. Jenna and the campus security officer hugged. The girls also agreed to help with a campaign to improve campus security's image among students. The officer expressed gratitude for the opportunity to participate in the conference because he worked night shifts and had not previously had a chance to follow up with a student in this way.

The conference also addressed tension that had arisen between the three students. Beth thought Jenna was mad at her for intervening that night and had not known how to talk this through. The conference helped Beth and Jenna to process the incident and the two agreed to get dinner together to work on their friendship. Gabby was disappointed that she did not know how to successfully help her long-time friend after seeing how Beth had so capably intervened. The opportunity to share their feelings helped bring the three of them closer together.

By convening Jenna with the various harmed parties and supporters, the RJ process gave her a voice in the decision-making process. The dialogue gave her the space to explain her actions, convey her remorse, and empower her to be an active member of the community – not a guest, but a student with the freedoms and responsibilities of campus membership.

Second learning outcome from fieldwork: active accountability: "I took responsibility"

Punishment is often framed in terms of accountability. When people are released from prison, you might hear them say that they have "paid their debt to society." But what was the payment? Braithwaite and Roche (2001) distinguish between passive and active accountability, arguing that punishments are often passive. For example, sitting in a jail cell does not demonstrate remorse or commitment to responsibility; it does not repair the harm that victims may have suffered. Similarly, expulsion from a campus is passive and does not engage a student in taking active responsibility for the harm they caused. A restorative approach obligates people who cause harm to make amends as best they can. Some harms can never be undone, but active responsibility signals a recognition of the harm and a commitment to restoration. In this case study, we see how one student sought to make amends after violating the campus sexual misconduct policy.

Anwen and Sameer met during their first semester at a small liberal arts college in the Pacific Northwest. They went on a date or two and then decided to remain friends. Fast forward to their second semester when they ran into each other at a party. Anwen noticed that Sameer was very intoxicated but danced with him anyway. He became more sexually aggressive, isolating her in a private room. She tried to leave, but all of her friends had already gone, and she did not have her dorm key or phone with her. Rather than assist her to get back to her room, Sameer persuaded her to go to his room instead. Once there, Anwen felt trapped and pressured into sexual activity she did not consent to and did not want. Afterwards, she said she walked "around for several days feeling disgust with myself, feeling a ghost hurt between my legs where he rubbed me, feeling dirty, blocking the thoughts."

Anwen stayed silent about her assault for the next three years. Throughout that time, she came into contact with Sameer on numerous occasions, especially through their roles as student orientation leaders. Her assault and their following interactions affected her both socially and academically. In the spring of her senior year, Anwen reported the incident to the campus conduct administrator. She specifically requested that it be handled through an informal resolution process that would let her meet with Sameer so she could share how much she had been hurt by him. Otherwise, she did not want him to be suspended or expelled, nor did she want to involve the local police.

The college did not have a restorative justice program in place, but the conduct administrator had participated in RJ training and thought an RJ process could help meet her request. He met with Sameer, told him of Anwen's complaint, and Sameer immediately admitted to the violation and expressed his deep remorse. He agreed that he did want to do whatever he could to meet Anwen's request and make up for what he had done. The administrator met individually with Anwen twelve times and Sameer seven times before bringing the two together. His conversations with Anwen were focused on regaining the power that she felt she had lost. The conversations with Sameer explored how he could take ownership and responsibility for his actions, and what he could do to repair the harm he caused.

The facilitated RJ dialogue lasted for two hours. It allowed Anwen to share the pain she felt. Initially, she had felt isolated and intimidated. Later, she started to blame herself for not calling security or ringing one of the blue lights on campus. She felt guilty thinking that she had led him on. These feelings of self-blame were triggered each time she saw him. Her role as an orientation leader was compromised due to his presence. Anwen's relationship with her new partner never felt whole because she prevented herself from feeling vulnerable with him. As a creative writing major, much of her work had been about the assault. She wanted Sameer to read her papers and write a response.

Active accountability for Sameer began with a commitment to fully hear about the harm he caused and to take responsibility. He agreed to be found formally in violation of the campus sexual misconduct policy and have a formal "conduct reprimand" in his file. Since Sameer had no other conduct charges in the three years since this incident and as it was just weeks before their graduation, the administrator decided that Sameer was not a threat to others and would not need to be suspended or expelled.

Collaboratively, they developed a list of remedies that best met Anwen's needs and the concerns of the institution:

- Reading and responding to Anwen's extensive writing about the incident.
- Writing an article openly discussing the misconduct for a student magazine that focuses on issues of gender and sexuality. She would use a pseudonym, but he wanted to use his real name.
- Teaching others about the incident. Both Anwen and Sameer agreed to present their story together at a campus bystander intervention workshop, focusing on how power,

privilege, emotional manipulation, and coercion help facilitate and perpetuate campus sexual misconduct.

- Collaborating with gender violence programming on campus to advocate for mandatory bystander intervention and other prevention training for all student athletes and Greek Letter organizations as well as developing strategies to encourage sincere and engaged participation by these students.
- Reaching out to students who provide peer support for sexual assault survivors to identify ways in which student offenders could speak with them and learn from them.
- Developing sexual violence prevention education programming for local middle and high school students.

After the RJ dialogue, Anwen and Sameer met regularly to plan their presentation and worked together to create a video where they recounted the night of the assault, each sharing what happened from their perspective. Sameer, after he graduated, continued to work with the conduct administrator for six months in order to finalize the community service project focused on prevention education in the local schools.

This case acted as a catalyst for bringing RJ to this college. It demonstrated to faculty, staff, and administrators that an event which created harm and fear within the community could result in greater knowledge and increased conversation. The remedies gave Sameer the opportunity to be actively accountable and ultimately created the space for Anwen to forgive him. At one of their shared presentations, Sameer stated, "I have raped. I am a rapist. Fuck Rape. We need to end rape." He said this in front of friends and fellow students, making himself extremely vulnerable, in an effort to create change and for others to learn from his actions. Sameer wanted people to see that although he was well known and well liked on campus, he had also engaged in unacceptable sexual misconduct. He wanted to shatter the concept that only bad people commit sexual assault – even he was capable of it. But he was also capable of personal change and being a catalyst for improving campus climate and culture.

Third learning outcome from fieldwork: interpersonal competence: "I talked it out"

People successfully coexist in a community when they listen to, understand, and respect the opinions, feelings, and preferences of those around them. A central goal in student development is social and emotional learning (SEL), which benefits students both socially and academically. Durlak et al. (2011: 406) provide evidence of the value of SEL and define it as "the process of acquiring core competencies to recognize and manage emotions, set and achieve positive goals, appreciate the perspectives of others, establish and maintain positive relationships, make responsible decisions, and handle interpersonal situations constructively." Restorative practices provide a space for open and honest conversation that brings participants a deeper understanding of those around them, helping them to develop interpersonal competence. A restorative circle was used for this purpose at a mid-sized, Mid-Atlantic public university in response to a bias incident with the football team.

A late-night argument occurred between five white and five black freshmen football players in their residence hall. Although it was clear to residence life staff that the conflict remained unresolved, they were unable to sort out the problem. The associate dean had been recently trained in restorative justice and explained the premise to his colleagues and the football coach. They agreed to organize a restorative circle as a way to better understand the nature of the conflict and seek resolution.

The dean gathered the ten players on a weekday evening. He explained that they would be using a circle process to help the group work through the ongoing tension. The teammates already knew each other well, so the dean asked them to begin by sharing something they would not likely know about each other. He modelled this by sharing challenges he faced when in college. Then he passed a talking piece so that each player would have a chance to speak sequentially around the circle. The first student to go said that his dad was an alcoholic who beats his mom on a regular basis. Another said that he had been adopted three times by three different families. Another said that he was struggling with an ongoing addiction to pain killers. Immediately, these players were being more vulnerable with each other than they had ever been before.

Next, the dean asked each to share their account of the night the conflict began. They shared that the conflict began over a girl, but escalated when a white player called one of the black players a "nigger." The next person to receive the talking piece was a student of colour, who said that they should forget about the slur because they are a team and need to move on. When the piece was passed to another student of colour, he said that he did not want to forget about it. His teammate hurt him by using the "N Word," and by saying it with such malice. He did not trust the player and was not willing to just get over it.

The talking piece reached the student who said the "N Word." He admitted what he had done and broke down crying. He said that he had used his intoxication as an excuse, but the truth was that he grew up in a poor trailer park where his family and neighbours used that word all the time. He apologized and asked what he could do to make things right. Once the teammates talked about the racial slur, they began to raise other issues that they had never before felt comfortable discussing, such as their friendships off the field and how they treated female students.

They committed to making a bigger effort to develop their relationships and spend more time together. They talked about needing to decrease their alcohol use. The players of colour told the student who used the "N Word" that it would take a long time for them to forgive him and he would need to work day in and day out to regain their trust.

The students left with a greater understanding of each other and better able to speak with each other openly and honestly. They learned more about each other's backgrounds and the struggles each faced. This increased their sense of connection with one other. They learned that it is okay, even for football jocks, to be vulnerable with their friends. The circle provided a safe environment for them to talk through their concerns and challenge each other to be accountable for their words and actions.

After the end of the circle, two of the students told the dean that they had never before shared what they said at the beginning of the circle. They asked to meet with him on a regular basis. Following the circle, the coach said it felt like he had an entirely new team. For the rest of the time these students were on campus, they would seek out the dean, share a "bro hug," and talk openly about how they were doing. This early success was instrumental to building what has now become a strong RJ program on that campus.

Fourth learning outcome from fieldwork: social ties to institution: "I belong here"

In Sampson and Laub's (1993) study of crime across the life course, an important predictor of juvenile delinquency was found to be school attachment: "[W]hen the bonds linking a youth to society – whether through the family or school – are weakened, the probability of delinquency is increased" (p. 122). The STARR Project provides evidence that restorative justice can strengthen students' connections to campus and sense of belonging. This case illustrates how a restorative process following a BB gun incident at a northeastern liberal arts college resulted in stronger social ties to the institution.

After a full day of summer term classes, Hugo and Dennis were invited to an off-campus barbeque. On their way, they stopped at Walmart to pick up supplies and stumbled upon the gun section, a display that was particularly mesmerizing for Hugo, an international student from France. They bought a BB gun for under $30, returned to campus to gather a few more things, and then left for the barbeque. Driving across campus, they tested their new gun by shooting at trees. Several people saw them and made frightened calls to the campus safety department that someone was shooting a handgun. The flurry of activity on the campus radios brought the incident to the attention of a facilities worker who saw the two students, jumped in his truck and chased them down. He escorted them to the campus safety office where they were met by local police and arrested for reckless endangerment and weapons violations.

The students admitted responsibility, and a restorative justice conference was arranged. Led by two restorative facilitators, the dialogue included Hugo and Dennis, a faculty support person of their choosing, a campus safety representative, and the facilities worker who chased them down. The facilitators first gave Hugo and Dennis a chance to explain what happened, what they were thinking at the time, and what they had thought about since the incident. They expressed their remorse, their fear regarding criminal charges and the possibility of suspension, and a willingness to do whatever they could to make things right. Hugo expressed confusion about guns in America. On the one hand, he had been told about gun rights and been amazed at how easy it was to make the BB gun purchase. On the other, he was shocked to be arrested for using what he thought was only a toy.

The facilitators then asked the harmed parties what happened from their perspective and to share their concerns over the incident. The campus safety representative shared what it was like to receive several panic-stricken calls from across campus from people who believed a school shooter was on campus. The facilities worker described himself as an avid hunter who immediately knew that the students were using a BB gun and was not personally afraid. He, in fact, was chasing the students down to protect them. As they were heading off-campus, he believed the local police, fearing lethal confrontation, "would shoot first and ask questions later." Hugo and Dennis were very surprised to learn how their actions caused panic and had put their own lives at risk. They expressed their embarrassment and then gratitude to the facilities worker for his intervention. They apologized to the harmed parties and committed to writing additional apology letters to other first responders in the situation. Later, both harmed parties said they appreciated the opportunity to participate in the process. Campus safety officers often write students up for violations but rarely hear about the outcome, let alone have a voice in the decision. Facilities staff are even less connected to students, and this individual believed he gained a better understanding of the situation and that he had made a positive difference for these two.

The students also talked about what it was like to be arrested and how they were treated at the police station. They had felt humiliated and threatened as the police interrogated them and led them to believe they would be facing serious criminal charges, jail time, and possible deportation for Hugo. Later, they reflected on how different the restorative conference was from the criminal justice process. While they were challenged to accept full responsibility, they felt supported. They believed their perspective and ideas mattered, which in turn helped them appreciate the perspectives of the harmed parties.

The group pondered what the students could do to take responsibility beyond apologizing. Since they had not understood the campus weapons policy, state laws about gun use, or much about the broader issue of gun violence, they decided to work to increase that knowledge among the student body. Hugo and Dennis agreed to research these issues and create an educational campaign for the campus community. Hugo additionally committed to making a presentation to the international student club.

In a situation like this, a traditional conduct policy might have suspended these students. In this process, however, a primary goal was to strengthen these students' connection to the college. Through support, mentoring, and taking leadership roles in an educational campaign, the students were challenged to fulfil an obligation for responsible community membership rather than be stigmatized and separated from the campus community. When the group learned that the incident and its aftermath caused Dennis to drop one of his summer classes, they explored the impact this had for completing his major requirements. His faculty support person agreed to supervise an independent study to make sure he could fulfil the requirement and graduate on time.

The students were able to build relationships with campus employees in the conference – the campus safety office, the facilities worker, and the faculty support person.. Some weeks after the restorative conference, the students stopped by the facilities office to thank the facilities worker for his support. Both students successfully completed their obligations. Neither got in trouble again. Hugo decided to join the campus restorative justice program and participated in facilitator training so that he could be a part of the team that works on cases like his. Both students, through their RJ process, were able to use their experience to strengthen their connections in the community and move past their incident successfully.

Fifth learning outcome from fieldwork: procedural fairness: "That was fair"

Procedural fairness as a learning outcome is based on the theory that students will follow the rules they understand and respect. Tyler (2006: 317) argues that "[t]he procedural justice model focuses on everyday rule following. It suggests that the key to motivating compliance based on internal social values is to maintain the legitimacy of the law and of legal authorities. To do so, legal authorities need to focus on exercising legal authority fairly." The restorative justice process allows for students to gain a better understanding of such rules, reducing the risk of recidivism and increasing trust in authorities. This is illustrated by a case involving a graduate student at a large public university in the southeastern US.

Tommy was a graduate student in an education administration program with a career goal of working in college student conduct administration. While taking courses, he obtained a position in the Office of Residential Life working on student conduct cases. This university had a strict substance abuse policy. If a student is found possessing drugs or alcohol, they receive a strike on their record. Additionally, the student must complete community service and attend a fee-based drug and alcohol education program. They are also placed on probation for one year. If a student receives a second strike while on probation, they are automatically suspended from school for at least one semester.

One night, students in a residence hall were having a party and were caught drinking by their resident advisor. They were reported, but because of the strict alcohol policy and a fear of being suspended, no one was willing to take responsibility for purchasing the alcohol. Several of the students were assigned to Tommy. Frustrated with the students and the amount of time it was taking to resolve the case, Tommy circumvented the adjudication process and found each of the students in violation of campus policy. Parents and lawyers began contacting the office in defence of their children and clients, causing a supervisor to scrutinize how the cases were being handled. A tracking feature in the case management software showed that Tommy had ignored the students' denial of responsibility and entered only that they had admitted guilt, undermining their ability to defend themselves. The supervisor confronted Tommy, and he admitted to the falsification as well as to an attempt to hide this by changing the online data later.

Tommy went through both the student and employee conduct processes. He was immediately banned from working on conduct cases. However, Tommy had heard of restorative justice and was hoping a restorative response might help him regain the trust of his colleagues and salvage his career aspirations. He requested a circle, which would allow him to explain himself fully and express his remorse to the people he affected. Circle participants included students he worked with, residential life staff members, and student conduct staff members.

During the circle, Tommy was able to share his deep regret for falsifying the conduct records. He explained that he had cut a corner because he believed the students were in violation of the alcohol policy. When people began to pay more attention to the case, he became nervous and changed the information. Throughout the circle, people supported him while explaining the impact that his decision and actions had on them. They believed his actions had undermined a crucial dimension of their office – that students would be heard fully and treated fairly. Without that, their work would only become more difficult. In addition, conduct and housing staff had to take on his workload. Many stated that they had lost trust in him but were willing to work with him to mend that. The circle concluded by creating a plan for Tommy to regain their trust. In addition to the restrictions on his job, he was asked to write a reflective paper discussing the impact of the incident. His paper focused on how this experience would affect him while applying to jobs. The participants also helped him reconfigure his job as a graduate assistant, without his role in student conduct. He would begin conducting presentations in the residence halls and with first-year students about the campus alcohol policy and how the office works with students to hear cases fairly.

The restorative process affirmed for Tommy the importance of procedural justice. By hearing how his actions affected others, he came to a deeper appreciation for why fairness in the conduct program was so important and how quickly its legitimacy can be undermined by missteps such as his. He also became an enthusiast for restorative justice through his direct personal experience of it in practice.

Tommy finished his master's degree and was able to get a job in student conduct. During the application process, his supervisor volunteered to be a reference and both were forthcoming about this incident. Tommy's experience and insight demonstrated to his new employer the effect that RJ had on this individual and was one of the principal reasons they hired him. His own positive experience inspired Tommy to implement RJ at his new university. This student went from thinking the rules did not apply to him to a deep understanding of how procedural fairness legitimizes a campus conduct system. But this was only achieved through the open, inclusive conversation that RJ creates.

Sixth learning outcome from fieldwork: closure: "I can move on"

The final student learning outcome of a restorative dialogue is closure. The goal is for a student to take responsibility for the misconduct and learn from the experience without allowing it to hinder future success. This is illustrated by a junior, named Jordan, at a large public university in the western US. Even minor conduct violations, such as the case illustrated here, can lead to emotional turmoil, causing a student to perseverate about the incident and be distracted from their studies (Mischel and DeSmet, 2000). Through a restorative process, this student was able to face up to his misconduct but also close the chapter and successfully move on.

Jordan and his friends "pre-gamed" – a form of binge drinking – together and then walked to a house party near campus. One stomped on a sprinkler on the campus grounds without damaging it. Jordan followed suit, but broke it, and water began gushing out. A witness got the attention of a nearby police officer, who wrote Jordan a citation for criminal mischief.

In a partnership between the city court and the university, Jordan was provided a restorative option as a form of court diversion. His charges would be dismissed if he successfully participated in an RJ dialogue and completed all remedies that the group developed. The RJ facilitator spoke to the director of irrigation about the incident and recruited the grounds manager, a campus police officer, and Jordan's father for the conference.

The RJ conference provided Jordan with the opportunity to see how a seemingly trivial act of vandalism could have significant consequences for his institution and the people who worked there. The grounds manager explained that they had been short-staffed and were struggling to make time for daily maintenance, let alone repairs. The sprinkler, which was broken months prior, was still not fixed. In a part of the West with almost no rain, a large area of grass was now dead. The irrigation director talked about the pride his department feels for maintaining a beautiful campus for students, faculty, staff, and members of the community. The officer expressed his frustration over the consequences of student criminal behaviour on campus. For Jordan, this was an eye-opening discussion; he simply never considered that his actions could have such an impact on others.

The most difficult aspect of the situation was the effect it had on Jordan's relationship with his father, which was affecting Jordan's ability to focus on his academic work. His family was very close and he had younger siblings who looked up to him. His father was angry and disappointed in Jordan, believing his behaviour to have been poor role-modelling. He had lost trust in his son and was worried about his future. As Jordan sat hunched over in his chair and staring at the floor, it seemed like this news was hard to hear.

Jordan wished to take responsibility for what he had done and offered to volunteer 20 hours of community service with the campus facilities office to help maintain the grounds. The group discussed how Jordan could learn to fix the sprinkler head. The harmed parties forgave him and Jordan seemed embarrassed but relieved. The campus staff said they were impressed that he was willing to meet them face to face and the officer noted that he could tell Jordan was doing everything he could to right the situation. Jordan said he did not want this incident to define him and that it did not reflect the way he would like to be seen by others.

As Jordan's father watched his son take responsibility and saw others forgiving him for his actions, his attitude towards Jordan began to change. He liked that Jordan wanted to make a positive impact on the community and work off his debt. He was relieved that the campus staff had forgiven Jordan, which made it possible for him to forgive Jordan, too. After everyone but the facilitators had left the conference, Jordan's father said he was proud of how Jordan had handled himself. This was the last thing Jordan needed to hear to fully move forward, and it seemed like a weight had been lifted from his shoulders. With a face-to-face reconciliation with his father and the university staff as well as a clear plan for taking responsibility, Jordan was able to put the incident behind him. The restorative process allowed Jordan to rectify the damage, repair his relationships, and find the closure necessary to get back to his studies.

Discussion: the future of campus restorative justice

Colleges and universities have become excellent laboratories for restorative justice. Beyond student conduct, faculties are publishing a wide stream of studies that explores the philosophy and practice of RJ across social sectors while building strong evidence of its effectiveness (Karp and

Frank, 2016a). Faculties are also using restorative practices to create more inclusive classrooms (Contemporary Justice Review, 2013). Numerous academic RJ centres conduct research and provide technical assistance to RJ practitioners in the criminal justice system and in K-12 schools (Karp and Frank, 2016a).

As the case studies illustrate, much of the focus of Campus RJ has been for incidents of student misconduct. While our literature review reveals that empirical studies of Campus RJ are limited, the research indicates positive outcomes and support for RJ among students, both among those who have participated as harmed parties and those who have caused harm. It is an approach that resonates among students who wish to have input into decisions that affect them and who may be sceptical of systems they believe replicate social inequalities and convey impersonal or arbitrary authority. Although sometimes caricatured by people who have not experienced RJ as an "easy out," actual participants find the process emotionally and intellectually engaging, serious, relevant, and challenging.

The case studies were selected from our fieldwork to illustrate how RJ works – when it is working well. Of course, not all conduct incidents are resolved to everyone's satisfaction. Much more needs to be learned about best practice and applications to complex situations that may include serious sexual harm, intimate partner violence, dangerous hazing, or bigoted acts of hate or discrimination. The cases hint at the tension between traditional punishment and the goals of RJ, especially when cases are simultaneously adjudicated on campus and in the courts. Should, for example, an accused student admit fault and try to take responsibility for their behaviour through a restorative process if that puts them at risk of prosecution in the criminal court? We know even less about the experience of harmed parties in the Campus RJ process. Although research on victims who participate in RJ in the criminal justice system is very positive (Strang et al., 2013), sometimes their participation takes place years after the crime. Such a waiting period is unrealistic for the short period students are in college. We would wonder, for example, if Anwen would have benefitted from the RJ process in the same way if she had done it in the weeks or months after her assault rather than three years later when she was a senior.

Restorative justice is proliferating across K-12 school communities (Armour, 2016) and more students will arrive on college campuses expecting to have restorative options available to them. As they bring this knowledge or learn about RJ on their campuses, they may also wish to serve as restorative mentors to youth during service-learning partnerships between universities and nearby K-12 school districts. We expect to see student support and participation in RJ grow in response to the movement in K-12 schools.

While conduct administrators often make use of RJ for minor conduct violations, they are also exploring wider application for more serious cases, such as the sexual assault incident described earlier. Some campuses create partnerships with local courts, so that students who are arrested in the community can participate in an RJ programme to resolve both the criminal complaint as well as the violation of the student code of conduct. Student affairs professionals are also using RJ to address campus climate issues, particularly surrounding racial tension (Mok, 2012). RJ can also be a method for prevention education and community building, often through circle dialogues in residence halls (Wachtel and Miller, 2013).

When RJ programmes are implemented in K-12 schools, one best practice is to use a "whole school approach" (Armour, 2016). This calls for training and use of RJ by students, faculty, and staff through a tiered system of application that includes community-building dialogues for everyone and targeted responses for those who get in trouble. The same philosophical approach can apply to the higher-education setting where full implementation of RJ would include widespread use of RJ practices in the classroom and in faculty scholarship; community building and problem-solving in residential life, athletics, student organizations, and service-learning community partnerships; and situations when faculty or staff cause harm, not just students (Acosta and Cunningham, 2014). Once a campus begins to experiment with RJ, it can discover a nearly endless array of possibilities.

References

Acosta, D. and Cunningham, P.G. 2014. Restorative justice to resolve learner and differential mistreatment, *Wing of Zock*, 20 March.

Ahlin, E., Gibbs, J.C., Kavanaugh, P.R. and Lee, J. 2015. Support for Restorative Justice in a Sample of U.S. University Students, *International Journal of Offender Therapy and Comparative Criminology*: 1–17. Doi: 10.1177/0306624X15596386.

Armour, M. 2016. Restorative Practices: Righting the Wrongs of Exclusionary School Discipline, *University of Richmond Law Review*, 50: 999–1037.

Baxter Magolda, M.B. 2008. Three Elements of Self-Authorship, *Journal of College Student Development*, 49: 269–284.

Blas Pedreal, M.L. 2015. Restorative Justice Programs in Higher Education, *The Vermont Connection*, 35: 38–46.

Braithwaite, J. and Roche, D. 2001. Responsibility and Restorative Justice. In G. Bazemore and M. Schiff (eds.) *Restorative Community Justice: Repairing Harm and Transforming Communities*, pp. 63–84.

Brenner, A. 2013. Transforming Campus Culture to Prevent Rape: The Possibility and Promise of Restorative Justice as a Response to Campus Sexual Violence, *Harvard Journal of Law & Gender*: 1–9.

Clark, K.L. 2014. A Call for Restorative Justice in Higher Education Judicial Affairs, *College Student Journal*, 48: 707–715.

Coker, D. 2016. Crime Logic, Campus Sexual Assault, and Restorative Justice, *Texas Tech Law Review*, 49: 1–64.

Contemporary Justice Review. 2013. Special Issue on Teaching Restorative Justice, 16(1).

CURJ (Colorado University Restorative Justice). 2016. *CU Restorative Justice (CURJ) 2015–2016 Academic Year Report*. Boulder, CO: University of Colorado Office of Student Conduct and Conflict Resolution. Available at www.colorado.edu/osccr/sites/default/files/attached-files/curj_2015-2016_report.pdf

Darling, J. 2011. *Restorative Justice in Higher Education: A Compilation of Formats and Best Practices*. San Diego: University of San Diego. Available at www.skidmore.edu/campusrj/documents/Darling-2011-campus-programs.pdf

Durlak, J., Weissberg, R., Dymnicki, A., Taylor, R. and Schellinger, K. 2011. The Impact of Enhancing Students' Social and Emotional Learning: A Meta-Analysis of School-Based Universal Interventions, *Child Development*, 82: 405–432.

Gallagher Dahl, M., Meagher, P. and Vander Velde, S. 2014. Motivation and Outcomes for University Students in a Restorative Justice Program, *Journal of Students Affairs Research and Practice*, 51: 364–379.

Goldblum, A. 2009. Restorative Justice from Theory to Practice. In J. Meyer Schrage and N. Geist Giacomini (eds.) *Reframing Campus Conflict: Student Conduct Process Through a Social Justice Lens*. Sterling, VA: Stylus Publishers, pp. 140–154.

Harper, S., Maskaly, J., Kirkner, A. and Lorenz, K. 2017. Enhancing Title IX Due Process Standards in Campus Sexual Assault Adjudication: Considering the Roles of Distributive, Procedural, and Restorative Justice, *Journal of School Violence*, 11: 302–316.

Ignelzi, M.G. 1990. Ethical Education in a College Environment: The Just Community Approach, *NASPA Journal*, 27: 192–198.

Kaplan, M. 2017. Restorative Justice and Campus Sexual Misconduct, *Temple Law Review*, 89: 701.

Kara, F. and MacAlister, D. 2010. Responding to Academic Dishonesty in Universities: A Restorative Justice Approach, *Contemporary Justice Review*, 13: 443–453.

Karp, D.R. 2009a. Reading the Scripts: The Restorative Justice Conference and the Student Conduct Hearing Board. In J. Meyer Schrage and N. Geist Giacomini (eds.) *Reframing Campus Conflict: Student Conduct Process Through a Social Justice Lens*. Sterling, VA: Stylus Publishers, pp. 155–174.

Karp, D.R. 2009b. Not with a Bang But a Whimper: A Missed Opportunity for Restorative Justice in a Plagiarism Case, *Journal of Student Conduct Administration*, 2: 26–30.

Karp, D.R. 2011. Spirit Horse and the Principles of Restorative Justice, *Student Affairs eNews*, 20 December.

Karp, D.R. 2013. *The Little Book of Restorative Justice for Colleges and Universities: Repairing Harm and Rebuilding Trust in Response to Student Misconduct*. Intercourse, PA: Good Books.

Karp, D.R. 2015. Restorative Justice at Dalhousie: A Reasoned Alternative to the 'rush to judgment', *Association for Student Conduct Administration Law and Policy Report*, 29 January.

Karp, D.R. and Allena, T. eds. 2004. *Restorative Justice on the College Campus: Promoting Student Growth and Responsibility, and Reawakening the Spirit of Campus Community*. Springfield, IL: Charles C Thomas.

Karp, D.R., Breslin, B. and Oles, P. 2002. Community Justice in the Campus Setting, *Conflict Management in Higher Education Report*, 3.

Karp, D.R. and Conrad, S. 2005. Restorative Justice and College Student Misconduct, *Public Organization Review*, 5: 315–333.

Karp, D.R. and Frank, O. 2016a. Anxiously Awaiting the Future of Restorative Justice in the United States, *Victims & Offenders*, 11: 50–70.

Karp, D.R. and Frank, O. 2016b. Restorative Justice and Student Development in Higher Education: Expanding 'offender' Horizons Beyond Punishment and Rehabilitation to Community Engagement and Personal Growth. In T. Gavrielides (ed.) *Offenders No More: An Interdisciplinary Restorative Justice Dialogue*. New York: Nova Science Publishers, pp. 141–164.

Karp, D.R. and Sacks, C. 2012. Research Findings on Restorative Justice and Alcohol Violations, *NASPA Knowledge Community Alcohol and Other Drug Newsletter*, Fall 2012.

Karp, D.R. and Sacks, C. 2013. Student Conduct, Restorative Justice, and Student Learning: Findings from the STARR Project (STudent Accountability and Restorative Research Project), *Association for Student Conduct Administration Law and Policy Report*, 28 March.

Karp, D.R. and Sacks, C. 2014. Student Conduct, Restorative Justice, and Student Development: Findings from the STARR Project (Student Accountability and Restorative Research Project), *Contemporary Justice Review*, 17: 154–172.

Karp, D.R., Shackford-Bradley, J., Wilson, R.J. and Williamsen, K.M. 2016. *Campus PRISM: A Report on Promoting Restorative Initiatives for Sexual Misconduct on College Campuses*. Saratoga Springs, NY: Skidmore College Project on Restorative Justice. Available at www.skidmore.edu/campusrj/documents/Campus_PRISM__Report_2016.pdf

Karp, D.R. and Shum, K. 2009. *Conflict Resolution Practices Member Survey*. College Station, TX: Association for Student Conduct Administration. Available at www.skidmore.edu/campusrj/karp-vitae-files/technical-reports/Conflict-Resolution-Practices-Member-Survey.pdf

Kirven, S.J. 2014. Isolation to Empowerment: A Review of the Campus Rape Adjudication Process, *Journal of International Criminal Justice Research*, 2: 1–15.

Koss, M.P. and Lopez, E.C. 2014. VAWA After the Party: Implementing Proposed Guidelines on Campus Sexual Assault Resolution, *CUNY Law Review*, 19 December.

Koss, M.P., Wilgus, J.K. and Williamsen, K.M. 2014. Campus Sexual Misconduct: Restorative Justice Approaches to Enhance Compliance with Title IX Guidance, *Trauma, Violence & Abuse*, 15: 242–257.

Llewellyn, J.J., Demsey, A. and Smith, J. 2015. An Unfamiliar Justice Story: Restorative Justice and Education, Reflections on Dalhousie's Facebook Incident 2015, *Our Schools/Our Selves*, 25: 43–56.

Llewellyn, J.J., MacIsaac, S. and Mackay, M. 2015. *Report from the Restorative Justice Process at the Dalhousie University Faculty of Dentistry*. Halifax, Nova Scotia, Canada: Dalhousie University.

McDowell, L.A., Crocker, V.L., Evett, E.L. and Cornerlison, D.G. 2014. Perceptions of Restorative Justice Concepts: An Evaluation of University Housing Residents, *Contemporary Justice Review*, 17: 346–361.

Meagher, P.J. 2009. *A Phenomenological Study of the Experience of Respondents in Campus-Based Restorative Justice Programs*, Ph.D. Dissertation. Bowling Green, OH: Bowling Green State University.

Mischel, W. and DeSmet, A.L. 2000. Self-Regulation in the Service of Conflict Resolution. In M. Deutsch and P.T. Coleman (eds.) *The Handbook of Conflict Resolution: Theory and Practice*. San Francisco, CA: Jossey-Bass, pp. 256–275.

Mok, H. 2012. UC Explores Restorative Justice in Improving Campus Climate, *UC Newsroom*, 27 January 2012.

Rinker, J.A. and Jonason, C. 2014. Restorative Justice as Reflective Practice and Applied Pedagogy on College Campuses, *Journal of Peace Education*, 11: 162–180.

Sampson, R.J. and Laub, J.H. 1993. *Crime in the Making: Pathways and Turning Points Through Life*. Cambridge, MA: Harvard University Press.Sebok, T. 2006. Restorative Justice on Campus: Repairing Harm and Building Community. In J.M. Lancaster and Associates (eds.) *Exercising Power with Wisdom: Bridging Legal and Ethical Practice with Intention*. Asheville, NC: College Administration Publications, pp. 63–76.

Sebok, T. and Goldblum, A. 1999. Establishing a Campus Restorative Justice Program, *California Caucus of College and University Ombuds*, 2: 12–22.

Strang, H., Sherman, L.W., Mayo-Wilson, E., Woods, D. and Ariel, B. 2013. Restorative Justice Conferencing (RJC) Using Face-to-Face Meetings of Offenders and Victims: Effects on Offender Recidivism and Victim Satisfaction. A Systematic Review, *Campbell Systematic Reviews*, 12.

Tyler, T.R. 2006. Restorative Justice and Procedural Justice: Dealing with Rule Breaking, *Journal of Social Issues*, 62: 307–326.

University of Colorado. 2016. *Annual Report of the Office of Student Conduct and Conflict Resolution 2015–2016*. Boulder, CO.

Wachtel, J. and Wachtel, T. 2012. *Building Campus Community: Restorative Practices in Residential Life*. Bethlehem, PA: IIRP.

Wachtel, T. and Miller, S. 2013. Creating Healthy Residential Communities in Higher Education Through the Use of Restorative Practices. In K.S. Van Wormer and L. Walker (eds.) *Restorative Justice Today: Practical Applications*. Thousand Oaks, CA: Sage, pp. 93–99.

Warters, B., Sebok, T. and Goldblum, A. 2000. Making Things Right: Restorative Justice Comes to Campus, *Conflict Management in Higher Education Report*, 1(1).

18

Restorative justice re-entry planning for the imprisoned

An evidence-based approach to recidivism reduction

Lorenn Walker and Janet Davidson

Introduction

This chapter furthers our knowledge and understanding of how a restorative justice approach to re-entry planning can be accomplished with an imprisoned population, and how such an approach is beneficial in reducing crime once the imprisoned are released. As will be demonstrated in this chapter, this approach creates an avenue for positive community health, lowered victimization, and reports of satisfaction by loved ones.

Specifically, this chapter discusses the background of this restorative justice effort with male and female imprisoned people in Hawai'i, and the manner in which the programme is delivered. The process studied provides imprisoned individuals the opportunity to meet with their loved ones to address reconciliation and to make self-directed re-entry plans for law-abiding lives. A public health, solution-focused, and restorative justice approach guided the development of the re-entry planning practice outlined in this chapter.

The chapter moves on to report on the study participants and overall methodology. In short, all adult inmates who took part in a restorative justice re-entry planning circle from 2005 to 2015 were included so long as they had at least three years of post-release time in the community at the time of study. This chapter then details the findings for the group of released inmates, who were tracked for three years. These findings were compared to two groups, imprisoned people who wanted but were unable to take the course, and all imprisoned people released in Hawai'i. This quasi-experimental study was conducted in 2016. The chapter ends with a summary of the findings and a discussion of implications and future directions.

This chapter contributes to the Handbook's key objective by reporting on new research findings of an innovative restorative practice, specifically restorative justice re-entry circles for imprisoned individuals. The information contained in this chapter should be useful to both practitioners looking to incorporate similar programmes and to researchers and policy makers seeking to build an evidence base for such programmes.

Hawai'i friends of restorative justice background

In 1980, Hawai'i Friends of Restorative Justice (Hawai'i Friends) incorporated as a non-profit in Honolulu to provide an intervention to divert juveniles in the justice system from court to an educational programme. Currently, Hawai'i Friends develops, provides, and studies pilot projects to assist both juvenile and adults in rehabilitating and healing from harm caused by crime and social injustice.

Hawai'i Friends works to generate evidence-based knowledge. The organization uses a public health approach in developing restorative and solution-focused responses to injustice and wrongdoing (Walker and Greening, 2010). It has worked with a wide variety of populations, including public housing communities (Walker, 2000); people harmed by crime, including those who did not know who harmed them and cases where no one was arrested (Walker, 2004); incarcerated people who did not commit the crimes that they were convicted and imprisoned for (Walker, 2015); homeless and foster youth (Walker, 2008); children of incarcerated parents (Walker, Tarutani and McKibben, 2015); and people who complete parole and those who helped them, including their families, parole officers, and judges (Walker and Kobayashi, 2015).

The organization also provides solution-focused mediation, restorative facilitation training, and a family law clinic for women incarcerated at the Hawai'i women's prison. It plans to publish an online legal resource and guidebook modelled after Root & Rebound's California re-entry programme for individuals returning to the community after incarceration (Root & Rebound, 2017).

Support for the re-entry circle approach

In 2005, Hawai'i Friends developed and began studying a re-entry planning process for adult incarcerated people (Walker and Greening, 2013). Effective re-entry for incarcerated people returning to the community is necessary to prevent repeat crime (Petersilia, 2004). The idea for Hawai'i's re-entry planning process came from John Braithwaite's (2004) "Emancipation and Hope" article about transition planning for youth emancipation. Called *Huikahi re-entry circles* in Hawai'i, the process provides an incarcerated individual the opportunity to apply for a meeting with their loved ones and a representative of the institution incarcerating them. The voluntary process gives an incarcerated individual autonomy and agency, recognized as necessary for successful re-entry planning (Taxman, 2004). Re-entry planning is an essential tool for "aiding re-entry" (Raphael, 2011: 192) and is needed by all incarcerated people returning to the community (Lattimore and Visher, 2013).

Throughout the United States, including Hawai'i, an extraordinary number of people are incarcerated and released daily. "More than seven hundred thousand inmates are released each year from the nation's state and federal prisons" (Raphael, 2011: 211), which is almost 2,000 people a day. According to Robert Merce, 89 people convicted of felonies were released monthly from Hawai'i state prisons for the fiscal year 2017 (personal communication, October 26, 2017), which is almost three people a day. Additionally, 1,033 people were released from Hawai'i jails during this same period. Merce has studied incarceration in depth in Hawai'i and is the primary author of the *Interim Report to the Legislature for the Regular Session, 2017*, prepared for the Hawai'i Legislative Task Force on Effective Incarceration Policies and Improving Hawai'i's Correctional System.

The re-entry circle process is approximately three hours long. Individuals apply to have a circle to meet with their loved ones, supporters, and an institutional representative. The circle is an interactive group process that focuses on an individual's unique goals and outlines steps for how they may attain them. The individual's basic needs for transitioning and re-entering the community are also addressed. Needs include reconciliation and how the individual might make amends and repair damaged relationships with their loved ones and community. A main objective of the re-entry circle is to address the healing needs of loved ones harmed by the individual. Other general necessities for an individual's law-abiding life, including housing, transportation, identification, physical and emotional health, education, leisure time use, and any other unique needs (e.g., divorce, immigration) are also planned for during the circle process.

From 2005 through October 2017, Hawai'i Friends provided 150 re-entry circles that 650 people participated in. The 650 participants completed surveys at the conclusion of each circle, which have been reviewed by Hawai'i friends. Surveys are distributed and collected after each circle by facilitators. Staff with Hawai'i Friends maintain these data in-house and routinely analyze and review the results, but no publications have resulted from these data analyses. To date, 100% of the 650 surveyed participants have indicated that they believe the re-entry planning circles they participated in were positive.

While the process was originally provided for men imprisoned by the state of Hawai'i, women, juveniles, individuals discharged from parole, those on state probation, and in federal custody and on federal probation in Honolulu have also used the process. A small federal pilot programme began in 2015 for individuals in custody to have a re-entry planning circle prior to their sentencing hearing in the Honolulu federal court. In 2017, the federal programme was expanded to individuals on probation under the Honolulu court's supervision and after sentencing. Other states replicating the programme have also used it for probationers and formerly incarcerated people. The circle process has been replicated or introduced in other states and countries, including California, New York, Washington, DC, Pennsylvania, North Carolina, Vermont, Japan, Spain, Finland, and Brazil.

Joan Petersilia, widely recognized as an expert in corrections and re-entry, has said: "Recidivism is an important, perhaps the most important, measure of correctional impact, but it is insufficient as a sole measure of the effectiveness of reentry programmes" (2004, p 12). While the study reported here examined recidivism, other ways that the re-entry circles have helped people harmed by crime and imprisonment have also be studied.

Children whose imprisoned parents have participated in the Huikahi re-entry circles have been studied. The circles have assisted the children and youth in healing from the emotional trauma associated with losing a parent to prison and has shown promise for helping them decrease their rumination and increase their optimism (Walker, Tarutani and McKibben, 2015). Women who have been abused have also experienced emotional recovery from participating in the re-entry circle process (Walker and Tarutani, 2017; Walker, 2017).

Re-entry circles as a public health approach

The re-entry circle process is based on public health learning principles. Many advocate for a public health approach to deal with a variety of problems that the criminal justice system ineffectively addresses, including: violence (Zimbardo, 2007), mass incarceration (Frost, Clear and Monteiro, 2017), substance abuse (United States Department of Health and Human Services, 2016), gambling (Korn and Shaffer, 1999), violence against women (Coker, 2016), and the re-entry of imprisoned people (Travis, 2005)

Public health approaches have been researched and found successful in reducing substance abuse (United States Department of Health and Human Services, 2016), gun violence (Webster et al., 2012), interpersonal abuse and violence, and child maltreatment (World Health Organization, 2010), which often underlie many crimes that cause incarceration.

Public health programmes work to prevent disease and promote healthy populations (Centers for Disease Control, 2014). There are three levels of public health prevention: primary, secondary, and tertiary. Ernest Drucker (2014: 388) explains how the criminal justice system could be improved at the three public health prevention levels:

> A new approach to criminal justice is needed, one based on public health and prevention: *primary prevention*, to shrink the system by changing drug laws and stopping mass arrests; *secondary prevention*, to reduce the harms of imprisonment by building education, job training, and humane treatment into our prisons; and *tertiary prevention*, restoring life and justice to those needlessly serving long sentences who pose no threat to public safety and cost us billions annually.

The Centers for Disease Control (CDC) (2014) explains that in applying the three levels of prevention to violence, primary prevention seeks to stop violence from ever occurring; secondary prevention provides immediate responses to violence, including medical care; and tertiary prevention helps people deal with the aftermath of violence, including victim trauma and offender rehabilitation (CDC, 2014).

The re-entry circles can be considered a tertiary prevention intervention. They assist imprisoned individuals in making amends with loved ones and in creating plans to meet their needs to desist from crime. The process also addresses trauma (Walker, Tarutani and McKibben, 2015) and can increase rehabilitation and criminal desistance.

In 1954, the World Health Organization (WHO) published criteria for developing public health practices. The WHO's *Expert Committee on Health Education of the Public*, considered and established practices for assisting people in learning healthy behaviours. The WHO committee recognized that autonomy and personal agency are vital for learning: "The aim of health education is to help people achieve health by their own actions and efforts" (1954: 4). The WHO understood that learning is "an active process" (1954: 4) in accord with Albert Bandura's research that *enactive learning* is the most effective learning approach (1997). The WHO also recognized that people learn when there is a focus on their specific goals, when their personal motivations are considered, and when a group-oriented approach is used.

The re-entry planning circle process applies the WHO's recommended learning criteria. The circles are driven by an individual's positive motivation to repair harm they have caused and their willingness to take responsibility for their future. The circles are conducted in a group process, they are self-directed and goal oriented, and they provide an active learning experience for participants. Finally, an important aspect of public health is that its practices should utilize and generate evidence-based knowledge (Jacobs et al., 2012).

Re-entry circles as a solution-focused approach

The re-entry circle process also applies a solution-focused approach. Solution-focused group processes have been studied and shown to decrease substance abuse (United States Department of Health and Human Services, 2012) and domestic violence (Lee, Uken and Sebold, 2004). Solution-focused group processes are considered to be evidence-based treatment for addressing substance abuse by the United States Department of Health and Human Services, 2012. Insoo Kim Berg, co-founder of solution-focused brief therapy, helped develop the re-entry circle process. She also helped develop a similar transition planning process, but without the reconciliation phase, for foster youth aging out of state custody (Walker, 2005).

Facilitating the circles with a solution-focused approach creates a positive experience for participants. Research indicates that "human cooperation . . . is best supported by positive interactions with others" (Rand et al.,2009: 1272). Group processes that are conducted by allowing participants agency (the processes are democratically driven), which the solution-focused approach provides, also generate more cooperation between participants than autocratic processes (Lewin, 1997). Autonomy is also key to the solution-focused approach, which is grounded in the belief that individuals are the best experts of their own lives (De Jong and Berg, 2012).

Re-entry circles and the application of restorative justice

Restorative justice initiatives have shown promise for reducing crimes for juvenile and adult offenders (Sherman and Strang, 2007), for reducing student misbehaviour (Fronius et al., 2016), and for reducing the negative effects of trauma that victims often suffer (New Zealand Government, 2016; Walker et al., 2016). 2015

The re-entry circles apply Howard Zehr's restorative philosophy for restorative practices (Walker and Greening, 2013). Zehr (2002: 58) believes that at its foundation restorative justice values respect, responsibility, and relationship:

> Ultimately, restorative justice boils down to a set of questions which we need to ask when a wrong occurs. These guiding questions are, in fact, the essence of restorative justice.

Guiding Questions of Restorative Justice

1   Who has been hurt?
2   What are their needs?
3   Whose obligations are these?
4   Who has a stake in this situation?
5   What is the appropriate process to involve stakeholders in an effort to make things right?

The reconciliation stage of the Huikahi circle process asks the following three questions based on Zehr's work: *Who was affected?* (by the behaviour and/or imprisonment of the incarcerated individual); *How were they affected?* (referring to those identified as affected by first question); and *What could be done to repair the harm?* Participants in a circle reflect on and openly discuss these questions. The discussion helps everyone understand each other's perceptions and experiences, which can help create empathy. Many circle participants have said that they appreciated this discussion, which was the first their family had concerning reconciliation. For an incarcerated individual to engage in the discussion, too, can show her or his loved ones, supporters, and community, that she or he is responsible and accountable.

Hawai'i Huikahi re-entry planning circle process – description of programme under study

There are four stages of the re-entry circle process: (1) an individual applies for a circle and is interviewed; (2) a circle is convened and a facilitator contacts and schedules the circle with participants; (3) a circle is held; and (4) a written plan resulting from the circle is prepared and delivered to the circle participants.

The re-entry circle process begins with an individual applying via a single-page application provided by the prison or institution supervising them. A facilitator interviews the applicant and discusses the process with them. People studied in this evaluation were interviewed in prison.

> The purpose of the interview is to ensure the applicant understands the nature of the circle, which is to make amends with loved ones, and to make a plan for reentry back into the community. Another goal of the interview is to increase the incarcerated person's confidence and their understanding that their efforts make a difference, and their behavior affects their futures.
>
> *(Walker and Greening, 2013: 29)*

Circle applicants provide contact information for the people that they would like to address reconciliation and make amends with, who they also hope will want to attend the meeting. The facilitator discusses the potential invitees with the imprisoned individual, and afterwards the interviewer contacts them. Only a few people identified by incarcerated individuals as potential circle participants have not been interested in attending.

While applicants are told that they need someone to attend their circle in order to have one, exceptions are made. A circle was provided for an imprisoned woman with only written information gathered from her sister (who could not attend the circle). Often loved ones and supporters cannot attend a circle for a number of reasons, including work, travel, and illness. In these situations, the facilitator telephones the person who cannot attend and asks the same questions that they would have been asked at the circle. Their responses are written down, printed out, and at the circle, placed on an empty chair, where they will stay until someone in the circle reads them aloud. The imprisoned woman, who had no loved one to personally attend her circle, instead had her sister's responses on an empty chair. A prison representative who knew her well participated in her circle and read her sister's responses during the circle. This process had an emotional impact on the imprisoned woman (she cried and expressed remorse).

During the interview, applicants are also informed that the circles are not provided to everyone who applies for them. Because resources are limited, a priority to provide the circles is made for those leaving the institution soonest or who have deadlines for parole or pardon requests. Circle applicants are also told that the "squeaky wheel gets the grease" and that individuals who continue to contact the facilitator are more likely to get a circle than those who do not. This could influence self-selection bias (Keeble, et al., 2015). The individuals more motivated to make amends with loved ones and a plan for their futures may be more likely to contact the facilitators. Also the fact that an individual needs to have a family member agree to come to a circle, distinguished from an individual who cannot get a family member to come, could indicate less support for the latter, which could influence recidivism (Wallace, et al., 2016).

After interviewing the circle applicant, and ensuring the individual understands the programme and circle process, the facilitator convenes the circle by contacting the potential invitees listed by the imprisoned individual. This can take significant time going back and forth with people and the prison on potential dates and times to hold the circle.

The third phase of the circle programme is conducting the circle, which follows the following agenda:

Welcome & Opening: The individual who applied for the circle opens it in a manner of her or his choosing (e.g., makes a statement, prayer, chant, and so on, and all in attendance introduce themselves and their relationship to the individual);

Purpose & Guidelines: The facilitator says the purpose of the circle is for reconciliation, healing, and to help the individual make a plan for success after leaving the institution; participants are also asked to speak one at a time to respect confidentiality;

Accomplishments: The incarcerated individual shares what they are most proud of having accomplished since their imprisonment, probation, parole, and so on;

Strengths: Participants each share what they like about the incarcerated person, what they think her or his strengths are, and the individual adds any additional strengths they have that were not mentioned;

Reconciliation: Group discusses who was affected by the individual's behaviour and/ or their incarceration, how they were affected, and what might be done to repair the harm;

Future (Goals): The incarcerated person shares how they would like their life to be different from the past, which describes their goals;

Identifying Resources for Basic and Unique Needs: The group brainstorms options for housing, finances, continued learning, employment, transportation, documents, emotional and physical health, leisure time, identifying the individual's supporters, other needs for successful living, and any unique needs; timelines for when tasks will be accomplished and also anyone who volunteers to assist in achieving any tasks is also described;

Determining the Next Circle Date: Schedule date for a follow-up circle if one is desired;

Circle Closing: Group participants compliment the individual who chose to have the circle, and she or he shares how the circle process was for her or him. Everyone completes a circle survey recording his or her experience with the process. Any allowable food and drink is provided at the conclusion of the circle or during the earlier short break.

The final stage of the circle programme is preparation and delivery of the plan generated at the circle to the participants. The facilitator prepares a written re-entry and transition plan based on the information gathered at the circle, including the individual's accomplishments, strengths, what she or he plans to do to repair any harm caused by past behaviour and or incarceration, and their plans to meet their goals and needs for a law-abiding life. The written plan, usually about six pages long, is delivered to the individual, the households of the circle participants, and to the institutional representative. The re-entry circle model is grounded in public health and applies solution-focused brief therapy and restorative justice (Walker and Greening, 2013).

The re-entry circle connection to desistance

The circle process promotes what desistance research shows is necessary for continued law abiding, including the ability to support oneself with meaningful activity, and having relationships with law-abiding supporters. These two factors are primary for staying crime and drug free (Maruna, 2006).

The re-entry circle also provides an individual with a platform for developing a new "self-narrative." Maruna reminds us that "a person's self-narrative identity can and does change throughout life" and "self-narratives should be understood as factors that help to sustain desistance" (2006: 42).

> The development of a self-story favourable to desisting from crime could be seen as 'hardening' the individual's resolve to stay out of trouble. This hardening of change, and not the moment of change, is the process that we are trying to understand when we study desistance".
>
> (Maruna, 2006: 42)

The circles set the stage in developing a "self-story favourable to desisting from crime." The circles begin with the incarcerated person describing their "accomplishments" that they are most proud of since they have been imprisoned, released on probation, parole, and so on. The circle participants then each share what they "like best" about the imprisoned person and what they believe her or his "strengths" are (Walker and Greening, 2013, pp. 38–41). After the individual's strengths have been identified, the individual discusses who was affected by their past misbehaviour and imprisonment. Loved ones affected, participating in the circle, also discuss this and add what the individual could do to help make things right and repair any harm. How "unrelated people and the community at large" were all also affected and what can be done to repair things for them is also discussed. All of this discussion contributes to a new positive "self-story" for the individual having the circle.

Much of the three-hour re-entry circle provides "a focus on individual-level transformation" and "individual-level change" that MacKenzie discusses as necessary for successful re-entry (2006: 124). The individual makes plans and timelines for maintaining sobriety, employment, health, relationships with loved ones, and so on. The circles set the stage for the person to tell a new story. The importance of telling stories is recognized as vital in planning: "Stories are the ineluctable context and stimuli to thinking and acting, for changing and for maintaining boundaries" (Michael, 1997: 16). Storytelling is a cognitive function that can help lead to change and improved behaviour.

The process also utilizes reality checks. For example, when the individual agrees to do whatever is discussed to repair harm, the facilitator uses "scaling questions" (Walker and Greening, 2013: 40). Scaling questions engage the individual in realistically accessing how confident they are that they will fulfil whatever they may agree to plan for during the circle. When an individual who has addiction problems promises to be clean and sober, the facilitator asks, "What gives you hope you will do that?"

Methodology of current study

This study evaluates the post-prison behaviour of 58 incarcerated individuals who participated in a Huikahi re-entry circle and 60 incarcerated individuals who wanted to take part in a Huikahi re-entry circle but were unable to do so. The experimental group in this study is comprised of those who received the Huikahi treatment, and the control group is those who were unable to participate in a circle.

The initial population under study was a list of all the incarcerated people who applied to participate in a re-entry circle between 2005 and 2015. In collaboration with the State Department of Public Safety, state identification numbers (SIDs) and prison release dates, were located for each individual.

There were two primary exclusion criteria for the final sample included in this study. First, incarcerated juveniles were excluded from this study; only adult results were studied. Access to the juvenile justice system and related statistics is heavily restricted, and the state only reports recidivism outcomes for the adult population.

Secondly, individuals who had not yet been released from prison and who had not been out of prison for three years were excluded from this study. The three-year window for follow-up was important for this study, as recidivism was measured by any new arrest within 36 months post-prison release. The conceptualization and operationalization of recidivism routinely used by the state of Hawai'i to assess recidivism rates for individuals released from prison was used in this study (any new arrest within 36 months post-prison release). Adopting the state measure of recidivism also allowed for a comparison of individuals receiving the re-entry circle treatment to those paroled statewide. The resulting study sample included adult individuals who participated in circles and had been released for at least three years before the time of the study.

Arrest data were obtained from the State of Hawai'i's Attorney General's criminal justice information system (CJIS). The date of prison release was obtained from the Hawai'i Department of Public Safety. Demographic data including gender, ethnicity, and age were obtained from both the CJIS and Department of Public Safety databases. Finally, a standardized survey was used in the re-entry circles. These surveys included measures of healing and overall satisfaction for the incarcerated participants, for their loved ones, supporters, and the prison representative who participated in the circles. The surveys were administered at each circle. Responses to those surveys are also included in this analysis for the experimental group only because the control group did not receive circles.

Study findings: demographics & outcomes

Demographic differences between the Huikahi and control group are presented in Table 18.1. As shown in the table, the control group had a significantly greater percentage of female participants (χ^2=3.190, p < .08). This is important because females typically exhibit lower recidivism rates than their male counterparts. There were not any significant differences in ethnicity or in age between the two groups. The average age of the Huikahi participants was 37.3 compared to 35.4 for the control group and the differences were not significantly different. No significant differences emerged in race of the Huikahi participants compared to the control group, as demonstrated in Table 18.1.

Table 18.2 displays a comparison of overall criminal histories for the Huikahi and control groups. While there are no significant differences between the two groups, the control group does demonstrate fewer average felony arrests and convictions, slightly more misdemeanour arrests and convictions, and a higher average for arrests and convictions for all severities.

Outcome analyses reveal that the circle participants performed significantly better than the control group in terms of post-prison adjustment (Figure 18.1). The Huikahi circle participants demonstrated a significantly lower recidivism rate of 43.1%, compared to 58.3% for the control group ($t = -1.660$, p < .05). Although unable to determine significant differences between the Huikahi group and state parole releases (raw data are needed for these calculations), the Huikahi

Table 18.1 Demographic characteristics of Huikahi circle participants

	Huikahi Participants (n=58)	Control Group (n=60)
Gender		
Male	72.4	56.7
Female	27.6	43.3
		(χ^2=3.190, p < .08)
Race		
Hawaiian/Part-Hawaiian	51.7	45.0
White	27.6	25.0
Filipino	12.1	11.7
Other	8.6	18.3
		(χ^2=2.407, p > .05)
Average Age	37.3	35.4
		$t = 1.083$, p > .05

Table 18.2 Criminal history summary for Huikahi and control group participants

	Huikahi Circle Participants	Control Group
	Average	
Total Felony Arrests	6.08	5.40
Total Felony Convictions	2.38	2.10
Total Felony Non-Convictions	3.50	2.73
Total Misdemeanour Arrests	3.45	4.83
Total Misdemeanour Convictions	0.60	0.98
Total Misdemeanour Non-Convictions	2.73	3.52
Total Petty Misdemeanour Arrests	1.78	2.70
Total Petty Misdemeanour Convictions	0.83	1.37
Total Petty Misdemeanour Non-Convictions	0.83	1.30
Total Arrests: All Severities	13.13	14.48
Total Arrests: Convictions	4.65	5.32
Total Arrests: Non-Convictions	7.55	7.75

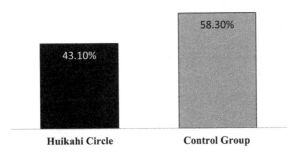

Recidivism Rates: Circle Participants versus Control Group

Note: t=-1.660, p < 0.5

Figure 18.1 Recidivism rates for Huikahi participants and control group
Note: T = −1.660, P < 0.5

group also exhibits substantially lower recidivism rates than the state group. Again, the Huikahi group demonstrated a recidivism rate of 43.1% compared to 56.4% for the state parole release group (Wong, 2011), using the same state definition for recidivism (Figure 18.2).

Table 18.3 exhibits the type of post-prison re-arrests for the Huikahi participants compared to the control group. The difference between the two groups is not statistically significant (χ^2 = 1.641, p > 05), but there are some interesting patterns nonetheless. The Huikahi participants had fewer felony, misdemeanour, or petty misdemeanour criminal arrests and were more likely to have a parole revocation or criminal contempt of court, as compared to the control group.

Table 18.4 also looks at post-prison re-arrests but uses the categories outlined in the state report on recidivism. Statistical significance cannot be calculated for this comparison, as these are two different samples, and we only had aggregate numbers for the state release group. However, the difference in recidivism rates is certainly substantial. Of those re-arrested within

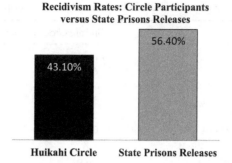

Recidivism Rates: Circle Participants versus State Prisons Releases

Figure 18.2 Recidivism rates for Huikahi participants compared to state parole releases

Table 18.3 Type of re-arrest (recidivating event) for Huikahi participants and control group – recidivists only

	Huikahi Circle Participants	Control Group
Arrest Type	*Percent*	
Felony Criminal Arrest	24.0	25.7
Misdemeanour or Petty Misdemeanour Criminal Arrest	16.0	28.6
Parole Revocation	40.0	28.6
Criminal Contempt of Court	20.0	17.1

Table 18.4 Type of re-arrest (recidivating event) for Huikahi participants compared to state releases – recidivists only

	Huikahi Circle Participants	State Releases
Arrest Type	*Percent*	
Criminal Re-arrest	17.2	15.2
Parole Revocation	17.2	37.6
Criminal Contempt of Court	8.6	3.6
No Recidivating Event within 3 Years	56.9	43.6

three years of release from prison, the state releases were slightly less likely to have a criminal re-arrest or criminal contempt of court, and more likely to have parole revocation compared to the Huikahi participants.

Discussion and conclusion

The results from this study show promising results for this restorative re-entry planning intervention, as applied in prison. Data indicate a reduction in recidivism three years after release, compared to similarly situated inmates. The study is unique in that it allowed for a quasi-experimental evaluation of the Huikahi re-entry circles on incarcerated populations as compared to a control group of individuals who applied to participate yet were ultimately unable to do so. This serves to eliminate some selection bias that would otherwise be present. The study provides evidence-based knowledge to help bridge the gap in restorative justice research that can contribute to criminology findings, especially concerning incarcerated people, which is an important objective of this Handbook.

Demographically, the participant group was significantly more male, with no differences in ethnic background or age. Although the control group demonstrated fewer average felony arrests and convictions, and slightly more misdemeanour arrests and convictions than the Huikahi participants, there was no significant differences in overall criminal histories between the groups prior to participation in the intervention.

The control group demonstrated statistically significantly higher recidivism rates than the Huikahi participants group, even though the control group had a significantly higher percentage of female inmates. Women tend to recidivate at lower rates (Snyder et al., 2016). The control group also had more felony and misdemeanour arrests than the Huikahi participants. The Huikahi group demonstrated more community supervision revocations as opposed to new crimes. The Huikahi group also demonstrated a lower recidivism rate compared to a cohort of state parole releases, using the same definition and measures of recidivism. Overall, the results support continued use and study of this intervention.

This re-entry model and aspects of it are transferable and have been replicated in communities outside Hawai'i. Psychologists, psychiatrists, social workers, teachers, lawyers, academics, prison staff, mediators and facilitators, and others who work with adults and juveniles incarcerated and on probation, have been trained on this model. Trainings have been provided in Japan, Finland, Spain, and Brazil. The model, in whole or in part, has been replicated in Rochester, New York (Dougherty et al. (2014); Washington DC (Collaborative Solutions for Communities, 2017); Santa Cruz, California (Assegued, 2016); Berkeley, California (personal communication with Ruth Morgan September 7, 2017), Pennsylvania (personal communication with Barbie Fischer, September 22, 2017), and Bermuda (personal communication with Yvette April Brown October 20, 2017).

Giving individuals the opportunity to set the course of their lives based on their strengths and their goals helps provide the variables identified for desistance. Opportunities to promote relationships with law-abiding others, finding employment, and discovering the platform to narrate a new reformed life story are desistance markers (Maruna, 2006). The re-entry process provides these opportunities.

There is also value in the re-entry circle process beyond its potential to reduce recidivism of imprisoned people. Qualitative and anecdotal evidence shows that even in cases where an imprisoned individual relapses and is re-incarcerated after a circle, their loved ones continue to appreciate the healing value of the circle process. The spouse of an imprisoned man who had a circle but relapsed and went back to prison, said: "It absolutely helped me heal. I had things I needed to say about how I was affected. The circle validated my feelings" (Walker and Greening, 2010: 69). Loved ones facing similar situations often express common sentiments.

This evaluation and other material from this Handbook will help address the needs of people and communities in the state of Hawai'i, and elsewhere, affected by crime and incarceration via the positive evaluation of re-entry circles. There is a promising link between the restorative practice evaluated in this study and reduced recidivism.

Phil Zimbardo, principal researcher of the *Stanford Prison Experiment*, who has studied psychology and corrections for decades (2007), "endorse[s] the widest possible utilization" of the re-entry circle planning process (Walker and Greening, 2013: 8). Government agencies, policy makers, and funders should endorse and support evidence-based practices in place of our current reactive and punitive system of incarceration. Evidence-based alternatives like this re-entry circle process are needed to help reduce recidivism, increase healing, and promote public safety.

Steven Raphael, University of California, Berkeley, public policy professor, has studied incarceration and re-entry in depth, and believes that: "Given the social and budgetary costs of crime and incarceration, programmes that have even modest effects are likely to pass cost-benefit tests" (Raphael, 2011: 213). It is irresponsible and constitutes a danger to society to release people from prison without ensuring they have adequate plans for meeting their needs for survival and criminal desistance. Funds should be reprioritized from imprisonment to re-entry for the safety and well-being of individuals and communities.

References

Assegued, V. 2016. A Juvenile Justice Process for the Family When Juveniles Are Freed from Incarceration. Available at Juvenile Justice Information Exchange. http://jjie.org/2016/08/03/a-restorative-justice-process-for-the-family-when-juveniles-freed-from-incarceration/. Accessed 1 September 2017.

Bandura, A. 1997. *Self-Efficacy: The Exercise of Control*. New York: W.H. Freeman and Company.

Braithwaite, J. 2004. *Emancipation and Hope*. Available at www.anu.edu.au/fellows/jbraithwaite/_documents/Articles/Emancipation_Hope_2004.pdf. Accessed 4 April 2017.

Centers for Disease Control and Prevention (CDC). 2014. Introduction to Public Health. In: *Public Health 101 Series*. Available at www.cdc.gov/publichealth101/public-health.html/. Accessed 10 May 2017.

Circles Program. [e-book] *Center for Public Safety Initiatives*, Rochester Institute of Technology. Available at https://books.google.com/books?id=pkKgCwAAQBAJ&lpg=PP1&pg=PR3#v=onepage&q&f=false. Accessed 27 June 2017.

Coker, D. 2016. Crime Logic: Campus Sexual Assault, and Restorative Justice, *Texas Tech Law Review*, 49: 147–210.

Collaborative Solutions for Communities. 2017. Our Work: What Is Healing Circle? *The Family Group Conference and Healing Circle*. Available at http://wearecsc.org/healing-circle/. Accessed 8 August 2017.

De Jong, P. and Berg, I, 2012. *Interviewing for Solutions*. Brooks Cole: Pacific Grove, CA.

Dougherty, J., Duda, J. and Klofas, J. 2014. Evaluation of Step by Step's Restorative Transition

Drucker, E. 2014. Restoring Justice: From Punishment to Public Health, Editors' Choice, *American Journal of Public Health*, 104: 388.

Fronius, T, Persson, H., Guckenburg, S., Hurley, S. and Petrosino, A. 2016. *Restorative Justice in U.S. Schools: A Research Review*. Available at https://jprc.wested.org/wp-content/uploads/2016/02/RJ_Literature-Review_20160217.pdf. Accessed 9 April 2017.

Frost, N., Clear, T. and Monteiro, C. 2017. *Ending Mass Incarceration: Six Bold Reforms to Rapidly Reduce Incarceration Without Compromising Public Safety*, Ernest Drucker, ed. New York: New Press.

Hawai'i Legislative Task Force On Effective Incarceration Policies and Improving Hawaii's Correctional System. 2017. *Interim Report to the Legislature for the Regular Session*. Available at www.courts.state.hi.us/wp content/uploads/2016/07/HCR_85_TASK_FORCE_INTERIM_REPORT.pdf. Accessed 23 July 2017.

Jacobs, J., Jones, E., Gabella, B., Spring, B. and Brownson, R. 2012. Tools for Implementing an Evidence-Based Approach in Public Health Practice, *Preventing Chronic Disease: Public Health Research, Practice, and Policy*. Available at <www.cdc.gov/pcd/issues/2012/11_0324.htm. Accessed 17 May 2017.

Keeble, C., Law, G., Barber, S. and Baxter, P. 2015. *Choosing a Method to Reduce Selection Bias: A Tool for Researchers, Open Journal of Epidemiology*. Available at <https://file.scirp.org/pdf/OJEpi_2015070913284831.pdf. Accessed 17 May 2017.

Korn, D. and Shaffer, H. 1999. Gambling and the health of the public: Adopting a public health perspective. *Journal of Gambling Studies*, 15: 289–365.

Lattimore, P. and Visher, C. 2013. The Impact of Prison Reentry Services on Short-Term Outcomes: Evidence from a Multisite Evaluation, *U.S. National Library of Medicine National Institutes of Health*. Available at www.ncbi.nlm.nih.gov/pubmed/24425806. Accessed 10 August 2017.

Lee, M., Uken, A. and Sebold, J. 2004. Accountability for Change: Solution-Focused Treatment with Domestic Violence Offender. *Families in Society: The Journal of Contemporary Social Services*, 85(4): 463–476.

Lewin, K. 1997. *Experiments in Social Space (1939): Resolving Social Conflicts & Field Theory in Social Science*, K. Lewin ed. Washington, DC: American Psychological Association.

Lewis, T. and Osborn, C. 2004. Solution-Focused Counseling and Motivational Interviewing: A Consideration of Confluence, *Journal of Counseling & Development*, 82: 38–48.

MacKenzie, D. 2006. *What Works in Corrections: Reducing the Criminal Activities of Offenders and Delinquents.* New York: Cambridge University Press.

Maruna, S. 2006. *Making Good: How Ex-Convicts Reform and Rebuild Their Lives.* Washington, DC: American Psychological Association.

Michael, D. 1997. *Learning to Plan and Planning to Learn.* Alexandria, VA: Miles River.

New Zealand Government. 2016. *Restorative Justice: Evidence Brief.* Available at www.justice.govt.nz/assets/Documents/Publications/evidence-brief-restorative-justice.pdf. Accessed 5 September 2017.

Petersilia, J. 2004. What Works in Prisoner Reentry? Reviewing and Questioning the Evidence, *Federal Probation Journal*, 68(2): 7–14.

Rand, D., Dreber, A., Ellingsen, T., Fudenberg, D. and Nowak, M. 2009. *Positive Interactions Promote Public Cooperation, Science.* Available at https://static1.squarespace.com/static/51ed234ae4b0867e2385d879/t/51fab972e4b07d5d9e43b4e9/1375385970593/positive-interactions-promote-public-cooperation.pdf. Accessed 10 July 2017.

Rapheal, S. 2011. Incarceration and Prisoner Reentry in the United States, *The ANNALS of the American Academy of Political and Social Science*, 635: 192–215. Available at http://journals.sagepub.com/doi/abs/10.1177/0002716210393321. Accessed 6 September 2017.

Root & Rebound Reentry. 2017. *Guidebook to Reentry.* Available at www.rootandrebound.org/guides-toolkits/. Accessed 22 July 2017.

Sherman, L. and Strang, H., 2007. *Restorative Justice: The Evidence*, London: The Smith Institute. Available at www.smith-institute.org.uk/wp-content/uploads/2015/10/RestorativeJusticeTheEvidenceFullreport.pdf. Accessed 16 May 2017.

Snyder, H., Durose, M. Cooper, A. and Mulako-Wangota, J. 2016. Bureau of Justice Statistics. Recidivism Rates of Prisoners with Selec ted Characteristics Released from Prisons in 30 States in 2005— Female and Male. Generated using the Prisoner Recidivism Analysi Tool – 2005 (PRAT-2005). Available https://bjs.gov/recidivism_2005_arrest/. Accessed 2 January 2018.

Taxman, F. 2004. The Offender and Reentry: Supporting Active Participation in Reintegration, *Federal Probation Journal*, 68(2): 49–55.

Travis, J. 2005. *But They All Come Back: Facing the Challenges of Prisoner Reentry.* Washington, DC: The Urban Institute Press.

United States Department of Health and Human Services. 2012. Substance Abuse and Mental Health Administration (SAMHSA), *National Registry of Evidence-Based Programs and Practices.* Available at http://legacy.nreppadmin.net/ViewIntervention.aspx?id=281. Accessed 7 August 2017.

United States Department of Health and Human Services 2016. *Facing Addiction in America: The Surgeon General's Report on Alcohol, Drugs, and Health.* Available at <https://addiction.surgeongeneral.gov/front-matter.pdf. Accessed 7 June 2017.

Visher, C.A. 2014. Unintended Consequences:Policy Implications of the NAS Report on Criminal Careers and Career Criminals, *Journal of Research in Crime and Delinquency*, 53(3). Available at http://journals.sagepub.com/doi/pdf/10.1177/0022427815603770. Accessed 7 September 2017.

Walker, L. 2000. Hawai'i Public Housing Implements Conferencing: A Restorative Approach to Conflict Resolution, *Journal of Housing & Community Development.* Available at http://lorennwalker.com/wp-content/uploads/2016/06/kalihi_article.html. Accessed 20 May 2017.

Walker, L. 2004. Restorative Justice without Offender Participation: A Pilot Program for Victims, *International Institute for Restorative Practices.* Available at www.iirp.org/library/lwalker04.html. Accessed 23 May 2017.

Walker, L. 2005. *E Makua Ana Youth Circles: A Transition Planning Process for Youth Exiting Foster Care.* Available at http://lorennwalker.com/wp-content/uploads/2016/06/E-Makua-Walker.pdf. Accessed 8 June 2017.

Walker, L. 2008. Waikiki Youth Circles: Homeless Youth Learn Goal Setting Skills, *Journal of Family Psychotherapy*, 19(1): 85–91.

Walker, L. 2015. Reentry Circles for the Innocent: The Psychological Benefits of Restorative Justice and Taking Responsibility in Response to Injustice. In T. Gavrielides (ed.) *The Psychology of Restorative Justice: Managing the Power Within*. Farmham: Ashgate.

Walker, L. 2017. Restorative Justice & Race Inequality, Hawai'i, USA. In T. Gavrielides (ed.) *Restorative Justice Case Studies*. London: RJ4ALL Publications, p. 25.

Walker, L. and Greening, R. 2010. Huikahi Restorative Circles: A Public Health Approach for Reentry Planning, *Federal Probation*, 74(1).

Walker, L. and Greening, R. 2013. *Reentry & Transition Planning Circles for Incarcerated People*. Honolulu, Hawai'i: Hawai'i Friends of Justice & Civic Education.

Walker, L. and Kobayashi, L. 2015. Restorative & Therapeutic Reentry Rituals. In M. Evans. (ed.) *Offender Release and Supervision: The Role of Courts and the Use of Discretion*. Netherlands: Wolf Legal Publishing.

Walker, L. and Tarutani, C. 2017. Restorative Justice and Violence Against Women: An Effort to Decrease the Victim-Offender Overlap and Increase Healing. In D. Halder and K. Jaishankar (eds.) *Therapeutic Jurisprudence and Overcoming Violence against Women*. Hershey, PA: IGI Global.

Walker, L., Tarutani, C. and McKibben, D. 2015. Benefits of Restorative Reentry Circles for Children of Incarcerated Parents in Hawai'i. In Gal and Faedi Duramy (eds.) *Promoting the Participation of Children Across the Globe: From Social Exclusion to Child-Inclusive Policies*. Available at https://ssrn.com/abstract=2666828. Accessed 10 October 2017.

Wallace, D., Fahmy, C., Cotton, L., Jimmons, C., Mckay, R., Stoffer, S. and Syed, S. 2016. Examining the Role of Familial Support During Prison and After Release on Post-Incarceration Mental Health, *International Journal of Offender Therapy and Comparative Criminology*, 60(1): 3–20.

Webster, D., Whitehill, J., Vernick, J. and Oarjer, E. 2012. *Evaluation of Baltimore's Safe Streets Program: Effects on Attitudes, Participants' Experiences, and Gun Violence*. Available at Johns Hopkins Center for the Prevention of Youth Violence Johns Hopkins Bloomberg School of Public Health. http://cureviolence.org/wp-content/uploads/2017/09/Safe-Streets-full-evaluation.pdf. Accessed 14 September 2017.

World Health Organization (WHO). 1954. *Expert Committee on Health Education of the Public, Technical Report Series, No. 89*. Available at http://apps.who.int/iris/bitstream/10665/40254/1/WHO_TRS_89.pdf. Accessed 11 July 2017.

World Health Organization (WHO) 2010. *Violence Prevention: The Evidence*. Available at http://apps.who.int/iris/bitstream/10665/77936/1/9789241500845_eng.pdf?ua=1. Accessed 17 August 2017.

Zehr, H. 2002. *The Little Book of Restorative Justice*. Intercourse, PA: Good Books.

Zimbardo, P. 2007. *The Lucifer Effect: Understanding How Good People Turn Evil*. New York: Random House.

19

Architecture and restorative justice
Designing with values and well-being in mind

Barb Toews

Introduction

In 2000, while facilitating a restorative justice workshop for a group of incarcerated men in a United States maximum security prison, my co-facilitator and I noticed that the men appeared angry and resistant to our topic of conversation, that of accountability for their crimes and empathy towards victims. In an attempt to create an atmosphere conducive to dealing with this difficult topic, we asked the men to imagine a room in which they could deal with their crimes. We created this room on paper; the men symbolically furnished the room with soft chairs, a bay window with a mountain view, a phone, books, plants, a fish tank, and children quietly playing. It looked like a mountain lodge. We called our creation the 'do-no-harm' room, a space in which the men could let their guard down, deal with their crimes, and face other areas of their lives in need of repair. From that point forward, if a man became resistant to class topics, we asked him to symbolically take a seat in the room. More often than not, his perspective would change. An image of a room, quite different from a prison, seemed to influence the degree to which these men would face themselves and deal with their crimes.

This experience began my inquiry into restorative justice and its relationship to the design of justice spaces. If an imaginary room could influence attitudes, I questioned what a real room, designed with restorative justice in mind, could do. Unbeknownst to me at that time, there already existed a rich history linking justice values to the design of justice spaces and significant research demonstrating the connection between environmental design and human physical, emotional, psychological, and behavioural health and well-being. When coupled with restorative justice theory, a new vision for architecture and design emerges: one that promotes restorative values and experiences, such as respect, accountability, and transformation. This new architecture seeks to provide values-based spaces in which to facilitate restorative justice practices while simultaneously creating the environmental conditions that promote well-being and transformation. Interaction with the design subsequently carries the potential to serve as a restorative experience or practice in and of itself.

This chapter explores preliminary insight into what this restorative justice design practice looks like. I begin with an examination of the values of and stakeholder experiences with justice architecture and the subsequent limitations of this architecture in meeting the needs of justice stakeholders. A new vision for architecture and design is then conceptualized through the intersection of the restorative justice philosophy, salutogenic design, and active engagement with justice stakeholders about their environmental preferences and needs. Architecture and design are contextual and cultural, and the vision discussed here emerges from contexts in the United States and to a lesser degree, Canada. The specific perspectives and design suggestions proposed in this chapter may not be applicable to other contexts and cultures. What the chapter offers, however, is a manner through which to explore environmental design across contexts and culture, and insight into the translation of restorative values into the built form. The specific restorative justice characteristics may serve as a jumping off point through which to engage in dialogue about restorative justice design across cultures.

Justice architecture and values

Architecture, including justice architecture and landscape architecture, has long been a values-based endeavour (Deming, 2015; Findley, 2005; Greene, 2006; Mulcahy, 2010) intended to give life to supposedly shared social values. Courthouses, for instance, have typically been designed to represent the rule of law and authority of the judge. Design elements include stone, brick, and other hard and opaque materiality, block like massing, and an often overwhelming and grand scale (Greene, 2006; Mulcahy, 2010). One cannot help but feel the power of the courts when inside or near a courthouse. The architecture of jails and prisons also communicates values and beliefs about offending and justice; an example is the now-closed Eastern State Penitentiary (ESP) in Philadelphia. When it opened in 1829, the prevailing belief was that offending was sinful behaviour that stemmed from spiritual deficits. Justice required penitence and the ESP architecture aimed to facilitate it. Solitary cells left the prisoner to himself to reflect. Skylight-type windows drew the prisoner's eyes up to God. Low doorways forced the prisoner to humble himself to enter and exit the cell (Johnston, 2000; Wener, 2012). These examples suggest that architecture is not neutral; it represents the beliefs and values of society. Indeed, these values change over time, as society changes. Courthouse design is now more representative of democratic ideals, such as transparency, accessibility, and civic engagement through the use of small-scaled buildings, a mixture of transparent and opaque materiality, and the inclusion of community spaces (Greene, 2006). Correctional facilities, especially the direct supervision model, are more normalized in appearance, with softer furnishings, colours, carpeting, and small podular living areas (Wener, 2012).

These architectural evolutions have ensured that modern architecture and design reflect values that society holds dear. However, this evolution has not addressed some fundamental shortcomings. Three shortcoming explored here include: the absence of victims in the theories that buttress the architecture; the removal of emotions from the design; and the way in which architecture and design communicates power and marginalization. These problems converge to the detriment to the victims, offenders, and communities impacted by or involved in crime.

Justice, within the dominant system, focuses on the offender, often at the exclusion of the victim and their needs to experience justice. Little has been done to understand victim needs when it comes to justice architecture, resulting in a less than ideal justice experience inside. Victims are typically relegated to the public galleries in the courtroom, seated behind a barrier that separates them from the judicial proceedings (Mulcahy, 2010). During proceeding breaks, they have few private spaces to which they can retreat and often find themselves in the courthouse hallways, at risk of interacting with the defendant and/or his or her supporters, or in public restaurants, surrounded an unknowing crowd and unable to talk or express emotions freely (Carey and Lowney, 2015; Toews, 2016a). A few lucky victims have access to secure and relatively private victim/witness rooms (Carey and Lowney, 2015). Victims also react negatively to the materiality of courthouses, experiencing the awe- and respect-inducing marble, stone, and ornate trappings as cold and a mismatch for their emotional state (Toews, 2016a).

This disconnect between the design and emotions is not unintentional. Criminal justice, especially as it occurs within the courthouse, is meant to be an "emotion-free zone" (Knight, 2014: 2), thus necessitating designs that reflect the supposed rationality of justice. Yet, as Kennedy and Tait state, "[a] court is not just a set of rooms, corridors and entrances, it is a social and emotional world" (cited in Missingham, 2003: 3). Emotions run rampant throughout the justice process, on the part of victims, offenders, their supporters, and justice professionals (Knight, 2014; Missingham, 2003). Victims bring the direct pain of the crime and a variety of emotions directed at the perpetrator (e.g. rage, forgiveness, or disgust). Perpetrators may feel afraid, bitter, or remorseful. Each of their supporters may harbour feelings of shame, anger, or defensiveness. Justice professionals also carry emotions in reaction to their clients (e.g. empathy, repulsion, or irritation). Correctional facilities are also emotional worlds, more than just rooms and corridors; the very fact that humans are confined inside and work within them make for an emotional experience. Yet, like courthouses, facility architecture and design rely on cold, hard, and unemotional materiality. When incarcerated people are asked to create spaces that would facilitate accountability or address their therapeutic needs, which require some degree of emotional literacy, they do not use cinder blocks and cement in their designs (Designing Justice+Designing Spaces, 2014, 2015a; Toews, 2016b).

The question surfaces of who makes the architectural decisions on behalf of society. According to Findley (2005), the act of building is in the hands of the wealthy and powerful, making them the most prominent clients with whom architects and designers collaborate. They have the money or influence to raise public and private funds to pay for buildings and/or have the authority to determine the function of the building or space (Findley, 2005). The power to determine the function extends to power to determine the form, or design, of the building or space. In the case of justice spaces, this typically means that justice authorities (e.g. police commissioners, judges and court administrators, and correctional administrators) make design decisions. Indeed, they bring a necessary birds-eye understanding of the infrastructure needs for justice to occur and carry the burden for attending to issues related to security, personnel, health standards, and public safety. Architects and justice authorities, however, rarely engage meaningfully with victims, offenders, and community members in the determination of the function or form of justice spaces. Anecdotally, we know that architects and justice authorities do ask justice stakeholders about their reaction to building designs, but this typically occurs after design decisions have been made, if not after buildings have been built, and it is typically done as an informal afterthought. Without the involvement of victims, offenders, and communities in the design for justice spaces, the function and form of the resulting buildings and spaces may be radically off-base and potentially negatively impact stakeholders experience with justice. Research suggests that violence survivors experience the courthouse design as cold, hard, and dead, experiences which largely stem from the materiality of the building (e.g. exteriors and interiors made of stone and marble). The grand scale and ornate decoration, rather than communicating respect for their experiences, communicates their insignificance to the justice process (Toews, 2016a).

Restorative justice: values and process

The restorative justice philosophy may offer a new vision for justice architecture that communicates a new set of values and addresses environmental limitations. Restorative justice seeks to do justice in a way that, among other things, attends to the human needs of victims, offenders, and communities, needs which are experienced physically, psychologically, emotionally, and spiritually. By addressing needs as well as obligations for repair, justice serves as a means through which to restore, or facilitate for the first time, wellness following a crime (Pranis, 2007). This wellness may take a variety of forms such as reduced trauma and stress symptoms, increased empathy, and improved social relationships (Sherman and Strang, 2007; Strang et al., 2013). Restorative justice values and processes play a pivotal role in the realization of these well-being outcomes.

Values

Proponents of restorative justice articulate a myriad of values inherent to restorative justice. For the purposes of this chapter, this discussion focuses on five values – respect, accountability/vindication, participation, transformation, and social justice – which allow for a comparison to the values represented in justice architecture. Restorative justice, first and foremost, *respects those most directly impacted by crime*, be they victims, offenders, or community members. Processes and practitioners seek to acknowledge the worth and dignity of all those impacted by crime and restore their humanity in the aftermath of crime. Respect surrounds the commitment to *meaningful accountability on the part of the offender and vindication on the part of the victim*. No longer singularly focused on punishment, restorative justice processes aim to repair the emotional, physical, psychological, and spiritual harms of the crime by holding the offender accountable and clearing the victim of [blame]. In order to achieve this repair, restorative justice processes call for the *participation of victims, offenders, and communities*. Victims speak to their experiences and needs for justice. Offenders actively take steps to address the harms. Communities gather to support victim and offenders and consider their own needs and obligations in response to the crime. Indeed, victims, offenders, and communities are considered experts in the justice process by the very nature of their involvement.

The reparation process is intended to contribute to an experience of personal and interpersonal *transformation* for all involved. This transformation may relate to, for instance, the repair or mitigation of harm, visions for a new life moving forward, or sense of peace. These values extend to the social world through a commitment to *social justice*. The restorative justice philosophy calls us to contextualize crime and other harmful behaviours within the reality of unjust social structures which give rise to crime and understand the social consequences of existing justice practices, especially on already marginalized groups of people. The justice response ideally aims to transform inequitable structures and do justice for the "common good"(Toews, 2006).

Process

Restorative justice processes, or practices, breathe life into the restorative values. There exist numerous types of restorative justice processes, such as victim offender dialogue in its many forms, circles to address interpersonal and community harms or facilitate an individual's re-entry after a period of separation, intergroup dialogues that explore experiences and understandings of justice, and micro-communities organized around restorative justice principles (Stutzman Amstutz, 2009; Anderson Hooker, 2016; MacRae and Zehr, 2004; Pranis, 2004; Toews and Harris, 2010). Indeed, the ways in which to practice the restorative justice philosophy are countless. There exists one commonality across them all that is critical when considering environmental design – they all actively and meaningfully invite participation from those most impacted by the crime. No longer bystanders to the justice process, impacted individuals and communities take the role of "experts" of the crime – its impacts, obligations, needs for justice, and the way to fulfil those obligations and address those needs.

Wellness-oriented design

The preliminary lens through which to explore architecture and design based on restorative justice is that of salutogenic design, which is concerned with designing to improve physical, emotional, and mental health. Victims seek healing from physical injuries, stress and trauma, and the emotional impacts of the crimes they experienced. Justice holds offenders accountable for their actions, which requires a degree of regard and empathy for others, and seeks to reduce recidivism, which may invite the offender to deal with substance abuse, mental illness, and past experiences with abuse and victimization. Justice employees, especially those who work inside correctional facilities, struggle with mental health issues such as burnout, fatigue, substance abuse, and suicide which impact their ability to do their job and their quality of life outside work hours. Environment design research offers insight into how the built and natural environments can positively influence health and wellness.

Much of what is known about salutogenic design in terms of the built environment comes from the design of healthcare spaces, such as hospitals. Design features most relevant for restorative justice architecture include access to small, quiet, and private living spaces as well as comfortable and flexible common/family spaces (Ulrich et al., 2008). Single-person bedrooms, such as those found in a hospital, foster privacy while also increasing and improving communication between patient, staff, and family. This increased communication leads to social support and satisfaction with care. Such support has been linked to improved progress towards health goals and reduced stress for both the patient and the family. Complementing the need for privacy is the need for social interaction and support. This need is frequently met through the availability of day rooms and lounges in which families and their loved one can gather; moveable furniture affords the family the flexibility to arrange the furniture according to their needs (Ulrich et al., 2008).

Access to and interaction with nature offer critical health benefits in most health and wellbeing domains. Nature views, for example, outside hospital windows have been shown to reduce pain and decrease healing time (Ulrich et al., 2008). Research also finds that interaction with nature in varied ways reduces stress, depression, and post-traumatic stress symptomology, and improves self-esteem (Cipriani et al., 2017; Genter et al., 2015; Wang and MacMillan, 2013). Nature access also relieves mental fatigue and positively influences cognitive functioning (Bratman et al., 2015; van den Berg et al., 2010). Kaplan argues that these nature-based experiences with relief and restoration are critical when engaging in highly demanding and exhausting tasks (1995) and for one's ability to actively and responsibly engage in community life (Kaplan and Kaplan, 2003). A small but growing body of literature explores justice stakeholders' environmental preferences (both built and landscape) and the impact of health-oriented design, especially as it relates to interaction with nature.

Victims

The bulk of the research addressing victims' environmental experiences focuses their preferences related to the interior and exterior spaces of domestic violence crisis shelters. Lygum et al. (2012, 2013) found that shelters users desired five design elements: (1) protection from outsiders and a sense of safety; (2) accessible and straightforward spaces and activities; (3) opportunities to engage with nature and be outside; (4) space for different activities and interactions, and that accounts for differences between adults and children; (5) play facilities for children. These spatial preferences influence environmental design characteristics such as fencing, backyard landscaping, paths, and seating. Earlier research also suggests that domestic violence survivors desire spaces that are aesthetically enriching and interesting (both inside and outside), have a home-like design in furnishing and appearance, and are located near social services. Such shelters are also controllable by and predictable to the individuals living in them and facilitate self-esteem and self-respect (Refuerzo and Verderber, 1989; Verderber, 2001). Ultimately, shelter designs should convey a "safe refuge . . . not an institution" (Refuerzo and Verderber, 1993: 53). The emergency shelter of the Pierce County YWCA (Tacoma, WA) provides an example of a shelter designed with survivor needs in mind. Families live in individual apartments, with private bathrooms and kitchens, which have been decorated like homes – for example, with comfortable and stylish furniture, modern colours, and throw rugs (YWCA of Pierce County, 2017).

Offenders

The exploration of health-oriented environmental design in the context of offenders largely focuses on the impact of nature-oriented interventions. At the most basic level, incarcerated individuals with views of nature from their cell windows experience less major illnesses and make fewer sick calls (West, 1986). More formally, incarcerated men and women who participate in horticultural programmes demonstrate improved social and emotional health, experience a sense of meaning, and gain vocational skills (van der Linden, 2015). Modern technology is bringing nature access inside the prison walls through the use of videos projected onto the walls of private rooms. Early results from pilot tests of these "blue rooms" (named for the colour of the wall on which the videos are projected) suggest that men who used the rooms had fewer disciplinary infractions than those who did not. The men also self-reported feeling calmer, an experience confirmed by staff perceptions, which contributed to better prisoner-staff relationships. The incarcerated individual chooses which video to watch and video analysis found that common video characteristics included a diversity of global landscapes, nature sounds, animals (with little human presence), sunlight, and wide open skies (Oregon Youth Authority, 2016). Iowa Correctional Institution for Women (ICIW) offers an example of a correctional campus in which the natural landscape has been intentionally designed to attend to health and well-being needs of incarcerated women. The prison "yard" consists of a one-acre garden (called the Multipurpose Outdoor Classroom, MOC) with walking paths, garden plots with prairie flowers indigenous to the area, an aspen trail with seating, and three open-air classrooms. A healing garden grows immediately outside the mental health unit, accessible to those with outside access and within view of the enclosed unit courtyard for those who do not. The campus also includes several acres of production gardens (Barron, 2015). Preliminary research, in which I am involved, is finding that the majority of women regularly use the MOC for a variety of individual and social activities and report that it improves their social and emotional health.

Justice professionals

Research to date has predominantly focused on the well-being of correctional staff. This focus is not unwarranted, as correctional employees experience high rates of stress, depression, substance abuse, and suicide (Ferdick and Smith, 2017), with some developing "corrections fatigue" due to the traumatic, organizational, and operational stressors inherent to correctional work (Denof et al., 2014). Research suggests that certain design characteristics contribute to compromised mental health, increased risk of physical assaults, and diminished sense of safety. These characteristics include, cluttered cell blocks, poor sanitation, minimal privacy, superfluous noise, and linear designs (Bierie, 2012; Steiner and Wooldredge, 2016). Research also suggests that staff physical health improves and stress lowers, however, when employees have access to nature, even if that access is as simple as viewing a mural with a nature scene (Farbstein et al., 2012). Another study, in which I am involved, found that approximately half of all correctional staff go outside during their work breaks, and 76% desire a designated outdoor space in which to decompress, relax, and cope with work stress. The preferred characteristics of this space includes trees, water, and flowers, along with music and/or other soothing sounds, good lighting, and seating (Wagenfeld et al., 2017). Again, we can look to ICIW for an example of a staff respite space. The recently built outdoor decompression area features a brick patio, built-in grills, and planters, surrounded by a privacy shield of trees (Barron, 2015). The National Institute of Justice recently affirmed the use of design solutions in response to staff health and well-being (Ferdick and Smith, 2017), which may lead to increased concern and redesign of the correctional environment with staff in mind.

Community

The community is a critical stakeholder in the restorative justice process, and little research exists connecting urban planning and community design to the justice context. The most notable, and perhaps the only, research done in this area, maps incarceration rates with neighbourhood characteristics (Spatial Information Design Lab, 2008). Maps revealed the existence of "million dollar blocks" – city blocks in which $1 million dollars is spent annually incarcerating its residents. In addition to being blocks that house low-income people of colour, land-use analysis showed that these blocks were filled with vacant and abandoned buildings, brown fields, waste treatment plants, and highway bypasses. They were void of green space. These findings suggest that those who are disproportionately at risk for incarceration have been denied access to design elements which could improve their health and well-being and reduce aggression, substance abuse, and other health concerns which contribute to crime, violence, and later incarceration.

Restorative justice design

Restorative justice design materializes restorative values and environmentally supports restorative processes in order to facilitate the personal, interpersonal, and social well-being goals. Indeed, given what we know about the impact of the environment on human health and well-being, spaces designed with restorative justice as their basis may serve as a restorative intervention in and of itself. But, what does a restorative justice design look like? How do we translate the restorative function into a restorative form? What does the design process look like as we seek answers to these questions? The answers to these questions merge through an integration of the strengths and limitations of current justice architecture, restorative justice theory, and evidence-based salutogenic design. The following discussion of restorative justice design begins with an exploration of the design process itself and then shifts to a preliminary framework for understanding restorative justice design characteristics.

Restorative design process

Just as restorative justice seeks to understand stakeholder needs and obligations, and design a justice process to address those needs and obligations, restorative design seeks to understand users' environmental needs as they relate to their justice interests, and to design a space that will meet those needs. A reframing of Zehr's restorative justice questions (Zehr, 2015) provide guidance for a stakeholder-engaged design process (Table 19.1).

Answers to these questions can be facilitated through restorative justice practices. For example, planners can use circle processes to solicit design insight, or they can use design techniques such as creating collages to visualize transformation (Designing Justice+Designing Spaces, 2015b). When restorative justice and design practices are used simultaneously, justice stakeholders experience the benefits of both approaches. Restorative justice practices create space for them to discuss their needs and obligations and link those to desired design aesthetics and characteristics. The design techniques may also contribute to an experience of social and personal restoration and transformation similar to that experienced in art-based therapeutic methods (Gamman and Thorpe, 2015; Leavy, 2009; Malchiodi, 2003).

Examples exist for this restorative design process being used, at least in part. Designing Justice+Designing Spaces (DJ+DS), an early initiative I co-created with designer Deanna van Buren to explore the relationship between restorative justice and design, grew out of the commitment to actively involve justice stakeholders in the creation of a vision for restorative justice design. Our early work entailed facilitating restorative justice classes and workshops inside county jails and state prisons. In these educational forums, incarcerated participants (and, in some situations, in collaboration with non-incarcerated students) learned about restorative justice and participated in mini-design labs, incrementally learning design skills. The culmination of these forums resulted in restorative justice design concepts for a variety of justice spaces, such as courthouses, re-entry campuses, and spaces for victim offender dialogue (for examples

Table 19.1 Questions to guide a restorative justice design process

Design creation

1. Who will be the users of the space – victims, offenders, support people, community members, justice professionals, others?
2. What are each of their justice needs and/or obligations?
3. What do these needs/obligations suggest about the goals to be achieved in the space?
4. What do the goals suggest about the design needed to achieve them?

Post-occupancy evaluation

1. How do each of the user groups perceive and experience the space, both inside and outside?
2. In what ways does the spatial design facilitate the achievement of the identified goals? What barriers exist?
3. What design modifications can be made to improve users' experiences and facilitate the achievement of identified goals?

Note: These questions represent an evolution of restorative justice design questions, initially developed for victims (Toews, 2018).

see Designing Justice+Designing Spaces, 2014, 2015a). My research with incarcerated women invited them to create 3-D models of jail life and ideal environments in which to address their personal and interpersonal issues (Toews, 2014; Toews, 2016b). More recent work with violence survivors used Peace and Justice Cards (Designing Justice+Designing Spaces, 2015b), a collection of 104 cards with different images on each one, to explore their experiences with the design of courthouse and preferences for places of respite (Toews, 2016a). DJ+DS, now a national design firm committed to restorative justice and peacebuilding design at multiple scales, conducts all phases of design work with community constituents through a variety of design-based workshops ("Designing Justice+Designing Spaces Home," 2017).

Design characteristics

My early vision of design revolved around metaphors of sanctuary and refuge, inspired by trauma literature and the implications of those metaphors for the design of correctional facilities. Many of these design "principles" were articulated more as values or the "feelings" to be experienced by the user rather than concrete design characteristics (Table 19.2).

Van Buren offered an early typology for restorative justice design based on her architecture and design experience (Van Buren, 2009). This typology contrasts the dominant justice architecture with that of architecture influenced by restorative justice (Table 19.3).

Through our individual work, collaboration, and engagement with incarcerated individuals, victims, and community members, the understanding of restorative justice design has evolved and matured. To date, we have identified ten design characteristics, or themes: access to nature; privacy and reflection; nesting; openness; fellowship; paths and long distance views; comfortable materiality; engaged spaces; family-oriented design; and home (Cooper Hewitt, 2016; Designing Justice+Designing Spaces, 2014, 2015a, 2016, Toews, 2014, 2016a, 2016b)

Access to nature

Victims, offenders, and correctional professionals alike all express their preference for natural elements, whether that be simply having nature within sight or having opportunities for direct

Table 19.2 Features of restorative space (Toews, 2006; see also Toews, 2017)

1. Orientation towards respect, care, trust, and humility
2. Ability to be in relationship
3. Opportunities for personal healing
4. Safety
5. Meaningful opportunities for accountability
6. Concern for self-worth and personal power
7. Mutual responsibility
8. Independence, productivity, and constructiveness
9. Understanding and acceptance
10. Creativity and positivity
11. Connection to nature and spirituality
12. Responsible decision making
13. Honesty and openness
14. Kindness and love
15. Nonviolence

Table 19.3 Comparing current and restorative justice architecture (van Buren, 2009; see also Toews, 2017)

	Current justice architecture	Restorative justice architecture
Siting	Centralised: One building at a central location	Decentralised: Small centres interspersed in the community
Massing	Monolithic: Represent authority through large size, hard, singular, and domineering building materials	Individuated: Represent restoration through small size, soft, varied, and welcoming building materials
Envelope	Opaque: Restricted and highly controlled access to interior spaces, people, light, and air; no views in or out; no organic artefacts; impermeable	Transparent: Open to community, collection of flexible private and public spaces; views in and out; presence of organic artefacts; permeable
Entry	Impermeable: Access to all interior spaces through security; assumption of security need; intimidating	Porous: Access to public interior spaces before security; no assumption of security; provide security in varied and welcoming way
Planning	Specific: Specific spaces for specific functions and processes; structured for security, control, and separation	Generic: Generic spaces for a variety of functions and processes; structured for safety, relationship building, and reflection
Interior	Institutional: Impersonal and formal	Intimate: Organic, domestic, and cultural; nourishing
Room	Centre: Participants face judge, sections and separations	Periphery: Participants face each other, circles, non-hierarchical

interaction with it. Access can also come through the materiality of the space (e.g., stone facades, wood floors). The desired forms of nature demonstrate the diversity that exists in nature in itself – trees, flowers, water, fresh air, open skies, grass, wood, daylight, and animals. The presence of and access to nature serves two roles for justice stakeholders. First, participants desired the restorative, relaxing, and rejuvenating experience that comes from being in nature and the way that could assist them emotionally and psychologically as they progressed through the justice system and the aftermath of crime or provide relief to a stressful work environment. Second, nature communicated symbolically for both offenders and victims. Live plants and moving water, for instance, represent hope, life, and the ability to transform, or re-bloom, and thrive after adverse experiences, be they surviving the murder of a loved one or returning home after a period of incarceration.

Privacy and reflection

The three stakeholder groups also desire the ability to experience privacy and control their interactions with others and what people know about them. For incarcerated individuals, privacy made it possible to cope with the very public aspects of institutional life as well as release emotions, especially anger and shame, and reflect on their lives and possible changes moving forward. Victims, with few places to which to retreat during court proceedings, sought spaces hidden and separate from the public life of the courthouse, the defendant, and the unknowing public outside the courthouse. They, too, wanted to express emotions as well as limit their interactions to just those who knew their experience and could offer support. Overall, for victims and offenders, privacy offers a means through which to reconnect with one's humanity, cope with their current reality, engage in meaningful interactions, and experience support.

Nesting

Design concepts, especially those created by incarcerated individuals, contain a unique characteristic in which people are contained (nested) within a space. This containment, however, is not like that of incarceration which serves to punish, dehumanize, and segregate. Not only do these spaces reflect principles of restorative justice design but the intent is to "hold" the individual, and by extension, hold their experiences in a way that is supportive, validating, and relational. Further, the design features which mark off spaces of containment are permeable, not impenetrable like cell walls. They may be constructed with translucent walls, big windows, cosy corners in larger rooms, and spaces nested within trees. These are spaces of "communion with self" (Designing Justice+Designing Spaces, 2016: 5), even though open and accessible to the outside world. This need for nesting also practically guides the placement of rooms within a building. For instance, a room in which dialogues are to occur would be surrounded by support spaces through which dialogue participants would walk through on their way to the dialogue room.

Openness

Stakeholders' desire for privacy and nesting is complemented with a desire for openness. Practically and materially, openness is achieved through such design elements as translucent surfaces, skylights and windows, low walls and doors. These elements make it possible for individuals to see what is going on around them outside the space that they are in. Openness is also achieved through interaction with nature (e.g. views of the sky, being in or seeing large swaths of the landscape). The openness achieved in this natural context reflected an experience of freedom, perspective, and playfulness.

Fellowship

Food and places to cook and eat play prominently for all stakeholders. This desire is, in part, practical; people need to eat and need places to cook and eat. Incarcerated individuals also expressed a desire to grow food and be involved in its growth. More importantly, however, this desire for food relates to a desire for relationships, fellowship, and breaking bread together. Victims, for instance, suggested a need for a type of fellowship as respite from court proceedings, especially fellowship centred around family relationships and the support experienced within them.

Paths and long distance views

Both victims and incarcerated individuals expressed a desire for long distance views (e.g. into the horizon) and paths, with a strong preference for these to occur within a natural environment. Physiologically, long distance views have been shown to facilitate attention restoration when an individual becomes fatigued (Kaplan, 1995), a restoration which could benefit anyone involved in justice proceedings or coping with an adverse situation. Stakeholders, especially victims, suggest a psychological impact, as well. Paths provide the experience of forward movement, which symbolically represent the individual's own emotional, physical, and spiritual forward, albeit likely circuitous, movement in the aftermath of the crime and justice process. The line of sight towards a horizon offers a future destination, even if it is not yet clear. As such, these paths and long distance views have the potential to offer a sense of hope for a better future.

Comfortable materiality

Stakeholders seek furniture, accessories, and colours that comfort and calm. This may be the couch that one just flops into, fuzzy pillows on a bed, or the soft petals of a flower. This comfort also shows up in worn surfaces (e.g. a wood floor showing years of being walked on or fabric that has been softened and faded with use). The narrative accompanying this attraction for worn surfaces and textures spoke to the way that patterns of wear demonstrated that an object could withstand the test of time, offering hope that a violence survivor could do the same.

Engaged spaces

Stakeholders desire spaces that are active and show signs of creativity and life. This is most evident in the entry ways of buildings, which are often seen as sterile and experienced as anxiety-producing. In one design workshop, community members created lobbies that contained day cares, libraries, gardens, and art spaces. They imagined themselves being made to feel welcome by greeters.

Flexible design

Design concepts and preferences consistently reflect the need for flexibility at the building and room scales, as well as in furnishings. There need to be spaces for individual, interpersonal, small and large group work and furniture to accommodate different numbers of people and meeting configurations. Rooms can serve different purposes – one time, hosting a victim offender dialogue consisting of 4–6 people and, at another time, an art class for 15. Such adaptable requires flexible floor plans.

Family-oriented design

Stakeholders wish to spend time with their families, including their children. For incarcerated individuals, this desire for family is to be expected given their isolation from these relationships. Victims also desired such relationships, especially for the support they offered. Victims, especially, spoke to how their children are impacted by crime and their desire for spaces where the children can play and receive care and support while, for instance, the adults attend court. Such child spaces relieved the emotional burden of worrying about the child and the financial burden of having to pay for childcare while attending justice related meetings and hearings. At the same time, some parents received solace from their children and having them in close proximity made it possible to see their child throughout justice proceedings.

Home

Design concepts frequently included the rooms, furnishings, and amenities of a house (e.g. beds, couches, living rooms, and kitchens). While practical, these features represented feelings of home. They communicated experiences of welcome, letting one's hair down, and being able to breathe. In many respects, restorative justice design culminates in this idea of "home," or "haven" as a violence survivor referred to it. It is not just a building; rather, it is that place where you can both deal with and get relief from chaos, uncertainty, and conflict. It is where you receive support and experience hope and possibility, even in the bleakest of moments.

These design characteristics are not mutually exclusive nor all that surprising. What is unique, however, is their consideration within the justice system and their application to the spaces in which justice occurs. Ongoing research and design work will further expand and clarify these design elements and contribute new understandings, as more people become involved in design processes. As this work has largely been done in the U.S., with one study conducted in Canada, these design elements may not generalize to other contexts or cultures. Any restorative design requires cultural humility and openness to the different ways in which culture influences how we understand and experience space and what constitutes meaningful design.

Exemplars

Much like restorative justice itself, restorative justice design exists on a continuum. One end of the continuum represents those spaces in which restorative design elements are ad hoc, coexisting with punitive or non-salutogenic goals and design elements. The ICIW natural landscape provides an example of this type of restorative justice design. At the other end are those spaces intentionally oriented towards restorative justice goals, use a restorative justice design process, and comprehensively include restorative justice design elements in the final built environment, including those preferred by stakeholders. Examples of these types of designs are presented next. In the middle resides those spaces which straddle the extremes by, for instance, designing to meet both punitive and restorative justice goals while involving stakeholders at various stages of the design process. The Johnson County Youth and Family Services Center is one such facility. This facility was designed and constructed with an intentional grounding in trauma and restorative justice philosophies, giving way to furnishings, art installations, and materiality that would address the developmental and justice needs of young offenders (Huskie, 2014, 2015). Candace House (Winnipeg, Manitoba, Canada), which seeks to provide a "comfortable, safe oasis" in which a victim could experience nourishment and encouragement away from the courthouse (Candace House, 2015), uses the environment to meet victim needs. Interviews and focus groups with violence survivors, Candace House representatives, and community partners solicited design input which is currently being used in the renovation of their newly purchased building (Toews, 2016a)

Two Designing Justice+Designing Spaces-affiliated projects exemplify designs that exist at the more comprehensive end of the design continuum – Near Westside Peacemaking Program and Restorative Justice City.

Near Westside Peacemaking Program

The Near Westside Peacemaking Program in Syracuse, NY, one of two peacemaking projects facilitated by the Center for Court Innovation, represents one of the first times that a peacemaking/restorative justice programme and the spaces in which that programme would occur were simultaneously designed, drawing on restorative justice principles and values. DJ+DS, with project collaborators, facilitated three two-hour community engagement design workshops, soliciting design input from 40 community participants. Prior to the workshop, participants were asked to bring with them an object, image, or material that represented a place of repair (vs. punishment), calm, and well-being. Van Buren began the workshop with a three-round circle process to solicit initial design information, using three prompts: Round (1) What values does your current justice architecture communicate?; Round (2) How are these values represented? and Round (3) Share a story about the image/object/material that you brought with you. The objects, forming a "peacemaking palette," "described the tactile and spatial qualities of nourishing and peaceful places in their lives" (Designing Justice+Designing Spaces, 2016: 3) Following the circle, participants diagrammed how a peacemaking centre would look, through the perspective of a victim, offender, and community member. Through this activity, participants visualized the placement of natural elements, meeting rooms, private and public spaces, and community resources, among other spatial features. The design characteristics that emerged through these activities, incorporated into the themes mentioned earlier, were published in a community engagement report which provided guidance for the design of the peacemaking centre (Designing Justice+Designing Spaces, 2016). An evaluation is current being planned, using the post-occupancy questions in Table 19.1.

Restorative Justice City

Concern for design extends beyond just those spaces for interpersonal and community-level processes. As evidenced by the research completed by The Spatial Design Information Lab discussed earlier, urban design and social and criminal justice intersect for the way design may marginalize and disadvantage already marginalized and disadvantaged groups of individuals. This intersection opens the possibility for urban design informed by restorative justice. Designing Justice+Designing Spaces is leading the way in this type of design through their development of the "restorative justice city", which integrates social and restorative justice in the design of the urban landscape and infrastructure. Inspired by Van Ness's vision for a restorative justice city (Van Ness and Strong, 2015), the recurring deaths of African American men at the hands of police, and the Black Lives Matter movement, DJ+DS aims to use the criminal justice infrastructure as a catalyst for exploring social injustice within urban centres and re-envisioning and rebuilding the urban infrastructure so that it promotes peace and equity. They do this by conducting data analysis to understand community issues and working with community partners and citizens to redesign the infrastructure in order to address those issues. Their work revolves around seven social justice domains (Table 19.4) (Designing Justice+Designing Spaces, 2017a).

Table 19.4 Restorative justice city paradigm (Designing Justice+Designing Space, 2017a, 2017b)

Shift from	Shift to	Proposed action
Individual orientation	Community orientation	Decentralize justice spaces and embed them in community spaces; involve community elders in interventions
Food desert	Food sovereignty	Increase access to healthy and affordable food; facilitate collaboration between food sovereignty and restorative justice advocates
Shouting	Listening	Facilitate dialogues through face-to-face meetings and use technological and art approaches when meetings are not possible or desired
Mistrust	Positive contact	Merge restorative justice processes with criminal justice ones and reform existing processes/structures to be restorative
Breaking the city	Healing the city	Use evidence-based design to transform justice and community spaces to lead to healthier outcomes
Just surviving	Being your best self	Co-create community services with those who will use the services; prioritize access to services as opposed to policing community
Environmental wasteland	Environmental justice	Use biophilic architecture and bring the natural wilderness into the concrete jungle

This introduction of social justice into the vision for a restorative justice city contributes to an intentional and comprehensive design vision that highlights the intersectionality between interpersonal, social, and criminal harms, justice, and prevention. Response to harm requires infrastructure to address the personal, interpersonal, and social/structural needs within the community. They are currently selecting a US city in which to pilot the Restorative Justice City process (Designing Justice+Designing Spaces, 2017b).

Conclusion

Restorative justice, as a new philosophical approach to justice that introduces new justice practices, requires a re-envisioning of our current justice architecture and design (Van Buren, 2009). This new restorative justice architecture and design seeks to create spaces that support the practices that occur within them by offering flexible and open spaces that accommodate processes involving small and large groups and public and private experiences. The design of these spaces may also enhance the justice experiences of victims, offenders, and community members, given the intersections between design characteristics and designs that facilitate health and well-being. Because justice stakeholders are treated as experts of their environmental needs and invited to actively engage in envisioning restorative justice designs, this transformative and restorative experience may even begin with the design process itself. Design carries the potential to be a new restorative justice practice.

Future work is necessary to fully conceptualize and evaluate the impact of restorative justice architecture and design, work ideally done with global collaboration. Examples exist worldwide of designs that are consistent with the restorative justice design principles introduced here. The Constitutional Court of South Africa, for example, built after the end of Apartheid, is "an invitation to newness and change. Whereas courts usually are known to be private and daunting, the Constitutional Court is happy, inclusive and open. One feels a participant here" (Law-Viljoen, B., 2006: 28). This newness, inspired by democracy, freedom, and transparency, evidences itself architecturally with glass windows, walls, and doors; views to the outside; passages connecting internal and external spaces; places of quiet retreat and public gathering; numerous gardens, courtyards, and nature imagery (Law-Viljoen, B., 2006). The Fambul Tok, a community peace and reconciliation process in Sierra Leone, occurs around a bonfire and follow-up activities include the selection and planting of a peace tree, around which community members gather for leisure, business, and conflict resolution ("How Fambul Tok works," 2017). The Norwegian prisons, Halden and Bastoy, offer designs that represent villages, with ready access to nature and outdoor activities and house-like settings, including dormitory-like rooms, common kitchens, and living spaces (Adams, 2010; James, 2013). We, in the US context, can learn much from these other settings and what it means to design spaces (and public policy) geared towards restorative and peace.

Victims, offenders, and community members live at the heart of restorative justice design and architecture. The men who created the do-no-harm room, introduced at the beginning of the chapter, only imagined what such a restorative space would look like. Through mindful consideration of what justice spaces look like and collaboration with justice stakeholders, designers, and architects, their vision and that of victims can become a reality.

References

Adams, W. 2010. Norway Builds the World's Most Humane Prison, *Time*, 10 May.
Amstutz, L.S. 2009. *The Little Book of Victim Offender Conferencing: Bringing Victims and Offenders Together in Dialogue*. Intercourse, PA: Good Books.

Anderson Hooker, D. 2016. *The Little Book of Transformative Community Conferencing*. New York: Good Books.

Barron, T. 2015. Iowa State Landscape Architecture Students Win National Award for Women's Prison Project, *Iowa State University News Service*. Available at www.news.iastate.edu/news/2015/09/30/iciw-asla

Bierie, D. 2012. The Impact of Prison Conditions on Staff Well-Being, *International Journal of Offender Therapy and Comparative Criminology*, 56(1): 81–95.

Bratman, G.N., Daily, G.C., Levy, B.J. and Gross, J.J. 2015. The Benefits of Nature Experience: Improved Affect and Cognition, *Landscape and Urban Planning*, 138: 41–50.

Candace House. 2015. Why We Do It. Available at www.candacehouse.net/whywedoit/

Carey, P. and Lowney, L. 2015. *Separate and Secure Waiting Area Task Force: Implementation Progress Report* (Prepared for Massachusetts Legislature). Boston, MA: Executive Office of the Trial Court.

Cooper, Hewitt. 2016. *By the People: Designing a Better America*. New York: Cooper Hewitt, Smithsonian Design Museum.

Cipriani, J., Benz, A., Holmgren, A., Kinter, D., McGarry, J. and Rufino, G. 2017. A Systematic Review of the Effects of Horticultural Therapy on Persons with Mental Health Conditions, *Occupational Therapy in Mental Health*, 33(1): 47–69.

Deming, E. 2015. *Values in Landscape Architecture and Environmental Design: Finding Center in Theory and Practice*. Baton Rouge, LA: LSU Press.

Denof, M., Spinaris, C. and Morton, G. 2014. *Occupational Stressors in Corrections Organizations: Types, Effects, and Solutions*. Washington, DC: National Institute of Corrections, U.S. Department of Justice.

Designing Justice+Designing Spaces. 2014. *Designing from the Inside Out: San Bruno Jail Workshop*. Oakland, CA: Designing Justice+Designing Spaces.

Designing Justice+Designing Spaces. 2015a. *Designing from the Inside Out: Santa Rita Jail Workshop*. Oakland, CA: Designing Justice+Designing Spaces.

Designing Justice+Designing Spaces. 2015b. *Designing Justice+Designing Spaces Toolkit*. Oakland, CA: Designing Justice+Designing Spaces.

Designing Justice+Designing Spaces. 2016. *Community Engagement Report: Near Westside Peacemaking Project*. Oakland, CA: Designing Justice+Designing Spaces.

Designing Justice+Designing Spaces. 2017a. Restorative Justice City. Available at http://designingjustice.org/restorative-justice-city/

Designing Justice+Designing Spaces. 2017b. *The Restorative Justice City Project*. Oakland, CA: Designing Justice+Designing Spaces.

Designing Justice+Designing Spaces Home. 2017. Available at http://designingjustice.org. Accessed 6 December 2017.

Farbstein, J., Farling, M. and Wener, R. 2012. Developing the Evidence for Evidence-Based Design, *Correctional News*. Available at www.correctionalnews.com/articles/2012/08/9/research-report-developing-the-evidence-evidence-based-design

Ferdick, F. and Smith, H. 2017. *Correctional Officer Safety and Wellness Literature Synthesis*. Washington, DC: Office of Justice Programs, US Department of Justice. Available at www.ncjrs.gov/pdffiles1/nij/250484.pdf

Findley, L. 2005. *Building Change: Architecture, Politics and Cultural Agency*. London: Psychology Press.

Gamman, L. and Thorpe, A. 2015. Could Design Help to Promote and Build Empathic Processes in Prison? Understanding the Role of Empathy and Design in Catalyzing Social Change and Transformation. In W. Jonas, S. Zerwas and K. von Amshelm (eds.) *Transformation Design: Perspectives on a New Design Attitude*. Basel, Switzerland: Birkhäuser, pp. 83–100.

Genter, C., Roberts, A., Richardson, J. and Sheaff, M. 2015. The Contribution of Allotment Gardening to Health and Wellbeing: A Systematic Review of the Literature, *British Journal of Occupational Therapy*, 78(10): 593–605.

Greene, F. 2006. The Image of the Courthouse. In S. Flanders (ed.) *Celebrating the Courthouse: A Guide for Architects, Their Clients, and the Public*. New York: W.W. Norton and Company, pp. 63–80.

How Fambul Tok Works. 2017. Available at www.fambultok.org/what-is-fambul-tok/our-process#ceremony

Huskie, B. 2014. Healing Designs Promote Better Overall Health for Youth, *Correctional News*, May–June: 34. Available at http://home.huskey-associates.com

Huskie, B. 2015. Trauma-Informed Juvenile Facilities: The Next Generation of Care, *Academy of Architecture for Justice Journal*, March: 1–3.

James, E. 2013. The Norwegian Prison Where Inmates are Treated Like People, *The Guardian*, 24 February.

Johnston, N. 2000. *Forms of Constraint: A History of Prison Architecture*. Chicago: University of Illinois Press.

Kaplan, S. 1995. The Restorative Benefits of Nature: Toward an Integrative Framework, *Journal of Environmental Psychology*, 15: 169–182. Available at https://doi.org/10.1016/0272-4944(95)90001-2

Kaplan, S. and Kaplan, R. 2003. Health, Supportive Environments, and the Reasonable Person Model, *American Journal of Public Health*, 93(9): 1484–1489.

Knight, C. 2014. *Emotional Literacy in Criminal Justice: Professional Practice with Offenders*. New York: Springer. Available at https://books.google.com/books?hl=en&lr=&id=TCvFAgAAQBAJ&oi=fnd&pg=PP1&dq=knight+emotional+literacy&ots=VCpdscvXD5&sig=tNj8adJgz1M_8kfj7_9-YCuoHdc

Law-Viljoen, B. 2006. *Light on a hill: Building the Constitutional Court of South Africa*. Parkwood, South Africa: David Krut Publishing.

Leavy, P. 2009. *Method Meets Art: Arts-Based Research Practice*. New York: Guilford Press.

Lygum, V., Stigsdotter, U., Konijnendijk, C. and Hojberg, H. 2012. Outdoor Environments at Crisis Shelters in Denmark, *Journal of Therapeutic Horticulture*, 23(22): 8–21.

Lygum, V., Stigsdotter, U., Konijnendijk, C. and Hojberg, H. 2013. Outdoor Environments at Crisis Shelters: User Needs and Preferences with Respect to Design and Activities, *International Journal of Architectural Research*, 7(1): 21–36.

MacRae, A. and Zehr, H. 2004. *The Little Book of Family Group Conferencing New Zealand Style*. Intercourse, PA: Good Books.

Malchiodi, C., ed. 2003. *Handbook on Art Therapy*. New York: Guilford Press.

Missingham, G. 2003. *User-Friendliness in the Public Realm: Architectural Psychology and Courts Facilities in Perth* (Prepared for the Department of Justice Western Australia). Melbourne: University of Melbourne.

Mulcahy, L. 2010. *Legal Architecture: Justice, Due Process and the Place of Law*. London: Routledge.

Oregon Youth Authority. 2016. *Nature Imagery in Prisons Project at the Oregon Department of Corrections*. Salem, OR: Oregon Youth Authority. Available at www.oregon.gov/oya/research/ResearchBrief-NatureImageryPrisonsProject.pdf

Pranis, K. 2004. *The Little Book of Circle Processes: A New/Old Approach to Peacemaking*. Intercourse, PA: Good Books.

Pranis, K. 2007. Restorative Values. In G. Johnstone and D. Van Ness (eds.) *Handbook of Restorative Justice*. Devon: Willan, pp. 59–74.

Refuerzo, B.J. and Verderber, S. 1989. Effects of Personal Status and Patterns of Use on Residential Satisfaction in Shelters for Victims of Domestic Violence, *Environment and Behavior*, 21(4): 413–434.

Refuerzo, B.J. and Verderber, S. 1993. In Support of a New Life: A Shelter for Victims of Domestic Violence, *Journal of Architectural and Planning Research*, 10(1): 40–58.

Sherman, L. and Strang, H. 2007. *Restorative Justice: The Evidence*. London: The Smith Institute.

Spatial Information Design Lab. 2008. *The Pattern: Million Dollar Blocks*. New York: Columbia University. Available at www.spatialinformationdesignlab.org/publications.php

Steiner, B. and Wooldredge, J. 2016. Individual and Environmental Influences on Prison Officer Safety, *Justice Quarterly*, 1–26.

Strang, H., Sherman, L., Mayo-Wilson, E., Woods, D. and Ariel, B. 2013. *Restorative Justice Conferencing (RJC) Using Face-to-Face Meetings of Offenders and Victims: Effects on Offender Recidivism and Victim Satisfaction: A Systematic Review*. (No. 12). Campbell Systematic Reviews.

Toews, B. 2006. *The Little Book of Restorative Justice for People in Prison: Rebuilding the Web of Relationships*. Intercourse, PA: Good Books.

Toews, B. 2014. *'Prospering in the trees': The Meaning of Privacy for Incarcerated Women*. Doctoral Dissertation.

Toews, B. 2016a. *Candace House: A Nourishing Haven: Report on the Ideas for the Design of Candace House*. Tacoma, WA: University of Washington Tacoma.

Toews, B. 2016b. This Backyard Is My Serenity Place: Learning from Incarcerated Women About the Architecture and Design of Restorative Justice, *Restorative Justice*, 4(2): 214–236.

Toews, B. and Harris, M.K. 2010. Restorative justice in prison. In E. Beck, N. Kropf and P. Leonard (eds.) *Social Work and Restorative Justice: Skills for Dialogue, Peacemaking, and Reconciliation*. Oxford: Oxford University Press, pp. 118–148.

Ulrich, R., Zimring, C., Zhu, X., DuBose, J., Hyun-Bo, S., Choi, Y.-S., . . . Anjali, J. 2008. A Review of the Research Literature on Evidence-Based Healthcare Design, *Health Environments Research and Design Journal*, 1(3): 61–125. Available at www.herdjournal.com/article/review – research – literature – evidence – based – healthcare – design

Van Buren, D. 2009. Restorative Justice Design: Developing New Typologies for Social Change. Unpublished manuscript.

van den Berg, A.E., Maas, J., Verheij, R.A. and Groenewegen, P. 2010. Green Space as a Buffer Between Stressful Life Events and Health, *Social Science & Medicine*, 70(8): 1203–1210.

van der Linden, S. 2015. Green Prison Programmes, Recidivism and Mental Health: A Primer, *Criminal Behaviour and Mental Health*, 25(5): 338–342.

Van Ness, D. and Strong, K. 2015. *Restoring Justice: An Introduction to Restorative Justice*, 5th ed. Waltham, MA: Anderson Publishing.

Verderber, S. 2001. Recent Trends in the Design of Shelters for Victims of Domestic Violence, *Loyola Law Review*, 47: 457–470.

Wagenfeld, A., Stevens, J., Toews, B., Jarzembowski, S., Ladjahasan, N., Stewart, J. and Raddatz, C. 2017. Addressing Correctional Staff Stress Through Interaction with Nature: A New Role for Occupational Therapy, *Occupational Therapy in Mental Health*. https://doi.org/10.1080/0164212X.2017.1385435.

Wang, D. and MacMillan, T. 2013. The Benefits of Gardening for Older Adults: A Systematic Review of the Literature, *Activities, Adaptation & Aging*, 37(2): 153–181. https://doi.org/10.1080/01924788.2013.784942

Wener, R. 2012. *The Environmental Psychology of Prisons and Jail: Creating Humane Spaces in Secure Settings*. New York: Cambridge University Press.

West, M. 1986. Landscape Views and Stress Response in the Prison Environment. Master thesis, University of Washington, Seattle.

YWCA of Pierce County. 2017. Emergency Shelter. Available at www.ywcapiercecounty.org/emergency-shelter

Zehr, H. 2015. *Changing Lenses: Restorative Justice for Our Times, 25th Anniversary Edition*. Newton, KS: Herald Press.

Part III
Thinking critically about restorative justice

20

Restorative justice in Chinese communities

Cultural-specific skills and challenges

Dennis S.W. Wong and Wendy C.Y. Lui[1]

Restorative justice (RJ) has gained significant recognition worldwide in recent decades. It is believed that RJ can provide opportunities for victims, offenders, and their supporters to voice their feelings and enable offenders to repair the harm to victims and related stakeholders (Bazemore and Umbreit, 1997; Boriboonthana and Sangbuangamlum, 2013; Johnstone, 2002; Liebmann, 2007; Maxwell, 2007; Presser and Van Voorhis, 2002; Van Ness and Strong, 2006; Walgrave, 2002; Zehr, 1990).

Over the past few decades, programmes based on the principles of RJ have been developed in response to the failures of traditional justice, which could not satisfy victims or reduce re-offending. We observed different methods of RJ practices developed to help offenders, especially juvenile delinquents, take responsibility for their criminal acts and appropriately repair the consequences of their actions (Chan, 2013; Johnstone and Van Ness, 2007; Lo et al., 2006; Maxwell and Morris, 1993; Van Wormer and Walker, 2013; Ward et al., 2014). In the youth services and education sector, we saw scholars integrating restorative practices into school settings, for example, by adopting RJ to handle cases of school bullying (Hopkins, 2004; Morrison, 2007, 2015; Wong et al., 2010).

In the Greater China region, including jurisdictions such as Hong Kong, Taiwan, and Mainland China, RJ has become a topic of interest among academics, social workers, criminal justice professionals, and governments over the last two decades. RJ is conceptualised as a new approach to crime prevention, victim support, and crime control. It is also assumed that the RJ process may empower crime victims, offenders, and communities to actively participate in resolving the impacts of crime in various Chinese communities (Berti, 2016; Di and Wu, 2009; Shi, 2008; Mok and Wong, 2013; Wong, 2016). This chapter first highlights recent developments in RJ in three jurisdictions in the Greater China region. To illustrate the healing impacts and skills application of RJ on adolescents, the chapter further describes how RJ can be applied to two cases.

Cultural-specific skills for the successful use of RJ in Chinese communities are analysed. It is noted from the case analyses that a wide range of traditional cultural values are in play during

1 The Research Grants Council of Hong Kong provided a grant to support this study (Project number: CityU/11409214).

a RJ conference. A careful plan to balance the power among decision makers and to adopt a multilayer conferencing approach might be a way to prevent the hierarchical dominance deeply rooted in the Chinese cultural context. With a clear description of RJ practices in each jurisdiction, readers may discover that there have been various innovative restorative practices in the Greater China region which are somewhat on par with the innovative RJ programmes operated in other locations. Literature on RJ in the Chinese language published in the region is abundant (Wong, 2016). Nevertheless, there are very few publications in the English language about Chinese RJ, and this chapter will represent a valuable addition to the growing literature.

Mainland China

Given the long history of mediation in Chinese communities, RJ has a broader meaning in China than in Western countries. It may include any form of alternative dispute resolution, alternatives to prosecution or sentencing, and community reintegration programmes. Practices related to RJ have been pioneered at various levels of the criminal justice system, including at the pre-court, during-court, and post-court levels in recent years. In Mainland China, RJ is currently connected with the arrangement of various disposals or measures, including RJ programmes for youth delinquents with conditional non-prosecution and those with suspended sentences, as well as RJ in the forms of people's mediation under People's Mediation Committees, judicial mediation, and criminal mediation (Wong, 2016).

Some developed provinces and cities have been aware of the benefits of RJ in treating delinquents for more than 15 years. Between 2001 and 2010, various RJ programmes for delinquents were pioneered under the mechanisms of suspended prosecution[2] or suspended sentences (Di and Cha, 2007; Dong, 2012; He, 2012; Shen and Zou, 2010; Yao, 2007; Zhai, 2011). For instance, RJ programmes such as Victim-Offender Mediation (VOM) and Victim-Offender Reconciliation (VOR) were used as additional measures in connection with suspended prosecution for diverting delinquents from formal criminal prosecution, or as additional conditions for rehabilitating offenders in connection with the use of suspended sentences (Shen and Antonopoulos, 2013; Wong and Mok, 2013; Wong, 2016). With the endorsement of the revised Criminal Procedure Law (CPL) in March 2012 (National People's Congress, 2012), RJ was formally recognised as an outcome-based and predisposal measure for rehabilitating youth offenders in China (Shen and Antonopoulos, 2013). In the revised CPL, conditional non-prosecution measures are encouraged for treating juvenile suspects who committed certain types of offences. The People's Procuratorate (Prosecutor's Office) is the organ responsible for administering the CPL. Chapter 2 of the Special Provision of the revised CPL clearly stipulates the use of criminal reconciliation and the duties of the convened administrative departments when a criminal suspect or defendant has shown true repentance and obtained victims' forgiveness through reconciliation. Apparently, the revised CPL endorses the new joint venture of conditional non-prosecution alongside criminal reconciliation. This formal recognition indicates that Western RJ practices are now generally welcomed in China (Di and Cha, 2007; Shen and Zou, 2010; Yao, 2007).

Since the formal endorsement of using RJ for young offenders, its introduction has been complimented, and recommendations to further improve the mechanism have been made (Li, 2014; Wei and Zhang, 2015; Yao, 2016; Wei, 2015; Research Group of Southwest University of Finance and Economics, 2016). Most literature focuses on refining the law or integrating RJ

---

2 'Suspended prosecution' has been renamed 'conditional non-prosecution' in the 2012 Criminal Procedural Law.

into the current criminal justice system, while discussions on the actual operation of cases are lacking. Empirical studies on the effectiveness of RJ practices in China are not readily available (Shen and Antonopoulos, 2013; Wong, 2016).

Taiwan

RJ came to prominence in Taiwan in the late 1990s. The Ministry of Justice (MOJ) established a committee to review criminal policy in 1997. In 1999, a White Book (Paper) on Prosecution Reform was published in response to growing problems in the justice sectors, such as an increase in serious crimes, constraints on judicial resources, and overloaded prisons (Ministry of Justice, 1999). To tackle these issues, a non-adversarial approach combined with the principles of both punishment and leniency was introduced. Mediation, deferred prosecution, and probation were recommended for offenders who committed minor offences (Huang and Chang, 2013). Since 2008, the MOJ has adopted RJ as its priority policy of criminal justice reform. Before the law reform, the government formally announced in 2010 a pioneer programme entitled the 'Restorative Justice Initiative' (RJI), which was conducted at the District Prosecutor Offices. Under existing criminal procedures in Taiwan, prosecutors are encouraged to adopt VOM to resolve disputes between conflicting parties before the case formally goes to trial in court. For this initiative, when victims and offenders participate in the RJ process, the proceeding of their criminal cases is not suspended. Based on existing legal mechanisms, including civil mediation, deferred prosecution, and plea-bargaining, once both parties reach an agreement, it cannot be sustained by law or taken as an important reference in criminal proceedings (Ministry of Justice, 2016: 27).

Since the announcement of the new initiative, a two-year pilot programme from September 2010 to August 2012 was first implemented in eight District Prosecutor Offices. In September 2012, the RJI programme was fully implemented in different parts of Taiwan, and continues today. The first author of this chapter was engaged in the pilot programme as a consultant and trainer on RJ practice (Wong, 2014). On behalf of the Centre for Restoration of Human Relationships, a non-governmental organisation (NGO) in Hong Kong that provides RJ training in the Greater China region, Wong and his associates were invited by the MOJ to train the first few teams of facilitators in Taiwan from 2009 to 2012. More than 300 participants with different backgrounds, including criminal justice personnel, psychologists, teachers, and social work professionals, were trained as certified facilitators through the pilot RJ system. The RJ operational manual and RJ handbook were subsequently developed (Ministry of Justice, 2016; Taichung District Prosecutor's Office, 2016). Based on these earlier efforts and good practices, the RJI programme was welcomed by the public.

By the end of December 2015, 1,254 cases had been referred from various sources to the RJI (see Table 20.1). Of the 1,254 cases, the Prosecutor Offices considered 1,086 (i.e. 87%) to

Table 20.1 Implementation of RJ in the cooperating District Prosecutors Offices from December 2010 to December 2015 in Taiwan

Items	Total (A = B + C)	Dropped Cases (B)	Accepted cases (C = D + I)	Finalised cases (D = E + H)		Withdrawn (H)	Being processed (I)
				Dialogue (E = F + G) 548			
				Agreement (F)	No agreement (G)		
Total	1254	168	1086	395	153	480	58

Source: Table extracted from Ministry of Justice (2016), p. 31

match the criteria for mediation after the initial assessments. Of these 1,086 cases, 548 (51%) entered into the final stage of dialogue. Of the 548 finalised cases, 395 (72%) were settled through an agreement, and 153 (28%) were closed without agreement. The Prosecutor Offices in individual districts have the freedom to select the types of cases to handle, although minor offense and juvenile crime cases are prioritised. By the end of December 2015, the types of cases that proceeded to the RJI were primarily offences related to the following: 'causing injury' (21%), 'domestic violence' (10%), 'negligently causing injury while performing occupational duties or activities' (10%), 'against sexual autonomy' (7%), 'manslaughter' (7%), 'against reputation' (6%), 'larceny' (6%), and 'against abandonment' (5%) (Ministry of Justice, 2016: 32).

Empirical surveys on the effectiveness of the RJ programmes in all districts are not available. However, based on a study of selected samples of participants, we do have a preliminary idea about the effectiveness of the pilot RJ project. The survey report published by the National Taipei University noted 388 qualified RJ cases in the period between September 2010 and May 2013. The research team sampled 40% (i.e. 158 cases) of the qualified cases for this study. For the 158 cases, 156 valid questionnaires were collected. The results indicated that RJ meetings were able to restore the psychological and tangible harm caused by offending behaviours. Nevertheless, it is a pity that no further information is available on whether RJ is more effective (or not) for juvenile cases than in others (Huang et al., 2014).

Hong Kong

Unlike Taiwan and Mainland China, the criminal justice system in Hong Kong is inherited from the British, as Hong Kong was a British colony before 1997. The minimum age of criminal responsibility remained at seven years from the late 1930s to 2003. In July 2003, the age was raised to ten. Various statutory measures exist to handle youth offenders such as police cautioning, community-based treatment options, and custodial sentencing. Nevertheless, no statutory restorative measure has yet been incorporated into the mainstream juvenile justice system in Hong Kong. However, NGOs endeavoured to develop innovative strategies to prevent misbehaving adolescents from delinquency and are willing to use restorative practices to desist delinquents from a criminal career.

In 2002, as attention on the use of RJ to handle juvenile offenders increased in many parts of the world, the decision of whether to implement the practice in Hong Kong eventually became a concern for the Hong Kong Government (Lo et al., 2003). A research team was formed that year to investigate whether the minimum age of criminal responsibility should be revised and whether alternative measures for treating juvenile offenders should be developed. As the samples of the study, the research team identified six jurisdictions representing various alternative practices in the juvenile justice system. The first author of this chapter was a member of the research team. In submitting the report to the Government, we proposed a number of pre-court restorative options, including the use of family group conferences for developing restorative plans to respond to juvenile offending (Lo et al., 2003). Despite these endeavours, the Hong Kong Government rejected our recommendations. Until today, a statutory RJ option has not been formally incorporated into the mainstream criminal justice system in Hong Kong.

However, over the past 15 years, many NGOs have worked hard to practice RJ outside the mainstream criminal justice system. For example, the Centre for Restoration of Human Relationships (CRHR) has practiced RJ since 2000. The CRHR is the most well known NGO to openly advocate RJ for juvenile delinquents in Hong Kong since the early 2000s. The first author of the chapter is the founding director of the CRHR. From 2001 to 2006, the CRHR trained teachers and social workers from 50 schools on how to adopt the Restorative Whole

School Approach (RWSA) to tackle the problem of bullying in Hong Kong (Wong, 2006). A longitudinal study confirmed the RWSA as a useful approach to decrease bullying behaviours in secondary schools (Wong et al., 2011). Over the years, the CRHR has contributed to training RJ conference facilitators in the Greater China region, and the centre has conducted at least 100 VOM or family group conferences since 2007. Most cases were evaluated as successful in terms of high participation and high satisfaction rates (Wong and Lo, 2011; Wong et al., 2012).

The Evangelical Lutheran Church Social Service Hong Kong (ELCSSHK) and the Methodist Centre (MC), an NGO in Hong Kong, also experimented with restorative practices for police-cautioned juveniles in 2004 and 2005. Modelled on restorative conferencing practices outside Hong Kong, social workers from the two organisations launched post-cautioning VOM for juveniles, victims, their family members, or supporters. A report on the evaluation of the ELCSSHK's services indicated that 37 of the 39 participants were highly satisfied with the results of the mediation. Juveniles who underwent the VOM admitted that they seemed to better understand their own faults and victims' feelings. All offenders agreed to make reparations for the victims voluntarily and are willing to restore relationships with the victims as well, as indicated in the evaluative study. The study concluded that juvenile offenders were reintegrated into the community and continued on to a normal life (Ho et al., 2007; Evangelical Lutheran Church Social Service Hong Kong, 2017). Similarly, since 2007, the MC has provided mediation services for juvenile offenders under the PSDS. The MC conducted research to capture the service impacts of the programme, finding positive results. For example, the results showed that nearly 70% of the offenders were willing to participate in the mediation, genuinely showed remorse, and apologised to the victims (The Methodist Centre, 2017). In the following section, through cases in a school and police setting, we identify useful skills applicable to delinquents and their families in Chinese communities.

Case illustration

Case 1: The Booger Boy case

This case pertains to two chubby boys, Frankie and Bobby, who were good friends and attended the same school. One day during recess, Bobby joined Frankie and his friends as usual. However, what happened next was not as usual. Instead of welcoming him as a friend, Bobby heard Frankie say, 'Stay away from Bobby!' Bobby wanted to play with his friends, and was angry about what Frankie had said, pushing him. Frankie fell back and grabbed Bobby's hands for balance. They both lost their balance and fell to the ground. Bobby's heavy body landed on top of Frankie, whose arm was badly injured. Feeling the excruciating pain surging through his arm, Frankie could not stand up. He was rushed to hospital afterwards for surgery on his arm, and needed stitches 10 inches long. He was hospitalised, and had a cast on his arm for some time before fully recovering. The case was initially referred to the school's social worker. As Bobby regretted his actions, he apologised instantaneously. Frankie, as a close friend, accepted. As far as the social worker was concerned, the case was closed. One thing left unresolved was the compensation Frankie's mother had asked for, although Bobby's mother could not afford to pay the amount.

During the RJ conference, it transpired that Frankie told his friends not to get close to Bobby because he saw Bobby pick his nose without cleaning his hands. Frankie did not intend to isolate Bobby from the group of friends. During the mediation, Frankie came to understand that Bobby was frightened of having no friends to play with, and his words were a huge blow, which triggered his reaction. Regarding the compensation, Frankie's mother initially asked for

$10,000, but Bobby's mother could only afford $3,000. During the process, the families' backgrounds were revealed, and each family heard about the other family's difficulties. Frankie's mother could not settle on a lesser amount because of pressure from her husband and mother-in-law. Their real concern was the need to witness a sign of regret from Bobby, who hurt the only male child in the family. Frankie's mother also came to understand that Frankie had said something that triggered the unintended fight. She also now knew more about the financial difficulties faced by Bobby's family. Bobby's father is the only breadwinner, and he must take care of seven family members, including older parents. Bobby's mother experienced depression after the accident and was sorry that they were not able to provide greater restitution to Frankie's family. With this understanding, the parties were willing to settle on terms that were mainly non-monetary in nature.

Factors underlying the success of RJ

Knowing that salient Chinese values such as 'filial piety', 'respect for parents', and 'family hierarchy' are still highly respected by most Chinese individuals, the facilitator strategically arranged separate meetings where issues pertaining to the peer relationship were first handled, and issues pertaining to compensation and face-saving between the adults were handled later. First, Frankie and Bobby met and allowed to finish apologising and forgiving. The second meeting, attended only by the mothers, focused on the amount of the compensation and enabled the parties to hear the stories from the other side. The facilitator used a telephone conversation to check on their thoughts before moving on to a third meeting, when the settlement amount was closer to what the parties expected. The facilitator did not rush to settle but asked both mothers to go home and discuss the issue with their husbands. The purpose here was to provide an opportunity for the women to show respect to their marriage partners. Maintaining law and order in Chinese communities relies heavily on the ethical values and moral standards proposed by Confucius, including 'the three bonds and five norms' (*sangang wuchang*). *Sangang* (three bonds) refers to appropriate vertical human relationships, namely, ruler – minister, father – son, and husband – wife. *Wuchang* refers to the qualities of horizontal human relationships (Mok and Wong, 2013). Allowing sufficient time for the woman to seek her husband's endorsement is considered an important element for the success of this mediation, wherein parties left the session with a positive hope, which was later supported by her family.

Fair, genuine, and voluntary participation: The facilitator allowed parties to engage in storytelling. The initial focus was on Bobby's act, which was wrong, and this part seemed settled, according to the social worker and mothers. However, the reasons behind the act remained unknown. The facilitator assisted the parties to more deeply examine the full version of the story to uncover the cause of the incident, which became an important factor for the final settlement. Although Frankie was the injured party, the facilitator did not view him only as a victim. Having heard the stories from both sides, it was clearer to both parties that they felt offended and victimised by others. When Frankie was not viewed as the victim, he ultimately shouldered his own responsibility. The final settlement agreement was not simply a payment of compensation, but a commitment by Frankie who wrote a card to his Grandma to accept his responsibility. As Grandma is the real decision-maker behind the scenes, the letter prompted her to accept an amount that was considered sufficient to her. In addition, the facilitator paid attention to the emotional needs of the parties. On the surface, Bobby's mother could not afford the compensation because of financial pressure. In fact, she suffered from mild depression and needed more support before making a decision.

A traditional Chinese way to heal wounds after surgery is for the patient to take a Chinese soup that is simmered with costly ingredients such as dried fish maw. Without this knowledge, it could be difficult for a facilitator to perceive why the initial claim was $10,000, which is much higher than the cost of hospitalisation. The pressure causing Frankie's mother to concede was from her mother-in-law, Frankie's Grandma, the primary decision maker. In Chinese tradition, family members consult elderly members about important decisions. It was later revealed that the grandma accompanied Frankie when he was hospitalised. Bobby's mother did not visit or send a fresh fruit hamper, which was almost a necessity in the local custom. The feeling of being belittled was the initial stumbling block for her to lower the compensation amount.

More important, Frankie is the only male descendent in the family hierarchy, and any injury meant a potential threat to the patriarchal domination and succession of the family, viewed as most important in Grandma's traditional perspective. In Chinese society, it is considered 'unfilial' to have no posterity, meaning having a male child. Grandma's thoughts in honouring the patrilineal descent system were of concern.

Another issue is the traditional Chinese family size: there are seven members in Bobby's family, with only one breadwinner. Bobby's mother is the only caretaker, caring for her parents and her in-laws in the same household. All household members live together on a common budget. Family members are bound, usually in custom, to support their aged family members. Telling the story of the families' background is one of the keys to move the other side to better understand the whole picture. The facilitator must have an awareness of family structure and custom. Balance in the family must be restored, and the justice to achieve that depends on the specific needs of the players in the family relationship (Gold et al., 2002; Zhang et al., 2009).

Case 2: Upset dad assaulted by insulted son

It was an ordinary evening when these events occurred. Mr Chan and his neighbour are friends in the same public housing estate and as usual, they lean against their front doors and casually chat after dinner. The conversation continues until late in the evening and Sunny, Mr Chan's son, seemed to have overheard part of the conversation, wherein his father was complaining about Sunny's addiction to online video games. To avoid being embarrassed, Sunny retreated to his room but could still hear his father blaming him. Sunny was concerned that if his father continued, he would feel shameful whenever he saw the neighbours, which upset him. With a surge of anger, Sunny rushed from his room and yelled at his father, hoping that he would stop. When his father tried to explain, Sunny could not stand it anymore, so he assaulted his father, then turned around and went to his room, slamming the door shut. A while later, he heard a crowd outside, and headed out to see what was happening. He saw the paramedics bandaging his father, who seemed to be unconscious. A policeman came over and told Sunny that Mr Chan injured his head, and they arrived after receiving a call from the neighbour. The policeman wanted to interview Sunny for a statement, which may lead to a criminal charge of assault occasioning actual bodily harm.

The case was referred to the Police Superintendent's Discretion Scheme, which provides for young persons aged less than 18 years who committed a criminal offence to be cautioned rather than being brought before a court. The young people are then placed under police supervision, rather than being convicted with a criminal record. This arrangement was agreed to by both Mr Chan and Sunny. The case was referred to mediation, which took place about a month after the incident. During this month, members of the family did not speak to each other at all. There was no chiding from the father, and not a word was spoken. They did not even discuss matters such as daily chores. The mediation session helped to break the ice between the two parties.

During the RJ conference, Sunny was given an opportunity to vent his grievances on how he played the role of a good son by managing his studies well, but the father did not seem to appreciate these actions. Rather, he picked on him and chided him for his habit of playing video games. He expressed how he would like to be recognised by his parents. The father, who was traditional, was also given a chance to discuss his real concerns and high expectations of his son. Sunny was born when he was old. In his old way of thinking, a good son simply studies hard after school, has dinner with the family every evening, and is obedient. To him, the son's behaviour of staying inside his room and not joining dinner and sometimes arguing back did not demonstrate the filial piety he expected. He was not aware that his words and acts hindered a closer relationship with his son. The mother was from a Chinese village and could not speak the local language well; therefore, she seldom spoke up. She relied fully on her husband in all aspects. After the incident, the mother became the go-between for the father and son. The RJ conference helped her to better understand her role in the family as well as the expectation of her as a loving mother who supports the family by being able to ease the tension if they are in a heated argument and communicate the needs of the father and son. Through the conference, the absent mom reappeared on the scene and was encouraged to play a more active role in the family.

Factors underlying success

One major feature of the RJ conference was that the parties were quiet in expressing themselves publicly and seemed to lack the ability to genuinely verbalise themselves well. This could be attributed to a common phenomenon among the Chinese, namely, that they are timid and inner-directed. The facilitator helped them to identify their most genuine needs and thoughts when the parties lacked the narrative skills to present them by themselves. The facilitator is able to look into their private zones – their feelings and beliefs, thoughts, and behaviours, and the background of each family member, which influences their thoughts. As the parties did not talk to each other much, there had been misunderstanding between them. Many clarification questions were asked to enlighten the parties on how incorrect they were in dwelling on their own taken-for-granted way of thinking. The facilitator asked the parties about the differences between their perception and the facts. For instance, Sunny thought that Mr Chan hated him, while in reality, Mr Chan's love for him had been wrongly expressed. In other words, Sunny's negative perception of his father was a misinterpretation of his father's true meaning. The skill of creating doubt was used to the same effect. When Mr Chan said he was worried that Sunny spent too much time playing video games, the facilitator challenged him by asking if this had caused any problems. Mr Chan had to admit that Sunny completed his homework, woke up on time every day, and did not miss classes. As such, he realised that it should not be a problem if Sunny was self-disciplined and managed his studies well. The thinking of both parties was transformed by obtaining new information from which to form a new perspective or lens.

The facilitator saw the need to reintegrate the mother into the family. Initially, the mother was absent from the scene in every respect. While she was present when the incident occurred, she did not say or do anything. The emergence of the mother's role helped to restore and rebuild the relationship between family members. The facilitator prepared the parties to deliver suitable apologies for their actions that hurt the other parties. Mr Chan had not given sufficient recognition to Sunny, and Sunny had been too impulsive, causing his father's injury. Mr Chan's character is typical of Chinese parents who traditionally ruled with absolute authority. Sunny resented this absolute authority, but was bound by Confucian filial obligations to honour his parents and unquestionably obey their commands (Goldin, 2014). This acquiescence is imminent in this case, where the father took for granted that he has the authority to expect the son to behave in a way he deemed right without considering it differently.

In this case, the mother also closely replicates the characteristics of a traditional Chinese woman, who should observe the 'the three obediences and the four virtues'.[3] Chinese women observe the male-dominated family silently. With regards to the case, the mother represented the most traditional type of woman in a Chinese family, because she was from a village and the traditional 'obedience' virtue was born with her in playing her role in the family. The RJ process helped her to realise her son's needs for her to play a more active role in the family and ease the tension between him and his father when needed.

Cultural-specific skills to heal young people and families

The two cases cited previously remind us that the Chinese always uphold salient traditional values, despite living in a contemporary world. Apart from the values of 'the three bonds and five norms' and 'the three obediences and the four virtues' mentioned earlier, Wong recently analysed Chinese literature on RJ, identifying cultural values that consistently appeared in the literature. These include 'repair harm done', a 'harmonious society', 'peace comes first', 'participation of all parties', 'avoiding litigation', 'forgiveness', and 'shaming' (Mok and Wong, 2013). Some of these salient Chinese values such as a harmonious society, peace comes first, and avoiding litigation may no longer be new to readers, because scholars have translated these values into English (Liu and Palermo, 2009; Trevaskes, 2010; Wong, 2014; Yuan and Di, 2015; Zhang, 2004). Bearing these values in mind, when facilitators facilitate a conference among the Chinese, we may need to pay more attention to engaging participants with cultural-specific skills to enhance the success of the mediation process such as building trust, respecting family values, balancing power, and ultimately aiming to restore relationships. In other parts of the globe, this has also been evidenced by the study on the use of RJ as a tool of conflict resolution for migrant minorities (Albrecht, 2010), and the effort in advocating a more personalised restorative justice vision of cultural differences suggested by Gavrielides (2014). Without the awareness of these salient values, facilitators could have missed the chance for overcoming impediments that hinder the progress of RJ practices.

Furthermore, appropriately arousing empathy among all members and moral repair of the offender is always useful (Ward et al., 2014). During the RJ conference, the facilitator must direct the offender towards reviewing his wrongdoings and raise the empathic intelligence of all participants by letting both parties understand each other's difficulties and feelings. Creating a sense of family or the 'we-feeling' fits the principles of building a harmonious society and peace comes first. Adults are more than willing to give a second chance to juvenile delinquents. This is the same for most Chinese families (Sheu and Huang, 2014). However, giving a chance does not mean tolerating wrongdoing at the expense of everything, and tolerance does not mean that young people will learn from their misbehaviours. One advantage of RJ is the opportunity

---

3 The Three Obediences and the Four Virtues (*samcong side*) were a set of basic moral principles specifically for women in Confucianism. The two terms ("three obediences" and "four virtues") first appeared in the Book of Etiquette and Ceremonial and in the Rites of Zhou respectively. The three obediences include to obey her father before marriage, her husband when married, and her sons in widowhood, and the four virtues (morality, proper speech, modest manner, and diligent work) of women in ancient China; spiritual fetters of wifely submission and virtue imposed on women in feudal society.

it provides victims to express their feelings, simultaneously enabling the offender to learn from his misbehaviours and make amends. This is a crucial procedure of the RJ process, in which the wrongdoer reflects on how shameful his behaviours are and grasps the opportunity to account for what he has done wrong and make appropriate reparations. In the appropriate re-integrative shaming process, genuine shamefulness would drive the engine of change for young people. Such a process is most usefully thought of as natural hooks for change that offer the young people the chance to re-enter the family and to regain their positive identify as productive citizens in the community (Braithwaite, 1989; Wong, 2013; Ward et al., 2014).

Conclusion

To conclude, similar difficulties and challenges were identified from the pilot stages of implementation in Taiwan and Mainland China. It is worth noting that some facilitators were not skilful in RJ practice. Motivation to participate in VOM or RJ conferencing was generally low for most cases, possibly because the RJ meetings were administered through the Prosecutor Offices or Courts in both Taiwan and Mainland China.

It is important to note that some judges and prosecutors in Mainland China who are running VOM share a dual identity (i.e. being adjudicators as well as government officials). The practice which allows judges or prosecutors to be the conference facilitator may lead to public concerns about the government's interference in managing disputes, as well as lack of impartiality during the conferencing process (He and Ng, 2013; Ng and He, 2014; Hu and Zeng, 2014). Notwithstanding the criticism, RJ practices are becoming more common in pre-sentencing and post-sentencing in both jurisdictions.

At the pre-sentencing stage, the prosecutor has the power to initiate RJ through the deferred or suspended prosecution mechanism. In addition, RJ can be used as a voluntary disposal in connection to a suspended sentence under the mechanism of the Court (He, 2012; Huang et al., 2014; Li, 2014; Wei and Zhang, 2015; Yao, 2016; Wei, 2015; Research Group of Southwest University of Finance and Economics, 2016; Wong, 2016). In Hong Kong, although RJ has not been formally incorporated into the mainstream criminal justice system, RJ scholars play a leading role in promoting its use. Furthermore, they play a leading role in advancing RJ skills in parts of Asia (Wong and Lo, 2011; Wong and Mok, 2013; Mok and Wong, 2013; Wong, 2014; Wong, 2016).

With respect to cultural-specific skills and challenges facing RJ practice, it is important to note that respectful elderly members in Chinese families are often invited to join dispute resolution meetings, and their opinion might be highly inferential (Boulle and Teh, 2000; Lee and Teh, 2009; Sheu and Huang, 2014). We can see from the Booger Boy case a modification from the traditional behaviour of succumbing to patriarchal power where paternal status is also enjoyed by senior women. The value of seniority (*zhangyou youxu*)[4] applies beyond the fraternal frame. With this inherent traditional value, those who are in the senior position will protect their junior ones, and in return, they expect the respect and obedience from those who are lower in the hierarchy (Barnes, 2006).

In the Chinese hierarchical structure, the primary order is that those who are in the senior positions are given more respect and authority. The importance of mothers over son or daughter also becomes more explicit, and their moral virtues are continuously respected along the

---

4 An emphasis in Mencius on the cultivation of virtues where the proper order is that the younger brother should behave toward his older brothers.

historical development of Confucian-Mencian thinking (Birdwhistell, 2007). It is noted from the case illustration that the absence of a most senior patriarchal figure may not result in the passage of power and authority to the son: the most senior woman can be accepted in a family as the authority. Senior women in a family predominated over junior men. Furthermore, women in the family could not be overlooked as one of the noteworthy Chinese traditional values and features that bear significance in an RJ conference. This practice wisdom should be kept in mind by those facilitators who are planning to run RJ conferences for Chinese adolescents where major decision makers are not simply those who attended the meeting. The ultimate decision makers are sometimes extended family members who act behind the scenes, making settlement decisions highly relevant to their inherent traditional values.

The two cases of RJ conference presented earlier have clearly illustrated that certain cultural nuances are ingrained in the Chinese culture. Nevertheless, it is premature to conclude that traditional Chinese values will absolutely affect the success or failure of the RJ conference. In this chapter, we do not attempt to use a broad-brush approach to stereotype the hierarchical influence of the authority figure in the Chinese families. Our findings are interim and are meant to inform this Handbook's up-to-date research and international coverage. Our use of case illustrations divulged certain distinctive values and practices in a Chinese family that we believe RJ facilitators should be cognizant of. Future study on how to maximise the effectiveness of RJ practices in the context of multicultural societies is deemed necessary. This chapter has opened the debate on RJ in Chinese communities, bridging a gap in the literature.

References

Albrecht, B. 2010. Multicultural Challenges for Restorative Justice; Mediators' Experiences from Norway and Finland, *Journal of Scandinavian Studies in Criminology and Crime Prevention*, 11: 3–24.

Barnes, B. 2006. *Culture, Conflict and Mediation in the Asia Pacific*. Maryland: University Press of America.

Bazemore, G. and Umbreit, M.S. 1997. *Balanced and Restorative Justice for Juveniles: A Framework for Juvenile Justice in the 21st Century*. Washington, DC: U.S. Department of Justice, Office of Justice Programs, Office of Juvenile Justice and Delinquency Prevention.

Berti, R. 2016. *Victim-Offender Reconciliation in the People's Republic of China and Taiwan*. New York: Palgrave Macmillan.

Birdwhistel, J. 2007. *Mencius and Masculinities: Dynamics of Power, Morality, and Maternal Thinking*. Albany: State University of New York Press.

Boriboonthana, Y. and Sangbuangamlum, S. 2013. Effectiveness of the Restorative Justice Process on Crime Victims and Adult Offenders in Thailand, *Asian Journal of Criminology*, 8: 277–286.

Boulle, L. and Teh, H.H. 2000. *Mediation – Principles, Process and Practice*. Singapore: Butterworths Asia.

Braithwaite, J. 1989 *Crime, Shame and Reintegration*. Cambridge: Cambridge University Press.

Chan, W.C. 2013. Family Conferencing for Juvenile Offenders: A Singaporean Case Study in Restorative Justice, *Asian Journal of Criminology*, 8: 1–23.

Di, X. and Cha, X. 2007. Research on Procedures of Criminal Mediation – From the Viewpoint of Restorative Criminal Justice. In X. Di and Z. Liu (eds.) *Theory and Practice of Restorative Criminal Justice*. Beijing: Qunzhong Publishing (in Chinese), pp. 64–102.

Di, X. and Wu, Y. 2009. The Developing Trend of the People's Mediation in China, *Sociological Focus*, 42(3): 228–245.

Dong, Y. 2012. Restorative Justice and Juvenile Justice Practices in the PRC, *Journal of Hebei Youth Administrative Cadres College*, 1: 5–9 (in Chinese).

Evangelical Lutheran Church Social Service Hong Kong. 2017. *Mission and Vision of the Project*. Available at http://iscr.elchk.org.hk/center_aboutus.php. Accessed 15 June 2017.

Gavrielides, T. 2014. Bring Race Relations Into Restorative Justice Debate: An Alternative and Personalized Vision of 'the Other', *Journal of Black Studies*, 45(3): 216–246.

Gold, T., Guthrie, D. and Wank, D. 2002. *Social Connections in China: Institutions, Culture, and the Changing Nature of Guanxi*. Cambridge: Cambridge University Press.

Goldin, P. 2014. *Confucianism*. Hoboken: Taylor and Francis.

He, X. 2012. A Preliminary Analysis of the Application of Restorative Justice in Juvenile Justice in China, *Legal System and Economics*, 323: 18–21 (in Chinese).

He, X. and Ng, K. 2013. In the Name of Harmony: The Erasure of Domestic Violence in China's Judicial Medication, *International Journal of Law, Policy and the Family*, 27(1): 97–115.

Ho, H.M., Chuk, W.H., Leung, W.H., Lam, H.Y., Lai, L.C. and Law, W.M. 2007. *Research Report on the Mediation Between Victims and Offenders*. Hong Kong: Social Service of the Evangelical Lutheran Church of Hong Kong.

Hopkins, B. 2004. *Just Schools: A Whole School Approach to Restorative Justice*. London and New York: Jessica Kingsley.

Hu, J. and Zeng, L. 2014. Grand Mediation and Legitimacy Enhancement in Contemporary China – The Guang'an Model, *Journal of Contemporary China*, 24(91): 43–63.

Huang, H.F. and Chang, L.Y.C. 2013. Evaluating Restorative Justice Programs in Taiwan, *Asian Criminology*, 8: 287–307.

Huang, L.Y., Sheu, C.J. and Huang, H.F. 2014. *The Study of the RJ Pioneer Project: A Focus on Indicators for Effectiveness Evaluation and Case Assessment*. Taipei: National Taipei University (in Chinese).

Johnstone, G. 2002. *Restorative Justice: Ideas, Values, Debates*. Cullompton: Willan.

Johnstone, G. and Van Ness, D. eds., 2007. *Handbook of Restorative Justice*. Cullompton: Willan.

Lee, J. and Teh, H.H. 2009. *An Asian Perspective on Mediation*. Academy Publishing, Singapore Academy of Law.

Li, J. 2014. A Brief Analysis of Conditional Non-Prosecution of Juvenile Delinquents, *Journal of Mudanjiang College of Education*, 149: 127–128 (in Chinese).

Liebmann, M. 2007. *Restorative Justice: How It Works*. London: Jessica Kingsley Publishers.

Liu, J. and Palermo, G. 2009. Restorative Justice and Chinese Traditional Legal Culture in the Context of Contemporary Chinese Criminal Justice Reform, *Asia Pacific Journal of Police & Criminal Justice*, 7(1): 49–67.

Lo, T.W., Maxwell, G.M. and Wong, D.S.W. 2006. Diversion from Youth Courts in Five Asia Pacific Jurisdictions: Welfare or Restorative Solutions, *International Journal of Offender Therapy and Comparative Criminology*, 50(1): 5–20.

Lo, T.W., Wong, D.S.W. and Maxwell, G.M. 2003. *Measures Alternative to Prosecution for Handling Unruly Children and Young Persons: Overseas Experiences and Options for Hong Kong*. Research Report from Youth Studies Net at City University of Hong Kong to the Security Bureau of the Hong Kong Government of SAR. Hong Kong: Youth Studies Net at City University of Hong Kong.

Maxwell, G.M. 2007. The Defining Features of a Restorative Justice Approach to Conflict. In G. Maxwell and J.H. Liu (eds.) *Restorative Justice and Practices in New Zealand: Towards a Restorative Society*. Wellington: Institute of Policy Studies, pp. 5–28.

Maxwell, G.M. and Morris, A. 1993. *Family Victims and Culture: Youth Justice in New Zealand*. Wellington: Institute of Criminology, Victoria University of Wellington.

The Methodist Centre. 2017. *Project Concord*. Available at www.methodist-centre.com/concord/tc. Accessed 15 June 2017.

Ministry of Justice. 1999. *White Book on Prosecution Reform*. Taipei, Taiwan: Ministry of Justice (in Chinese).

Ministry of Justice. 2016. *The Current Situation and Prospects of the Republic of China's Initiative in Restorative Justice*. Taipei, Taiwan: Ministry of Justice.

Mok, L.W.Y. and Wong, D.S.W. 2013. Restorative Justice and Mediation: Diverged or Converged?, *Asian Journal of Criminology*, 8: 335–347.

Morrison, B. 2007. Schools and Restorative Justice. In G. Johnstone and D.W. Van Ness (eds.) *Handbook of Restorative Justice*. Cullompton: Willan, pp. 325–350.

Morrison, B. 2015. Restorative Justice in Education: Changing Lenses on Education's Three Rs, *Restorative Justice: An International Journal*, 3(3): 445–452.

National People's Congress. 2012. *Criminal Procedure Law*. Available at www.cecc.gov/resources/legal-provisions/criminal-procedure-law-of-the-peoples-republic-of-china. Accessed 15 June 2017.

Ng, K. and He, X. 2014. Internal Contradictions of Judicial Mediation in China. *Law and Social Inquiry*, 39(2): 285–312.

Presser, L. and Van Voorhis, P. 2002. Values and Evaluation: Assessing Process and Outcomes of Restorative Justice Programs, *Crime & Delinquency*, 48(1): 162–188.

Research Group of Southwest University of Finance and Economics. 2016. On the Role of the People's Procuratorate in Restorative Justice: The Experience of Shuangliu District, Chengdu, *Juvenile Delinquency Prevention Research*, 6: 28–52 (in Chinese).

Shen, A. and Antonopoulos, G.A. 2013. Restorative Justice or What? Restorative Justice in the Chinese Youth Justice System, *European Journal of Crime, Criminal Law and Criminal Justice*, 21: 291–315.

Shen, Y.L. and Zou, Z. 2010. Relationship Between Restorative Justice and Juvenile Justice. In J.X. Wen, X.H. Di and Z.W. Ji (eds.) *New Direction for the Preventive Measures of Juvenile Criminal Justice*. Beijing: Qunzhong Publishing, pp. 733–750. (in Chinese).

Sheu, C.J. and Huang, H.F. 2014. Restorative Justice in Taiwan's Aboriginal Societies: The Example of the Atayal Tribe, *Restorative Justice: An International Journal*, 2(3): 260–279.

Shi, Y. 2008. On Restorative Justice Practices in China: Status, Challenge and Future of the Victim Offender Reconciliation System, *Frontiers of Law in China*, 3(2): 294–323.

Strang, H. and Braithwaite, J. 2000. *Restorative Justice: Philosophy to Practice*. Surrey: Ashgate.

Taichung District Prosecutors Office. 2016. *Working Manual on Restorative Justice*. Taichung, Taiwan: Taichung District Prosecutors Office (in Chinese).

Trevaskes, S. 2010. The Shifting Sands of Punishment in China in the Era of 'harmonious society', *Law & Policy*, 32: 332–361.

Van Ness, D.W. and Strong, K.H. 2006. *Restorative Justice: An Introduction to Restorative Justice*, 3rd ed. Newark, NJ: LexisNexis Matthew Bender.

Van Wormer, K. and Walker, L., eds. 2013. *Restorative Justice Today: Practical Applications*. Loa Angeles: Sage.

Walgrave, L. 2002. Restorative Justice and the Law: Socio-Ethical and Juridical Foundations for a Systematic Approach. In L. Walgrave (ed.) *Restorative Justice and the Law*. Cullompton and Devon: Willan, pp. 191–218.

Ward, T., Fox, K.J. and Garber, M. 2014. Restorative Justice, Offender Rehabilitation and Desistance, *Restorative Justice: An International Journal*, 2(1): 24–42.

Wei, J.H. and Zhang, J. 2015. On the Rational Construction of Case Handling Mechanism for Procuratorial Organs Under the Background of Non-Adult Criminal Policies, *Journal of Political Science and Law*, 32(5): 87–93 (in Chinese).

Wei, X.W. 2015. Theoretical Basis for Conditional Non-Prosecution of Juvenile Offenders, *Academic Exchange*, 258(9): 103–107 (in Chinese).

Wong, D.S.W. 2006. Tackling School Bullying Behavior By Restorative Justice. In P. Hunag (ed.) *Restorative Justice Forum II*. Beijing: Qun Zhong Publishers, pp. 84–98.

Wong, D.S.W. 2013. Restorative Justice for Juvenile Delinquents in Hong Kong and China, In K.S. Van Wormer and L. Walker (eds.) *Restorative Justice Today: Practical Applications*. Thousands Oaks, CA: Sage, pp. 53–62.

Wong, D.S.W. 2014. Harmony Comes First: Challenges Facing the Development of Restorative Justice in Asia, Restorative Justice: *An International Journal*, 2(1): 1–8.

Wong, D.S.W. 2016. Restorative Justice at Different Levels of the Criminal Justice System in China: Challenges and Paths Forward, *Restorative Justice: An International Journal*, 4(1): 10–26.

Wong, D.S.W., Cheng, C.H.K., Ngan, R.M.H. and Ma, S.K. 2011. Program Effectiveness of a Restorative Whole-School Approach for Tackling School Bullying in Hong Kong, *International Journal of Offender Therapy and Comparative Criminology*, 55(6): 846–862.

Wong, D.S.W. and Lo, T. 2011. The Recent Development of Restorative Social Work Practices in Hong Kong, *International Social Work*, 54(5): 701–716.

Wong, D.S.W. and Mok, L.W.Y. 2013. Evolution of Restorative Justice Practices for Juvenile Offenders in the People's Republic of China. In J. Liu, S. Jou and B. Hebention (eds.) *Handbook of Asian Criminology*. New York: Springer, pp. 393–406.

Wong, D.S.W., Mok, L.W.Y. and Au Yeung, T.Y. 2012. Application of Restorative Justice in Juvenile Justice in Hong Kong and Mainland China, *Crime and Criminal Justice International*, 19: 73–103.

Yao, J.L. 2007. The Practice and the Future of Restorative Justice in China, *Journal of Social Sciences*, 8: 114–120 (in Chinese).

Yao, L. 2016. Institutional Transformation and Optimization of Measures in the Transition of Models of Judicial Administration for Juvenile Delinquents, *Law Review*, 195: 79–85 (in Chinese).

Yuan, X. and Di, X. 2015. Harmonizing or Restoring Justice? A Study of Victims' Experiences Meeting with Their Young Offenders in China, *Social Work Review*, 4: 75–92.

Zehr, H. 1990. *Changing Lenses: A New Focus of Crime and Justice*. Scottsdale: Herald Press.

Zhai, Z. 2011. The Application of Restorative Justice in Administrative Detention, *Journal of Chinese People's Public Security University (Social Sciences Edition)*, 150: 108–113 (in Chinese).

Zhang, L., Messner, S.F., Liu, J. and Zhuo, Y.A. 2009. Guanxi and Fear of Crime in Contemporary Urban China, *British Journal of Criminology*, 49: 472–490.

Zhang, X.Z. 2004. *A Restorative Justice Audit of the Chinese Criminal Justice System*. Dissertation submitted on 1 September 2004, MSc Criminal Justice Policy at the Department of Social Policy, LSE. London: LSE.

21

Is changing lenses possible?

The Chilean case study of integrating restorative justice into a hierarchical criminal justice system

Isabel Ximena González Ramírez

Introduction

The purpose of this chapter is to test whether Howard Zehr's 1980 call for "a change of lenses" is possible for restorative justice by evaluating its strengths and weaknesses in hierarchical, top-down criminal justice. To this end, let us consider the Chilean criminal justice system as a case study.

Today, restorative justice is manifested in Chile in an incipient manner only. Pilot projects have been implemented, but derivation from the formal criminal system is infrequent due to a complete lack of awareness of the existence and usefulness of this procedure. In this chapter we ask: What would the consequences be in an accusatory criminal justice system such as the Chilean one, if penal mediation were used as an alternative outcome? This question is a necessary one to ask ourselves in light of citizen dissatisfaction produced by the univocal answers the criminal system offers today and growing demands for justice and security.

We propose the main hypothesis for the study as: "In a criminal system such as Chile's, the normative regulation of criminal mediation as an autonomous alternative promotes justice and limits the State's discretionary power in deciding whether to submit to investigation, formalization or trial. This decision is based on criminal characteristics and refers to mediation according to uniform, pre-established criteria".

To address this topic, we begin the present chapter with a section describing the development of criminal mediation in Chile. In the second section we analyze how the normative incorporation of criminal mediation could affect the principles of public criminal action: opportunity and legality procedure principles. A third section shows the criminal mediation model used in Chile, and a fourth section contains operators' perceptions regarding the consequences of normatively regulated criminal mediation.

Our research design is descriptive and exploratory, with the qualitative, dogmatic and comparative methodology that is characteristic of legal science (Corral Talciani, 2008: 62). We used secondary source information such as legal regulations, recommendations by international organizations and doctrine.

Herein, we will review and compare how criminal mediation has been implemented in countries with common and continental legal systems. For this comparison, we used England and France for the Common Law systems and the Continental Law systems, respectively.

In addition to this, we applied information recollection techniques, regarding practitioners' opinions and perceptions. To this end, we held semi-structured interviews (Creswell and Plano, 2011), addressed at prosecutors, defence attorneys, judges and mediators of public centres in four of the country's regions, selected due to their high number of mediations.

The present study is indispensable for Latin America since even though there has been legislation about criminal mediation in countries such as Argentina, Costa Rica, Colombia, Venezuela, Ecuador and Bolivia (Parra Urdaneta et al., 2009), these countries have lacked uniform regulations and comprehensive treatment in their legal systems, and as yet there are no conclusive studies regarding the consequences.

Criminal mediation in Chile requires a new approach, one that is more institutionalized than the current system. The legal system in Chile requires more thorough normative regulation as an independent alternative to its current criminal processes in order to achieve its full judiciary potential. Therefore, it would be necessary to carefully regulate the implementation of these norms in the criminal system, to avoid discriminatory decisions in the derivation of such, on behalf of equality for all citizens before the legal system (Gonzalez and Fuentealba, 2013). This allows for the diversification of criminal treatment, through collaborative methods, which comply with criminal processes and Restorative Justice principles.

Development of criminal mediation in Chile

Considering that Chile's criminal justice system, like that of most Latin American countries, is characterized by a lack of community participation in conflict resolution processes, we affirm that the restorative justice model in Chile is only partially restorative, according to McCold and Wachtel's theory (2003), and centres on dialogue between parties, using a bilateral system and some characteristics based on the VORP model (Díaz, 2012:61).

We will use our own definition for this study, without prejudice to the multiple dogmatic definitions that have been given to criminal mediation, which we conceive as: "A restorative mechanism in which parties pertaining to a crime-based conflict seek the recognition of damage caused unto the victim and the possibility of reparation, according to their needs and the options available to the offender, during a voluntary encounter within a protected space guided by an impartial third party, aiming to restore individual and social balance, reintegrating both parties to a healthy social co-existence"[1]

In Chile, criminal mediation has been considered as a complement to the penal system and in some cases, as a substitute to trial and its respective consequences for collaborative ways of solving crimes, yet it has not achieved national validation, which has led to a decrease in the Public Prosecutor's Office referrals to the mediation system each year (González, 2016). The foregoing is due to the fact that this mechanism is not socially recognized as an alternative to criminal processes in Chile's legal system, for since it is not regulated normatively, it does not allow for quantitative and qualitative evaluations, nor are the results monitored to improve implementation.

Considering that Chile has had an inquisitive procedural history and started its transition towards a criminal accusatory, oral and public system 17 years ago, implementing the principle

---

1 Self Definition.

of opportunity, with a distinctive continental influence, we can affirm that today Chile needs public policy, legislative procedures and institutionally defined criteria for mediation case selection and an appropriate methodology for treatment.

Considering these effects, we should evaluate the possibility and requirements of incorporating normative criminal mediation in order to expand the forms of criminal treatment, with collaborative methods that comply with due process principles in criminal and restorative justice procedures.

Thus, this intervention cannot be carried out at such an early stage that it impedes guarantees of due process to the accused, which clarifies facts to the victim, nor too late that it stigmatizes the offender, provoking societal feelings of impunity regarding crime by directly compensating the victim, socially reintegrating the offender and restoring the damage caused.

Despite the fact that the legal systems of Continental and Common Law share ideological and legal roots, the differences between them are varied. The common feature in France and England is that criminal action is undertaken following authorities' initiative (Glaeser and Shleifer, 2002: 1193 and ss).

In England these participatory practices – understood as self-governance and democratization – curiously remain, even after the consolidation of governmental central power. The opposite occurred in France due to the weakness of the central government (Hendler, 2006:17).

As a result, the continental system in France established a judicial system operated by professional judges strongly controlled by the crown (Hendler, 2006:17), while a relatively independent jury system was consolidated in England (Glaeser, Shleifer, 2002: 1194), given its resistance to state structure (Anitua, 2004: 69), as well as people's distrust towards the government (Horvitz, López, 2005: 111).

The differences between these legal systems allow us to explain how restorative justice conflict resolution mechanisms have become greatly diffused in countries with traditional Common Law with fewer applications of these in countries with the Continental System (Márquez Cárdenas, 2012).

Within the prosecution bodies in the UK's criminal justice system are Her Majesty's Police Service and the Crown Prosecution Services (Creswell and Plano, 2011) Here, not only lawyers, but also laymen are allowed to intervene, supporting the fact that the State is not the absolute owner of the conflict (Cheliotis, 2011: 110). This is in contrast with the Continental System, where only the Attorney General's Office is the representative of penal action (Carnevali, 2005). For this reason, restorative practices in the UK's criminal justice system have not been settled due to imposition of the law but due to the community's conviction and self-action (Hoyle, Young, 2002: 533), unlike the Continental System (Díaz, 2012).

A characteristic of the French model, which is a mixed model with both inquisitive and accusatory aspects, is that criminal mediation has incidence, and may be applicable in different types of infringement.

Therefore, procedure and jurisdiction will differ according to the crime (Solaro and Paul Jean, 1987). In this context, criminal mediation began to slowly gain ground in the 1980s, and was consolidated in the 1990s by means of a law which recognized and validated it (Cesano, 2010), applying the principle of opportunity and making legal procedure more flexible. This can be observed in the country's high rate of cases without prosecution, which are approximately 80% of criminal investigations initiated (Cesano, 2010).

However, the freedom of French attorneys to apply the principle of opportunity is not absolute, as it must be subjected to the parameters established by the law. The dispositions contained in articles 40, 40–1 and 40–2 of the Criminal Procedure Code allow alternative outcomes or composition measures. The attorney may decide to suspend public action if it turns out that such a measure is capable of ensuring damage reparation and putting an end to the conflict (Loi n° 93–2 du 4 janvier 1993). This recognition was made by adding a final paragraph to article 41–1 of the criminal procedure code (Legifrance.gouv, 2017), incorporating a procedure that obliges the Attorney General of the Republic to analyze several aspects, including the type of crime, its penalty and whether the criteria for mediation established by law may be achieved, whether such a decision would (1) ensure damages to the victim be repaired, (2) put an end to the problem caused by the crime, and (3) contribute to the perpetrator's reintroduction to society.[2]

In these cases the prosecutor, prior to deciding on the exercise of public action, either directly or by means of a judicial police officer, a delegate or mediator, may ask the perpetrator to repair the damage, encourage the parties to reach a settlement or attempt a mediation between the perpetrator and the victim, thus suspending the need for public action.

According to the criteria that permit mediation in France, these must be clearly stated and recognized, and must constitute a minor offense. The most common cases of mediation are: insults, threats, disruption of public order, moderate violence, theft and damage to property, and non-payment of alimony.[3]

Criminal mediation is carried out in France by public officers of the judiciary system and by a representative of an authorized association. Parties may be assisted by an attorney. If mediation is rejected, the prosecutor is free to exercise criminal action. If mediation is successful, the prosecutor simply archives the case. Without prejudice to the foregoing, the prosecutor may still prosecute the offender, in the case of new information, and always in the case of non-compliance (Díaz López, 2011).

Not only are mediation opportunities greater in England but the types of officials who can propose and approve them are also more varied. In France this is limited to a single body: the prosecutor (Fleiner, 2005).

The comparative methodology shows that the greater occurrence of restorative mechanisms in countries with Common Law is due to the ideologies that motivated their implementation, inspired by different ways of conceiving and imparting justice. Therefore, the reasons for mass implementation, which do not require normative regulation, are not applicable in countries with continental jurisdiction, due to their strong adherence to the principle of procedural legality (Mera-Ballesteros, 2009) and their greater tendency to obey authority.

Nonetheless, unlike in France, where attempts have been made for stricter regulations regarding criminal mediation, in continental countries where it has been established in generic form, without incorporating the exact requirements for its implementation, as in the case of Argentina; we can see that it has been the target of criticism, in the sense that its ambiguous regulation affects the principle of procedural legality and may affect the principles of due process (Del Val, 2012). Our comparison of criminal mediation in Latin American countries such as Argentina and Chile showed, among other findings, that in countries where it has been normatively regulated, such as Argentina, its implementation is more widespread, whereas in the case of Chile it is not formally implemented and thus remains a foreign concept for citizens (González, 2016).

2 Article 41, last paragraph from C.P.P
3 Legal information and administrative Direction, 2015

By this, we understand Chile needs public policy, legislative procedures and institutionally defined criteria to select mediation cases as well as an appropriate methodology to treat them. To this end, it is necessary to assess the usefulness of and requirements for normatively incorporating criminal mediation in order to expand the ways crime is treated, using collaborative methods that comply with the due process principles of procedural legality and restorative justice.

One of the examples that Chile should consider when implementing criminal mediation is the experience of France, which has stricter regulations than other regions, leaving the prosecuting entity little space for free initiative, thereby granting actors in the legal system and the citizenship as a whole, clear understanding of the consequences of submitting to this collaborative process.

Introducing criminal mediation: the principles of public criminal action

It is necessary to briefly analyze the principle of opportunity to evaluate the impact of incorporating criminal mediation as an independent alternative, in which, according to Davalos, (2016: 13), there are two opportunity models where: a) criminal procedures do not recognize legality principles. In this case, opportunities constitute the general system. Thus, the discretionary powers of the Public Prosecutor's Office allow the prosecution to withdraw and restrain accusations.

And b) opportunities constitute an exception, adopted by the German criminal procedure ordinance, which establishes legality principle as a rule. Constituting opportunities as exceptions limits the discretionary powers of the Public Ministry, to whom it grants the possibility to reject criminal prosecution only when the law allows it. Therefore, when restorative mechanisms operate under the powers granted to the persecutor, opportunities may be used as a exceptions.

With respect to not dealing with the regulated opportunity as a true opportunity, authors such as Cafferata (2010: 32–33) state that the attribution which the principle of opportunity grants the Public Ministry includes that of limiting criminal prosecution in its objective and subjective extension, supported by the foundations of this principle, convening penalty extension by agreement between accuser and accusee. Therefore, in the continental system, when restorative mechanisms operate by virtue of powers granted to the persecuting organ expressly or tacitly, we find ourselves facing the principle of opportunity as an exception.

When criminal justice in Latin America began a modernization process more than 15 years ago, moving from an inquisitive criminal system to an accusatory, oral and public system (Horvitz and López, 2003:31), the principle of opportunity was incorporated in the criminal process. This process incorporates, among other manifestations, alternative outcomes, using criteria relevant to system efficiency, such as self-compositional mechanisms, in the case that preventive criteria and public interests in legal sanctions are not compromised (Horvitz and López, 2003: 50 ss.).

When alternatives are defined by the doctrine, there seems to be confusion between termination processes and restorative resolution mechanisms, which are far from identical, since collaborative solutions play a much more important role, because they include a conflict management process between parties, which is distinct from alternative mediation methods.

Thus, the principle of opportunity or discretion of public action requires the implementation of selection mechanisms, where the application of criminal mediation has been framed in countries where there is no legal recognition of this.

The principle of opportunity constitutes an exception in continental court systems, where the prosecution procedure is affirmed and the victim is denied their role in the process, thus representing a crime, not a personal hostility towards the latter, but rather against the established order (Anitua, 2004: *69*).

Under the mandatory principle, the Public Ministry is exclusively subject to criminal law, in terms of the procedural matters that regulate its prosecution and processing powers, and in terms of substantive matters, whereas with the principle of opportunity, the Public Ministry is subject to the same law, which regulates its competencies and powers, but these same rules authorize it to escape – to a greater or lesser extent, with judicial control – from substantive criminal law when promoting penal action, and to incorporate opportunity.

Chilean constitutional order does not include the principle of mandatory prosecution, nor does it prohibit the principle of opportunity. Art. 83 mandates the Public Ministry to exercise public criminal action "in the manner provided by law", enabling the legislator to determine discretionary margins. By principle of mandatory prosecution, we allude to the Attorney's duty to initiate and continue the criminal prosecution of all known crimes, being unable to suspend, interrupt or cease prosecution at its discretion (Rodríguez Vega, 2013).

This is why for Ferrajoli, (1995: 33), when going from an inquisitive procedure to an adversarial one, the process' main objectives remain the same. Sanctions made by the justice system fulfil the purpose of public order and aim to satisfy general prevention expectations. Thus in penal processes in Latin America, criminal mediation is used for certain types of offence – those of little importance with low penalties – unlike Common Law, where negotiation can be used as a legal solution in a wide range of crimes. However, differences between these two main legal families (Common Law and Continental Law) are attenuated by transitions from the continental system to a contradictory model, incorporating restorative practices from Common Law systems.

Nevertheless, the principle of opportunity assumes an exceptional character faced with procedural legality, which limits the prosecuting body's performance and imposes the obligation to initiate prosecution rather than suspending or ceasing it, at discretion.

In this way, in Latin America the principle of legality is applied, which may be understood as "The State's automatic and inevitable reaction, through the relevant bodies, when faced with the hypothesis of an offense being committed, is to investigate it, call a trial, and enforce a penalty as applicable" (Buteler, 1998:17).

It bears mentioning that in the field of criminal policy, the principle of opportunity has often been viewed as contrary to legality, which is not absolute, for if the law grants the attorney both powers of investigation and the power not to initiate an investigation, or to temporarily suspend one (Aguad et al., 2011), and legally determines the conditions of this decision, therefore it is the law, not the prosecutor, who applies discretion.

In this context, the common characteristic of criminal mediation is that a judge ensures approval AGREEMENTS as an alternative way out. In this way, it plays the role of judge in charge of sentencing, authorized to exercise jurisdictional functions, extinguishing penal action. For this reason, some tendencies are less inclined to use criminal mediation, affirming that when it is not expressly regulated, it allows violating principles of procedural legality (Del Val, 2012). Thus, it has been understood that criminal mediation, when not regulated and the criteria for the selectivity of infractions is NOT determined in advance, publicly and transparently, AFFECTS principles of procedural legality. (Langbein, 1974).

From the perspective of Hassemer (2003: 8), one of the main foundations of the principle of legality would be equality before law, to the extent that one of the purposes for it to work would be to avoid arbitrariness and discrimination in the prosecution of crimes. All citizens who are in identical conditions would be subject to equal treatment, without making capricious distinctions of who has the power to decide on criminal actions, possibly endangering the division of powers with opportunistic selectivity of legal norms.

In this line, the principle of procedural legality emphasizes the idea of the legal rights system and the opportunity system as effective, (Horvitz, López, 2003:45)[4] making the regimes of criminal action and rules related to political content a subject of political legislation. On the other hand, it is necessary to clarify whether it corresponds to criminal law to determine in which cases the criminal justice system should not intervene, as Hassemer says, affirming that the opportunity system is not the correct instrument for decriminalization. Respect for rule of law will depend on whether cases are determined with absolute precision, because the vague formulation of opportunity law destroys the principle of legality (Hassemer, 1998:8).

From this perspective, "deviation" by the prosecution, may lead the State to fail in its duty to avoid arbitrariness and discrimination in the prosecution of crimes (Hartmann, 2010:202). However, criminal mediation must not be an obstacle to equality before the law, given that the defence of the legality principle represents a partial and unrealistic claim of equal treatment, which cannot be achieved through the practice of criminal prosecution (Langbein, 1974: 442). Supporting this line of thinking, Maier (2008:343) maintains that given that prosecution obligation did not exist for many centuries, giving priority to the private criminal prosecution model, action by the prosecution is but one possible model, which in some way weakens the indispensable aspect of the procedural legality principle.

Ratifying the above, but from another perspective, Binder (2000:77), argues that public criminal action must be designed in a more complex way, given that there are social interest cases, in which the State should not be limited to criminal prosecution. Thus it can be argued that the relationship between private and public action must be dynamic, and it does not make sense for the State to assume only the exercise of this action and then abandon the victim for exceeding it (Binder, 2009).

Despite the link between the principle of mandatory criminal action and substantive legality, there is no identity between them (Rodriguez, 2013). However, the legality principle, which is constitutionally enshrined in Latin America with negative formulae, which prohibits punishment and imposes penalties that are not provided for in laws before crime commissions, in no case dissociates from it. This means that all those who commit a crime must be punished with the penalty determined by law. Therefore, victim-offender mediation in Chile cannot affect the principles of legality. However, opportunity principle, which allows for the uniform use of this mechanism by all citizens must also be respected.

Criminal mediation model in Chile

The mediation model used in Chile is managed by professionals who participate as mediators and not volunteers in Continental systems (*Judicial Health Project and Community Mediation*, 2008), as opposed to what happens in Common Law models, where the participation of volunteers as mediators in the processes is not just usual practice but part of project ideology (Gavrielides, Artinopoulou, 2012).

With respect to the judicial Common Law models, such as VORP, the mediator is a community volunteer and not only follows the role of guiding and facilitating dialogue between parties but also represents the community in the process. This explains the volunteers being representatives of different age ranges, ethnicities, cultures and socio-economical classes that

---

4 Consider in art. 83 of the Chilean Political Constitution, were establishes the exercise of the penal action should abide to what the Criminal Procedural Code in the Constitutional Law of the Public Ministry

form part of the specific community from which the victims and offenders originate (Dagger, 2013).

This model also shares some characteristics with the Christian tradition of restorative justice, typical of the Zher theory (1990), in which direct mediation prevails, in contrast to practices developed in Common Law countries with indirect interventions to surrogate victims, close communities and community leaders.

In addition, it is part of the Latin American model to carry out previous individual sessions, a common VORP model feature, where these sessions fulfil an important symbolic function (Eiras, 2008).

The small number of mediated cases over the last 15 years in Chile allows us to affirm that although the practice of restorative justice exists in Latin America, it is still marginal and is not completely institutionalized. Statistics from Judicial assistance corporations indicate that derivation from the Prosecution Offices to the mediation centres decreases on a daily basis (González and Fuentealba, 2015).

Furthermore, unlike other countries such as New Zealand, the emergence of restorative justice has consisted in a policy called "top-down", raised from experts and/or authorities of the criminal justice system and not demands arising from the community and/or citizens, as in Common Law countries (Díaz, 2012).

A total of 60.8% of legal cases were effectively mediated in Chile during the last ten years, which lies within international parameters. Where Chile ranks lowest is in the level of agreements reached, possibly influenced by a low quality of referrals by the Attorney General to Criminal Mediation Centres, which are mostly disposable cases for the prosecutor, for not having antecedents and precise locations of the suspects (Gonzálezet al., 2015).

Thus, we maintain that the bilateral model of criminal mediation used in Chile has given good results, without prejudice to the low quality and importance of cases derived from the Public Ministry, which does not validate this form of terminating criminal proceedings because it affects their ranking in terms of the time taken to close processes, since they are not established as an alternative. Parties must then ratify the agreement in a hearing, which unnecessarily lengthens the closing process.

Nor do the judges value this model, ruling that the procedural terms used during criminal mediation only record that a reparatory agreement was reached, in some cases.

In this context, we observe some good practices of broad derivation to the criminal mediation system. We can cite the Argentine model of the Federal Province of Buenos Aires, where there is an integral system for the admission of criminal cases, in which the complainant and accused approach the public system with an offer, coordinated in a physical space (legal office, or criminal mediation and litigation system).

This allows mediation services to be widely used. In respect to the legislative model for normative regulation of criminal mediation processes, the most complete and coherent continental system to which Chile is integrated is the French, which is very accurate in its description, in terms of origin, requirements, implementation, consequences of achieving or not achieving agreements and compliance or non-compliance with them.

Operator perceptions regarding consequences of criminal mediation regulation

Information gathering techniques were applied in the field work carried out in Chile, consisting of in-depth interviews with a sample selected in four Chilean cities: Iquique, Valparaíso, Santiago and Temuco, chosen for the significant statistical experiences in penal mediations these localities present in relation to the rest of Chile, regarding Prosecutors (4), Judges (4), Defence attorneys (4) and criminal mediators (4). For interview analysis, the selected sample was labelled according to significance, and then the information was integrated, establishing relationships between the categories obtained and the postulated theoretical foundations.

The objectives of the field work were: to detect the perceptions of operators regarding consequences of normative regulation, criminal mediation and contents to be regulated in the Chilean legal system, as autonomous alternatives.

Among the advantages were: massive and uniform application of criminal mediation, allows systems to decongest and achieve better solutions between parties than they would obtain through the courts, creating previous instances which provide better solutions and justice.

However, the application of this restorative mechanism requires that it be regulated, in order to not affect procedural legality and place limits on opportunities, which is possible provided that such legislation was presented in a comprehensive and consistent manner to the criminal legislation of the country to which it applies.

This means saving on unnecessary resources of investigating and judging bodies, to be able to focus on efficient solutions for crimes of greater social connotation, which cannot be solved through collaborative mechanisms, because the parties are not found in adequate conditions or because the crimes committed have an important implication on public interests.

In addition, the parties involved participate in conflict solutions, with more empowered victims (Baruch Bush and Folger, 1995) and citizens that do not leave with a sense of impunity, as with the alternative, in which there is no collaboration.

On the other hand, criminal mediation offers a more functional solution for victims, repairing damages immediately and not only punishing the accused with spaces to reflect on the responsibility of the offenders and their interest on damage caused. Criminal mediation offers equal conditions between parties and a more humanizing process, centring the person before punishment (mediators and judges).

Another benefit of regulating criminal mediation is that it gives greater confidence to the community and credibility in the justice system. The fact that mediation is regulated allows a judicial certainty to exist regarding what can happen with this new system and provides equal access to each and every one of the people involved (judges and prosecutors).

On the other hand, and within the same opportunity systems regulated today, a greater quantity and quality of alternatives can be achieved through a mediated process, which, when regulated, is more likely to be used. Some prosecutors propose that: "Victims, when arriving with exalted emotions to the control audience, prevent agreements being reached, a situation which is mitigated by mediation". In addition, the accused are given a space for reflection and awareness of their actions, which helps prevent future recurrences.

In this way, criminal mediation regulation would allow greater formality and objectivity to be incorporated into this process, respecting the principles of due process and preventing the

Table 21.1 Development of restorative justice in Chile

	Iquique	Santiago	Valparaíso	Temuco
Mediator	2	2	2	2
Defender	1	1	1	1
Judge	1	1	1	1
Prosecutor	1	1	1	1
Total	20 subjects			

implementation of mediation favouring a situation of inequality between the parties and due process violations, as currently happens without regulation. Today all parties, in equal conditions, do not have the same access to a collaborative solution. This possibility is only offered arbitrarily to a few.

On the other hand, the fact that the consequences relating to the termination of penal action are not regulated discourages criminal mediation, the manner of terminations of criminal proceeding when there is a mediated agreement, its executive value and the situation it operates against for non-compliance (González, 2017).

At a transversal level, actors of the legal system believe that normative regulation of criminal mediation would allow greater use of this resource by citizens, achieving greater credibility and facilitating the consensus of networking.

Chile has a legalistic culture, therefore change in public policies on how to resolve crimes should not be left to the discretion of the prosecuting agency. Laws should establish necessary conditions for the application of this new system.

In this way, criminal mediation standardization would raise the Chilean justice standard, returning power to citizens, but taking care not to let the "soft hand" prevail in countries that greatly privilege punishment (Gonzalez and Fuentealba, 2013).

Disadvantages of regulating criminal mediation have not been identified, except for the cultural shock that this mechanism may produce with retributive expectations of citizens, which may encourage unsatisfactory solutions, in the face of extensive judicial processes, accepting mediation as the lesser evil.

In relation to whether criminal mediation configures an independent option or occupies an alternative option in force, there are different opinions and experiences. If it is treated as an independent option, this mechanism could be validly registered, and qualitative and quantitative studies of its findings could be made possible, allowing its monitoring and terminating cases faster than with the alternative options in progress. The current way to validate these mechanisms is through a complex procedure, since they require agreement ratifications in judicial hearings, which lengthens the process. Therefore, it is proposed that the mediator be a minister of faith in the acceptance and signing of agreements by parties and that the court may approve the agreement without requiring the presence of the parties.

Conclusion

It seems necessary that a country like Chile normatively regulate criminal mediation, because to solve criminal conflicts, legal systems require deeper procedures than the rapid negotiations granted currently between prosecutors and defendants. Solutions must have collaborative processes, regulated with objective criteria, with a sufficient number of professional experts and clarity in process stages, which citizens can access under equal conditions as a minimum guarantee for its implementation.

An alignment exists between judicial operators, inasmuch as the best time for criminal mediation is that closest to the date of the crime, which has a better impact on the entire system. However, incorporation prior to formalization may advance the resolution of the conflict and avoid judicialization, placing mediation in a stage of investigation, allowing it to be part of the penal system, but outside trials, giving authorities greater control with respect to guarantees of due process and system decongestion.

However, minority opinions state that "to be called criminal justice, mediation must take place when offenders are accused and informed of their responsibilities". Others maintain that "criminal justice must be transversal to the criminal process, applicable at every moment, before the criminal process, in a parallel manner, and even when the trial has ended with a conviction".

There are diverse opinions and experiences on the matter regarding whether to configure criminal mediation as an independent option or as an already established alternative option. If they are used as an independent option, this mechanism can be validly registered and carried out in qualitative and quantitative studies, allowing follow-ups and faster terminations than the alternative options already in progress.

In addition, the failure to reach an agreement in the mediation process should reactivate criminal action, in order to continue advancing procedurally and satisfy the needs of the victim, since the impossibility of returning to the judicial system can provoke withdrawal from mediation when victims perceive the possibility of losing their rights.

Regarding organizations that should be in charge of the derivation of causes for criminal mediation, options are varied; the essential is that it does not depend on the discretion of the prosecutor, which is necessary to have a neutral and impartial entity and a regulation that requires derivation to mediation in all cases unless there is explicit legal prohibition.

Without prejudice to the opinion of prosecutors that the Public Ministry should be the deriving entity, since they have all the information, carry out the investigations and are in charge of the principle of opportunity, this option allows arbitrary decisions, which depend on the confidence that prosecutors have in criminal mediation, as has happened in pilot projects in Chile and other countries in Latin America.

Mediators, prosecutors and judges consider that referrals may also be handled by police or investigators, as the first entity to be informed of the crime, allowing for a less bureaucratic process, where mediation would be applied over a period of time closer to the event. However, this option has detractors, because these interested parties in prosecution lack impartiality.

For this author, the option of referral by the Prosecutor's Office or the Police would be appropriate only if it were submitted to laws which require derivation of crimes to mediation, with express legal exceptions, and with the obligation of these entities to inform parties on the existence and benefits of mediation.

Regarding the crimes to which criminal mediation must be applied, there is still reluctance on the part of actors to assume the implementation of this mechanism to all crimes, which requires greater use of this mechanism and analysis.

However, there is a large majority of actors in the system who agree to using this mechanism for all crimes, except in cases expressly restricted by law, related to psychological circumstances of the parties and the type of crime, as is the case of violent crimes, those that provoke great social connotations and when public interest is compromised, having to justify the reason for non-derivation of a crime to mediation formally.

Finally, according to experiences in countries which have regulated criminal mediation and the opinion of interviewed actors, a protocol is required for its application which exhaustively defines conditions for its use, the value of the agreements and the future of criminal action in case there is no agreement, among other aspects. In this way, a better alignment of information for the parties involved will be achieved, preventing processes from being judicialized.

In terms of management, care must be taken that these processes do not affect the investigation time that prosecutors have as parameters to carry out their investigation.

In general, most experiences resulted in having to generate instruments to raise awareness of criminal mediation for penal system officials and citizens, through inter-institutional work.

One of the most important difficulties in this issue is the absence in Latin America of municipal networks strengthened to offer paid employment and/or community work for the accused, allowing them to offer compensation to those affected by crimes, whether economic or symbolic, as well as the possibility of medical treatments necessary to guarantee adequate future behaviours by the offender.

Finally, it is necessary to consider a special item in the national budget for the implementation and monitoring of criminal mediation practices (Project "Judicial Health and Community Mediation", 2009), mediator training and a registry maintained by the Ministry of Justice, who should periodically evaluate the quality of registered mediators, as in the case of mediation solicited as a family.

We highlight the Argentine model used in the federal province of Buenos Aires as a good practice, for its broad referral to mediation practices in the criminal system.

In this case, the victim, upon reaching the public system, is offered care and information through a specialized victims unit, a Mediation Centre and a litigious system, which facilitates the use of mediation.

Chile should follow France's legislative model for the normative regulation of mediation practices as an example, because it is the most complete and coherent with the continent's cultural system. This model is quite rigorous in its description, requirements, forms of implementation and consequences.

To conclude, it is important to affirm that the hypothesis suggested in this study is the following: "The normative regulation of criminal mediation as an independent alternative, in a criminal justice system such as Chile, will gain popularity for uniform use, promoting justice and discretion, limiting the power of authorities to decide whether to submit a criminal act to investigation, formalization, trial, or refer to criminal mediation, with previously established criteria". It was possible to confirm this hypothesis through our study analysis.

Additionally, we can affirm that it is possible to "change lenses", or change the way in which criminal mediation is seen today in Chile. For this, it is necessary for Chile to exhibit a cultural change, which goes hand in hand with the normative regulation of criminal mediation practices, considering its implementation at a national level to be included in the national budget as a special item.

Bibliography

Aguad, D., Bazán, N., Bianciotti, D., Gorgas, M. and Olmedo, B. 2011. *La regulación provincial del principio de oportunidad*. Córdoba: Academia Nacional de Derecho, Instituto de Ciencias Penales.

Allen, R. 2002. Alternatives to prosecution. En M. Mc Cconville, y G.wilson (eds.) *The Handbook of the Criminal Justice Process*. Oxford: University Press, pp. 32–41.

Anitua, G. 2004. *Enfoque histórico-comparado*. Buenos Aires: Publicaciones Universidad de Buenos Aires.

Baruch, B., y Folger, J.P. 1995. *La promesa de la mediación*. Buenos Aires: Gránica.

Beltrán, A. 2014. Justicia Restaurativa y Mediación Penal en los Modelos Anglosajones, *Revista de l' Institut Universitari d' Investigació en Criminologia i Ciències Penals de la UV*, 11(1989–6352): 28–44.

Binder, A. 2000. *Ideas y materiales para la reforma de la justicia penal: De La Formulación A La Praxis*. Buenos Aires: Editorial Ad-Hoc.

Binder, A. 2009. *Introducción al Derecho Procesal Penal*, 2° edición, Buenos Aires: Ad Hoc.

Buteler, J.A. 1998. *Los problemas constitucionales y procesales que plantea el principio de oportunidad en el Derecho Argentino*. En 12 Jornadas Nacionales de Derecho Penal. 9 de noviembre 1998. Mendoza: Editorial Universidad Nacional de Cuyo.

Cafferata, N.J. 2000. *Cuestiones actuales sobre el Proceso Penal*, 3ª ed., Editores del Puerto, Buenos Aires.

Carnevali, R. 2005. Las políticas de orientación a la víctima examinadas a la luz del derecho penal, *Revista de Derecho de la Pontifica Universidad Católica de Valparaíso*, XXVI, Semestre I: 27–39.

Cesano, J.D. 2010. *El nuevo Derecho Procesal Penal, entre el fortalecimiento de las garantías y la evitación del castigo*. Lima: Editorial Ara.

Cheliotis, L. 2011. The Perils of Non-Adversarialism, *Journal of Criminology*, 8(1), *Comentary on Freiberg European*, Enero-abril: 108–112.

Creswell, J. and Plano, C. 2011. *Designing and Conducting Mixed Methods Research*. Thousand Oaks, CA: Sage Publications.

Corral, H. 2008. *Cómo realizar una tesis en Derecho*. Santiago. Editorial Jurídica de Chile.

Dagger, R. 2013. Republicanism and the Foundations of Criminal Law. In R. Duff y S. Green (eds.) *Philosophical Foundations of Criminal Law*. Oxford: Oxford University Press. May-Agosto, pp. 44–66.

Dávalos, J.I. 2016. La mediación penal como método alternativo de resolución de conflictos: resultados actuales en la República Argentina. Ultima visita junio. Available at www.derechoycambiosocial.com/revista022/mediacion_penal.pdf

Del Val, M.T. 2012. *Gestión del conflicto penal*. Buenos Aires: Editorial Astrea.

Díaz Gude, A. 2012. La Experiencia de la Mediación Penal en Chile, *Revista Política Criminal*, 5(9). Santiago: Universidad de Talca, pp. 1–67.

Díaz López, J. 2011. Propuestas para la práctica de la mediación penal: Delitos patrimoniales cometidos entre parientes y responsabilidad penal de las personas jurídicas, *Revista para el Análisis del Derecho*. Barcelona: Dret, julio: 38–59.

Eiras, U. 2008. *¿Dónde está la víctima? Apuntes sobre victimología*. Buenos Aires: Editorial Histórica.

Eiras, U. 2012. Justicia Restaurativa en Mediación Penal. In Ministerio de Justicia (ed.) *Congreso: Un aporte a la Cohesión Social*. Santiago: Minju, Noviembre, pp. 22–40.

Entrevista semiestructurada efectuada a Fiscal de Valparaíso. 2017. *En Estudio Exploratorio de Opiniones de los Operadores Jurídicos del Sistema Procesal Penal en Chile, sobre la Necesidad y Consecuencias de Regular Normativamente la Mediación Penal*. Universidad Central de Chile.

Ferrajoli, L. 1995. *Derecho y Razón: Teoría del Garantismo Penal*. Madrid: Editorial Trotta. Trad. Ibañez P.

Frances Lecumberri, P. 2012. El principio de oportunidad y la justicia restaurativa, *Revista para el análisis del Derecho*, N° 4. Barcelona, In Dret, abril:1–42.

Fleiner, T. 2005. *Common Law and Continental Law: Two Legal Systems*. Proyecto de investigación. Suiza: Agencia Suiza de Desarrollo y Cooperación.

Gavrielides, T. y Artinopoulou, V. 2007. *Restorative Justice Theory and Practice: Addressing the Discrepancy*. Helsinki: European Institute for Crime Prevention and Control, affiliated with the United Nations (HEUNI).

Gavrielides, T. y Artinopoulou, V. 2012. *Using Restorative Justice with Street Group Violence*. London: IARS.

Glaeser, E. and Shleifer, A. 2002. Legal Origins, *Quarterly Journal of Economics*, 117(4): 1193–1229.

González, I. 2016. *Justicia restaurativa: herramientas para el cambio desde la gestión del conflicto*. Santiago: Ril editores.

González, I. and Fuentealba, S. 2013. La mediación penal como mecanismo de Justicia Restaurativa. *Revista de Derecho y Ciencia Política*. Universidad Católica de Temuco, 4(3), Temuco: 175–210.

González, I. and Fuentealba, S. 2014. *Es necesario incorporar formalmente mecanismos propios de la Justicia restaurativa en el sistema penal chileno*. En I. González and Universidad Central de Chile (ed.) Herramientas para el cambio desde la gestión del conflicto. Santiago: Ril editores, pp. 23–105.

González, I., Fuentealba, S. and Cordova, M. 2015.Protocolo de atención de casos de mediación Penal en el Centro de Mediación Negociación y Arbitraje de la Universidad Central de Chile. En *Revista La Trama*, N° 45, Mayo. Buenos Aires: Florencia Brandoni. Available at www.revistalatrama.com.ar/contenidos/larevista_articulo.php?id=312&ed=45

González Ramírez, Isabel. 2017. Justicia Restaurativa: Herramientas para el cambio desde la gestión del conflicto, La Mediación Penal y su desarrollo normativo, Editorial Tirant Le Blanch, España, pp. 23–105.

Hartmann, A. 2010. The Practice of Tater-Opfer- Ausgleich. In Germany, Budapest, Conference European Best Practices of Restorative Justice, Conference Publication. Londres: IARS Publications.

Hassemer, Winfried, 1988. *La persecución penal: legalidad y oportunidad En Revista Jueces para la Democracia*, N° 4. Trad. Cobos Gómez de Linares, Madrid, pp. 8–11.

Hassemer, W. 2003. *Crítica al Derecho Penal de Hoy: Norma, Interpretación, Procedimiento: Límites de la Prisión Preventiva*. Buenos Aires: Editorial Ad-Hoc.

Hendler, E. 2004. *Las garantías penales y procesales: Enfoque histórico-comparado*. Buenos Aires: Editores del Puerto.

Hendler, E. 2006. *El juicio por jurados: Significados, genealogías, incógnitas*. Buenos Aires: Editores del Puerto.

Horvitz, M.I. y López, J. 2003. *Derecho procesal penal chileno*, Tomo 1. Santiago: Editorial jurídica de Chile.

Horvitz, M.I. y López, J. 2005. *Estado de Derecho y Reformas a la Justicia*, Santiago: Edición conjunta Universidad de Chile, Heilderberg University y California Western School of Law.

Hoyle, C. and Young, R. 2002. Restorative Justice: Assessing the Prospects and Pitfalls. In M. McConville and G. Wilson (eds.) *The Handbook of the Criminal Justice Process*. Oxford: Oxford University Press, pp. 525–548.

Langbein, J. 1974. Controling Prosecutorial Discretion in Germany, *The University of Chicago Law Review*, 41(3): 439–467.

López Masle, J. 2012. Debido proceso en Chile; hacia un principio generador de reglas. En A. Bordalí (coord.) *Justicia Constitucional y Derechos Fundamentales*. Santiago: Editorial LexisNexis.

Maier, J. 2008. Balance y propuesta del enjuiciamiento penal del siglo XX. En el mismo (ed.) *Antología: El Proceso Penal Contemporáneo*. Lima: Palestra Editores, pp. 343–365.

Márquez Cárdenas, A. 2012. La Mediación como Mecanismo de Justicia Restaurativa, *Revista Prolegómenos: Derechos y Valores*, XV(29): 149–171.

McCold, Paul y Wachtel, T. 2003. *En busca de un paradigma: una teoría sobre Justicia Restaurativa*. Ponencia presentada en el XIII Congreso Mundial sobre Criminología, del 10 al 15 de agosto de 2003, Río de Janeiro, Brasil.

Mera-Ballesteros, A. 2009. Justicia Restaurativa y proceso penal garantías procesales: límites y posibilidades, Revista *Ius et Praxis*, 15(2): 165–195.

Parra Urdaneta, S., Fernández González, M.A., Morales Manzur, J. y Párraga. 2010. El sistema penal venezolano desde la perspectiva de los medios alternos de resolución de conflictos: una mirada garantista. Revista Luz Universidad de Zulia, *Capítulo Criminológico*, 38(1): pp. 35–62.

Rodríguez Vega, M. 2013. Principios de obligatoriedad y discrecionalidad en el ejercicio de la acción penal, *Revista de Derecho*, XXVI(1): 181–208.

Solaro, C. y Paul, J. 1987. El proceso penal en Francia, *Jueces para la democracia*, 2(2), semestre. Disponible, julio 2017. Available at https://dialnet.unirioja.es/descarga/articulo/2525740.pdf

Zárate campos, M. 2004. *Comentarios de los acuerdos reparatorios: algunos comentarios a partir de las nociones de reparación y negociación*. En Revista de Derecho y Humanidades, N° 9: 125–146.

Zehr, H. 1990. *Changing Lenses: A New Focus for Crime and Justice*. Scottdale, PA: Herald Press.

No reference is provided for "Some prosecutors propose that: "Victims, when arriving with exalted emotions to the control audience, prevent agreements being reached, a situation which is mitigated by mediation".

22

Is restorative justice possible through the eyes of lay people? A Polish evidence-based case study

Anna Matczak

Introduction and research strategy

This chapter aims to contribute to the Handbook's key objective of pushing the barriers of criminological scholarship by examining restorative justice within the Polish context of a post-socialist, post-transformation society. My intention for this chapter is to present selected findings from my doctoral study to challenge the scope and viability of restorative justice and encourage examining its preconditions through lay people's understandings of punishment and justice. In order to explore whether, and to what extent, restorative justice is possible through the eyes of lay people, one must therefore look beyond the legal basis and formal logistics which have been already in place for many years. I used Poland as my case study, but the findings are relevant to the international reader.

My research aims to account for the complexity of lay people's views on crime, punishment and justice insofar as these help us to understand their views on restorative approaches to justice. It also aims to investigate their interpretations and the underlying 'drivers' of those attitudes – the constructed knowledge that exists within this specific post-socialist, post-transformation, European context. Taking into account the complexity of the subject and the social, political and economic background that might explain study participants' views, it was important to use a research method that did not impose upon the participants' expectations or prior inferences but that elicited expressions of the views in participants' own words (Crossley, 2002).

Qualitative research, in the form of focus groups and in-depth interviews, was chosen because it allows greater opportunity for participants to express their opinions in more depth (Noaks and Wincup, 2004). In my study, I explore how 65 lay Polish people and four mediators understand punishment and justice, and how their narratives inform the viability of restorative approaches to punishment and justice. The sampling strategy was based on theoretical requirements and considerations. Having reviewed the literature on restorative justice and lay people's views on crime and sanctions, a number of break characteristics needed to be taken into account in order to sample study participants: age, gender, geographic location, and prior experience of the criminal justice system, as research suggests these factors could influence participants' views on crimes, punishment and justice.

In consequence, my research was carried out in two settings: one rural, the other urban. In each setting, I set up the following focus groups: one group of young and one of older participants (unisex) and one group of female-only, and one of male-only participant groups (mixed age). The main fieldwork was carried out between April and September 2013. I began this by conducting ten focus groups, initially in the rural and then urban locations, and then between July and September 2013, I undertook 41 in-depth interviews with focus group participants as well as additional interviews with people who did not participate in group discussions. In May and June 2015 an additional ten interviews were undertaken with lay people who had experience of the Polish criminal justice system. Table 22.1 presents an overview of the number of participants in the research and the form of fieldwork in which they appeared.

The structure of this chapter is as follows. I will firstly introduce the Polish context and discuss the value of lay opinion in criminology. Based on my research findings, I will then argue that while the projections of criminal justice perceptions onto victim-offender mediation may be seen as the main obstacle to the development of restorative justice in Poland, participants' confidence in unpaid work, seen as a symbolic feature of Polish society, could serve as an avenue to develop restorative practice further.

The Polish context

Poland is predominantly known for its socialist past. The time of 'real socialism' or communism that is considered as the time between 1944–1989, can be argued as the period when the Stalinization, or Sovietization, of the Polish criminal law and criminal justice system was one of the most distinctive 'products' of the communist regime (Krajewski, 2002). As the separation of powers into legislative, executive and judicial branches was non-existent, the communist authorities aimed at subordinating the criminal justice system in order to: legitimize the activity of the Party,[1] eliminate political opponents and supervise citizens and their property. The collapse of the communist regime in 1989 resulted in rapid regime change carried out in the form of multiple transformations.

Table 22.1 Sampling and research strategy for the fieldwork

Form of fieldwork	Number of participants	Number of interviews/focus groups
Exploratory research – interviews with mediators	4 interviewees	4 interviews
Focus groups	41 FG participants	10 focus groups
In-depth interviews	– 27 interviews with FG lay participants – 14 interviews with new lay (non-FG) participants – 10 interviews with people who had experience with the Polish criminal justice system	51 interviews
Total	69 participants	55 interviews & 10 focus groups

1 The Polish United Workers' Party (*Polska Zjednoczona Partia Robotnicza*, PZPR) was the Communist party which governed the Polish People's Republic from 1948 to 1989.

Post-1989 was a time when the shape and condition of the Polish penal landscape went through a transformation. Restorative justice, introduced in the form of victim-offender mediation, was part of these political ambitions to change the Polish penal reality and join the international community in the West. Given that the concept was introduced at a time when Polish society was dealing with the socialist legacy and creating a new democratic reality, it was also hoped that victim-offender mediation could serve as a fast-track remedy and act as an ancillary mechanism to reduce the sudden spike in court workloads after the fall of communism. In other words, victim-offender mediation was believed to be a remedy for the crisis of the criminal justice system, and widely practised (Cielecki, 2009; Juszkiewicz, 2010; Politowicz, 2012).

The Polish model of victim-offender mediation is now closely interwoven with the criminal justice system. However, it is neither a typical alternative out-of-court procedure nor a diversion practice. The Polish legislation envisages three referring bodies that can send cases to mediation: police officers, prosecutors and judges (courts) and penitentiary judges at the post-sentence stage (Bieńkowska, 2009). Bieńkowska (2009) has observed that under the current circumstances, the Polish model of victim-offender mediation constitutes a practice that runs parallel to the traditional inquisitorial system of adjudicating cases. Once a decision about referring a case to mediation is made, the proceedings are adjourned for a mediation encounter to take place outside of the court setting (and the court case is neither suspended nor discontinued). Another characteristic feature is the 'legal status' of a mediation agreement (Bieńkowska, 2009). Although mediation outcomes are always scrutinized by a judge, mediation agreements are not legally binding like court decisions. Furthermore, there is no legal provision to execute mediation outcomes (such as financial reparation or unpaid work) (ibid.).

The number of cases referred to mediation in Poland is relatively small,[2] and victim-offender mediation, with a few exceptions, has been recognised as a 'dead institution' in Poland (Rękas, 2003). Restorative justice might be a convenient solution in an increasingly globalized world, however. As discussed by Jones and Newburn (2007), the transnational transfer of penal policies is equally shaped by the national, political cultures and institutions. In the case of Poland, it may well be that the exceptionally limited interest in victim-offender mediation and paucity of anticipated outcomes of the practice might have deeper sociocultural roots.

Lay people

I believe that there is value in lay opinion in criminology. Therefore, I approach punishment and justice as social activities – which echoes the argument that stories about crime and punishment are entangled with people's daily routines, and as a result are lodged in their cultural imagination (see Garland and Sparks, 2000). People's engagement with punishment and justice is now seen as a new approach to democracy, in which lay people, as citizens, are expected to be more responsible for, and engaged with, the work being delivered by criminal justice institutions (Roberts, 2014). Additionally, restorative justice also indicates a more active role for lay people, as lay involvement means that people are given back a 'direct and hands-on control of justice decision making' (Dzur, 2008:202) that creates a chance for them as a community to experience the process of conflict resolution themselves. In the Polish context, lay people are seen as *Homo post-Sovieticus* (see Kania, 2012), whose perceptions of punishment and justice need to be analysed along with the legacy of

---

2 According to Polish Ministry of Justice statistics, in 2015 there were only 4,046 cases referred to mediation, out of which 2,530 were successfully completed. Data available at http://mediacja.gov.pl/Statystyki.html accessed 14.11.2017.

the previous socialist system, their nostalgic sentiments for 'the socialist world that was lost' and their bitter disappointment with the post-1989 changes.

Criminal justice projections – limitations to restorative justice

Restorative justice, since its conception, is interwoven with punishment and justice. This 'uneasy' relationship reflects Gavrielides's concept of restorative justice fault lines that contribute to the concept's ambiguity and complexity (see Gavrielides, 2008). Although restorative justice has been introduced and mainly discussed by restorative justice scholars as an alternative vision of justice administration, most restorative justice interventions worldwide operate within formal criminal justice systems. Dzur (2011:371) argues that it is both a strength and weakness that restorative justice originated in conventional justice institutions, as without criminal justice agencies it would have been difficult to put restorative justice practices in motion.

Dzur's argument is especially important for the Polish context, in which victim-offender mediationis closely situated within and dependent on the criminal justice establishment. Likewise, my participants' perceptions of victim-offender mediation were significantly intertwined with and echoed their views on the Polish criminal justice system. The viability of restorative justice depends on many factors. However, drawing on these lay perspectives, my contention is that understanding of and the confidence in restorative encounters might also depend on how someone's perceives the traditional criminal justice system and projects those perceptions onto any alternative conflict resolution.

Post-1989 (in)justice

People's chronic distrust of the Polish justice system is one of the key characteristics of the Polish legal culture (Kurczewski, 2007). What was, however, evident in my research was that the hasty transition from socialism to democracy and from a centrally planned to free-market economy has remarkably influenced my participants' perceptions of justice administration and the Polish institutions involved in these processes. In my study, it is participants' perceptions of sentencing as being different for the poor and the rich that reflect a wider sense of social (in) justice and the post-1989 consequences of the transformation struggle. The perception of 'sentencing inadequacy' was discussed alongside the importance of being in possession of money, and the following quotation comes from an interviewee who contrasted his opinion with the so-called 'sad' Polish reality, in which the value of money is high:

AM: *What is most important when it comes to sentencing?*
        When it comes to sentencing . . . The circumstances of the incident. Whether this person is aware
        of one's actions, consequences, whether is willing to submit oneself to penalty. Yes, it should depend
        on this. Unfortunately, in our country it depends on whether this person has money or not, and
        this is sad.

[male interviewee, 23 years old, urban area]

A similar observation was found in a quantitative study conducted in 2002/2003 where the money element, second after lawyers' services, was mentioned by survey respondents as something that matters the most in the Polish justice system (Kurczewski, 2007). Limited trust in the efficiency and fairness of the Polish criminal justice system might also be interwoven with certain materialistic/consumerists attitudes which were reported by Szymanowski (2012) along with the sudden inflow of material goods after 1989.

The understanding of justice as a privilege of the rich, and as oppression for the poor led my participants to believe in the alleged built-in inequality of 'Polish justice'. The rich were perceived as the ones who first of all accumulated their wealth through fiddles and skulduggery, made the best connections and now can afford to pay financial penalties as well the best lawyers, and in consequence they appeared as unreachable by the Polish justice system:

P33:   *From the one who stole a bottle worth 12 (PLN), they would take damn everything, and the one who stole millions using a scam gets nothing.*

P32:   *Because there is a linkage between political, business elites and the courts. I know people who work at the Prosecutor's office; sometimes we drink vodka in the garden. So what he said is this: there are some situations when you can do something and no one is bothered. For example my friends' daughter died when she was 18 years old. She went camping with other people and apparently she drowned. There were fifteen people from one class, it was a post-graduation camp and these kids were children of prosecutors, judges, directors of big companies. And while we were sitting and drinking vodka in the garden this prosecutor told me that my friends shouldn't waste money on lawyers because they would achieve nothing. So there is a linkage between political, business elites and the courts. And as P33 said earlier, there is no democracy . . .*

P33:   *There is none, no democracy and no justice in the courts.*

              [focus group with male participants in their early sixties, urban area]

Participants' perception of disproportionate or inadequate sentencing clashes with the still present 'culture of favours' – another characteristic relic among post-communist societies where social order has been particularly grounded in informality, reciprocity and networks. The participants' perception of the divide between the poor and the rich in the Polish justice system aptly reflects the post-1989 divide between Polish people who did and did not benefit socially and economically from the transformation (see Czarnota, 2009), and their ambivalent legal culture that facilitates the application of 'double legal standards' (see Kurczewski, 2007). The post-1989 times of transition in Poland brought not only the privatization of property and the reduction of state involvement in the economy but it was also a time that attracted a significant increase in white collar crime (Jasiński, 1999). A description of the immediate post-1989 events was detailed by Staniszkis (1999) as a privatization of the state that also meant the exploitation of considerable state resources and institutions for private ends. She argued that post-socialist economies were prone to international organized crime due to general chaos, blurred lines between legitimate and illegitimate businesses, well-established cultures of corruption, clientelism, poorly defined property rights, currency and foreign exchange fluctuations and opportunities for safe money laundering. The process of dismantling the socialist system was, according to Staniszkis (1991), a controlled power conversion process which is a conversion of political assets of the nomenklatura into economic ones. Furthermore, Skąpska (2009) compared the post-1989 privatization and implementation of economic freedoms to colonialism, when the conquistadors participated in the accumulation of capital in order to legalize it, and later became prestigious, law-abiding entrepreneurs.

Channelling economic insecurities

This unequal post-1989 privatization of property not only strongly affected the sense of social justice that, as my research demonstrates, was projected onto people's understandings of the administration of justice but also contributed to participants' perception of victim-offender mediation as being that of a business-like meeting, with the promise of compensation as a primary advantage. In my study, reparation through the mediation process was more likely to gain people's support when harm falls into the category of property loss or criminal damage rather than psychological injury or death. Such perception of mediation does not fully reflect the restorative concept, and the following quote from a male interviewee interestingly illustrates this point:

> *Where mediation would be effective, for example . . . let's say that the victim agrees to, for example, to get something repaired, the offender smashed through the victim's fence for example. What I am saying is based on my own experience and what I have seen, and for example, it is not necessary to take the police and court's time, you know. The offender accepts it: I was driving too fast, my car skidded, I damaged the fence, how much does it cost? . . . and someone estimates that 1000zl – here you are, I pay 1000zl and this is how they sort things out. And in this case they don't get involved, the police can fine him for careless driving, but neither the prosecutor is involved nor the case is continued, because there are more important things and the case is sorted.*
>
> [male interviewee, 65 years old, rural area]

However, one Polish female mediator remarked on how frequently victims come to mediation sessions and demand enormous financial compensation and how 'this attitude' still surprises her:

> [Laugh] *and the other thing is about the victims, hmm oh they are various people. It depends what happened, because it depends on the case and how big is the harm that was caused. But sometimes they smart off, they know that they could be quids in . . . What do you think Miss how much I can gain out of it?* [Laugh]
>
> [Mediator1/I]

In one of the in-depth interviews, a 31-year old male interviewee living in an urban area explored possible explanations for the perception of victim-offender mediation as a negotiation of interests:

> *I think that this* [mediation] *would be great, but unfortunately in many cases . . . with such a strange you know, strange Polish mentality, I don't know, triggered by frustration you know, salary frustration, it could lead to the situation where the victim, despite already having received . . . restitution for the damage, somehow still tries to scrounge and . . . still stands fast to gain something else . . .*
>
> [male interviewee, 31 years old, urban area]

Firstly, similar observations to the view taken by some of my study participants were made by Tränkle (2007:402), who says: '[T]he first risk is that the mediation process may be reduced to a simple negotiation of interests [. . .] some victims try to make money by claiming more compensation than would be appropriate'. A similar remark was made by Fellegi (2010) in the context of the Hungarian system of mediation. She observed that cases with no financial loss are rarely referred to victim-offender mediation, and the Hungarian authorities underestimate the significance of non-material reparation. This observation is analogous to the one that appears in the report on restorative justice in New Zealand, also based on focus group discussions with lay people (Ministry of Justice, 1996). The authors warn that the success of restorative practice can be challenged by the vindictive attitudes of some of the people. In terms of people's support for restorative practices, research demonstrates that restitution and compensation are key issues that attract significant support among lay people (see Ministry of Justice NZ, 1996; Roberts and Hough, 2005), but there is still little known about the nature of this support.

Secondly, the aforementioned quotations demonstrate that mediation encounters and the perception of harm do not happen in a social vacuum. Walklate (2005:174) has argued that some socio-economic conditions might facilitate restorative justice, while others might not. The reflections on 'strange Polish mentality' and 'salary frustration' open the door to a broader understanding of the socio-economic context in which the Polish victim-offender mediation operates. This craving for financial gain can be viewed as a consequence of post-1989 political and economic policies and the transformation from a socialist to a market society. Under the guise of interest in restorative practice, such as mediation, there is a risk of pursuing individual intentions to perceive mediation more as a practice to gain compensation and perhaps seek a degree of economic justice. Under these circumstances, restorative practice may be perceived as an opportunity for 'channelling economic insecurities' and perhaps seeking economic justice – something that poses a substantial obstacle to further development of restorative justice in Poland and might be an impediment elsewhere, too.

Lawyers v. mediators

Another interesting element of the relationship between the Polish criminal justice system and victim-offender mediation is the juxtaposition between the role of mediators and lawyers in the process of mediation. When it comes to achieving justice, my participants placed hope in 'merciless' lawyers who knew perfectly how to navigate litigants, prevaricate and search for loopholes in the law to win their clients' cases. The image of lawyers as 'money-mad, heartless sharks' whose presence in court is perceived to be necessary has long been argued by Friedman (1989). Given participants' sense of division between the rich and the poor, and their confidence in the value of money, it is also interesting to observe how lawyers equally appeared as people who could provide safety and surety that defendants have to pay for. The following excerpt from an interview with a senior male illustrates how lawyers' accessibility and availability was discussed against the theme of financial means:

> We have been complaining a lot about the functioning of the courts. We tend to say the mills of God grind slowly, yet they grind exceedingly fine. This applies to some deistic sayings, but you have to wait, for example civil cases take years to conclude. It takes years to get someone convicted. And this is not good about our criminal justice system. When it comes to convictions, it's been said that we shouldn't dispute them, but when you compare some of them, for example appropriation of property and murder, when someone gets so many years or months, it's just a pure misunderstanding, right? You just need to have a really good lawyer, which simply means you need to have money to pay him and then your sentence is just symbolic. Fortunately, I don't know it from my experience but from what I hear from my friends and friends of friends etc. In my opinion, our judiciary does good between E and C. That's how I think.
>
> [male interviewee, 72 years old, urban area]

The 'necessary presence' of lawyers in people's narratives requires further elaboration. Kurczewski (2007, 2009) has highlighted that lawyers used to be greatly trusted by the Polish public. He explains this confidence by the fact that under socialism lawyers were widely known and respected, as they performed an overarching mission of protection from injustice and political oppression. Secondly, he says, they played a key role in introducing and leading post-1989 transformation changes. However, I doubt whether this interpretation has broader implications. It is questionable whether lay people were familiar with the incarceration of all high-profile political opponents, or who was behind the implementation of post-1989 policies. Therefore, it is better to ask what place in the life of the community the legal profession had. Undoubtedly, there was a profound difference between the role played by the legal profession in the West and the Soviet countries. While advocates in the West established their position through a long tradition of independent and courageous affirmation of the rights of the individual, the Soviet lawyers were expected to act as 'bold defenders of socialist truth and justice' (Razi, 1960). Their role to defend the rights of the individual was greatly limited to the areas of strictly private matters such as divorce, alimony or housing (ibid.). These type of court cases frequently attracted financial compensation, and this is something that could better explain participants' confidence in lawyers.

Despite low confidence in the Polish criminal justice system, study participants perceived lawyers to be part and parcel of the administration of justice and their presence a safeguard in mediation encounters. Interestingly, one of the interviewed mediators, who was trained as a lawyer, said that a legal background should be a precondition to entering the profession of mediation because the nature of Polish mediation is highly legally dependant:

> When it comes to mediation in criminal cases there has to be a requirement of having a law degree. It does matter, really. You see, at least I know how to read the Penal Code and how to interpret its sections. I don't want to sound like I am downgrading their professions but if it is up to a pedagogue, or sociologist, I'm not sure whether they can explain to people what they can expect from mediation.
>
> [Mediator 1]

Fellegi (2007), based on her research in Hungary, has interestingly argued that such a close relationship between the criminal justice system and restorative practice can result in the over-professionalization of restorative practices, or 'lawyerization' of victim-offender mediation. However, not only the process of lawyerization might be seen as a hindrance to the development of restorative justice but also the mutual antipathy between the two professions. This was very interestingly illustrated by the same mediator:

> It might be a conspiracy theory, but that's how I see it, perhaps it is because of the lawyer lobby who doesn't like us, mediators. It's about money. I have a friend who is a lawyer. When he gets a client, who is a defendant, he would give the client such a fright that the poor fella goes home to his family, they raise money and he brings 5 000 PLN [approximately £1000]. If my friend referred this case to mediation, for which the State pays a mediator 140 PLN [approximately £28], then he had 5 000 PLN disappeared from the table. It's a conflict of interests. He will never tell his client: go and see a mediator because it's worth it. Instead, for 5 000 PLN, he will pretend that he can do everything to win his case. Generally speaking no one has an interest in mediation, but mediators themselves [laugh].
>
> [Mediator 1]

Participants' confidence in lawyers might indicate that some people are not necessarily interested in resolving 'conflicts' themselves, and despite limited trust in justice institutions, people might still stick to the logic and principles of a penal procedure, and again, project courtroom/traditional justice perceptions onto how they view restorative justice. In my research, this was manifested in participants' perception of mediation as a 'business-like settlement' that would be 'most beneficial' if assisted by lawyers. The nature of lay people's views might further indicate that the functioning of a majority of restorative justice practices is, and will remain, dependent on the criminal justice agencies and the perception of the traditional justice mechanisms. I therefore argue that, given the close relationship between the Polish criminal justice system and victim-offender mediation, participants' overall disappointment with the system and their projections onto victim-offender mediation should be seen as a significant obstacle to the viability of restorative justice in Poland.

Unpaid work – the window of opportunity for restorative justice

While the low confidence in, and the projections of, the Polish criminal justice system might be seen as an obstacle to popularizing victim-offender mediation further, according to my research, increasing the work element in mediation outcomes perhaps would bring better chances for success. What was of one of the most significant interests in my doctoral research was the question of whether Poland as a post-communist and post-transformation society has the potential to be receptive to the restorative function of punishment. In my research, unpaid work was overwhelmingly viewed as the most appropriate and beneficial form of punishment. When discussed in the form of a community sanction, unpaid work was seen as a vehicle that could enhance remorse, activate the feeling of guilt among offenders and in consequence attract restorative perspectives.

Participants' trust in work as a response to crime was built on a number of intertwined themes. One of the themes that recurred throughout participants' accounts was how work, as reparation, can help offenders to restore their relations with their respective communities. Such a restorative tone can be found in the following quotation, where a more humane approach towards offenders ('educate and talk to offenders') was indicated in the discussion with male participants:

AM: *I am wondering what you think about sending people to prison. Imprisonment as punishment? You started saying that we should talk to offenders, am I right?*

P32:   *Of course we should. They should be given punishments, do not isolate them, how to put it? . . . Educate them.*

P33:   *Rehabilitation.*

P32:   *This type of rehabilitation, where they report to a certain meeting place or work, sort of . . . or workshops, where they could realize . . . that they can return to society through work! Oh! This way, I would see it this way, not to lock them up in prisons and have nothing out of this. The State pays without making him realize . . . and he could be educated . . . he doesn't participate in generating national income, I would never be in favour of prisons. For some big offences, murders, robberies yes, but otherwise . . .*

[focus group with male participants in their sixties, urban area]

One of the advantages of work as a community service was that work could serve as a better means to redeem one's wrongdoings:

I would also prefer them to work. Wherever there are any needs, shortfalls, where there is no money to finance some public works, they should work there, ho-hum, whoever can afford to pay, won't feel the restriction. And the ones who can't afford to pay, so to speak, it's a bit of a vicious circle for them and what next? How to force him to . . .? He got a fine but doesn't pay, he is sent to prison and what? He should get a chance to rehabilitate himself through some community work. There are so many needs, for example in orphanages, you can arrange a lot of things, it is just important that they work and become helpful.

[female interviewee, 66 years old, urban area]

In my research some participants said that work could generate some sort of 'thinking processes' in offenders that could teach them a lesson and affect their future decisions and actions. The just-described 'thinking processes' involves acknowledging one's actions, taking responsibility and feeling remorseful, which correspond with the core restorative justice objectives. Restorative justice has long been argued for as a process of respectful dialogue, where offenders are held accountable for their actions, harm is repaired and offenders are reintegrated into society (Zehr and Mika, 1998). One of the important features of restorative justice is the expressions of remorse that are essential components of any restorative practice (see Roberts and Hough, 2005; Stalans, 2002). This observation was made in one of the interviews, where it was indicated that work can enhance remorse in offenders, leading to their reintegration into society:

> *First thing, unpaid work means a lesson in remorse and cooperation with other people. That's what I think.*

[female interviewee, 20 years old, urban area]

Another interesting outcome of the data analysis is the participants' view that work might activate a feeling of guilt, and so break the denial of responsibility among offenders – something known as neutralization techniques. These techniques were described by Sykes and Matza (1957), who argued that most delinquency is based on justifications for crime that protect the individual from self-blame and the blame of others after the wrongdoing. When there is no disapproval from the social environment, these rationalizations are lightly neutralized and the individual can engage in further delinquency. A similar understanding of the issue appeared in conversations with young study participants living in an urban area, in which one of them shared his view that work can be seen as an avenue for the offender to realize the consequences of his actions and, as a consequence, prevent any denial:

> AM: *Fine. Those of you who indicated the second option as the better one [in relation to a case scenario], so what was it exactly that appealed to you? Was it that he acknowledged his guilt, that he wrote an apology letter, or that he would get a financial penalty because he agreed to compensate all the damage, or that he would do unpaid work? What was it . . .//*
> P21: *That he acknowledged his guilt, and that he agreed to cover damages.*
> P24: *Essentially the fact that he would compensate financially, and that he would work for a bit as this way he could feel that he had done something wrong. If he apologized and only gave it back, that wouldn't be enough.*

[focus group with university students, urban area]

Although this view was mainly articulated among young study participants, there is some indication that lay people might perceive work as a powerful sanction to disable the neutralization techniques described by Sykes and Matza (1957). Finally, some participants expressed that victim-offender mediation could gain people's interest if it was made clear that there would be a work element to it:

> P40: *I would consider mediation if only this 'turd' does some unpaid work.*
> P41: *Or replace your roofing felt.*
> P40: *At his expense.*

[focus group with male participants in their late thirties, urban area]

Looking at unpaid work as a potential restorative justice enhancer is contrary to some of the restorative literature, which suggests that there is a risk of branding community work as a restorative practice (see Bussu, 2016). Nevertheless, due to the ingrained nature of, and strong support for, community service in my study, I align myself with Fellegi (2010), who argues that in Central Eastern European societies, community service can be seen as the basis for further development of restorative justice. According to Fellegi, community work has a more established structure in those countries; what is needed is to strengthen the process conceptually and provide relevant practitioners with a better understanding of the restorative concept in order to convey restorative ideas through community service (ibid.). Such an approach would reflect Daly's (2002) argument that the introduction of restorative justice in various contexts should incorporate degrees of 'cultural appropriateness'. Only such an understanding of restorative justice will make restorative practices flexible towards and accommodating of cultural differences. Although I argue that the origins of participants' support for unpaid work might be distinctive for the Polish context, the nature of this support might have relevance in other countries, too.

Work in the Polish context

The Polish context of work as a sanction corroborates the idea that punishment is a social process that is not only a reaction to crime. Punishment can be seen as a social artefact with social causes and social effects, shaped by various social forces, with its own historical tradition and cultural styles – as well as being intended to perform various instrumental roles (Garland, 1991, 2012). Quite early in my fieldwork it was apparent that participants' deep-seated and overwhelming confidence in unpaid work, articulated through many well-known work-related Polish sayings, reflects wider social and cultural specificities. As a distinctive symbol in Polish social imagery, work in participants' narratives has revealed a deeply embedded peasant mentality as well as still-vivid perceptions of socialist 'working people'.

Work as punishment has a long tradition in many other countries. In the literature (Durnescu, 2008; Robinson et al., 2013), it is argued that performing work of benefit to the community by wrong-doers has evolved over the years in all European jurisdictions and, alongside electronic monitoring or community justice innovations, unpaid work has become one of the new forms of community sanction. Western research suggests that most members of the public are unconvinced about the productiveness of community-based measures on the basis that they are not tough enough (Roberts, 2002). For instance, despite the fact that improving confidence in community penalties has become a central concern for British policy makers (see Casey, 2008), British people and criminal justice professionals remain sceptical about the advantages of community penalties (Maruna and King, 2008). My study participants' support for work in the community resonates with findings from the 2005 European Survey on Crime and Safety, which shows that 49% of survey respondents in Poland opted for community service in contrast to 34% who chose imprisonment. By comparison, in the United Kingdom the support for unpaid work was 29% and 52% favoured imprisonment (see Maffei and Markopoulou, 2013).

Drawing on Garland's definition of punishment and its applicability in examining the peculiarity of a society's penal landscape, I consider [unpaid] work as a tool that unlocks a broader picture in the Polish context. Firstly, the failures of the nineteenth-century uprisings led to the belief that the best initiative to remedy the political situation was to renew Polish society and revert to the defence of national interest through social, economic and cultural initiatives – something that had already been somewhat of a tradition in Poland and was known as 'organic work' (*praca organiczna*) (Blejwas, 1970). The tenets of 'organic work' aimed at neutralizing the revolutionary attempts to restore Poland's independence, and instead, encouraging capitalistic entrepreneurship and improving the economic well-being of the nation (ibid.). Secondly, Andrzej Leder, in his historical study entitled *An over-dreamed revolution: an exercise in historical logic*[3] (2014), drew on Charles Taylor's general concept of social imagery, and investigated contemporary values and symbols through which Poles imagine their society. According to Leder, work, among many other features, has always served as a distinctive symbol in Polish social imagery that stems mainly from both peasant heritage and experience of the socialist regime. He observes that the time of communism served as a social incubator where work as a symbol of Polish social imagery was strengthened and was the strongly advocated ideal of the 'working people', further preserving the agricultural attitude. The class of *Homo Sovieticus* – the new Soviet people – was composed of workers who were mainly of peasant descent (ibid.).

The foregoing discussion suggests that confidence in work, of many sorts, has a long tradition in the Polish context, and that Poland may be considered as a society with a certain historical receptiveness to work. Participants' narratives on work as a sanction included certain traces of restorative orientation towards punishment; therefore, the proponents of restorative justice would do well to address the relationship between punishment and the concept of restorative justice. The restorative practice of community work can be seen as a restorative measure that may produce a restorative pain – the type of pain that is welcomed and justified, and that is a natural by-product of a restorative practice that aims to cleanse, restore, construct, repair and reintegrate (Gavrielides, 2016).

Concluding remarks

The results of my study show that sociopolitical and economic context matters when exploring the functioning of restorative practices. This chapter has demonstrated that lay people's understandings of punishment and justice can add an interesting perspective to our well-established understanding of how restorative justice is possible in various societies. A number of lessons can be drawn from the Polish case in order to explore people's views on punishment and justice, understand the viability of restorative practices and analyse the extent to which people's attitudes towards punishment and justice are such that restorative justice could work. Poland's socialist past, change of political regime, post-communist 'accession' to the international community in the West and high level of religiosity (among many other factors) make Poland a fascinating object of study that can, at the same time, offer insights about restorative justice in other societies.

Restorative justice scholars are fond of imagining a world built on the universal principles of restorative justice (Roche, 2006:235), but restorative justice would probably do better if we promised less (Daly and Immarigeon, 1998) and accepted that every society has its own restorative justice story to tell. Although my research is not a classical restorative justice thesis, it echoes Daly's (2002) argument about telling the 'real RJ story', its 'cultural appropriateness', or in other words, its preconditions. In addition, Braithwaite (2003:1) has strongly encouraged the realization that restorative justice is about struggling against injustice in the most restorative manner possible and thus also within the rigidity of the criminal justice system.

This chapter demonstrates that there are a number of cultural values and attitudes that might be seen as prerequisites for restorative justice success (or failures) in Poland and other countries, too. Ragin and Becker (1928:225) long ago observed that 'the two main problems social scientists face as empirical researchers are the equivocal nature of the theoretical realm and the complexity of the empirical realm'. As they would suggest, my scholarly intention for this Handbook was to use the Polish case to sharpen and refine the question on the viability of

3 Polish original: *Prześniona rewolucja: ćwiczenie z logiki historycznej.*

restorative justice and to show how lay views can shed light on the possibility of restorative justice in the Polish context.

As argued in this chapter, the way lay people perceive criminal justice processes and agencies might influence their understandings and receptiveness to restorative practices. In my research, low confidence in the criminal justice system and support for the involvement of lawyers was projected onto participants' understandings of victim-offender mediation – something that should be considered as an obstacle to the development of restorative justice in the Polish context. However, work in the form of community service might indeed be of assistance to the possibility of restorative practice in post-socialist countries, as it attracts significant support on the part of lay people. In sum, lay views on punishment and justice greatly assist in exploring the factors that might influence the development of restorative justice in the Polish context and point to directions for future research elsewhere.

References

Bieńkowska, E. 2009. Mediacja w sprawach karnych i nieletnich: kiedy organ procesowy moze (a nawet powinien) odwołać się do postępowania mediacyjnego (Mediation in Criminal and Youth Cases: When the Authorities Can (and Even Should) Refer to a Mediation Proceeding?). In L. Mazowiecka (eds.) *Mediacja* (Mediation). Warszawa: Wolters Kluwer.

Blejwas, S.A. 1970. The Origins and Practice of 'Organic Work' in Poland: 1795–1863, *The Polish Review*, 15(4): 23–54.

Braithwaite, J. 2003. Principles of Restorative Justice. In A. Hirsch, J. Roberts, A.E. Bottoms, K. Roach and M. Schiff (eds.) *Restorative Justice and Criminal Justice: Competing or Reconcilable Paradigms*. Portland, OR: Hart.

Bussu, A. 2016 In Need of a Cultural Shift to Promote Restorative Justice in Southern Europe, *Contemporary Justice Review*, 19(4): 479–503.

Casey, L. 2008. *Engaging Communities in Fighting Crime: A Review*. London: Cabinet Office.

Cielecki, T. 2009. Bezdroża mediacji. In L. Mazowiecka (eds.) *Mediacja* (Mediation). Warszawa: Wolters Kluwer.

Crossley, M.L. 2002. Could You Please Pass One of Those Health Leaflets Along?: Exploring Health, Morality and Resistance Through Focus Groups, *Social Science & Medicine*, 55(8): 1471–1483.

Czarnota, A. 2009. Transitional Justice, the Post-Communist Post-Police State and the Losers and Winners. An overview of the Problem, *Silesian Journal of Legal Studies*, 1: 11–20.

Daly, K. 2002. Restorative Justice, the Real Story, *Punishment and Society*, 4(1): 55–79.

Daly, K. and Immarigeon, R. 1998. The Past, Present, and Future of Restorative Justice: Some Critical Reflections, *The Contemporary Justice Review*, 1(1): 21–45.

Durnescu, I. 2008. An Exploration of the Purposes and Outcomes of Probation in European Jurisdictions, *Probation Journal*, 55(3): 273–281.

Dzur, A. 2008. *Democratic Professionalism, Citizen Participation and the Reconstruction of Professional Ethics, Identity and Practice*. Pennsylvania: Pennsylvania State University Press.

Dzur, A. 2011. Restorative Justice and Democracy: Fostering Public Accountability for Criminal Justice, *Contemporary Justice Review*, 14(4): 367–381.

Fellegi, B. 2007. *Building and Toning: An Analysis of the Institutionalisation of Mediation in Penal Matters in Hungary*. Available at www.europeana.eu/portal/en/record/92040/BibliographicResource_3000094572386.html?l%5Bp%5D%5Bq%5D=what%3A%22restorative+justice%22&l%5Br%5D=10&l%5Bt%5D=29&q=what%3A%22restorative+justice%22

Fellegi, B. 2010. *The Restorative Approach in Practice: Models in Europe and in Hungary: European Best Practices of Restorative Justice in the Criminal Procedure. Conference Publication*. Budapest: Ministry of Justice and Law Enforcement of the Republic of Hungary.

Garland, D. 1991. Sociological Perspectives on Punishment, *Crime and Justice*, 14: 115–165.

Garland, D. 2012. Punishment and Social Solidarity. In J. Simon and R. Sparks (eds.) *The Handbook of Punishment and Society*. London: Sage.

Garland, D. and Sparks, R. 2000. Criminology, Social Theory and the Challenge of Our Times, *British Journal of Criminology*, 40: 189–204.

Gavrielides, T. 2008. Restorative Justice – The Perplexing Concept: Conceptual Fault-Lines and Power Battles Within the Restorative Justice Movement, *Criminology and Criminal Justice*, 8(2): 165–183.

Gavrielides, T. 2016. Restorative Pain: A New Vision of Punishment. In T. Gavrielides and V. Artinopoulou (eds.) *Reconstructing Restorative Justice Philosophy*. London: Routledge.

Jasiński, J. 1999. Crime: Manifestations, Patterns, and Trends of Crime; 'Traditional' Versus 'New' Crime; Juvenile Crime; Fear of Crime, *European Journal of Crime, Criminal Law and Criminal Justice*, 7(4): 374–386.

Jones, T. and Newburn, T. 2007. *Policy Transfer and Criminal Justice: Exploring US Influence Over British Crime Control Policy*. Maidenhead: Open University Press.

Juszkiewicz, W. 2010. Reparation as a Mitigating Circumstance When Imposing a Sentence – Mediation in Poland. In *European Best Practices of Restorative Justice in the Criminal Procedure*. Conference Publication. 27–29 April 2009. Budapest.

Kania, E. 2012. Homo Sovieticus – „jednowymiarowy klient komunizmu", czy „fenomen o wielu twarzach"? (Homo Sovieticus – 'a single-dimensional client of communism' or a 'multifaceted phenomenon'?), *Przegląd Politologiczny*, 3: 157–170.

Krajewski, K. 2002. Punitywność społeczeństwa. In J. Czapska and H. Kury (eds.) *Mit represyjności albo o znaczeniu prewencji kryminalnej* (The Myth of Represiveness, or the Meaning of Criminal Prevention). Krakow: Zakamycze.

Kurczewski, J. 2007. Prawem i lewem. Kultura prawna społeczeństwa polskiego po komunizmie (Either Rightly or Like a Crook: Legal Culture of Polish Society After Communism), *Sociological Studies*, 2(185): 33–60.

Leder, A. 2014. *Prześniona rewolucja: Ćwiczenie z logiki historycznej* (A Dreamed Revolution: An Exercise from the Historical Logic). Warszawa: Wydawnictwo Krytyki Politycznej.

Maffei, S. and Markopoulou, L., eds. 2013. New European Crimes and Trust-Based Policies, *FP7 Research Project Report*, 2: 21–42.

Maruna, Sh. and King, A. 2008. Selling the Public on Probation: Beyond the Bib, *Probation Journal*, 55(4): 337–351.

Ministry of Justice New Zealand. 1996. *Restorative Justice: A discussion paper*. Available at www.justice.govt.nz/publications/publications-archived/1996/restorative-justice-a-discussion-paper-1996

Noaks, L. and Wincup, E. 2004. *Criminological Research: Understanding Qualitative Methods*. London: Sage Publications

Politowicz, K.A. 2012. Mediacje w postępowaniu karnym wykonawczym. In M. Tabernacka and R. Raszewska-Skałecka (eds.) *Mediacje w społeczeństwie otwartym* (Mediation in an Open Society). Wrocław: Gaskor.

Ragin, Ch. and Becker, H. 1928. *What Is a Case?: Exploring the Foundations of Social Inquiry*. Cambridge: Cambridge University Press.

Rękas, A. 2003. *Mediacje w Polsce na tle doświadczeń państw Unii Europejskiej*. In *Mediacje w krajach Unii Europejskiej i Polsce* (Mediation in Poland and other EU Countries). Konferencje i Seminaria, 4(48):04. Biuletyn Biura Studiów i Ekspertyz Kancelarii Sejmu. Warszawa: Kancelaria Sejmu Available at http://biurose.sejm.gov.pl/teksty_pdf_03/kis-48.pdf

Roberts, J.V. 2002. Public Attitudes to Community-Based Sanctions. In J.V. Roberts and M. Hough (eds.) *Changing Attitudes to Punishment: Public Opinion, Crime and Justice*. Cullompton: Willan.

Roberts, J.V. 2014. Clarifying the Significance of Public Opinion for Sentencing Policy and Practice. In J. Ryberg and J.V. Roberts (eds.) *Popular Punishment: On the Normative Significance of Public Opinion*. New York: Oxford University Press.

Roberts, J.V. and Hough, M. 2005. *Understanding Public Attitudes to Criminal Justice*. Maidenhead: Open University Press.

Robinson, G., McNeill, F. and Maruna, Sh. 2013. Punishment in Society: The Improbable Persistence of Probation and Other Community Sanctions and Measures. In J. Simon and R. Sparks (eds.) *The SAGE Handbook of Punishment and Society*. London: Sage.

Roche, D. 2006. Dimensions of Restorative Justice, *Journal of Social Issues*, 62(2): 217–238.

Skąpska, G. 2009. The Rule of Law, Economic Transformation and Corruption After the Fall of the Berlin Wall, *Hague Journal on the Rule of Law*, 1: 284–306.

Stalans, L. 2002. Measuring Attitudes to Sentencing. In J.V. Roberts and M. Hough (eds.) *Changing Attitudes to Punishment: Public opinion, Crime and Justice*. Cullompton: Willan.

Staniszkis, J. 1991. *The Dynamics of the Breakthrough in Eastern Europe: The Polish Experience*. Berkeley: University of California Press.

Staniszkis, J. 1999. *Post-communism: Emerging Enigma*. Institute of Political Studies. Warsaw: Polish Academy of Sciences

Sykes, G.M. and Matza, D. 1957. Techniques of Neutralization. A Theory of Delinquency, *American Sociological Review*, 22(6): 664–670.

Szymanowski, T. 2012. *Przestępczość i polityka karna w Polsce: w świetle faktów i opinii społeczeństwa w okresie transformacji*. Warszawa: Wolters Kluwer.

Tränkle, S. 2007. In the Shadow of Penal Law: Victim-Offender Mediation in Germany and France, *Punishment & Society*, 9(4): 395–415.

Walklate, S. 2005. Researching Restorative Justice: Politics, Policy and Process, *Critical Criminology*, 13: 165–179.

Zehr, H. and Mika, H. 1998. Fundamental Concepts of Restorative Justice, *Contemporary Justice Review*, 1: 47–55.

23

Restorative justice as a colonial project in the disempowerment of Indigenous peoples

Juan Marcellus Tauri

Introduction

Indigenous peoples' experience of the restorative justice (RJ) industry has been marked by a number of strategic decisions and practices that have made the relationship uncomfortable for both parties. One particularly problematic set of behaviours is the partiality shown by some members of the industry for utilising elements of Indigenous life-worlds in the manufacture and marketing of RJ products. The strategic deployment of Indigenous cultural practices, along with a willingness to standardise practice to align justice practice and outcomes with those of the public service, has seen the movement increasingly accepted within the folds of the criminal justice system. However, the industry's failure to deliver on many of its promises, most especially as a source of jurisdictional empowerment for Indigenous peoples, means that it is increasingly viewed as a *colonial project* within the settler colonial state's attempts to manage Indigenous peoples.

This chapter offers an Indigenous critique of the settler colonial state's current reliance on the importation and dissemination of restorative justice programmes, including conferencing forums and sentencing circles, as preferred responses to the related intractable problems of Indigenous over-representation in the criminal justice system and Indigenous resistance to settler colonial governance. We argue that recent Indigenous experience of the globalised RJ industry diminishes the efficacy of exaggerated claims made by RJ advocates about the transformative properties of RJ products and their ability to satisfy the demands of Indigenous peoples for jurisdictional self-determination.

The stated aim of the Handbook is, in part, to provide 'a comprehensive and authoritative review of research in new and contested areas', whilst bringing 'much needed attention to grey areas of practice'. This modest offering endeavours to meet these aims by enhancing our understanding of the impact the RJ industry has on Indigenous peoples based on the experiences of Indigenous peoples themselves. This is important given that Indigenous peoples are a criminal justice 'client group' whose views have thus far been severely neglected, and even ignored, by many RJ researchers, advocates and practitioners. At first glance, one might say that the Indigenous critique of RJ offered here is nothing 'new'. This is a fair point when we consider that the first published critiques informed by Indigenous perspectives began appearing in the mid-1990s (see Blagg, 1997; Cunneen, 1997; Lee, 1997; Tauri, 1998). To date there has been a demonstrable lack of response to this body of work from RJ advocates. However, of late this largely conceptual and theoretical critique has been supported by Indigenous-led empirical research that reveals the disempowering impact RJ practices are having on Indigenous individuals and communities (see Moyle, 2013, 2014; Moyle and Tauri, 2016). This development means that the Indigenous-informed critique can no longer be ignored. We demand a meaningful response from the RJ industry, especially to our challenge that its members move past the mystification and romanticisation of its policies, programmes and practice, and demonstrate the value to us as a meaningful response to our social justice needs. This challenge is particularly important given that we have our own processes for dealing with social harm, and evidence that the globalisation of RJ has impacted the ability of some Indigenes to implement their own processes (see Tauri, 2014).

Restorative justice and the globalised crime-control market

Ruminating on the growth in popularity of RJ throughout the 1990s, Freiberg (2001: 273) argued that if a primary goal of a social response to crime is to reinforce and reaffirm social solidarity, then preventative measures should facilitate and solidify civic co-operation. Furthermore, 'bottom-up', community-centred initiatives and other techniques of crime control should induce core communitarian values such as "mutuality, interdependence, reciprocity and trust". There are powerful analogies here with the somewhat surprising success of the restorative justice industry since its theoretical and conceptual (re)birth in the late 1980s (see Braithwaite, 1989) and early 1990s (see Zehr, 1990), surprising in terms of the fact that the industry arose amid the expansion of the neo-liberal, carceral state (Gray, 2005; Griffin, 2012; Levrant et al., 1999; Wacquant, 2009). Frieberg (2001) further contends that 'success' in this context equates to being successful in capturing the public's imagination, as opposed to delivering on comparatively more substantive outcomes, such as reducing crime, increasing public safety and empowering disaffected communities. It could also be argued that the RJ industry, through its promises to deliver accountability to offenders, empowerment to victims and a reduction in recidivism leading to cost savings for government – some which have been meet in part (for example, see Bonta et al., 2002) but nowhere near the transformative levels advocates claim (see Wood, 2015) – was successful in capturing the policy sector's imagination, thus securing policy, legislative and financial support. Finally, success might also be measured in terms of profit for the growing restorative justice industry as it increasingly penetrates into, and competes on, the globalised crime-control market (Tauri, 2016).

Over the past two decades, the restorative justice industry has been successful in expanding its share of the increasingly globalised crime-control market. This success has been driven in part by Western governments' insatiable appetite for crime-control products, be they 'new', rehashed and/or regurgitated (for example, boot camps, see Tauri, 2016). The evidence of the significant part played by RJ on the globalised market is unmistakable. Miers (2007: 447), for one, has noted that 'viewed globally, informed observers estimate that, by 2000 there were some 1,300 (RJ) programmes across 20 countries directed at young offenders'. By 2010, there were at least 9,000 publications on restorative justice (Cunneen and Hoyle 2010: 101). Muncie (2005: 42) further attests to the impact of the global demand for RJ products when he writes that 'indeed it is also clear that youth justice in England and more widely across Europe has also been informed by contra penal trajectories such as those derived from the import of restorative justice conferencing pioneered in New Zealand and Australia'. Lastly, the increasing globalisation of RJ is further evidenced by the fact that the United Nations (2002), the European Union (see Gavrielides, 2016) and the Council of Europe (2005) have signalled their full support for the introduction of RJ principles and initiatives within international criminal justice systems.

To lay the foundation for the analysis that is to follow, it is worthwhile considering the factors that might help explain the success of the RJ industry on the globalised crime-control market. Frieberg (2001) contends that in the first instance, the industry offers appropriate and enforceable consequences for offenders, most often in the form of forced participation and acts of contrition that enable practitioners to demonstrate that offenders are 'taking responsibility' for their conduct (Acorn, 2004). These design elements have ensured that the industry's marketing activities resonate with the 'tough-on-crime' rhetoric of conservative advocates (see Levrant et al., 1999), including commentators in the late 1990s and early 2000s advocating for a return to 'shaming' practices to encourage desistance from crime (Harris and Maruna, 2006). We further argue that its increasing popularity was partly due to the fact that much of the rhetoric of RJ advocates appealed directly to the social justice warriors who populate various schools within criminology. Especially influential were empirically weak promises of increased community involvement in the criminal justice system, and images of hordes of offenders being diverted away from a rapacious, violent criminal justice system (Kitossa, 2012; Tauri and Webb, 2012). And lastly, the increasing global influence of the industry can be explained through the fact that its adherents have often promised the criminal justice mother lode to settler colonial states who are grappling with the interrelated intractable problems of Indigenous over-representation and Indigenous critiques of settler colonial justice. In response, RJ entrepreneurs have developed and marketed what they claim to be 'Indigenous inspired' and 'derived' justice forums such as conferencing and sentencing circles that concur with the communitarian sensibilities of Indigenous peoples everywhere (for examples of this type of 'orientalist' marketing, see Maxwell, 2008; for a critique see Blagg, 1997 and Tauri, 2014).On all three claims, restorative justice advocates have demonstrably over-promised and under-delivered, most especially in their claim to be able to deliver culturally appropriate forums and reduce crime and social harm (Hansen and Antsanen, 2012; Suzuki and Wood, 2017; Wood, 2015). We will argue here that the exaggerated claims of RJ advocates, both in terms of the industry's crime reduction capabilities, and the 'Indigenousness' of signature interventions like the family group conferencing (FGC) forum, have greatly reduced its potential to deliver radical transformation of the criminal justice experience of the dispossessed, those individuals and communities that Ruggiero (2000) describes as the 'social waste' of contemporary Western jurisdictions. Instead, it has gradually morphed into a Colonial Project that bolsters the settler colonial state, largely at the expense of Indigenous peoples' desires for jurisdictional self-determination (Jackson, 1992; Tauri, 2016).

Before we move to the main arguments of this chapter, let me deal briefly with the last of the claims just introduced, the supposed indigeneity of the RJ industry's programmes and their deliverance of the settler colonial state from the intractable problem of Indigenous over-representation in the criminal justice system.

Exaggeration, mystification and the restorative justice industry

In previous work, we have critiqued the exaggerated claims of the RJ industry in relation to its supposedly 'Indigenous-derived' policies and products (see Tauri, 2014). Over the past 15 years, the industry's continued mystification of the FGC forum has been heavily critiqued by critical Indigenous and non-Indigenous scholars alike, including Blagg (1997) and Cunneen (1997) in the Australian context; Lee (1997), Rudin (2005) and Victor (2007) presenting

Indigenous Canadian perspectives and Love (2002), Moyle (2013, 2014;) Moyle and Tauri (2016) and Tauri (1998, 2004, 2014, 2016) from a critical Māori perspective. Much of the work of these scholars has collectively exposed a number of significant issues with the RJ industry, including that much of the empirical research on Indigenous satisfaction is exaggerated, largely based on glorified customer satisfaction surveys (most particularly in New Zealand; for examples of this approach see Maxwell and Morris, 1993 and Maxwell et al., 2004) and closed-ended interview methods that restrict Indigenous participants' from openly critiquing state-sanctioned forums (see Tauri, 2011). Furthermore, their work also demonstrates that reported Indigenous experiences of RJ programmes often do not match the glowing reports of meaningful cultural appropriateness or their ability to meet Indigenous aspirations for self-determination, often reported in academic literature and the pronouncements or RJ advocates (for detailed discussion of the exaggerated claims of 'cultural sensitivity' and juridical empowerment for Māori in the New Zealand context, see Love, 2002; Moyle, 2013, 2014; Tauri, 1998, 2004; and also Walker, 1996).

A related issue is that much of the government-sponsored research highlights the co-optive and indigenised character of the FGC process (see Tauri, 2011) which all too often results in the marginalisation of whānau (family) members, cultural practices and 'cultural experts' (for example, in the New Zealand context regarding FGC practice, compare Maxwell and Morris, 1993 and Tauri, 1998 and Maxwell et al., 2004 and Tauri, 2004). Lastly, it has been argued that both the FGC process and the legislation that introduced it were influenced by the settler colonial states' need to be seen to be doing something constructive in the face of a perceived rise in juvenile offending, particularly amongst Māori youth, and ongoing criticism by Māori of the Eurocentric bias of the formal system (Richard, 2007; Tauri, 1998; see discussion later on the role of RJ as a contemporary colonial project).

Some may argue that the politics that underpin the development of RJ-related policies and interventions, such as the co-option of aspects of Indigenous life-worlds, is not as important as the 'success' such forums provide. Success in relation to the FGC-style forums includes the meaningful (re)integration of Indigenous and other marginalised youth back into their families and communities. The impact of RJ forums is supported by concentrated efforts by the central government to enhance the socio-economic profile of said communities who have, for example, been 'transformed' through their schools being properly resourced and their once-depleted labour markets now offering 'real' job opportunities and liveable incomes for residents. There is little evidence of any of this happening in any of the settler colonial jurisdictions, most especially for Indigenous peoples. There is also little evidence that the massive expansion of the RJ industry within the globalised crime-control market has had a significant impact on Indigenous over-representation in criminal justice. And finally, it should also be noted that we have had little return on the investment we have made in the RJ industry. To date, there has been little or no compensation for the significant amount of the philosophical and ideological silage our sociocultural context(s) have provided to the industry's programme design and marketing activities (Tauri, 2014).

Thus one has to ask the obvious question: if the RJ industry is not providing us with a set of policies and interventions that alleviate the intractable problem of Indigenous over-representation, and if it is failing to support us to achieve judicial self-determination, then what purpose does it serve? What, if anything is it achieving, especially for us? To that question we now turn, and in doing so we argue that a primary role of the contemporary, globalised, co-opting (and co-opted) RJ industry, in relation to the dual intractable problems of Indigenous over-representation and Indigenous radicalism, is its acting as a Colonial Project that supports the settler colonial states' continued subjugation of Indigenous peoples.

Colonial projects in the contemporary moment

> Colonialism is not simply a historical artifact that has no bearing on contemporary events.
>
> —Elizabeth Comack (2012: 66).

We have previously argued that many of the adherents of the discipline of criminology operate without a theory of colonialism, meaning a critical analysis of the impact that colonialism had on Indigenous peoples as part of a critical analysis of the drivers of over-representation. Equally true is the fact that they also fail to consider colonialism's continued impact on Indigenous peoples through the manufacture of *contemporary colonial projects* that support the settler colonial states' continued domination of Indigenes (Tauri, 2014, 2017). The portrayal of colonialism as an historical artefact, as an event with little bearing on our understanding of contemporary social issues, is spurious, for as Monture-Angus (2007: 207) once argued, colonialism is "a living phenomenon. . . . The past impacts on the present and today's place of Aboriginal peoples in Canadian society cannot be understood without a well-developed historical understanding of colonialism and the present-day trajectories of those old relationships". Comack (2012) demonstrates that in both Canada and Australia, foundational narratives have been developed in support of the colonial project of dispossession. These narratives highlight the 'civilising ethos' of the colonial intent, made real by the offer of the gift of Western knowledge to primordial, stone age peoples (see also Cunneen, 2011 and Merry, 2000). Much the same can be said about the RJ industry, especially since so many of its adherents are constantly mythologising and exaggerating its links to Indigenous epistemologies (Tauri, 2014). This conduct alone would provide the basis for an argument that the industry can and should be considered a colonial project that supports the settler colonial state in it continued war of manoeuvre against Indigenous peoples (Tauri, 2017). But before we consider the contemporary moment, and our argument that RJ constitutes a colonial project, we should first consider the role of colonial projects as key processes that facilitated the colonial subjugation of Indigenous peoples.

Colonial projects and colonisation

Colonial and settler colonial attempts at dominating the Indigenous Other rely on a range of social control technologies, or what Thomas (1994) refers to as colonising projects. According to Bhabha (1994: 94–120), one such technology or project is *stereotype*, which entails the use of language and signifiers (linguistic or symbolic) that denote a fixity in the ideological construction and (re)presentation of the Indigenous Other (or indeed, of any identified 'problem population'): '[I]t connotes rigidity and the unchanging order as well as disorder, degeneracy and daemonic repetition . . . [it is] a form of knowledge and identification that vacillates between what is always "in place", already known, and something that must be anxiously repeated'. Thus we read of various stereotypes about Indigenous peoples designed to primordialise them, to represent them as having unalterable *states of being*, whether of mind, physicality and/or social mores. These stereotypes are exemplified in ideological constructs such as 'the savage Red Indian', the 'drunk Aboriginal', the 'sexually insatiable Black slave', the 'happy but dim, guitar strumming Maori' and so on (Kidd, 1997). The colonial project of *stereotype* transcends the physicality and intellectual boundaries of the Indigenous Other and provides fixity of their supposed uncivilised beliefs, social behaviours and institutions, exemplified in the child-like nature of our nativistic and/or pan-theist religious systems (Fitzpatrick, 1992), or the quaint, myth-based processes they use for responding to social harm (Jackson, 1992). The role that colonial projects like stereotype have in the negative Othering of Indigenous peoples cannot be overstated, as Bhabha (1994: 100) demonstrates when he writes that:

> colonial discourse [is] an apparatus of power and its predominant strategic function is the creation of a space for a 'subject peoples' through the production of knowledges in terms of which surveillance is exercised whilst seeking authorisation for its strategies by the production of knowledges of coloniser and colonised which are stereotypical but antiethically evaluated. *The objective of colonial discourse is to construe the colonised as a population of degenerate types on the basis of racial origin, in order to justify conquest and to establish systems of administration and instruction.*
>
> *(emphasis added)*

The localised and partial nature of colonial projects allows for variations in the effect that colonisation has on Indigenous peoples, where the impact may vary relating to different projects, whilst allowing for the overall impact – social and cultural dislocation – to manifest (Proulx, 2003; see also Tauri, 2014 for a full discussion of the concept of colonial projects).

As reported by Tauri (2014), a significant project in the colonial context was the 'civilising mission', a key driver of which was the purposeful destruction of the native residing within the Indigenous person, and his or her replacement by a civilised, Westernised Christian (Cunneen, 2011). The civilising mission in colonial contexts like New Zealand and Australia involved an ideological and policy-based pincer movement involving education and religious institutions. Over time, colonial education policies forbade the teaching of Indigenous culture and language, policies given particular potency with the advent of Mission Schools and the forced removal of Indigenous children to church-run, education establishments (Cunneen, 2011; Milroy, 1999). In the Canadian context, the residential school system began in the 1870s and lasted as an official component of Federal education policy until the 1980s. The policy involved a network of schools nationwide, run by Catholic, Anglican, Presbyterian and United Churches. Many thousands of Indigenous children were removed and spent their formative years in these schools. Milroy (1999) relates how the system was a church-state partnership, with the Department of Indian Affairs providing the funding, setting of standards and practices and exercising direct legal control over the Indigenous children who were considered wards of the state.

Similarly, Cunneen (2011) relates that in the Australian context, Australia Aboriginal children were forcibly removed from their families and communities as part of a policy programme aimed at their assimilation, an exercise that lasted over six decades. In some states and territories of Australia, Aboriginal children were placed in church-run establishments, whilst in others, such as New South Wales, the institutions were the responsibility of the colonial state. However, regardless of the source of authority, church or state, the focus of pedagogy and curriculum was the same – to kill the 'native within' (NISATSIC, 1997), as Cunneen (2011: 5–6) relates when he writes that:

> [b]oth the Canadian and Australia authorities saw the removal process as part of a civilising mission and spiritual duty to uplift the 'natives'. By today's standards the assimilationist 'civilising' process would be condemned as ethnocide or cultural genocide and properly considered as a state crime.

Combined with criminal justice policy and practice, modes of domination such as residential schools and forced removal of children provide powerful examples of how colonial discourse and practice 'organised social existence and social reproduction' in the colonial context (Proulx,

2002: 42; see also Foucault, 1977). And, as demonstrated by Tauri (2013, 2014), they also provide concrete processes for the continued subjugation of Indigenous peoples within the settler colonial context, both past and present.

Contemporary (settler) colonial projects

> Colonialism has not disappeared; it has just taken on new forms in contemporary times.
>
> —Elizabeth Comack (2012: 79).

In previous work, we have outlined the various strategies and processes deployed by the settler colonial state, supported by the Western academy and various justice industries, through which colonialism is perpetuated in the contemporary moment (Tauri, 2016). These strategies and processes include the continued refinement and use of the racialised discourses discussed earlier, although refined and redeployed in the modern context. So, whilst we still have the 'drunk Indian', we must now contend with the depiction of Indigenous peoples as 'welfare dependent' and, perhaps the most invidious of all, our representation as the 'criminal other'. Other notable projects include our structural exclusion from the labour and housing markets, and a range of social exclusionary projects in the social welfare and child care and protection sectors (Moyle, 2013). But perhaps the most potent, contemporary colonial project is the racialised, violent criminal justice system (Comack, 2012; Fyfe, 2010; Weitzer, 2000).

Proulx (2003: 43–51) describes how some of the key colonial projects of the assimilationist phase of colonisation, such as the residential school programme in Canada, have either ceased to be used or had their form and delivery significantly altered. Albeit, whilst education and child care and protection processes remain important social control institutions, it can be argued that the form in which these colonial projects are delivered has altered. The process through which change takes place will be examined during our discussion of RJ as an exemplar of a contemporary colonial project.

In both the New Zealand and Canadian context, we can measure the cessation of specific colonial projects, such as residential schools in Canada and the legal assault on Māori cultural transmission, with the move from assimilationist discourse and policies towards integrative, then multicultural, and of late, self-determination/reconciliation rhetoric and policy (Short, 2003; Tauri, 1999). The fact that specific colonising projects and strategies went *out of style* or were refashioned is unsurprising, as every colonial epoch produces projects that support the continuation of colonialist hegemony. However, what is more enduring is the interconnected nature of colonial (and settler colonial) governance; a highly sophisticated, multilayered, intersectional process that involves interrelationships between the state (made up of the legislature, Cabinet, the policy-making and service delivery institutions), and civil society (Proulx, 2003).

Within the settler colonial edifice, Woolford (2013) imagines the process of colonial government as a highly sophisticated mesh made up of interlocking levels, from the outer meta-level, to meso and micro levels, each containing colonial projects of varying complexity and interconnectedness. The former are key edifices of the colonial context and provide the superstructure upon which settler colonialism is built and continues to thrive (Tauri, 2016). At this level, we find the institutions of social control, including education, child care and protection, and health services. It is also the level at which we find a colonial project of particular potency, the criminal justice system. The potency of this macro-level colonial project comes from the authority it derives from being the site of the contemporary, neo-liberal states' deployment of legitimated violence to facilitate social order within the body politic (Haleh Davis, 2011).

The implementation of a Western European legal jurisdiction and criminal justice system were fundamental platforms of the colonial enterprise (Merry, 2000; Proulx, 2003; Tauri, 1998). As a sub-component of the legal system, criminal justice was a powerful colonial project in two specific ways: (1) it ensured that the definitions of what constitutes crime, social harm and victims were based on Eurocentric interpretations of those terms; and (2) it provided a ready platform for the deployment of structural violence by the state against Indigenous peoples who could not, or chose not, to adhere to Western standards of behaviour – most especially those who dared challenge the hegemony of the colonial state, or who were simply residing on good pastoral and/or mineral-rich land (Comack, 2012; Tauri, 2013).

Other powerful colonial projects intersect, feed off and support one another in this manner. For example, Friederes (2000: 215–219) describes the intersections between government and economic policies supportive of corporations as well as the activities that created and maintain welfare dependency on Indigenous reserves. These activities provided significant stimuli for the urban migration that occurred amongst many Indigenous communities in the settler colonial context from the 1950s onwards (Gale, 1981; Thorns and Sedwick, 1997). In turn, this phenomenon brought with it the social, cultural and economic dislocation of Indigenous communities, the results of which are summarised by Proulx (2003: 53), who writes that:

> [t]he colonial and postcolonial colonial context . . . has destroyed Aboriginal social orders, stability and cultural integration leading to a disjunction between ends and means within Aboriginal cultures resulting in crime and social disorder. Assimilationist social policy and laws, coupled with culturally different judicial philosophies and practices, are central to this process.

It would be unwise to imagine that the colonial context lies in the past, as historical moments and memories that we only need now reflect upon with regret and without a sense of individual or collective ownership. For Indigenous peoples residing in settler colonial jurisdictions, colonialism is a technology of control seemingly without end. It is, at this time, only the processes through which it is being *managed* that have changed, that have been altered and that have been sometimes resurrected. And from all this shape-changing, reconfiguration and renewal by the settler colonial state and its supporting academies has arisen a particularly virulent form that reflects the contemporary configuration of colonialism beautifully, and that is the RJ industry (Tauri, 2014).

Restorative justice: a contemporary colonial project?

Criminal justice in all its programmatic manifestations, be it prisons, policing, courts, sentencing practice, the policy process and so on has long played an instrumental role in the settler colonial states' management of Indigenous peoples. Many theories have been offered to explain the disproportionate over-representation of Indigenous peoples in settler colonial criminal justice systems, but in terms of the development of legislation and policy, the most influential theories emanate from administrative and authoritarian criminology, where the explanatory focus is on the pathological, deviant individual Indigenous offender and his or her criminalising culture (for example, see Marie, 2010; Newbold, 2000; Weatherburn, 2010, 2014). Missing from most of the analysis of these forms of criminology is any meaningful discussion of colonisation, or the conduct of crime-control agencies and agents (Tauri, 2016). As Comack (2012:

86) argues, '[E]xplaining the disproportionate incarceration rates of Aboriginal people [by the] crime-producing conditions in their families and communities tells only part of the story. Left out of the equation is the role of the criminal justice system in the production of crime', and for Indigenous peoples, its role in propelling their continued over-representation through support for the settler colonial states as a contemporary colonial project. Until recently, the role of the RJ industry was also exempt from our critique of the criminal justice system's role in the suppression of Indigenous peoples. However, over the past decade the critical Indigenous gaze has firmly focused on the industry, and in particular upon some of its most celebrated 'successes', most notably the FGC forum.

The family group conference and the construction of a contemporary colonial project

> [W]e live in an era of postmodern imperialism and manipulations by shape-shifting colonial powers; the instruments of domination are evolving and inventing new methods to erase Indigenous histories and senses of place. Therefore, 'globalisation' in Indigenous eyes reflects a deepening, hastening and stretching of an already-existing empire.
>
> —Alfred and Corntassel (2005: 601).

Despite the contested nature of the findings of research on the FGC process and its empowerment (or not) of Māori, what is evident is that over the past decade the FGC has become an increasingly popular commodity on the globalised crime-control market and a key player in the expansion of the restorative justice industry's portion of that market. This is particularly evident in the settler colonial jurisdictions of Canada, Australia and the US, and also in the colonial power that is now the UK, where there recently has been a significant uptake in scripted FGC-style RJ initiatives (see House of Commons, 2016). As noted earlier, all three jurisdictions have high rates of Indigenous over-representation in their criminal justice systems, and all three have been dealing with the hegemonic challenge derived from the interrelated intractable problems of Indigenous cultural revival and the radicalisation of Indigenous politics (Bonner and Sykes, 1975; Poata-Smith, 1996; Richardson, 1989; Troy, 2007; Warrior, 1996). Evidence exists that New Zealand's FGC forum and its Australian derivative were purposely and at times aggressively marketed in other settler colonial jurisdictions, especially Canada (Richards, 2007; Tauri, 2016). The marketing of these products was aided by the fact that much of the academic literature uncritically promoted origin myths that the forum, and RJ more generally, was founded upon Indigenous justice ideals, philosophies, and was designed to empower Indigenes, and so forth (for example, see Consedine, 1995; LaPrairie, 1996; Maxwell and Morris, 1993; Olsen et al., 1995 and Umbreit and Stacey, 1996. For more contemporary manifestations of the reiteration of the myths, see Maxwell, 2008; Ross, 2009 and Waites et al., 2004).

Undoubtedly, the exportation of the FGC forum to various Western jurisdictions has been heavily influenced by the marketing strategies discussed earlier. Particularly important is the fiction that the FGC product provides a forum that empowers Māori/the Indigenous Other, and signals the ability of the imposed criminal justice ordering to culturally sensitise itself. Further mythologising includes the claim that because the conferencing process and Māori justice practice have 'restorative elements', the conferencing process therefore provides Māori with a culturally empowering process for addressing their justice needs (Olsen et al., 1995). And lastly is the claim that the conferencing process empowers Māori to deal with their youth offenders in culturally appropriate ways (Maxwell and Morris, 1993). This process of claims making and myth construction is supported by the co-option and the purposeful utilisation of selected Indigenous cultural practices (such as 'circles'), as a key component of the marketing strategy for these types of RJ products across Western European jurisdictions, and more recently across Asia and Latin America (Scuro, 2013; Tauri, 2013).

A brief survey of the academic and marketing literature on conferencing in these countries highlights the importance placed on the supposed 'indigenousness' of the FGC forum (see Olsen et al., 1995; Maxwell, 2008). The strategies being utilised by policy entrepreneurs and purchasers (meaning government agents) to both market, standardise and legitimise the forum are based on an orientalist assumption that Indigenous peoples residing within the various jurisdictions are fundamentally 'the same' in terms of cultural practices and philosophies. As a result, the belief is that all or any interventions that includes elements of the cultural context of an Indigenous people will somehow be acceptable to other Indigenous peoples (see Blagg, 1997; Tauri, 2004). In response to these arguments, we have countered that the FGC forum signifies the co-option of Māori cultural practices to add colour to what is essentially a Eurocentric, Western justice process. The forum signifies the continued willingness of the state to disempower Māori by employing their justice processes whilst denying them a significant measure of jurisdictional autonomy.

The myths espoused by the RJ and policy sectors have been contested by authors such as Love (2002); Moyle (2014) and Tauri (1998, 1999, 2004), who point out that the commentators' own empirical research does not support their glowing reports of the forums' ability to empower Māori. In fact, much of the government-sponsored research underlines the co-optive nature of the FGC forum and the marginalisation of whānau members and 'cultural experts' (for example, compare Maxwell and Morris, 1993 and Tauri, 1998 and Maxwell et al., 2004 and Tauri, 2004). However, despite the contested nature of the findings of research on the FGC process and its empowerment (or not) of Māori, what is evident is that in the past decade, FGCs and 'conferencing' style initiatives have become a popular commodity on the international crime-control policy market (see Barnsdale and Walker, 2007; Duekmedjian, 2008; House of Commons, 2016; Scuro, 2013; Tauri, 2017). Whilst the spread has covered many Western jurisdictions, it appears to be a particularly popular appropriation in the settler colonial jurisdictions of Canada, Australia and the US.

This now brings us to the question of what has been the impact of all this globalising, indigenising and standardising evolution in RJ policy and practice on Indigenous peoples. Elsewhere, we have revealed the micro-level impact of this activity on Indigenous peoples in Canada, most especially the preference shown by Federal and Provincial institutions for the bastardised, imported FGC forum (see Tauri, 2009; see also Palys and Victor, 2005; Victor, 2007). This preference in turn has impacted the development of policies and programmes based on Indigenous responses to social harm (Tauri, 2014).

Of late, our attention, along with Māori social worker and activist Paora Moyle through her Master's and PhD-related research, has turned to exposing the experiences of RJ interventions, of Māori social work practitioners, and youth offenders and their family members. In brief, what Moyle's work (2013, 2014; and Moyle and Tauri, 2016) reveals is a widely held dissatisfaction amongst Māori with the way in which the FGC forum is run in the New Zealand context. Most especially problematic for the 15 practitioners, and the 28 youth and family members, were the many contradictions between the supposedly 'Indigenous and RJ foundations' of the forum, and their lived experience of it. More specifically, both sets of participants, practitioners and participants alike, expressed disquiet at what they often described as a tokenistic approach to Māori cultural philosophy and practice. This perspective is effectively summarised in the following comments from research participants:

> The family group conference is about as restorative as it is culturally sensitive . . . in the same way Pakeha [European] social workers believe they are competent enough to work with our people . . . Pakeha think they're the natural ordinary community against which all other ethnicities are measured.

And

> Whakapapa [genealogy] is intrinsically linked to the development of tamariki [children] but unfortunately it's something that this system does not recognise let alone value . . . I've seen FGCs run without any whānau showing up and then it's their fault for not caring enough . . . and that's what the Court report will show.

And finally:

> For me the FGC process does not begin until we've had our whakamoemiti [words of praise] . . . for us (Maori), it would not be appropriate to do so . . . But often the rush of the FGC diminishes the importance of the karakia [prayer] and other tikanga [rules of proper conduct] processes . . . I've heard some whānau say no to the karakia because they know it is unappreciated.

The experiences of Moyle's research participants reveals that the FGC forum does not always live up to the restorative principles and philosophies, or deliver the restorative outcomes, that many RJ advocates and practitioners claim it is designed to do. Their experiences offer an insight into the disconnect between myth making and fictional rhetoric that RJ advocates often employ regarding the movement's ability to offer products that deal effectively with the social justice needs of Indigenous peoples and that aid in reducing their over-representation in criminal justice statistics. We contend that the industry has so far failed to deliver on the promises it has made to deliver more culturally appropriate justice practice, and a measure of jurisdictional empowerment that allows Indigenous peoples a greater role in dealing with the offending and victimisation of our own. When you combine that failure with evidence that some of its members are purposefully and strategically utilising elements of Indigenous life-worlds to enhance the marketability of their products, then you quickly come to the realisation that at present we must consider the industry to be working as a colonial project in the service of the settler colonial state.

Concluding comments

As an Indigenous scholar, I hold little hope that the RJ movement will one day prove itself to be of significant value to Indigenous peoples. My pessimism is based on observations of the way members of the industry go about their work. Especially problematic is the fact that the consistent use of elements of the Indigenous life-world by RJ advocates cannot be considered an unintended consequence of the marketing activities of the industry. The marketing of RJ products is underpinned far too often by the reiteration of unsupported myths designed to demonstrate the 'indigenousness' of what is ostensibly a white, middle class-dominated crime-control business for this to be considered as anything other than the purposeful employment of Indigenous knowledge and practice for the advantage of the industry (Cunneen, 2008; Tauri, 2014). And so restorative justice advocates continue to bastardise Indigenous philosophies and sociocultural practices and to mislead the 'market' about the level of 'Indigeneity' of their products. This activity continues despite a decade or more of sustained Indigenous, and non-Indigenous, critiques of this behaviour (for example, see Blagg, 1997; 2008; Cunneen, 1998, 2008; Love, 2002; Tauri, 1998, 2004, to name but a few). To date, there has been little response to this critique. Indeed, I would suggest that the situation is worse than that: it appears the more we reveal the unethical conduct of members of the RJ movement with regard to Indigenous peoples, the more our critique is ignored. So why the lack of response to the Indigenous critique? Why do members of the RJ industry continue to co-opt elements of Indigenous life-worlds and continue to exaggerate the Indigenous foundations of both their movement and some of its key products? These questions provide the basis for an interesting and informative research project. Until that is done, we can only speculate, as I will do now.

It is now well established that members of the RJ 'community' aggressively marketed their RJ wares, most especially derivatives of New Zealand's FGC forum, on the increasingly globalised crime-control market (Tauri, 2016). It has further been established that the marketing was most aggressive in those settler colonial contexts suffering from the dual intractable problems of Indigenous over-representation and the radicalisation of Indigenous political activity (Tauri, 2014). This should come as no surprise to anyone who has engaged with the RJ lexicon that exploded from 1990 to the late 2000s. Much of this material contained oft-repeated claims of the Indigenous foundations of RJ policies and philosophies and forums imbued with the ancient teachings and practices of Indigenous peoples (Tauri, 2014). That the RJ movement is now accepted as a legitimate player on the globalised crime-control market, and treated by the settler colonial states as a viable partner in its continued domination of crime control, owes much to the development and marketing of the industry's supposedly 'Indigenous products'. In part, this may explain why so many RJ advocates, in particular those responsible for bastardising Indigenous peoples' philosophies and practices, remain silent in the face of increasing critique of their practice. And why would they not choose to remain so? For right now they have the support of the state to design, implement and 'evaluate' their products. In return, and to ensure their products are 'marketable' to the biggest funder of crime control, they modify them, continually designing out or softening the restorative 'bits' in order to make them more palatable to the tough-on-crime stance that dominates governmental response to social harm in most Western jurisdictions (Roach, 2012; Rudin, 2005; Suzuki and Wood, 2017; Tauri, 2009). In such a policy environment as this, what is a little bit of noise from a small group of stroppy coloured folk, when the industry has been accepted into the governmental fold and is eligible to receive taxpayers' monies? After all, they know better than we do what our communities need, right?

Wrong. From a critical Indigenous perspective, the response to the deceit, the myth making and condescension of the RJ industry towards us is obvious: if you continue to use our philosophies and practices without our input and consent; if you continue to use 'our stuff' to line your own pockets and to further your careers without respectful engagement with us; if you continue to exaggerate the 'Indigenousness' of your products and ignore our critique of your conduct, then you are a hypocrite who is not living up to so-called principles of the restorative justice movement to which you belong. You will also do serious damage to the movement itself in being able to work to achieve the transformative potential its members claim it is capable of. But perhaps just as important to a movement founded on social justice principles and aims, you will soon cease to be of any consequence to one of the most disaffected, disenfranchised communities residing in the settler colonial context.

Earlier we acknowledged that two of the aims of this Handbook were to provide a comprehensive review of "new and contested areas" in RJ, and to shine a light on significant 'grey areas of practice'. In response to these aims, this offering was formulated to inject an Indigenous perspective into one of the key 'contested areas' of RJ-related scholarship, namely, the value the industry brings to marginalised communities residing in Western jurisdictions. It has also been designed to once again offer an empirically informed perspective on what the author considers to be one of the significant 'grey areas' of RJ theorising, policy formulation and practice, namely, the Indigenous experience of all this activity. I say 'once again' because whilst it has been written with these key aims in mind, it was also written for another purpose, which is to cajole, to embarrass and/or to prompt RJ advocates and practitioners to respond to the Indigenous critique of RJ. In truth, the 'debate' over the value of RJ to Indigenous peoples is neither an intellectual or empirical contest at all because, as stated earlier, the majority of theoreticians, advocates and practitioners have thus far ignored Indigenous criticism of their activities. For there to be a 'contest', there would actually have to be a debate, and so far the only debate that is taking place is between like-minded, RJ advocates who are conveniently ignoring the Indigenous experience whilst they convince each other how well they are doing 'saving the natives'.

It must also be acknowledged that the impact that RJ is having on Indigenous communities is very much a 'grey area' of research and practice. And yet despite the absence of firm, empirical evidence, RJ advocates continue to make claims about RJ programmes, like how the FGC and other conferencing formats are 'capable of meeting the needs of Indigenous peoples' because of some magical, mythical alignment between these programmes and our 'ways of doing justice'. Indigenous-led research that has been privileged here, by Moyle, Victor and others, inserts an empirically informed edge to our critique and also acts as a thinly veiled challenge to the RJ to up its game when making claims about the 'added value' of its activities for our communities.

I have from time to time been asked if RJ offers anything of value to Indigenous peoples, if we 'want' it, if it can play a meaningful part in how Indigenous communities respond to social harm that occurs in our communities. I usually answer these questions with a two-part response, the first being direct and to the point, which is, that it is hard to formulate a response because there has been very little RJ 'delivered' in Indigenous communities across all settler colonial contexts. Most of what passes for RJ programmes experienced by Indigenous peoples are state-controlled standardised criminal justice interventions where the RJ elements have been exaggerated to create the illusion of communitarianism. And secondly, I answer by saying that rather than having to identify a position on the validity of the use of RJ by or in Indigenous communities, it is for RJ advocates and practitioners to demonstrate why we should consider implementing and utilising their Western, Eurocentric policies and programmes when we have our own processes and institutions for responding to social harm.

Reference

Acorn, A. 2004. *Compulsory Compassion: A Critique of Restorative Justice.* Vancouver: University of British Columbia Press.
Alfred, T. and Corntassell, J. 2005. Being Indigenous: Resurgences Against Contemporary Colonialism. *Politics of Identity*, IX: 597–614.
Barnsdale, L. and Walker. 2007. *Examining the Use and Impact of Family Group Conferencing.* Edinburgh: Scottish Executive.
Bhabha, H. 1994. *The Location of Culture.* London: Routledge.
Blagg, H. 1997. A Just Measure of Shame? Aboriginal Youth and Conferencing in Australia. *British Journal of Criminology*, 37(4): 481–501.

Blagg, H. 2008. *Crime, Aboriginality and the Decolonisation of Justice.* Sydney: Hawkins Press.

Bonner, N. and Syke, B. 1975. *Black Power in Australia.* South Yarra: Heinmann Educational Australia Pty Ltd.

Bonta, J., Wallace-Capretta, S., Rooney, J. and Mcanoy, K. 2002. An Outcome Evaluation of a Restorative Justice Alternative to Incarceration. *Contemporary Justice Review,* 5(4): 319–338.

Braithwaite, J. 1989. *Crime, Shame and Reintegration.* Cambridge: Cambridge University Press.

Comack, E. 2012. *Racialised Policing: Aboriginal People's Encounters with the Police.* Winnipeg: Fernwood Publishing.

Consedine, J. 1995. *Restorative Justice: Healing the Effects of Crime.* Wellington: Ploughshare Publishing.

Council of Europe. 2005. Resolution #2: On the Social Mission of the Criminal Justice System – Restorative Justice. *26th Conference of European Ministers of Justice,* Helsinki, 7–8 April.

Cunneen, C. 1997. Community Conferencing and the Fiction of Indigenous Control. *Australian New Zealand Journal of Criminology,* 30: 292–311.

Cunneen, C. 2008. Indigenous Anger and the Criminogenic Effects of the Criminal Justice System. In A. Day; M. Nakata and K. Howells (eds.) *Anger and Indigenous Men.* Leichhardt: Federation Press, pp. 37–46.

Cunneen, C. 2011. *State Crime, the Colonial Question and Indigenous Peoples.* Sydney: University of New South Wales.

Cunneen, C. and Hoyle, C. 2010. *Debating Restorative Justice.* Oxford and Portland, OR: Hart.

Deukmedjian, J. 2008. The Rise and Fall of Rcmp Community Justice Forums: Restorative Justice and Public Safety Interoperability in Canada. *Canadian Journal of Criminology and Criminal Justice,* 50(2): 117–151.

Fitzpatrick, P. 1992. The Impossibility of Popular Justice. *Social and Legal Studies,* 1: 199–215.

Foucault, M. 1977. *Discipline and Punish.* New York: Vantage.

Frieberg, A. 2001. Affective versus Effective Justice. *Punishment and Society,* 3(2): 265–278.

Friederes, J. 2000. Revelation and Revolution: Fault Lines in Aboriginal-White Relations. In M. Kalbach and W. Kalbach (eds.) *Perspectives on Ethnicity in Canada: A Reader.* Toronto: Harcourt Canada Ltd, pp. 207–237.

Fyfe, J. 2010. Blind Justice: Police Shootings in Memphis. In S. Rice and M. White (ed.) *Race, Ethnicity and Policing.* New York: New York University Press, pp. 368–381.

Gale, F. 1981. Adjustment of Migrants in Cities: Aborigines in Adelaide, Australia. In G. Jones and H. Richter (ed.) *Population Mobility and Development: Southeast Asia and the Pacific.* Canberra, Australia: Australian National University, pp. 283–303.

Gavrielides, T. 2016. Repositioning Restorative Justice in Europe. *Victims and Offenders,* 11(1): 71–86.

Gray, P. 2005. The Politics of Risk and Young Offenders' Experiences of Social Exclusion and Restorative Justice. *British Journal of Criminology,* 45(6): 938–957.

Griffin, D. 2012. Restorative Justice, Diversion and Social Control: Potential Problems. *Paper was Presented at the National Conference on Young People and Crime: Research, Policy and Practice at the Centre for Social and Educational Research, the Dublin Institute of Technology,* Ireland, 13 September.

Haleh Davis, M. 2011. A New World Rising: Albert Camus and the Absurdity of Neo-liberalism. *Social Identities: Journal for the Study of Race, Nation and Culture,* 17(2): 225–238.

Hansen, J. and Antsanen, R. 2012. The Pedagogy of Indigenous Restorative Justice. *The Quint: An Interdisciplinary Quarterly from the North,* 5(3): 29–40.

Harris, N. and Maruna, S. 2006. Shame, Sharing, and Restorative Justice: A Critical Appraisal. In D. Sullivan and L. Tifft (eds.) *Handbook of Restorative Justice: A Global Perspective.* London and New York: Routledge, pp. 452–462.

House of Commons – Justice Committee. 2016. *Restorative Justice: Fourth Report of Session 2016–17.* London: House of Commons.

Jackson, M. 1992. The Colonisation of Maori Philosophy. In G. Oddie and R. Perret (eds.) *Justice, Ethics and New Zealand Society.* Auckland: Oxford University Press, pp. 1–10.

Kidd, R. 1997. *The Way We Civilise: Aboriginal Affairs – The Untold Story.* Brisbane: The University of Queensland Press.

Kitossa, T. 2012. Criminology and Colonialism: Counter Colonial Criminology and the Canadian Context. *Journal of Pan African Studies*, 4(1): 204–226.

LaPrairie, C. 1996. *Examining Aboriginal Corrections in Canada*. Ottawa: Ministry of the Solicitor General.

Lee, G. 1997. The Newest Old Gem: Family Group Conferencing. *Justice as Healing*, 2(2): 1–3.

Levrant, S., Cullen, F., Fulton, B. and Wozniak, J. 1999. Reconsidering Restorative Justice The Corruption of Benevolence Revisited? *Crime and Delinquency*, 45(1): 3–27

Love, C. 2002. *Māori Perspectives on Collaboration and Colonisation in Contemporary Aotearoa/New Zealand Child and Family Welfare Policies and Practices*. Paper presented at the Policy and Partnerships Conference, Wilfrid Laurier University, Waterloo, June.

Marie, D. 2010. Maori and Criminal Offending: A Critical Appraisal. *Australian and New Zealand Journal of Criminology*, 43(2): 283–300.

Maxwell, G. 2008. Crossing Cultural Boundaries: Implementing Restorative Justice in International and Indigenous Contexts. *Sociology of Crime, Law and Deviance*, 11: 81–95.

Maxwell, G. and Morris, A. 1993. *Family, Victims and Culture: Youth Justice in New Zealand*. Wellington: Victoria University of Wellington.

Maxwell, G., Robertson, J., Kingi, V., Morris, A. and Cunningham, C. 2004. *Achieving Effective Outcomes in Youth Justice*. Wellington: Ministry of Social Development.

Merry, S. 2000. *Colonising Hawai'i: The Cultural Power of Law*. Princeton, NJ: Princeton University, Press.

Miers, D. 2007. The Internationalisation of Restorative Justice. In G. Johnstone and D. Van Ness (eds.) *Handbook of Restorative Justice*. Devon: Willan, pp. 447–467.

Milroy, J. 1999. *A National Crime: The Canadian Government and the Residential School System 1879 to 1986*. Winnipeg: The University of Manitoba Press.

Moyle, P. 2013. From Family Group Conferencing to Whanau Ora: Māori Social Workers Talk about their Experiences, unpublished Master's thesis, Massey University.

Moyle, P. 2014. Maori Social Workers' Experiences of Care and Protection: A Selection of Findings. *Te Komako, Social Work Review*, 26(1): 5–64.

Moyle, P. and Tauri, J. 2016. Maori, Family Group Conferencing and the Mystifications of Restorative Justice. *Victims and Offenders*: Special Issue: The Future of Restorative Justice? 11(1): 87–106.

Monture-Angus, P. 1999. Considering Colonialism and Oppression: Aboriginal Women, Justice and the 'theory' of Decolonisation, *Native Studies Review*, 12(1): 63–94.

Monture-Angus, P. 2007. Racing and Erasing: Law and Gender in White Settler Societies. In S. Bolaria and S. Hier (eds.) *Race and Racism in 21st Century Canada: Continuity, Complexity and Change*. Peterborough, ON: Broadview Press, pp. 197–216.

Muncie, J. 2005. The Globalisation of Crime Control – The Case of Youth and Juvenile Justice: Neoliberalism, Policy Convergence and International Conventions. *Theoretical Criminology*, 9(1): 35–64.

Newbold, G. 2000. *Crime in New Zealand*. Palmerston North: Dunmore.

NISATSIC. 1997. *Bringing them Home: Report of the National Inquiry into the Separation of Aboriginal and Torres Strait Islander Children from their Families*. Sydney: Human Rights and Equal Opportunity Commission.

Olsen, T., Maxwell, G. and Morris, A. 1995. Maori and Youth Justice in New Zealand. In K. Hazlehurst (ed.) *Popular Justice and Community Regeneration: Pathways to Indigenous Reform*. Westport: Praeger, pp. 45–66.

Palys, T. and Victor, W. 2005. *Getting to a Better Place: Qwi: Qwelstom, the Stó:lo and Self-Determination*. Ontario: Law Commission of Canada.

Poata-Smith, E. 1996. He pokeke uenuku i tu ai: The Evolution of Contemporary Māori Protest. In P. Spoonley, D. Pearson and C. Macpherson (eds.) *Nga patai: Racism and Ethnic Relations in Aotearoa/New Zealand*. Palmerston North: Dunmore Press, pp. 97–116.

Proulx, C. 2002. *Re-claiming Justice and Community: The Community Council Project of Toronto*. Unpublished PhD thesis, McMaster University, Hamilton, ON.

Proulx, C. 2003. *Reclaiming Aboriginal Justice, Community and Identity*. Saskatoon: Purich Publishing Ltd.

Richards, K. 2007. *'Rewriting History': Towards a Genealogy of 'Restorative Justice'*. Unpublished PhD thesis, University of Western Sydney, Sydney.

Richardson, B. 1989. *Drumbeat: Anger and Renewal in Indian Country*. Toronto: Summerhill Press Ltd.

Roach, K. 2012. The Institutionalisation of Restorative Justice in Canada: Effective Reform or Limited and Limiting Add-on? In I. Aertsen, T. Deams and L. Robert (eds.) *Institutionalising Restorative Justice.* New York: Routledge, pp. 167–193.

Ross, R. 2009. Searching for the Roots of Conferencing. In G. Burford and J. Hudson (eds.) *Family Group Conferencing: New Directions in Community-centered Child and Family Practice.* New Jersey: Transaction Publishers, pp. 5–14.

Rudin, J. 2005. Aboriginal Justice and Restorative Justice. In E. Elliot and R. Gordon (eds.) *New Directions in Restorative Justice: Issues, Practice, Evaluation.* Devon: Willan, pp. 89–114.

Ruggiero, V. 2000. *Crime and Markets: Essays in Anti-criminology.* Oxford: Oxford University Press.

Scuro, P. 2013. Latin America. In G. Johnstone and D. Van Ness (eds.) *Handbook of Restorative Justice.* Cullompton: Willan, pp. 500–510.

Short, D. 2003. Reconciliation, Assimilation, and the Indigenous Peoples of Australia. *International Political Science Review*, 24(4): 491–513.

Suzuki, M. and Wood, W. 2017. Co-option, Coercion and Compromise: Restorative Justice in Victoria, Australia. *Contemporary Justice Review*, 20(2): 274–292.

Tauri, J. 1998. Family Group Conferences: A Case Study of the Indigenisation of New Zealand's Justice System. *Current Issues in Criminal Justice*, 10(2): 168–182.

Tauri, J. 1999. Explaining Recent Innovations in New Zealand's Criminal Justice System: Empowering Māori or Biculturalising the State? *Australian New Zealand Journal of Criminology*, 32(2): 153–167.

Tauri, J. 2004. *Conferencing, Indigenisation and Orientalism: A Critical Commentary on Recent State Responses to Indigenous Offending.* Paper presented at The Qwi: Qwelstom Gathering: 'Bringing Justice Back to the People', Mission, British Columbia, 22–24 March.

Tauri J. 2009. An Indigenous Commentary on the Standardisation of Restorative Justice. *Indigenous Policy Journal*, 20(3), online.

Tauri, J. 2011. *Criminology and the Disempowerment of First Nations in Settler Societies.* Paper presented at Crime, Justice and Social Democracy: An International Conference, Queensland University of Technology, Brisbane, 25–28 September.

Tauri, J. 2014. Settler-colonialism, Criminal Justice and Indigenous Peoples. *African Journal of Criminology and Justice Studies*, 8(1): 20–37.

Tauri, J. 2016. *The State, the Academy and Indigenous Justice: A Counter-colonial Critique.* Unpublished PhD thesis, University of Wollongong.

Tauri, J. 2017. Indigenous Peoples and the Globalisation of Crime Control. *Social Justice: A Journal of Crime, Conflict and World Order*, 43(3): online.

Tauri, J. and Webb, R. 2012. A Critical Appraisal of Responses to Māori Offending. *International Indigenous Policy Journal*, 3(4): Article 5 (online).

Thomas, N. 1994. *Colonialism's Culture: Anthropology, Travel and Government.* Melbourne: Melbourne University Press.

Thorns, D. and Sedgwick, C. 1997. *Understanding Aotearoa/New Zealand: Historical Statistics.* Palmerston North: Dunmore Press.

Umbreit, M. and Stacey, S. 1996. Family Group Conferencing Comes to the U.S: A Comparison with Victim Offender Mediation. *Juvenile and Family Court Journal*, 47(2): 29–38.

United Nations. 2002. *Declaration of Basic Principles on the Use of Restorative Justice Programmes in Criminal Matters.* Geneva: The Economic and Social Council.

Victor, W. 2007. *Indigenous Justice: Clearing Space and Place for Indigenous Epistemologies.* Ottawa: National Centre for First Nations Governance.

Wacquant, L. 2009. *Punishing the Poor: The Neoliberal Government of Social Insecurity.* Durham and London: Duke University Press.

Waites, C., MacGowan, M., Pennell, J., Carlton-LaNey, I. and Weil, M. 2004. Increasing the Cultural Responsiveness of Family Group Conferencing. *Social Work*, 49(2): 291–300.

Walker, H. 1996. *Whanau (family) Decision Making: Why Do they Not Trust Us?* Paper presented at the Under Construction: Building a Better Future for Colorado's Children and Families Conference, Denver.

Warrior, R. 1996. *Like a Hurricane: The Indian Movement from Alcatraz to Wounded Knee*. New York: New York Press.

Weatherburn, D. 2010. Guest Editorial: Indigenous Violence. *Australian and New Zealand Journal of Criminology*, 43(2) pp. 197–198.

Weatherburn, D. 2014. *Arresting Incarceration: Pathways Out of Indigenous Imprisonment*. Canberra: Aboriginal Studies Press.

Weitzer, R. 2000. Racialised Policing: Residents' Perceptions in Three Neighbourhoods. *Law and Society Review*, 34(1): 129–155.

Wood, W. 2015. Why Restorative Justice Will Not Reduce Incarceration. *The British Journal of Criminology*, 55(5): 883–900.

Woolford, A. 2013. The Next Generation: Criminology, Genocide Studies and Settler-Colonialism. *Revista Critica Penal y Poder*, 5: 163–185.

Zehr, H. 1990. *Changing Lenses: A New Focus for Crime and Justice*. Scottsdale: Herald Press.

24

Does restorative justice reduce recidivism?

Assessing evidence and claims about restorative justice and reoffending

Ellie Piggott and William Wood

Introduction

Since the 1990s, restorative justice (RJ) has emerged as a popular alternative to more traditional responses to criminal behaviour. At present, restorative programmes and policies have been implemented, trialled, or planned in all regions of the world, including Australasia, America, Europe, Africa, and Asia. The global rise of RJ has followed from a growing number of claims regarding its ability to achieve high levels of victim involvement, participant satisfaction, procedural justice, offender accountability and compliance (Hoyle et al., 2002; Latimer et al., 2005; McCold and Wachtel, 1998; McGarrell et al., 2000), and lower rates of reoffending (Bonta et al., 2006; Bradshaw and Roseborough, 2005; Nugent et al., 2003; Latimer et al., 2005; Sherman et al., 2015a, 2015b). While there is considerable debate whether the reduction of recidivism should be a legitimate goal of RJ (Robinson and Shapland, 2008), crime reduction is nonetheless a significant policy concern. That is, reoffending reduction is a key measure of the effectiveness of criminal justice initiatives and an overall performance indicator of a criminal justice system across most public departments (Cunneen and Luke, 2007: 197). Consequently, within a policy context, it is essential to test the empirical claim that RJ can positively effect change in offending behaviour (Hayes, 2005: 79).

Substantial research literature has aimed to determine whether participation in RJ reduces reoffending. However, such evaluation research has failed to report consistent findings. Although a number of studies have found that RJ programmes can reduce post-intervention offending (Allard et al., 2009; Baffour, 2006; Bergseth and Bouffard, 2007, 2013; Daly et al., 2013; de Beus and Rodriguez, 2007; Hayes, 2005; Luke and Lind, 2002; McGarrell et al., 2000; McGarrell and Hipple, 2007; Sherman et al., 2000), others have reported no significant effect (Jeong et al., 2012; McCold and Wachtel, 1998; Piggott, 2015; Shapland et al., 2008; Smith and Weatherburn, 2012). A small number of studies have also found RJ to *increase* the likelihood of reoffending (Bonta et al., 1983; Roy, 1993; Sherman et al., 2000; URSA Institute, 1993).

These mixed findings can be attributed to substantial differences between RJ programmes in policy and practice. Currently, there is little consensus on what constitutes RJ (Daly, 2016) and, therefore, on what constitutes an RJ intervention. As a result, a diverse range of programmes – which differ in ways that are both theoretically and empirically related to reoffending – have been assessed by RJ evaluators. The conflicting results reported in RJ evaluations can further be attributed to wide variation in study design and methodological challenges, largely pertaining to: (i) how best to control for potential bias and form a fair and equivalent comparison group, and (ii) how best to measure recidivism.

This chapter aims to provide a concise but thorough explanation of the contradictory findings reported in RJ evaluation research. The chapter offers readers a critical overview of current evidence and claims regarding RJ's ability to reduce reoffending. We first examine how restorative programmes differ in ways theoretically and empirically related to recidivism and assess existing evidence from English-speaking countries of what is currently known and not known about RJ and reoffending. We then examine current methodological limitations and differing research approaches in controlling for potential bias and forming equivalent comparisons within studies assessing the influence of RJ on recidivism. Finally, we discuss current methodological issues within RJ research related to the measurement of reoffending, before providing concluding remarks and directions for future research.

Variation in restorative justice programmes

There is currently little agreement among practitioners, researchers, and academics regarding the definition of RJ. What precisely constitutes a "restorative" intervention remains subject to rigorous debate (Daly, 2016). Consequently, the label of "restorative justice" has been applied to a diverse range of programmes. While some scholars have argued that it may be not be possible or even preferable to reach an agreed definition of restorative justice, current variation in theory and practice make assessing the evidence of RJ's ability to reduce reoffending challenging. Different types of restorative interventions are likely to have different impacts on recidivism (Strang and Sherman, 2015: 16). Even within specific types of RJ practices, restorative justice conferencing (RJC) for example, differences between programmes are still likely to impact estimates of reoffending. In this section, we assess what is empirically known about how, for whom, and in what context different RJ practices may or may not effectively reduce reoffending.

Involvement of victims

One element of RJ interventions that appears to affect post-intervention offending is the level of victim participation. The efficacy of direct victim involvement is supported by Sykes and Matza's (1957) neutralization theory and Collins's (2004) interaction ritual theory. RJ processes that involve direct participation of victims via face-to-face meetings appear to undermine offenders' abilities to employ neutralization techniques, particularly "denial of harm" and "denial of victim", because it is difficult for offenders to deny the existence of victims and injury caused when evidence to the contrary is placed squarely in front of them (Braithwaite, 2002). However, if a victim chooses not to participate, or participate only indirectly, it is much easier for an offender to maintain such denials. This is supported by findings from Maxwell and Morris (2001), who found that juvenile offenders who met and/or apologized to their victim during their conference were less likely to receive a reconviction. Similarly, Shapland et al. (2008) found that serious adult offenders who wanted to meet their victim were also less likely to be reconvicted. Findings from Hayes, McGee and Cerruto (2011) and Shapland et al. (2008) also suggest that offenders who were more successful in desisting from crime reported being impacted by hearing the harms and consequences of their actions from victims. Given these findings, RJ interventions with direct victim participation may be likely to have a greater impact on offender behaviour post-intervention compared to RJCs that do not.

Collins's (2004) interaction ritual theory further suggests that the presence of victims in RJ interventions influences post-intervention offending. Collins (2004: 111) asserts that interaction rituals (IR), such as RJ interventions, encourage individuals to conform to law-abiding behaviour through social solidarity and strong collective emotion. The four ingredients required for a successful IR include: (i) the physical presence of all participants, (ii) the exclusion of non-participants (via physical or psychological barriers), (iii) a collective focus on a common purpose, and (iv) a shared mood or emotional experience (Collins, 2004). According to Rossner (2011), if all these conditions are met during an IR, conversational and bodily rhythm develops between participants, resulting in a mutual sense of group membership and a long-term boost in positive feelings such as confidence, enthusiasm, and elation that serves to recommit those present to the shared morality of the group. Rossner's (2013) reanalysis of RJCs from the Canberra Reintegrative Shaming Experiments (RISE) (Sherman et al., 1998) examined differences between conferences in three core elements of a successful IR: reintegration, solidarity, and emotional energy, finding that RJCs achieving high levels of solidarity and reintegration resulted in a decrease in both the prevalence and frequency of rearrest of young offenders. To our knowledge, only one study, by Bouffard et al. (2017), has found that juvenile offenders who had direct contact with their victim took significantly less time to reoffend than those who had no, minimal, or indirect victim contact. However, this study utilized exceptionally small sample sizes, a problem we discuss later in more detail.

Given these findings, there is also some doubt as to the effectiveness of RJ to reduce reoffending for victimless crimes such as drug possession, public intoxication, dangerous driving, or crimes against corporations, governments, or community organizations which frequently lack an identifiable victim.

Involvement of communities of care

Another element of some restorative practices that is frequently argued to reduce reoffending is the inclusion of offender support persons, or what RJ advocates term "communities of care". Both Hirschi's (1969) social bond theory and Braithwaite's (1989) theory of reintegrative shaming support this claim. According to social bond theory, RJ practices that include an offender's community of care offer a means of strengthening or repairing (damaged) relationships with conventional others and, in turn, normative society (Hirschi, 1969). Braithwaite's (2002: 154) concept of "reintegrative shaming" is similar, as its emphasis is placed on those who have the most meaningful relationships with the offender. Braithwaite (1989: 87) also contends that offenders' desires to maintain the social approval of their significant others motivates them to conform more than does the indeterminate threat of legal sanctions or the opinion of justice officials. Consequently, both theories suggest that RJ programmes which do not engage agents of informal social control are not theoretically equivalent in terms of reducing reoffending compared to those that do. While many RJ interventions involve the participation of offender support persons, at least in principle, other programmes only include an offender, a victim, and a neutral mediator.

Evidence supporting these theoretical pathways of reduced offending is, however, limited. At present, research suggests that offenders perceive RJ as more reintegrative than court processing (Strang et al., 2011), particularly when it encompasses existing positive social attachments (Kim and Gerber, 2010), and that the perceived experience of social disapproval and reintegration predicts feelings of shame and guilt in offenders (Harris, 2006). But to date there remains limited empirical support linking informal social control, reintegrative shaming, and/or the presence of communities of care during RJ and recidivism. However, some evidence suggests juvenile offenders who feel socially supported and not stigmatically shamed during their RJC experience a significant reduction in post-RJ offending (Maxwell et al., 2004; Maxwell and Morris, 2001).

Procedural justice

Another element of RJ practices that some argue plays a role in reducing reoffending is that of procedural justice. According to Tyler's (1990) theory of procedural justice, offenders who are afforded the opportunity to actively participate in the decision-making process and have a "voice" in the resolution of the conflict are more inclined to perceive a justice intervention as fair and respectful. This, in turn, leads offenders to perceive justice officials and the justice system as legitimate and, consequently, to be more likely to obey the law (Tyler, 1990). Current evidence suggests that compared to those who attend traditional court processing, offenders that participate in RJ report higher levels of perceived procedural justice (Shapland et al., 2007) and greater levels of respect for police, the law, and the justice system (Strang et al., 2011). Further evidence indicates that offenders who attend RJ and (consequently) perceive the law as legitimate are less likely to reoffend (Daly, 2003), and that this perception is shaped by higher ratings of procedural justice (Tyler et al., 2007). Moreover, additional research shows that when young offenders are treated with fairness and respect, are involved in the decision-making process, and outcomes are achieved by genuine consensus, they are less likely to reoffend following RJ (Hayes and Daly, 2003; Maxwell et al., 2004; Maxwell and Morris, 2001).

Offender eligibility criteria

In RJ practice, programme eligibility criteria dictate whether an offender may be referred to a specific programme. These criteria vary significantly from one intervention or programme setting to another. As a result, a wide array of different offending populations have been examined within RJ evaluation research. Although many researchers have utilized offending and demographic variables as covariates, fewer have assessed whether the impact of RJ programming on recidivism differs according to these characteristics. Existing evidence indicates that offence type, prior offending history, age, gender, and ethnicity influence the effectiveness of RJ on reoffending (Allard et al., 2009; Bergseth and Bouffard, 2007; Hayes, 2005; Hayes and Daly, 2004; Maxwell et al., 2004; McCold and Wachtel, 1998; Sherman et al., 2000; Strang et al., 2013). While an in-depth review of existing research is beyond the scope of this chapter, research relating to age and offence type requires some attention as some evidence appears to be in the opposite direction of conventional practice. In most jurisdictions, RJ is typically only available to young, minor, and/or non-violent offenders with little to no criminal history (Weatherburn and Macadam, 2013: 3). Despite this, evaluations of the Bethlehem, Pennsylvania, and Restorative Policing Experiment (Hayes, 2005; McCold and Wachtel, 1998) and RISE Experiments (Sherman et al., 2000) have reported significant reductions in rearrests for violent offenders one-year post-conference, but no significant reductions for property offenders. A recent meta-analysis of ten randomized experiments by Strang et al. (2013) also found RJCs to work better for violent offenders than property offenders in lowering recidivism. RJCs were also found to be more effective for adults than young people in reducing post-intervention offending.

Variation in restorative models and practice

RJ interventions have been categorized into a series of distinct models, including victim-offender mediation, community reparative boards, RJC, and circle sentencing. Even within these distinct models, however, programmes may differ in ways that may impact future offending. While some interventions of even the same model, for example, RJC, may only include a written apology, financial restitution, or community service within the terms of outcome agreements, other programmes may further include counselling or other rehabilitative programmes. Some programmes utilize comprehensive conference preparation and follow-through for offenders, while others do not. Programmes also accept referrals at different points within the justice system (i.e. pre-court diversion, pre-sentence, or post-sentence).

Summary

As illustrated, due to substantial differences found between "restorative" programmes, it is not analytically useful to think of RJ as a singular concept or practice. Hayes (2005: 96) noted over a decade ago that "given the diverse range in [RJ] practice, we should expect equal diversity in the ways [RJ] influences offenders and their behaviour". Since that time, we have greater evidence that some RJ interventions are effective in reducing recidivism, but we are still far less certain about how, for whom, and in what contexts RJ programmes work. Unfortunately, there remains a strong focus on "what" (i.e. outcomes), but less of a focus on "why" (i.e. mechanisms) restorative interventions work to reduce reoffending. Thus, the ability to account for measurable programme differences is vital in moving forward in knowledge on RJ and reoffending. Towards this end, readers must "take stock" of programme characteristics that are theoretically or empirically related to post-intervention offending prior to drawing conclusions regarding the effectiveness of an intervention, while researchers should endeavour to better understand the mechanisms at work underneath the label of "restorative justice".

Methodological issues forming an equivalent comparison

In the previous section, we discussed existing research and theory on what we know and don't know about the ability of RJ to reduce reoffending. In this section, we describe and analyse the methodological approaches and problems currently found in RJ evaluation research.

Apart from some simulation modelling research (e.g. Stewart et al., 2008), research on RJ and recidivism can be divided into two categories: comparison studies and variation studies. Comparison studies seek to test the effectiveness of RJ in reducing reoffending compared to court and/or other justice processes (Hayes and Daly, 2004: 169). Variation studies assess how differences *within* the RJ experience, such as feelings of remorse, an apology to the victim, involvement in the decision-making process, and level of procedural justice, predicts later variation in offending (Hayes and Daly, 2004: 169). Of the two, comparison studies are more common in RJ research.

To date, a number of meta-analyses and reviews suggest that, on average, RJ is more effective in reducing recidivism compared to comparison groups (Bonta, et al., 2006; Bradshaw and Roseborough, 2005; Nugent et al., 2003; Latimer et al., 2005; Sherman et al., 2015a, 2015b). Authors of other reviews and meta-analyses (e.g. Hayes, 2007; Sherman and Strang, 2007; Wilson et al., 2017) contend that current evidence of RJ's crime reduction potential is promising but remains inconclusive. Still others assert that due to significant methodological limitations (Livingstone et al., 2013; McGrath, 2008; Weatherburn and Macadam, 2013), and well-known threats to validity (McCold, 2008: 9), current research lacks reliable evidence to support RJ's purported ability to reduce reoffending.

The problem of selection bias

One significant threat to validity facing comparison research is selection bias. This occurs when researchers select groups for comparison that are not equivalent on baseline characteristics that are known or expected to affect reoffending outcomes. Due to this bias, there is a problem for researchers in determining what reoffending outcomes may be a result of initial group differences or a "selection effect", and what outcomes may be a result of an RJ intervention or a "treatment effect".

In RJ evaluations, selection bias occurs largely as a result of programme eligibility criteria and referral decisions by justice officials. Such decisions are not necessarily haphazard and are often a result of existing laws or other constraints. For example, as established, RJ is most typically used for minor and/or non-violent offenders with little to no prior offending history. But at present there are limited RJ options available for repeat offenders who commit serious and/or violent crimes (Weatherburn and Macadam, 2013: 3). Consequently, offenders who are eligible for RJ referral may have a lower risk of reoffending than those who are not, and differences reported in recidivism between RJ and non-RJ samples, such as court-referred offenders, may simply be a product of pre-existing group differences in criminogenic risk (Luke and Lind, 2002: 2).

Selection bias is a widely-recognized problem within the RJ literature (Bergseth and Bouffard, 2007; Hayes, 2005, 2007; Livingstone et al., 2013; McGrath, 2008; Weatherburn and Macadam, 2013). Some comparison studies have not attempted to account or control for possible selection bias. Most researchers, however, have used a range of different methods to isolate the treatment effect of RJ from a potential selection effect. We discuss each of these strategies in turn next.

One strategy used by comparison researchers to address the problem of selection bias is purposive (or selective) sampling (e.g. Allard et al., 2009; Bergseth and Bouffard, 2007, 2013; Luke and Lind, 2002). To control for initial group differences, researchers selectively sample specific types or groups of offenders such as only first-time or property offenders. However, as evidenced by Bergseth and Bouffard (2007), purposive sampling based on one characteristic (e.g. referral offence type) can rarely achieve adequate balance among groups on other key factors related to reoffending. Consequently, researchers have had to rely on additional methods of controlling for selection bias.

The most common method used to address selection bias is statistically controlling for initial group differences through multivariate analyses (e.g. Daly et al., 2013; de Beus and Rodriguez, 2007; Jeong et al., 2012; Luke and Lind, 2002; McGarrell and Hipple, 2007). These techniques allow researchers to control for the effects of measured covariates on reoffending outcomes. Studies utilizing this method examine RJ outcomes using a retrospective study design, meaning that researchers use existing administrative data to determine whether those who reoffended did so as a result of prior intervention and/or prior exposure to risk or protective factors. Retrospective studies have the benefit of being both time- and cost-effective due to the immediate availability of study data. However, these studies are limited in that they can only control for variables that have been collected by administrative agencies and to the degree in which they are accurately recorded. Therefore, without access to a minimum set of control variables – for example, prior offending history, offence type, age, gender, and ethnicity (Nagin, Cullen, and Francis, 2009: 136) – pre-existing group differences may remain undetected by researchers. Moreover, even with methodologies in place to control for pre-existing differences, imbalance can remain between groups on key demographics and offending characteristics (e.g. Sherman et al., 2000).

A third strategy used to address selection bias is the matching of offenders on predictors of reoffending and/or programme referral (e.g. Little, 2015; Piggott, 2015; Smith and Weatherburn, 2012; Shapland et al., 2008). This approach involves selecting pairs of subjects based on matching "like for like" comparisons between offenders. As an observational method, matching shares most of the same strengths and limitations as multivariate analyses in dealing with selection bias. However, an approach such as Propensity Score Matching (PSM) has been argued to be a superior method in that it allows researchers to determine the extent to which the statistical model has adequately eliminated selection bias (Austin, 2011: 417). However, studies that use PSM may lack external validity. Findings may not be generalizable to other offending populations, jurisdictional contexts, and time periods as the matching process may exclude a large proportion of offenders (Little, 2015: 288). For this same reason, potential treatment effect can be lost.

A fourth method used to address selection bias is random allocation of offenders to treatment (i.e. RJ intervention) and comparison (i.e. non-RJ intervention) conditions (e.g. Baffour, 2006; Hayes, 2005; Jeong et al., 2012; McCold and Wachtel, 1998; McGarrell et al., 2000; McGarrell and Hipple, 2007). Random allocation is considered the "gold standard" for estimating treatment effects on outcomes, as it ensures that offenders across conditions are equivalent on both measured *and unmeasured* confounders (Austin, 2011: 399). Randomized controlled trials (RCTs) do not eliminate selection bias altogether, for example, within the RISE experiments (Sherman et al., 2000), offenders randomly assigned to conferencing significantly differed from offenders assigned to court on offending history and self-reported binge-drinking (McGrath, 2008: 319). Nevertheless, RCTs do increase the probability that any individual differences between offenders are equally distributed among groups (McCold, 2008: 13). Despite being considered the most reliable means of controlling for group differences, RCTs are rare in RJ research, as prospective, longitudinal research designs are costly and exceedingly time-consuming. Random assignment is also ethically and procedurally difficult, as it requires that some offenders be denied the opportunity to participate in a potentially superior condition (i.e. the treatment condition) on the basis of chance (Little, 2015: 40). Also, RCTs have been criticized for the artificial conditions they may create because, in practice, justice officials do not refer offenders to restorative programmes on a random basis but consider the history of the offender and the nature of the crime prior to determining eligibility (Hayes 2005: 80).

Regardless of what method is employed to control for potential selection bias, comparative studies which have small sample sizes are unlikely to achieve equivalence on observed and unobserved covariates across samples (Farrington and Welsh, 2006: 60). Therefore, results from RJ evaluations with 50 or fewer offenders per group should be interpreted with caution due to poor internal validity (Farrington and Welsh, 2006: 60).

The problem of self-selection bias

Another methodological challenge in comparison research is self-selection bias. As offenders may decide whether to voluntarily participate or "self-select" into RJ, it is likely that only those most amenable to RJ will choose to do so (Bergseth and Bouffard, 2007: 435), with the effect that offenders who consent to participate in RJ have likely moved closer towards desistence than those who decline (Shapland, Robinson, and Sorsby, 2011: 178). Consequently, group differences in reoffending found in some RJ evaluations may be a result of offenders' decisions to participate rather than the effects of the programme itself.

To control for these motivation effects, some researchers have conducted analyses on an intention-to-treat (ITT) basis. ITT seeks to measure the effect of *referral* to an RJ intervention, as opposed to the RJ programme itself. In other words, RJ samples are comprised of offenders who receive a referral (or random assignment) to RJ, regardless of whether they participate or fulfil the requirements of the programme. In addition to accounting for motivation effects, ITT also standardizes follow-up periods for all offenders within a research sample (Hayes, 2005: 83), thus ensuring a fairer comparison between treatment and comparison groups (Sherman, et al., 2000: 10). In a policy context, analysing data on the basis of ITT has been argued to produce findings that may be more practically relevant to both justice officials and policy makers than as-treated analyses, as not all referred offenders will consent to participate in RJ (Sherman, Strang, and Woods, 2000: 10). Despite these advantages, ITT analysis has only been conducted by a small number of researchers (e.g. Bergseth and Bouffard, 2007, 2013; Jeong et al., 2012; McCold and Wachtel, 1998; McGarrell et al., 2000; McGarrell and Hipple, 2007; Piggott, 2015; Sherman et al., 2000; Smith and Weatherburn, 2012).

Some RJ researchers have been critical of the use of ITT analyses. In instances where a large proportion of RJ-referred offenders decline to participate, ITT design arguably provides little information about the effectiveness of the programme in reducing recidivism, because a high number of declines dilute a potential treatment effect (Gupta, 2011: 110). When this occurs, ITT analysis provides, at best, a conservative estimate of reoffending and, at worst, a type II error (i.e. a false negative finding). Therefore, when possible, researchers conducting ITT analyses should report reoffending outcomes for three distinct samples: a treatment (or as-treated) (i.e. offenders who participated and completed the requirements of RJ), ITT (or decline) (i.e. offenders who were referred to RJ), and the comparison group. This provides readers with estimates of both the efficacy of RJ programming and RJ policy. But to our knowledge, only two studies have done this. McCold and Wachtel (1998) reported significant differences in rearrest rates between violent juvenile offenders who agreed to participate in a RJC (20%) and those who declined (48%). Conversely, Smith and Weatherburn (2012) found no significant differences between ITT and as-treated groups of young offenders in post-conference offending.

Unfortunately, many studies on RJ and recidivism have only compared RJ groups and traditional court processing groups, without considering self-selection bias. This problem may be exacerbated by additional eligibility conditions in some programs, such as an admission of guilt. To account for such bias, several studies have compared offenders who participate in RJ interventions against offenders who are eligible but do not participate in RJ in order to ensure an equivalent comparison (e.g. de Beus and Rodriguez, 2007; Jeong et al., 2012; McCold and Wachtel, 1998; McGarrell et al., 2000; McGarrell and Hipple, 2007; Piggott, 2015; Shapland et al., 2008; Sherman et al., 2000; Smith and Weatherburn, 2012). However, as argued by Hayes (2005: 81), while only examining offenders who meet RJ eligibility requirements (e.g. voluntary consent and admission of guilt) maintains equalization across RJ and comparison groups, it also significantly reduces the generalizability of study findings, as both samples are similar in ways theoretically related to recidivism.

Problems in variation studies

While comparison studies have been criticized for comparing non-equivalent groups, variation studies have been criticized for not utilizing comparison altogether. When treatment and control groups are equivalent on baseline characteristics, observed differences in outcomes can be attributed to the treatment. Thus, "[E]ven the most comprehensive long-term measurement and analysis of reoffending is of limited value without the use of an appropriate control group" (Cunneen and Luke, 2007: 201). Consequently, some scholars contend that because variation studies do not provide evidence about how RJ programmes perform compared to other justice processes, any found effects on recidivism may be due to confounding variables. Hayes (2005: 82) notes, however, that the primary goal of variation research is not the isolation of treatment effects but instead an improved understanding of how and why RJ reduces reoffending.

Summary

Many comparison studies of RJ and reoffending remain plagued by biased samples. Due to small sample sizes and high risks of selection and self-selection bias, some RJ evaluations have produced promising, but methodologically suspect, conclusions regarding the impact of RJ on reoffending. As studies significantly vary in their success in achieving fair and equivalent comparisons, it is unsurprising that the recidivism rates reported by such evaluations also vary. Among other inherent methodological flaws, the threats to validity introduced by biased samples considerably contribute to the conflicting evidence found within RJ literature. Consequently, before establishing the effectiveness of an RJ intervention, it is vital that readers first inspect the evaluation for any biases that are likely to inflate its treatment effect.

Methodological issues measuring recidivism

The final substantive issue we consider in this chapter is the problem of how researchers measure reoffending. To date, RJ scholars have outlined several unresolved methodological issues regarding the accurate evaluation of recidivism within RJ research. Most of these challenges are not unique to RJ but are common issues in all criminological evaluations. We discuss these issues in turn next.

Identifying reoffending

As it is not possible to directly measure reoffending, researchers must rely on data sources, largely administrative data and self-report data, to provide proximal estimates (Payne, 2007: 9). In RJ evaluation research, a reoffence or "indicator event" has been variously defined as:

1   Officially recorded police contact such as police arrest or apprehension (e.g. Daly, 2003; Hayes and Daly, 2003, 2004; McGarrell, et al., 2000; Rossner, 2013);
2   System contact, including formal cautioning, RJ attendance, court appearance, or imprisonment (e.g. de Beus and Rodriguez, 2007; Little, 2015; Luke and Lind, 2002);
3   Finalization of criminal justice sanction (e.g. finalization of formal caution, RJ programme, or court case) (e.g. Daly et al., 2013; Smith and Weatherburn, 2012);
4   Proven offence (e.g. Luke and Lind, 2002);
5   Criminal conviction (e.g. Maxwell and Morris, 2001; Shapland et al., 2008); and,
6   Any post-intervention self-reported criminal behaviour (e.g. Hayes et al., 2011, 2014; Hoyle et al., 2002).

All of these measures of reoffending are proxies, and each has limitations. Most RJ researchers have used official records from administrative agencies, primarily police and courts, to approximate recidivism (Payne, 2007). It is widely recognized, however, that official data significantly underestimates crime, as only a small percentage of offences are identified and processed through the criminal justice system. As summarized by McCold (2008: 12), "crimes are unfounded by the police, withdrawn by prosecutors, dismissed and suspended by judges". Consequently, reoffending assessed at later points in the system is increasingly subject to underestimation as a result of cumulative decisions by law officials (McCold, 2008: 17).

As police represent an offender's first point of contact with the criminal justice system, policing records may provide the most accurate assessment of reoffending (Payne, 2007: 34). However, policing practices can also skew recidivism measurements by focusing on specific people and offences (Maxwell and Morris, 2001: 244); through decisions about whether and how to process offenders (Payne, 2007: 23), or by over-charging offenders in anticipation of a plea bargain (Payne, 2007: 34).

Prior to appearing in court, offenders must first be apprehended and charged by police. Consequently, court data inherits the limitations of official police records (Payne, 2007: 27). But, court data may also further distort estimates of reoffending in various ways. As a case progresses further through the court system, the greater the likelihood that repeat offending will be underestimated and offenders will be incorrectly labelled as non-recidivists (Payne, 2007: 32). At court appearance, offenders may appear before a separate court and remain undetected by evaluators (Payne, 2007: 35). They may also have their court cases diverted or deferred, have cases pled down or dismissed, or have lengthy continuances – all of which may result in significant underestimates of the true extent of reoffending (Payne, 2007: 27–35). At court finalization, case processing time is more likely to be longer and police charges are more likely to have been negotiated away or withdrawn due to lack of evidence. Therefore, official records of conviction may reflect an even more substantial underestimate of reoffending.

Aside from administrative records, the other form of data used by RJ evaluators to estimate reoffending is self-reported data. This type of data is often seen as a more reliable source for approximating recidivism, as it can identify offending behaviour that has or may never be detected by criminal justice officials (McCold, 2008: 11). Self-report data, however, has its own limitations. Reoffending may be underestimated due to respondents' unwillingness or inability to accurately recall events, overestimated due to respondents' exaggeration of criminal activity, or otherwise skewed due to respondents' poor understanding of survey items (Payne, 2007: 20). Nevertheless, recent reviews suggest that self-reported measures of offending are both reliable and valid (Jolliffe and Farrington, 2014; Piquero et al., 2014).

Defining reoffending

In addition to considerable variation in the identification of a reoffence, RJ evaluators have also applied differing offence inclusion and exclusion criteria to indicator events. These methodological decisions may significantly influence how reoffending is both defined and measured. For example, only some researchers have excluded pseudo-offences, or officially recorded offences which occur during the follow-up period but result from offences committed prior to the RJ intervention. The same is true for breaches of justice offences such as violation of bail conditions, court orders, good behaviour bonds, or parole, and for trivial offences such as unpaid fines, driving offences, and public transport offences. Additionally, only a minority of RJ evaluators have excluded juvenile status offences from their definition of reoffending. Because these acts are only illegal due to the minority status of the young offender, their inclusion within recidivism analyses is unlikely to produce meaningful estimates of RJ's ability to reduce reoffending.

Operationalizing reoffending

Once offending data is obtained and the indicator event is defined, researchers must then decide how to operationalize recidivism. Within RJ research, the most common recidivism measure is prevalence of reoffending. This dichotomous measure (reoffence/non-reoffence), however, "fails to take into account either the relative seriousness or frequency of subsequent offending" (Maxwell and Morris, 2001: 245), thus leaving researchers with little insight into RJ's impact on desistance from crime. Existing literature suggests that desistance is a process, not a binary change from offender to ex-offender (Maruna, 2001). Therefore, the lack of measures sensitive to this in most RJ evaluations leaves important questions unanswered as to whether RJ can foster "turning points" in offenders' lives.

While several studies have relied only on prevalence of reoffending, many have employed additional measures. These include:

1   Frequency, or the average number or rate of reoffences per reoffender within a sample (e.g. Allard et al., 2009; Bergseth and Bouffard, 2007; Daly et al., 2013; Little, 2015; Luke and Lind, 2002; McGarrell and Hipple, 2007; Piggott, 2015; Shapland et al., 2008; Sherman et al., 2000; Smith and Weatherburn, 2012);
2   Seriousness, or the percentage of reoffenders in a sample who committed a more serious offense than their index offence (e.g. Bergseth and Bouffard, 2007; Little, 2015; Piggott, 2015; Smith and Weatherburn, 2012); and,
3   Time to reoffending, or the average number of days taken to reoffend per reoffender within a sample (e.g. Allard et al., 2009; Baffour, 2006; Bergseth and Bouffard, 2007; 2013; Daly et al., 2013; Hayes, 2005; Jeong et al., 2012; Luke and Lind, 2002; McGarrell and Hipple, 2007; Piggott, 2015; Smith and Weatherburn, 2012).

But only a handful of studies have utilized all three (e.g. Bergseth and Bouffard, 2007; Little, 2015; Piggott, 2015; Smith and Weatherburn, 2012). When considered together rather than in isolation, such measures of recidivism arguably provide the best means of assessing the influence of RJ on desistence in comparison research.

After recidivism measures are selected, researchers must then make a series of methodological decisions regarding the reoffending follow-up period. Within RJ research, there is a broad variation in the length of time in which offenders are observed, ranging from approximately 12 months to 12 years. This variation has produced different recidivism estimates across RJ evaluations – the longer an offender is observed, the more likely that a reoffence will be detected (Richards, 2011: 6). Short follow up periods such as 12 months may thus underestimate reoffending. When utilizing court data, long-term follow-up periods are also required to capture serious recidivism due to lengthy processing delays. However, as the influence of justice interventions on later offending is mediated by factors such as family dysfunction, deviant peers, and substance abuse, the impact of RJ on reoffending is expected to gradually decrease or cease over time (Richards, 2011: 7). Therefore, as evidenced in research by Jeong et al. (2012) and Sherman et al. (2015a), RJ is unlikely to have a lasting effect on repeat offending following a decade. So, RJ evaluations that employ observation periods longer than two years but less than ten may offer the best estimates of recidivism.

To assess RJ's long-term impact on reoffending, it is also recommended that investigators analyse recidivism at multiple points in time. However, most studies have only measured reoffending at one point in time. This is made more problematic by that fact that while studies may appear to estimate recidivism for a single standardized period, the exact observation period may vary considerably between each offender within the sample (Payne, 2007: 46). As offenders are referred to RJ programmes and enter studies at different points within a research time frame, several studies have followed the reoffending of offenders over differing or unequal periods of time (ranging from a few months to some years). Such data is problematic, as offenders are provided unequal opportunities or "time at risk" to reoffend (Sherman, Strang, and Woods, 2000: 5). To address this, researchers can standardize time at risk for each offender within their sample or, alternatively, assess reoffending using suitable statistical techniques that can appropriately handle censored data, such as survival analysis (Hayes, 2005: 84). But not all researchers have done so. As a result, it is possible that these studies have reported inaccurate estimates of RJ's ability to reduce recidivism.

Analysing reoffending

Once researchers have formed decisions regarding indicator events, recidivism measures, and follow-up periods, they then need to conduct appropriate statistical analyses and draw valid conclusions from the results. In RJ research, these conclusions may be influenced by the interpretation of statistical significance. While most RJ evaluators have used the conventional significance level of .05, a few studies have employed a .10 or even a .15 alpha. These scholars have argued that, while the conventional alpha level of .05 is preferable for theory testing, employing this "conservative" threshold within a policy context may result in a type II error. Sherman et al. (2000: 8) argue that rather than imposing an arbitrary cut-off of statistical significance when reporting research findings, p-values should instead be interpreted by the reader. This argument is echoed in a position paper from the American Statistical Association (Wasserstein and Lazar, 2016), which recommends that regardless of the significance level achieved, all p-values should be reported to allow for proper inference. However, reporting exact p-values as opposed to conventional ranges (e.g. $p<.05$ or $p>.05$) is not standard practice in RJ research. For these reasons, some RJ evaluators who have used more conservative alphas and reported p-value ranges may have potentially rejected promising interventions. Conversely, reporting a significant decrease in reoffending based on a p-values such as .165 (i.e. 83.5% probability that group differences are not due to chance) (Sherman, Strang and Woods, 2000: 21) may be equally misleading.

Finally, the types of statistical tests used to evaluate reoffending may lead to different conclusions. It is beyond the scope of this chapter to discuss the variety of statistical tests utilized in RJ research. Rather, we wish to point out that there remains debate among RJ researchers as to the appropriateness of some tests in estimating recidivism. For example, as argued by Smith and Weatherburn (2012: 3), the use of t-tests, such as those employed by Sherman at al. (2000) and Shapland et al. (2008), may be problematic, as they assume a normal distribution. As offending rates typically are highly positively skewed (as most offenders have no recontact and few offenders have multiple recontacts), t-tests may result in spurious findings (Smith and Weatherburn, 2012: 3).

Summary

Like most evaluations in criminology, studies assessing the crime reduction potential of RJ are fraught with methodological limitations regarding the accurate identification, definition, operationalization, and analysis of recidivism. To date, there is wide variation in reoffence definitions, recidivism measures, observation periods, and alpha levels. These differences have likely substantially contributed to the variable outcomes reported across RJ studies. Therefore, before the effectiveness of an RJ programme can be determined, readers must critically review evaluations for methodological flaws that are expected to significantly over- or underestimate the true extent of recidivism.

Conclusion

Research assessing the crime reduction potential of RJ is plagued by substantial variation in programme models, methodological approaches, and quality of evidence. Many RJ interventions evaluated by RJ researchers differ in ways that are theoretically and empirically related to reoffending. It is thus unsurprising that research outcomes reported in RJ evaluations are equally varied (Hayes, 2005: 96). Consequently, readers and researchers must "take stock" of intervention differences prior to compiling results of evaluations, as RJ programmes are not always appropriately comparable. However, this is often difficult due to the inadequate reporting of programme policy and practice in many studies on RJ and reoffending. Therefore, greater transparency in RJ evaluation research regarding what interventions entail is needed. McCold (2008: 23) argues that for findings to be comparable across programmes – and for the knowledge and practice of RJ to evolve – programme elements that are likely to affect the effectiveness of a RJ intervention must be reported. Existing theory and evidence suggests these elements include the level of victim involvement, participation of support persons, perceptions of procedural justice, and programme eligibility requirements.

The methodological rigour of RJ evaluation research has been criticized for well over two decades. This chapter has argued that despite this, a number of methodological issues have persisted among studies examining the impact of RJ on reoffending. As established, these shortcomings pertain to challenges around forming of an equivalent comparison and measuring reoffending. Due to the significant heterogeneity in programme models and research design found in the RJ literature, the positive conclusions reported within some reviews of RJ's ability to reduce recidivism are thus questionable. Likewise, many reviews of RJ evaluation research are largely unhelpful in determining the influence of RJ on reoffending, as they do not review studies of a homogenous RJ model or systematically exclude poor-quality research. In response to these apparent flaws, some scholars have exclusively reviewed RCTs of RJ interventions that adhere to a specified programme definition (e.g. Livingstone et al., 2013; Sherman et al., 2015a, 2015b). Although these systematic reviews may provide more meaningful conclusions regarding the potential of RJ to reduce reoffending, such strict inclusion criteria excludes the majority of RJ evaluation research and, therefore, a potential treatment effect. As such, there is clear need for further systematic reviews of evaluations examining a homogenous RJ programme ranked by methodological strength. Reviews such as these would provide a strong basis for rating the overall quality of evidence and strength of recommendations presented by RJ evaluators.

This chapter also concludes that due to the continuing methodological limitations found within the RJ literature, there is an urgent need for additional and improved RJ research. While experimental or prospective longitudinal studies may provide the best means of assessing the effect of RJ on reoffending, given their significant financial costs, lengthy time frames, and ethical encumbrances, such studies cannot be relied upon as the primary basis of knowledge on RJ's ability to reduce crime. Therefore, evaluators must learn how to better accurately estimate the effect of RJ on recidivism within these methodological and real-world constraints. Future research must not only address well-known threats to validity, such as selection bias but must also attempt to better account for the impact of research design characteristics, which are still not entirely understood (Bergseth and Bouffard, 2007: 437). Moreover, future research should aim to go beyond "what" works and assess how, for whom, and in what context RJ programmes work to reduce reoffending. Such evidence is required to inform and improve the future of RJ practice.

Given the substantial variation in RJ practice, methodological approaches, and quality of evidence found in existing research, the question of "does restorative justice reduce recidivism?" is currently, at best, an unanswerable one and, at worst, a potentially misleading one. We can state with some degree of certainty that, overall, evaluation research suggests RJ interventions generally perform at a minimum just as well as traditional court processing in lowering reoffending. Beyond this, claims that "restorative justice" reduces reoffending cannot withstand the problems of variation in practices and methodological limitations inherent in much of the existing research. Smaller claims to this effect related to specific programmes within rigorous evaluative research exist (e.g. Baffour, 2006: Bergseth and Bouffard, 2007; 2013; McGarrell and Hipple, 2017), but so do findings of no effect on recidivism (e.g. Jeong et al., 2012; Piggott, 2015; Smith and Weatherburn, 2012). If a more definitive consensus on the potential of RJ to reduce reoffending is to be found, it will require increased definitional clarity (Daly, 2016), greater transparency regarding programme characteristics (McCold, 2008), and better attention to overcoming existing methodological limitations.

References

Allard, T., Stewart, A., Chrzanowski, A., Ogilvie, J., Birks, D. and Little, S. 2009. *The Use and Impact of Police Diversion for Reducing Indigenous Over-representation*. Canberra, ACT: Criminology Research Council. Available at www.criminologyresearchcouncil.gov.au/reports/15-0708.pdf.

Austin, P.C. 2011. An Introduction to Propensity Score Methods for Reducing the Effects of Confounding in Observational Studies, *Multivariate Behavioral Research*, 46(3): 399–424. Available at http://dx.doi.org/10.1080/00273171.2011.568786.

Baffour, T.D. 2006. Ethnic and Gender Differences in Offending Patterns: Examining Family Group Conferencing Interventions Among At-risk Adolescents, *Child and Adolescent Social Work Journal*, 23(5–6): 557–578. Available at https://doi.org/10.1007/s10560-006-0075-4.

Bergseth, K.J. and Bouffard, J.A. 2007. The Long-term Impact of Restorative Justice Programming for Juvenile Offenders, *Journal of Criminal Justice*, 35(4): 433–451. Available at http://dx.doi.org/10.1016/j.jcrimjus.2007.05.006.

Bergseth, K.J. and Bouffard, J.A. 2013. Examining the Effectiveness of a Restorative Justice Programme for Various Types of Juvenile Offenders, *International Journal of Offender Therapy and Comparative Criminology*, 57(9): 1054–1075. Available at http://dx.doi.org/10.1177/0306624X12453551.

Bonta, J.L., Boyle, J., Motiuk, L.L. and Sonnichsen, P. 1983. Restitution in Correctional Half-way Houses: Victim Satisfaction, Attitudes, and Recidivism. *Canadian Journal of Corrections*, 25(3): 277–294. Available through: Griffith University Library www.griffith.edu.au/library.

Bonta, J., Jesseman, R., Rugge, T. and Cormier, R. 2006. Restorative Justice and Recidivism: Promises Made, Promises Kept? In D. Sullivan and L. Tifft (eds.) *Handbook of Restorative Justice: A Global Perspective*. London: Routledge. pp. 108–120.

Bouffard, J.A., Cooper, M. and Bergseth, K.J. 2017. The Effectiveness of Various Restorative Justice Interventions on Recidivism Outcomes among Juvenile Offenders, *Youth Violence and Juvenile Justice*, 15(4): 465–480. Available at http://dx.doi.org/10.1177/154120 4016647428.

Bradshaw, W. and Roseborough, D. 2005. Restorative Justice Dialogue: The Impact of Mediation and Conferencing on Juvenile Recidivism, *Federal Probation*, 69(2): 15–21. Available through: Griffith University Library www.griffith.edu.au/library.

Braithwaite, J. 1989. *Crime, Shame and Reintegration*. Cambridge: Cambridge University Press.

Braithwaite, J. 2002. *Restorative Justice and Responsive Regulation*. Oxford: Oxford University Press.

Collins, R. 2004. *Interaction Ritual Chains*. Princeton: Princeton University Press.

Cunneen, C. and Luke, G. 2007. Recidivism and the Effectiveness of Criminal Justice Interventions: Juvenile Offenders and Post Release. *Current Issues in Criminal Justice*, 19(2): 197–210. Available through: Griffith University Library, www.griffith.edu.au/library.

Daly, K. 2003. Making Variation a Virtue: Evaluating the Potential and Limits of Restorative Justice. In E. Weitekamp and H. Kerner (eds.) *Restorative Justice in Context: International Practice and Directions.* Devon: Willan, pp. 95–122.

Daly, K. 2016. What Is Restorative Justice? Fresh Answers to a Vexed Question, *Victims and Offenders*, 11(1): 9–29. Available at http://dx.doi.org/10.1080/15564886.2015.1107797.

Daly, K., Bouhours, B., Broadhurst, R. and Loh, N. 2013. Youth Sex Offending, Recidivism and Restorative Justice: Comparing Court and Conference Cases, *Australian and New Zealand Journal of Criminology*, 46(2): 241–267. Available at http://dx.doi.org/10.1177/0004865812470383.

de Beus, K. and Rodriguez, N. 2007. Restorative Justice Practice: An Examination of Program Completion and Recidivism, *Journal of Criminal Justice*, 35(3): 337–347. Available at http://dx.doi.org/10.1016/j.jcrimjus.2007.03.009.

Farrington, D. and Welsh, B. 2006. A Half Century of Randomized Experiments on Crime and Justice, *Crime and Justice*, 34(1): 55–132. Available at http://dx.doi.org/10.1086/500057.

Gavrielides, T. 2008. Restorative Justice – The Perplexing Concept: Conceptual Fault Lines and Power Battles Within the Restorative Justice Movement, *Criminology and Criminal Justice*, 8(2): 165–183. Available at https://doi.org/10.1177/1748895808088993.

Gupta, S.K. 2011. Intention-to-treat Concept: A Review, *Perspectives in Clinical Research*, 2(3): 109–112. Available at http://doi.org/10.4103/2229-3485.83221.

Harris, N. 2006. Reintegrative Shaming, Shame, and Criminal Justice, *Journal of Social Issues*, 62(2): 327–346. Available at http://dx.doi.org/10.1111/j.1540-4560.2006.00453.x.

Hayes, H. 2005. Assessing Reoffending in Restorative Justice Conferences, *The Australian and New Zealand Journal of Criminology*, 38(1): 77–101. Available at http://dx.doi.org/10.1375/acri.38.1.77.

Hayes, H. 2007. Reoffending and Restorative Justice. In G. Johnstone and D.W. Van Ness (eds.) *Handbook of Restorative Justice*. Devon: Willan, pp. 426–444.

Hayes, H. and Daly, K. 2003. Youth Justice Conferencing and Reoffending, *Justice Quarterly*, 20(4): 725–764. Available at http://dx.doi.org/10.1080/07418820300095681.

Hayes, H. and Daly, K. 2004. Conferencing and Re-offending in Queensland, *The Australian and New Zealand Journal of Criminology*, 37(2): 167–191. Available at http://dx.doi.org/10.1375/0004865041188906.

Hayes, H., McGee, T. and Cerruto, M. 2011. Explaining Continuity and Change in Offending Behaviour After a Restorative Justice Conference, *Current Issues in Criminal Justice*, 23(2): 127–143. Available through: Griffith University Library, www.griffith.edu.au/library.

Hirschi, T. 1969. *Causes of Delinquency*. Berkeley, CA: University of California Press.

Hoyle, C., Young, R. and Hill, R. 2002. *Proceed With Caution: An Evaluation of the Thames Valley Police Initiative in Restorative Cautioning*. York, UK: Joseph Rowntree Foundation. Available at www.jrf.org.uk/file/36675/download?token=2wPeK1LY&filetype=full-report.

Jeong, S., McGarrell, E.F. and Hipple, N. 2012. Long-term Impact of Family Group Conferences on Re-offending: The Indianapolis Restorative Justice Experiment, *Journal of Experimental Criminology*, 8(4): 369–385. Available at http://dx.doi.org/10.1007/s11292-012-9158-8.

Jolliffe, D. and Farrington, D.P. 2014. Self-reported Offending: Reliability and Calidity. In G.J.N. Bruinsma and D. Weisburd (eds.) *Encyclopedia of Criminology and Criminal Justice*. New York: Springer-Verlag, pp. 4716–4723.

Kim, H.J. and Gerber, J. 2010. Evaluating the Process of a Restorative Justice Conference: An Examination of Factors that Lead to Reintegrative Shaming, *Asia Pacific Journal of Police and Criminal Justice*, 8(2): 1–19. Available through: Griffith University Library www.griffith.edu.au/library.

Latimer, J., Dowden, C. and Muise, D. 2005. The Effectiveness of Restorative Justice Practices: A Meta-analysis, *The Prison Journal*, 85(2): 127–144. Available at http://dx.doi.org/10.1177/0032885505276969.

Little, S.B. 2015. *Impact of Police Diversion on Re-offending by Young People*. PhD Griffith University. Available through: Griffith University Library, www.griffith.edu.au/library.

Livingstone, N., Macdonald, G. and Carr, N. 2013. Restorative Justice Conferencing for Reducing Recidivism in Young Offenders (aged 7 to 21), *The Cochrane Database of Systematic Reviews*, 2, (CD008898). Available at http://dx.doi.org/10.1002/14651858.CD008898.pub2.

Luke, G. and Lind, B. 2002. *Reducing Juvenile Crime: Conferencing Versus Court (Crime and Justice Bulletin No. 69)*. Sydney, NSW: Bureau of Crime Statistics and Research New South Wales. Available at www.bocsar.nsw.gov.au/Documents/CJB/cjb69.pdf.

Maruna, S. 2001. *Making Good: How Ex-convicts Reform and Rebuild their Lives*. Washington, DC: American Psychological Association.

Maxwell, G., Kingi, V., Robertson, J. and Morris, A. 2004. *Achieving Effective Outcomes in Youth Justice Research: Final Report*. Wellington, New Zealand: Ministry of Social Development. Available at www.msd.govt.nz/documents/about-msd-and-our-work/publications-resources/research/youth-justice/achieving-effective-outcomes-youth-justice-full-report.pdf.

Maxwell, G. and Morris, A. 2001. Family Group Conferences and Reoffending. In: A. Morris and G. Maxwell (eds.) *Restorative Justice for Juveniles: Conferencing, Mediation and Circles*. Oxford: Hart, pp. 243–263.

McCold, P. 2008. Protocols for Evaluating Restorative Justice Programmes, *British Journal of Community Justice*, 6(2): 9–28. Available through: Griffith University Library www.griffith.edu.au/library.

McCold, P. and Wachtel, B. 1998. *Restorative Policing Experiment: The Bethlehem, Pennsylvania Police Family Conferencing Project*. Pipersville, PA: Community Service Foundation. Available at www.iirp.edu/pdf/BPD.pdf.

McGarrell, E.F. and Hipple, N.K. 2007. Family Group Conferencing and Re-offending Among First-time Juvenile Offenders: The Indianapolis Experiment, *Justice Quarterly*, 24(2): 221–246. Available at http://dx.doi.org/10.1080/07418820701294789.

McGarrell, E.F., Olivares, K., Crawford, K. and Kroovand, N. 2000. *Restoring Justice to the Community: The Indianapolis Juvenile Restorative Justice Experiment*. Indianapolis, IN: Hudson Institute, Crime Control Policy Center. Available at www.ibarji.org/docs/mcgarrell.pdf.

McGrath, A. 2008. The Effect of Diversion From Court: A Review of the Evidence, *Psychiatry, Psychology and Law*, 15(2): 317–339. Available at http://dx.doi.org/10.1080/13218710802001447.

Nagin, D.S., Cullen, F.T. and Jonson, C.L. 2009. Imprisonment and Reoffending, *Crime and Justice*, 38(1): 115–200. Available at http://dx.doi.org/10.1086/599202.

Nugent, W.R., Williams, M. and Umbreit, M.S. 2003. Participation in Victim Offender Mediation and the Prevalence and Severity of Subsequent Delinquent Behavior: A Meta-Analysis, *Utah Law Review*, 1: 137–166. Available throuh: Griffith University Library, www.griffith.edu.au/library.

Payne, J. 2007. *Recidivism in Australia? Findings and Future Research* (Research and Public Policy Series No. 80). Canberra, ACT: Australian Institute of Criminology. Available at www.aic.gov.au/media_library/publications/rpp/80/rpp080.pdf.

Piggott, E. 2015. *Conferencing and Cautioning: A Comparison of Police Diversion in Reducing Re-contact by First-time Indigenous Juvenile Offenders in South Australia*. Adelaide, SA: Office of Crime Statistics and Research. Available at www.ocsar.sa.gov.au/docs/research_reports/OCSAR_Research_Report_Caution_vs_Conference_Referral.pdf.

Piquero, A.R., Schubert, C. and Brame, R. 2014. Comparing Official and Self-report Records of Offending across Gender and Race/Ethnicity in a Longitudinal Study of Serious Youthful Offenders, *Journal of Research in Crime and Delinquency*, 51(4): 526–556. Available at http://dx.doi.org/10.1177/0022427813520445.

Richards, K. 2011. *Measuring Juvenile Recidivism in Australia* (Technical and Background Paper No. 44). Canberra, ACT: Australian Institute of Criminology. Available at www.aic.gov.au/media_library/publications/tbp/tbp044/tbp044.pdf.

Robinson, G. and Shapland, J. 2008. Reducing Recidivism: A Task for Restorative Justice?, *British Journal of Criminology*, 48(3): 337–358. Available at https://doi.org/10.1093/bjc/azn002.

Rossner, M. 2011. Reintegrative Ritual: Restorative Justice and Micro-sociology. In: S. Karstedt, I. Loader, and H. Strang (eds.) *Emotions, Crime and Justice*. Oxford: Hart, pp. 169–192.

Rossner, M. 2013. *Just Emotions: Rituals of Restorative Justice*. Oxford: Oxford University Press.

Roy, S. 1993. Two Types of Juvenile Restitution Program in Two Midwestern Counties: A Comparative Study, *Federal Probation*, 57(4): 48–53. Available through: Griffith University Library www.griffith.edu. au/library.

Shapland, J., Atkinson, A., Atkinson, H., Chapman, B., Dignan, J., Howes, M., Johnstone, J., Robinson, G. and Sorsby, A. 2007. *Restorative Justice: The Views of Victims and Offenders: The Third Report From the Evaluation of Three Schemes* (Ministry of Justice Research Series 03/07). London: Ministry of Justice. Available at www.restorativejusticescotland.org.uk/Restorative-Justice.pdf.

Shapland, J., Atkinson, A., Atkinson, H., Dignan, J., Edwards, L., Hibbert, J., Howes, M., Johnstone, J., Robinson, G. and Sorsby, A. 2008. *Does Restorative Justice Affect Reconviction? The Fourth Report from the Evaluation of Three Scheme* (Ministry of Justice Research Series 10/08). London: Ministry of Justice. Available at www.restorativejustice.org.uk/sites/default/files/resources/files/Does%20restorative%20 justice%20affect%20reconviction.pdf.

Shapland, J., Robinson, G. and Sorsby, A. 2011. *Restorative Justice in Practice: Evaluating What Works for Victims and Offenders*. London: Routledge.

Sherman, L.W. and Strang, H. 2007. *Restorative Justice: The Evidence*. London: The Smith Institute. Available at www.iirp.edu/pdf/RJ_full_report.pdf.

Sherman, L.W., Strang, H., Barnes, G.C., Braithwaite, J., Inkpen, N. and Teh, M. 1998. *Experiments in Restorative Policing: A Progress Report on the Canberra Reintegrative Shaming Experiments (RISE)*. Canberra, ACT: Australian Institute of Criminology. Available at www.aic.gov.au/media_library/aic/rjustice/ rise/progress/1998.pdf.

Sherman, L.W., Strang, H., Barnes, G., Woods, D.J., Bennett, S., Inkpen, N.,. Newbury-Birch, D., Rossner, M., Angel, C., Mearns, M. and Slothower, M. 2015a. Twelve Experiments in Restorative Justice: The Jerry Lee Program of Randomized Trials of Restorative Justice Conferences, *Journal of Experimental Criminology*, 11(4): 501–540. Available at http://dx.doi.org/10.1007/s11292-015-9247-6.

Sherman, L.W., Strang, H., Mayo-Wilson, E., Woods, D.J. and Ariel, B. 2015b. Are Restorative Justice Conferences Effective in Reducing Repeat Offending? Findings From a Campbell Systematic Review, *Journal of Quantitative Criminology*, 31(1): 1–24. Available at http://dx.doi.org/10.1007/ s10940-014-9222-9.

Sherman, L.W., Strang, H. and Woods, D.J. 2000. *Recidivism Patterns in the Canberra Reintegrative Shaming Experiments (RISE) (Final report)*. Canberra, ACT: Australian Institute of Criminology. Available at www.aic.gov.au/media_library/aic/rjustice/rise/recidivism/report.pdf.

Smith, N. and Weatherburn, D. 2012. *Youth Justice Conferences versus Children's Court: A Comparison of Re-offending (Crime and Justice Bulletin No. 160)*. Sydney: Bureau of Crime Statistics and Research New South Wales. Available at www.bocsar.nsw.gov.au/Documents/ CJB/cjb160.pdf.

Stewart, A., Hayes, H., Livingston, M. and Palk, G. 2008. Youth Justice Conferencing and Indigenous Over-representation in the Queensland Juvenile Justice System: A Micro-Simulation Case Study, *Journal of Experimental Criminology*, 4(4): 357–380. Available at http://dx.doi.org/10.1007/ s11292-008-9061-5.

Strang, H. and Sherman, L. 2015. The Morality of Evidence: The Second Annual Lecture for Restorative Justice: An International Journal, *Restorative Justice*, 3(1): 6–27. Available at http://dx.doi.org/10.1080/ 20504721.2015.1049869.

Strang, H., Sherman, L.W., Mayo-Wilson, E., Woods, D. and Ariel, B. 2013. Restorative Justice Conferencing (RJC) Using Face-to-Face Meetings of Offenders and Victims: Effects on Offender Recidivism and Victim Satisfaction: A Systematic Review, *Campbell Systematics Reviews*, 9(12): 1–59. Available at http://dx.doi.org/10.4073/csr.2013.12.

Strang, H., Sherman, L.W., Woods, D. and Barnes, G. 2011. *Experiments in Restorative Policing: Final Report on the Canberra Reintegrative Shaming Experiments (RISE) (Final Report)*. Canberra, ACT: Australian Institute of Criminology. Available at www.aic.gov.au/criminal_justice_system/rjustice/rise/final. html.

Sykes, G.M. and Matza, D. 1957. Techniques of Neutralization: A Theory of Delinquency. *American Sociological Review*, 22(6): 664–670. Available through: Griffith University Library, www.griffith.edu. au/library.

Tyler, T.R. 1990. *Why People Obey the Law*. New Haven: Yale University Press.

Tyler, T.R., Sherman, L., Strang, H., Barnes, G.C. and Woods, D. 2007. Reintegrative Shaming, Procedural Justice, and Recidivism: The Engagement of Offenders' Psychological Mechanisms in the Canberra RISE Drinking-and-driving Experiment, *Law and Society Review*, 41(3): 553–585. Available at http://dx.doi.org/10.1111/j.1540-5893.2007.00314.x.

URSA Institute. 1993. *Final Evaluation Report: Community Involvement in Mediation of First and second Time Juvenile Offenders Project of the community Board Program of San Francisco*. Washington, DC: U.S. Department of Justice. Available through: Griffith University Library. Available at www.griffith.edu.au/library.

Wasserstein, R.L. and Lazar, N.A. 2016. The ASA's Statement on p-values: Context, Process, and Purpose, *The American Statistician*, 70(2): 129–131. Available at http://dx.doi.org/10.1080/00031305.2016.1154108.

Weatherburn, D. and Macadam, M. 2013. A Review of Restorative Justice Responses to Offending, *Evidence Base*, 1: 1–20. http://dx.doi.org/10.21307/eb-2013-004.

Wilson, D.B., Olaghere, A. and Kimbrell, C.S. 2017. *Effectiveness of Restorative Justice Principles in Juvenile Justice: A Meta-analysis*. Fairfax, VA: George Mason University. Available at www.ncjrs.gov/pdffiles1/ojjdp/grants/250872.pdf.

25

Restorative justice compared to what?

Annalise Acorn

Introduction

I go back and forth on restorative justice. Years ago, I wrote a book that opened with the story of my conversion from true believer to sceptic: an account of how my enthusiasm for restorative justice had given way to deep distrust of its seductive promise (Acorn, 2004). In the 13 or so years since that book was published, I've done a bit of backsliding. I've turned again from committed critic to cautious, partial, selective supporter. That is to say, at least, that I've come to believe that in evaluating restorative justice, context is everything. Moreover, I am now firmly of the view that it is impossible to say whether restorative justice is good or bad in any given context without looking carefully at the realistically available alternatives. One must always ask the question: restorative justice compared to what? In this sense, it is not possible to evaluate any restorative process in isolation or even intrinsically. One must also always ask, what were the actually available alternatives? Even if a restorative response looked at in isolation was not very good, it may still have been better than everything else on offer as a response to the wrongdoing in question. And different contexts offer different, sometimes better, sometimes far worse, alternatives.

As scholars, we sometimes despair over whether our work has any impact. But worse still than the possibility of no impact at all is the possibility that one's work will be used to scuttle projects and possibilities that one actually considers deeply and urgently valuable. In an article published in 2008, David Milward reminded me of that possibility. In it he identified many of my own and others' criticisms of restorative justice and highlighted the probability that these critiques might be used to justify the rejection by Canadian courts and other government institutions of restorative justice for Indigenous offenders (2008). He wrote, "The criticisms that have been made against restorative justice can provide additional justification to not further accommodate, or even roll back, Aboriginal justice projects" (2008: 151). With admirable commitment to truth and justice, however, Milward ultimately saw the criticisms as helpful to Indigenous communities in the sense that they provided the impetus for refining arguments in favour of restorative justice and also in promoting restorative programmes that responded to fair

Contextualizing the Supreme Court of Canada's Restorative Aspirations in *R. v. Gladue* criticisms, particularly those that were concerned with victim safety and the power imbalance between victim and offender. (Milward, 2008) Though it has been a long time coming, this chapter is an attempt, first, to acknowledge the force of Milward's arguments, and then also, I hope, to repudiate any attempt to use my own work as ammunition against restorative justice in the context of Indigenous offenders in Canada.

The point of this chapter, then, is to argue that one context in which restorative justice is decidedly better than the alternatives is that of Indigenous criminal offenders in Canada. In keeping with the aims of this Handbook, to give scholars access to discussions around contested areas in restorative justice internationally, and to support innovative restorative justice initiatives, I intend to try to show here that even principled objections to restorative justice, persuasive in other contexts, are largely unpersuasive in the Indigenous context. The Supreme Court of Canada in its 1999 decision in R. v. Gladue had a grasp on this truth. In that case, the court articulated aspirations to incorporate Indigenous understandings and practices of restorative justice into the Canadian courts' response to crimes committed by Indigenous offenders. The uptake of Gladue in the Canadian courts has been disappointing (Milward and Parkes, 2011; Roach, 2009; Rudin, 2007–8; Rudin, 2009; Roach, 2010; Friedland, 2016; Maurutto and Hannah-Moffat, 2016). As Megan Berlin notes, in the Indigenous context "Restorative justice sits in a limbo between overwhelming theoretical support and disappointingly inconsistent practical implementation" (2016: 3). One of the core problems with implementation of Gladue has been the failure of the Canadian state to fund and support restorative responses to Indigenous crime and the failure of the Canadian courts to become full and honourable participants in those responses (McMillan, 2016).

Given the international scope of this Handbook, it is my hope that the analysis here will be of interest to those elsewhere also seeking to forge responses to Indigenous crime. The Supreme Court of Canada's initiative in Gladue, and indeed the Canadian Legislature's initiative in enacting s. 718.2(e) of the Criminal Code are, to the best of my knowledge, unique. And while those initiatives have met with limited success at the practical level, the theory behind them, and the express legislative and judicial acknowledgement of the need for restorative approaches to sentencing for Indigenous offenders, may be of interest internationally.

My intention here, therefore, is to examine the Supreme Court of Canada's decision in R. v. Gladue and to test its restorative aspirations against what I find to be generally persuasive and principled objections to restorative justice generally. First I will outline the decision and highlight some of the Court's insights about the relevance of restorative practices to a just response by the Canadian state to Indigenous crime on the part of Indigenous offenders. I then intend to focus on two criticisms of restorative justice, both of which I consider valid in critiquing restorative justice generally but unpersuasive in the context of Indigenous offenders in Canada.

The first criticism is that restorative justice is insufficiently retributive, that it does not give offenders their just deserts. Second, I will examine the criticism that restorative justice is a privatization of the criminal law through which the state abdicates its responsibility for criminal justice and unfairly outsources the task of responding to crime to victims and communities.

As I analyze each of these objections to restorative justice in the context of Indigenous offenders in Canada, I will continue to pose the question, restorative justice compared to what? What are the realistically available alternatives against which we should evaluate the value of restorative justice? In posing these questions, I will try to explain why restorative justice makes sense in relation to Indigenous offenders in Canada and why a restorative approach to criminal justice in the Indigenous context should be part of a broader move towards reconciliation and repair of relations between settler society and Indigenous communities.

The Supreme Court of Canada making restorative sense in *R. v. Gladue*

Jamie Gladue killed her fiancé on her 19th birthday. She was Indigenous.

Ms. Gladue was initially charged with second degree murder but pleaded guilty to manslaughter and was given a sentence of three years imprisonment along with a ten-year weapons prohibition. The Supreme Court's decision in her case is in relation to an appeal of that sentence. In it, the Supreme Court interpreted section 718.2(e) of the *Criminal Code of Canada* which provides,

> 718.2(e) all available sanctions, other than imprisonment, that are reasonable in the circumstances and consistent with the harm done to victims or to the community should be considered for all offenders, with particular attention to the circumstances of Aboriginal offenders.

At the court of first instance, no attention at all had been given to Ms. Gladue's circumstances as an Indigenous person. She was living in an urban setting, and the lower court seemed to view that as a sufficient reason to bypass section 718.2(e)(*Gladue*, 1999). On appeal, the question was whether section 718.2(e) meant that the court had to look at all Indigenous offenders' circumstances as Indigenous people or whether courts could judge that no such inquiry was necessary. The court examined the legislative history of the provision and rejected the prosecution's interpretation that the section did not apply in the present case. Rather, upon a careful review of the history of Indigenous peoples in relation to the Canadian state, the legacy of residential schools and the circumstances of extreme poverty suffered by many Indigenous people in Canada as well as the alarming rates of over-incarceration of Indigenous people in Canada, the Court found that the provision was remedial. From there, they concluded that it was mandatory for Canadian courts in sentencing Indigenous offenders to inquire into their individual circumstances as Indigenous people and to consider the effect those circumstances have on the offender's culpability and the appropriate understanding of the principle of proportionality in the case of Indigenous offenders.

In addition to mandating an inquiry into any Indigenous offenders' circumstances, the Supreme Court went on to say that in sentencing Indigenous offenders, the court ought to be drawing on the principles and practices of restorative justice. While the aspiration to incorporate restorative justice in sentencing applied to all offenders, the need for a restorative approach was particularly urgent in relation to Indigenous offenders both because of the history of Indigenous peoples in Canada and because Indigenous legal traditions were grounded in principles of restorative justice. The Court wrote, "[M]ost traditional aboriginal conceptions of sentencing place a *primary* emphasis upon the ideals of restorative justice. This tradition is extremely important to the analysis under *s. 718.2 (e)*" (1999) (emphasis in the original).

The Court was careful not to homogenize Indigenous legal traditions, recognizing that they varied widely. However, the Canadian criminal justice system's failure with Indigenous people, as evidenced by the shocking rates of over-incarceration of Indigenous peoples in Canada, and the fact that restorative processes were more consistent with the values of traditional Indigenous cultures were seen as key. The Supreme Court of Canada wrote,

> In general terms, restorative justice may be described as an approach to remedying crime in which it is understood that all things are interrelated and that crime disrupts the harmony which existed prior to its occurrence, or at least which it is felt should exist. The

appropriateness of a particular sanction is largely determined by the needs of the victims, and the community, as well as the offender. The focus is on the human beings closely affected by the crime.

(1999)

The import, then, of the Court's decision in *Gladue* was essentially that section 718.2(e) was to be interpreted as requiring not merely that the particular circumstances of Indigenous offenders should be considered but that restorative responses to Indigenous offenders that emphasize healing as a core element of justice should be prioritized when sentencing Indigenous offenders. The Court's interpretation of 718.2(e) therefore was not to give what has come to be derisively referred to as a "race-based discount" (*R. v. Ipeelee* at paras 64, 70, 75 and 126; 2000 Turpel-Lafond), but rather to direct the court to consider first the offender's particular circumstances as Indigenous persons and secondly to craft alternatives to incarceration through principles of restorative justice, particularly those informed by Indigenous understandings of the role of healing and repair of relations as core responses to wrongdoing.

The decision in *Gladue* attempted to initiate a tectonic shift, at least in aspiration, of the Canadian judiciary in their approach to Indigenous offenders. It is a shift which is still in very slow process (Roach and Rudin, 2000; Rudin, 2007–8; Pfefferle, 2008; Stephens, 2007; Roach, 2009; Roach, 2010; Milward and Parkes, 2011; Friedland, 2016; Maurutto and Hannah-Moffat, 2016). But the direction of that very slow shift appears at least to be towards acknowledging the role colonialism, residential schools, poverty and addiction and the like suffered by Indigenous people *through the direct fault of the Canadian state* have played in Indigenous offending (Rudin, 2009). One plate of that shift has been the recognition that incarceration is very often neither just nor effective as a response to Indigenous offenders. Another even more essential plate of the shift, however, is the recognition that in crafting a just and effective response to Indigenous offenders, the Canadian criminal justice system must begin to embrace, support, and participate in restorative practices, particularly those that are culturally relevant to Indigenous communities. Both of these plates need to move. Again, neither is moving very quickly, and resistance to and failure of resources for the implementation of the profound insights in *Gladue* are endemic (Roach and Rudin, 2000; Stephens, 2007; Roach, 2009; Roach, 2010; Milward and Parkes, 2011; Maurutto and Hannah-Moffat, 2016; Hewitt, 2016).

Following this decision, however, the need for a *Gladue* analysis has become a key concept in sentencing for Indigenous offenders (Friedland, 2016; Hewitt, 2016). Courts are required to look at what have come to be referred to as "Gladue factors" (Pfefferle, 2008; Friedland, 2016). There is a restorative aspect even to this information-seeking element of the SCC's decision in *Gladue*, an aspect that goes beyond the usual look into any offender's circumstances as a way of assessing culpability and proportionality. The Gladue report aspires to deep understanding of the ways in which an offender is situated in an Indigenous community that has been impacted by colonialism, racism, poverty, addiction, and of course, the legacy of the residential schools (Hewitt, 2016). There have been varying degrees of resistance on the part of the government to fund Gladue reports. (Milward and Parkes, 2011; Berlin, 2016) And defence counsel often struggle under extreme time and resource constraints to come up with information necessary to impart to the court their client's particular circumstance. (Milward and Parkes, 2011; Berlin, 2016).

But inasmuch as implementation of the "Gladue Report" aspect of the Court's interpretation of section 718.2(e) has been partial and inadequate, the restorative justice aspect of that interpretation, the sense that 718.2(e) requires the courts, with the support of the state, to craft restorative justice responses to Indigenous crime as alternatives to incarceration, has been even more difficult to realize (Hewitt, 2016).

In an article published shortly after the Supreme Court's decision in *Gladue* entitled "Sentencing within a Restorative Justice Paradigm: Procedural Implications of *R. v. Gladue*," then Saskatchewan Provincial Court Judge Mary Ellen Turpel-Lafond set out the challenges of implementing the Supreme Court's decision, which stressed the need for the Court to take an active and creative approach to crafting restorative alternatives to incarceration (1999). Turpel-Lafond wrote, "It is imperative that counsel, both Crown and defence, take the initiative to adjust their practice to reflect the requirements of the decision. For example, simply citing the decision and suggesting to a court that it should take into account 'the *Gladue* factors' is not a standard of practice which should be countenanced" (1999: 37). Turpel-Lafond articulated the significant demands that the *Gladue* decision, if implemented properly would make on the prosecution, defence counsel, the courts as well as the surrounding communities. Turpel-Lafond articulating the extent of the challenge wrote,

> The *Gladue* decision has brought the notion of healing into the mainstream as a principle that a judge must weigh in every case involving an Aboriginal person in order to build a bridge between their unique personal and community background experiences and criminal justice.
>
> *(1999: 35)*

Turpel-Lafond went on to cite the ways in which the courts with the assistance of both the Crown and defence counsel would need to become aware and assist in accessing programmes in the community that would offer restorative alternatives to incarceration for Indigenous offenders (1999).

With this sense of the aspirational aspects of the decision in *Gladue*, let us now turn to some critiques of restorative responses to crime and ask whether they are persuasive in the context of Indigenous crime.

Just deserts and the colonial state

To be a thoroughgoing supporter of restorative justice, one has to reject the idea of retributive punishment, or what is sometimes called the "just deserts" theory of punishment. That is the idea that infliction of suffering on a wrongdoer can be a moral good. This idea extrapolates a norm of reciprocity. The wrongdoer has made others suffer and thus there is a need to reciprocate – to make that wrongdoer suffer proportionately in relation to the suffering they have caused. This retributive ideal gets scant support in academic circles these days. People tend to view retribution as having unsavoury associations with the notion of revenge (Nozick, 1981; Markel, 2001).

H.L.A. Hart's utilitarian rejection of retributive suffering has been profoundly influential. Hart took the view that the suffering inflicted by punishment was *always* a negative value that had to be made up for by other potential benefits of punishment and was *never* a good in itself (Hart, 2008).

However scant the support for retributivism is in the current literature, there is a certain lay resistance, one I generally endorse, to restorative justice on the ground that it is insufficiently punitive and is, therefore, unjust (Acorn 2015). The idea that our response to wrongdoing should not be about the infliction of suffering proportionate to that caused by the offender, but rather that it should be about healing seems too kind to offenders. This criticism is especially compelling when mixed with scepticism about the offender's *bona fides* in the restorative process. Letting the offender off the hook when he or she may be feigning remorse is unfair. Focusing on the suffering of the offender rather than that of their victim seems doubly unjust.

The restorative justice response to this criticism has been ambivalent (Kwochka, 1996). Some restorative advocates thoroughly reject any idea that an offender deserves to suffer; others commend restorative justice for its ability to deliver a meaningful kind of suffering (Gavrielides, 2013). But the desert-based critique of restorative justice rejects both the claim that suffering for the offender ought to be replaced with a superior paradigm of healing, and the claim that restorative justice *does* deliver appropriate punitive suffering. The desert-based critique compares restorative justice unfavourably to a punitive system in which the offender is subjected to objectively measurable hard treatment proportionate to the suffering the offender has caused.

A further assumption behind the desert-based critique, however, is that the state meting out that punishment is in a position of moral authority to do so. The state has a privileged position structurally and morally from which to deliver deserved suffering and hence to do justice (Nozick, 1981; Markel, 2008).

No matter how compelling, retributivism is, it is far less so in the context of Indigenous offenders *in their relation to a colonial Canadian state*. Indigenous peoples have been exploited and victimized by the Canadian state through the use of legal and political power for a very long time. (TRC Report, 2015) Witness the attempted cultural genocide that was the residential schools as well as the litany of broken treaty promises. (TRC Report, 2015) And from this history of betrayal and abuse two points emerge. First, as recognized in *Gladue*, much of Indigenous offending has state-sponsored violation and dispossession of Indigenous people as root cause (1991). Second, because the Canadian colonial state was the agent of that violation and dispossession, the state is profoundly compromised in its status as a moral authority capable of meting out even deserved punishment to Indigenous offenders.

Most obviously, Indigenous people who were physically and sexually abused in the residential schools as part of the Canadian state's programme of cultural genocide are at high risk of becoming abusers themselves (*R. v. H.G.R.* 2015, TRC Report, 2015). While such Indigenous offenders remain, in some sense, responsible for their actions, the criminal culpability of these offender is reduced, not just because they were victims of abuse but because that abuse was perpetrated *by the Canadian state* in pursuit of the state's policy and political objectives aimed at domination and destruction of First Nations. The logic of retributivism collapses under the weight of these circumstances. It is a moral impossibility to conclude that the Indigenous offender who suffered so terribly at the hands of the Canadian state in the residential schools deserves to suffer still more at the hands of that same Canadian state if they fail to stem the well-nigh inevitable progression towards becoming an abuser themselves.

Not only is the Indigenous offender's culpability in question but the state's moral authority as dispenser of deserved suffering is hopelessly compromised (Nowlin, 2004). Having inflicted the wounds that led to the Indigenous person becoming an offender, having failed to make amends to the Indigenous person to compensate and heal those wounds, the state simply lacks the moral authority either to be the arbiter of just desert or a legitimate agent of punitive suffering.

Let's re-pose our key question in the Indigenous context. Restorative justice compared to what? Here we no longer have a case of restorative justice being unfavourably compared to the meting out of deserved suffering on a fully responsible offender by a morally upright authoritative state. Rather, here restorative justice compares decidedly favourably to a situation in which a state, *directly* responsible for the background conditions that led to the crime, a state that ought to have done so but did not commit resources to help heal the wounds it inflicted, treats the offender as though none of that happened, as though it is in no way complicit in the offender's wrongdoing, and proceeds to inflict additional suffering on the Indigenous offender, compounding the brokenness of Indigenous communities. Compared to that, restorative justice is better.

In short, then, however compelling retributivism may be where the relation between state and offender is one of legitimate political authority to wrongdoer, the circumstances of colonialism displace that presumed relation and demand the logic of healing and reconciliation rather than the logic of reciprocal suffering for Indigenous offenders.

The privatization of crime and the shirking of state duties

A second criticism of restorative justice, and here again, it is one that I am generally inclined to agree with, is that restorative justice, by offloading crime onto victims, offenders, and their communities, wrongly relieves the state of its duty to deal with criminal offenders. It is the state's job to deal with crime, not the victim's. Restorative justice privatizes a public problem. Thus Gerry Johnstone notes that while some people might be grateful for the opportunity to participate in a restorative process:

> [I]it is just as likely that many victims would prefer to delegate this decision-making process wholly to officials and professionals. Rather than experiencing this as the state stealing their conflict (cf. Christie, 1977 – whose words on this have become a mantra of the restorative justice movement), it is just as plausible that many victims would experience this as the state fulfilling its proper function.
>
> *(Johnstone, 2017)*

So restorative justice (a process where victims and communities have to expend scarce time and energy responding to crime and trying to work towards right relation) is perceived as comparing unfavourably to a situation where the state uses its resources and fulfils its core role of responding to crime (Gavrielides, 2018). But while this logic is often compelling, especially in the context of urban property crime where no antecedent relationship exists between victim and offender and no such relationship is desired in the future, it is less so in the context of Indigenous offenders.

First of all, in the Indigenous context, especially when victims are also Indigenous, the community affected by the crime is often very real and sometimes badly broken (Adjin-Tettey, 2007; Berlin, 2016). The work of healing in the community is urgently needed. And again the state is in a morally compromised position. The idea that the Canadian state might simply step in and deal with the situation through punishment is completely untenable. The brokenness of so many Indigenous communities, ravaged as they have been by the legacy of colonialism, residential schools, and the resultant social problems, demands a healing response that involves victims, offenders, and the whole community. But the best reading of *Gladue* also envisions *the state itself* through funding and through the courts as working towards becoming honourable and good-faith participants in that restorative process.

What *Gladue* doesn't do is envision the state simply handing over crime to Indigenous communities to sort things out by themselves. As we have seen, what *Gladue* envisions is the court, with the help of both the prosecution and the defence, drawing on the principles of healing and restoration of relation to craft alternatives suitable to the circumstances of the Indigenous offender in collaboration with Indigenous communities.

At least part of the problem with the implementation of the Court's restorative aspirations in the aftermath of *Gladue*, however, was that the *Gladue* decision *itself* did not implement those aspirations or model a restorative approach to sentencing in Jamie Gladue's case (Roach, 2000). There were some aspects of Gladue's own conduct after the offence that could have been interpreted as having reparative significance, though such significance was not articulated or analyzed by the courts. Gladue had named her son Reuben Ambrose Beaver in honour of her deceased partner. She had taken alcohol and substance abuse counselling. It's possible that these actions might have been given meaning within a restorative framework. But in the Supreme Court's decision they were not. Thus, unfortunately, the decision in *Gladue* itself did not point the way to how courts might breathe life into the restorative rhetoric. The Supreme Court's follow-up decision in *R. v. Ipeelee*, while it affirmed the applicability of *Gladue* to serious offences, did not further elucidate the courts' role in crafting restorative solutions.

Ideally, however, in the Indigenous context, restorative processes initiated and supported through the state apparatus of the criminal justice system take place as part of the reconciliation envisioned by the Canadian Truth and Reconciliation Commission. A commitment by the Canadian government to fund, create, and support restorative alternatives to incarceration for Indigenous peoples under the *Gladue* reasoning could be a powerful demonstration of Canada's commitment to reconciliation (Hewitt, 2016). The Final Report of the Truth and Reconciliation Commission of Canada contains the following calls to action,

> 30. We call upon federal, provincial, and territorial governments to commit to eliminating the overrepresentation of Aboriginal people in custody over the next decade, and to issue detailed annual reports that monitor and evaluate progress in doing so.
>
> 31. We call upon the federal, provincial, and territorial governments to provide sufficient and stable funding to implement and evaluate community sanctions that will provide realistic alternatives to imprisonment for Aboriginal offenders and respond to the underlying causes of offending.

Gladue should be read as standing in reinforcing relationship to these calls to action. Of course, it is these governments as whole entities, and not just the courts in isolation, that need to act and coordinate action. Courts need to be able to rely on and to communicate with government bodies making funding decisions as well as those implementing and evaluating the restorative programmes. Indigenous communities, elders, offenders, and victims need to be involved in these programmes and processes. But the obligation to fund restorative community sanctions and to work with communities to build viable alternative responses rests squarely with the Canadian state as part of the obligation to reconciliation as envisioned by the Commission's report. The funding of the prison system is unquestioned as a core state function (Hewitt, 2016). The state's obligation to fund restorative alternatives to prison in the Indigenous context should come to be viewed as equally fundamental to the state's core responsibilities.

Of course, any restorative solution to crime is going to put significant burdens on the communities involved. This can be especially taxing for small Indigenous communities. (Milward, 2008; Berlin, 2016). This makes it even more evident that the state needs to be involved in funding initiatives to support restorative alternatives within communities.

Thus, courts should be wary of sentimentalizing Indigenous communities, seeing them as infallible restorative agents. Indigenous communities are as prone as anyone else to getting things wrong, missing the mark in search of ways to genuinely repair relations. Indeed, as Megan Berlin points out, Indigenous communities may lack the resources and the training to come up with and implement restorative solutions effectively. (2016: 13) The reasoning in *Gladue* suggests, however, that it is part of the courts' and the state's responsibility to remain in conversation with Indigenous communities as co-participants and to work together towards restorative solutions in a way that takes victims safety, dignity, and healing seriously while also providing reintegration and healing for the offender.

One might well argue that restorative justice, even well funded by the Canadian state and administered through the Canadian courts, is a bad alternative compared to full recognition of Indigenous sovereignty in relation to crimes committed by Indigenous peoples. The restorative justice envisioned in *Gladue*, where the Canadian state is still largely in charge, might compare unfavourably to leaving the response to Indigenous crime entirely to Indigenous communities. While the state might have some obligation to fund Indigenous restorative processes, courts ought not to be seen as having a supervisory role over solutions crafted within the Indigenous community.

I do not argue against full Indigenous sovereignty as the first-best alternative for addressing Indigenous offenders. Perhaps it is. However, assuming the conditions that we are for the most part faced with now, where Indigenous offenders come under the jurisdiction of the Canadian criminal courts and their sentencing is done under the auspices of those courts, those courts ought to embrace their role as participants and supporters of the restorative practices. Further, the state must, as an obligation of reconciliation, fund that participation generously.

Pursuing the restorative vision of *Gladue*: one failure and one success

Let me now elaborate on two instances of collaborative experiments in restorative solutions where Canadian courts and Indigenous communities have partnered, one, in my view a failure, and the other a success. By way of failure, I will look at the 2015 British Columbia Supreme Court case of *R. v. H.G.R.*. I will then look generally at the First Nations Court in British Columbia, which I consider a successful model (albeit an underfunded one). I will conclude by pointing out why I think the First Nations Courts in British Columbia should be seen as an example of best practices of restorative justice building partnerships between Canadian state institutions and Indigenous communities.

i   *R. v. H.G.R.*: or what's a Canadian court to do when Indigenous restorative justice is aggressively punitive?

H.G.R. was a 69-year-old Indigenous survivor of physical and sexual abuse at a residential school. He was a hereditary chief of a band of the Haida people in British Columbia. He was charged with and pleaded guilty to three counts of sexual interference, that is, touching a person under the age of 16 for sexual purposes (Criminal Code section 151). The psychiatric report described the nature of his offences as limited and described his level of risk as low. It noted that H.G.R. had symptoms of Post Traumatic Stress Disorder arising out of the abuse he had suffered in the residential school.

The psychiatric report to which the court had access noted further, "I have assessed many men who have gone through the Indian residential school system, and a significant proportion have themselves become sexual abusers of children. The potential links between being abused and becoming an abuser are many" (*R. v. H.G.R.*, 2015). The psychiatrist noted, "[H]is overall attitudes and orientation vis-à-vis people and society is generally pro social and lawful" and recommended that H.G.R. should receive basic education in "sexuality, child abuse and inter-personal boundaries". The psychiatric report went on to say,

> He will also benefit from ventilation and support within a therapeutic relationship, so that his grief and anger can be dealt with in a direct manner, rather than continuing to fester. Ideally, his therapist would also be of First Nations background, as the sexual and physical

abuse occurred in the context of cultural and spiritual deprivation, a very important factor if healing is to occur, but one that is very difficult for an "outsider", no matter how well-meaning, to integrate into therapy . . . Ideally, [H.G.R.] would embark on individual therapy only after an intensive program that specifically deals with the abused–abuser link that is run by and for First Nations, such as Tsow-Tun-Le-Lum on Vancouver Island. I have seen remarkable results from that program.

(R. v. H.G.R., 2015)

The issue before the BC Supreme Court was a defence application for an order requiring a *Gladue* report. The Court ultimately rejected this request, holding that the psychiatric report contained sufficient information regarding H.G.R's Indigenous background such that there was no need to order a separate *Gladue* report.

Earlier on in the sentencing process, however, the court had heard from the justice coordinator for the Prince Rupert Aboriginal Community Services Society who had suggested a restorative justice process that would take place with three band members, including one other hereditary chief. H.G.R. agreed to participate in the process. The judge, probably anticipating a too-lenient result, made clear that the court "was not bound in any fashion by such a process or any recommendations arising from it" (*R. v. H.G.R.*, 2015).

H.G.R. met with the three band members, and victim impact statements were read. H.G.R. and his supporters spoke about his past in the residential school. H.G.R. expressed remorse and deep sadness that having been victimized as a child he went on to victimize others. At the conclusion of the conference, the participants performed a ceremony whereby H.G.R. was stripped of his Indigenous name as well as his status as a hereditary chief. The panel then went on to make the following three further recommendations to the court:

1 All regalia and anything pertaining to the tribe and the [respondent's tribal name] be returned to the Gitlaan tribe.
2 That a cleansing/healing feast be held and [H.G.R.] will fully or partially fund the feast. [H]owever [H.G.R.] will not be in attendance for the feast. It will be for the tribe to try to make amends to the victims and their families.
3 After sentencing, the panel requested permission from the court to have a media release. They would like the community to be aware that this is something that happened and how it was handled within their tribe. In the hopes that it will encourage victims to come forward as well as encourage other tribes to deal with their members who are involved with the law. They have stated they will only use [H.G.R.'s] name and how they dealt with the charges against him at the circle.

(R. v. H.G.R., 2015)

H.G.R.'s lawyer, Terrence La Liberté Q.C., took the position that what had taken place did not qualify as a restorative process at all. It was a shaming. Further, La Liberté Q.C. had hoped that the restorative justice conference would yield additional information in the nature of *Gladue* factors that would assist the court in its deliberation. No such information came out in the course of that process. La Liberté Q.C. pointed to the failure of the so-called restorative process as further support for his application that the court order a Gladue report. Crown counsel Ms. Freda Zaltz argued that the "offender was fully informed of the nature of the tribal meeting, including its potential results, and consented to the process nevertheless". No details of what H.G.R. had been told about the nature or possible outcomes of the restorative process are set out in the judgement. This is unfortunate because, to evaluate the methods used to persuade both victims and offenders to participate in restorative alternatives, and to formulate ethical standards for those processes, more needs to be known about what court actors are saying in the course of obtaining consent from the parties to participate in restorative justice. Nevertheless, the prosecution took the view that H.G.R. had given informed consent and that such consent foreclosed any objection to the process or its outcome.

In the course of the decision to deny the defence application for a Gladue report, the court made no comment *at all* about the ceremonial stripping of H.G.R.'s tribal name and status. Nor did it comment on the three further recommendations for punitive sanctions against H.G.R. – seizing H.G.R.'s regalia, requiring him to pay money damages for the cost of the feast from which he would be excluded and, of course, lifting the publication ban to allow the press release, all of which would have required the court's participation. The judge avoided these issues altogether. The judge simply related the positions of both counsel and then ignored all questions as to the adequacy and legitimacy of the process. And, of course, he refused to order the Gladue report for H.G.R. Ultimately the court sentenced H.G.R. to four months imprisonment plus three years probation, a term not more lenient than one would expect in the case of a non-Indigenous offender, even one with far less sympathetic circumstances. (2009, *R. v. Oldford*, 2008 *R. v. D.A.M*).

H.G.R. got the worst of both worlds: from the Canadian courts he received incarceration and lengthy probation without the benefit of a Gladue report. From the band conference he received treatment arguably better calculated to stigmatize, exclude, and inflict retributive suffering than to reintegrate and heal.

So what ideally ought the Canadian criminal justice system to have done here? If the Haida sense of justice is retributive and endorses shaming, (Lee, 2016) what business is it of the colonial courts to question their punitive measures? Would it not be yet one more act of colonial arrogance for the court as an arm of the Canadian state to use its authority to repudiate this Indigenous response to a member of their own community who has admittedly harmed other vulnerable members? Is it beyond the legitimate scope of the court's authority to criticize or supervise such processes? Would the court have had jurisdiction to impose the additional sanctions recommended by the band panel? Would such sanctions have violated the offender's constitutional rights? Would evidence about any underlying political tensions in this Indigenous community that might elucidate the nature and outcome of the purportedly restorative process have been relevant and admissible in the judicial proceeding?

Could the court have heard evidence, for example, on who benefitted from stripping H.G.R. of his status as a hereditary chief? If it were proved that band members participating in the restorative process had a conflict of interest, what ought the upshot of that to have been in the judicial process? Should the judge have entered into a conversation with the band members about the dignity interests and procedural rights of the offender? What kind of a conversation ought to have taken place between the band panel and the BC Superior Court in the aftermath of this purportedly restorative process? How could the Court have fulfilled an ideal of being both deferential and supervisory?

In *Gladue* itself, the Supreme Court's reasoning was anchored in the sense that traditional Indigenous culture provides an authoritative source for restorative justice (1999 para 70). Yet this commitment to acknowledging Indigenous traditional culture as a source of wisdom about restorative justice cannot mean that colonial courts, while seized with the matter, have no business questioning Indigenous practice. There is no absolute epistemic authority of Indigenous restorative tradition that should insulate Indigenous actions from scrutiny even by the Canadian courts as partners in the restorative process. A conversation about the dignity interests of the offender and the meaning of healing and reintegration ought to have taken place `between the courts, the band panel, defence, and Crown counsel as well as other members of the community.

I do not say that there is good reason to trust the Canadian courts' ability to partner with Indigenous communities in crafting more genuinely restorative solutions. The inherent paternalism in the notion that the court should be in a position to disqualify Indigenous solutions as not properly restorative is abhorrent. Nevertheless, where restorative processes are initiated under the auspices of the Canadian courts, those courts ought still to have a mandate to protect the procedural rights as well as the dignity interests of the accused (Pavlich, 2017). Again, H.G.R.'s case documents a complete failure of conversation between the Indigenous community and the courts. The outcome was in no way restorative. The goal should be towards reciprocal and mutual scrutiny, where all parties, including Indigenous communities and courts, participate in dialogue and struggle in good faith towards meaningfully restorative solutions.

ii   First Nations Court of British Columbia: a best practice of "happy medium?" (McDonald, 2017)

There are a number of specialized Indigenous courts in Canada that deal exclusively with Indigenous crime using restorative practices (Bryant, 2002; Milward, 2008; Ministry of Justice British Columbia, 2016; Hewitt, 2016; Maurutto and Hannah-Moffat, 2016; McMillan, 2016; Friedland, 2016; Department of Justice Government of Canada, 2017). Many of them provide hopeful strategies for realization of the tectonic shift promised in *Gladue*. But since our example of failure comes from British Columbia, I will find a ray of hope in BC as well and focus on the British Columbia First Nations Court. This court provides a hopeful alternative to these failures of restorative solutions to the problem of Indigenous crime. The BC First Nations Courts are a branch of the Provincial Courts of British Columbia and are referred to as "Gladue Courts" (Legal Services Society, 2017). They are charged with the task of addressing over-representation of Indigenous people in the criminal justice system. (McDonald, 2017) Four First Nations Courts exist in BC, one in New Westminster, Duncan, Kamloops, and North Vancouver (Legal Services Society, 2017). Anyone who identifies as Indigenous and is either applying for bail or pleading guilty to a criminal offence can apply to have their case heard by the First Nations Court. While the court is still woefully underfunded (Friedland, 2016) (each court sits only one day per month) and woefully "overlooked" (McDonald writes, "Barristers with 20 years' call are unaware of its existence" (McDonald, 2017), the court structure and sensibility is genuinely restorative.

During a sentencing hearing, the court hears from the victim and offender as well as counsel for the prosecution and the defence. Offenders do not go into the restorative process unrepresented. Further, the offender's family, friends, and other support people are encouraged to be present, as are elders, social workers, and counsellors (Legal Services Society of British Columbia, 2014). Again, in line with best practices of restorative process, the victim and victim's support group are also encouraged to be present, as are police officers, probation officers, and anyone else impacted by the case. The process of the court strives to ensure that everyone is heard. As is explained on the First Nations Court website, "Each person will be given a chance to speak. After everyone has had a chance to speak, the judge will work with everyone to come up with a healing plan" (Legal Services Society, 2017).

In addition to involving the whole community in the creation of a healing plan, the BC First Nations Court is also active in providing follow-up contact with offenders. Offenders return to the court once a month to check in with elders and discuss the progress they have made with healing and repair. They face the community and are cross-examined by elders about their adherence to the plan (Legal Services Society, 2017). The prospect of being sent back to the conventional court exists, but a breach of the healing plan does not necessarily result in a referral back to the conventional courts (McDonald, 2017). Lapses are sometimes dealt with through continued supervision by the court. Some of the healing plans include tasks for the offender such as learning their Indigenous language or researching the offender's own family history (McDonald, 2017).

When completed successfully, the process is also meaningfully reintegrative for offenders. As McDonald notes, "At the end of the offender's healing plan, the judge places a blanket embroidered with traditional symbols around the individual's shoulders to acknowledge the offender's new life" (2017). The offender's dignity is honoured, their sense of belonging is affirmed, and a pathway to meaningful change is supported by the court and the surrounding community. While not fully independent of the Canadian court system, the First Nations Courts do not raise the same crisis of legitimacy that arises for Indigenous offenders in the conventional colonial courts. (McDonald, 2017; cf Cupido, 2017). Further, all the difficulties offenders have in getting courts to recognize *Gladue* rights in the conventional courts are eliminated in the First Nations Courts, as *Gladue* reports are ordered as a matter of course. The BC First Nations Courts, then, do provide a restorative process which, compared to everything else on offer for Indigenous people in Canada, appears to be an appealing alternative that should be supported fully and wholeheartedly by the Canadian state as a move towards reconciliation with Canada's Indigenous people.

Conclusion

This Handbook aspires to inform scholars and practitioners about current controversies and innovations in restorative justice globally. To that end, I have focused on one such controversy in Canada and its attendant attempts towards reform. I have scarcely scratched the surface of the many debates around restorative justice and Indigenous crime that have followed the Supreme Court of Canada's decision in *R. v. Gladue* in this country.

What I have tried to do, however, is to demonstrate how the historical context of Indigenous peoples in their relation to the Canadian colonial state ought to inform one's evaluation of restorative justice in the Indigenous context. The legacy of colonialism disarms the logic of many otherwise persuasive objections to a restorative approach to crime. Therefore, so long as the Canadian courts are involved in responding to crime committed by Indigenous peoples, those courts should continue to try to partner in good faith with Indigenous communities to forge meaning restorative solutions that secure the safety of victims while repairing the lives of offenders and the vitality of Indigenous communities. Indigenous communities should be given meaningful support by the Canadian state, at least commensurate with the usual costs of the criminal court process and incarceration, to carry out the restorative alternatives to incarceration of Indigenous offenders. While Indigenous communities should not be sentimentalized or idealized as holding perfect knowledge of restorative responses to crime, the actors in the court system should remain in meaningful conversation with those communities and all should stay present and committed to the struggle to forge healing solutions to Indigenous crime through truth-telling.

References

Acorn, A. 2004. *Compulsory Compassion: A Critique of Restorative Justice*. Vancouver: University of British Columbia Press.

Acorn, A. 2015. "Son Be a Dentist": Restorative Justice and the Dalhousie Dental School Scandal, *Harvard Negotiation Law Review*, 2 October 2015 Available at www.hnlr.org/wp-content/uploads/Acorn. HNLR-Article.pdf. Accessed 16 August 2017.

Adjin-Tettey, E. 2007. Sentencing Aboriginal Offenders: Balancing Offenders' Needs, the Interests of Victims and Society, and the Decolonization of Aboriginal Peoples, *Canadian Journal of Women and the Law*, 19(1): 179–226.

Berlin, M. 2016. Restorative Justice Practices for Aboriginal Offenders: Developing an Expectation Led Definition for Reform, *Appeal: Review of Current Law and Law Reform*, 21: 3–20.

Bryant, M.E. 2002. Tsuu T'ina First Nations Peacemaker Justice System, *LawNow*, 26(4): 27–30. Criminal Code of Canada. R.S.C., 1985, c. C-46.

Cupido, M. 2017. An Independent Indigenous Court-Panel Discusses Successes and Challenges of Akwesasne Court, *The McGill Daily*, 23 January. Available at www.mcgilldaily.com/2017/01/an-independent-indigenous-court/. Accessed 16 August 2017.

Department of Justice Government of Canada. 2017. *Gladue Practices in the Provinces and Territories*. Available at www.justice.gc.ca/eng/rp-pr/csj-sjc/ccs-ajc/rr12_11/p2.html. Accessed 16 August 2017.

Friedland, H. 2016. Navigating Through Narratives of Despair: Making Space for the Cree Reasonable Person in the Canadian Justice System, *University of New Brunswick Law Journal*, 67: 269–312.

Gavrielides, T. 2018. Victims and Offenders' Perceptions and Experiences of Restorative Justice: The Evidence from London, UK *Current Volume*.

Gavrielides, T. 2013. Restorative Pain: A New Vision of Punishment. In T. Gavrielides and V. Artinopoulou (ed.) *Reconstructing Restorative Justice Philosophy*, Farnham: Ashgate, pp. 311–337.

Hart, H.L.A. 2008. *Punishment and Responsibility: Essays in the Philosophy of Law*, 2nd ed. Oxford: Oxford University Press.

Hewitt, J.G. 2016. Indigenous Restorative Justice: Approaches, Meaning & Possibility, *University of New Brunswick Law Journal*, 67: 313–335.

Johnstone, G. 2017. Restorative Justice for Victims: Inherent Limits? Forthcoming in *Restorative Justice: An International Journal*.

Kwochka, D. 1996. Aboriginal Injustice: Making Room for a Restorative Justice Paradigm, *Saskatchewan Law Review*, 60: 153–188.

Lee, J. 2016. Haida Strip Two Hereditary Chiefs of Titles for Supporting Enbridge, *Vancouver Sun*, 17 August 2016. Available at http://vancouversun.com/news/local-news/haida-strip-two-hereditary-chiefs-of-titles-for-supporting-enbridge. Accessed 18 November 2017.

Legal Services Society. 2017. *What's First Nations Court?*. Available at http://aboriginal.legalaid.bc.ca/resources/pdfs/pubs/Whats-First-Nations-Court-eng.pdf. Accessed 16 August 2017.

Legal Services Society of British Columbia. 2014. *Aboriginal Legal Aid in BC*. Available at http://aboriginal.legalaid.bc.ca/rights/firstNationsCourt.php. Accessed 16 August 2017.

Legal Society of British Columbia. 2017. Cknúcwentn First Nations Court: Heartwarming and Effective. The Factum My Law BC [blog] 20 July. Available at http://factum.mylawbc.com/2017/07/20/cknucwentn-first-nations-court-heartwarming-effective/. Accessed 16 August 2017.

Markel, D. 2001. Are Shaming Punishments Beautifully Retributive? Retributivism and the Implications for the Alternative Sanctions Debate, *Vanderbilt Law Review*, 54: 2157–2243.

Maurutto, P. and Hannah-Moffat, K. 2016. Aboriginal Knowledges in Specialized Courts: Emerging Practices in Gladue Courts, *Canadian Journal of Law and Society*, 31(3): 451–472.

McDonald, A. 2017. Maintaining a Happy Medium between the Criminal Courts and First Nations, *The Advocate*, 75(2): 195–198.

McMillan, L.J. 2016. Living Legal Traditions: Mi'kmaw Justice in Nova Scotia, *University of New Brunswick Law Journal*, 67: 187–210.

Milward, D. 2008. Making the Circle Stronger: An Effort to Buttress Aboriginal Use of Restorative Justice in Canada against Recent Criticisms, *International Journal of Punishment and Sentencing*, 4(3): 124–158.

Milward, D. and Parkes, D. 2011. Gladue: Beyond Myth and Towards Implementation in Manitoba, *Manitoba Law Journal*, 35(1): 84–110.

Ministry of Justice British Columbia. 2016. *Specialized Courts Strategy*. Available at http://www2.gov.bc.ca/assets/gov/law-crime-and-justice/about-bc-justice-system/justice-reform-initiatives/specialized-courts-strategy.pdf. Accessed 16 August 2017.

Nowlin, C. 2004. Taking Aboriginal Justice Beyond Gladue: Canadian Criminal Law in Conflict with Human Rights, *Saskatchewan Law Review*, 67: 59–96.

Nozick, Robert. 1981. *Philosophical Explanations*. Cambridge, MA: Harvard University Press.

Pavlich, G. 2017. Restorative Justice and the Rights of the Accused. Forthcoming in *Restorative Justice: An International Journal*.

Pfefferle, B.R. 2008. Gladue Sentencing: Uneasy Answers to the Hard Problem of Aboriginal Over-incarceration, *Manitoba Law Journal*, 32(2): 113–143.

Provincial Court of British Columbia. 2015. *Cknucwntn First Nations Court, Kamloops*. Available at www.provincialcourt.bc.ca/enews/enews-20-10-2015. Accessed 16 August 2017.

R. v. D.A.M. [2008] NBQB 353.

R. v. Gladue. [1999] 1 S.C.R. 688

R. v. H.G.R. [2015] 3 C.N.L.R. 168

R. v. Ipeelee. [2012] 1 SCR 433

R. v. Oldford. [2009] NLTD 124.

Roach, K. 2009. One Step Forward, Two Steps Back: Gladue at Ten and in the Courts of Appeal, *Criminal Law Quarterly*, 54(4): 470–505.

Roach, K. and Rudin, J. 2000. Gladue: The Judicial and Political Reception of a Promising Decision, *Canadian Journal of Criminology*, 42(3): 355–388.

Rudin, J. 2007–2008. Incarceration of Aboriginal Youth in Ontario 2004–2006 – The Crisis Continues, *Criminal Law Quarterly*, 53(2): 260–272.

Rudin, J. 2009. Addressing Aboriginal Overrepresentation Post-Gladue: A Realistic Assessment of How Social ChOnge occurs, *Criminal Law Quarterly*, 54(4): 447–469.

Stephens, M. 2007. Lessons From the Front Lines of Canada's Restorative Justice Experiment: The Experience of Sentencing Judges, *Queen's Law Journal*, 33(1): 19–78.

Truth and Reconciliation Commission of Canada. 2015. Honouring the Truth, Reconciling for the Future: Summary of the Final Report of the Truth and Reconciliation Commission of Canada. Available at www.trc.ca/websites/trcinstitution/File/2015/Findings/Exec_Summary_2015_05_31_web_o.pdf. Accessed 16 August 2017.

Turpel-Lafond, M.E. 1999. Sentencing Within a Restorative Justice Paradigm: Procedural Implications of *R. v.* Gladue, *Criminal Law Quarterly*, 43(1): 34–50.

Part IV

The future of restorative justice

26

Restorative justice and the therapeutic tradition

Looking into the future

Gerry Johnstone

Introduction

Restorative justice advocates frequently invoke Nils Christie's (1977) idea that, in large-scale societies, conflicts – which are valuable commodities – tend to be stolen by state officials and lawyers. One of the key merits of restorative justice, on this view, is that it returns conflicts involving crime to their rightful owners: the direct victims of criminal acts, the perpetrators, and the family members and friends of both.

The extent to which restorative justice has actually succeeded in rescuing conflicts from 'that capricious old fox' that is criminal justice has been questioned by, amongst others, George Pavlich (2005: 105). Pavlich, who also writes in this Handbook, shows how restorative justice advocates simultaneously promote alternative visions of justice from those which underpin contemporary criminal justice arrangements *and* defer to and rely upon key aspects of existing criminal justice systems.

This chapter aims to contribute to the Handbook's objectives by raising a different, and much neglected, question concerning how successful the restorative justice movement has been in retrieving conflicts from those whom Christie calls 'professional thieves'. It questions the extent to which the social movement for restorative justice has succeeded in wresting conflicts from the grip of 'treatment personnel'. It will be suggested that not only has the restorative justice movement been less successful in this regard than it sometimes imagines; in important ways the movement has augmented a process whereby therapeutic language, objectives and practices have expanded into everyday life (Furedi, 2004) and fortified the 'therapeutic state' (Nolan Jr., 1998).

In outlining this argument, the chapter suggests that the social movement for restorative justice can be fruitfully understood as encompassing and blending two quite different viewpoints. Both are opposed to the viewpoint, which underpins much criminal justice practice, that offenders have violated the state's laws, that for this they must be punished, and that the state must take charge of this process (Zehr, 2015: 101). However, from this common starting point, they diverge significantly. One 'restorative' viewpoint is that, in the aftermath of crime, the parties directly involved and most directly affected should deliberate and decide what needs to be done to restore justice and a sense of security. The other 'restorative' viewpoint is that, in the aftermath of crime, our priority should be not to add to the human suffering that has occurred but to heal. For shorthand, the first of these viewpoints will be referred to as the 'participatory justice' viewpoint, the second as the 'healing justice' viewpoint. The argument of the chapter is that the presence of the healing justice viewpoint within the restorative justice movement makes the latter attractive as a vehicle through which treatment personnel and the therapeutic culture can maintain their grip on our society's understanding and handling of crime.

Christie, participatory justice, and restorative justice

Christie was an advocate of participatory justice or, to use a term he preferred, 'conflict participation' (1981: 35). Put very simply, his view was that in the process for handling a conflict the parties to the conflict should be at the centre of things (Christie, 1977: 2). They must have the opportunity to talk and to be listened to. Above all, they must be allowed to decide what is relevant, that is, what complaints, arguments, facts, and so on are pertinent to the process of handling the conflict (e.g. in the case of a crime, how blameworthy the perpetrator was) (ibid: 8). But, in modern society, the idea of leaving people to handle their own conflicts tends to be regarded as dangerous. There is a fear that the parties will resort to private vengeance and that vendettas will flourish (ibid: 1). For these reasons, modern societies tend to delegate the handling of conflicts to state officials, lawyers, and treatment professionals. These professionals then tend to monopolise the process of handling conflicts. Concomitantly, conflicts increasingly become seen as bad things, and the process for handling them increasingly becomes defined as 'conflict resolution' or 'conflict management'.

As a result of this development, the many opportunities which conflict provides, and especially opportunities for norm-clarification, become lost. It is no longer possible to stage 'a political debate in the court'; there is no longer 'a continuous discussion of what represents the law of the land' (ibid: 8). And because there is no personalised encounter between the parties to the conflict, the 'victim' and the 'offender' never come to know each other; hence they resort to classical stereotypes when seeking to make sense of the actions and situation of the other party (ibid: 8–9).

An important question is whether restorative justice represents some sort of a 'return' to the participatory justice which Christie cherished. In certain respects it clearly does. In restorative justice, the perpetrator and victim of a wrongful act have an opportunity to participate in their own case. They get to talk, and they get to be listened to. Also, they have a personalised encounter which, ideally, humanises them to each other. And, as in the participatory justice imagined by Christie, the focus is on the victim's losses, and there is a discussion of restitution. Offenders, by participating actively in discussions about how they could make good the losses of their victims, also gain the possibility of being forgiven (ibid: 9).

However, as I have noted elsewhere (Johnstone, 2002: 145), most restorative justice proponents and practitioners do not go as far as Christie in important respects. Few advocate, or would encourage to take place during a restorative justice encounter, the sort of political debate about crime that Christie advocates. These encounters take place within the law of the land; they are not opportunities to discuss what the law actually is. And, my guess is that few restorative justice proponents and practitioners view conflicts – at least those arising from serious wrongdoing – in quite the same positive light as Christie proposed. Most would have little problem with the idea that when crime or 'internal conflict' occurs, we should deal with it in a way that enables personal and moral growth to take place. But it seems inconsistent with the emphasis of restorative justice upon reducing recidivism (O'Mahony and Doak, 2017: 175–195) to suggest that our societies have too little crime and internal conflict, or that we should organise our societies in such a way that conflict is nurtured. These caveats aside, it seems reasonable to characterise restorative justice as an embodiment of the ideal of participatory justice. However, before concluding that such a characterisation is accurate and adequate, we need to excavate other features of the restorative justice viewpoint.

Christie's critique of treatment

Christie – and those who have followed his approach[1] – regarded lawyers as particularly good at stealing conflicts (1977: 4). With characteristic eloquence, he manages in one paragraph to construct a vivid image of how lawyers distort conflicts by highlighting arguments and facts that their clients regard as irrelevant, and suppressing those that their client thinks are central to the conflict (ibid). This sort of claim deeply impresses many restorative justice advocates and practitioners, who regularly depict restorative justice as an alternative to legal justice and are fond of contrasting 'genuine' restorative encounters with the 'lawyer's games' that take place in the courts.

What is sometimes less noticed is that Christie regarded the 'theft' of conflicts by lawyers as less pernicious than their theft by treatment personnel. At least with lawyers, there is no attempt to disguise the fact that they are in the business of handling conflicts (ibid: 4). When the case is a criminal one, state officials seek to attach blame to and impose pain upon the alleged perpetrator; the defence lawyer, on the other hand, tries to get the opposite outcome (i.e. they try to exonerate their clients or, failing that, to secure a less severe sentence). The entire criminal legal process is organised around the assumption that it is a process for the handling of conflicts. According to Christie, treatment personnel, on the other hand, adopt a non-conflict perspective. They seek to convert 'the image of the case from one of conflict to one of non-conflict' (ibid: 4). In a treatment relationship, one party – the healer – seeks to help the other party to achieve a goal that both agree is desirable: the restoration of health. What Christie implies is that when the relationship between a professional and an offender is constructed as a treatment relationship, the treatment professional's role becomes to *help* the offender to achieve a goal that the offender, if they were thinking rationally, would agree is desirable: to cure the offender of the tendency, and perhaps even the desire, to do things prohibited by the criminal law.

In a later work, Christie (1981) elaborates on the dangers of 'treatment for crime'. He suggests that the treatment perspective eliminates all rationale for arguing for limits to the pain that can be inflicted upon an offender. To illustrate this, he uses an example of a change in policy towards public drunkards in Norway. The story goes that there were many demands for public drunkards to be incarcerated – to keep them off the streets and out of circulation. However, efforts to meet these demands were hampered by the conflict perspective embodied in criminal law. Within a conflict perspective such incarceration is considered to be against the interests of the public drunkards, who would prefer to be free. Hence, it was necessary to prove that the behaviour of public drunkards was so disgusting that they deserved to be incarcerated for a long time. Proving this was quite difficult. However, then the relationship between the state and public drunkards became redefined as a treatment relationship. As a result, it became possible to conceive of state officials and public drunkards as sharing a desirable goal: the cure of the public drunkards of their illness. To achieve this shared goal, it was decided that public drunkards required long periods of incarceration. No matter how painful this was for public drunkards, they could not reasonably object to a measure that was designed to benefit them: So:

> What could not justly be done in the name of punishment could not be objected to if it were carried out as treatment. Treatment might also hurt. But so many a cure hurts. And this pain is not intended as pain. It is intended as a cure.
>
> *(Christie, 1981: 6)*[2]

It follows that to the extent that restorative justice embodies a treatment perspective upon crime, it has failed, according to the terms of Christie's analysis, to rescue conflicts involving crime from the most pernicious professional thieves. Far from returning conflicts to those to whom they belong, restorative justice will be contributing to the professional theft of conflicts. Moreover, it will be complicit in the most serious of these acts of theft: the theft by those who are not satisfied – as are the lawyers – with simply stealing conflicts, but who wish to 'define conflicts away' (Christie, 1977: 5).

So does restorative justice embody a treatment perspective? As a prelude to answering this question, this chapter will now look at the nature of the therapeutic tradition in penal systems.

The therapeutic tradition in penal systems

What follows is a the briefest of summaries of a long and very complicated historical transformation in the way criminal conduct was discussed, viewed, and handled in modern societies.[3] It will be illustrated with examples from British penal policy, but given this Handbook's international scope, examples from other modern societies would be plentiful.

During the nineteenth century, a change occurred in the language used in discourses of crime policy and penal practice (Johnstone, 1996). New terms to refer to offenders began to emerge. These terms were less openly pejorative than the more commonly used terms, and they had different connotations. One example of this is the language used to refer to 'habitual drunken offenders'. These were people who tended to be repeatedly convicted of offences involving drunkenness, such as 'being found drunk in public'. Throughout the nineteenth century, the authorities and various moral and social reform organisations regarded this group as manifesting a serious social problem (in general, see Harrison, 1994; Johnstone, 1996: 25–78). But, in the second half of the nineteenth century, new words began to appear in their discussions. The first law making drunkenness a crime, passed in 1606, was entitled An Act to Repress the Odious and Loathsome Sin of Drunkenness. Until the middle of the nineteenth century, such language was still deemed adequate. However, in a series of parliamentary inquiries into the problem, starting in 1872, habitual drunkards were increasingly referred to as 'inebriates' and sometimes as 'dipsomaniacs'.[4] By 1879, legislation targeting this group was called 'the Inebriates Act' (ibid).

These terms were considered, by those who used them, to convey a 'medical' understanding of the phenomenon of habitual drunkenness. Habitual drunkards, it was suggested, behaved as they did because they suffered from a disorder – inebriety or dipsomania – which destroyed their 'will' and hence and robbed them of their ability to control their drinking behaviour (in addition to Johnstone, 1996, see Valverde, 1998). This new understanding gave rise to new policies. Previously, those convicted of drunkenness offences were ordered to pay fines or sentenced to a few weeks in prison. Some reformers argued that such punishments were wholly inadequate; they were based on the assumption that public drunkenness was a vice that could be dealt with by punishment. To the contrary, they suggested, the inebriate suffered from a disease, allied to insanity, which needed to be treated by medical measures (see Johnstone, 1996: 57). Hence, it was proposed that inebriate reformatories should be constructed to which inebriate 'patients' could be sent for the 'treatment' designed to 'cure' them (see also Radzinowicz and Hood, 1990: chapter 9). The actual treatment proposed was a long period spent in a disciplined, orderly environment; the claim was that by living in such an environment, the patient's will could be restored and they would be able to control their drinking conduct.

To give one more example, a similar shift occurred in the language used to describe those who were increasingly regarded as constituting a 'criminal class'; a group who made their living by crime. In Britain, some estimated that this group comprised up to 15 per cent of the population and that they were responsible for hundreds of thousands of crimes every year.[5] From the second half of the nineteenth century, members of this group were increasingly referred to as 'moral imbeciles' and 'moral defectives'. The implication was that they suffered from a congenital mental disorder which prevented them from developing 'moral sense', defined as the faculty which normal people used to appreciate the distinction between right and wrong. This group were portrayed as analogous to 'imbeciles' or 'mental defectives' (i.e. people who, due to some disorder of the brain, had never developed their intellectual capacities). 'Moral imbeciles' or 'moral defectives' suffered from no such defect of understanding. They were perfectly capable of reasoning and had an 'intellectual' grasp of the distinction between right and wrong. But they could not really grasp moral principles – they had no *feeling* for the distinction between right and wrong. Again, this new understanding gave rise to new policy proposals. In the case of moral imbeciles, many suggested that since their moral defect was inborn and hence incurable, they needed to be locked up permanently. But advocates of this policy insisted that this was not a punishment for past wrongdoings but a matter of social protection: just as dangerous lunatics needed to be kept locked in asylums, so people lacking moral sense could not be set at liberty to commit further crimes.

Hand in hand with the developments just described, new types of people became involved in the task of managing offenders. Medical doctors took on a larger role in prison administration and prison doctors increasingly became consulted as experts on offending conduct and its management (Sim, 1990). The 'alienists' who managed asylums for the insane also played an increasing role in the handling of troublesome people who, according to these new understandings, occupied a nebulous position between the insane and the mentally normal offender. These groups brought new working ideologies – developed in their work with the ill, the infirm, and the insane – into the world of crime policy and penal practice.

The wholesale 'medicalisation' of society's approach to the criminal lawbreaker, which has been advocated by many penal reformers since the late nineteenth century, never transpired. But through the twentieth century therapeutic vocabularies, ideas, policies, practices, and personnel become firmly established within the field of penal practices. Throughout the twentieth century, they were developed and modified. 'Inebriates' became redefined as 'alcoholic' offenders; 'moral imbeciles' became 'psychopathic offenders', then 'sociopathic offenders', and later offenders suffering from a 'personality disorder' (Johnstone, 1996: 79–100, 133–175). More nuanced conceptions of the disorders which many offenders were deemed to suffer from were developed. More sophisticated causal theories emerged, some inspired by psychoanalysis and some by other branches of psychiatry, psychology, and biology. A wide range of therapeutic interventions were experimented with. And new therapeutic professions – psychotherapists, social psychiatrists, psychiatric social workers, behavioural psychologists, and so on – became involved in the treatment of offenders.

By the 1950s and 1960s, what had started out as a rather authoritarian approach – in which the main point of treating offenders was simply to render them less of a danger or a nuisance to respectable society, and in which the methods of 'treatment' advocated seem, at least by later standards, to be disciplinary and harsh – had diversified considerably. Indeed, some of the ideas, policies, and practices developed under the rubric of penal treatment were informed by socially radical perspectives. To illustrate this, let us look again at policies towards habitual drunken offenders.

By the 1960s, despite decades of reform efforts, most of those repeatedly arrested for drunkenness offenders were still being dealt with through fines and short periods of imprisonment. Almost a century after a therapeutic alternative to the 'penal revolving door' was first advocated, fresh efforts were made to develop a treatment regime for these 'alcoholic offenders'.

However, the explanations of the behaviour of these people had developed significantly since the nineteenth century. Tim Cook (1969) who was a driving force behind the establishment of a new network of treatment facilities, pointed to very harmful experiences alcoholic offenders typically suffered in their early years; experiences which resulted in a range of emotional and personality problems. These problems resulted in their having difficulties in forming and sustaining normal social relationships in adulthood. Many became extremely socially isolated. Heavy drinking – and the thin social relationships that existed amongst 'skid row alcoholics' – was turned to as a substitute for the sociability that most of us take for granted. Treatment of the habitual drunkard therefore needed to be focussed not so much on their drink problem (which was just a symptom) but upon a complex of emotional and social problems that prevented them from living normal lives. These included an inability to enter into and to sustain a normal adult relationships, apathy and an inability to take responsibility for one's own life, and chronic and acute feelings of guilt, anxiety, inadequacy, and rejection.

According to Cook, many of these alcoholic offenders actually welcomed the highly authoritarian structure of control typical of prisons. Within such a structure, they were relieved of the need to take responsibility for their own lives and decisions. Much of the anxiety of living in society was relieved. The problem, however, was that after a few weeks in this environment, they were returned to a social situation which they simply could not manage. Inevitably, they returned to 'skid row' and – at some point – another prison sentence.

To break this cycle, Cook sought to establish a range of institutions between the total control of the prison and the total liberty of normal society. So, for instance, on release from prison, an alcoholic offender would live in a hostel, where they would still be subject to a significant level of observation and control but would have more freedom – and more responsibility – than they had in prison. In such an environment, they would become more socialised and develop a greater capacity for personal responsibility. Whilst living in the hostel, they would also receive counselling, crisis intervention, training, guidance, and advice on seeking housing and employment. Hostels, it was proposed, should be run along the lines of therapeutic communities (similar proposals were made around the same time for so-called 'psychopathic' offenders). For instance, the residents would be encouraged to develop their own codes of conduct and to make their own decisions on how breaches of this code were to be handled. The idea, basically, was that by living in such an environment – with its careful balance of permissiveness and control, external authority, and participation – habitual drunkards could be gradually integrated into the normal community (Johnstone, 1991). Even then, however, there would be various other institutions, such as shop-fronts, to which recovering alcoholic offenders could go if they felt the need for support.

Attacks on the therapeutic tradition

The therapeutic tradition in penal systems had, from the outset, been criticised by morally conservative commentators who rejected and found dangerous the notions that many offenders lacked personal responsibility for their misdeeds and that they required treatment rather than punishment. However, during the 1960s and 1970s, other voices joined in this attack upon the ideology of penal treatment. Some highlighted the practical failure of therapeutic interventions into the lives of offenders (i.e. they argued that these interventions seldom cured offenders of their criminal tendencies).[6] However, the idea of offenders as sick people requiring treatment also came under attack from more radical voices in the debate about criminal justice, including, as we have seen, Nils Christie. This 'radical' critique of the therapeutic tradition has many interweaving strands. Some of these strands, moreover, seem inconsistent with others. Yet it is possible to capture its general thrust (see Johnstone, 1996: 10–16).

The idea that criminal conduct is a symptom of some underlying illness or disorder was criticised on the ground that it ignored the fact that crime does not exist independently of the judgements society makes about behaviour; hence the therapeutic tradition suppressed questions about the validity of the moral and political judgements involved in calling something 'crime' (this seems to be close to the heart of Christie's idea that treatment professionals deny that what they are dealing with are conflicts). It was argued further that criminal behaviour is almost always the result of some choice on the part of offenders, no matter how much these choices are constrained and conditioned by forces beyond their control, and that the causes of crime are more social than biological or psychological (ibid: 10–12). Critics of the therapeutic tradition also claimed that policies based on this erroneous notion were not only ineffective and futile but could be very harmful. In the name of therapy, many offenders were subjected to hazardous and dehumanising procedures. Sometimes these procedures did indeed change the personalities of offenders, so that they were deprived of their very personhood or, as Nicholas Kittrie (1973) put it, of 'the right to be different'. And, as we have seen Christie argue, the therapeutic approach was criticised on the ground that it tended to result in offenders – or even those who were predicted to become offenders – being subjected to various deprivations of liberty that could not be justified as punishments for crimes they had committed.

Whilst some of those who made these criticisms saw the rise of the therapeutic tradition in penal practice as a mistake, others regarded its rise as more sinister. According to this perspective, treatment professionals did not just unwittingly suppress questions about the validity of the moral and political judgements involved in labelling conduct as criminal; rather, the suppression of deviant moral and political viewpoints was part of the reason for the dissemination of the idea that crime could be understood as an illness (see, for example, Box 1980). And therapeutic interventions were often depicted as part of a conspiracy to subdue or even alter the personalities of those who thought and acted in ways that normal society found troublesome. And, as we have seen Christie strongly imply, the 'illegitimate' deprivations of liberty which some offenders were subjected to in the name of therapy were not simply the result of an over-enthusiasm for the treatment approach. Some argued that therapeutic ideologies were actually devised and propagated in order to throw a cloak of therapeutic respectability over what would otherwise have been exposed for what it truly was: the illegitimate confinement of those whom mainstream society deemed to be troublesome or unacceptably different (Johnstone, 1996: 14–16).

Restorative justice and the therapeutic tradition

Following the seeming decline of the therapeutic tradition in penal systems in the 1970s, something of a vacuum was created (see Crow, 2001: 30; Garland, 1990: 6–8). Arguably, a significant part of this vacuum has been filled by restorative justice. But did restorative justice, when it stepped into the space previously occupied by treatment, bring about a radical break with the therapeutic tradition in penal systems, or did the restorative justice movement inherit therapeutic language, objectives, practices, and personnel that were left in that space that it occupied? In order to address these questions, we need to look at the language, objectives, practices, and personnel of the restorative justice movement.

The meaning of 'restoring' victims

First, it must be recognised that restorative justice differs sharply from the therapeutic tradition in penal systems in the emphasis it places, at last in its rhetoric (see Johnstone, 2017), upon crime victims. Until the 1970s, the therapeutic tradition in penal systems was entirely offender-focussed. Within the discourse of restorative justice, on the other hand, 'restoring' victims gets equal attention. However, even here, or perhaps especially here, there is an important continuity between the therapeutic tradition and restorative justice.

Whilst the discourse of restorative justice emphasises the need to 'restore' victims of crime, what is meant by 'restoring' is often vague. This term could be, and within restorative justice discourse is, construed in multiple ways. At least two of these ways can be explained without making any resort to therapeutic language or practices. One way of thinking about what restoration involves is to conceive of it as involving compensation or restitution to the victim. According to this conception, the crime victim has suffered losses or injuries for which they need to be compensated. Whereas conventional criminal justice systems typically ignore this need, and sometimes even prevent it being met (by, for instance, imposing a fine upon an offender rather than ordering the offender to use what limited means they have to pay restitution), a restorative criminal justice would prioritise the need to make good the losses of the victim. The move to restorative justice, on this interpretation of 'restoring', represents a move towards a more 'civil law' approach to criminal wrongdoing – a 'civilising' of criminal justice (Cornwell et al., 2013: 26–27). Alternatively, one might think of crime victims as people whose rights have been violated. Hence, 'restoring' crime victims might mean vindicating the victim's rights. One usual way of attempting to vindicate the rights of crime victims in modern society is to punish those who violate them. Restorative justice might be understood as an alternative – and, according to its advocates, superior – way of vindicating the rights of crime victims.

Within the discourse of restorative justice there is, however, a third way of construing 'restoring' in the context of restoring victims. And as the restorative justice movement has developed, this third way has become more and more prominent. This third way involves giving 'restoring' a decidedly therapeutic meaning: crime victims have suffered 'trauma' and restoring them means 'healing' them.

The discourse of restorative justice is replete with references to the 'trauma' suffered by crime victims (for example, and most notably, see Zehr, 2015: 25–38). And this is meant quite literally. Restorative justice theory and practice are heavily informed by research literature on the impact of crime upon the well-being of its victims. One review of this literature (Shapland and Hall, 2007) points to a range of ways in which crime victims tend to suffer as a result of the crime committed against them. In addition to financial losses, victims often suffer psychologically, socially, and physically. In particular, many suffer from long-term depression, sleeplessness, and anxiety. These feelings often result in unhealthy changes to their lifestyle; and these changes further exacerbate the victim's psychological trauma. As society has 'recognised' the traumatic impact of crime upon its victims, various therapeutic services have emerged to meet the needs of victims for healing (see the literature reviewed in Johnstone and Brennan, 2014). Nowadays, there are many public sector and voluntary organisations which offer victims support, advice, and counselling in order to help them to get better following their traumatic experience.

A central theme in restorative justice discourse is that not only do criminal justice systems not do enough to promote the recovery of crime victims from the trauma they have suffered but in significant ways they compound their injuries (Zehr, 2015: 36). Accordingly, restorative justice is advocated as a way of handling crime that is based on full cognizance of the fact that victims are traumatised people in need of healing and which makes promoting the psychological recovery of victims a priority for criminal justice systems (Van Ness and Strong, 2015: 3–4).

Moreover, those involved in developing the practice of restorative justice have drawn heavily on psychological theories and therapeutic ideas. For instance, at the heart of restorative justice practice is the 'lay encounter': a meeting in which lay people – victims, offenders, family members and friends of both, and community members – meet to deliberate about the harm that has been caused by a crime and about what needs to be done to repair this harm (Rossner, 2012: 971–972). As with the concept of 'restoring', there are multiple ways of conceiving the purposes of these encounters and of thinking about their dynamics. But one of the most prominent ways of discussing encounters is in therapeutic terms. Hence, there is a large emphasis on the expression of emotions during a restorative justice encounter. Indeed, Meredith Rossner, who has researched these encounters deeply (see Rossner, 2013), suggests that 'the emotional element of restorative justice may be its defining characteristic' (Rossner, 2012: 972). In a restorative encounter, emotional expression is encouraged and facilitated in order that those who participate can undergo a transformation from trauma to recovery (Johnstone, 2002: 116–134). One function of the restorative encounter is to enable victims to witness genuine remorse being expressed by the person who harmed them. This enables them to move from anger and resentment towards forgiveness. But, as is repeatedly emphasised in the restorative justice literature, forgiveness – if and where it occurs – is valued because it is healthy. Harbouring long-term feelings of anger, hatred, and resentment is regarded as problematic because it is bad for the health of crime victims. A process which enables victims to express and let go of these emotions, and to move towards forgiveness, is central to their recovery from trauma. Hence, restorative justice is frequently described as 'healing justice'.

'Restoring' offenders

Bazemore and Bell (2004: 120) state that most restorative justice practitioners are unenthusiastic about 'professional treatment' models. The restorative view of the offender, they suggest, cannot be easily reconciled with 'a "medical model" perspective that views offenders primarily in terms of deficits and "thinking errors"' (ibid). I suggest that this captures well the attitude of many restorative justice proponents and practitioners towards 'treatment'. However, in what follows, I will also suggest that this expressed attitude towards the therapeutic tradition does not reflect the way many restorative justice proponents and practitioners actually view offenders and actually think about the appropriate response to them. In order to make this argument, I will first briefly revisit some of the central assumptions of the therapeutic tradition in penal systems.

For all its internal diversity, the therapeutic tradition is held together by the following assumptions. First, many offenders behave as they do because they are in some sense 'damaged'. For instance, some are lacking in the ability to exercise normal levels of control over their conduct. Some seem to lack an appropriate grasp of the distinction between what is morally right and wrong; whilst they are capable of understanding this distinction at a cognitive level, they don't quite appreciate – at an emotional level – what is wrong about certain ways of behaving. Many seem to have a deeply rooted lack of a normal sense of self-responsibility; indeed their offending conduct is just one part of a wider lifestyle characterised by irresponsibility. Second, the best response to such offenders is a therapeutic one. They need interventions that are designed to strengthen their self-control, develop their 'moral sense', and instil a capacity for responsibility. Third, there is an underlying assumption that it is in the interests of both those who offend and members of the society who are affected by their behaviour that offenders receive such therapeutic intervention. Although, on the surface, there may be a conflict of interest between offenders and society, at a deeper level their interests are aligned. Offenders will benefit from being helped to become both more law-abiding and more 'social'; society will benefit since not only will it have less troublesome behaviour to contend with but it will be strengthened by having the offender returned to it a productive citizen. In society's dealing with offenders, there can be win-win outcomes.

With this in mind, let us look now at the goals and assumptions, with regard to offenders, which underpin restorative justice interventions. First, the following statement, by Carolyn Hoyle (2010), arguably provides an accurate account of how restorative justice proponents and practitioners actually view most of the offenders who take part in restorative justice encounters. She argues that restorative justice 'puts the offence (or other harmful behaviour) in the context of relative deprivation, dysfunctional relationships, poor educational or health services, or failures of those in authority to identify or respond effectively to evident criminogenic factors' (ibid: 12). She goes on to suggest that restorative processes are organised to enable participants 'to see beyond the label of "offender" to a sometimes confused and vulnerable person who may have been harmed by his or her experiences as much as he or she has harmed others' (ibid). Such a view of offenders is, I suggest, entirely consistent with the way offenders are viewed within the therapeutic tradition in penal systems. And when we look at the objectives of restorative justice encounters, with regard to offenders who participate in them, we will see that these objectives are also therapeutic.

One of the key ideas behind the restorative justice encounter is that many perpetrators of criminal wrongdoing do not quite understand that there is something wrong with what they have done. They tend to think of their offences as breaches of abstract societal rules rather than acts which bring pain and suffering to other people (Zehr, 2015: 39–50). Hence, one of the key purposes of organising an encounter between an offender and a victim is to enable the offender to hear, directly from the victim, about consequences of their conduct which they had not previously considered: the pain and suffering that occurs in the lives of their victims. This, it is hoped, will trigger an emotional transformation within the offender. Whereas previously their stance was one of indifference, they will now experience remorse or shame. However, as Braithwaite and Strang (2000) suggest, often this will not work. The reason is that 'the offender has *learnt a callousness* that protects him from experiencing any shame in the face of hearing these consequences' (ibid: 215, emphasis added). They then go on to suggest how an encounter can be organised to create the possibility of an 'indirect emotional dynamic' which will 'get behind the offender's emotional defences' and allow them finally to experience remorse (ibid).

The view of offenders here, as people who have, presumably through faulty learning, developed a callousness that shields them from an appreciation of the consequences of their behaviour, and hence enables them to hurt other people without experiencing any pangs of conscience, is remarkably similar to the way so-called 'psychopathic' offenders – or 'offenders with personality disorders' – were described in the therapeutic discourse of the 1960s (Craft, 1966; see Johnstone, 1996: 157–175). And the two discourses share the therapeutic objective of overcoming this emotional disorder, enabling offenders to experience 'moral emotions' such as shame and remorse.

This continuity between the therapeutic tradition and restorative justice becomes even clearer if we consider recent writings on restorative justice, such as Wallis (2014). Wallis describes a similar dynamic, suggesting it has the potential to elicit 'empathy' within offenders. It is worthwhile looking, albeit briefly, at his discussion, as I assume it is one which reflects well the thinking of many in the restorative justice movement.[7]

Wallis argues that empathy stops people from harming others (ibid: 21). So, he goes on, for a crime to be possible, the 'person responsible must have no empathy for the person they are harming, at least at the moment the crime is committed' (ibid). Wallis then goes on to support and illustrate this claim by reference to research from the discipline of developmental psychopathology. This research suggests that all people can be located on an empathy spectrum. On a scale of zero to six, with zero representing zero degrees of empathy, and six representing high degrees of empathy, most people score 2–4 (i.e. the empathy curve is bell shaped). Drawing on this research, Wallis suggests that people with 'zero degrees' of empathy have a personality disorder which has its roots in early childhood: '[T]hese individuals typically experienced trauma as a result of early abuse, insecure attachment and neglect, which interrupted the development of healthy empathy' (ibid). Further, the research Wallis draws upon 'has identified a neurological 'circuit' where empathy is located, and shown that prolonged exposure to stress and trauma can lead to specific regions in the brain becoming underactive or abnormal' (ibid). The upshot is that years of 'extreme childhood unhappiness' result in a person for whom low or zero empathy is a stable personality trait (ibid: 22). Although these people are not predestined to offend, their lack of empathy enables then to commit offences more easily; indeed 'they are 'able to commit acts of great cruelty with no remorse' (ibid: 21). Hence a high percentage of people in penal custody are people who have such a personality disorder (ibid: 22).

Wallis's book goes on to explain how restorative justice has the potential to raise empathy levels in 'persons responsible'[8] for criminal wrongdoing. In other words, restorative justice has the potential to cure personality disorders which lie at the root of much offending behaviour, although in Wallis's work, as in the discourse of restorative justice more generally, the term 'healing' seems to be preferred to curing (ibid: 178). But, if the trauma which people who offend is to be properly recognised and treated, and they are to be brought to 'the moment of healing', it is important that restorative justice is facilitated by experts. In order to heal people with low degrees of empathy through restorative encounters, the facilitators of these encounters require a high degree of knowledge and skill, which in turn requires training (ibid: see p. 179). If it is to fulfil its therapeutic purpose, it seems that restorative justice encounters can no longer be entrusted to pure lay people. The implication of Wallis's work is that, within restorative justice, the 'participatory justice' viewpoint must be subsumed within the 'healing justice' viewpoint.

Conclusion and implications for the future of restorative justice

This chapter has argued that, far from wresting conflicts from the grip of treatment personnel, restorative justice – in its discourse and practice – has adopted much of the language and many of the assumptions and objectives of the therapeutic tradition in penal systems. When it occupied part of the vacuum created by the seeming decline of the therapeutic tradition in penal systems, it did not so much provide a stark alternative to the therapeutic tradition as develop that tradition in new directions. If this argument is persuasive, those in the restorative justice movement need to rid themselves of, or at least radically revise, the notion that restorative justice – as it is currently imagined and practised – returns conflicts from the professional thieves who have stolen them to ordinary people to whom they really belong. Rather than challenge the ideology of treatment personnel, the contemporary restorative justice movement has provided the ideology of treatment with a new outlet. A more general implication of this argument is that, rather than being seen as a radically new paradigm in criminal justice, restorative justice needs to be understood as a continuation and development of the therapeutic tradition in penal systems which first emerged in the nineteenth century. Indeed, it might even be suggested that the restorative justice movement has enabled the therapeutic tradition to survive the full-scale attack to which it was subjected in the 1960s and 1970s.

By highlighting this fact, this chapter aims to bring to the surface an important choice facing the restorative justice movement about its future development. Should the movement continue to develop itself around the 'healing justice' viewpoint, or should it renew its efforts to break with older paradigms of crime and justice by shedding the therapeutic language, assumptions, objectives, and practices which it has adopted? As the chapter has argued, at the moment the movement seems to be unaware that it faces this choice. Advocates and practitioners of restorative justice regard crime and related forms of wrongdoing through a therapeutic lens, whilst at the same time disparaging the therapeutic tradition and insisting that the restorative justice movement is retrieving conflicts from 'professional thieves' – including treatment personnel – and returning them to the ordinary people to whom the conflicts really belong.

To be clear, the aim of this chapter is to reveal a contradiction in the way restorative justice advocates and practitioners think and act; it makes no attempt to argue for a particular resolution of this contradiction. But it does suggest that in order to resolve this contradiction and hence develop a more coherent future direction, the restorative justice movement needs to be engaged more deeply with questions about the merits of the therapeutic tradition in penal systems and with discussions of therapeutic culture. If the restorative justice movement continues to adopt a highly disparaging attitude towards the therapeutic tradition in penal systems, as Christie (writing in the mid-1970s when the radical attack on treatment was at its most ferocious) did, then – to be consistent – the movement should purge itself of therapeutic language, assumptions, and objectives. However, as the chapter suggests in its brief account of the development of the therapeutic tradition in the twentieth century, such a disparaging attitude towards treatment tends to be based on a caricature rather than upon an accurate image of the ideas of therapeutic professionals about offenders and their treatment. The therapeutic tradition is a diverse one, and it embodies many progressive assumptions, attitudes, and objectives.

That being said, the therapeutic tradition should not be endorsed uncritically. Frank Furedi, whose work was referenced at the outset of this chapter, has written a scathing critique of therapy culture (Furedi, 2004). He shows how therapeutic language and practices have expanded into everyday life and become part of our cultural imagination. We increasingly interpret all our encounters, experiences, and relationships through a therapeutic script. We increasingly see ourselves as emotionally vulnerable beings, constantly at risk of suffering emotional damage from difficult encounters and experiences. We increasingly seek and act upon the therapeutic advice in our efforts to manage our lives, whether our goal is to manage our anger better, deal with stressful situations (such as being the victim of crime), or become more successful in our relationships and enterprises. Furedi sharply disagrees with those (including many leading advocates and practitioners of restorative justice) who think this development has empowered people by increasing their emotional intelligence (cf. Goleman, 1996). Rather, Furedi argues – echoing Christie's point about treatment professionals defining conflicts away – that the therapeutic ethos constitutes a regime of social control which has deeply disturbing authoritarian consequences.

Furedi's work – which forms part of a long tradition of sceptical and critical writing about therapeutic culture (see, for instance, Rieff, 1966) – provides an important and interesting critical perspective on one of the most dominant of the cultural scripts which people in modern societies draw upon (usually without being conscious of the fact) to talk about and think about and their experiences, lives, and relationships. However, it is a highly polemical account which arguably needs to be balanced by more neutral and sympathetic readings of the triumph of the therapeutic. Advocates and practitioners of restorative justice may well want to address such accounts and argue that they place too much emphasis upon the problematic aspects of therapy culture and concomitantly underemphasise or misrepresent its more progressive elements, such as those embodied within the practice of restorative justice. But to do this, the restorative justice movement would need to recognise that restorative justice *is* a new form of therapy for offenders and crime victims, and is not – as the movement sometimes like to think of itself – a radically new paradigm of crime and justice. Hence, the crucial point of this chapter is that the social movement for restorative justice, far from challenging therapy culture, has arguably been permeated by that culture and is indeed a major transmitter of therapeutic ideologies.

Notes

1 Bottoms (2003: 80–83) discusses the impact Christie's paper has had upon the development of restorative justice thinking and describes it as 'a foundational text'. Similarly, Braithwaite (1999: 5) describes Christie's essay as 'the most influential text' of the restorative justice movement.
2 Cf. Gavrielides (2013).
3 This account is drawn from the author's previous work *Medical Concepts and Penal Policy* (1996). Given the summary nature of this account, references will mainly be to this earlier work, rather than to the primary historical materials upon which it is based. To avoid repetition, unless indicated otherwise, the source for what follows is Johnstone (1996). Other general accounts of the transformation described here can be found in Conrad and Schneider (1980), Garland (1985), Kittrie (1973), Prins (1980), Radzinowicz and Hood (1990), and Sim (1980).
4 On the following, see (Johnstone, 1996: 25–78).
5 On the following, see (Johnstone, 1996: 103–156).
6 The mantra 'nothing works', attributed to Martinson (1974), tends to be directed at therapeutic interventions in particular.
7 It appears in a book about restorative justice which is endorsed by leading figures in the restorative justice movement as an important contribution to the field. Wallis is a 'senior practitioner' who has 'facilitated hundreds of restorative meetings' and is a 'consultant for the new Restorative Service Quality Mark' (Wallis 2014: from the blurb).
8 As in the therapeutic tradition, many restorative justice advocates and practitioners prefer to avoid morally pejorative language when labelling those who commit criminal offences and other wrongs.

Bibliography

Bazemore, G. and Bell, D. 2004. What is the Appropriate Relationship between Restorative Justice and Treatment? In H. Zehr and B. Toews (eds.) *Critical Issues in Restorative Justice*. Monsey, NY: Criminal Justice Press.

Bottoms, A. 2003. Some Sociological Reflections on Restorative Justice. In A. von Hirsch, J. Roberts, A. Bottoms, K. Roach, and M. Schiff (eds.) *Restorative Justice and Criminal Justice: Competing or Reconcilable Paradigms*. Oxford: Hart, pp. 79–113.

Box, S. 1980. Where Have all the Naughty Children Gone? In National Deviancy Conference (ed.) *Permissiveness and Control: The Fate of the Sixties Legislation*. London: Palgrave Macmillan, pp. 96–121.

Braithwaite, J. 1999. Restorative Justice: Assessing Optimistic and Pessimistic Accounts, *Crime and Justice: An Annual Review of Research*, 25: 1–127.

Braithwaite, J. and Strang, H. 2000. Connecting Philosophy and Practice. In H. Strang and J. Braithwaite (eds.) *Restorative Justice: Philosophy to Practice*. Aldershot: Ashgate, pp. 203–220.

Christie, N. 1977. Conflicts as Property, *British Journal of Criminology*, 17(1): 1–15.

Christie, N. 1981. *Limits to Pain*. Oxford: Martin Robertson.

Cook, T. 1969. Existing Facilities. In T. Cook, D. Gath and C. Hensman (eds.) *The Drunkenness Offence*. Oxford: Pergamon Press.

Conrad, P. and Schneider, J. 1980. *Deviance and Medicalization: From Badness to Sickness*. St. Louis, MO: Mosby.

Cornwell, D., Blad, J. and Wright, M. 2013. *Civilising Criminal Justice*. Hook: Waterside Press.

Craft, M. 1966. *Psychopathic Disorders and their Assessment*. Oxford: Pergamon Press.

Crow, I. 2001. *The Treatment and Rehabilitation of Offenders*. London: Sage.

Furedi, F. 2004. *Therapy Culture: Cultivating Vulnerability in an Uncertain Age*. London: Routledge.

Garland, D. 1985. *Punishment and Welfare: A History of Penal Strategies*. Aldershot: Gower.

Garland, D. 1990. *Punishment and Modern Society: A Study in Social Theory*. Oxford: Oxford University Press.

Gavrielides, T. 2013. Restorative Pain: A New Vision of Punishment. In T. Gavrielides and V. Artinopoulou (eds.) *Reconstructing Restorative Justice Philosophy*. Farnham: Ashgate, pp. 311–336.

Goleman, D. 1996. *Emotional Intelligence: Why It Can Matter More than IQ*. London: Bloomsbury.

Hoyle, C. 2010. The Case for Restorative Justice. In C. Cunneen and C. Hoyle (eds.) *Debating Restorative Justice*. Oxford: Hart.

Harrison, B. 1994. *Drink and the Victorians*. London: Faber and Faber.

Johnstone, G. 1991. Between Permissiveness and Control: Community Treatment and Penal Supervision, *Law and Critique*, 2(1): 37–61.

Johnstone, G. 1996. *Medical Concepts and Penal Policy*. London: Cavendish.

Johnstone, G. 2002. *Restorative Justice: Ideas, Values, Debates*. Cullompton: Willan.

Johnstone, G. and Brennan, I. 2014. Victim-Offender encounters for Restorative Dialogue: A Review. Available at http://restorative-justice.eu/bb/wp-content/uploads/sites/3/2016/02/WS-1.-D1.3b-VOM-review.pdf.

Johnstone, G. 2017. Restorative Justice for Victims: Inherent Limits, *Restorative Justice*, 5(3): 382–395.

Kittrie, N. 1973. *The Right to be Different; Deviance and Enforced Therapy*. Baltimore, MD: Penguin.

Martinson, R. 1974. What Works? – Questions and Answers about Prison Reform, *The Public Interest*, 35: 22–54.

Nolan, Jr., J. 1998. *The Therapeutic State: Justifying Government as Century's End*. New York: New York University Press.

O'Mahony, D. and Doak, J. 2017. *Reimagining Restorative Justice: Agency and Accountability in the Criminal Process*. Oxford: Hart.

Pavlich, G. 2005. *Governing Paradoxes of Restorative Justice*. London: Glasshouse Press.

Prins, H. 1980. *Offenders, Deviants, or Patients*. London: Tavistock.

Radzinowicz, L. and Hood, R. 1990. *The Emergence of Penal Policy in Victorian and Edwardian England*. Oxford: Clarendon Press.

Rieff, P. 1966. *The Triumph of the Therapeutic: Uses of Faith after Freud*. Chicago: University of Chicago Press.

Rossner, M. 2013. *Just Emotions; Rituals of Restorative Justice*. Oxford: Oxford University Press.

Rossner, M. 2017. Restorative Justice in the Twenty-First Century: Making Emotions Mainstream. In A. Liebling, S. Maruna and L. McAra (eds.) *The Oxford Handbook of Criminology, Sixth Edition*. Oxford: Oxford University Press, pp. 967–989.

Shapland, J. and Hall, M. 2007. What We Know about the Effects of Crime on Victims, *International Review of Victimology*, 14: 175–217.

Valverde, M. 1998. *Diseases of the Will: Alcohol and the Dilemmas of Freedom*. Cambridge: Cambridge University Press.

Van Ness, D. and Strong, K. 2015. *Restoring Justice: An Introduction to Restorative Justice*, 5th ed. New York: Routledge.

Wallis, P. 2014. *Understanding Restorative Justice: How Empathy Can Close the Gap Created by Crime*. Bristol: Policy Press.

Zehr, H. 2015. *Changing Lenses: Restorative Justice for our Times (25th Anniversary Edition)*. Harrisonburg: Herald Press.

27

True representation

The implications of restorative practices for the future of democracy

Ted Wachtel

Beyond broken

True representation is the underlying goal of democracy, yet that goal has proven elusive. Consider the comments of eight-term U.S. Congressman Steve Israel from Long Island, New York, who chose not to run for office after 16 years in the legislature. "I don't think I can spend another day . . . begging for money. I always knew the system was dysfunctional. Now it is beyond broken (Hulce, 2016)."

Americans should not be surprised. Political parties and partisan elections have been the handmaidens of corruption and divisiveness since the founding of the republic.

George Washington predicted in his farewell speech (1796), after eight years as America's first president, that political parties "are likely, in the course of time and things, to become potent engines, by which cunning, ambitious, and unprincipled men will be enabled to subvert the power of the people and to usurp for themselves the reins of government."

Not just in America, but in democratic republics around the globe, current opinion surveys reveal that voters everywhere see their elected representatives as primarily concerned with enriching themselves:

- A Transparency International survey of 114,000 people in 107 countries found that only 23 percent believed their governments were effectively dealing with corruption (2013).
- In the US in 1958, about 75% of Americans expressed trust in their country's government "most or all of the time."
- In 2017, only 20% of Americans trust their government "most or all of the time."
- Merely 29% describe their elected officials as "very" or "fairly honest."
- 74% of Americans feel that elected officials don't care about what people think (Pew Research Center, 2017).

Alvin O'Konski, a U.S. Congressman from 1943 to 1973, claimed that most lawmakers "are bought, sold, signed, sealed and delivered." (UPI Archive, 1984). Veteran Washington journalist Robert G. Kaiser's book title sums it all up – *So Damn Much Money: The Triumph of Lobbying and the Corrosion of American Government* (2009).

Professional politicians have stolen our decision making. Throughout the world, politicians pursue wealth and power by selling favourable decisions to the highest bidder. The remedy to rampant corruption may lie in filling our legislatures with randomly selected citizens – a process that has its origins in ancient Athenian democracy.

This chapter will address the critical question that such an approach raises – whether groups of ordinary people can make good decisions, better than the professionals. Research and experience with restorative practices such as family group conferences, restorative conferences and circle sentencing provide meaningful evidence that ordinary people can make good decisions about issues that affect them and their community of care better than professionals. This chapter argues that, along with similar outcomes from business management research and deliberative democracy experiments, restorative practices can point to the potential of making government more truly representative.

Against elections

Sadly, corruption plagues all of the world's electoral democracies. If the election process has become hopelessly corrupt, why should we keep selecting our representatives by voting in elections? Might there be another way?

In the United States and throughout the world, we have come to define democracy by the act of voting. Voting in elections, as Flemish author David Van Reybrouck points out in his widely translated book *Against Elections: The Case for Democracy* (2013), means that each citizen has power for only one minute every few years. We give our vote and we delegate our power.

Van Reybrouck and others suggest that instead of professional politicians, we might be better served by selecting ordinary citizens by lottery to serve in legislatures. The process is called "sortition," "election by lot" or the Greek term "demarchy."

American philosopher Alexander Guerrero, in an article with a similar name ("Against Elections"), which will be published as a book in 2018, sought to refine the Athenian process into a workable modern context. He has coined a new term with the forthcoming book's subtitle: *The Lottocratic Alternative*.

Instead of a unicameral or bicameral legislature that deals with all areas of policy, in Guerrero's "lottocracy" there would be a series of single-issue legislatures, with members selected by lottery. Each lottocratic legislature would focus on an individual policy area – agriculture, consumer protection, defence, education, environmental protection, financial services regulation, healthcare, taxation – rather than trying to deal with all of those areas in general. By specializing the legislative process, lottocracy makes it easier for citizen legislators to learn what they need to know to make informed decisions.

Guerrero's suggested model includes 300 members in each single-issue legislature, although there could be any number. He proposed that the legislators be randomly selected for three-year terms. Each year, the 100 of the longest-serving representatives in each legislature would retire and 100 newly selected representatives would take their place, a process analogous to the U.S. Senate's six-year cycle of three biennial elections.

The advent of digital meeting services that bring hundreds of people together via the Internet in live face-to-face meetings, while still in their homes, makes it possible for ordinary people to serve as representatives to a legislature largely from a distance. The biggest disruption of a citizen legislator's personal life would be an initial and then an occasional week or weekend gathering to be attended in person at a central location.

Individual involvement in the legislature could be only a part-time responsibility – like that of corporate board members working about five hours a week, largely from home, with appropriate compensation, support services and legal boundaries and protocols to protect, as needed, the home-based legislators from overzealous lobbyists, including intrusive friends and family members. Just like military or jury duty – serving in the legislature would be seen as a responsibility of citizenship in a democratic society.

By combining lottocratic legislatures with digital meeting technology, we may satisfy many of the concerns about direct democracy raised years ago by Australian distinguished professor John Braithwaite: "There are just too many decisions and too many people for participatory democracy to be feasible. Besides, few of us want to spend our lives in the endless meetings it would require. The expanding impracticability of all affected citizens participating in important decisions that affect their lives has reinforced the dominant view that representative democracy is all that is feasible (1999b)."

"At the same time, if Madison or Jefferson returned to America today they would be disappointed at how remote government is from the people, at how much power governments, and worse, democratically unaccountable corporations, exercise in ways that educated citizens dimly understand (1999b)."

Guerrero recognizes that while there could be many variations, the most critical feature of his lottocratic alternative is the selection of legislators by lottery. His concern with election by vote is that, "In the presence of widespread citizen ignorance and the absence of meaningful accountability, powerful interests will effectively capture representatives, ensuring that the only viable candidates – the only people who can get and stay in political power – are those who will act in ways that are congenial to the interests of the powerful."

The ancient Athenian democracy avoided this problem by selecting their jurors and legislators by lottery, only using elections to choose about ten percent of their public officials. Mostly executives and administrators, they were chosen for their ability to carry out the policies that the legislatures decided – not to make policy – the opposite of the approach now used in most democracies. (Wachtel, 2017)

The Athenian experience with direct democracy persisted for almost two centuries, with some ups and downs. It ended, not because of weaknesses in the Athenian democratic process, but because the Greek city states were conquered by Phillip, king of Macedonia and father of Alexander the Great. And so the civilized world returned to its reliance on the rule of kings and queens for many centuries.

When a newly independent America ended the rule of the English king, the founders who wrote the U.S. Constitution in 1787 did not imitate the Greek tradition of choosing legislators by lottery. The founding fathers decided that, unlike Athens, legislators would be elected by competitive ballot although, just like Athens, only men with property were eligible to vote – not women, men without property, or slaves.

The infamous "Three-Fifths" compromise adopted by the Constitutional Convention gave slave states like Virginia extra congressional districts based on counting three-fifths of the slave population toward awarding the number of representatives. Selection by lottery surely would have complicated the discussion further. More likely, sortition was never considered.

The biggest benefit of sortition and lottocracy is the absence of expensive election campaigns funded by the wealthy and powerful, which gives them more influence over legislation than the voters have. Choosing legislators by random lottery dramatically changes the game – reducing the influence of political parties while guaranteeing that, year after year, a truly representative cross section of the citizenry makes its own decisions.

"Can large groups of ordinary people make better decisions than professional politicians?" Of course, we must satisfactorily answer this question before we change our method of choosing legislators. (Wachtel, 2017).

Braithwaite on democracy and restorative practices

John Braithwaite recently wrote that "decision by vote destabilizes in ways that can threaten other values, including truth. This is because politicians often win by being more adept at lying than their adversary."

Braithwaite is especially concerned that we have imposed competitive elections on new nations with unintended but often terrible consequences.

> It is a pathology of elections doing more harm than good in the very places where, according to our political theories, democracy is the imperative remedy. . . . As with sudden decolonization, quick fix elections allowed populist tyrants to garner votes by sowing ethnic division, thereby seizing power in the aftermath of conflict, criminalizing the state, and fomenting future coups and civil wars.
>
> *(2017)*

In the 1999 speech mentioned earlier, in which Braithwaite pondered the limitations of direct democracy, he also pointed out that restorative practices had implications for democracy. Just as Nils Christie, the late Norwegian criminologist, in his landmark essay "Conflicts as Property," accused lawyers and court professionals of stealing our conflicts, Braithwaite suggests that professional politicians expropriate our opportunities for active responsibility and decision making.

> The lived experience of modern democracy is alienation. The feeling is that elites run things, that we do not have a say in any meaningful sense. . . . Circles and conferences, in contrast, teach active responsibility.
>
> *(Braithwaite, 1999b)*

Braithwaite pointed out that restorative justice provides deliberative engagement opportunities, such as "listening to the arguments and the experiences of others and then reflecting on their needs and aspirations for decent outcomes." He envisioned that restorative practices could help to salvage participatory democracy, to be employed in criminal offending, child protection, bullying incidents, nursing home inspections – and beyond – to problems like unemployment, homelessness and educational failure (1999b).

Family Group Conferences (FGC)

The 1989 Child, Young Persons and Families Act that implemented the "family group conference" was New Zealand's response to the indigenous Maori population's outcry about their children being taken unnecessarily from their homes in child abuse and juvenile delinquency cases. No one could have predicted the revolutionary impact of the new law, now employed in many jurisdictions in North America (National Center on Family Group Decision Making, 2017) and Europe (European Network on Family Group Conferences, 2017). The law granted families the right to meet and develop an alternative plan before any child is removed from his or her home.

The most radical feature of this law is its requirement that, after social workers and other professionals brief the family on the government's expectations and the services and resources available to support their plan – the professionals must leave the room. This "family alone time" or "family private time" is when the extended family and friends of the family have an opportunity to take responsibility for their own loved ones. Never before in the history of the modern interventionist state has a government showed so much respect for the rights and potential strengths of families. (Smull, Wachtel and Wachtel, 2012)

The critical question about family group conferences is similar to the critical question raised by direct democracy. "Can groups of ordinary people make better decisions than professional social workers?" Social workers typically don't think so, but there is a growing body of research which supports the proposition.

A review of research by the American Humane Association (AHA) on the use of FGDM (the North American term for FGC) in child protection found that families did at least as well as the experts, if not better. "When compared to traditional child welfare practices, child safety plans developed collaboratively by families, their support networks, and child welfare system representative are more likely to keep children safe, result in more permanent placements, decrease the need for foster care, maintain family bond and increase family well-being."

The AHA report also found that FGDM create effective solutions for even the most challenging child welfare situations, including neglect, domestic violence, substance abuse and sexual and physical abuse regardless of factors such as age, race, ethnicity or level of involvement in the child welfare system (Merkel-Holguin, 2005).

A similar review undertaken for the government of Scotland was more cautious, finding that "FGC was viewed as an ethically sound and practically effective way of working with families whose strengths and resources often remain untapped by mainstream practice." As for saving money, "[T]he available evidence indicates that FGC is likely to be cost neutral or to provide savings" (Barnsdale and Walker, 2006).

Not surprisingly, the best outcomes were when the conferences were of the highest quality. Eigen Kracht Centrale, a Dutch non-profit organization, has developed a reliable and cost-effective approach that has delivered more than 12,000 conferences – using non-professionals trained as coordinators. Independent coordinators help resist the tendency of the system and its professionals to take back the decision-making power from families.

"Research shows that Eigen Kracht conferences are effective, even in complex situations where youth care is involved, in cases of domestic violence, as well where so-called multi-problem families are concerned. The costs are relatively low, clients are satisfied and in most cases the quality of the plan that families make is good, according to families as well as professionals. Most plans are executed, the problems are solved and escalation is prevented. In many cases, Eigen Kracht is effective as well as cost saving. This is because families use their own resources; instead of applying for residential care, as professionals might do, they arrange for help at home and for foster care instead of residential youth care" (Eigen Kracht Centrale, 2004–2009).

In a cost analysis of a range of cases, from residential care, foster care and non-residential cases, an Eigen Kracht conference dramatically reduces the cost of services. The 'per file' cost of services averaged €8900 (in Euros), including the cost of the conference itself, in cases handled through Eigen Kracht. Comparable cases handled without an FGC averaged €16,180 in services provided per case – almost twice as much (Eigen Kracht Centrale, 2004–2009).

In New Zealand itself, the net effect of the new law, according to former New Zealand Judge Fred McElrea, "was that many expensive institutions were able to be closed, and court sittings dealing with young people were greatly reduced."

New Zealand has moved away from the idea that experts know best. Rather, it engages families, empowering them to guide outcomes. Nor has New Zealand allowed social workers to limit which child gets a conference, resulting in well over 100,000 conferences since the law went into effect. McElrea points out that the outcome has been unquantified, but that it has realized "substantial savings – not only in dollar terms, but also in terms of the unintended damage that those institutions can cause" (2012).

In FGCs, groups of ordinary people can achieve better outcomes than professional social workers.

Restorative conferences

I first became aware of restorative conferences in 1994 when Terry O'Connell, an Australian police officer speaking at an event in Pennsylvania, described how he had been inspired by the New Zealand FGC to invent a conference process that enabled police officers to divert young people from court.

He wrote a script to facilitate restorative conferences between offenders, victims and their family and friends, with a set of questions that seemed to satisfy everyone's needs while establishing boundaries for police officers who might be tempted to participate in the discussion. Police were instructed to just stick to the written script and ask the questions; don't intrude into the discussion by the participants. O'Connell explained that the questions encourage participants to talk about their own experience and thereby foster a shared understanding of how everyone has been affected by an incident. (Wachtel, 1997)

Evaluations of thousands of restorative conferences by varied researchers, in varied settings, with varied offenses and in varied countries, have reliably demonstrated that more than 90 percent of all participants – victims, offenders and their supporters – express satisfaction and a sense of fairness with the process (McCold and Wachtel, 2002). Other research has indicated that restorative conferences reduce re-offending rates (Sherman and Strang, 2007).

Research suggests that victim needs alone provide sufficient justification to hold restorative conferences – even it does not reduce re-offending. Dr. Caroline M. Angel, a lecturer in criminology at the University of Pennsylvania, studied the impact of restorative conferencing on post-traumatic stress symptoms in victims of burglary and robbery in London, UK (Angel, 2005). "The most striking thing was that conferences reduced symptoms of post-traumatic stress disorder," she said. Six months after the crime, victims who participated in conferences reported 40 percent less stress than those who did not participate. "What you have here is a one-time program that's effective in producing benefits for the majority of people . . . I thought that was an incredibly important public health benefit." (Porter, 2006)

Restorative conferences, by engaging groups of ordinary people in participatory learning and decision making, satisfy everyone affected by a crime more reliably than courts or mental health professionals.

Sentencing circles

Judge Barry Stuart of the Yukon Territorial Court in Canada pioneered the sentencing circle in 1992 when he invited the family and friends of Philip Moses to advise him on how to deal with the accused, who lived in their rural community. (Leonardy, 1998: 278). In Stuart's written decision, he pointed out how the criminal justice system feeds on its own failures, absorbing more and more resources as the problems it deals with grow worse. "The state, despite spending at least a quarter of a million dollars on Philip in the past 10 years, has worsened his chances for rehabilitation and lessened public security" (Cayley, 1998: 9).

He described judicial wisdom as an illusion:

> The judge presiding on high, robed to emphasize his authoritative dominance, armed with the power to control the process, is rarely challenged. Lawyers, by their deference, and by standing when addressing the judge, reinforce to the community the judge's pivotal importance. All of this combines to encourage the community to believe judges uniquely and exclusively possess the wisdom and resources to develop a just and viable result. They are so grievously wrong. . . . Whatever their intentions, circuit counsel can never know Philip as well as his family or others within his community.
>
> *(Duhaime, 2012).*

Sentencing circles have not been widely implemented nor has there been much evaluation. However, Judge Barry Stuart's own experience demonstrated that when judges deal with offenders whom they hardly know, groups of ordinary people can achieve better outcomes than court professionals.

Fair process

When authorities do things *with* people, whether reactively – to deal with crisis – or proactively, the results are better than when those in charge do things *to* people or *for* people – without their engagement. This fundamental thesis is evident in a *Harvard Business Review* article about the concept of *fair process* producing effective outcomes in business organizations (Kim and Mauborgne, 1997).

Professors Kim and Maugborne developed the concept of fair process, whose central idea is that "individuals are most likely to trust and cooperate freely with systems – whether they themselves win or lose by those systems – when fair process is observed."

The three principles of fair process are:

- Engagement – involving individuals in decisions that affect them, by listening to their views and genuinely taking their opinions into account
- Explanation – explaining the reasoning behind a decision to everyone who has been involved or who is affected by it
- Expectation clarity – making sure that everyone clearly understands a decision and what is expected of them in the future

Fair process relates to how leaders handle their authority in all kinds of professions and roles, from parents and teachers to managers and administrators. The original 1997 "Fair Process" article in *Harvard Business Review* was based on research into strategic decision making in 19 multinational companies (Kim and Maugborne, 1997).

The research concluded, "Managers who believed the company's processes were fair displayed a high level of trust and commitment, which in turn engendered active cooperation. Conversely, when managers felt fair process was absent, they hoarded ideas and dragged their feet."

In subsequent field research, the authors identified the three principles of fair process and affirmed their findings. Two contrasting case studies from their research illustrate the significance of restorative practices values in organizations:

Volkswagen – In the summer of 1992, at Volkswagen's Puebla, Mexico, manufacturing facility, workers turned down a contract recommended both by their union and the company, despite a generous 20 percent wage increase offer. The "union's leaders had not involved employees in discussions about the contract's terms," especially a number of unexplained work rule changes that the workers feared. A massive walkout cost the company about 10 million dollars per day, and disrupted its optimistic plans for the US market.

Siemens – On the other hand, troubled Siemens Nixdorf Informationssysteme had cut 17,000 jobs by 1994, when Gerhard Schulmeyer, the new CEO, held a series of meetings, large and small. In these, he personally explained to 11,000 of the company's remaining 32,000 employees the bleak outlook and the need to make deep cuts. He asked for volunteers to come up with ideas to save the company.

The initial group of 30 volunteers grew to 9,000 employees and managers who met mostly after business hours, often until midnight. They offered their ideas to executives, who could choose to fund them or not. Although 20 to 30 percent of their ideas were rejected, the executives explained the reasons for their decisions, so people felt the process was fair. By the next year, the company was operating in the black again and employee satisfaction had doubled, despite the drastic changes under way – "a transformation notable in European corporate history (Kim and Maugborne, 1997)."

These two contrasting case studies illustrate the advantages of engaging the collective intelligence of large groups of ordinary people in the decision-making process.

The wisdom of crowds

Perhaps the most compelling argument for the benefits of large-group decision making comes from author James Surowiecki in *The Wisdom of Crowds*, which both *Forbes* and *Business Week* magazines chose as "best business book of 2004." (Library Thing website, 2017, Forbes.com, 2004)

Surowiecki claims that large groups, given the right conditions, make better decisions than experts. He describes the surprising wisdom of large groups – from the famous 1906 county fair ox-weight-guessing contest, reported by British scientist Francis Galton, in which the average of the 787 individual guesses was exactly right, better than any expert guess – to stock index funds which rely on the collective decisions of buyers and sellers that annually outperform more than half of all professional stock-pickers. It is as if, when we collate all the individual decisions of a great many human beings, we integrate their strengths, weaknesses and diverse opinions to achieve a more accurate perspective. It is like stringing together a large number of desktop computers to create a powerful supercomputer.

Surowiecki defined the three critical conditions for effective large-group decision making:

- Diversity of opinion
- Independence of judgement
- Decentralized decision making

Ironically, political parties cannot satisfy any of those three critical conditions. They cannot allow diversity, independence or decentralization without losing control of legislative decision making.

Representing a very narrow demographic, the average state legislator in the United States is a white male Protestant in his sixties with a graduate degree and a business background (Kurtz, 2015). In the current U.S. Congress, more than half of all senators and more than a third of all representatives are lawyers (Manning, 2016). The American Democratic and Republican parties are highly centralized and demand conformity from the lawmakers they support. In every legislative body in America, there is a specialized party official called the "whip," whose job is to keep individual legislators from exercising their own judgement and straying from their political party's position on any issue.

Because of the dominance of political parties, no American legislature – and presumably no legislature anywhere in the world – satisfies the three critical criteria necessary for good large-group decision making.

Deliberative polling

Surowiecki directs us to the remarkable work of James Fishkin, whose deliberative polling experiments come closest to demonstrating the role of a citizen legislature (2004: 259–272).

Are ordinary people competent to serve as legislators, given that so many voters seem to make their choices based on superficial knowledge and the influence of attack ads? James Fishkin's Deliberative Polling research brings people together in what might be described as "weekend legislative sessions" and demonstrates how Surowiecki's three conditions allow large groups of ordinary citizens to make thoughtful and informed decisions about complex issues.

While it is unlikely that we will choose our legislatures by lottery anytime in the foreseeable future, greater use of Deliberative Polling can move governance toward true representation. Two stories illustrate the potential and the limitations of Deliberative Polling in developing public policy.

In 1996 in Texas – a leading gas and oil state – Fishkin was asked to organize a Deliberative Poll within eight rural electric districts, surveying a randomly selected sample of customers on their opinions about wind and solar power.

First polled by telephone, each respondent was invited to a gathering, in which they heard from speakers with varied contrasting views on alternative energy and had the chance to ask questions. Then they met in small groups to have discussions.

In advance of the event, they were sent briefing books that gave them time to study a variety of perspectives, and at the end of the weekend, they were asked to vote again. What was remarkable was that participants – once they had a chance to study the issues – shifted their opinion in a way no one had anticipated: they favoured paying higher rates for electricity if it comes from alternative energy.

On the other hand, a 2012 Deliberative Poll about nuclear energy in Japan was ignored when the political party that sponsored the poll lost the next election. This illustrates the limits of authentic public decision making when professional politicians stay in control.

Having conducted more than 70 polls in 24 countries, Fishkin's participant groups range in size from 200 to as high as 466 – equivalent to many legislative bodies.

Fishkin believes that Deliberative Polling would be a productive way to move beyond America's polarized politics. Fishkin says:

> It works best when you have hard choices. . . . Despite what you see and read, this is not a nation of extremists. What you see on TV, and in most polling, is an impersonation of public opinion. The actual public isn't really like that, especially when it is given something more than sound bites and distorted political messaging. If you give people real choices and real consequences, they will make real decisions.
>
> *(Klein, 2010)*

The fear most expressed by critics of citizen legislators is that "reason and evidence won't change our minds." Research results from a variety of experiments indicate that even after learning "the truth," participants often reject the evidence and cling to their unfounded opinions (Kolbert, 2017). From the unscientific questioning of immunization against diseases to White House spokesperson Kellyanne Conway's assertion of "alternative facts," thoughtful reasoning seems to be giving way to "fake news."

The ability of individuals to step outside their "web of belief" (Quine and Ulliane, 1978) and accept new facts is hindered by our loyalty to the group in which see ourselves. Truth often depends on context. Citizens who are chosen to be part of a deliberative democracy experiment, however, seem to see themselves in a new context and take their responsibility very seriously. They rise above partisanship and show a willingness to pursue the truth, even if it clashes with their existing beliefs.

"The public is very smart if you give it a chance," says Fishkin, after 20 years of deliberative democracy. "If people think their voice actually matters, they'll do the hard work, really study their briefing books, ask the experts smart questions and then make tough decisions. When they hear the experts disagreeing, they're forced to think for themselves. About 70% change their minds in the process." (Klein, 2010)

Concluding thoughts: true representation projects

U.S. President George Washington was right. As he predicted in 1796, political parties have become the engines by which cunning, ambitious, and unprincipled men have usurped for themselves the reins of government – not only in America but around the globe. However, a growing body of evidence from restorative practices and related disciplines suggests that, under the right conditions, ordinary people can make better decisions than professional politicians. Sortition or election by lot, which originated in ancient Greece, may prove to be the best way for modern democracies to achieve true representation.

Congruent with this Handbook's international ambition for a restorative justice movement that stretches the boundaries of the field, sortition is a natural extension of restorative practice principles. It moves the field beyond its widely known use in criminal justice and school settings to new frontiers. Doing things "with" people, rather than "to" them or "for" them, sortition engages people directly in making their own decisions instead of relying on professionals chosen by traditional adversarial elections that foster conflict, misunderstanding and gridlock.

True representation projects are needed to advocate for the potential uses of sortition demonstrated by James Fishkin's experiments and other means of engaging citizens directly in decision making, accompanied by thoughtful evaluation. Although sortition represents a radical change in modern democracy – with unknown consequences – there are many opportunities to study the process, not just in government, but in organizations, both non-profit and profit-making.

Consider, for example, the silly election conducted by a large national charitable organization to which I belong. The leadership sent me a ballot with the names and brief biographies of several candidates for the organization's board of directors and asked me to vote for my preferred candidates. Based on their written description only, I still have no meaningful idea who these people are – really.

It's pretty much the same with the political candidates in elections. Who has time to learn all the names and backgrounds of all the local, state and national candidates for all the varied offices? We must go to work every day, run our errands, look after our families. Further complicating our learning are information sources that contradict one another in an era of "fake news." Who has the time or means to make knowledgeable choices in elections – really?

On the other hand, what if the national organization selected a random sample of a couple of hundred of its members to serve as an electoral committee. The group would consider its own nominees, as well as suggestions from the organization's leadership. The committee would hear the candidates speak, ask questions and in small groups discuss the merits of the respective board members. On the basis of actual face-to-face meetings (using digital media to make the process affordable), and thoughtful discussion, a truly representative group of members would choose the board.

Or perhaps the national organization could ask a representative group of members to ponder policy issues that are otherwise confined to discussion by the board members. The discussions can be livestreamed to an audience of interested members who might be polled or permitted to submit written comments.

My own efforts, described in my BuildingANewReality.com website, will include in-person and online groups convened to discuss "True Representation" and other ways in which restorative practices can be applied in new areas, including governance, enterprise and non-school learning. We hope to engage interested participants by asking them to guide the direction of future conversations, including possible action steps that they may want to support. We will experiment with the new large-meeting technology that allows collaborative conversations without anyone leaving their home (Wachtel, 2017).

Similarly, an electoral committee of stockholders of a profit-making corporation might be selected randomly to carry out the selection of the board of directors. Currently in large corporations, the CEO and the board serve their own interests, instead of those of the stockholders. The median annual pay for corporate board members in the US is now a quarter of a million dollars per year, although board members work less than five hours per week, with many board members serving on multiple corporate boards. It's evident that stockholders lack true representation as well (Pfeiffer and Wallack, 2015).

In Northeast Friesland, on Netherlands' northern coast, the Scionsburg Hospital went bankrupt in 2014, much to the dismay of the residents of the province. Anke Siegers was hired to mediate among the varied interest groups because there was a crisis and no apparent solution. To ensure that the negative spiral of public opinion could be broken, she insisted on a "bottom-up" process, called "Community Processing," so that all stakeholders were directly involved, in a way that allowed everyone to participate in and to observe the process.

Anke Siegers and her colleagues created 22 interest groups based on needs and values, including hospital administration, insurance companies, local government, staff and community. Livestream technology made it possible for 16,000 people to watch the 14-hour marathon negotiation by the 22 representatives, which produced a detailed plan signed by all parties. The transparency of the process, with everyone able to observe the negotiation by video, prevented the kind of rebellion that all too often occurs, for example, among the members of a union, who reject the decision of their representatives because they were not privy to the ups and downs of the negotiation. On January 26, 2015, the hospital reopened with the positive support of all its stakeholders, a remarkable outcome in a world where conflicting views are rarely reconciled in a satisfying and lasting way (Wachtel, 2017)

In a similar fashion, local, state and national governments can randomly select representative groups to deliberate on especially contentious problems and make recommendations for the actual legislature. The deliberative poll in Texas, mentioned earlier, convened a representative group of citizens from eight rural electric districts. The fact that they chose alternative energy as a favoured option encouraged Texas, known as the gas and oil state, to go from last to first in wind power among the 50 US states (Wachtel, 2017).

In another type of experiment in the United States, the government might create a single-purpose randomly selected legislature of 435 representatives, one from each congressional district, as a demonstration project, with funding and staff all dedicated to creating legislation on a single controversial issue – like gun control. The commission process used in 2005 to deal with a controversial list of US military base closings only allowed Congress the option of a "yes" or "no" vote on the commission's proposed list. Such an experimental single-issue, single-house lottocratic body could be created with a similar mandate. Congress would have to accept or reject the proposed legislation without amendment. (Wachtel, 2017).

Consistent with favourable research outcomes with restorative conferences, family group conferences, business management and in deliberative democracy experiments – engagement and participatory decision making by ordinary citizens will likely prove more effective than decisions by professional politicians. After all, we need only to remind ourselves that a new reality in governance would not be competing with perfection. The democratic process in countries around the world is no longer a deliberation. Rather, it is an auction.

References

Angel, C.M. 2005. Crime Victims Meet their Offenders: Testing the Impact of Restorative Justice Conferences on Victims' Post-traumatic Stress Symptoms. [Dissertation], University of Pennsylvania. Abstract retrieved from http://repository.upenn.edu/dissertations/AAI3165634/

Barnsdale, L. and Walker, M. 2006. *Examining the Use and Impact of Family Group Conferencing: Executive Summary*. Edinburgh, Scotland: Scottish Executive. Available at www.scotland.gov.uk/Publications/2007/03/26093721/2

Braithwaite, J. 1999a. Restorative Justice Is Republican Justice. In G. Bazemore and L. Walgrave (eds.) *Restorative Juvenile Justice: Repairing the Harm of Youth Crime*. Monsey, NY: Criminal Justice Press, pp. 103–126.

Braithwaite, J., August 5–7, 1999b. Democracy, Community and Problem Solving. *Proceedings of the Building Strong Partnerships Conference*, Burlington, VT. Available at www.iirp.edu/eforum-archive/4227-democracy-community-and-problem-solving

Braithwaite, J. 2017. Criminal Justice That Revives Republican Democracy, *Northwestern University Law Review*, 111(6): 1507–1524.

Cayley, D. 1998. *The Expanding Prison: The Crisis in Crime and Punishment and the Search for Alternatives*. Toronto: House of Anansi Press.

Duhaime, L., 2012. *The Good and the Bad: Judge Stuart's R v. Moses Legacy*. 22 December. Available at www.duhaime.org/LawMag/LawArticle-1252/The-Good-and-the-Bad-Judge-Stuarts-R-v-Moses-Legacy.aspx.

Eigen Kracht Centrale. 2004–2009. Netherlands Website. Research was originally reported in English but page is not currently accessible. Available at www.eigen-kracht.nl/what-we-do/

European Network on Family Group Conference. Available at www.fgcnetwork.eu/en/the-network/. Forbes.com. 8 December 2004.

Forbes.com's Business Books of the Year. Available at www.forbes.com/2004/12/08/cx_da_1208bizbooks.html

Guerrero, A. A. 2014. Against Elections: The Lottocratic Alternative, *Philosophy & Public Affairs*, 42: 135–178.

Hulse, C., 2016. Steve Israel of New York, a top House Democrat, Won't Seek Re-Election, *The New York Times*. 5 January. Available at http://nyti.ms/29WS4NW

Kaiser, R. G. 2009. *So Damn Much Money: The Triumph of Lobbying and the Corrosion of American Government*. New York: Vintage Books.

Kim, W.C. & Mauborgne, R. 1997. Fair Process: Managing in the Knowledge Economy, *Harvard Business Review*, 75(4): 65–75.

Klein, J. 2010. How Can a Democracy Solve Tough Problems?, *New York Time Magazine*, 2 September.

Kolbert, E. 2017. That's What You Think, *New York The New Yorker*, 27 February.

Kurtz, K., 2015. *State Legislatures Magazine*. Washington, DC: National Conference of State Legislatures. 1 December. Available at www.ncsl.org/research/about-state-legislatures/who-we-elect.aspx

Leonardy, M. 1998. *First Nations Criminal Jurisdiction in Canada*. Saskatoon: Native Law Centre.

Library Thing Website. 2017. Business Week Top Ten Books of the Year. Available at www.librarything.com/bookaward/Business+Week+Top+Ten+Books+of+the+Year

Libin, K. 2009. *Sentencing Circles For Aboriginals: Good Justice?* Toronto: National Post, Available at www.nationalpost.com/news/story.html?id=1337495&__federated=1

Manning, J., 2016. *Membership of the 114th Congress: A Profile*. Washington, DC: Congressional Research Service, 5 December.

McCold, P. and Wachtel, T. 2002. Restorative Justice Theory Validation (From Restorative Justice: Theoretical Foundations. In E. Weitekamp and H.J. Kerner (eds.) *Restorative Justice in Context: International Practice and Directions*. Cullompton: Willan, pp. 110–142.

McElrea, F.W.M., 2012. Twenty Years of Restorative Justice in New Zealand. 10 January. Available at www.tikkun.org/nextgen/twenty-years-of-restorative-justice-in-new-zealand

Merkel-Holguin, L. 2005. FGDM: An Evidence-Based Decision-Making Process in Child Welfare, *Protecting Children*, 10(4): 2–3

National Center for Family Group Decision-Making. Available at www.ucdenver.edu/academics/colleges/medicalschool/departments/pediatrics/subs/can/FGDM/Pages/FGDM.aspx

Pew Research Center. 2017. *Public Trust in Government: 1958–2017*. Washington, DC, 3 May. Available at www.people-press.org/2017/05/03/public-trust-in-government-1958-2017/

Pfeiffer, S. and Wallack, T. 2015. The Board Game: Few Hours, Soaring Pay For Corporate Board Members. *The Boston Globe*, 2 December. Available at www.bostonglobe.com/business/2015/12/01/good-work-you-can-get-corporate-directors-among-highest-paid-part-time-employees-america/rYHPP7ozPXU0AG8VSo37MM/story.html

Porter, A. 2006. *Restorative Conferences Reduce Trauma from Crime, Study Shows*. Bethlehem, Pennsylvania: International Institute for Restorative Practices eForum. Available at www.iirp.edu/eforum-archive/4348-restorative-conferences-reduce-trauma-from-crime-study-shows

Quine, W.V. and Ullian, J.S. 1978. *The Web of Belief*. Columbus, OH: McGraw Hill Education.

Sherman, L. and Strang, H. 2007. *Restorative Justice: The Evidence*. London: The Smith Institute. Available at www.iirp.edu/pdf/RJ_full_report.pdf

Smull, E., Wachtel, J. and Wachtel, T. 2012. *Family Power: Engaging and Collaborating with Families*. Bethlehem, PA: International Institute for Restorative Practices.

Surowiecki, J. 2004. *The Wisdom of Crowds*. New York: Doubleday.

Transparency International. 2013. *Global Corruption Barometer Report*. Berlin, Germany. Available at www.transparency.org/gcb2013/report

UPI Archive. 1984. Former Congressmen Criticize Congress, 1 January. Available at www.upi.com/Archives/1984/01/01/Former-congressmen-criticize-Congress/6507441781200/

Van Reybrouck, D. 2013. *Against Elections: The Case for Democracy*. London: The Bodley Head.

Wachtel, T. 1997. *Real Justice*. Pipersville, PA: The Piper's Press

Wachtel, T. 2017. *BuildingANewReality.com* website. Pipersville, PA.

Washington, G., 1796. Farewell Address, 19 September. Available at http://avalon.law.yale.edu/18th_century/washing.asp

Wikipedia, Defense Base Realignment and Closure Act of 1990. Available at http://bit.ly/1Nsp9PW.

28

The best is yet to come

Unlocking the true potential of restorative practice

Terry O'Connell

Introduction

Although we assume that for any practice to be effective it must be rigorous and explicit, that largely has not been the norm within the restorative justice or restorative practices movement. Many practitioners struggle to provide a clear rationale for the processes they use or an explanation for why the process works and is capable of consistent and reasonably predictable outcomes.

It is important to briefly examine where the restorative movement is now and what has changed since the 'restorative' word first entered the criminal justice lexicon. Almost two decades ago McCold (2000: 2) observed that restorative justice had something unusual and universal to offer:

> The evolution of restorative justice as a paradigm is more akin to a process of discovery rather than invention. Practice has always led the theoretical developments, as a kind of social physics was being uncovered. Facilitators of restorative processes regularly observe a personal and social transformation occur during the course of the process. There is often the strong sense that something significant is occurring which has very little to do with the facilitator and operates at a subconscious level among the participants. Restorative processes create the possibility for the physics of this social transformation to operate.

Daly (2015: 3) confirmed McCold's observation:

> The popularity of the idea has affected a broad range of humanities and social science disciplines (including law, linguistics, politics, psychology, sociology, philosophy, religious studies, international relations, as well as criminology and criminal justice). Thus, analysis of definitions, practices, and effects takes different forms, depending on analyst's disciplinary field and research interest.

The past 20 years have witnessed an exponential increase in the use of restorative processes. Those interested tend to view them as a technique or strategy. A few see this practice as integral to everything they do (Gavrielides, 2007). The former group see restorative practice as another 'tool', whereas the latter group view restorative practice as their 'tool box'.

The basic prerequisites for any practice to be considered explicit involve identifying a particular need and then clarifying how and why a particular practice is able to provide predictable outcomes.

To support this contention, the chapter will explore four key ideas:

1   Limitation of existing restorative practices
2   The significance of the Wagga restorative experience
3   Development of an explicit restorative practice framework
4   Restorative case studies

Limitation of existing restorative practices

The main limitation of most restorative practice is its lack of explicitness. The significant interest shown by such diverse disciplines/professions suggests that each share a common challenge, how to effectively engage others. Most practitioners struggle when asked about what restorative processes have to offer. Few practitioners are able to provide a simple explanation to a relatively straightforward question. I consistently hear the same response: 'I have never been asked that question before.' I suspect their initial interest in restorative was its innate appeal, one that resonated strongly with a belief in human dignity.

'What influences your practice, and how you practise?' This question challenges practitioners. Practice (noun) meaning is influenced by specific elements or characteristics:

*   Philosophy
*   Values and beliefs
*   Theory
*   Clarity on outcomes

Explicit[1] practice is when a practitioner is able to provide a detailed explanation of the constituent elements of his or her toolbox and how these then influence how they practise (verb). It is not implied that implicit practice doesn't work but instead suggests that its potential is limited. Adding restorative to any existing practice that is *implicit* won't help it to become *explicit*.

Donald (2004: 7) observed that:

> practitioners in family work were able to articulate what works but often unable to articulate why and therefore unable easily to replicate what works.

A consequence of the limitation of implicit restorative practice is definitional confusion and practice that lacks rigour, coherence and congruence. Restorative practice is often discussed in isolation to (practitioners') existing practice and seen as an alternate with a strong 'behavioural' focus. Daly (2015) argues that the question of restorative justice's future is dependent upon it

---

1 Explicit means 'stated clearly and in detail, leaving no room for confusion or doubt' [www.google.com. au/?gws_rd=ssl#q=explicit+meaning].

being defined concretely as *a justice mechanism*. I suggest that definitional issues are integral to explicit practice and that implicit practice presents the greatest challenge to restorative practice realising its potential.

The restorative literature, however, consistently reports encouraging outcomes, something that Daly (2015: 2) observed:

> [D]espite no 'clear-cut definition,' outcomes are 'very promising.' Whatever could this mean? Put another way, over two decades of research on RJ show apparently 'promising' outcomes for a justice activity that cannot be defined.

I argue that the problem has to do with implicit practice, not just definitional clarity. This raises an issue about the research and development phase of restorative processes so far. Unlike Daly, I think it has hardly begun. I surveyed (O'Connell, 2015) 15 experienced restorative practitioners[2]:

* How do you define restorative justice/practice?
* If your definition has changed over time what has influenced those changes?
* What are the key words you believe are essential in any definition of restorative justice/ practice?

Respondents did not mention victims or offenders (Gavrielides, 2015). Most talked about 'restorative' being integral to their daily lives, both personally and professionally. Most said that initially restorative was viewed as a strategy, but that over time they have come to realise that it was integral to their practice.

Most mentioned the following words in their definition: relationships, dialogue, safety, harm and connections. One definition strongly resonated with my own thinking and practice. Mark Vander Vennen[3] provided the following definition:

> Restorative Practice is a way of thinking and being, focused on creating safe spaces for real conversations that deepen relationship and create stronger, more connected communities.

In what continues to be an evolving restorative landscape, ambiguity will always exist in relation to definitions,[4] programmes and models when (restorative) practice is not explicit. The following issues have added to this confusion:

* Practice preceding theory
* Questionable working assumptions
* Constraints of existing systems and structures
* Restorative viewed as an alternate
* Interdisciplinary practice contradictions
* Failure to recognise non-contemporary practice

2 From a variety of disciplines – teachers, police, counsellors, youth workers, psychologists, social workers, correctional officers, and so on.
3 Mark Vander Vennen is the Executive Director of the Shalem Mental Health Network in Ontario, Canada.
4 It is important to note that there is a strong view that RJ might not benefit from definitions (see Gavrielides, www.theogavrielides.com/1st-international-symposium-on-rj)

The next section looks at how a particular restorative experience became the catalyst for the development of a unique and explicit restorative practice framework.

The significance of the Wagga restorative experience

Wagga Wagga is a New South Wales regional city roughly at the midpoint between Sydney and Melbourne. It became well known in the 1990s as the Australian town where police developed a restorative justice approach for dealing with young offenders. It is widely accepted that this development owes its inspiration to New Zealand where Family Group Conferences were legislated in the late 1980s (Thorsborne, 2016).

It is, however, important to revisit this history because the restorative developments in Wagga were primarily about policing reform (Moore, 1997). The young offender focus was an example of the change process that had considerable traction prior to any knowledge of the New Zealand juvenile justice reform (McDonald, J and Ireland, S 1990). Moore (1997) recognised this and suggested that Wagga was probably the only policing jurisdiction in New South Wales capable of 'making this happen.'

It was the process used to engage all stakeholders that was at the heart of Wagga's success. This process was heavily influenced by my personal policing style. Prior to providing an explanation of why this was so, the following quote from Justice James Wood (1997) provides an insight into the culture within the NSW Police Service at the time the Wagga experience was unfolding:

> At the core of many of the problems that have emerged lies the traditional approach of the Service to its staff: they have largely been developed in a conditioned, inward-looking environment which has been characterised by command and control, autocracy and suspicion of new ideas.

Police were highly sceptical and well versed in sabotaging any attempt at reform. Police history is replete with failed attempts at change: community policing, problem-solving policing and many more (Bradley, 1996). What may surprise is my claim that the Wagga restorative experience with young offenders was always going to happen. We had already developed a principled operating framework to inform and guide our practice when dealing with young offenders well before hearing about the New Zealand restorative developments (MacDonald and Ireland, 1990). It confirmed what I intuitively knew about 'process'.

The question is often asked, 'How did you get to work out the script?'[5] The assumption beginning that I had replicated the New Zealand conference protocols. This was not so, as I had no knowledge of their protocols. Rather, with six months of facilitating many restorative cautions, I had developed a 'conference script' that remains largely unchanged[6] today. I suggest the answer has a lot to do with 'intuitiveness' that came from my life experiences as well as what I describe as a universal 'innateness' about the human condition.

Setting the scene – restorative formation

One of ten children, I was the youngest boy, son of a hard-working (railway) engine driver. My first memorable restorative encounter was as a nine-year-old when my dad took me to

---

5 A script prescribes the order of proceedings and the questions asked in a restorative conference. 'Unscripted' conferences are less structured, although technically the proceedings are still guided by some form of script.
6 The first transcripts of conferences recorded by Moore reveal a consistent use of script protocols.

the neighbour so I could apologise for lobbing a firecracker in my neighbour's yard. I listened, cried and said sorry. I look back on what I now realise was a great learning opportunity. My first serious 'formal' restorative policing encounter happened in June 1973. I was responding to a fight in a community hall. I managed to remove Gary (14 years) from the hall. In the process Gary 'king hit' me, knocking me to the concrete path.

What happened next, in hindsight, has proven to be a watershed moment in my policing. Gary was a troubled young lad who had been charged on two previous occasions with assault. He was on a 'good behaviour' bond – a further breach would have resulted in juvenile detention for at least 12 months. I took Gary to his home, and the following afternoon met him and his mum at the police station. We were seated on three chairs in a very small room sitting close to one another in a circle. Gary's mum burst into tears when she noticed my bruised right eye. Gary's head was down.

I clearly remember the questions I asked. The first was directed at Gary's mum, 'What has this been like for you?' It evoked an immediate outpouring of painful emotions. 'Tell me about Gary.' His mother talked about Gary growing up and then mentioned that he had 'lost it' after his father had been killed some 14 months earlier. I turned to Gary, who at this stage was in tears. 'Tell me about your dad.' Gary talked about his dad and how he (Gary) struggled to deal with the pain of losing his dad. We then talked about what happened the previous night.

He said how deeply ashamed he felt and apologised. Gary said that for the first time he realised how he had hurt the person he most loved, his mother. The issue of greatest concern for his mum was trust. We then talked about putting in place something that would help Gary succeed so that he could prove to himself, his mum and me that he could be trusted. Some 15 years later, I bumped into Gary at a football reunion in the same community hall where he had assaulted me. Gary thanked me for helping him turn his life around. He was now a 29-year-old father of two with a good job – life was good.

The original encounter with Gary unsurprisingly attracted lots of comment and interest from my police colleagues. During my nearly 30 years of policing, I learned that dialogue and persuasion delivered consistently better outcomes than confrontation and fear (Tyler, 2006). I can recall on at least five occasions being assaulted in the course of my policing duties, yet somehow I managed to deal with each incident without resorting to a formal charge.

Relational engagement and policing reform

Joining the New South Wales Police Service just after my twenty-first birthday was an important decision. I had left school when I was 14, successfully completed an electrical trade and learned a lot about life as I worked in remote locations, often in harsh conditions. Like most, I felt policing was a career where it was possible to make a difference in the lives of others.

In 1990, following my promotion, I was appointed the Sergeant in Charge of the Wagga Community Beat Policing Unit. I had responsibility for 12 constables and a sergeant. I had just completed a Bachelor of Arts (Community Social Welfare) at the local Charles Sturt University. I was also a senior elected official of the largest Australian police union (16,000 members).

My appointment was an ideal opportunity to create a different policing experience. I knew that respectful dialogue was critical to engagement. Rather than direct, I facilitated. Our first two days as a newly formed Unit involved circle processes. Initially each staff member was asked to respond to a number of questions, some of a personal nature and then generally about their policing experiences.

This proved significant. It was the first time that these police had been asked for their views about policing. More importantly, they learned how to be vulnerable with one another through sharing personal information and venting their frustrations[7] about their day-to-day policing challenges. I had designed a two-day schedule so that the group could learn how to engage with one another, and importantly, collaborate on the development of an operational blueprint to guide our group's activities over the next two years.

Youth crime was identified as a priority. I then questioned them about this issue:

- How are we presently dealing with this issue?
- What is working and what is not?
- What needs to change to begin addressing this issue?

This discussion[8] revealed that the group felt that the courts were far too lenient. This began another round of questions:

- How does increasing the punishment help young people to make better choices?
- What are the factors that influence offending?
- What is the offender and victim experience of the court process?
- What do we need to change?
- What can we change?

We decided to survey all Wagga police in order to gauge their perceptions about youth crime and how to improve police responses. Sixty surveys were circulated, and all were returned. Most police felt the courts were not 'tough enough'. Within two weeks, we had developed an Operational Strategic Plan.

One important strategy involved obtaining a 'policing mandate' from the Wagga community. I coordinated the planning and implementation of this event that took place within our first three months. Over 300 community members and police participated. Importantly, each member of our Unit had the responsibility to research, plan and facilitate one session. The final session was dedicated to having the community identify the priorities it wanted our Unit to focus on over the next two years. Youth crime was the number-one priority.

As I look back, I recognised the importance of 'changing' the conversation with my colleagues. New stories were being told. I had created an environment that allowed police to:

- Make sense and meaning of policing;
- Work out what was most important in how they viewed policing;
- Identify what needed to change in policing, and their part in this change process;
- Learn how to build and sustain healthy collegial relationships.

Consolidating the Wagga script

The script was a guide to assist others to facilitate restorative meetings involving victims, juvenile offenders and families following a crime. It provided a structure for proceedings: when participants should be invited to speak and the questions that should be asked. The script delivered consistently similar and positive outcomes regardless of the nature of the incident, number of participants involved or other variables. Early evidence showed that it was working (O'Connell, 1993; Moore and O'Connell, 1994).

---

7 Their frustrations were largely about the experience of working in a 'toxic' police culture.
8 The discussion revealed previously unstated assumptions.

Why it worked, however, was not clear. This changed following the introduction of two complementary theories. The first involved the notion of 'reintegrative shaming' developed by John Braithwaite (1989), who advocated utilising shame in a positive and constructive way with a focus on strengthening an offender's links to his or her community. Key was communicating the unacceptability of the behaviour whilst at the same time acknowledging the intrinsic worth of the individual.

Masters (1997: 15) suggested:

> [W]ithin reintegrative shaming, maintaining a positive regard for oneself, for one's identity, rests upon other people. Reintegrative shaming draws from social psychology; resting on the uncontroversial statement that each and every person's identity is primarily constructed from how other people treat them.

Braithwaite suggested that as individuals, we are interdependent, constantly seeking validation and approval from those around us. We now had a way to explain the communitarian nature of the Wagga experiment. Braithwaite's theory emphasised a number of key points that supported the script's protocols:

- Social disapproval is strongest from significant others.
- Reintegration involves respectful and inclusive rituals.
- It is important to distinguish between behaviour and the person.

Braithwaite's theory, however, failed to provide an adequate explanation of shame as an emotion (Scheff and Retzinger, 1994), something that Braithwaite (1998: 20) acknowledged:

> [A] profound deficiency of Braithwaite's (1989) theory is that is it just a theory of shaming, with the emotion of shame left sadly under theorised.

Silvan Tomkins's *Psychology of Affects* (Nathanson, 1992) provided a theory that explained why we observed a consistent and similar pattern of emotions in every restorative encounter. Moore's (1993) discovery was an important step towards understanding why the 'script' worked:

> [W]e have found a psychological theory that fits the empirical evidence from conferences. It is a theory that provides a sophisticated psychological counterpart to the theory of reintegrative shaming; it helps to explain why the role of shame in the conference is positive and constructive rather than oppressive.

Silvan Tomkins's work has dominated theoretical discussion on restorative processes (Nathanson, 1992; Kelly, 2012; George, 2014; Thorsborne, 2016). It is detailed and can be difficult to understand. I intend to offer a very rudimentary explanation of those aspects of Tomkins's theory that have helped my practice evolve.

Basically, the 'central blueprint' Tomkins developed provides a set of (biological) rules that shape and govern our emotional well-being. He says we are hardwired to experience innate affects. Tomkins contends we are at our emotional best when we are able to:

1   Maximise positive affects.
2   Minimise negative affects.

3   Maximise the expression of affect.
4   Maximise the power and ability to do more of 1–3

(Kelly, 2009)

Tomkins identified nine affects:

- Interest-Excitement
- Enjoyment-Joy
- Surprise-Startle
- Distress-Anguish
- Anger-Rage
- Fear-Terror
- Disgust
- Dissmell
- Shame-Humiliation

Shame is the 'affect' that lets us know that something has interrupted our positive affects of interest and/or enjoyment (Kelly, 2012). Shame is the central social regulator that according to Nathanson (1992) draws our attention to something we don't want to know about ourselves. Dealt with positively, shame is an opportunity for growth. Nathanson's Compass of Shame describes how we react negatively to shame – each pole involves specific behaviours intended to reduce or manage the shame feeling:

- Withdrawal (isolating oneself; not speaking)
- Avoidance (addictive behaviours – drugs/alcohol; gambling)
- Attack Self (self-loathing; self-harm)
- Attack Others (Violence; blame others)

As our thinking and practice evolved towards a universal vision for restorative processes, understanding shame has proven to be the 'game changer'.

Nathanson's (1992) community 'blueprint' (adapted from Tomkins's blueprint) suggests that community does best when it is able to:

1   Share and reduce negative emotions (best achieved by listening and acknowledging);
2   Share and promote positive emotions (achieved by affirming);
3   Encourage expression of emotions in order to experience 1 & 2; and
4   Do more of 1, 2 and 3 (essential for building and maintaining good relationships).

The script's structure, sequencing and nature of the questions was shown to satisfy those conditions prescribed in each blueprint.

Questions asked of wrongdoer:

- What happened?
- What were you thinking at the time?
- What have you thought about since?
- Who has been affected by what you did?
- In what way?
- What do you think you need to do to make things right?

Questions asked of other participants:

- What did you think when you realised what had happened?
- What impact has this incident had on you and others?
- What has been the hardest thing for you?
- What do you think needs to happen to make things right?

The diagram in Figure 28.1 shows the alignment between the theories and the script protocols.

The Wagga script is now referred to as the IIRP Conference script (O'Connell et al., 1999). It is the only restorative conference facilitator script with an explicit theoretical practice foundation and validated by empirical evidence (McCold, 2000). The next section will explore Wagga's broader influence in the development of an explicit restorative practice framework

Development of an explicit restorative practice framework

In the mid-1990s, restorative conferences were being embraced in many countries. I was often asked about the high conference participation rates in Wagga conferences and how I managed to 'convince' people to participate. These questions indicated two things: facilitators believed that the conference process was where the 'magic' happened and that it was the art of persuasion that was going to influence participation rates.

It took nearly 12 months after I had developed the 'script' to realise that success of the conferences I facilitated was built on preparation prior to the meeting. Using the questions (from the script), I was able to 'restoratively' engage participants. The conference became a seamless extension of that (preparation) process. It was never likely to fail, as participants had already experienced the power of the restorative questions. Importantly, it meant that the 'restorative

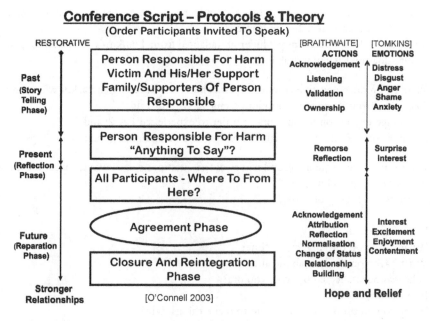

Figure 28.1 Conference script – protocols and theory

experience' was available to all, not just those who participated in a conference. It became clear to me that the restorative questions had enormous potential, well beyond the conference process.

In early 2000, I printed thousands of (business-sized) cards with the restorative questions on both sides as shown in Figure 28.2.

By then, the questions were shown to have application in any human interaction. This would not have surprised Tomkins given he had developed what I think is the 'defining' theory on human motivation, Human Being Theory (Thorsborne, 2016). I realised the questions provided the 'relational foundation' for restorative practice. Developing an explicit restorative practice framework was key to how I explained, used and shared my practice. It provided a 'template' so others could learn how to integrate restorative practice into their day-to-day practice (see Figure 28.3).

Figure 28.3 shows the various 'elements' that contribute to creating the conditions prescribed in Nathanson's blueprint. There is nothing sequential about this diagram. The arrows attempt to illustrate the resonance and congruence between the various elements that ultimately shape the process (practice). An attempt will now be made to explain how this is possible. Note: the key elements of Figure 28.3 are underlined in the following explanatory process.

Logical practice analysis

I coined the phrase 'Logical Practice Analysis' (LPA). I needed a logical way to describe my practice. LPA means:

- Logical – clear, considered, reasonable, follows certain rules
- Practice – detailed, explicit, sequential, consistently delivers desired outcomes
- Analysis – capable of detailed examination, scrutiny and validation

---

Restorative Questions I

When things go wrong.
What happened?
What were you thinking of at the time?
What have you thought about since?
Who has been affected by what you have done? In what way?
What do you think you need to do to make things right?

Restorative Questions II

When someone has been hurt.
What did you think when you realised what had happened?
What impact has this incident had on you and others?
What has been the hardest thing for you?
What do you think needs to happen to make things right?

Figure 28.2 Restorative questions

Source: Real Justice, www.iirp.org or www.realjustice.org

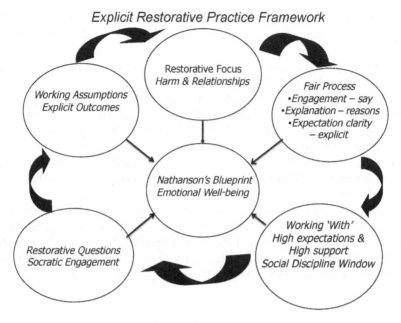

Figure 28.3 Explicit restorative practice framework

The following is an example of the sort of questions I ask myself prior to assisting an individual experiencing disruption in their life:

- What is happening for this individual at this moment?
- How did this person get into this space?
- What does this person need now and beyond?
- To what extent does this person understand what is happening in their life?
- What can I contribute?

Earlier I mentioned the significance of shame. Shame interrupts positive affects, and without exception, the shame impediment is the reason why individuals feel some degree of disconnection, with themselves and others. These insights provided further clarity on what I have always believed (about the primacy of relationships) but importantly, validated what I knew to be true. Through a logical process of cause and effect relationships (Business Directory, 2017) I developed a set of <u>working assumptions</u> to frame my practice:

- Relationships help shape our identity, from which we derive life's meaning.
- Those who are not able to deal with vulnerability tend to struggle with relationships.
- Creating the conditions that help others to deal honestly with their vulnerability is an important step towards building trust and a more positive experience.
- Silvan Tomkins's blueprint for individual psychological and emotional wellness prescribes the conditions needed for this to happen.
- The Restorative Questions developed by O'Connell (1993) provide a 'template' that helps achieve these conditions.

Over the past 27 years, I have been privileged to facilitate many restorative processes for serious crime or incidents involving severe trauma. The great majority have not involved offenders (or anyone connected with offenders). I discovered that these victims shared similar experiences as a result of their trauma:

• Struggled with their shame
• Felt disconnected from themselves and others
• Locked into an emotional 'holding pattern'; felt powerless to disrupt
• Professional assistance made little difference
• Looked to (blamed) others for answers – offenders and systems

When developing the restorative questions, I was very aware of the questions I should ask victims. Crime was mostly about opportunity. Victims rarely featured in an offender's thinking. Yet I heard the victim cry 'why me?' It was personal. The restorative questions (Side 2) were designed exclusively to encourage those experiencing shame to talk about their experience. For example, the most powerful question, 'What's been the hardest thing for you?' evokes a strong emotional response because it gets to the core of an individual's vulnerability (Thorsborne, 2016).

I understood the practical implications of Tomkins's work. I recognised the similarities in the processes used to engage Gary and his mum, my Wagga police colleagues and the many restorative processes I had facilitated over the years. Every experience in their own way replicated Tomkins's blueprint. I knew that creating the conditions that allowed people to sit with the discomfort of their vulnerability made it likely that they would be open to sharing emotions. This was the key to obtaining good outcomes because those involved were able to:

• Make sense and meaning of their lives;
• Identify what was most important in all that was happening;
• Work out what needed to change and their part in this change process, and importantly;
• Learn how to build and sustain healthy relationships.

Chan Kim & Mauborgne's (1997: 66) article on fair process added an important dimension to my practice. They suggested that for something to be 'fair' three guiding principles needed to be satisfied:

• Engagement – opportunity to be heard, taken seriously and opinion valued
• Explanation – understanding the rationale for decisions or practice
• Expectation clarity – understanding expectations

Engagement reinforced my belief about the importance of 'being heard and understood'. Explaining and sharing my practice supported the ideal that 'others are experts in their own lives'. Establishing expectations emphasised the importance of respectful and collaborative processes. I realised from their stories that those experiencing crisis innately understood this was about relationships, shame, being heard and fairness – those were the words they used. Very few, however, understood what was happening (at an emotional level), even though they were experiencing a raft of negative emotions. Whilst I knew that shame was an important impediment and that a fair and respectful process was needed, rather than tell them what I knew, I asked questions. This 'Socratic' engagement style (Phillips, 2002) allowed them to work it out.

Maria was a 28-year-old woman who had been sexually abused when she was young. In our initial conversation, I inquired about her frequent use of the word 'shame' and how she dealt with it. Maria said that she managed her shame by (her words) *withdrawing, attacking herself, big-time avoidance and getting angry with others*. I then showed her Nathanson's Compass of Shame and she burst into tears, saying, '*Do you mean I am normal? Why didn't the mental health professionals tell me this?*' Maria's insight into shame is not unusual. It is a regular experience when there is a rudimentary understanding of Tomkins and shame.

Shame is rarely understood, and its treatment varies. Brown (2011) discovered shame as she struggled to understand the relationships between vulnerability and connection. Brown found that those who embraced vulnerability felt they were worthy of 'loving and belonging' and shared three distinct common characteristics (with those who struggled with vulnerability):

- Courage – courage to be imperfect; able to tell their story with their whole heart
- Compassion – were able to be kind to themselves before being kind to others
- Connection – this was a result of authenticity; willing to let go of who they wanted to be and to accept who they are

Shame is what keeps us in and out of relationships. As restorative facilitators, we should aim to create the conditions that allow shame to be experienced as an opportunity for growth. Relationship style is fundamental to how we engage and facilitate any restorative encounter. The final element of our explicit framework is the Social Discipline Window (see Figure 28.4).

The notion of working 'with' others involves establishing high expectations and high levels of support. Low expectations and high support means doing things 'for' others. High expectations and low support results in doing things 'to' others. Low expectations and low support means 'not' doing anything. Relationships do best when we establish clear expectations within

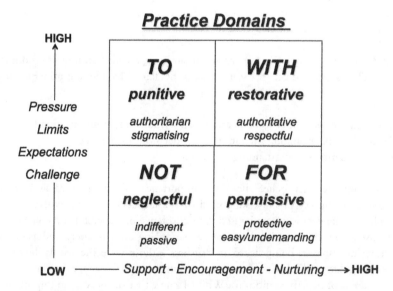

Figure 28.4 Practice domains

Source: Adapted from *Social Discipline Window*, Paul McCold and Ted Wachtel, 2000.

a supportive context where the focus is on engagement, collaboration and possibilities. Vander Vennen (2016) argues that:

> the window engages our 'internal working model' for understanding relationships and moves it towards becoming explicit. And once explicit, our way of being in relationship with others can change.

A unique feature of our explicit practice framework is that the following elements appear on printed and laminated A4 posters:

- Restorative questions (also on business-sized cards)
- Compass of Shame
- Restorative Practice – basic tenets being 'harm and relationships'
- Practice Domains

These posters and the Hoberman Sphere (used to simulate the influence of shame in how we open or close) make up our Restorative Practice kit. In summary, the key features of our explicit practice framework are:

- Has a clear practice rationale
- Is easily explained and shared
- Able to consistently deliver on intended outcomes
- Provides a common language and practice for building relational capacity

A number of case studies will now be shared to illustrate the power of this restorative framework.

Restorative case studies

In late 1993, I transferred to Sydney with the intention of replicating the Wagga experience throughout NSW Police Service. I was awarded a Churchill Fellowship in 1994 and this resulted in some important restorative developments, including:

- Meeting and working with Professor Donald Nathanson in Pennsylvania (US).
- Ted Wachtel started the Real Justice organisation (now IIRP).
- Thames Valley Police Service (UK) received restorative justice training.
- RISE project in Canberra (Sherman et al., 1994).

The following case studies are examples of how our explicit restorative framework influenced practice.

Restorative school communities

MacKillop primary school (NSW) was the first school where I trained teachers, students and parents. I had previously worked only with teachers. It was the explicit practice framework that appealed to the school's principal, Liz O'Callaghan (2005); the most critical element was the restorative questions. In order to embed the restorative questions in their practice, students, teachers and parents were given copies of RP cards. Posters were placed in every classroom. Two large restorative signs were placed in the playground.

Things changed markedly following the introduction of restorative practice. Playground and classroom incidents reduced. Teacher practice became more explicit. School culture was peaceful. Parents reported that relationships had improved at home. Students were better at dealing with conflict. A small group of students were interviewed six years after leaving the school and reported that their restorative experiences had a significant influence on their own relationships.

Rozelle Public School's (NSW) restorative journey was similar. Principal Lyn Doppler described restorative as a 'way of being and relating'. Staff, students and parents were encouraged to use restorative language and to practice explicitly when relating, thinking and learning together. The school received the Director-Genera's Award for Outstanding Achievement in Being and Learning Together.

Doppler (2011) identified the explicit restorative practice framework as the key to engagement:

- Strong linkages with Quality Teaching – aligns with the three dimensions of the Quality Teaching Framework: quality learning environment, intellectual rigour and significance (NSW QTF).
- It helped teachers be more deliberate and explicit in employing their own best practice.
- Student achievement increased in all learning areas with standardised testing.
- Data on student engagement matrix indicated a more motivated and engaged student population.
- Student suspension rates dramatically reduced.

Restorative organisation

Re-Engage Youth Services was recognised by BRW (*Business Review Weekly*) as the 6th best Australian Workplace (September 2016). Re-Engage's restorative journey began in 2010 with ten staff. By 2017 there were 76 staff and a caseload of a thousand 'at risk' young people and families. Their 'four pillars' philosophy was a relational foundation for change. It involved being 'restorative' with:

- Self
- Colleagues
- Young people and families
- Community

My initial meeting with Re-Engage was interesting. Loymeyer (2015: 3) provides an insight on this discussion:

> In our first meeting we encountered something completely unexpected: Terry didn't initially volunteer information. Instead, he relentlessly asked questions:
>
> - Tell me about your practice?
> - You mentioned that you use a coaching model. What is this about?
> - You have regular structured staff meeting. What form do these take?
> - What do you talk about? What do you hope to achieve from these meetings?
> - What are some of your practice challenges?
> - What does success look like when working with young people and their families?

A restorative culture developed. Policies and procedures changed. Circle processes were a daily occurrence. Collegial relationships strengthened. Discussion on success and failure was seen as crucial to improving practice. Critical incidents were dealt through collegial processes without involving other professionals. Case management quality improved. Staff turnover was minimal. Performance management was a rare event. A restorative narrative developed. The 'restorative kit' was in daily use. Restorative cards were given to young people and families.

Restorative family support agency

Goulburn Family Support Service (GFSS) has been working with vulnerable families since 1978. Their restorative journey began in 2000 when introduced to restorative conferencing. Today GFSS uses an *explicit restorative practice framework response* when dealing with family violence. This practice has a number of key elements:

- Explicit Affective Engagement – initial process of stories, expressing emotions, assessment, focus on harm and relationships.
- Compass of Shame – how shame can trigger behaviours that impede relationships.
- Social Discipline Window – examination of relationship styles.
- Explaining Tomkins's 'Blueprints for Life' and Kelly's 'Blueprint for Relationships'.
- Fair Process – explaining practice and theory is key to helping others to understand emotions and behaviours.

Processes vary depending upon the needs of couples or families. Flexibility is key. A family conference is used occasionally. Therapeutic and learning engagement is central to their practice (Donald 2004: 130):

> In my observations and reflections on the practice of Goulburn Family,
> learning comes from healing in therapy. Healing comes from a human or emotional engagement of the worker and the client from the start supported by application of a range of technical or cognitive tools provided by the worker.

GFSS appears to be the only Australian community agency that involves all parties impacted by family violence. Outcomes are very encouraging (Broderick et al., 2012)

Restorative community probation officer

Grahame Chaseling worked for NSW Corrections for 30 years. Grahame's restorative journey started in 2000 when he trained as a conference facilitator. In 2004, Grahame became a Community Corrections officer with a view to using restorative practice when supervising offenders. He developed The Game (Wachtel, 2006) to ensure that all mandated offender programmes had a restorative focus.

He shared his practice with offenders and their families. He handed out restorative question cards. Pre and post sentence reports were framed using the restorative questions with input from offenders and families. Grahame engaged offenders so that they began to understand themselves and the importance of relationships. Whilst there was no formal evaluation, anecdotal offender feedback consistently reported stronger relationships.

Terry O'Connell

Restorative aged care facility

Maranatha House is a small rural aged care facility in Wellington (NSW). Leadership and staff embraced restorative practice in 2015. Since that time, this facility has undergone a quiet transformation (Wachtel, 2016). General Manager Debra Wells attended an IIRP forum and left convinced that the restorative questions had something to offer her workplace.

Restorative practice has evolved over the past two years from an initial focus on 'things that went wrong' towards building a stronger culture of care. Some of the key features are:

- Restorative language and practice is shared with staff, residents and their families.
- Staff circles are used regularly for general discussions, feedback, problem solving and information giving.
- Individual care plans are developed collaboratively with residents, families and staff.
- Restorative circles are used to deal with resident or family concerns or complaints.
- Staff relationships are strong, with a number of staff reporting that their (family) relationships had improved.
- Residents and families felt valued and respected.

Restorative policing

In 1995, I was invited by Assistant Commissioner Christine Nixon to explore restorative justice's potential use within Human Resources (NSW Police Service). Within 12 months I had established the Restorative Justice Group, a small unit that had adapted restorative process to resolve workplace conflicts and grievances. Our early success of dealing with complicated personnel and welfare issues was noticed. We began focusing on police reform. We designed and implemented a Behavioural Change programme for operational police. It was underpinned by restorative justice principles.

Waratah and Shaolhaven were two of five locations that had embraced our Behavioural Change programme. Both stood out like 'beacons' when compared with every other police command within NSW, on almost every measure.

Crime reduction in Waratah was a result of significant improvement (Collins, 1998) in the following areas:

- Rationalisation and improvement in work practices;
- Employee satisfaction and motivation; and
- Public satisfaction and police responsiveness.

Discussion

The success of each case study was directly attributable to the process practitioners used to engage one another. The concept of being 'explicit' in their day-to-day practice proved both challenging and exciting. Being able to articulate and then share their practice with others opened up many new (practice) possibilities. Practitioners learned how to manage their own vulnerability. They learned about fair process and the important role shame has in their lives. They understood how the restorative questions helped shape respectful conversations. Stronger relationships were an outcome of emotional connection. Relational capacity was enhanced. All had experienced a process that improved their emotional well-being. They learned how to replicate this modelling in their own lives and with those they were assisting.

438

The explicit practice framework was shown to have provided consistent opportunities for each 'community' to begin to:

- Make sense and meaning of what was happening;
- Identify what was most important;
- Work out what needed to change, and their part in this change process; and
- Learn how to build and sustain strong relationships.

Most significant was the fact that the practitioners involved learned to have the 'right' conversation, one that allowed them to collaborate with their colleagues and others. The satisfaction that practitioners gained from knowing why their practice was making a difference could not be overstated:. the result was improved confidence, certainty and consistency in their day-to-day practice. Practitioners reported that by sharing their story of change (that resulted from them embracing an explicit restorative practice framework) considerable interest and inquiry was generated from other practitioners.

The 'right' conversation ensures a logical and rigorous approach to practice. It began with understanding what the needs were, how they developed and what was likely to make the difference. The challenge was to then find the practice capable of creating the conditions that allowed others to experience the difference. This logical approach provided a context to rigorously test what practice was capable of consistently providing the required outcomes. It created a 'level practice arena' where the only real measure was whether a practice was able to provide those outcomes. The case studies demonstrated how explicit restorative practice was consistently able to deliver positive outcomes for everyone involved.

Conclusion

As a general proposition, the case for 'explicit practice' is uncontroversial. It should therefore not be surprising that close examination of most relational practice reveals a lack of explicitness. No claim is made that the explicit restorative practice framework discussed in this chapter provides the complete answer to what is needed to strengthen the restorative movement's broader societal influence. However, what this explicit framework offered was a practice capable of consistently delivering positive outcomes (as shown with each case study).

Explicit practice will position the restorative movement in a unique place, one that has the potential to attract attention and to influence mainstream thinking and practice. It can influence bureaucratic reform by reducing the dominance of government and professionals. Explicit practice will greatly enhance the role of individuals and families in helping themselves.

We must continually look for opportunities to expand the role of restorative justice and other restorative practices – beyond token or situational reparative processes to a strategic approach that has broad application in everyday life. There is little doubt the 'best is yet to come'.

References

Braithwaite, John. 1989. *Crime Shame & Reintegration*. Cambridge: Cambridge University Press.
Braithwaite, John. 1998. 'Restorative Justice: Assessing an Immodest Theory and a Pessimistic Theory.' In *Crime and Justice – A Review of Research*. Chicago: University of Chicago Press.
Broderick, S. and Bazeley. 2012. *Outcomes of the Explicit Affective Practice*. The Ian Potter Foundation. Available at http://gfss.ned.org.au/.
Brown, B. 2011. Power of Vulnerability. *TED Talk*. Available at www.ted.com/talks/brene_brown_on_ vulnerability

Business Directory. 2016. Available at www.businessdictionary.com/definition/assumptions.html. Accessed 10 August 2017.

Chan Kim, W. and Mauborgne, R. 1997. Fair Process: Managing in the Knowledge Economy, *Harvard Business Review,* July–August.

Collins, Deborah. 1998. *Evaluation of the Behavioural Change Program of the NSW Police Service.* Sydney, Australia, Internal Police Service Document.

Daly, K. 2015. What Is Restorative Justice? Fresh Answers to a Vexed Question, *Victims & Offenders,* 11(1): 9–29. DOI: 10.1080/15564886.2015.1107797.

Donald, J. 2004. *A Policy Framework For a Knowledge Based Society: Families and Knowledge.* Master's Thesis, Deakin University.

Gavrielides, T. 2007. *Restorative Justice Theory & Practice: Addressing the Discrepancy.* HEUNI: Helsinki.

Gavrielides, T. 2015. Available at www.theogavrielides.com/product-page/offenders-no-more.

George, G. 2014. Affect and Emotion in a Restorative School. In V. Kelly, and M. Thorsborne (eds.) *The Psychology of Emotion in Restorative Practice: How Affect Script Psychology Explains How and Why Restorative Practice Works.* London: Jessica Kingsley Publishers.

Kelly, V. 2009. A Primer of Affect Psychology. Available at www.tomkins.org/uploads/Primer_of Affect_Psychology.pdf. Accessed 14 July 2017.

Kelly, V. 2012. *The Art of Intimacy and the Hidden Challenge of Shame.* Maine, ME: Maine Authors Publishing.

Loymeyer, B. 2015. Taking Restorative Practices Seriously. *Presented at the International Institute of Restorative Practices 2014 World Conference,* Bethlehem, PA.

MacDonald, J. and Ireland. 1990. *Can It Be Done Another Way?* Sydney, New South Wales Police Service [Internal Report].

Masters, G. 1997. Reintegrative Shaming in Theory and Practice: Thinking About Feeling in Criminology. Thesis submitted for Ph.D Department of Applied Social Science, Lancaster University England.

McCold, P. 2000. Toward a Mid-range Theory of Restorative Criminal Justice: A Reply to the Maximalist Model, *Contemporary Justice Review,* 3(4): 357–414.

McCold, P. and Wachtel, T. 2003. In Pursuit of Paradigm: A Theory of Restorative Justice IIRP, *E FORUM,* 12 August.

Moore, D. and O'Connell, T. 1994. Family Conferencing in Wagga: A Communitarian Model of Justice. In C. Alder and J. Wundersitz (eds) *Family Conferencing and Juvenile Justice: The Way Forward or Misplaced Optimism?* Canberra: Australian Institute of Criminology.

Moore, D. 1997. Emotions and the Ethics of Justice and Care. Thesis submitted for Ph.D., Faculty of Humanities, Griffith University.

Nathanson, D. 1992. *Shame and Pride: Affect, Sex and the Birth of Self.* New York. W.W. Norton.

NSW Department of Education. 2003. *Quality Teaching Framework.* Discussion Paper.

NSW Parliamentary Handsard. 1998. 28 October, p. 17.

O'Callaghan, L. 2005. The MacKillop Model of Restorative Practice. *Presentation at 5th IIRP International Conference,* Penrith.

O'Connell, T. 1993. Wagga Wagga Juvenile Cautioning Program: It May be the Way to Go!. In L. Atkinson and S. Gerull (eds.) *National Conference on Juvenile Justice.* Canberra: Australian Institute of Criminology.

O'Connell, T. 2003. Why the Real Justice Conference Script. *Presentation at Fourth International Conference on Conferencing,* Veldhoven, Netherlands.

O'Connell, T. 2015. The Best Is Yet To Come – Unlocking Restorative Practice's True Potential. *Presented at International Institute of Restorative Practices 2015 World Conference,* Bethlehem, PA.

O'Connell, T. and Ritchie, J. 1999. *Restorative Justice and the Contest Between the Relational and Institutional Paradigms.* Paper presented to Restorative Justice Conference and Civil Society Conference, Australian National University, Canberra, 16–18 February.

O'Connell, T., Wachtel, B. and Wachtel, J. 1999. *Conferencing Handbook: The New Real Justice Training Manual.* Pipersville, PA: The Piper's Press.

Phillips, C. 2002. *Socrates Cafe: A Fresh Taste of Philosophy.* New York: W. W. Norton & Company.

Scheff, T. and Retzinger, S. 1994. *Bloody Revenge: Emotions, Nationalism and War*. Chicago: The University of Chicago Press.

Sherman, L.W., Braithwaite, J. and Strang, H. 1994. Reintegrative Shaming of Violence, Drink Driving and Property Crime: A Randomised Control Trial. Appendix: Technical Proposal. Funding Application, Canberra: Australian National University.

Thorsborne, M. 2016.Affect and Script Psychology Restorative Practice, Biology and a Theory of Human Motivation. In B. Hopkins (ed.) *Restorative Theory in Practice: Insights into What Works and Why*. London: Jessica Kingsley Publishers.

Tyler, T. 2006. *Why People Obey The Law*. Princeton: Princeton University Press.

Vander Vennen, M. 2016. Towards a Relational Theory of Restorative Justice. In Belinda Hopkins (ed.) *Restorative Theory in Practice: Insights Into What Works and Why*. London: Jessica Kingsley Publishers.

Wachtel, T. and McCold, P. 2000. Restorative justice in everyday life. In J. Braithwaite and H. Strang (eds.) *Restorative Justice in Civil Society*. New York: Cambridge University Press, pp.117–125.

Wachtel, J. 2006. *The Game: Restorative Community Supervision for Adult Offenders*. Restorative Practices E-Forum, September 20 2006. Available at www.iirp.org

Wachtel, J. 2017. A Nursing Home that Feels Like Home, *IIRP News*, May 18. Available at www.iirp.org

Wood, J. 1997. Royal Commission into the New South Wales Police Service, Final Report Volume Ii: Reform.

29

The new generation of restorative justice

Carl Stauffer and Johonna Turner[1]

Introduction

It is a daunting task to be asked to write about the future of Restorative Justice (RJ). Despite our continual immersion as practitioners and professors in the work of RJ, it would be presumptive for us to make any predictive claims on the future direction of RJ as a movement. To be part of the RJ movement in this time is like being thrust into the strong currents of a deep river that twists and turns as it is carried along by the powerful force of rapids, waterfalls and whirlpools. The RJ movement is expanding and growing at a breath-taking rate. It is almost impossible to keep track of the proliferation of new theory, research and practice applications in the field. At best, we can lay claim to being part of this "adventure", and as such we will aim to share our research, observations, experiences and vision for what RJ as a movement could look like in the next generation.

To that end, in this chapter we will take a cursory glance at the origins, history and evolution of RJ as a practice-driven field now becoming an international social movement. We will mine the lessons learned by the *Zehr Institute for Restorative Justice*[2] from the past three years of intentionally listening to and engaging with the people who make up RJ as a movement in the North American context and beyond. We will then bring in the voices and visions of three contemporary RJ movement leaders in the US gathered through one-on-one interviews. Finally, in our concluding reflections, we will grapple with the idea of RJ as not only a social movement but as a social justice movement and identify the critical questions that are core to this identification. In keeping with the aims of this Handbook, we address the relationship between RJ and social justice as a new and contested area of research, and the implications of this relationship for innovative practice. Most of the experience and evidence that we reference comes from the US, but the claims and contributions we make are relevant for readers around the world.

Before going further, we, as the co-authors, feel it is essential that we "locate" ourselves in the context of the RJ movement and are transparent about what we bring to this conversation. I (Carl) am a white, middle-aged male who carries a US passport and is reminded regularly that I have lived in and benefited from my white privilege for most of my life. I consider myself on a journey to becoming an ally to those who have been marginalized, oppressed and dominated by the injustice of global structural racism. Having been born to US church workers in the midst of the Vietnam war, I am no stranger to the injustice of direct and systemic violence. I came to academia having spent the first half of my life in practice both domestically and internationally. I formally entered the RJ field in 1991, providing non-profit services to the US criminal legal system. Following that, I lived and worked in South Africa for 16 years, where I worked with the RJ applications in the criminal legal system, civil society and in the South African Truth and Reconciliation Commission. For a decade, I travelled to multiple countries engaging with RJ applications at the level of national war-to-peace reconstruction efforts (also called transitional justice). I come to this work of building an international RJ social movement with an expansive, hopeful vision which stems from the many innovative, bottom-up, indigenous and hybrid approaches to RJ that I have witnessed here in the US and around the world.

I (Johonna) came to the RJ movement from a deep-rooted commitment to social justice activism and organizing, more broadly. As a black woman born and raised in a working-class family in the United States, I am intimately familiar with the violence of white supremacy, patriarchy and class oppression. As a heterosexual university professor with a terminal degree, I am also well acquainted with multiple dimensions of privilege. Two overlapping vocational paths led to my current place as a tenure-track professor at a small Christian liberal arts university. In 1998, I began my career as an educator, working primarily with African-American and Latinx youth within informal educational environments. For about a decade, I was also deeply engaged in community education, youth leadership development and grassroots organizing in Washington, DC, particularly in relation to issues of safety and justice. I first learned about RJ in the early 2000s while engaged in a grassroots intergenerational organizing campaign that successfully transformed the District of Columbia's juvenile justice system. However, I came to connect especially closely with organizations and leaders in the prison abolitionist, feminist anti-violence and transformative justice movements. It was leaders in these movements that helped me to draw from my own experiences of violence, including my identity as a survivor of childhood sexual abuse, as sources of great insight and wisdom. My faith and spirituality further undergird my tenacity for seeking justice in healing. As a result of these paths, I hold deep vision and values for a RJ movement that is led by those directly impacted by direct and structural violence, inextricably connected to broader movements for social justice and invested in challenging oppression in all its forms.

Restorative justice as field of practice: an overview of its origins, history and evolution

Origins

The practice of RJ predates its nomenclature. For millennia, communities around the world have used relational practices of addressing harm and settling disputes that center on values, principles and strategies that we now associate with RJ such as accountability, safety and community engagement as well as storytelling and healing. Hadley (2001) makes the case that most societies had a mix of punitive and restorative approaches to justice within their histories. Colonialism around the world has erased many of these histories. In addition, many communities' engagement with what is now known as RJ are not reflected in mainstream literature, particularly communities that are marginalized as the result of racism and other systems of oppression. For these reasons, we distinguish between the origins of RJ as praxis and its origins as a contemporary field of practice documented in scholarly and grey literature. Here, we focus particularly on the latter.

The contemporary RJ field was birthed amid humble beginnings in 1974 in the small town of Elmira, Ontario, Canada (Northley, 2004; Kelly, 2006). It originated out of the frustration of a probation officer, Mark Yantzi, who longed for a more effective way to deal with two youths who under the influence of alcohol had destroyed some property inside and outside of 22 homes in a single neighborhood. Yantzi, a member of a local Mennonite Church and a colleague, Dave Worth, a church volunteer with the Mennonite Central Committee, had been meeting with other concerned church and community members to engage in an ongoing exploration of what it means to live out their faith – the justice of Jesus – in their work as systems professionals and volunteers. When this vandalism case emerged, it was a perfect opportunity to experiment with the ideas that this group had been wrestling with in their Bible studies and other dialogues about alternative approaches to justice within their community. The risky "ask" made of the Judge, Gordon McConnell, was simple, yet powerful: take the two young people door to door and require them to meet each of the persons living in the homes of the properties that they vandalized. In the meeting, invite them to apologize and offer to make restitution. Judge McConnell, using his discretion, granted permission, and the results were so astounding that the idea literally spread around the world. The DNA of RJ, its values and practices in a contemporary application were wired in at this juncture (e.g. encounter, amends, reintegration and inclusion) (Van Ness and Strong, 1997).

History

In the early decades of the RJ field, the dominant white hegemony did what it knew best. Enthralled with the "magic" of the interpersonal transformation that occurred in this newfound field of practice, it worked diligently to make RJ into a better social service – this meant more professionalized, more specialized, more technically complicated, more time-efficient and more outcomes-solutions based. However, in the process, at least five critical matters were neglected:

- Firstly, by focusing on the practical applications alone, the field neglected the production of social theory, analysis and research that would help to understand the significance of RJ beyond its interpersonal benefits.
- Secondly, by enshrining RJ as a therapeutic, social service model, the field focused on the pathologies of individual behavior and failed to sufficiently name and deconstruct the structural injustices that drive people to harm others and the institutional violence that represses many communities, and especially formerly colonized communities of color (e.g. through the use of critical theory and intersectional analysis of race, gender, class, sexuality and beyond).
- Thirdly, by allowing RJ to be identified by, and dependent on, the contemporary criminal legal system for case referrals and funding, the field failed to give credence to the many other socio-political sectors and institutions of society in which RJ could flourish.
- Fourthly, by channelling its energies into building RJ non-profits/NGOs, relying on private donor funds and pushing through small legislative changes, the field lost sight of how it was being divided, forced to compete and co-opted by government systems in order to expand the means of surveillance and social control, and to fulfil their own punitive ends.
- Fifthly, by pursuing the establishment of RJ as a specialized academic discipline and professional practice, the field failed to acknowledge the deep restorative wisdom, moral philosophy and profound worldview of our customary traditions and indigenous "elders" who have been practicing reparative justice and peacemaking circles for eons (Gavrielides, 2005, 2013; Gavrielides and Artinopoulou, 2013).

Indeed, it is precisely these five listed oversights that reflect the tensions between RJ as one of many options to be chosen from a professional menu of social services, and RJ as a broad-based social movement with collective impact on individuals, communities and institutions writ large. In reality, this debate about RJ as a social service or a social movement presents an unnecessary polemic. The function of strong, localized, and intersectional practice is to provide the direction, guidance and restraint for social movements to progress with the necessary equanimity. In other words, social movements and social practice have a symbiotic relationship.

Evolution from social practice to social movement

Out of this fomentation, the stage was set for an international RJ social movement to emerge. In 1990, Dr Howard Zehr published his seminal work on RJ as a "paradigm shift" laying the foundation for a new way to understand crime and punishment. Zehr's work was instrumental in popularizing different ideological responses to social harm that grew out of diverse social movements of the 1960s, 1970s and 1980s, as well as the synthesis and cross-fertilization of these ideas. Following the publication of Zehr's *Changing Lenses*, a series of RJ anthologies appeared on the scene touting sections and chapters on topics such as "Creating Restorative Systems", "Community Justice Initiatives", "Governance Systems", "Social Justice" and "Transformation of Perspectives, Structures and Persons" (Braswell et al., 2001; Johnstone, 2001; Toews and Zehr, 2004; Pavlich, 2005; Gavrielides, 2007; Sullivan and Tifft, 2008; Woolford, 2009). Umbreit and Armour (2011) described the potential of the RJ social movement as follows:

> By drawing upon many traditional values of the past, from many different cultures, we have the opportunity to build a far more accountable, understandable, and healing system of justice and law that can lead to a greater sense of community through active victim and citizen involvement in restorative initiatives.
>
> *(p. 29)*

Interestingly, a decade earlier, Sullivan and Tifft (2001), argued for RJ vis-à-vis social justice with a genuine passion that is more akin to the narrative discourse of the current RJ social movement:

> But, as we look over the landscape of existing programs of RJ, we continue to see a lack of concern over the structural conditions, the political-economic foundations that determine whether the personal integration and reintegration of a person into his or her community will be possible. . . . How can a person find support to heal amid social arrangements that have little or no ability to meet personal needs, indeed, that are structured to deny the meeting of essential needs? We suggest here that, if our efforts to achieve RJ are real, then we must have a concern for transforming those social arrangements that disallow personal growth. That is, we are talking about transformative justice, a RJ that seeks to affect social-structural, institutional arrangements, while simultaneously helping those whose lives have been affected by interpersonal harms.
>
> *(preface, ix and x)*

In the United States over the past ten years, a rising set of voices are speaking into the US RJ social movement with prophetic clarity and authenticity. They are speaking into issues of mass incarceration (Davis, 2003; Alexander, 2012; Mauer and Jones, 2013; Stevenson, 2014), the "school-to-prison pipeline" and racial disproportionality in suspension and expulsion rates in the school system (RJOY, 2015; Ginwright, 2016), and into police violence and transforming the historical harms of slavery and the Native American genocide through truth-telling, reparations and healing (Davis and Scharrar, 2017; Hooker, 2016; Hooker and Czajkowski, 2012; Jenkins, 2006).

Internationally, the RJ movement has taken uneven and varied expressions (Galaway and Hudson, 1996). From North America, the RJ concepts, practices and legislation quickly spread to Europe, Australia and New Zealand and then to every continent. A cursory "snapshot" of international RJ activity reveals that Intensive RJ applications in schools are spreading in locations like South Korea, Taiwan and Russia, to name but a few. Aside from Europe and New Zealand, comprehensive national RJ legislation was enacted in Jamaica in 2012. Regional RJ projects in the criminal legal systems of Nepal, India, Sri-Lanka and Bangladesh are being piloted. Hybrid Western-Indigenous approaches to community harms are being implemented in Pakistan (Braithwaite and Gohar, 2014), Bangladesh (Asadullah, 2016), Libya (Elmangoush, 2015), Burundi, Zambia, DRC (Juma, 2012) and Uganda, to name a few. Restorative Transitional justice efforts have been rolled out in South Africa, Rwanda, Sierra Leone, Liberia, Cambodia and East Timor. Brazil, Mexico and South Africa all have active national RJ movements addressing harms across multiple sectors in their societies.

Social movement theory

If we are going to make the claim that RJ is a social movement, then it is necessary that we embed it in social movement theory. In the broadest terms, social movement theory can be divided into four different categories of thought: Political Opportunity Theory, Resource Mobilization Theory, New Social Movement Theory and Frame Analysis Theory. All four of these categories help explain the rise of the RJ as a social movement.

Political Opportunity Theory includes the study of the "collective mind" of the crowd and what is commonly referred to as mob psychology (Le Bon, 1895), the study of the politics of mass society especially as it relates to the rise of fascism and totalitarianism (Kornhouser, 1959), the argument for rational choice as a determining factor in collective action (Olson, 1965) and what has been termed political process theory (McAdam et al.,1996), which maintains that social movements are embedded in political contexts and are galvanized by "structures of political opportunity". Political opportunities include new potential allies, splits among powerholders, new government processes and/or new "ideological dispositions" of those in power.

The RJ social movement is filling political gaps and expanding political opportunities across the world. We are currently experiencing a global upsurge in authoritarian governments and at the same time the very institutions that support these authoritarian impulses are imploding (e.g. the criminal legal, political, economic, educational systems). Politicians, civil servants, activists, organizers, teachers, lawyers, business leaders and the like are coming to the RJ movement saying they are tired of the adversarial approach to work, they are tired of always fighting, and they are looking for alternatives. RJ is offering alternative ways of being and doing that speak directly to the punitive, hierarchical, divisive, "win-lose" and "us/them" mentality of the abuse of power. The political opportunity for the values and practices of RJ could not be more clear than it is now.

Resource Mobilization Theory suggests that socio-political movements are only sustained when there is sufficient mobilization of four key resources – human engagement, communications media, influence over third-party stakeholders and those who control funding (Lipsky, 1968). Research indicates that the very nature of the NGO-Industrial-Complex works against movement-making and that most of these limitations revolve around the non-profit funding structures. According to Heideman (2013: 135), the reasons for this are:

- Donors see projects as units of peacebuilding.
- Donors are novelty seekers (always in search of new ideas and new locations).
- This results in premature abandonment of successful projects.
- Difficulties in securing long-term funding.
- Favouring of countable events over relationship building.

Despite these findings, welcoming signs from a number of key funders indicate a willingness to engage with the RJ social movement on two points: To work toward maximum impact (e.g. structural or systemic change), and to consider longer-term funding arrangements moving away from one to three-year grant cycles and toward five-to-ten-year cycles, or decadal thinking.

The key point here is not that we should avoid building RJ programs (within non-profits or NGOs), but if we do start programs, they should no longer be imagined outside of functioning coalitions where multiple local organizations join together across a myriad of sectors to impact whole communities. Recent research on "local social forums" found that "[o]verall, local social forums are used as tactical and cultural collective action repertoires by actors, redefining the boundaries of social resistance and its practices" (Dufur, 2013: 235).

New Social Movement Theory (Larana et al., 1994; INCITE!, 2007; Pollack et al., 2011; Branch and Mampilly, 2015) posits that there is now a shift away from ideology toward identity- or issue-based organizing in current social movements. This theory focuses on the interplay of cultural change and social movements and how each influences the other for the purpose of social transformation. The RJ social movement is less about coming to agreement on what justice means and more about how RJ can meet the justice needs of all people and especially those from historically marginalized communities. De-colonization and white privilege demands us to walk in solidarity across the barriers of race, gender and class to name the structural violence of our history and its current manifestations in our societal structures both public and private. It calls us to be uncomfortable and vulnerable and to intentionally "sit in the fire" of the hard truth being spoken by those who have suffered and have been fighting for generations to overcome structures that have repressed and oppressed them from birth. It requires us to act together across all divides in order to change and eliminate these harmful structures once and for all. It requires us to seek out new spaces to live, work, worship and socially inhabit across racial/ethnic, political and economic boundaries in order to press into the better world we want to see.

Frame Analysis Theory (Hunt et al., 1994; Fine, 1995) emphasizes the importance of creating a popular messaging or social narrative framing that will convince the public to join or support a movement's cause. RJ has a compelling vision in the idea of intergenerational justice that heals. One of the key reasons why our contemporary legal system is failing is because of its preoccupation with the past (who's to blame) and the present (how to administer pain/punishment), with little or no regard for the future healing needs of both the harmed and the harmdoers and their respective communities. The current legal system has failed us precisely in the fact that it is unable to cast a vision or provide the appropriate future-view that would motivate those who have committed wrongs and those who have been wronged to step into the risky, liminal space of transformational change and healing. It is our contention that RJ provides an ethical and moral framework for justice that not only effectively interrupts injustices from the past and in the present but also lays a foundation for a healing social justice that can be transmitted to the next generation for the future. This is a message worth framing.

The next generation project – a restorative justice case study

The Zehr Institute for Restorative Justice set out to accompany the burgeoning RJ social movement in four ways. First, we engaged in a facilitated consultation with a select group of influential "thought leaders" from across the field – mostly US domestic and a few international. Second, we hosted a public conference to explore what the "containers" of this social movement might look and feel like. Third, we conducted a Listening Project in six sites (hubs) across the US and Canada in order to gather and document the voices of a cross section of everyday RJ practitioners in the movement. Finally, we have embarked on publishing an RJ anthology that amplifies the breadth and depth of this RJ social movement through the insights and stories of people on the ground (publication set for 2018). The express aim of this three-year project was to impact the field of RJ by putting our energies into framing and building a movement for social justice.[3] The overall three-year project goals were:

- To facilitate dialogue between and with diverse RJ communities and related social justice movements
- To influence the evolution of the RJ field as a social justice movement
- To give exposure to innovative RJ approaches, applications and practices

Year one

In 2015, we invited a gathering of 36 key figures in the RJ movement from the UK, US, Canada, DRC and Pakistan. Together we journeyed together through a Transformative Scenario Building process (Kahane, 2012) where we created, analyzed and debated four scenarios of how the RJ movement might progress in the future. As a group, we developed a cross-sectional matrix that interrogated the impact (marginal or significant) and the coherency (unified or scattered) of a RJ social movement (see Table 29.1). Then we had participants work in small groups

Table 29.1 Four possible future scenarios of growth for the RJ social movement

	Coherent Movement	Scattered Movement
Significant Impact	Scenario #1: *Ecosystem* We are surrounded by a strong RJ ecosystem characterized by diversity and self-sufficiency that exists parallel to the current criminal legal system. There are many different water sources and indigenous plant life that represent and reinforce coherent sets of principles, values and norms. Not a centralized, top-down coherence model.	Scenario #2: *Community Gardens* We are connected through a network of local RJ programs. Small groups (neighbourhoods, families, schools, etc.) have multiple and self-chosen ways of responding justly to harms. There is not a whole "RJ system", rather, people have a choice – society is more equal and less hierarchical.
Marginal Impact	Scenario #3: *Honey Bees & Beehives* RJ is highly coordinated, organized and transformative. Its coherency lies in its shared values and assumptions of practice. However, resources and practices remain highly concentrated in particular insular locales.	Scenario #4: *Restored Natural Habitat* RJ springs up (like vines or deep-rooted plants) among the ruins of our current legal system. It is spontaneous, organic, free, multiple in its expressions and as a result it is less ordered, controlled and institutional – and also less measurable.

and do a SWOT analysis (Strengths, Weaknesses, Opportunities and Threats) of each of these scenarios. Each scenario was given a name by a group that represented a metaphor or analogy of that scenario. It was of interest to note that all the names had to do with ecology and the natural environment. What emerged from this dialogue is the realization that among this small representative group of leaders who were all deeply committed to RJ, we each possess different perceptions of what this growing RJ social movement was and how it worked and should be channelled or expanded into the future.

Year two

In 2016, we hosted a public conference on building the RJ movement. We purposefully set out to design a unique conference event. We had 172 attendees consisting of practitioners, academics, activists, organizers and funders. The schedule was full with 52 sessions for trainings, workshops, seminars and presentations and involving theatre, drama, circles, mind-body exercises, youth spaces and panels, professional storytelling performances and the use of open space technology processes. The express goals were clear: we wanted the exchange of ideas and collaborative partnering and networking to go forward in a stimulating but unhindered space. We wanted to simulate the look and feel of a social movement in action. In essence, we were exploring a satisfying container for a RJ social movement – one that provided enough order and boundary to give meaning but not too much to obstruct the free flow of energy and the impulse to self-organize when a group of creative, passionate, motivated people come together to create a more just world.

Year three

In 2017, we conducted an RJ Listening Project that provided ground-level understanding of how RJ has developed, is practiced and is evolving regionally. The wisdom of local RJ practitioners was central to: (a) understanding the current landscape of RJ, (b) offering regional direction and recommendations that emerge from local social context, people and history, (c) examining successes and challenges that are area-specific and identifying issues that are movement-specific. The collective knowledge from these six listening sessions has helped to clarify and strengthen the direction of the broader Restorative Justice movement. We convened six listening sessions in select, cross-cutting RJ regional "hubs" across the US and Canada, and engaged a total of 130 people. The highlights of the project report include:[4]

General consensus: There was an overwhelming sense by all participants that RJ is alive and well, expanding in scope and needing more connection and coordination among its practitioners and organizations. There was strong affirmation to acknowledge and partner together with the two roots of RJ: the Indigenous and the Western. It is paramount that Westerners in RJ learn from the Indigenous who do not see "RJ" (a foreign term) as separate from their holistic life world view. Indigenous practitioners share a focus on community and healing and a clear resistance to top-down imposed systems of "best practices" or other external control that dictate how justice is done. Finally, all expressed a deep commitment to uphold the quality of RJ work and a desire to fully embody its values.

Tensions: The language of "Restorative Justice" is used and understood differently by RJ practitioners and programs with often divergent attitudes toward the legitimacy of existing institutions and culture: from providing a social service to the criminal legal system, to changing the societal paradigm of justice, to guiding a social justice movement, to embracing a restorative lifestyle. Some RJ practitioners ascribe to RJ accreditation and professional evidence-based practice to uphold the quality of the work, while many voices we heard saw these criteria as "elitist" and "classist" – forms of neo-colonization by outside powers that disregard and even disrespect local knowledge and practice in the name of "efficiency" or "effectiveness".

Strategies: Many communities exhorted the RJ movement to teach and practice RJ values using a bottom-up "Pillars of Wisdom" frame rather than a top-down, prescriptive "Best Practices" frame. Generally, there appeared to be a clear demand for increased opportunities for RJ training that is pedagogically transformative, low cost and visible, and that has a popular appeal. There was a great deal of affirmation to intentionally "center" Indigenous wisdom, foundational values and current practices. A clarion call was sounded to saturate the field with anti-racism and anti-oppression education and with opportunities for RJ facilitators to do personal transformative work and to hold circles on racial justice issues, especially for white practitioners. A strong challenge was given: coordinate and multiply RJ efforts without mirroring the status-quo, top-down national structures. This will require innovation and adaptability. There was considerable support for the formation of local and regional RJ "hubs", decentralized national networks and a RJ fund to bolster local community-based RJ organizations and initiatives. People welcomed the idea to consider and discuss the meaning of co-optation by systems, institutions and hierarchical structures and how to counter these threats. Finally, in whatever is built, make RJ values, relationships and equity the guiding ethos.

Recommendations

In the end, the following top recommendations (see Figure 29.1) were proposed. Each of these recommendations have been discussed in considerable detail in the RJ Listening Project Final Report.

The reflections and recommendations that emerged from the Zehr Institute's three-year *Next Generation Project* are also reflected in one-on-one interviews we conducted with contemporary RJ practitioners.

Voices and visions of contemporary restorative justice practitioners

While the RJ Listening Project illuminates the dimensions, or shapes, of current and future generations of RJ, it is the voices of contemporary RJ practitioners that give these shapes color and vibrancy. We interviewed a small sample of contemporary RJ practitioners. Interview

---

1. *Support Indigenous peacemaking and restorative justice practices, as determined by Indigenous communities in their own context (i.e., a strong bottom-up approach).*
2. *Support movement building:*
   a. *Create decentralized structures such as national networks and regional coalitions or hubs.*
   b. *Develop a restorative justice fund that supports mid-size regional and local community-based restorative justice organizations.*
3. *Support the full integration of social justice values – anti-oppression and specifically anti-racism – into the restorative justice movement.*
4. *Support quality trainings and maintain the integrity of practices in restorative justice.*
5. *Support sustainable funding and resource allocations that maximize impact and involve long-term program/project design, implementation monitoring and evaluation plans (5–10 years).*

Figure 29.1 Recommendations from the Listening Project Final Report

transcripts were analyzed by two outside coders to identify common themes. Here, we high-light the voices and perspectives of three practitioners who lead RJ organizations, programs or initiatives in the US: Dana Coles, Jodie Geddes and Sonya Shah. Women of color are at the forefront of social movements working to dismantle the prison industrial complex (Templeton, 2004). As women of color, Coles, Geddes and Shah reflect the sustained leadership of women of color within efforts to not only reduce or eliminate mass incarceration but also provide healing and redemptive strategies for safety and justice within communities most impacted by punitive policies and practices.

Dana Coles, as the co-director of the community conferencing program for Prince Georges County, Maryland, manages the administration of cases, including processing referrals, coordi-nating intake for new cases and talking with potential participants about the conferencing pro-cess. In addition to facilitating selected cases each month, she also recruits, trains and supports a large pool of volunteers who prepare and facilitate the majority of cases the program takes on.

Jodie Geddes, as the first community organizing coordinator of Restorative Justice for Oakland Youth (RJOY) in Oakland, California, designs and leads education and training pro-grams for young people at the intersection of community organizing and RJ, and supports education and training for neighborhood groups in RJ approaches. Geddes is also helping to lead RJOY's national project to map and network truth-telling, racial healing, and repara-tions initiatives throughout the US, particularly initiatives that address historical harms against African-Americans. In addition, Geddes is Board President of Coming to the Table, a national organization that provides leadership and resources "to acknowledge and heal wounds from racism rooted in the U.S. history of slavery".

Sonya Shah is the founding director of the Ahimsa Collective, a network of people creat-ing an alternative way to address violence and heal trauma that is driven by relationships, not systems, and that is grounded in a restorative justice and peacemaking approach. The collective works with survivors of sexual trauma, people who have committed sexual violence inside and outside of prison, and systems professionals such as corrections officers and law enforcement officials. They also equip and connect the RJ movement through facilitator trainings, RJ work-shops, and research and writing. Working in conjunction with the Zehr Institute for Restora-tive Justice, Shah served as lead facilitator of the RJ Listening Project (described earlier). She is also an associate professor at the California Institute for Integral Studies.

We spoke one on one with these leaders engaged in very different kinds of RJ practice about what RJ means to them, where they believe RJ thinking and practice must deepen and how they conceptualize the "new generation of RJ". By highlighting their voices and visions, our goal is to better amplify important voices and visions that are not yet adequately represented in RJ scholarship but that substantially reflect leadership within the contemporary RJ move-ment, particularly at the grassroots level. In addition, the practitioner perspectives we feature here both underscore and expand the discussion on RJ as a social movement unfolded in the previous sections. Moreover, they make the case that the continuance of RJ as a social move-ment is insufficient; it is imperative that the RJ movement, in its successive generations, exist as a movement for social justice.

Defining restorative justice

Shah, Geddes and Coles integrated three elements in their definition of RJ: an abiding concern for relationships and belonging, the cultivation of personal healing and attention to structural and systemic harms. For Sonya Shah, RJ is a relational, community-driven process to address both interpersonal and systemic harm – but also much more. According to Shah, "[I]t's a whole philosophy – that's really about dismantling all these ways that we have been harmed and all these ways we can heal." Moreover, it transcends philosophy. "For me," Shah explained,

> Restorative justice is lifestyle and creating [a] sense of belonging that deeply centers our relationships. It serves as our humble antidote to capitalism, modernity, racism, historical trauma, all of these systems and histories that are meant to tear people apart, tear at the fabric of who we are.

Jodie Geddes similarly emphasized relationships and connection within her definition of RJ:

> There is a way that you want to be deeply connected with people whether that's in the world or in your family, but there's also these systems that don't allow for us to be as deeply connected as we would like to be. It's also a way for us to build deeper relationships with community and each other that's healthy.

It is noteworthy that both Geddes and Shah name deep connection with people in the context of systemic and historical harms as integral to their conceptualization of RJ.

For practitioner Dana Coles, RJ "*is a way to address – in some instances, in many instances – an underlying issue that goes well beyond just the incident or harm that happened*". As an example, Coles described cases often referred to her program in which young people have stolen basic necessities from grocery stores and drug stores:

> [A] lot of times they're stealing deodorant. They're stealing soap. . . . They're trying to meet a need that isn't being met. . . . They don't need to have a record because they stole a bar of soap. We need to address the need that they have.

Here, Coles points especially to the structural causes that lie at the root of much harm, and RJ as a process for acknowledging, identifying and meeting these needs.

Definitions of RJ continue to be contested, but too often the key concepts and contours that make their way into academic scholarship reflect the ideas of those with multiple forms of systemic power and privilege. It is essential for RJ practitioners to adopt a dual perspective that is not only attentive to interpersonal harm and accountability but also cognizant of systemic harms and the structural roots of crime (Napoleon, 2004). It is evident that Shah, Geddes and Coles hold this dual, or multidimensional, perspective on what RJ is and the contributions it offers to praxis. This perspective also surfaced within their reflections on deepening RJ and describing new generations of RJ movement building.

Deepening restorative justice

The three restorative practitioners that we spoke with outlined a vision for deepening RJ in two distinct areas. They assert that the contemporary RJ movement must become much more culturally conscious and more structurally responsive (Dyck, 2006). While there were calls for deepening additional dimensions of RJ practice (e.g. by fostering greater connections and linkages to additional justice movements), these two areas were emphasized the most. We provide a brief discussion of their responses around the issue of cultural consciousness and then focus much more extensively on attention to structural concerns.

Culturally conscious

Many RJ practitioners trace the roots of RJ to indigenous communities (e.g. Native American communities such as the Navajo in North America, the Maori people in New Zealand) and emphasize these origins in their scholarship and practice (e.g. when introducing processes such as peacemaking circles to new groups). While this was recognized as important and valuable, there was also a cautionary note about the tendency to exoticize and homogenize the indigenous roots of RJ, and deny the profound cultural nuance present among such practices. In Shah's words, the indigenous history of RJ in North America is "varied, it's complex, it's nuanced, you know. And has its own life force and organic-ness to it, right?" Recognizing this complexity is essential.

In addition, many cultural groups in the United States, particularly communities of color, desire to understand how RJ is rooted in their own history and traditions. As Coles laments,

> We're taught from other native perspectives. We're not taught from the African perspective any part, and I'm sure there are probably thousands of different African restorative practices that can be chosen, and none of those have been presented to us. . . . We just want some kind of connection to our ancestry.

Developing and highlighting histories of RJ from around the world will enable more individuals and communities to embrace the practice as relevant to their own cultural identity. Shah suggests that we must also go beyond this:

> We have to create RJ processes that center relationships, have ritual, and are about healing and justice. We do this by bringing own histories into the room and creating new practices that aren't co-opted. We're bringing ourselves, we're bringing our traditions, we're bringing our hurt and pain, and then we're trying to figure out how do we be in this wacky, multicultural, crazy world.

This work of bringing in multiple histories while writing history anew may be especially important for multicultural spaces.

Culture is often defined as "the way we do things around here." Coles emphasized the importance of RJ practitioners adopting their practice to reflect the culture of the communities in which they work, especially when the practitioners are a part of those same communities. As an African-American RJ practitioner working in a predominantly African-American locality, Coles has adopted the techniques she learned in training to better reflect her own racial-ethnic culture and that of the participants she regularly engages. "That's where I think we need to go with RJ, is not just making generic — especially if you're dealing with whole groups of people, which tend to be the case because a lot of harm and crime are dealt intra-culturally, you know? They're dealt intra-racially", Coles said. Her culturally conscious practice of RJ includes being attentive, creative and responsive to dynamics such as the use of language (e.g. the specific words used to ask a question), patterns of dialogue, eye contact and ways of expressing honour and affirmation.

Structurally responsive

Restorative justice is often introduced within US communities and institutions as a solution to the structural inequities that characterize federal, state and local criminal legal systems. The recognition of structural racism and its central role in funnelling African-American, Latinx, Native and South Asian youth into juvenile detention centres and adult prisons has led to the development of youth-focused RJ diversion programs and RJ organizations. The creation of Restorative Justice for Oakland Youth and the Key Bridge Community Conferencing Program in Prince George's County, Maryland, are two examples. Dana Coles, who leads the latter, stressed the tendency of school resource officers to define the actions of students of color perceived as insubordinate or defiant as criminal – a pattern that not only reflects structural racism (even when the adults are also people of color) but also structural power imbalances between youth and adults. Coles and Geddes see RJ processes as particularly useful for shifting these intergenerational power dynamics.

As a community organizer, Jodie Geddes experiments with the possibilities that RJ practice presents for identifying and disrupting traditional hierarchies of power that often determine who makes decisions for entire communities and whose experiences and perspectives are reflected in discourse and policies on public safety. During a circle process with the members of a neighborhood crime prevention council (NCPC), she asked the participants to share a time that they felt excluded:

> One of the reasons for that particular question was for them to think about people that are not in the circle process. . . . Are those voices on the margin? . . . To really begin to name that there are people who are really not showing up in the space, and those things are directly linked to power, which we have to acknowledge. And so I had a follow-up meeting with one of the co-chairs of that NCPC, and we're going to do follow-up circle processes.

While in practice RJ has the ability to challenge existing power imbalances, deploying RJ processes in this way requires practitioners to have an intersectional anti-oppression lens.

Shah and Geddes use the language of an "anti-bias lens," an "anti-racist lens" and an "anti-oppression analysis" to call out the necessity of seeing and naming the ways in which structural racism, patriarchy, heterosexism, xenophobia, adultism and other systems of oppression have led to any given harm and the responses to it, and how they function as ongoing sources of structural violence and harm. Shah and other members of the Ahimsa Collective bring this analysis into all of the work that they do. According to Shah, "Understanding the inequity and oppression has to be interwoven into everything." Both Shah and Geddes are adamant that racial justice and special attention to anti-black racism must be brought to the center of RJ movement building. Too many practitioners still lack, in the words of Geddes, "a lens around equity, and a really clear understanding of the way that racism has worked as a part of systems, and the foundation of the United States".

While Shah concedes that the movement as a whole "hadn't done enough to really unearth the structural piece," she believes that it is now headed in that direction. Geddes concurs, and envisions that furthering this direction will not only impact the analysis and vision of RJ practitioners but also have an effect on their approach to basic process decisions:

> When restorative justice begins to really hold an anti-bias lens, the voices that are on the margin are really becoming a part of that circle, right? When we think about power and hierarchy in circle process, it doesn't automatically go away because we're sitting in circle, right? It's about where are people sitting, who's the first person that's talking in circle, or who are even the facilitators of the circle process? Where is the circle being held? It goes down to all those details to really inform our lens of how we're living circle process and how the process goes. And I do think that more people are starting to do that investigation.

For these leaders, it is an investigation that begins with self.

As Shah explains, **"[W]**hite people who started doing RJ without a racial justice analysis or an anti-oppression analysis are kind of like, how do I do it? How do we integrate racial justice into restorative justice? . . . Actually it's your own unearthing, it's not how do we – it's how do you unearth all your relationships to racism so that you can do RJ from a more racially integrated place?" Geddes talks about the need for people "to do an investigation of themselves and their own practices, including herself, "because I think people can make the assumption that because I'm a black woman I don't make mistakes around prejudice and misunderstanding, but those things can still exist". In yet another moment of self-reflection, Geddes framed RJ as a way to "check myself . . . to check my educational privilege, and more and more my financial privilege, my economic privilege". As women of color located in a multiracial urban center with a strong history of social justice activism, the reflections of Geddes and Shah demonstrate what it looks like to infuse RJ with social justice values and principles from an intersectional framework.

Funding emerged as a focal point in the emergent conversation on RJ and structural inequality. Coles contends that "right now community conferencing as we are supposed to be practicing it, according to our grant funding, is for youth. . . . We're tied to that, as far as what we get money for, how we use that money, how we use our resources. But we'd like to expand it so that we can use restorative practices for the adult population in the county as well." Investing in RJ organizations and programs like Coles's – that is, those within communities of color led by practitioners of color, and powered by the members of their communities, also have incredible potential to shift structural disparities and leadership dynamics within the RJ movement as a whole. However, Geddes points out that funding streams can also water down the concentration of social justice practice when people enter the field primarily because "foundations can give your organization money for it". Shah continues to grapple with the complexities of resourcing the work of the Ahimsa Collective in ways that fully reflect her social justice vision and values: "I think that's the hardest place for me, how can we create this other funding source, other creative funding models . . . I would say there's these ways that we're embedded, structurally, in the violence of capitalism that feels impossible [to escape]." Shah has found some reprieve by moving away from non-profit organizational models that rely exclusively on paid staff. We cover this issue in greater detail within the next section.

Describing the new generation

The RJ leaders we interviewed shared diverse perspectives on who or what constitutes a "new generation of RJ". According to Coles, "Today's practitioners are the new generation, and that's who's evolving the practice." She sees previous generations of practitioners producing scholarship and engaged in university teaching, and a new generation constituted by contemporary practitioners like herself. Not only are these practitioners generating new ways to think about and practice RJ but they are also united in their opposition to incarceration as a solution to social problems: "I think for the first time in, at least in the US, we really are realizing that prisons aren't the answer," Coles attests. She continued:

> Imprisoning people is really about making money, and not about correcting bad behavior. It's not even about punishment. And I think this new generation of RJ and practitioners is onto that.

Even as practitioners took the lead in forming RJ as a bona fide field of practice in the early decades, once again we see it is the practitioners (organizers, activists and peacebuilders) who seem to be taking the lead to envision and model what RJ will look like for the next generation.

Affirming an increased focus on sexual violence and anti-prison perspectives within some spheres of the RJ movement, Shah described an RJ workshop panel she organized of survivors who are leading RJ work around sexual violence. Because the experiences of survivors of gender-based violence continue to receive scant attention in the criminal legal system, the overwhelming tendency is to call for increasingly severe punishment for people who commit sexual violence, Shah explains. She is among a vanguard of contemporary RJ leaders who insist that it is possible, even critical, to center the voices and experiences of survivors while also decrying punitive responses: "It's a very counter-narrative idea to be like, don't lock them up and throw away the key . . . well, the problem is, nobody's paying attention to survivors of sexual trauma, child sexual abuse and rape . . . all of these stories need a lot of space and healing, and at the same time it doesn't mean we need to lock more people up." In many ways, this perspective reflects a multidimensional and intersectional approach, as well as theoretical and visionary agility. With such agility, contemporary RJ practitioners are able to hold in one hand the reality of severe interpersonal violence, particularly intimate violence, and in the other hand the reality that incarceration keeps cycles of violence intact, and work for a world where neither are present. They are also bringing much more sophisticated consideration of trauma and trauma healing. As Geddes put it, "[F]olks are also in a space where they're really thinking about healing. Like, deep healing. And so restorative justice [offers] a way to do the healing, and the healing is what gets us free." Healing, liberation and freedom are core concepts in the lexicon of many new generation leaders.

Shah pushed back against the temptation to identify new generations of RJ using a narrative frame that presents history as linear and successive. Rather, new generations might be understood as both a return to the indigenous roots of the movement as well as a renewed legitimization of what has already been present – grassroots practitioners, particularly leaders of color, who have for decades been working at restorative and transformative strategies for safety and justice with attention to structural and systemic harms, cultural legacies of trauma and resilience, and a holistic, intersectional and visionary praxis. This tradition of practitioners, organizers and community leaders see themselves as part of multiple justice movements. And while this is not new, various generations are continually making new linkages to issues, interests and inquiries that have not been seen as integral to RJ movement building before. For example, Geddes noted that increasingly, people working from a RJ framework "are really thinking about what it means to restore relationship with our land, and I see some of that coming up in my conversations with folks around – particularly around RJ and truth and reconciliation". Geddes imagines that deeper connections between the RJ movement and the environmental racism movement will emerge from these explorations.

Geddes, who works primarily with teenagers and young adults, thinks about this demographic when she imagines a "new generation of RJ". Geddes contends: "There's a generation of young people that are really being deeply invested in restorative justice, and that are actually asking the questions for us to challenge the process." Geddes uses popular education approaches to help young people articulate their own political analysis and vision, while also exposing the young people within RJOY to the progressive theories and freedom dreams of movement leaders such as Angela Y. Davis. This is but one way that Geddes pursues what she calls "community restor-ganizing", the intersection of community organizing and RJ. Geddes notes this synthesis as another feature of the contemporary movement landscape, of a new generation of RJ: "What we're seeing is a deeper relationship between restorative justice and community organizing. More organizers are beginning to name restorative justice as a part of their practice. And I know that folks from Black Lives Matter have also been talking about restorative justice." As RJ leaders and organizations progressively draw from elements of community organizing, they come to invest more heavily into developing a base of members to build the movement.

Restorative justice work powered by voluntary community participation, rather than paid professionals, is indicative of this shift. Shah and Coles reveal the centrality of voluntary leadership and labor from local communities to RJ values and principles. For the community conferencing program that Coles directs, she says:

> [W]e utilize volunteers who live in our community, who give their time up to this process, who take the time to train. . . . A lot of our people do work full-time jobs and still take on this work, because they're passionate about it.

Coles is one of two paid staff in her community conferencing program in a large metropolitan area. They handle approximately 90 cases each year by relying on 20 trained volunteer facilitators. Coles strongly encourages anyone who plans to start new programs to train community members "to reach out to people in the community and use volunteers as their facilitators". This approach, according to Coles, is central to spreading the advancement and promotion of RJ:

> Because those volunteers have other communities that they're a part of . . . they have all kinds of other communities that they are in touch with, and are a part of that they can get the word out about this work. About this opportunity. About this way of handling harm and conflict.

It is here that we see the intersections between resource mobilization and political process theory in the development of social movements. Working off an "asset-based" approach to community organizing, the vision of RJ has captured the imagination of local leaders who volunteer their time and their energy to facilitate RJ processes in order to emancipate themselves, their families and their neighbourhoods. And at the same time they use their social-political networks as the means to spread the message about the liberatory power of RJ beyond their local contexts.

Sonya Shah describes additional benefits of reliance on community members who volunteer their time to provide facilitation, rather than a team of paid staff. Shah's Ahimsa Collective operates on the margins of the non-profit world as a network in which there are a few paid core members, but the majority of practitioners in the collective give their time. According to Shah, "When commitment is not based on monetary currency, but commitment is based on a sense of belonging and a sense of really true caring for each other, it's actually ridiculously strong." Shah recounts:

> I remember having this conversation with one of the facilitators . . . she's an elder black woman who's been doing this sort of work for a really long time in our community and I've known her for a long time. . . . When I approached her about facilitating, I was like, so, you know, you're worth so much more than this, but this is just a thousand dollars for the year as a token of affection for you and a sense of respect for what you offer. . . . And she just said to me, that means more than you know, and at the same time, it does help to keep the PGE lights on. I think she captured the sentiment exactly, which is, I'm doing this because I trust you, I love you, I know you. . . . And yeah, a little token of affection is also important.

The Ahimsa Collective values voluntary work in a way that pays special attention to "the sacredness of giving time", Shah said. The importance of voluntary labor, rather than reliance on paid staff, is further evidence of the existence and potential of RJ as social movement rather than social service, or professional field of practice alone.

Conclusion

Drawing from social movement theory, we have argued that RJ can be understood as a contemporary social movement and presented key contours and questions of this movement based on new research. Our research also supports the claim that the integrity and liberatory potential (Harris, 2010) of the RJ movement would be maximized by its existence and expansion as a contemporary movement for social justice. Therefore, it is imperative that we connect with and anchor our work in relation to ongoing grassroots struggles for safety, justice, liberation and healing in relation to a myriad of identities and issues. Many of the contemporary leaders that we spoke with through consultations, conferences, focus groups and one-on-one interviews are already engaged in this work.

RJ as a social movement will effectively accomplish its vision: by nurturing the safe space for truth-telling, accountability and trauma healing to occur, by offering a non-violent alternative to state-sanctioned retributive violence and therefore breaking the cyclical nature of generational revenge, by providing the platform for building community through the transmission of grassroots organizing and social reciprocities – bonding, bridging and linking capital (Flora and Flora, 2008), and finally by integrating social justice values and vision.

New generations of RJ require integration of an anti-oppression lens, which facilitates opportunities to challenge interpersonal and relational power imbalances that reflect structural and societal arrangements of power and privilege. Practicing RJ with social justice values enables movement beyond victim/offender binaries, enabling visionary practice that centres the narratives and needs of victims and survivors but also calls for alternatives to state violence for people who have committed harms, including severe harms. New generations of RJ movement building are also powered by community and volunteer engagement, not strictly paid professionals. Moreover, the leaders of today's RJ emphasize personal healing and transformation; it is healing as a practice of freedom.

As further practitioners, peacebuilders and organizers engage with RJ movement building for social justice, it will be especially important for us to grapple with a set of critical questions within our organizations and collectives, and in the field at large. These include:

- Who controls what is defined as RJ? Whose voices are being ignored?
- What counts as a harm in RJ practice? How do we see individual harms, collective harms, structural harms?
- How do we account for and address the structural and societal roots of interpersonal harms?
- Who is centred as victims, harmed persons, harmed groups? Who continues to be marginalized? How do we change this?
- What is the relationship of the RJ movement to the state? Whose interests are reflected?
- What does RJ offer when the state is the harm-doer?
- How might RJ be utilized as a framework to challenge systems of oppression, including white supremacy, patriarchy, heterosexism and global capitalism while addressing its internalized, interpersonal and structural manifestations?

Attention to social justice will require us to revisit these and other questions as we deepen our analysis and broaden our vision to inform new generations of innovative RJ practice.

Notes

1 We would like to acknowledge the tremendous research assistance of Hannah Kim, Brenna Case and Jennifer Lee.
2 The Zehr Institute for Restorative Justice was founded in 2012 under the auspices of the Center for Justice & Peacebuilding at Eastern Mennonite University – (zehr-institute.org).
3 This project was made possible through a three-year funding grant (2015–2017) generously provided by the Porticus Foundation, and the Listening Project was supplemented by a grant from the Open Philanthropy Project.
4 These highlights were adapted from a one-page summary written by David Belden, who masterfully edited the Listening Project Final Report. Available at: www.zehr-institute.org/publications.

References

Alexander, M. 2012. *The New Jim Crow – Mass Incarceration in the Age of Colourblindness*. New York: The New Press.

Asadullah, M. 2016. Victor's Justice or Restorative Justice: Exploring the Value of Participation for Bangladesh's Future Reconciliation Process, *Contemporary Justice Review*, 19(13): 347–362.

Braithwaite, J. and Gohar, A. 2014. Restorative Justice, Policing and Insurgency: Learning From Pakistan, *Law & Society Review*, 48(3): 531–561.

Branch, A, and Mampilly, Z. 2015. *Africa Uprising: Popular Protest and Political Change*. London: Zed Books.

Braswell, M., Fuller, J. and Lozoff, B. 2001. *Corrections, Peacemaking and Restorative Justice*. Cincinnati, OH: Anderson Publishing Co.

Davis, A. 2003. *Are Prisons Obsolete?* New York: Seven Stories Press.

Davis, F. and Scharrar, J. 2017. Reimagining and Restoring Justice: Toward a Truth and Reconciliation Process to Transform Violence Against African-Americans in the United States. In M. Silver (ed.) *Transforming Justice, Lawyers and the Practice of Law*. Durham, NC: Carolina Academic Press.

Dufur, P. 2013. Practices of Local Social Forums: The Building of Tactical and Cultural Collective Action Repertoires. In P. Coy (ed.) *Research in Social Movements, Conflicts and Change*, Vol. 36. Bingley: Emerald Group Publishing, p. 235.

Dyck, D. 2006. Reaching Toward a Structurally Responsive Training and Practice of Restorative Justice. In D. Sullivan and L. Tifft (eds.) *Handbook of RJ: A Global Perspective*. London and New York: Routledge, pp. 527–543.

Elmangoush, N. 2015. Customary Practice and Restorative Justice in Libya: A Hybrid Approach, *USIP*, Special Report 374, May 28.

Fine, G. 1995. Public Narration and Group Culture: Discerning Discourse in Social Movements. In H. Johnston, and B. Klandermans (eds.) *Social Movements and Culture*. Minneapolis, MN: University of Minnesota Press.

Flora, C. and Flora, J. 2008. *Rural Communities: Legacies and Change*, 2nd ed. Boulder, CO: Westview Press.

Galloway, B. and Hudson, J. (eds.) 1996. *Restorative Justice: International Perspectives*. Monsey, NY: Kugler Publications & Criminal Justice Press.

Gavrielides T. 2005. Some Meta-theoretical Questions For Restorative Justice, *Ratio Juris*, 18(1): 84–106. DOI: 10.1111/j.1467–9337.2005.00287.x.

Gavrielides, T. 2007. *Restorative Justice Theory and Practice: Addressing the Discrepancy*. Helsinki, Finland: European Institute for Crime Prevention and Control.

Gavrielides, T. 2013. Restorative Pain: A New Vision of Punishment. In T. Gavrielides and V. Artinopoulou (eds.) *Reconstructing Restorative Justice Philosophy*. Farnham: Ashgate, pp. 311–337.

Gavrielides, T. and Artinopoulou, V. 2013. *Reconstructing Restorative Justice Philosophy*. Farnham: Ashgate.

Ginwright, S. 2016. *Hope and Healing in Urban Education*. London and New York: Routledge Publishers.

Hadley, M. (ed.) 2001. *The Spiritual Roots of Restorative Justice*. New York: SUNY Press.

Harris, A.P. 2010. Book Review, Beyond the Monster Factory: Gender Violence, Race, and the Liberatory Potential of Restorative Justice, *Berkeley Journal of Gender and Law*, 25: 199.

Heideman, L. 2013. Pathologies in Peacebuilding: Donors, Ngos and Community Peacebuilding in Croatia. In P. Coy (ed.) *Research in Social Movements, Conflicts and Change*, Vol. 36. Bingley: Emerald Group Publishing Limited, p. 135.

Hooker, D. 2016. *The Little Book of Transformative Community Conferencing*. New York, NY: Good Books.

Hooker, D. and Czajkowski, A. 2012. *Transforming Historical Harms: Coming to the Table*. Harrisonburg, VA: Eastern Mennonite University.

Hunt, S., Bedford, R. and Snow, D. 1994. Identity Fields: Framing Processes and the Social Construction of Movement Identities. In E. Larana, H. Johnson and J. Gusfield (eds.) *New Social Movements: From Ideology to Identity*. Philadelphia, PA: Temple University Press.

INCITE! Women of Color Against Violence, eds. 2007. *The Revolution Will Not be Funded*. Cambridge, MA: South End Press.

Jain, S., Bassey, H., Brown, M. and Kalra, P. 2014. Restorative Justice in Oakland Schools – Implementation and Impacts [pdf]. Oakland, CA. Available at www.ousd.org/cms/lib/CA01001176/Centricity/Domain/134/OUSD-RJ%20Report%20revised%20Final.pdf. Accessed 8 January 2018.

Jenkins, M. 2006. Gullah Island Dispute Resolution: An Example of Afrocentric Restorative Justice. *Journal of Black Studies*, 37: 299–319.

Johnstone, G. 2001. *Restorative Justice: Ideas, Values, Debates*, 2nd ed. New York: Routledge.

Juma, M. 2012. Community-Based Approaches to the Reintegration of Self-demobilised Child Soldiers: The Case of the Democratic Republic of Congo. In I. Derluyn, C. Mels, S. Parmentier and W. Vandenhole (eds.) *Re-Member: Rehabilitation, Reintegration and Reconciliation of War-Affected Children*, Vol. 11 of the Transitional Justice Series. Cambridge: Intersentia, pp. 377–401.

Kahane, A. 2012. *Transformative Scenario Planning*. San Francisco, CA: Berrett-Koehler Publishers. Inc.

Kelly, R. 2006. *From Scoundrel to Scholar – The Russ Kelly Story*. Self-published. Available at www.volumesdirect.com/detail.aspx?ID=2955.

Kornhauser, W. 1959. *The Politics of Mass Society*. Glencoe: The Free Press.

Larana, E., Johnson, H. and J. Gusfield, eds. 1994. *New Social Movements: From Ideology to Identity*. Philadelphia, PA: Temple University Press.

Le Bon, G. 1895. *The Crowd – A Study of the Popular Mind*. Kitchner, ON: Batoche Books.

Lipsky, M. 1968. Protest as a Political Resource, *American Political Science Review*, 62: 1144–1158.

Mauer, M. and Jones, S. 2013. *Race to Incarcerate: A Graphic Retelling*, 3rd ed. New York: The New Press.

McAdam, D., McCarthy J. and M. Zaid (eds.) 1996. *Comparative Perspectives on Social Movements*. Cambridge: Cambridge University Press.

Napoleon, V. 2004. By Whom, and By What Processes: Is Restorative Justice Defined, and What Bias Might this Introduce? In: H. Zehr and B. Toews (eds.) *Critical Issues in Restorative Justice*. Monsey, NY, Cullompton and Devon: Criminal Justice Press and Willan, pp. 33–45.

Northey, W. 2004. Restorative Justice and Spiritual Origins, November 19. Available at http://m2w2.com/wp/wp-content/uploads/2009/08/rj-spiritual-origins-nov-2004.pdf. Accessed 4 September 2012.

Olsen, M. 1965 and 1971. *The Logic of Collective Action*. The President and Fellows of Harvard College.

Pavlich, G. 2005. *Governing Paradoxes of Restorative Justice*. New York: Routledge-Cavendish & Glass House Press.

Pollack, K., Byman, D. et al. 2011. *The Arab Awakening*. Washington DC: The Brookings Chapter.

Stevenson, B. 2014. *Just Mercy – A Story of Justice and Redemption*. New York: Speigel & Grau Publishers.

Sullivan, D. and Tifft, L. 2001. *Restorative Justice – Healing the Foundations of Our Everyday Lives*. Monsey, NY: Willow Tree Press.

Sullivan, D. and Tifft, L., eds. 2008. *Handbook of Restorative Justice*. London and New York: Routledge Press.

Templeton, R. 2004. She Who Believes in Freedom: Young Women Defy the Prison Industrial Complex. In V. Labaton and D. Lundy Martin (eds.) *The Fire this Time: Young Activists and the New Feminism*. New York: Anchor, pp. 254–277.

Toews, B. and Zehr, H., eds. 2004. *Critical Issues in Restorative Justice*. Monsey, NY: Criminal Justice Press.

Umbreit, M. and Armour, M. 2011. *Restorative Justice Dialogue: An Essential Guide for Research and Practice*. New York: Springer Publishing Company.

Van Ness, D. and Strong, K. 1997. *Restoring Justice: An Introduction to RJ*. London: Routledge.

Woolford, A. 2009. *The Politics of Restorative Justice: A Critical Introduction*. Winnipeg: Fernwood Publishers.

Zehr, H. 1990. *Changing Lenses: A New Focus for Crime & Justice*. Scottsdale, PA: Herald Press.

30

Transforming powers and restorative justice

George Pavlich

Introduction

Reckoning with the past is inescapable when imagining possible futures. Reflecting on what Nietzsche (1967) might have called the 'lowly beginnings' of restorative justice, I am drawn to elapsed promises of community mediation and its pledge to install new ideas and techniques of justice beyond courtrooms (e.g. mediations, conferences, panels and later circles). Prefiguring what would later appear under the amorphous banner of 'restorative justice' (Johnstone, 2011; Zernova, 2007), these promises were born from a critique of the state's inaccessible, alienating, and crime-focused justice. But what exactly was targeted by this critique? In my search for a dissertation topic, I decided to find out by observing – as per the sociology of law – law 'in action' rather than 'on the books'. Seated quietly in a lower court, I recall vividly the speedy presentation and disposition of 'cases' that one by one displaced a neatly kept stack of files (this was, after all, the 1980s). Each was methodically placed in the waiting hands of an administrator who adroitly filled out forms to reflect court decisions: pleas, judgements, warrants for arrest, bail conditions, sentencing, fines, incarceration orders and so on. The pile would be replaced, Sisyphus like, by another the following day. To be sure, such bureaucratic processes moved numbers efficiently through the courts, but they reduced people's complex anxieties and relations to reams of paper, with brown folders leading the way through criminalizing processes. One recalls the anxious faces of the people called to this justice – contoured by unequal class, gender and race profiles – as they followed in the wake of 'their' files (Latour, 2010).

No doubt, such observations echoed the officious, accusatorial institutions to which early alternative dispute resolution critics directed their concerns (e.g. Salem, 1985; Sander, 1976). Like others at the time (Merry and Milner, 1993), I was intrigued – even buoyed – by the aspiration to secure popular, neighbourhood justice, replacing the 'law in action' witnessed (see Llewellyn and Philpott, 2014; Sander, 1990). However, soon enough, disjunctions between aspiring community promises and practices led me to ponder fragmenting promises of justice (Pavlich, 1996). If early restorative calls to replace criminal justice were later attenuated (see

Aertsen et al., 2006; Woolford and Ratner, 2003), today renewed opportunities for alternatives to a criminal justice have emerged. Wood and Suzuki put it this way:

> Given the ideological implosion that is occurring in the United States and elsewhere (particularly with policy makers) of the tough-on-crime policies that have dominated criminal justice over the last quarter century or more, restorative justice represents an attractive alternative to the vacuum left in the wake of this implosion.
>
> *(2016: 160)*

Indeed, since restorative justice has thrived by shoring up a 'law and order' empire facing growing symbolic crises, one may ask this question: what earlier promises of community and neighbourhood justice were conceded in a restorative bid to complement such criminal justice? And what might these eclipsed promises suggest about the prospects for transformative, locally enunciated patterns of justice in the future?

With such questions in mind, the current chapter first recalls a selected genealogy of restorative ideas that reveals three key early promises. Curtailed by the sheer weight of programmatic struggles for survival, these promises remained largely unfulfilled in the cut and thrust of real politics for counter-powers in state-legitimated arenas of control (Walgrave, 2003). Regardless, there is value in returning to them, if only to consider what outshone restorative lineages might offer to those seeking alternate visions of justice today. Reassessing foundational community justice of past aspirations, that is, may allow us to consider paths not taken in the search for justice that do not by reflex summon notions of crime, criminals and mass punishment (Wacquant, 2010). Of course, these selected promises are not here presented as comprehensive, but are instead evoked to address the limits of present justice forms and to imagine outlines within which future visions of justice might be conceived.

Community becomes restorative justice

Useful accounts on the rise of restorative justice obviate repeating that general story (Johnstone, 2011; Zernova, 2007; Aertsen et al., 2006; Walgrave, 2003; Strang and Braithwaite, 2001; Wright, 1996). A less recounted strand of this story, however, considered whether developing informal alternatives to formal justice would ever be feasible (Matthews, 1988; Abel, 1982). To be sure, early advocates of community justice, alternative dispute resolution and neighbourhood justice sought to reclaim conflict from the state's expanding courtrooms (Shonholtz, 1984; Sander, 1976). Their aim was precisely to 'divert' cases out of state justice to communities. More than simply extending dispute resolution options, such diversions would resist growing state intrusions into people's lives, simultaneously renewing spontaneous civil societies and rekindling what appeared to some as the dying embers of participatory democracy (Shonholtz, 1988).

Against such promises, left-leaning critics argued that under the banner of 'community', informal justice had enabled the state to expand its reach by regulating disputes previously not even on its radar (Matthews, 1988; Hofrichter, 1987; Abel, 1982). Whereas 'minor' neighbourhood disputes had escaped state regulation, a new post-Fordist ethos sought to bring them under the control of community authorities (Baskin, 1988). In the process, social control networks expanded and assembled new kinds of 'offenders' in more finely woven regulatory meshes (Cohen, 1985). Thus, critics alleged that the promises of the informal, community justice movement, in effect, helped floundering welfare states to deal with intractable fiscal and legitimacy crises. By 'decarceration' and 'privatizing' its control operations, the state might thereby recast unpopular coercive controls in a more agreeable form (Abel, 1982). It could also exercise sovereign powers remotely by funding, populating and sanctioning selected community justice programmes (Pavlich, 1996). In this justice ethos, states only funded compliant community 'experiments' and authorized the people who were allowed to run – and even participate in – them (Hofrichter, 1987).

Some critics were also quick to counter hegemonic criminal justice ideologies that shored up exploitative social relations, and thereby perpetuated capitalist inequalities (Hofrichter, 1987; Abel, 1982). Many viewed informal claims to alternative justice as a ruse: under the guise of supposedly retracting capitalist state control from individual lives, this new justice imperceptibly expanded the state's capacity to reach into more areas of social life (Christie, 2015; Baskin, 1988; Cohen, 1985). In the process, informal justice helped to legitimize state control, precisely as crises began to reveal ideological cracks and exposed its rank oppressions (see Abel, 1982). So instead of informal justice enabling progressive social change – by retracting state control and opening possibilities for non-alienated political actors to emerge – it actually retarded transformative possibilities. By expanding state control, that is, such justice stifled potentially revolutionary community opposition (Hofrichter, 1987).

These debates might retrospectively suggest neoliberal divisions surfacing around a clash between advocates and critics of community mediation, informal justice, neighbourhood justice or alternative dispute resolution (Wacquant, 2010; Hofrichter, 1987). But as such descriptors were absorbed into the umbrella vagueness of 'restorative justice', subsequent iterations narrowed discussion to 'maximalist' (Walgrave, 2003) versus 'purist' (Strang and Braithwaite, 2001) visions of how to transform state approaches – from within or without criminalizing institutions (Acorn, 2004). If the maximalists sought to change criminal justice from within, the purists called for the latter's replacement. Drawing on concepts like 'reintegrative shaming', the plan was to replace an emphasis on punishing and excluding people with an endogenous form of justice (Braithwaite, 1989). However, as maximalist visions took pragmatic form on the ground, as it were, the dangers of state absorption and co-optation became clear; compromises were made that allowed successful programmes to nestle comfortably within criminal justice lexicons and forms (Wood and Suzuki, 2016; Pavlich, 2005). In the process of making such accommodations, restorative justice deserted notions of popular alternatives and became increasingly wedded to criminal law's lexicons – crime, offenders and victims (London, 2011). Thus, whereas the initial aspirations of community panels prioritized popular justice beyond criminalization (Blagg, 2005; Merry and Milner, 1993; Shonholtz, 1988), later versions of 'community justice' were increasingly tied to the prevention and management of crime (Clear et al., 2011; Karp and Clear, 2002; Clear and Karp, 1999).

In the event, though, narrowing discussions to dichotomous claims either 'for or against' state expansion or retraction in justice arenas seemed to me excessively reductive: it reified what was after all a complex, unfolding and dynamic political ethos. Drawing on selected themes in Foucault's (1980, 1979, 1978) work, I argued instead that critique could highlight the complex and changing power relations that were in the process of changing the very ideas and practice of justice in Western contexts (Pavlich, 1996). Even if those powers did little to curtail the vast overcriminalization that confronts us today (Husak, 2009), they reflected new ways for criminal and restorative measures to work in complementary ways to govern crime, or more appositely 'govern through crime' (Simon, 2007). This approach made explicit the consequent fragmentations as sovereign power was governmentalized and shaped by new disciplinary powers (Pavlich, 1996). It also showed how confluences of these hybrid powers complemented one another to form a changing control landscape, even as restorative advocates continued to claim a paradigmatic shift away from criminal justice (Zehr, 2015). It was indeed revealing that even supposed 'alternatives' premised themselves on basic concepts of the very justice they claimed to challenge (e.g. crime, victim, offender, criminal harm). Such may be the lot of counter-powers, and the resilient 'imitor paradox' they inevitably face, especially when seeking to replace culturally hegemonic political forms, such as with the criminal justice systems (Pavlich, 2005). Regardless, this paradox suggests less an abject failure of restorative promises and more an indication that all power relations are beset by intrinsic dangers.

From this, one detects the importance of critical vigilance, of actively seeking out and naming dangerous potentials – even if unintended – within unfolding power configurations. The key issue was this: justice could never be secured by either uncritical advocates, or by advocating critics. Instead, it seemed more productive to insist on naming and maintaining a close watch over emerging powers, social limits and the exclusions produced in the wake of encounters between powers and counter-powers. In the spirit of this critical vigilance, the next section of the chapter re-examines three promises to restrict unfettered criminalization by criminal justice institutions: (1) calling for justice outside of criminalizing tendencies; (2) focusing on relations to pursue the transformations of a social or community justice; and (3) challenging notions of criminal justice that helped to define the state's sovereign powers. These are closely related promises, but in retrospect they remained unfulfilled in different ways. Each also suggests new ways to reactivate calls for justice beyond hegemonic reflexes to criminalize unequally that still constrain our concepts and practices of justice (Alexander, 2010).

Three past promises in future prospect

Promise 1: Justice beyond criminalization

In efforts to distinguish restorative from criminal justice, as seen earlier in this chapter, advocates of the former initially rallied around ideas of neighbourhood or community justice. Yet this was later more influentially framed by Zehr (2015, 2002) as a 'paradigm shift' with the markedly 'different lenses' of a restorative justice. Whereas criminal law used accusatorial methods to judge the legal guilt or innocence of accused persons, restorative justice sought communal measures to 'repair the harms' of crime as a primary focus (Johnstone, 2011, 2003). The one was seen as an abstracted legal approach, the other required the direct involvement and active participation of all parties to a dispute (Zernova, 2007). The latter's assumption was that the harms of broken relations between people were best calibrated, and responses agreed to, by those affected. From this vantage point,

> Crime is a violation of people and relationships. It creates obligations to make things right. Justice involves the victim, the offender, and the community in a search for solutions which promote repair, reconciliation, and reassurance
>
> *(Zehr, 2015: 183).*

In other words, what had to be controlled was not simply the abstracted 'crimes' defined by statute or code, nor an amorphous 'criminal' targeted for authorized vengeance and retribution (see Johnstone and Van Ness, 2007). Rather it was concrete persons who did something wrong by harming other 'people and relationships' and often in profound ways (Zehr, 2015: 183, 187). Addressing the complex needs, responsibilities and duties of all participants was deemed essential to restoring 'right relations' that promised to reduce repeated enactments of social harm. On the strength of this logic, restorative justice challenged the combative and even 'criminogenic' form that criminal justice had assumed (Zehr, 2015).

In the event, the subsequent promise to 'divert' social conflicts away from criminalizing structures was limited, as the restorative movement's success depended on serving as a 'complementary alternative' to criminal justice (Smith, 2011; Law Reform Commission of Canada, 1977). This may have propelled its global influence, but it also subordinated its initiatives, first, to what was considered 'crime,' and then, to the 'harms' or 'obligations' that criminal behaviour generated (Zehr, 2015). Consequently, it positioned itself as an accomplice to expanding industries directed at 'crime' (Christie, 2013; Matthews, 1988). Indeed, restorative justice's remarkable expansion may make claims about 'diverting cases', but this is less a diversion to a radically different kind of justice and more as an option authorized and largely funded by an increasingly heterogeneous and expanding 'crime-control industry' (Christie, 2013). Like other trades, that industry's future was tied to continually shoring up, and indeed expanding, its criminalizing operations (Tauri, 2016). There were, of course, many ways to do this, and its institutions pursued some options vigorously, including by increasing the number of statutes under which persons could be criminalized (Farmer, 2016). But these state forms also linked up with, and supported themselves through, 'complementary' versions of restorative justice that they authorized, funded and populated. In return, restorative measures worked within expanded police, courts and mass incarceration institutions. Ideas about diverting, replacing and shrinking criminal justice were sidelined as restorative ideas and practices followed omniscient visions of crime, criminals and victims (Woolford, 2009; Woolford and Ratner, 2003).

If diversionary promises of community justice, then, remained unfulfilled, they could in future be redirected to reduce the scope of criminalization and punishment. Specifically, diversion might be revitalized by engaging sociopolitical rationales and practices as gateways to criminal justice (Pavlich, 2000). In that way, restorative justice could directly engage the ideas and practices that populate unequal criminal justice systems. Focusing on the initiating rituals by which criminal accusation translates complex life to narrow idioms of criminal law would call restorative attention to the moments that inaugurate vast criminalizing enterprises (Pavlich, 2018a). Furthermore, engaging the accusatory rituals that call people to account (e.g. as criminals, offenders, victims) could have profound social ramifications, just as reviving diversionary aspirations might highlight the work of gatekeepers and gatekeeping rituals at thresholds to criminal justice. Since these accusatory processes seldom attract direct attention, no doubt exacting political advantage from that silence, a future opening could spawn restorative justice initiatives to reduce the size of criminal justice systems by restricting their entryways. Such initiatives could then narrow the scope of what and who is criminalized by attending to the size and inequalities of the gates through which accused persons must pass in order to face state criminalization.

This sort of justice might also recognize explicitly its role in forming social limits and summoning new targets for governance. Of course, the latter would avoid an all-too-prevalent reflex to border social forms through practices centred on crime, criminals and their punishment. If there be democratically framed reasons for criminalizing highly destructive social events, they will be comparably few when set against the vast and unequal flows that criminalize as a reflex (Ball, 2009). Regardless, a future restorative justice might curtail dominant cultural impulses to criminalize by attending to rituals that call regulatory targets to account. Given the variable forms destructive social behaviour might take, this kind of justice could develop social rituals that do not simply frame complex societal events as criminalizable individual culpability. But that leads us directly to the next promise, which was to target and transform collective structures (inequality, alienation, marginalization, exclusion, etc.) behind destructive social forms (Rosenblatt, 2015).

Promise 2: Deal with damaged relations by transforming social forms

More specifically, an early promise of restorative justice advocates was not simply to focus on the actions, intentions or guilt of individual offenders but to also pay attention to the victims and the communities harmed by criminal acts (Zehr, 2015; Braithwaite, 1990). Broadening rituals of justice to include identities beyond criminal justice's emphasis on 'guilty' individuals also called for local changes to social relations that produced harm (Johnstone and Van Ness, 2007). By concentrating on healing harms agreed to by those affected by destructive acts, and restoring 'right relations' between them, restorative practices were intended to work off participants' varied needs. One strand of such thought promised to offer transformative kinds of justice (Bazemore and Schiff, 2001; Bush and Folger, 2004; Law Commission of Canada, 1999). Even those who spoke of crime, sought to do so broadly; namely, by considering its 'interpersonal' nature in a 'full' context – 'moral, social, economic and political' (Zehr, 2015: 184). Community justice advocates were also clear that 'communal' rather than mere individually focused responses were important to addressing 'criminal' matters with a greater chance of lasting peace (Hoyle, 2010). In such calls, one senses an emphasis placed on social transformations, not simply restorations to the very relations that generated problematic behaviour in the first place. In other words, social reform and change was very much part of the initial philosophy and promise to fundamentally recast our approaches to justice and damaged relations (Gavrielides and Artinopoulou, 2013).

In the event, however, an opportunity to expand the regulation of harmful actions beyond individualized conceptions of criminal and victim was missed. Instead, restorative rituals increasingly devoted attention to the 'needs' of victims and offenders following a crime, and indeed the hypostatized visions of 'the community' that they were imagined as sharing (Pavlich, 2005). This approach largely (though not entirely) eclipsed the possibility of responding to social disruptions beyond idioms of individual criminal culpability. Whatever the merits of such thinking in certain cases, it assumed criminal justice conceptions of participant identities as offenders, victims or communities. In rendering itself subservient to such regulatory objects, restorative justice entered a Mephistophelean pact with a price. The pact was to complement criminal justice; the price included sacrificing a promise to develop a paradigmatically different justice focused on changing 'interpersonal' social relations behind injurious events. In foregoing that promise, restorative justice did not fully develop as a social movement in pursuit of social justice, nor did it actively develop as a counter-power in search of ways to change complex relational structures that shaped destructive acts, actors or perhaps even the exclusionary (punishment orientated) impulses of criminal justice.

But perhaps it is possible to recover from that unfulfilled promise vestiges of what might have been, and which could be taken up in future. Specifically, the vast exclusionary justice landscapes confronting us nowadays might be approached as complex sociopolitical arenas capable of varied development (Woolford, 2009). Given the sheer dominance of criminal justice horizons in our lives, most people conceive of crime through abstracted laws, and some may even take as obvious the need to address such crime via individually conceived victims, offenders and their collective assimilation within communities or states. But we should also recognize the contingency of these assumptions: none is an *a priori* being – each is a contingent product of a pervasive reflex to govern in the name of crime (Simon, 2007). Bearing that contingency in mind, one could refuse basic criminal justice assumptions to name, and ask different questions of, powers that might work under a broad banner of justice. What sociopolitical identities do particular rituals claiming the name of justice demand? Must these be individually conceived? Do their ritualized processes address local conflicts and yet also attend to wider social matters that could prevent their reoccurrence? Common rituals of restorative justice (e.g. conferences) are seldom directed at fundamental social transformation, especially when they deal with the aftermath of 'crime' through individual victim and offender identities, alongside assumptions of fixed, consensual communities (Moyle and Tauri, 2016; Tauri, 2009; Stubbs, 2009; Blagg, 2005).

Of course, this is not to deny devastating traumas of victimization experienced by those harmed, or even the background biographical ruptures experienced by some that harm others (Strang, 2002; Dignan, 2005). But social precepts may blur distinctions between identities. Moreover, imagining a stable 'community' as a common and consensual field behind either or both might seriously misconceive the collective foundations that yield social trauma. In any case, such recognitions do suggest the possibility of a 'paradigm shift' that could approach justice as an engagement with the social complexes behind destructive collective harms. Of course, how exactly such harms are defined is always to be worked out politically in historical contexts, and restorative justice might provide for rituals that enable diverse voices to assist communal deliberations of such limits (Braithwaite, 1990; Gordon, 1997). Even so, recalling restorative justice's promise to deal with social conflict via interpersonal relations in their 'full' moral, political social and legal contexts reminds us that simply replicating criminal justice's individualized conceptions of responsibility and harm seems to lose sight of, or at least marginalize, the underlying social foundations of destructive interpersonal conflict.

If, however, justice's aim is to transform social relations that ushered in harmful events, then its rituals may be expected to focus on identifying and changing these relations. Pursuing 'right relations' seems to require paths that assist all parties to work through the pain and disempowerments of victimization, while recalibrating 'being with' others in ways that avoid future recurrences of social action that destroys sociality (Pavlich, 2009; Nancy, 2000). Equally, focusing on social change in the aftermath of such events might signal a different target for justice that focuses not on individuals but that which lies 'in between', namely, the relations that generate specific kinds of subjects, whether victims or offenders, neighbours or enemies, or other identities (Pavlich, 2018b; Esposito, 2010). The altered focus might then see restorative governance exploring social limits in order to redress structures of unequal marginalization that generate interpersonal ruptures.

From an earlier promise, then, restorative justice might revive a focus on social formulations of wrongdoing and recognize the significance of transforming problematized aspects of society. No doubt this approach would require a shake-up of institutions concerned with setting limits to social forms in the name of sovereigns and their criminal justice, refusing expanding crime-control industries that blithely criminalize subjects as a routine response to social perceptions of limit infraction. As a counter-power to this justice, restorative initiatives might then develop governing rituals centred on social rather than criminal justice, emphasizing the relational foundations 'between' individuals, recognizing that people *become* (i.e. they are not fixed beings) through instances of 'being with' (the social) through fluid relational histories (Nancy, 2000). Locating responsibility in social relations that yield historical individuals and identities could be accommodated by developing new rituals, namely, ones that enable plural voices to narrate perspectival stories that re-imagine being differently with others. They might also pursue visions of 'inoperative' communities (Nancy, 1991) conceived as always on the way to becoming rather than as closed ontological absolutes (Pavlich, 2018b). Regardless, by emphasizing the relational and fluid nature of communal patterns, it may be possible to pursue a socially transformative justice whose rituals are directed, say, to redressing specific powers that shape social inequalities (e.g. race, class and gender – see Alexander, 2010; Gavrielides, 2014). The overarching aim here would be to enhance, rather than erode, variegated social relations and attachments.

Promise 3: Pluralizing justice beyond imperial and colonial sovereignty

At somewhat of an admitted stretch, one might detect in restorative attempts to recover silenced forms of conflict resolution an implicit challenge to sovereign powers allied with criminal justice (Braithwaite, 1990). For instance, restorative justice's 'origin myths' influentially traced restorative justice to pre-colonial, and indigenous ideas/practices of conflict resolution (Tauri, 2016; Gavrielides, 2011; Daly, 2002). There is much wrong with such moves, as they misappropriated pre-modern and indigenous ideas of conflict resolution (Tauri, 2009; Hewitt, 2016; Stubbs, 2009), overlooked whether complex indigenous formulations could ever be authentically reconciled to restorative techniques (Cunneen, 2007), and failed to recognize that a global expansion of restorative techniques at times hindered indigenous self-determination (Tauri, 2016). Yet for all that, one might recover in silenced ideas and repressed rituals of justice, together with restorative uses of disciplinary and pastoral powers beyond sovereignty (Pavlich, 1996), a vague and implicit critique of sovereign power. Hence, an initial promise was to do something about the injustices of sovereign sponsored powers that criminalized so many subjects through disaffecting institutions (McGillis, 1997). Restorative justice was to challenge the abstract, often incomprehensible, logic of juridical lexicons that estranged people from justice, and so seek 'justice without law' (Auerbach, 1984). In short, the search for justice through participatory community development promised more than the resolution of conflict; it was also to revitalize civic participation (Braithwaite, 2002a, Shonholtz, 1988).

But as restorative justice increasingly adopted criminal justice lexicons, clear challenges to the injustices of state criminalization and intimidating sovereignty abated. More and more, restorative adherents focused on defining the kind of 'option' restorative justice might provide within the ambit of criminal justice. If such developments muted promises to substitute the injustices within state's vast criminalizing empires, they also stifled ideas of popular justice. Indeed, whereas local ideas of justice were initially embedded in the deployment of early community panels (Merry and Milner, 1993), that sense was conspicuously absent in later iterations of 'community justice'; as noted, now communities were condensed to spaces that could eliminate 'crime' through prevention and crime-reduction efforts (Clear and Karp, 1999; Karp, 1998). Consequently, the moment was lost to reflect in more subtle ways on the interactions between powers of imperial and settler-colonial sovereignty, fixed communities united in their rallies against crime and how popular (globally expansive) restorative measures might avoid serving either or both.

Instead of grappling with the complexities posed by local, plural and often competing visions of justice, then, the global ambitions of restorative justice were secured by becoming marginal add-ons to criminal justice systems (Wood and Suzuki, 2016). As noted, co-optation rather than resistance marked such power arrangements, and they evinced how restorative programmes depended on the state's criminal justice concepts, institutional authorization, and funding and referrals (police, courts, prisons). Rather than pluralizing local forms of justice, such arrangements tended towards worldwide homogeneity; a paradoxical situation in which restorative counter-powers were mobilized as local alternatives, but now from *within* dominant criminal justice cultures. These alignments sacrificed the promise of plural, local justice that changed harm-generating social relations and contested the criminalizing dimensions of sovereign powers.

Even so, the earlier pursuit of popular justice, to limit the state's sovereignty-orientated criminal justice, suggests a possible line for future development. There are examples and ideas that illustrate possible ways to think about justice along these lines. The Zwelitemba model in South Africa provided for visions of justice beyond the courts, within the hands of local groups, but yet was governed by a constitution to avoid dangers that haunt all communal power relations (Froestad and Shearing, 2012). The programmes included measures aimed at social transformation, while offering local responses, different from sovereign criminalizing justice. By way of another example, Braithwaite (2002a) suggests that restorative justice understand its role as part of 'responsive regulation' with broad 'standards' rendering it subservient to republican forms of democracy (Braithwaite, 2002b). One may or may not agree with that 'civic republicanism', and whether it actually challenges neoliberal forms of sovereignty; but there is surely purchase in calling for non-dominating restorative processes that promote civil freedoms and restrain dominating powers. Indeed, he argues thus:

> [A] programme is not restorative if it fails to be active in preventing domination. What does this mean in practice? It means that if a stakeholder wants to attend a conference or circle and have a say, they must not be prevented from attending. If they have a stake in the outcome, they must be helped to attend and speak. This does not preclude special support circles for just victims or just offenders; but it does mandate institutional design that gives every stakeholder a meaningful opportunity to speak and be heard. Any attempt by a participant at a conference to silence or dominate another participant must be countered.
> *(Braithwaite, 2002b: 565)*

He also calls thus for plural forms of justice in an environment responsive to active communities and self-defining local voices:

> Evidence and innovation from below instead of armchair pontification from above should be what drive the hopes of restorative justice to replace our existing injustice system with one that actually does more to promote justice than to crush it. It would be a less tidy justice system, but tidiness seems decisively not a good candidate for a justice standards framework.
> *(Braithwaite, 2002b: 576).*

Inevitably, such dynamism requires allowance for plural visions of justice that would enable diverse voices to frame justice and pursue transformed social relations, all working under the restraining banner of civil order – ironically once an aspiration of criminal law, now too largely abandoned (see Farmer, 2016). Whatever one makes of these examples, they suggest prospects for thinking about the future of restorative justice beyond a current reliance on unequal criminalizing powers that define and punish criminals in the name of state (sovereign) authority – whether deriving from legacies of imperial or settler-colonial political forms.

This suggests another important possibility. Reflecting on how restorative and indigenous traditions in Canada and New Zealand had previously been framed, Zehr acknowledges that he 'did not adequately realize in those early days what a tremendous debt restorative justice owes to many indigenous traditions' (Zehr, 2015: 234). More generally, though, he calls for restorative justice to 'legitimate and reclaim the restorative elements in our traditions – traditions that were often discounted and repressed by Western colonial powers' (2015: 236). If appropriately considered, and framed, such indigenous traditions might indeed form part of challenges to the criminalizing powers of settler-colonial sovereignty. They could also be understood as mapping political forms of self-determination appropriate to local context, as well as plural rituals of justice to serve local contexts. Just as crime-focused law at the Cape of Good Hope at the turn of the 19th century was instrumental in defining settler-colonial sovereignty, so one might understand how criminal justice survives – despite its notable failure and exacting costs – because it helps to define contemporary state sovereignty (Pavlich, 2013). Perhaps the most promising dimension of a local justice that recognizes its socially transformative mission lies in appropriately enabling the recovery of lost rituals and idioms marginalized by settler-colonial sovereignty – akin to the quest to assert indigenous law (Napoleon and Friedland, 2016; Borrows, 2002). Here one might question alignments of criminal law and settler-colonial sovereignty in order to re-imagine plural patterns of justice that recalibrate dominant forms of governance. Such governance might seek rituals and idioms that promote rather than erode local social bonds, engage rather than stifle critical voices, enable rather than prevent indigenous self-determination and question rather than blindly serve sovereign forms of criminal justice.

All such initiatives would recognize that constant critical vigilance is required to thwart the dangers that continuously beset power formations – no power relations escape potential perils. Whether such vigilance is sought through struggles over rights, standards, constitutional limits, laws, treaties and the like, the important matter rests with restraining powers, and actively enabling diverse voices to show the effects thereof. However, there is also value in not overplaying the role of restorative justice in all this. As Zehr perceptively puts it,

> Restorative justice at its best is a compass, pointing a direction, but not a detailed map describing how to get there. Ultimately, what is most important about restorative justice may not be its specific theory or practice but the way it opens a dialogue, an explanation, in our communities or societies about our assumptions and our needs.
>
> *(Zehr, 2015: 231)*

Conclusion

The previous discussion has surveyed some early ideas behind a global restorative justice complex. Working off the idea that justice terrains are contoured by diverse ideas and power relations, the chapter began by repudiating the value of 'for or against' restorative or criminal justice debates when imagining possible futures for this movement. Recognizing instead the intricate power relations at play within justice domains, and their direct insinuation into mindsets, it critically explored three promises that positioned restorative justice as a counter-power to the pervasive powers of criminal justice. Highlighting early aspirations to contest and replace aspects of criminal justice indicated paths not taken by foremost strands of the movement. In returning to such promises, though, one might see possibilities for reinvigorating future political engagements with justice. We saw how, first, the quest for justice without criminalization, by diverting cases from courtrooms, was attenuated by restorative successes; but it also implied possibilities for future engagements with a politics of criminal accusation that reduces entryways to criminal justice. Secondly, promising to broaden responses to socially destructive events beyond criminal justice's emphasis on crime, criminals and victims showed prospects for re-engaging social relations behind such events – suggesting the value of pursuing a fluid communal justice that calibrates how to 'be with' in other ways. Finally, an unfulfilled restorative promise to replace criminal justice measures behind settler-colonial and imperial sovereign powers opens possibilities for imagining rituals that actively promote contextual social bonds through inclusion, enable indigenous self-determination and question rather than blindly serve sovereign forms of criminal justice.

Throwing forth ideas of a future from the horizons of a present inevitably proceeds through supposition. But it also points, as per one of the aims of this collection, to possibilities for conceiving of and practising restorative justice that rework all but forgotten promises. Yet one should at least be clear on this point: the previous discussion has not sought to unearth an imagined purity of purpose. Nor has it summoned autochthonous solutions calling for a return to pure origins gone awry. Rather, the intent has been to excavate three more or less neglected lines of descent as a way to rethink key early promises and their prospects. Historical calculations of justice, whether criminal, restorative, community or popular, can never capture the boundless promise of justice that always gestures to other ways of 'being with' (Derrida, 1992). But we cannot escape situated calculations, either. So, as we negotiate between the limits of a finite now and infinite promises of what may be, the preceding is offered as a way to enunciate limited possibilities of what may now come to be.

References

Abel, Richard L., ed. 1982. *The Politics of Informal Justice*. Studies on Law and Social Control. New York: Academic Press.

Acorn, Annalise E. 2004. *Compulsory Compassion: A Critique of Restorative Justice*. Vancouver: UBC Press.

Aertsen, Ivo, Daems, Tom and Robert, Luc, eds. 2006. *Institutionalizing Restorative Justice*. Cullompton and Portland, OR: Willan.

Alexander, Michelle. 2010. *The New Jim Crow: Mass Incarceration in the Age of Colorblindness*. New York: New Press.

Auerbach, Jerold. 1984. *Justice Without Law?* Oxford: Oxford University Press.

Ball, Jennifer. 2009. *Doing Democracy with Circles: Engaging Communities in Public Planning*. St. Paul: Living Justice Press.

Baskin, Deborah. 1988. Community Mediation and the Public/Private Problem, *Social Justice* 15(1):742–786.

Bazemore, S. Gordon, and Schiff, Mara, eds. 2001. *Restorative Community Justice: Repairing Harm and Transforming Communities*. Cincinnati: Anderson.

Blagg, Harry. 2005. *A New Way of Doing Justice Business?: Community Justice Mechanisms and Sustainable Governance in Western Australia*. Background Paper, no 8. Perth, W.A.: Law Reform Commission of Western Australia.

Borrows, John. 2002. *Recovering Canada: The Resurgence of Indigenous Law*. Toronto: University of Toronto Press.

Braithwaite, John. 1989. *Crime, Shame, and Reintegration*. Cambridge: Cambridge University Press.

Braithwaite, John. 1990. *Not Just Deserts: A Republican Theory of Criminal Justice*. Oxford: Clarendon Press.

Braithwaite, John. 2002a. *Restorative Justice & Responsive Regulation*. Oxford: Oxford University Press.

Braithwaite, John. 2002b. Setting Standards for Restorative Justice, *British Journal of Criminology*, 42: 563–577.

Bush, Robert, A. Baruch and Folger, Joseph P. 2004. *The Promise of Mediation: The Transformative Approach to Conflict*. San Francisco, CA: Jossey-Bass.

Christie, Nils. 2013. *Crime Control as Industry*. London: Routledge.

Christie, Nils. 2015. Widening the Net, *Restorative Justice*, 3(1):109–113.

Clear, Todd R., Hamilton, John R. and Cadora, Eric. 2011. *Community Justice*, 2nd ed. New York: Routledge.

Clear, Todd R. and Karp, David R. 1999. *The Community Justice Ideal: Preventing Crime and Achieving Justice*. Crime and Society. Boulder, CO: Westview Press.

Cohen, Stanley. 1985. *Visions of Social Control*. Cambridge: Polity Press.

Cunneen, Chris. 2007. Reviving Restorative Justice Traditions? In Gerry Johnstone and Daniel W. Van Ness (eds.) *Handbook of Restorative Justice*. Collumpton: Willan, pp. 113–131.

Daly, Kathleen. 2002. Restorative Justice: The Real Story, *Punishment and Society*, 4(1): 55–79.

Derrida, Jacques. 1992. Force of Law: The Mystical Foundation of Authority. In Drucilla Cornell, Michel Rosenfeld, and David Gray Carlson (eds.) *Deconstruction and the Possibility of Justice*. New York: Routledge, pp. 3–67.

Dignan, James. 2005. *Understanding Victims and Restorative Justice*. Maidenhead: Open University Press.

Esposito, Roberto. 2010. *Communitas: The Origin and Destiny of Community*. Cultural Memory in the Present. Stanford: Stanford University Press.

Farmer, Lindsay. 2016. *Making the Modern Criminal Law: Criminalization and Civil*. Oxford: Oxford University Press.

Foucault, Michel. 1978. *The History of Sexuality*, Vol. 1. New York: Pantheon Books.

Foucault, Michel. 1979. *Discipline and Punish: The Birth of the Prison*. New York: Vintage Books.

Foucault, Michel. 1980. *Power/Knowledge: Selected Interviews and Other Writings, 1972–1977*. New York: Vintage Books.

Froestad, Jan and Shearing, Clifford. 2012. *Security Governance, Policing, and Local Capacity*. Boca Raton: CRC Press.

Gavrielides, T. 2011. Restorative Practices: From the Early Societies to the 1970s. *Internet Journal of Criminology*. ISSN 2045–6743.

Gavrielides, T. 2014. Bringing Race Relations into the Restorative Justice Debate, *Journal of Black Studies*, 45(3): 216–246.

Gavrielides, Theo and Artinopoulou, Vasso. 2013. *Reconstructing Restorative Justice Philosophy*. Farnham: Routledge.

Gordon, Bazemore. 1997. The 'Community' in Community Justice: Issues, Themes, and Questions for the New Neighborhood Sanctioning Models, *The Justice System Journal*, 19(2): 193–228.

Hewitt, Jeffery G. 2016. Indigenous Restorative Justice: Approaches, Meaning & Possibility. *University of New Brunswick Law Journal*, 67: 313–335.

Hofrichter, Richard. 1987. *Neighborhood Justice in Capitalist Society: The Expansion of the Informal State*. New York: Greenwood Press.

Hoyle, Carolyn, ed. 2010. *Restorative Justice: Critical Concepts in Criminology*. Critical Concepts in Criminology. London: Routledge.

Husak, Douglas. 2009. *Overcriminalization: The Limits of the Criminal Law*. Oxford: Oxford University Press.

Johnstone, Gerry, ed. 2003. *A Restorative Justice Reader: Texts, Sources, Context*. Cullompton: Willan.

Johnstone, Gerry. 2011. *Restorative Justice: Ideas, Values, Debates*, 2nd ed. Abingdon: Routledge.

Johnstone, Gerry and Van Ness, Daniel W., eds. 2007. *Handbook of Restorative Justice*. Cullompton: Willan.

Karp, David R. 1998. *Community Justice: An Emerging Field: Rights and Responsibilities*. Lanham, MD: Rowman & Littlefield.

Karp, David R. and Clear, Todd R. 2002. *What Is Community Justice?: Case Studies of Restorative Justice and Community Supervision*. Thousand Oaks: Sage.

Latour, Bruno. 2010. *The Making of Law: An Ethnography of the Conseil d'Etat*. Cambridge: Polity Press.

Law Commission of Canada. 1999. *From Restorative Justice to Transformative Justice: Discussion Paper*. Ottawa: Law Commission of Canada.

Law Reform Commission of Canada. 1977. *Diversion*. Ottawa: Minister of Supply and Services Canada,.

Llewellyn, Jennifer J. and Daniel Philpott. 2014. *Restorative Justice, Reconciliation, and Peacebuilding*. New York: Oxford University Press.

London, Ross. 2011. *Crime, Punishment, and Restorative Justice: From the Margins to the Mainstream*. Boulder, CO: First Forum Press.

Matthews, Roger, ed. 1988. *Informal Justice?* Sage Contemporary Criminology. London: Sage Publications.

McGillis, Daniel. 1997. *Community Mediation Programs: Developments and Challenges*. Darby, PA: Diane Publishing.

Merry, Sally Engle and Milner, Neal, eds. 1993. *The Possibility of Popular Justice: Case Study of Community Mediation in the United States*. Ann Arbor: University of Michigan Press.

Moyle, Paora and Tauri, Juan Marcellus. 2016. Māori, Family Group Conferencing and the Mystifications of Restorative Justice, *Victims & Offenders*, 11 (1): 87–106.

Nancy, Jean-Luc. 1991. *The Inoperative Community*. Theory and History of Literature 76. Minneapolis, MN: University of Minnesota Press.

Nancy, Jean-Luc. 2000. *Being Singular Plural*. Meridian, Crossing Aesthetics. Stanford: Stanford University Press.

Napoleon, Val, and Friedland, Hadley. 2016. An inside Job: Engaging with Indigenous Legal Traditions through Stories, *McGill Law Journal*, 4: 725–730.

Nietzsche, Friedrich. 1967. *The Will to Power*. New York: Knopf Doubleday.

Pavlich, George. 1996. *Justice Fragmented: Mediating Community Disputes Under Postmodern Conditions*. London: Routledge.

Pavlich, George. 2000. Forget Crime: Accusation, Governance and Criminology, *Australian & New Zealand Journal of Criminology*, 33(2): 136–152.

Pavlich, George. 2005. *Governing Paradoxes of Restorative Justice*. London: GlassHouse Press.

Pavlich, George. 2009. Being Accused, Becoming Criminal. In Don Crewe and Ronnie Lippens (eds.) *Existentialist Criminology*. London: Routledge, pp. 53–69.

Pavlich, George. 2013. Cape Legal Idioms and the Colonial Sovereign, *International Journal for the Semiotics of Law*, 26: 39–54.

Pavlich, George. 2018a. *Criminal Accusation: Political Rationales and Sociolegal Practices*. London: Routledge.

Pavlich, George. 2018b. Promised Communities and Unrestored Justice. In Brunilda Pali and Ivo Aertsen (eds.) *Restoring Justice and Security in Intercultural Europe*. Oxford: Hart, pp. 297–313.

Pue, W. Wesley, and Wright, Barry. 1988. *Canadian Perspectives on Law & Society: Issues in Legal History*. Carleton Library Series, no 152.

Rosenblatt, Fernanda Fonseca. 2015. *The Role of Community in Restorative Justice*. London: Routledge.

Salem, Richard. 1985. The Alternative Dispute Resolution Movement: An Overview. *The Arbitration Journal*, 40(3): 3–11.

Sander, Frank. 1976. Varieties of Dispute Processing, *Federal Rules Decisions*, 70: 79–90.

Sander, Frank. 1990. ADR Explosion, Perfection and Institutionalization, *ABA/Dispute Resolution*, 26: 1–46.

Shonholtz, Raymond. 1984. Neighborhood Justice Systems: Work, Structure and Guiding Principles, *Mediation Quarterly*, 5: 3–30.

Shonholtz, Raymond. 1988. Community as Peacemaker: Making Neighborhood Justice Work, *Current Municipal Problems*, 15: 291–330.

Simon, Jonathan. 2007. *Governing through Crime: How the War on Crime Transformed American Democracy and Created a Culture of Fear*. New York: Oxford University Press.

Smith, Roger. 2011. Developing Restorative Practice: Contemporary Lessons from an English Juvenile Diversion Project of the 1980s, *Contemporary Justice Review*, 14(4): 425–438.

Strang, Heather. 2002. *Repair or Revenge: Victims and Restorative Justice*. Oxford: Oxford University Press.

Strang, Heather, and Braithwaite, John, eds. 2001. *Restorative Justice and Civil Society*. Cambridge: Cambridge University Press.

Stubbs, Julie. 2009. *Restorative Justice, Gendered Violence, and Indigenous Women*. Oxford: Oxford University Press.

Tauri, Juan Marcellus. 2009. An Indigenous Perspective on the Standardisation of Restorative Justice in New Zealand and Canada, *Indigenous Policy Journal*, 20 (3).

Tauri, Juan Marcellus. 2016. Indigenous Peoples and the Globalization of Restorative Justice, *Social Justice*, 43(3): 46–67.

Wacquant, Loïc. 2010. Crafting the Neoliberal State: Workfare, Prisonfare, and Social Insecurity, *Sociological Forum*, 25(2): 197–200.

Walgrave, L. 2003. *Repositioning Restorative Justice*. Cullompton: Willan.

Wood, William R. and Masahiro Suzuki. 2016. Four Challenges in the Future of Restorative Justice, *Victims & Offenders*, 11(1): 149–172.

Woolford, Andrew. 2009. *The Politics of Restorative Justice: A Critical Introduction*. Halifax, NS: Fernwood.

Woolford, Andrew, and Ratner, R.S. 2003. Nomadic Justice? Restorative Justice on the Margins of Law, *Social Justice,* 30(1(91)): 177–194.

Wright, Martin. 1996. *Justice for Victims and Offenders a Restorative Response to Crime*. Winchester: Waterside Press.

Zehr, Howard. 2002. *The Little Book of Restorative Justice*. The Little Books of Justice & Peacebuilding. Intercourse, PA: Good Books.

Zehr, Howard. 2015. *Changing Lenses: Restorative Justice for Our Times*. Kitchener: Herald Press.

Zernova, Margarita. 2007. *Restorative Justice: Ideals and Realities*. Aldershot: Ashgate.

31

Extending the reach of restorative justice

Martin Wright[1]

Introduction

This Handbook began by exploring directions for restorative justice theory and then looked at evidence about its operation in various settings. Critical examinations were made of actual experiences, and this concluding chapter looks at some aspects of implementing the restorative justice ideal more widely through society. After a note on terminology, it will consider restorative values, especially empathy, respect and dialogue. Methods of restorative practice are summarized, and then structures for implementing them, either within existing organizations or by civil society agencies within communities. This leads to a broader vision of restorative communities, cities or even countries, in which the usual way of making decisions or resolving differences is to use restorative methods, including expressing thoughts and feelings, summarizing in neutral language and focusing on the future together with processes such as mediation (direct and indirect), conferencing and circles.

Restorative justice comes in different forms, and the word 'restorative' itself is acquiring an extended meaning, including practices and concepts such as dialogue, participation, empathy and others. What's in a name? Numerous terms are in use, with similar, overlapping meanings: mediation, alternative (or appropriate) dispute resolution, victim-offender mediation, restorative justice, restorative practices (or approaches), community (or family group) conferencing. They all share the same 'big tent' as regards their values; the differences lie in the methods used by practitioners and the structures through which they are delivered. Generally, I will use 'restorative practices' as the overarching term, 'mediation' for dialogue between two parties with a facilitator, 'conferencing' or 'circles' for work with groups and 'restorative justice' or 'victim-offender mediation' when the criminal justice system is involved.

This chapter will explore some of these varieties of restorative experience and suggest that they have much in common, showing how their application is spreading from criminal justice to schools, workplaces, management and broader aspects of social organization.

---

1 Thanks to Annette Hinton, Corinne Rechais and Mark Finnis for comments and information; responsibility for any errors is, of course, mine.

Restorative values

Firstly, let us consider restorative values, especially empathy, fairness and respect. We start with the word 'restorative', which has acquired an aura of meaning beyond the dictionary definition. As Ted Wachtel, contributor to this Handbook, has said, restorative processes are based on the principle that human beings are happier, more cooperative and productive, and more likely to make positive changes to their behaviour when those in positions of authority, such as managers or teachers, do things

- *with* them (combining high expectations and high support) rather than
- *to* them (top-down imposed change, control or even punishment, with little support) or
- *for* them (support with little control) (Wachtel T, 2013: 8).

The basic value of restorative justice is empathy, as expressed in respectful dialogue, often guided by a third person, and many would add the desirability of community involvement in the process (of which more will be discussed later). Restorative practices aim to ensure a fair process, involving people in decisions that affect them. As regards respect, this applies even in victim-offender mediation, where one party has clearly harmed the other: the mediator still tries to distinguish the person, the human being, from the act (the crime, harmful act or mistake).

Even the same word may be understood differently by different people. Some politicians seem to interpret restorative justice as consisting mainly of reparation or unpaid work, while for practitioners the dialogue is the essential feature. Radical feminists have objected to the use of mediation in cases of domestic violence, apparently because their image of mediation is a one-to-one encounter in which the man might dominate the woman: 'Feminists also claim that the typical marriage structure embodies a general power imbalance between the wife and husband, and that this consequently manifests itself in divorce mediation' (Mirzaie, 2016). This objection takes no account of safeguards, such as requiring the man to attend an anti-violence programme beforehand, or other methods such as shuttle mediation, in which the parties do not meet, or at least not until the facilitator is satisfied that it is safe. Hoyle (2010) points to the strengths of another method, 'conferencing', in which family members and other supporters are also present; and even she does not refer to yet another model, used extensively in Austria, in which a male and a female mediator listen to the couple separately and then describe their respective points of view with both of them present. They see their behaviour through someone else's eyes and are given the opportunity to correct or modify their story. This distancing makes it harder for the perpetrator to use 'neutralization' techniques to deny the seriousness of his conduct. It is not claimed that this method can be used in all cases, but there has been a high degree of satisfaction from women who have experienced it (Liebmann, 2007: 290–293; see also Gavrielides, 2015).

Restorative justice methods

Restorative practice is not just a matter of dispute resolution: it can also be preventive. As Karen Erwin, former president of the Mediators' Institute of Ireland, points out,

> Although mediation is frequently thought of as a way of helping to resolve disputes it can be used very effectively in dispute prevention. Whether this is in Elder Mediation, succession planning, joint ventures or boardroom strategy, the same principles apply and the process helps what might be otherwise difficult discussions to take place in a safe space.
>
> *(Erwin, 2010)*

Techniques of participative decision making may prevent the dispute from arising in the first place. For children, writers like Adele Faber and Elaine Mazlish (1980) have described how to win cooperation from children by trying to imagine what it feels like to be on the receiving end of blame, put-downs, sarcasm and so on. Instead, parents can describe the problem (leaving the child to draw her own conclusions about what she needs to do), avoid long harangues, describe their feelings, allow the child to make choices or even write them a note.

It is surprising how many situations can be addressed by variants of those three non-blaming, non-punitive questions: What happened? Who was affected? What is needed to make things better?

For big meetings, a basic method is to divide a large group into smaller ones, each if possible containing representatives of differing viewpoints, so that everyone can have a say; or a small group can discuss in the centre of the room with the rest listening; individuals from this outer circle can move to the centre to make a point.

Many restorative practitioners have great faith in the power of the circle: the dynamics are different from those produced by sitting round a rectangular table, let alone confronting an authority figure who is on a daïs or behind a desk. Carolyn Boyes-Watson (contributor to this Handbook) describes, for example, how the Roca programme for young people in a deprived part of Boston, Massachusetts, uses circles for talking (sharing ideas and experience), conflict and peacemaking (including gangs), support (for a person undergoing a challenging experience), healing (after neglect or trauma), ceremonies (to celebrate an achievement) or as part of the 'visioning' and organization of the programme itself. For participants, coming to an agreement about the circle's guidelines is itself an educative process; for staff, circles (without tables or papers) encourage hard questions about the agency's mission, whereas because a bureaucracy doesn't encourage speaking up, it cultivates grumbling (Boyes-Watson, 2008: 63).

Circles, too, are not new. Group psychotherapy relies on circles in which each person may be influenced not by a professional but by his or her peers, who have confronted the same demons themselves. It was pioneered at the Henderson Hospital in southwest London, unfortunately closed in 2008, and at Grendon prison in Buckinghamshire, long before the word 'restorative' acquired its present meaning.

Mediation works on a combination of the rational and the emotional. The rational is encouraging people to focus on their real interests rather than their dug-in positions and to hear the other person's point of view by such techniques as 're-framing in neutral language' and even asking each person to summarize the other's point of view. It is set out in Fisher and Ury's well-known *Getting to yes* (1991). On the international level, it is described in Roger Fisher's *Beyond Machiavelli* (1996), and a parallel approach is described in Elworthy and Rifkind's *Making terrorism history* (2006).

The emotional component is to provide a space in which people can express their feelings safely and can begin to feel empathy for each other. Mediators can't make it happen, but they can create conditions where it can happen more easily.

Non-violent communication (Rosenberg, 1999) combines the two, using rational clarity to describe emotions and make respectful requests. Non-violence combines idealistic values with calculating pragmatism, because in many situations, it can be argued, it is the best policy (Kurlansky, 2007). It could be argued that despite the hostile treatment of the inhabitants of Gaza by the Israeli military, non-violent resistance would have been their wisest strategy instead of retaliating by firing rockets into Israel. Twisting a lion's tail is a brave act of defiance but can be counterproductive. However, non-violent resistance cannot guarantee success; Mazin Qumsiyeh (2011) describes a long history of non-violent resistance by Palestinians to Israel, which has not yet resolved the conflict. This could be because the civil resistance was punctuated by acts of violence, to which the occupying power responded (disproportionately as many would argue); or it could be that some régimes do not respond even to complete non-violence.

My favourite example of 're-framing' concerns a conflict between Christian chiefs and Muslim chiefs in northern Nigeria.

> One hundred of the four hundred people in the community had been killed, and three of the people who were eventually persuaded to meet knew that someone who killed their child would be in the room. Rosenberg began by asking those on each side to express their needs. One of the Christian chiefs shouted at the Muslims: 'You people are murderers!' Rosenberg re-framed that: 'Chief, are you expressing a need for safety that isn't being met? You would hope that things could be resolved with non-violence, correct?' He said, 'That's exactly what I'm saying.'
>
> Rosenberg asked if a member of the other tribe would repeat what the chief from the first tribe had said, to make sure he had heard. One of them screamed, 'Why did you kill my son?' Rosenberg repeated his summary of what the first chief was feeling and needing; eventually the chief was able to do so.
>
> Then he asked the other chiefs what were their needs. One of them said 'They have been trying to dominate us for a long time, and we're not going to put up with it any more.' Rosenberg again summarized: 'Are you upset because you have a strong need for equality in this community?' 'Yes.'
>
> After about an hour of shouting, each side had heard just one need of the other, when one chief exclaimed, 'Marshall, we can't learn this in one day. And if we know how to talk to each other, we don't have to kill each other.' Several of them volunteered to be trained.
>
> *(Summarized from Marshall Rosenberg (1999)*

Restorative justice is being widely discussed in the context of criminal justice. In Ireland, for example, the National Commission on Restorative Justice recommended that it could have valid and effective application in the Irish criminal justice system. using victim-offender mediation, family group conferencing or reparation panels (National Commission, 2010).

A discussion of restorative approaches would not be complete without addressing the subject of punishment. Both practitioners and theorists are coming to realize that punishment, in the conventional sense of threatening to inflict pain (Gavrielides, 2005; 2013b), and doing so if the other person behaves in a certain way, has at best a limited effectiveness (Wright, 2008, ch. 2). Faber and Mazlish (1980, ch.3) devote a whole chapter to alternatives to punishment, which are restorative although they do not use that terminology. Belinda Hopkins (2004, ch. 7) also stresses the need to move on from punitive methods, based on fear, to restorative ones.

In short, they are not merely specialist techniques to be applied by professional mediators in specific circumstances, but potentially part of a sea change in the way people relate to each other. Advocates of restorative practices stress that before introducing this great new idea, it is worth looking at one's existing practice to see how restorative it already is. In some cases restorative practice (RP) will merely refine the structure of what people already do – but in others it revolutionizes it.

Structures

In organizations

School or college students or employees in a business may participate in creating the conflict-resolving structure itself and the action to be taken when conflicts nevertheless arise. Circles can be used not only as a response to crime or conflicts but as a regular part of a young person's development (Boyes-Watson, 2008: 63). Belinda Hopkins advocates circles for every part of the school community, both as regular 'circle time' and for problem solving, with the students themselves developing the ground rules at the beginning of a year (Hopkins, 2004). Ron and Roxanne Claassen (2008), in California, similarly, have evolved and practised a system of school discipline that is restorative from the start: students are asked to state their goals, the teacher informs them of hers and they agree on a flowchart of ten steps that will be taken in the event of student-teacher conflict. These are restorative but increasingly interventionist; only the final one, which is hardly ever reached, involves the school's authority structure. Even this is applied as restoratively as possible, for example, not demanding expulsion but arranging transfer to another school (Claassen and Claassen, 2008).

The International Institute for Restorative Practices (IIRP) maintains that 'individuals are most likely to trust and cooperate freely with systems – whether they themselves win or lose by those systems – when fair process is observed' (Costello, 2010). It stresses, however, that this does not mean that restorative management forfeits the prerogative of making decisions and establishing policy, nor taking all decisions by consensus or winning people's support through compromises to accommodate everyone; management still has to manage but builds trust and commitment, producing voluntary cooperation by sharing the knowledge and creativity of the staff.

As an everyday example of how things could be different, let us look at a typical non-restorative organization and its grievance procedure. The basic grade workers will be line-managed by a supervisor, who in turn will be line-managed, and so on. The danger in this authoritarian style is that suggestions are seen as criticism, and questions as insubordination. The grievance procedure will say things like 'If you have a grievance, raise it with your line manager; if it relates to him or her, raise it with the next in line', and so on. There is a natural tendency for the senior manager to support the line manager, unless the latter is clearly in the wrong. The procedure is adversarial: Upheld or Not Upheld; it does not encourage recognition of 'faults on both sides' or recommendations for improvements within the organization. If the grievance is upheld, relations between the employee and the manager will suffer; if not, the employee is likely to feel more aggrieved. The grievance can continue in this way up the chain of command to the board of management, with the possibility of additional causes for dissatisfaction if the employee feels that the procedure itself has not been satisfactory. The procedure may provide for a final hearing, possibly by the chairman of the board, who again will be under pressure to support the management. After that, if the employee still felt unfairly dealt with, he or she could apply to a tribunal; this in itself would be harmful to the organization's reputation and the morale of other staff, whether or not the grievance was upheld.

In a restorative organization, the grievance is less likely to arise in the first place. Suppose, as a typical case, an employee wants extra time off (which will affect other people's workload), or feels that their own workload has been increased unreasonably. The matter would be raised initially in a circle meeting, which would try to find a way of meeting everyone's needs. Sometimes agreement might still not be reached. Then the manager would have to make a decision, but only after listening to the wisdom of the circle, so that further action is less likely to be needed. However, if the employee felt that decision was unfair or contrary to company policy, an independent mediator would interview him or her, and then the manager, to explore what could be a settlement that would meet the needs of the employee, the manager and the organization. There could be some 'shuttle diplomacy', if necessary, and then they would be invited to meet in a mediation session. As always with mediation, this would not focus on the details of what actually happened (perceptions often differ) or who was to blame; instead they would ask both parties to concentrate on a workable arrangement for the future. Of course, no one suggests that there would be a 100 percent success rate. Ultimately someone has to make a decision, but all the indications are that this approach would be much more likely to improve performance and morale.

In communities

Finally, there are different ways of delivering mediation and restorative practices to the community: through practitioners in private practice, by training people within the system (teachers, managers, police) and by community-based mediation services, using trained volunteer mediators. Civil and commercial mediation are developing to meet demand as they become better known, with the help of organizations such as the Mediators' Institute of Ireland, and similarly in the UK, the more recently created Civil Mediation Council.

The provision of restorative practices through the statutory sector is more problematic. They are likely to have a robust management structure and until the current crisis more secure funding. For example, in juvenile justice in England and Wales, mediators are likely to be in a small minority (perhaps of one) in a large youth-offending team whose dominant ethos is still that of conventional criminal justice. Youth offender panels have restorative elements in that victims can be invited to take part, and the focus is on a constructive action plan for the young person; they also involve the community by using trained volunteers as panel members. But these receive only minimal training in restorative principles, and few victims take part (Fonseca Rosenblatt, 2015). The legislation can make a big difference: in New Zealand, the Children, Young Persons and their Families Act 1989 built family group conferencing into the juvenile justice system, and Northern Ireland has followed suit (with the Justice (Northern Ireland) Act 2002), and has achieved good victim participation (Jacobson and Gibbs, 2009).

As regards delivery of restorative practices through the community, in England and Wales we hoped that politicians would recognize that this fits well with the new, though not very clearly spelt out, idea of the 'Big Society'. This was an initiative of the then prime minister, David Cameron; we were not sure what he meant by community participation, although there were suspicions that it was not unconnected with cuts in public expenditure on staff, and the idea seems to have faded away. However, a restorative approach has room for involvement of members of the public at all levels. It includes parents, extended family and other supporters who attend a family group conference (FGC), where they can not only help to reach agreement or confront a young person with the effects of his actions on other people but also contribute to making an action plan and support him or her in putting it into effect. In the New Zealand model of FGC, after social workers have provided information about locally available resources, they withdraw, allowing 'private family time' in which the family can work out its own solution. In one case in the Netherlands, for example, where a Turkish father objected to his daughter's adopting Western culture, his sister (the girl's aunt) used the private time to explain to him 'You are an OK father, but you are living in another country now.' What could never be accepted if said by a social worker could be said by a family member in the absence of professionals (Wachtel, 2007).

Mediators can be trained volunteers. The service can be provided by a voluntary (non-government) organization, usually a registered charity, whose management often includes volunteers and officers of statutory agencies. The community has a role outside the actual mediation. When someone has committed a crime and offers to make reparation, the community in the form of, for example, a local charity can provide an opportunity for community service; local employers can provide paid work if the person needs it to keep out of trouble and perhaps pay compensation. If the person needs work skills or life skills, there is a need for suitable programmes, provided by voluntary organizations or the local authority (for which the local community has voted). All of this contributes to a restorative society.

In England and Wales there are a number of local community mediation services; unfortunately, since the national organization Mediation UK closed in 2008, no one knows how many (Gavrielides, 2013). In addition to neighbourhood mediation, they can be a focus for other work in schools, workplace mediation, hate crimes and others. I understand that a few have also been established in Ireland.

The use of volunteers should not be regarded as providing a substandard service. Experience in the UK, Norway, the Netherlands and Poland has shown that volunteers can be capable mediators, and between them they can bring the perspectives of more different cultures (and sometimes languages) than would be possible with paid staff alone. An example comes from a multicultural city in the north of England. The case was provided anonymously by a mediator working for a restorative justice service in London.

> The owner of a shop complained of harassment. She sold alcohol, and the mosque next door objected. She was a Sikh, and her partner, who was Black British, had converted to Islam, but did not observe the prohibition of alcohol. She felt that the elders of the mosque did not respect her; they refused to talk to her, as a woman, but only spoke to her partner. Younger, radical members of the mosque threatened her; on one occasion she had to barricade herself in upstairs, and the young people stole from her shop.
>
> Two imams and two mosque members who knew the young Muslims agreed to meet her with the mediators (her partner had left meanwhile). The mediators were a volunteer (a Hindu) and the manager of the community mediation service (a Christian who had converted to Buddhism). She spoke about her fears, and said that she was already isolated from her family because of her non-Sikh partner, and this made it worse. She felt entitled to sell what she wanted to, and to live free from threats. The mosque elders agreed, and the others promised to speak to the young radicals. She in turn would not promote alcohol so conspicuously. During the meeting, the Muslims did speak to her directly, and they agreed to nominate an elder to whom she could speak if there were any problems in future. The people concerned recognised each other's humanity, and a potentially serious situation was calmed with no involvement of the criminal justice system.

A community mediation service, unlike, say, a youth-offending team, is entirely committed to restorative principles. Its mediators will not have to take off one 'hat' (or a policeman's helmet) and put on the hat of a mediator: they will already be wearing it. The mediation service will, ideally, be affiliated to a national body, which will require local services to be accredited and comply with a code of restorative principles and practice; this seal of approval should reassure statutory agencies when considering referring cases to them, and also funders. Until now, the Restorative Justice Council in England and Wales has concentrated on accrediting individual mediators; in my view, this is necessary but not sufficient, and it is good to know that they have begun to introduce accreditation of mediation services. (Traffic lights are very desirable, but they are no use if there aren't any cars!)

Some people are sceptical about the use of volunteers, but it is suggested that restorative practices should not only be the preserve of a new brand of professionals but should be available to everyone. To make an imperfect analogy, we don't want specialist health food shops for the enlightened élite, with junk food shops for everyone else. Everyone should have healthy food and understand why. Of course, we will often want sugar, starch, alcohol and so on, and in small quantities we may even need them. With a healthy diet, we will go to the doctors less often, but they should not worry – they will still be needed, and so will mediators! In Norway, for example, the law setting up a nationwide network of mediation centres, funded by local authorities, requires mediators to be lay people, supervised by staff or a senior mediator. There are about 700 in a population of just under five million (Andersen, 2013). In the Netherlands, the organization *Eigen Kracht* ('Our Power') also uses about 500 independent coordinators, from 72 ethnicities; they are paid a fee, and each case takes up to 30 hours for preparation and the family group conference itself. Cases they deal with include community conflicts, evictions, schools, domestic violence and other crime. The programme is seen as enabling citizens to keep control over decisions affecting their lives without being dependent on the state. In a phrase reminiscent of President Lyndon Johnson's Great Society and its Office of Economic Opportunity in the 1960s, Rob van Pagée, the director of *Eigen Kracht*, says that people who were considered part of the problem can become part of the solution.

In Northern Ireland, community-based restorative justice has been running for about 20 years, but there are fears that some of its work will be taken over by the statutory criminal justice system. It is hoped that a role can be found for both.

An example of how these ideas can grow is the city of Hull, in north-east England. This summary draws on the account by Marian Liebmann (2015; also a contributor to this Handbook). Its population is 280,000, including 57,000 young people. There is high unemployment, partly as a result of the decline of the fishing industry. Collingwood Primary School, which had been in difficulties, adopted restorative practices, and in two years was rated excellent. Endeavour High School (secondary) followed. Their statistics over the period Spring 2007–July 2008 are impressive:

Collingwood primary school

- 98.3% fewer classroom exclusions
- 75.0% fewer racist incidents
- 86.7% punctuality improvement

Endeavour high school

- 45.6% fewer verbal abuse incidents
- 59.4% fewer physical abuse incidents
- 50% fewer theft incidents
- 62.5% fewer days staff absence (saving over £60,000 in 8 months)

Other schools adopted restorative practices, and Hull decided to train 23,000 people who work with young people in restorative practices, as the next step to becoming a restorative city. The chief of police, previously oriented to obtaining the maximum penalties, accepted that a restorative approach can be more effective in preventing re-offending. He did so despite a system of key performance indicators which does not give credit for incidents resolved restoratively. Among youth workers, the aim is to create a common language and values, and to be not merely reactive but proactive and preventive, and to try to feel what it is like from the child's point of view.

The programme started with practice, but is now thinking strategically. The aim is to build-in the use of circles, not hold one only when there is a problem. At least twenty agencies or groups of agencies have been trained, including schools, fostering and adoption, a children's centre for under-5s, youth clubs, church groups, housing, police and more. The Hull Centre for Restorative Practices has run regular practice forums for specific agencies to ensure quality assurance, maintain standards, support practice and develop it. Lead practitioners monitor, support and challenge practice in organizations. Regular courses are advertised to bring in new staff, and restorative practices are included in staff induction in many places. Some schools insist that staff do training within a certain time period of starting the job. It is hoped that all this reduces the possibility of a RP-trained member of staff feeling isolated in a non-restorative organization. The aim is for restorative practices to be embedded, not an add-on.

Although there is no community mediation centre in Hull, there is a family mediation service; some statutory and community agencies trained in the use of restorative practices offer mediation, and some of them use volunteer mediators.

Liebmann (2015) describes a different strategy used in Bristol, with a series of planning meetings of local and national agencies, and Brighton & Hove has also brought organizations together to 'build a restorative city' (Read, 2017). The county of Norfolk has a police-led initiative to become a restorative county. Leeds uses the term 'child-friendly city', acknowledging the value of starting while they are young and letting the restorative idea spread as they grow older. In West Lancashire, a first step has been made in which a group of schools pays into a limited company which they have set up to provide training and support for young and adult mediators. Children transfer their skills to their families, and the area has the lowest exclusion rate in Lancashire. The group works alongside other agencies such as the police. The case was provided anonymously by a mediator working for a community-based restorative justice service.

> In one case, parents complained about an elderly woman, 'Annie', whose house children passed on the way to school. They alleged that she threw things at them. The police said they couldn't do anything. A meeting was held with her, the children and their parents. She told them how she felt isolated and threatened, and the children admitted that they threw the first stones, and called her a witch. The matter was resolved without bringing criminal charges, and a group of parents gave Annie's daughter flowers and a cake on her birthday.

This case is interesting because the criminal justice system would probably have categorized Annie as the 'offender' and the children as 'victims'; even if the full story came out, it might only mitigate her 'offence' on grounds of provocation, rather than reclassify her as the victim.

Elsewhere in the world, some traditional communities have customary conflict resolution techniques from which we could learn. The Ojibway community in Hollow Water, Manitoba, for example, discovered widespread sexual abuse. Rather than disrupt the community by asking the Canadian authorities to prosecute, which could have led to the perpetrators being imprisoned hundreds of miles away and then returned as outcasts, traditional healing methods were used, which led to a recidivism rate of two per cent, as against the national average of 13 per cent (Sawatsky, 2009 ch. 4). In other places, the traditional methods have been weakened but are being reintroduced as a way of resolving conflicts over natural resources. In South Kordofan, Sudan, the aid charity SOS Sahel International has found that agricultural problems lead to conflict, and the conflict aggravates the problems. They are therefore training key individuals in conflict management skills which will help communities to defuse potential conflict situations. These individuals include traditional leaders, women and youth, and the training focuses on different approaches to managing conflict such as via negotiation and mediation (SOS International UK, 2010).

Conclusion

On the basis of the theory and experience described in this Handbook, how can restorative practice develop?

The possible areas for conflict are, of course, as varied as human life itself, from living in a family to international disputes, and the principles involved are uncannily similar, such as treating people with respect, listening to them, helping them to listen to each other, moving from positions to interests, looking to the future more than the past and helping them to find face-saving choices acceptable to both sides. As contributions to this volume have shown, many of the building blocks of both the theory and the practice of a restorative society are already in existence; the challenge is to make them universally available.

The movement has started in schools, so that children from the outset are familiar with restorative processes. Community mediation services, established as non-profit agencies, help to resolve disputes between local residents or within families; they can also spread knowledge of restorative principles and practice in their localities. An important part of their work is restorative justice, summarized by Tim Read in his account of Brighton & Hove as a restorative city: '[W]hatever has happened to you that has caused you harm, you will be offered a restorative service' and 'the person who caused you harm [can be enabled] to hear of the impact of their behaviour and get support to reduce the likelihood of that behaviour happening again' (Read, 2017). If both people are willing, the response to harmful behaviour need not involve the criminal justice system, or restorative justice can be used in addition. Communities could benefit by the creation of a network of such community-based services, professionally run and accredited but mainly using trained volunteer mediators.

In organizations such as schools and businesses (and even charitable agencies), restorative methods such as circles and non-violent communication may help to avoid conflicts in the first place or resolve them before they become serious. We may even be seeing the beginning of a move away from line management to management with circles, although there will still be a need for a leader to ensure that the circles take place. For example, cooperative enterprises such as the Mondragon Corporation in Spain or the Scott Bader Chemical Company in the United Kingdom, and numerous smaller ones, have been operating for many years. Wherever possible, decisions will be reached by a restorative process in the first place. Mediation is increasingly used to resolve industrial conflicts and disputes between commercial organizations. In this context, professional mediators come into play, and the relationship between community mediation and private practice needs careful thought.

The next stage could be a more restorative style of government; rule by a single party with a simple majority does not lend itself to this, but systems based on coalitions are a step in that direction. After violent internal conflicts, some three dozen countries have followed South Africa in establishing truth and reconciliation commissions. Finally, in the international sphere, the word 'mediation' is now commonly used, but this highlights one of the dangers faced by the restorative movement at all levels: when mediators are not neutral, do not have the temperament or the training to be facilitators, or have power and are not prepared to use it, the process they undertake is not likely to be restorative and, more significantly, is not likely to succeed.

As more and more people experience the benefits of restorative practices, it is not hard to envisage that they will spread. This has the potential to be a successful 'bottom-up' movement; but to be effective and remain true to restorative principles it needs a system at national and local levels for quality control, selection, support and supervision of facilitators, especially in the case of volunteers. Mediators are showing that they have the capacity to deal with ever more complex conflict situations in order to assist people in creating agreement. A national 'umbrella body' would also be in a position to urge policy makers to provide necessary legislation and resources, but should resist any governmental tendency to take control. It would promote research and theory to accompany practice and consider basic principles, including legal and ethical issues when deciding how to handle a new situation. Children will grow up to become restorative parents, employers and politicians. Then we shall be on the way to seeing restorative communities, cities, counties, *départements, Länder, oblasti* . . . and even countries.

Let me end by referring back to my example of reclaiming the desert in Sudan. Over the last two or three decades, the big challenge has been learning how to live in harmony with the planet; the next challenge for us all is to learn to live in harmony with each other.

References

Andersen, P. 2013. Development of Restorative Justice Practices in Norway. In D. J. Cornwell, J. Blad and M. Wright (eds.) *Civilising Criminal Justice: An International Restorative Agenda for Penal Reform.* Hook: Waterside Press.

Boyes-Watson, C. 2008. *Peacemaking Circles and Urban Youth: Bringing Justice Home.* St. Paul, MN: Living Justice Press, pp. 58–65.

Claassen, R. and Claassen, R. 2008. *Discipline that Restores: Strategies to Create Respect, Co-operation, and Responsibility Ion the Classroom.* South Carolina: Booksurge Publishing. Available at www.booksurge.com

Costello, Bob 2010. Workshop on Restorative Supervision, *IIRP Conference,* Hull, October.

Elworthy, S. and Rifkind, G. 2006. *Making Terrorism History.* London: Rider.

Erwin, K. 2010. MII E-zine 2(2) June 2010. Available at www.themii.ie/onlinemarketing/ezine4.htm. Accessed 2 November 2010.

Faber, A. and Mazlish, E. 1980. *How to Talk So Kids Will Listen and Listen Do Kids Will Talk.* New York: Avon Books.

Fisher, R, and Ury, W. 1991. *Getting to Yes: Negotiating an Agreement Without Giving In,* 2nd ed. London: Random House.

Fisher, R. et al. 1996. *Beyond Machiavelli: Tools for Coping with Conflict.* New York: Penguin Books.

Fonseca Rosenblatt, F. 2015. *The Role of Community in Restorative Justice.* London and New York: Routledge.

Gavrielides, T. 2015. Is Restorative Justice Appropriate for Domestic Violence Cases?, *Social Work Review,* XIV, nr. 4/2015: 105–121.

Gavrielides, T. 2013. Where Is Restorative Justice Heading?, *Probation Junior,* 5(1): 79–95.

Gavrielides, T. 2013b. Restorative Pain: A New Vision of Punishment. In T. Gavrielides and V. Artinopoulou (eds.) *Reconstructing Restorative Justice Philosophy.* Farnham: Ashgate, pp. 311–337.

Gavrielides, Theo. 2005. Some Meta-theoretical Questions for Restorative Justice, *Ratio Juris,* 18(1): 84–106.

Hopkins, B. 2004. *Just Schools: A Whole School Approach to Restorative Justice.* London and New York: Jessica Kingsley Publishers.

Hoyle, C. 2010. The Case for Restorative Justice. In C. Cunneen and C. Hoyle (eds.) *Debating Restorative Justice.* Oxford and Portland, OR: Hart, pp. 75–81.

Jacobson, J. and Gibbs, P. 2009. *Out of Trouble: Making Amends – Restorative Youth Justice in Northern Ireland.* London: Prison Reform Trust; Campbell, C., Devlin, R., O'Mahony, D., Doak, J., Jackson, J., Corrigan, T. and McEvoy, K. 2005. *Evaluation of the Northern Ireland Youth Conference Service* (NIO Research and Statistical Series: Report No. 12). Belfast: Queen's University, Institute of Criminology and Criminal Justice. Available at www.nio.gov.uk/evaluation_of_the_northern_ireland_youth_conference_service.pdf

Kurlansky, M. 2007. *Non-violence: The History of a Dangerous Idea.* London: Vintage Books.

Liebmann, M. 2007. *Restorative Justice: How It Works.* London and Philadelphia, PA: Jessica Kingsley Publishers.

Liebmann, M. 2015. Building the Restorative City. In Theo Gavrielides (ed.) *Offenders No More: An Interdisciplinary Restorative Justice Dialogue*. New York: Nova Science Publishers.

Mirzaie, R. 2016. Divorce Mediation for Women: An Examination of Feminist Critiques. *Dispute Resolution Journal*, 71(3).

National Commission on Restorative Justice. 2010. *Final Report*. Dublin. Available at https://restorative-justice.org.uk/sites/default/files/resources/files/National%20Commission%20for%20Restorative%20Justice%20final%20report%20-%20Ireland.pdf. Accessed 4 December 2017.

Qumsiyeh, M. 2011. *Popular Resistance in Palestine: A History of Hope and Empowerment*. London: Pluto Press.

Read, T. 2017. Building a Restorative City: The Brighton & Hove Story, *Resolution* (Restorative Justice Council), 61, Autumn, 4–5.

Rosenberg, M. 1999. *Non-violent Communication: A Language of Compassion*. DelMar, CA: PuddleDancer Press.

Sawatsky, J. 2009. *The Ethic of Traditional Communities and the Spirit of Healing Justice: Studies From Hollow Water, the Iona Community and Plum Village*. London and Philadelphia: Jessica Kingsley Publishers.

SOS Sahel International UK 2010. *Assessment of Resource-Based Conflict Flashpoints Along the Babanusa-Muglad-Abyei Livestock Corridor South Kordofan, Sudan*. Oxford: SOS Sahel.

Wachtel, J. c.2007. Making the Circles Bigger: The Netherlands. Eigen Kracht Holds its 1000th Family Group Conference. Available at www.familypower.org/library/eigenkracht.html. Accessed 3 November 2010.

Wachtel, T. 2013. *Dreaming of a New Reality: How Restorative Practices Reduce Crime and Violence, Improve Relationships and Strengthen Civil Society*. Pipersville, PA: The Piper's Press, p. 8.

Wright, M. 2008. *Restoring Respect for Justice: A Symposium*, 2nd ed. Hook: Waterside Press.

Epilogue

Restorative justice with care and responsibility: new directions in restorative justice theory, practice and critical thinking

Theo Gavrielides

Our journey together has almost come to an end. I conclude it with this Epilogue. Its structure is simple, reflecting its dual objective of first summarising the key points that were made by the Handbook's expert authors, and then proceeding with my own reflections. The first part of the Epilogue draws from the authors' abstracts to succinctly present their contributions. The second part concludes the Handbook with my own contribution.

Restorative justice theory: the next steps

History is a mirror reflecting on our future, Greek historian Thucydides once said. Thus, it was fitting for this Handbook to start with a historical account of restorative justice. In chapter 1, Boyes-Watson critically reviews the modern history of the restorative justice movement by deconstructing the legal, political and social agendas that have contributed to the programmes, principles, practices and philosophy of restorative justice. It is common to note that the principles and practices of restorative justice are not new, because elements of this contemporary philosophy can be found in Indigenous and non-Western conflict resolution and within major religious traditions (see Gavrielides, 2011). This chapter also examined the reservoir of ideas retrieved from the past, demonstrated how these ideas were refashioned to serve diverse agendas and concluded with an overview of the contemporary context within which restorative practices are situated.

Maglione then proceeded with a highly normative account of restorative justice, aiming to push its theoretical boundaries. Drawing on Foucault, Blanchot, Agamben and Butler, Maglione's chapter explored themes related to the idea of a non-sovereign justice. In particular, he argued that in times when the neo-liberal/neo-conservative political rationality structures multiple spheres of human life, radical political and social theories strive to envision alternative forms of resistance and disentanglement. These intellectual endeavours touch on critical subjects such as identity, power, justice and love. Maglione argues that reflections on the re-articulation of the relationship between ethics and politics have showed the capacity to generate a range of realistic utopias against the current state of global politics. These variegated efforts often share a critique of sovereignty as a paradigm of political action based on domination and offer implications of how to respond to transgressions of collectively established modes of conduct. The chapter reflects on how radical political and social inquiry can enhance a new frontier of justice in the framework of imaging and practising challenges against exclusionary political rationalities.

Skelton then explored what common ground exists between restorative justice and human rights by considering their genesis and theoretical underpinnings. Recent writing in this field was critically examined to determine the conceptualisation of rights that best coexists with restorative justice in all its complexity. The chapter also examined what risks are possibly posed to victims and offenders' rights, particularly when restorative justice is run parallel to, or is interlinked with, the criminal justice system. Skelton reminds us that victims may face risk of coercion to participate in restorative justice processes and threats to their physical or psychological integrity, and may be left without a civil remedy. Offenders may also be coerced into participation and may be negatively affected by net-widening and disproportionality. They may also be required to relinquish certain rights that they have in the criminal justice system such as the right to remain silent and the right to legal representation. Beyond due process concerns, the chapter also discussed broader human rights issues such as human dignity, social justice and power relationships between participants. The rights of particularly vulnerable victims and offenders were also considered.

In the next chapter, Courakis and I argued that social justice constitutes an important, new challenge in criminal justice policy. Using the concepts and principles of social solidarity and meritocratic fairness, the chapter argues that the task of social justice is twofold. First, to enhance the social rights that are considered to be essential for the decent living of citizens. Secondly, to create the conditions needed in order to ensure that opportunities deemed necessary for a successful career are given to those who have the skills and ability to take advantage of them. This chapter aimed to advance restorative justice theory by linking it with social justice and by contending that both can play an important role for justice at three levels: legislative, judicial and correctional. The chapter argues that social justice can function as a model of criminal justice policy beyond restorative justice, especially in relation to financial crimes. Social justice can also prove to be particularly effective for social crime prevention by improving standards of living, with emphasis on vulnerable social groups. It can also cope with nepotism, bureaucracy and corruption, which may hinder meritocratic social mobility and the optimal functioning of justice institutions.

Subsequently, Cohar brought us back to basics by reviewing Indigenous traditions of peacemaking. He argues that peacemaking, peacebuilding and peacekeeping need different approaches in the contemporary world, but all can be achieved by using Indigenous systems of justice. Gohar uses Jirga (Pakistan/ Afghanistan's Indigenous conflict resolution system) as an example. He uses evidence from Jirga practices to suggest that when involving all stakeholders in peacemaking and peacekeeping, the chances of achieving effective conflict resolution are increased. Gohar argues that these practices have common characteristics throughout the world. However, he concludes that for these practices to be truly effective, one must combine them with restorative justice values. He also warns us that traditional systems are often sidelined in favour of modern ways of conflict resolution and peacebuilding. But the chapter contends that peacemaking problems tend to find their solution where they originated from.

Mackay responded to Cohar's empirical claims by developing a normative argument to differentiate restorative justice from peacemaking. He presents a novel framework for analysing conflict and disputes resolution within a threefold typology of temporal focus, the socio-political locus of conflict and the axis of consent-coercion. His framework is grounded in a model of peacemaking, which is based on a legal-ethical argument applying neo-Aristotelian theory and discourse ethics. Mackay argues that clarity about how different methods of conflict and dispute resolution and management fit into this framework allows us to make better decisions about which methods to employ in particular situations. The chapter contributes to the Handbook's ambitions for a normative push of restorative justice by concluding with an application of a new typology through the medium of the model of law and literature to a well-known story, leading to a reflection about motivation and recognition of the other in the resolution of conflicts.

The last chapter of the Handbook's first Part argues that theories underpinning restorative justice overlap significantly with work around addiction recovery, in particular, the concept of recovery capital. Kawalek, Edwards and Best claim that while both restorative justice and recovery capital are relatively new movements, the former has a longer-standing history and a greater application in practice settings. They proceed with a comparative review of the concepts, assessing how the theories and practices align, as well as how each framework may inform the other. The authors argue that recovery is enhanced when social capital is built, establishing previously non-existent social networks and accessing support networks and resources in the community. The chapter points out that a key component of recovery theory is community capital and the importance of community attitudes and resources as a predictor of recovery longevity. The effective implementation of these principles may facilitate the generation of a virtuous cycle enhancing the well-being of disputants and their communities, and providing sustainable pathways to effective reintegration by building capital in communities and creating a therapeutic landscape for restoration and rehabilitation.

Restorative justice practice: the evidence

The second part of the Handbook starts with a chapter I authored, arguing that there is a need for an up-to-date, evidence-based picture on victims and offenders' perceptions and experiences of restorative justice. I used London (England) as my case study to illustrate this need. The chapter argues that recent changes in legislation in England and Wales have allowed restorative justice to be used at all stages of the criminal justice system, presenting it with both opportunities and challenges. As part of these developments, I presented the findings of a research project that I conducted in 2016–2018. In particular, the findings were drawn from an online quantitative survey with 66 victims and 44 offenders, followed by 11 qualitative, in-depth victim interviews and a focus group with seven victims and practitioners. The data pointed out a number of assumptions and caveats that persist within the restorative justice movement, and which must be addressed in order to ensure that further investment in restorative justice yields benefits to all those whose lives are blighted by crime. The experiences and perceptions of London victims and offenders are used as a platform for wider learning for the international reader of this Handbook.

Subsequently, Hartmann gave an overview of the latest research on the significance of restorative justice for victims of crimes. Relevant theories were critically reviewed from victims' perspectives, and new arguments and empirical evidence were identified within this framework. Hartmann also looked at the implications of the European Commission's Victims' Directive for restorative justice both in Europe and internationally. Using unpublished data from his recent research, Hartmann also reviewed the merits and weaknesses of restorative justice for victims looking at variants such as type of crime, gender, age and social class.

Terry then proceeded with an investigation of a controversial area of restorative practice. Having worked on the issue of child sexual abuse for many years, Terry argues that theoretically, a restorative justice approach could help address harm to victims of child sexual abuse through voluntary and honest dialogue. She acknowledges that previous studies have shown that those who were sexually assaulted as youths may exhibit increased levels of depression, anxiety, suicidal ideation, substance abuse, eating disorders, anger, resentment, low self-esteem, shame and self-blame. Additionally, child sexual abuse victims often have difficulty trusting others and forming intimate, interpersonal relationships. These psychological, emotional, physical and behavioural effects can be debilitating to some and permeate all aspects of their lives in both the short and long term. Terry argues that while there are many restorative justice options available to assist crime victims generally, there are few options for helping victims of child sexual abuse. The restorative justice programmes that do exist lack consistency in definition, approach and application, and there is little evaluation of their efficacy. Her chapter examines the research that does exist on restorative justice approaches for victims of child sexual abuse, and discusses policy implications based on what is known.

Bolitho then looked at another much-neglected practice area. She rightly points out that despite the prevalence of disability in both offender and victim populations and the various human rights treaty obligations on many Western states, little research explores what it means for criminal justice interventions, including restorative practices. Her chapter begins to address this gap by presenting new and unpublished data from a study of 74 victim offender conferences in a government-operated post-sentencing programme for adults following serious crimes in New South Wales (Australia). Within this sampling population, Bolitho carried out an in-depth study of 16 cases involving disabled people (15 cases of offenders, seven cases of victims and six cases that involved both disabled victims and offenders). The study was conducted using 15 departmental case files, seven observations and 35 in-depth interviews with participants. While the nature of disability varied, mental health issues were present in all cases. The findings are revealing. The chapter contends that if practitioners have the capacity to manage the inherent and complex power dynamics in cases involving disability, then a priority for the restorative movement is the sharing of knowledge, strategies and resources and the development of an evidence base around best practice. Bolitho argues that the creation of enabling spaces for those with disability is in keeping with the philosophy and aims of the restorative justice movement as well as human rights obligations.

Clamp then looked at the lessons of restorative policing for future practice. She argues that restorative policing has experienced somewhat of a tumultuous journey. She uses the 1990s pilot in Wagga Wagga (Australia) as a successful case study, which she believes has not been replicated elsewhere. She then proceeds to interrogate the reasons for this failure. She argues that the operationalisation of restorative justice within contemporary policing environments with the pressures of austerity and public accountability naturally lends itself to quantity over quality resolutions. She also claims that both the champions and evaluators of contemporary restorative policing schemes have prioritised learning from failure over success. The chapter also argues that if we return to the origins of the restorative policing model, we will remind ourselves that good practice takes time, investment and collegiality. Clamp concludes that only once these internal resources are secured can true restorative policing that benefits the community take place. The chapter warns the international reader that limits to that realisation come from surprising quarters. Indeed, Clamp raises some uncomfortable questions about the state of the field, if restorative policing was 'allowed' to work.

In chapter 13, Hayden investigated yet another contested practice area. She looked at the phenomenon of intimate partner violence and the potential of restorative justice. To this end, she used her research with 29 non-randomised participants (eight victims, six perpetrators and 15 key informants). None had experienced restorative justice, but a number of victims and perpetrators expressed a wish that they had. None of the total participants excluded it as suitable for all intimate partner violence cases. Seventy-nine percent of the total sample considered that the availability of restorative justice for these cases would increase reporting. Using its original findings, the chapter contributes to the Handbook's ambitions by arguing that restorative justice is seen by intimate partner violence victims and perpetrators as a safer option. The chapter also suggests that restorative justice could improve relationships sooner and could benefit children more, while delivering a speedier justice. The chapter, however, also points out qualities that can made restorative justice less safe for intimate partner violence cases. The chapter proposed ways of increasing safety, including participants having realistic expectations of the process and outcomes, the use of specialised facilitators, voluntary attendance, timing, commitment to honesty and the presence of support people. Power and reporting were reconceptualised, and the voices of men, who are seldom heard, were included.

Doak and O'Mahony then presented the latest evidence on restorative justice conferencing. They argue that this practice differs from other forms of restorative justice in terms of both its practical operation as well as its theoretical underpinnings. First developed in New Zealand and Australia during the 1980s, conferencing has rapidly grown in popularity on the international platform, and a number of jurisdictions now prioritise it as the primary response to juvenile offending. This chapter presented an overview of the theory and practice of restorative conferencing, before proceeding to analyse a number of major evaluative studies that have been carried out in Australia, New Zealand and Northern Ireland. Doak and O'Mahony believe that while the evidence to date suggests that conferencing holds a number of clear advantages for victims, offenders and the community over orthodox criminal justice interventions, a number of important challenges remain in regards its use in serious and 'problematic' cases (such as sexual offending and domestic abuse). They also feel that there is a need to overcome structural and attitudinal barriers which have hitherto prohibited the development of conferencing. The chapter makes a number of suggestions as to how such barriers might be overcome to ensure that conferencing fulfils its maximum potential as a criminal justice intervention.

In chapter 15, Reisel and Carroll's work in healthcare settings in the UK is put in the context of restorative justice to challenge yet one more grey area of implementation. Using original data from their direct experiences, the authors argue that there are significant conflicts in the health sector that are often not adequately dealt with via the courts. Additionally, the spiralling costs of litigation indicate that more needs to be done to bring resolution earlier and without resorting to costly legal processes. Their research indicates several benefits from using restorative justice in healthcare settings. For patients, the benefits would be timely attention to their complaint and the opportunity to affect quality improvement in the relevant setting. For clinicians, the benefits would also be significant, as such cases could provide learning that would benefit them and their future patients. Finally, for hospitals, the investment needed to train staff would be minuscule compared to even one case of litigation. The chapter concludes by arguing that restorative justice in the healthcare settings internationally would be valuable and have far-reaching beneficial effects.

Subsequently, the role of restorative justice for traffic congestion and road rage conflicts was explored through a case study by Liebmann. The chapter was based on original data that was collected from the innovative project 'Road Sharing – A Restorative Approach', which was conducted during 2015 in Bristol (England). This was set up after concerns had been raised about the increasing numbers of conflicts relating to road usage. Seventy-one people attended 11 small group meetings of mixed road users. The restorative model that was used for these meetings was that of peacemaking circles, enabling everyone to have a voice. The pilot results were positive. For example, instead of regarding different road users as enemies and competitors, this project harnessed listening and consideration of other views, leading to what the author names as 'a cooperative ethos'. Aligned with the Handbook's vision of pushing the boundaries of criminology and restorative justice, this chapter concludes that the Bristol pilot model of restorative working could be applied to other situations, such as hard-to-reach groups with fixed world views and incidents of road rage.

Karp and Schacter then presented their research on student misconduct. Paradoxically, universities are institutions with ancient traditions and hierarchical power relations. However, they are also known to be sites of progressive thought and proving grounds for emerging social movements. As the authors argue, universities allow for creative experimentation and academic freedom, but at the same time enforce rigorous compliance to academic standards and 'politically correct' speech. That is why Karp and Schacter were right to ask whether restorative justice has any place in this sea of liberated students and challenging ideas. Their chapter is based on original evidence from a restorative justice project that was applied for student misconduct ranging from academic dishonesty to violent assault. The project was run in the US, focusing on the needs of harmed parties and fostering student development. The chapter also explored promising applications of restorative justice to contentious campus issues, including race relations and sexual assault. Its potential to address faculty or staff conflict and misconduct was also considered.

Staying within the US, Walker and Davidson presented their recent work on using a public health approach for increasing desistance of formerly incarcerated people. Their chapter was based on a study that reviewed recidivism outcomes for adult men and women who participated in restorative circles and were imprisoned in two Hawai'i state prisons. The review covered at least three years after their release. Their unpublished data showed promising results, with significantly lower recidivism for the 58 individuals in the experimental group that had circles compared to the 60 individuals in the control group who applied for a circle but did not have one. The results indicate that restorative circles can repair harm and damaged relationships, rendering much better recidivism rates while addressing the desistance needs of individuals transitioning from prison.

Toews concluded this part of the Handbook with an original investigation of the relationship between restorative justice and designing. It is true that architecture and the design of justice buildings, such as courthouses and correctional facilities, have long represented the ideals of justice philosophies. Toews argues that with each evolution of social understandings of justice and offending, the design of justice buildings has also changed. That is why the increasing use of restorative justice raises questions about how the design of spaces in which justice occurs can better reflect restorative values, such as respect, healing and transformation. The chapter illustrates that there is growing interest and collaboration among restorative justice practitioners, architects and landscape architects to design such restorative spaces. It also presents preliminary principles for the design of spaces informed by the restorative justice philosophy and used to facilitate restorative justice practices. These principles emerge following an examination of the values manifested in existing justice architecture and natural landscapes and draw on research findings regarding the impact of environmental design on health and well-being. The chapter includes examples of real-world architecture and landscape projects that either directly use restorative justice values and principles in the creation of the environment or offer insight into the design of spaces informed by restorative justice.

Thinking critically about restorative justice

It is important for anyone who is studying, practising, researching or writing about restorative justice to be open to all sorts of views and possibilities. I have argued elsewhere that the restorative justice movement would do far better if it stopped obsessing over proving its superiority over the criminal justice system and focused more on evaluating and correcting its own flaws and practices (Gavrielides, 2007). A more international approach is also needed for wider cultural perspectives on restorative justice.

Wong and Lui opened this part of the Handbook by shedding some light on restorative justice practices in a geographical area that has long been neglected by the vast extant literature. With real-cases illustration, this chapter compares and contrasts programme goals, models, procedures and skills central to restorative interventions in three Chinese communities, including Hong Kong, Taiwan and mainland China. The chapter contributes to the Handbook's international targets and ambitions by opening a window into the specific developments of a range of restorative interventions for youth offenders in Chinese communities and argues that some culture-specific principles and skills are essential elements for the success of restorative practice independently of location. The authors' lessons from the implementation of restorative justice in Chinese communities are transferable across the globe, and thus they conclude with a critical account of future directions of restorative justice for the international community.

Ramirez then tested whether Howard Zehr's call for 'changing lenses' is ever possible for restorative justice by evaluating its strengths and weaknesses in a hierarchical, top-down criminal justice system. She uses the Chilean criminal justice system as a case study as well as her original research. This was based on an exploratory descriptive design and qualitative research methods. Secondary sources were also combined with data from fieldwork using a sample drawn from Chile's legal operators. She explains that in Chile, restorative justice appears in the form of penal mediation but without being institutionalised or normatively developed. She argues that innovative pilot projects have been implemented sporadically, but these have not had enough exposure that would have allowed them to be validated by legal operators and the citizenry. Her data confirm that penal mediation is the most appropriate mechanism for introducing restorative justice into hierarchical criminal justice systems such as the Chilean. The chapter argues that in order for penal mediation to realise its true potential, an effective establishment of normative legislation is needed. Ramirez believes that this must also be the case for any hierarchical inquisitorial criminal justice system in the world.

Matczak's chapter then takes us to Poland, bringing to light the restorative justice experience in a post-socialist, post-transformation society. The findings of her study challenge the scope and viability of restorative justice and encourage examining its preconditions through lay people's understandings of punishment and justice. Matczak claims that one of restorative justice's central hopes was to establish an alternative system of crime resolution that would eliminate the infliction of pain. However, the nature of lay people's views might indicate that the functioning of restorative practices is, and will remain, dependent on criminal justice agencies and that there is a need to address better the notion of punishment in restorative encounters. Her chapter is based on original research findings that were collected through in-depth interviews and focus groups with 69 lay Polish people. The chapter demonstrates how participants' perceptions of the Polish justice system, the police and unpaid work can facilitate understanding a number of factors that might influence the development of restorative justice. The Polish experience is indeed transferable across the restorative justice movement, and Matczak's critical perspective opens a window into a more honest restorative justice worldwide.

I was positively charged by Tauri's critical analysis of restorative justice as a colonial project in chapter 23. Utilising unpublished findings from recent research projects on Indigenous experiences of the imposition of restorative justice programmes in Canada and New Zealand, Tauri offers an Indigenous critique of the settler colonial state's current reliance on the importation and dissemination of restorative justice policies and conferencing forums as its preferred response to the related intractable problems of Indigenous over-representation in the criminal justice system. He claims that Indigenous people's experience of the restorative justice industry has been marked by a number of strategic decisions and practices that have made the relationship uncomfortable for both parties. His chapter argues that members of the industry purposely utilise elements of Indigenous life to enhance the marketability of their restorative justice products. Tauri believes that the industry has become a significant colonial project within the settler colonial state's ongoing regulation of Indigenous peoples. Tauri challenges the restorative justice movement by concluding that recent Indigenous experience of the globalised restorative justice industry are not aligned with the transformative properties of restorative justice policies and interventions.

Wood and Piggott then critically examined the question of whether restorative justice can reduce reoffending. They argue that since the increasing institutionalisation of restorative justice, there has been a growing focus by policy makers and interest by researchers on its ability to reduce reoffending. To date, however, evaluation research has failed to report consistent findings. They argue that these mixed results can be attributed to substantial variation in restorative justice programmes. They believe that many programmes differ in ways that are theoretically and empirically related to offending. The conflicting results found in evaluations can be further attributed to the wide variation in study design and significant methodological limitations, largely pertaining to how best to control for potential bias and form a fair and equivalent comparison group and measure reoffending. Through a concise but thorough exploration of existing findings reported in available evaluation research from English speaking countries, they provide readers with a user guide for understanding and critically assessing current evidence on effects of restorative justice in reducing reoffending.

It was fitting to conclude this part of the Handbook with an account from a long-standing sceptic of restorative justice, and thus I was honoured to have Acorn's critical, legal contribution. She reminds us that it is impossible to say whether restorative justice is good or bad in any given context without looking at the alternatives. She asks 'restorative justice compared to what?' Acorn argues that one context in which restorative justice is decidedly better than the alternatives is that of Indigenous criminal offenders in Canada. In this chapter, Acorn tests the judgement of the Supreme Court of Canada in *R. v. Gladue (1999)* that strongly endorses restorative justice in sentencing of Indigenous offenders against what she considers to be generally persuasive and principled objections to restorative justice. Acorn gives reasons why neither the objection that restorative justice is insufficiently retributive nor the objection that restorative justice is an abdication of state responsibility are persuasive in the Indigenous context.

The future of restorative justice

Gerry Johnstone, editor of this Handbook's predecessor (Johnstone and van Ness, 2006), opens this final part of the Handbook with his reflections on the future of restorative justice. According to Johnstone, if asked to explain the essence of restorative justice in one or two sentences, many advocates and practitioners might employ Christie's formula about the state and its actors stealing conflicts (1977). Johnstone believes that this formula misrepresents the role which treatment professionals and their working ideologies have played in shaping the discourse and practice of restorative justice. The chapter starts by looking more closely than has become usual at Christie's renowned remarks about the state stealing conflicts, and in particular at what he has to say about treatment. It then argues that the therapeutic tradition in penal practice has suffered from being mischaracterised, and offers a revised image of this tradition. On this basis, the chapter goes on to argue that restorative justice can be located firmly within the therapeutic tradition in penal practice, albeit it makes some important innovations within it. Whilst critical of the notion that restorative justice emerged from outside the therapeutic tradition and is sharply opposed to it, this chapter is intended not as a critique of restorative justice but as a more accurate placement of it. Crucially, it suggests that in going forward, the restorative justice movement can benefit from a better understanding of its affinities with the treatment tradition in penal practice.

Wachtel, a veteran in restorative practice, proceeds with a critical exposition of the implications of restorative justice for the future of democracy. He claims that just as Christie accused lawyers and court professionals of stealing our conflicts, professional politicians have stolen our decision making. Wachtel believes that throughout the world, politicians pursue wealth and power by selling favourable decisions to the highest bidder. The remedy to rampant corruption may lie in filling our legislatures with randomly selected citizens – a process called sortition or election by lot, which has its origins in Athenian democracy. The critical question is whether groups of ordinary people can make good decisions, better than the professionals. Wachtel articulates a vision whereby restorative practices can provide significant evidence that ordinary people can make good decisions in issues which affect them and their community of care. Using evidence from the extant literature combined with the author's decades of restorative justice observations, the chapter argues that along with similar outcomes from business management research and deliberative democracy experiments, restorative practices can point to the potential of making governance more truly representative.

Subsequently, O'Connell, a pioneer in restorative justice conferencing, helps us to unlock restorative practice's true potential by sharing his field expertise. He claims that during the last four decades, we have seen restorative justice evolve from a specialised criminal justice reform policy – bringing victims, offenders and others together in response to a crime – to a generalised range of practices, proactive and reactive, formal and informal, that unlock the potential to enhance all human social interaction. The chapter explores the history of the restorative conference process that the author pioneered in 1991 in Wagga Wagga (Australia) to argue that restorative justice will achieve its greatest and most enduring impact by becoming increasingly explicit – integrating diverse possibilities within existing restorative terminology and practice – but at the same time expanding the paradigm. O'Connell emphasises the critical importance of explicit practice if the restorative movement is to achieve its true potential. He argues that by adopting the most fundamental, yet broadest hypothesis – that doing things 'with' people is better than doing things 'to' them or 'for' them – we recognise that relationship building is not just a technique for effective restorative justice but provides the underlying rationale for a healthier civil society.

Stauffer and Turner then speak openly and critically about the new generation of restorative justice. They argue that restorative justice as an academic and professional discipline is facing at least three critical transitions: defining its identity, expanding its transformative practice and sustaining its adaptability. While controversial, a critical number of voices are predicting that restorative justice may either fade away or be co-opted by the established legal system. At the centre of this concern is the danger of viewing restorative justice as only one of many professional services in our menu of social welfare responses to criminal justice reform. In this chapter, the authors argue for an understanding of restorative justice as a social movement. As such, this chapter aims to contribute to the Handbook's key objective by highlighting popular, bottom-up expressions of restorative justice emerging from communities around the world who find themselves at the margins of mainstream justice.

Pavlich then speaks about the transforming powers that surround restorative justice and justice internationally. Exploring prospects of a politically transformative future tied to a restorative past, this chapter returns to three unfulfilled promises in the movement's past. First, it recalls how restorative justice called for 'changing lenses' and diverting people away from an exclusionary, disempowering and increasingly vast criminal justice system. Secondly, it scrutinises the critique that restorative justice has tended to deploy power relations paradoxically tied to the very criminal justice arenas that its moral claims abjured. Finally, it examines restorative justice as a critique of sovereign justice that silenced pre-modern and Indigenous forms of conflict resolution. Working with key insights generated by these critiques, the chapter proposes that restorative justice could in future reclaim a fresh transformative moral and political role, namely, as a social movement in search of inclusive, non-criminalising governance that renovates entry-ways to criminal justice systems. Its aim might then be to reduce the number of people selected and admitted as 'criminals' to growing criminal justice arenas and to renew the pursuit of wide-ranging ways to govern wrongdoing that augment, rather than disrupt, social bonds.

It was appropriate to conclude this part of the Handbook with a contribution from one of the longest-serving, living restorativists, Martin Wright. In his chapter, varieties of restorative practice as well as the values, methods and structures for implementing them are outlined. Wright reminds us that the main restorative justice values are based on empathy, usually expressed in dialogue. Looking into the future, his chapter illustrates how these ideas are slowly growing into the concept of the 'restorative city'. This concept, he claims, is beginning to happen, at first in schools and other work with young people, and spreading to other parts of society such as the workplace, where it is suggested that restorative practice could replace conventional line management. The chapter also argues that there is a place for professional mediators, especially in the world of commerce and international relations. He also argues in favour of establishing networks of locally based restorative services, starting with young people who may indeed hold the best hope for the future.

Restorative justice with care and responsibility

I must now conclude this Handbook by paving a clear path for future directions. Like (Acorn, 2004), I go back and forth with restorative justice. Maybe it is our legally trained brains that keep pulling us back to basic questions of rule of law and the division of public and private legal affairs.

But one conclusion is certain following the work of this Handbook. If restorative justice is to survive the next few decades of unpredicted world financial, political and societal changes, and place itself in a strong position for challenging the available justice options, then it must do so with care and responsibility.

Restorative justice with care

In writing for this Handbook, Skelton is right that anyone who is unfamiliar with the true restorative justice notion would be uncomfortable with its disregard for substantive and procedural due process legal rights. However, I dare to claim that a closer scrutiny of the restorative justice normative promise and of the good practices that have manifested it will help us understand that these safeguards are irrelevant and unnecessary in the world of proper restorative justice. I believe that we feel the urge to demand them, simply because we have been experiencing justice within a punitive matrix of power manifestation and just deserts. This is also the paradigm within which we have primarily experienced restorative justice, including its application without care.

And I am not talking about the kind of care that we put as criminal justice agents, lawyers and servants of justice, making sure that in the adversarial or inquisitorial criminal justice battle all available weapons have been considered. I am talking about a different kind of care.

Restorative justice is relational. It is premised on the assumption that we are all connected and through this relationship we ultimately care not just about ourselves but also for others. I have called this the 'social liaison' that bonds individuals in a relationship of respect for others' rights and freedoms (Gavrielides, 2005, 2013). Restorative justice assumes that this liaison has always been with us, simply because of our humanity. Individuals are not really strangers, and that also includes victims and offenders who are not really enemies but connected living entities who care about each other. That is also why in restorative processes, victim and offender must be treated as equal and free individuals, responsible for their actions and decisions. They are not strangers, but related, because the 'social liaison' connects them. They have come together to care for that liaison that needs restoration.

Under this matrix, victim and offender are seen as two sides of the same coin. The offender is not dealt with as a parasite of society, but as 'one of us'. Offenders distort the social liaison, but this does not make them our enemy. On the contrary, their actions are seen as an opportunity to prevent greater evils, 'to confront crime with a grace that transforms human lives to paths of love and giving' (Braithwaite, 1999).

Despite the risk of sounding idealistic, I believe that we have all experienced this social liaison. We cannot see it, but we feel it in moments of danger, or of extreme happiness, even with the most random people. One personal example that I recall is when the 7th July 2005 multiple London bombings took place. I remember walking over London Bridge in the evening of the bombings. There was no public transport, so all Londoners had to walk home that day. The bridge was packed with sad faces. Most heads were down, but when lifted up they would search for someone else's eyes. We would look in each other's eyes and search desperately for a connection. It did not matter whether I had met those people I looked at or not. And yet, I was drawn to them. I wanted to tell them that we would get through this and that they are not alone – that I cared. I wanted to tell them that we are all the surrogate victims of our city's attack, and that they were now safe. I wanted to share my own feelings of loss and sadness. I also wanted them to tell me that they cared about me, and that I was safe.

> Systems, or integral wholes, are wholes which have at least one special sort of partition. This is characterised by the fact that its members are united by a special relation (or set of relations); they form a family. Families are defined in terms of binary relations.
>
> (Barnes, 1991: 13)

The broken social liaison, or what Barnes called the 'special relation' between individuals and their community, is the focus of restoration within the restorative justice matrix. Zehr spoke about this liaison in a different way. He used the phrase 'wound in human relationships' and he spoke about actions that 'create an obligation to restore and repair' (Zehr, 1990). This is also similar to what Wright said: 'The boundary between crime and other harmful actions is an artificial and constantly changing one' (Wright, 1996). This is also where my legally trained mind found comfort, and where the division of public and private law affairs collapsed. It is because of this inherent care that the restorative justice matrix assumes that human rights legal safeguards are irrelevant. This care is indeed manifested through a much stronger network of human rights values such as equality, dignity, respect, fairness and involvement in decision making. These are the values and the minimum standards that must be applied when manifesting the ethos of restorative justice.

To sum up, if restorative justice is to be further normatively developed and its practices expanded, then we must do so by placing its caring aspect at the centre of our attention. The Greek Sirens of funding, praise and awards must be silenced if the power games of the current criminal justice matrix are to be overcome. Non-believers in the existence and significance of this inherent caring element of the restorative justice matrix will struggle to understand, theorise, legislate or implement it. And my research and evaluation experience of restorative justice has taught me that there have been practices, laws and policies that prioritised power over care. And I fear for the victims and offenders who are offered this uncaring restorative justice. This failure of the restorative justice movement may explain the fall of restorative justice in the historical continuum (Gavrielides, 2011) as well as its struggles with current administration. But we have identified it now, and watching it is the first step in eliminating it. As we become the watchers, we must ask what sort of restorative justice we want.

Restorative justice with responsibility

The question 'what sort of restorative justice we want' brings me to my second concluding point. Restorative justice must be carried out with responsibility. It is not a soft option – in fact, it is a practice that intends to drill down into the darkest places of our hearts and minds. I am not surprised that in this Handbook Johnstone asked for a more direct association of restorative with therapeutic practices. And I must admit that in all my observations, studies, readings and evaluations of restorative practice, one variant was always present (independently of the harm that was being restored, the parties' characteristics, the location or the stage in which the process was introduced). This constant variant was that of pain. Pain is a hard and difficult venture for the parties in conflict, and I associate it in restorative justice with at least three concerns.

My first concern is about the restorative justice offer to the parties in conflict. If this offer is not carefully balanced and executed with care, it may result in several problems. For instance, if restorative pain is not organically developed through mutual feelings of trust among participants, it may end up being coercive, similar to state-inflicted punishment. The literature on coerced restorative practices and their consequences is rich, and I refer you to it. Moreover, if the specific needs and circumstances of the involved parties are not carefully assessed, the restorative pain may end up re-victimising them, causing further harm and unnecessary, complex pain.

The second concern relates to language, which is the key tool used to identify, extract and externalise restorative pain. The dangers associated with any dialogue-based approaches are well documented. For instance, Wind noted: 'While language can offer hope in the healing process, it may also profoundly exacerbate the trauma' (Wind et al., 2008: 251). For language to be healing, it needs to be reordered and reimagined away from the world of retriggering and into a world where siblings, parents, and others engage in conversations of acceptance of trauma and its ongoing consequences.

The third concern relates to the pain itself. Although pain in restorative justice can be constructive, cleansing and honest, it is still tough. Hume's discussion on the paradox of tragedy comes to mind. 'It seems an unaccountable pleasure, which the spectators of a well-wrote tragedy receive from sorrow, terror, anxiety and other passion, which are in themselves disagreeable and uneasy' (*Of Tragedy – Four Dissertations*). With this statement, Hume helps us to understand why pain as received through the restorative process in the form of sorrow, anxiety, fear, pity and various other passions, is still welcomed by all parties involved.

And when I speak of restorative justice, I do not mean the quick fixes that have gradually been introduced to serve alien ends. Klamp, among other authors of this Handbook, spoke about the reasons that drive funding and support for this kind of service. I am referring to the complex and in-depth restorative processes that aim to consciously inflict voluntary pain with care, and through the imposition of constructive pain achieve catharsis.[1] These practices are not many, but they do exist, and this Handbook, especially Part II, presented evidence on new and contested areas with real case studies of implementation. Therefore, for the sake of brevity and space, I will not present practical examples here.

Greek tragedies have taught us that in order to generate catharsis, we first need pain. Pain creates responsibility. But let's take a step back. Aristotle spoke about this kind of catharsis (see *Poetics*), which aims to awaken feelings of fear and pity. These feelings are necessary and welcomed, as the upsetting process is purgative and engenders a sense of catharsis at the removal of debilitating emotions otherwise built up and trapped inside. Aristotle argues that this type of pain reminds us that life itself is something fundamentally painful and in need of justification, of redemption from suffering. Using his medical training, Aristotle asserted that catharsis is a 'form of homeopathic treatment – curing emotion by means of an emotion like kind but not identical' (Woodfin and Groves, 2006: 157).

In referring to Aristotle's Dialectic Method, Hegel also explains that catharsis works as a thesis that moves to its opposite, the antithesis, by principle of negativity (1910). It is via this negative that a new state, called synthesis (Abdulla, 1985), is arrived at through the clash of the two opposite forces. This new state of synthesis, while sharing traits of both thesis and antithesis, produces a discovery of the two opposite forces, or a 'reconciliation of the two' (Abdulla, 1985). Hegel believes that all things are related and nothing can stand in isolation. He claims that everything in one way or another influences and is being influenced by the forces around it. He moves on to explain that the dialectical procedure that results in catharsis could be transferred into restorative justice and that our restorative pain reveals conflict ideas or beliefs not as disjunctions, but as conjoined. Such is the synthesis, a category of becoming, rebuilding and restoring.

Catharsis as pursued by the restorative dialogue is an important transformative discovery. Like the spectators of a Greek tragedy, the parties in a restorative process will go through tragic, dramatic experience and pass catharsis, only then to realise that catharsis is not the final state in itself but rather a reaching to the state of synthesis, recognition, understanding or discovery. It is a glimpse of the moment of sublimation. Aristotle reminds us that these are the types of moments that affirm the beauty of life, the connection between individuals and then between the individual and their community.

I have written about catharsis and its relationship with 'restorative pain' elsewhere (Gavrielides, 2005, 2013). Here, what I will retain is that like care, pain is also inherent in restorative justice. Neither care nor pain can be transferred. Pain must also be voluntary, private and personal. Without pain, there is no catharsis, and without catharsis there is no transformation. Without care there are also risks, and a possibility for further harm, vengeance and the manifestation of trivial and punitive feelings of power, profit and control.

1 Catharsis derived from the Greek word κάθαρσις meaning 'to cleanse'.

This is where responsibility kicks in. But perhaps to the surprise of the reader, I do not place this responsibility on the state and its criminal justice machinery. This would be a fallacy and an oxymoron, since restorative justice is relational.

Responsibility lies with the parties themselves and their communities, as these are represented through the facilitator, their friends and family, their connected entities. As free individuals, parties in conflict have rights that need to be respected and protected. But they also have obligations (Braithwaite, 2002), among which includes restoring the power imbalance that the harm had distributed within the community. Therefore, what restorative justice calls them to do is to restore the broken liaison that used to bond them. To this end, they willingly engage in a rather painful process of transformation and personal investment. This is why restorative justice must also be carried out with *personal* responsibility.

Restorative justice, of course, assumes that parties are mentally competent and hence morally culpable actors, who are willing to take responsibility for their own actions, not only to the parties directly injured, but also to a wider community. So what about individuals who cannot be willingful morally culpable actors? Here, we must identify the frontiers and limitations of restorative justice.

Restorative justice makes one more assumption. It takes individuals to be dependent on their communities, and vice versa. Communities are dependent on the preservation and restoration of the social liaison. When inflicting pain through the restorative justice dialogue, the parties involved bear responsibility to honour their interdependence. Parties must remember that in pursuing (restorative) justice, this must not be for their own ends. Their lives gain meaning from the aggregation, and their happiness is linked to the existence of the aggregation that witnesses it. That is why the restoration of their relationship becomes of such importance so as to justify pain and as a result enjoy the fruits of catharsis.

It appears that when translating this into action, restorative justice assumes a kind of relationship between people, which is difficult to accept, or even comprehend in modern Western societies. Sullivan et al. (1998) argued that restorative justice promotes a social ethic 'that differs radically from that prevalent in our current political economy' (p. 16). Accordingly, many restorativists suggest that we try to understand this relationship by looking at small or Indigenous communities such as the Navajo Nation, not by comparing it with what we live today in our societies (where the 'social liaison' is less visible).

But again, isn't this a bit far-fetched? How can we expect our modern societies to transform themselves into Indigenous models of community living? The answer is very simple. We must learn to view community through the restorative justice lenses. It is far more than a place. This does not mean that we have to change the structure or sizes of our communities; what it does mean is that we have to change the normative idea that we have planted in our minds of what constitutes community.

Now, bearing in mind the assumption of the pre-existence of a social liaison, the central characteristic of a restorative community is that it provides the environment for growing human relations. This creates further layers of responsibility, only this time not for the parties in conflict. The existence of this kind of community is the prerequisite for the liaison that relates individuals and hence justifies restorative pain.

However, this community must also bear responsibility in instilling a sense in individuals to respect and protect the liaison. It must be responsible for also keeping a liaison between itself and the individual, not a liaison of control and power but of care. More importantly, parties need to be guided and supervised by an impartial third party chosen by the community, such as a mediator.

Finally, it is important to add that the community 'wants reassurance that what happened was wrong, that something is being done about it, and that steps are being taken to discourage its recurrence' (Zehr, 1990: 195). To reiterate, restorative justice embraces the human rights ideals of individual freedom and liberty. Consequently, the community aims to protect humans' relations by giving them the voice and choice to amend and restore their broken liaison. The community can supervise them, but should not control them. However, as Johnstone (2001) notes, 'the community must be prepared to become involved in the resolution of conflict' (p. 14). In fact, in the mind of a restorativist, government cannot effectively address crime without the moral authority and informal social control provided by the community.

One final thought

In my many years of studying restorative justice, I have come to conclude that all those who practise or write about true restorative justice genuinely believe that it is wiser to strengthen our relationship with offenders rather than weaken it (e.g. by ostracising them). That is why it makes sense to show them that we care about them. That is also why it is important that restorative justice is exercised with care within its own matrix of human rights principles and safeguards. Accordingly, offenders must be provided with opportunities and encouragement to (1) understand the harm they have caused to victims and their community, and (2) develop plans for taking appropriate responsibility. This is when the self-infliction of restorative pain through community care and personal responsibility becomes paramount.

If restorative justice is carried out with care and responsibility as described in this Handbook, then the pursuit of catharsis and the experience of restorative pain will be accepted and indeed be welcomed as natural by-products of the restorative dialogue. Care and responsibility go hand in hand in restorative practice and ethos. But caring for others, especially those who have harmed us, is not easy. Furthermore, accepting responsibility for our own self-inflicted pain is a complex and high moral demand. Whether this path for restorative justice is a clear one, I will leave to you to judge.

I am certain that it is not an easy one, and this may explain why in my many years of researching and writing on restorative justice, the genuine practices that I have encountered have been scant. I am not a minimalist who views restorative justice through the narrow lenses of face-to-face encounters and strict ground rules. In fact, I have advocated for the diversity and malleability of restorative justice, as its practice must be driven by local needs and people's given realities. But we must be honest abouts its limitations, and indeed take our own responsibility as a restorative justice movement.

At the same time, there is nothing wrong with leading our lives restoratively or running our schools, businesses, interpersonal relationships and parenting styles using restorative justice values. These are all manifestations of the restorative justice ethos. But they are not delivering alternative criminal justice.

In conclusion, if these manifestations of the restorative justice ethos work for the betterment of our relationships with others, prevent conflicts or even restore relationships, then restorative justice is a good and moral option. If offering restorative justice as a formal route to justice, and indeed if it is viewed by parties as an alternative route to criminal justice, then one must do so with care and responsibility.

References

Abdulla, A. 1985. *Catharsis in Literature*. Bloomington: Indiana University Press.
Acorn, A. 2004. *Compulsory Compassion: A Critique of Restorative Justice*. Vancouver: University of British Columbia Press.

Barnes, J. 1991. Partial Wholes. In J. Paul (ed.) *Ethics, Politics, and Human Nature*. Cambridge: Basil Blackwell, pp. 1–23.

Braithwaite, J. 1999. Restorative Justice: Assessing Optimistic and Pessimistic Accounts, *Crime and Justice*, 25: 1.

Braithwaite, J. 2002. *Restorative Justice and Responsive Regulation*. New York: Oxford University Press.

Christie, N. 1977. Conflicts as Property, *British Journal of Criminology*, 17(1): 1–15.

Gavrielides, T. 2007. *Restorative Justice Theory & Practice: Addressing the Discrepancy*. Helsinki: HEUNI.

Gavrielides, T. 2011. Restorative Practices: From the Early Societies to the 1970s. *Internet Journal of Criminology*, ISSN 2045–6743 (Online).

Gavrielides, T. 2013. Restorative Pain: A New Vision of Punishment. In T. Gavrielides and V. Artinopoulou (eds.) *Reconstructing Restorative Justice Philosophy*. Farnham: Ashgate, pp. 311–337.

Gavrielides, Theo. 2005. Some Meta-theoretical Questions for Restorative Justice, *Ratio Juris*, 18(1): 84–106.

Hegel, G. 1910. *The Phenomenology of Mind*. New York: Palgrave Macmillan.

Johnstone, G. 2001. *Restorative Justice: Ideas, Values, Debates*. Cullompton: William Publishing.

Sullivan, D., Tifft, L. and Cordella, P. 1998. The Phenomenon of Restorative Justice: Some Introductory Remarks, *Contemporary Justice Review*, 1, 7–20.

Wind, L., Sullivan, J. and Levins, D.J. 2008. Survivors' Perspectives on the Impact of Clergy Sexual Abuse on Families of Origin, *Journal of Child Sexual Abuse*, 17(3–4), 238–254.

Woodfin, R. and Groves, J. 2006. *Introduction: Aristotle*. Icon Books: Cambridge.

Wright, M. 1996. *Justice for Victims and Offenders: A Restorative Response to Crime*. Winchester: Waterside Press.

Zehr, H. 1990. *Changing Lenses: A New Focus for Crime and Justice*. Scottdale, PA: Herald Press.

Index